UNM
GALLUP

Zollinger Library

# Energy for
# the 21st Century

# Energy for the 21st Century

A Comprehensive Guide to
Conventional and Alternative Sources

**Second Edition**

**Roy L. Nersesian**

*M.E.Sharpe*
Armonk, New York
London, England

To friends of the family—
Taffy, Daisy, Rue, Heather, Ginger, Quincy, Marco, and Maya

**Library of Congress Cataloging-in-Publication Data**

Nersesian, Roy L.
  Energy for the 21st century : a comprehensive guide to conventional and
alternative sources / Roy L. Nersesian.—2nd ed.
      p. cm.
  Includes bibliographical references and index.
  ISBN 978-0-7656-2412-3 (cloth : alk. paper)—ISBN 978-0-7656-2413-0 (pbk : alk. paper)
  1. Power resources. 2. Energy policy. I. Title.

  HD9502.A2N465 2010
  333.79—dc22                                                              2009037417

Printed in the United States of America

The paper used in this publication meets the minimum requirements of
American National Standard for Information Sciences
Permanence of Paper for Printed Library Materials,
ANSI Z 39.48-1984.

∞

CW (c)  10   9   8   7   6   5   4   3   2
CW (p)  10   9   8   7   6   5   4   3   2   1

# CONTENTS

# LIST OF TABLES AND FIGURES

## TABLES

## FIGURES

# PREFACE

Many of life's greater expectations remain unfulfilled, but on a more mundane level our lives are ones of fulfilled expectations. We expect that the radio alarm will awaken us in the morning, that there will be light when we turn on the light switch, that water will flow when we turn on a faucet, that the food in the refrigerator will still be cold, that the burner on the stove will fry an egg. We expect a newspaper at our front doorstep and something to look at if we turn on the television. If we commute we expect that the bus or train will be running, or that the car will run, and that the gas station will be open for refueling. In our office, we expect that the mail will be delivered, that the computer boots up when we turn it on, that our e-mail has received all messages that had been sent to us, and that there is a dial tone when we pick up the telephone. There is an endless list of fulfilled expectations that are necessary for our modern way of life to continue for another day.

All this depends on energy: electricity for the lights, refrigerator, computer, and communications; natural gas or electricity for the stove; gasoline or diesel fuel for the car, bus, and train; jet fuel for the airplane; heating oil or natural gas to heat a home or a building. Electricity itself is derived for the most part from burning coal, natural gas, and oil, and to a lesser extent, nuclear and hydropower. A rather miniscule, but growing, contribution is made from alternative sources such as wind, solar, geothermal, and biomass. Of these, biofuels and wind have made the most progress in becoming a meaningful alternative supply of energy, yet such progress is only a very few percentage points of overall energy demand. This still leaves the bulk of energy demand for electricity generation to be fulfilled by conventional means. Despite all the hoopla, the hydrogen economy—the Green Answer to the world's burgeoning energy needs—has far to go technology-wise before being commercially feasible.

This book examines the role of the principal sources of energy, both in the aggregate and by specific types (biomass, coal, oil, natural gas, hydro and nuclear power, and sustainable sources), for a balanced view of energy. Nations exhibit enormous variance in energy consumption both in amount and the degree of reliance on different types of energy. Moreover, their energy plans to satisfy future needs vary markedly. Energy diversity on a national level is too great for the global community of nations to adopt a common policy approach to energy. The only international convention that deals with energy issues is the Kyoto Protocol, currently under revision. However, one can argue that the Protocol is more environmental in orientation in that its primary concern is reducing greenhouse gas emissions. But in complying with the Protocol nations will tend to favor natural gas, nuclear and hydro, and wind and solar over coal and oil.

Having divergent and perhaps mutually exclusive energy policies prevents integration into a single, coherent, and consistent policy toward energy; the world will have to live with a portfolio of energy policies that fit each nation, not one that applies globally. Although it may be possible to develop regional energy policies, such as in the European Union or North America, even here there is a great deal of diversity among individual nations on their dependence on various types of energy and their aims in establishing energy goals.

I have tried to present a balanced view on energy without succumbing to the temptation to tell one side of the story. I have probably failed from time to time. In preparing to write the book I discovered to my amazement divergence of opinion rather than consensus on simple matters such as where does oil come from, the relationship between global warming and the rising concentration of carbon dioxide in the atmosphere, and whether we are running out of oil. My approach has been to try to represent both sides of a point, although I do show partiality at times such as when I leave out the views of those who espouse that energy is infinite, that consumption does not matter, and that pollution though a nuisance is nothing to be concerned with.

I would like to express my gratitude to Richard Howard, who read the manuscript and made a number of suggestions, particularly in giving Gulbenkian, an individual who disdained oil exploration, production, refining, and distribution, his due in developing the oil industry. I would like to mention Neal Dougherty and John Altenau as lifelong friends and supporters. My thanks go to Fred Kelly, Dean of the Leon Hess Business School at Monmouth University, and Albert Brassand, Director of the Center for Energy, Marine Transportation, and Public Policy at the School for International Affairs, Columbia University, for their support along with student assistance from Ophelia Karavias and Rahiba Sami.

I accept all errors as my responsibility. However, I would like to warn the reader that there is a wide range of opinion on energy issues. Some are far from settled, and others are more like questions begging for answers. Lastly I plan to make good the promise I made to Maria, my wife, that I will spend more time with her and less with the computer, a promise which I've failed to keep in the past.

# Energy for
# the 21st Century

# 1

# ARE WE ON EASTER ISLAND?

Energy is a natural resource and, for the most part, finite. Exhaustion of fossil fuels (coal, oil, and natural gas) is not imminent, although we may be at the onset of negotiating a slippery slope with regard to oil production. Interestingly, we have a history of responding to finite natural resources in danger of exhaustion. We exhausted forests in Europe at the start of the Industrial Age in our quest for making glass and metals, and we nearly drove whales to the point of extinction during the nineteenth century in our quest for whale oil. Fortunately, we found ways to avert what could have been a terminal crisis. The forests in Europe were saved from the axe by the discovery of coal as an alternative to wood in glass- and metal-making. Whales were saved from extinction by finding an alternative source for their oil for lighting in the form of kerosene. In the twentieth century we took effective action to rejuvenate a threatened species of marine animal life, but at the same time we discovered the technology to strip-mine the open oceans of fish life. As we exhaust open-ocean fishing, an alternative has been found in aquaculture or fish farming. Aquaculture is similar to relying on sustainable biofuels whereas open-ocean fishing, when fish are caught faster than they can reproduce, is similar to exhausting fossil fuels.

In the case of energy, it is true that immense energy reserves have been found that have kept up with our horrific appetite for energy, making mincemeat of Theodore Roosevelt's prediction, from the vantage point of the early twentieth century, that we will soon exhaust our natural resources. A key question facing us is whether the future pace of discovery can keep ahead of our growing appetite for energy; that is, will Roosevelt ultimately be proven right? Just because we run short of a natural resource does not necessarily mean that we can find an alternative. That is the tragedy of Easter Island.

## EASTER ISLAND

Easter Island is over 2,000 miles from Tahiti and Chile. To the original inhabitants, Easter Island was an isolated island of finite resources surrounded by a seemingly infinite ocean. What happened on Easter Island when it ultimately exhausted its finite resources is pertinent because Earth is an isolated planet of finite resources surrounded by seemingly infinite space. Whether we admit it or not, we are in danger of exhausting our natural resources. Rough, and some deem optimistic, estimates are forty years for oil, sixty years for natural gas, and a one hundred twenty years for coal. These are not particularly comforting when viewed from the perspective of a six thousand year history of civilization. Like the Easter Islanders who had nowhere to go, this is our home planet now and for the foreseeable future. Space travel is a long way off, and flying off to Mars to escape a manmade calamity on Earth is not a particularly inviting prospect.

Examination of the soil layers on Easter Island, or Rapa Nui to the present inhabitants, reveals an island with abundant plant and animal life that existed for tens of thousands of years. Around

400 CE, the island was discovered and settled by Polynesians, who originally named the island Te Pito O Te Henua (Navel of the World). The natives survived on the bounty of natural animal and plant life on the island and fish in the surrounding waters. Critical for survival was the eighty-foot tall Easter Island palm that provided sap and nuts for human consumption and canoes for fishing. The palms also provided the means to move the massive stone Moai, stone figures for which the island is famous, which now stand in mute testimony to an ecological catastrophe that unfolded around 1500. By then, the estimated population had grown to somewhere between 10,000 and 15,000 inhabitants.

This sounds like an awful lot of people descended from a few settlers, but this is the nature of exponential growth. If a party of ten people originally settled on Easter Island and grew at a relatively modest 1 percent per year (about the current growth rate in world population), the number of Easter Islanders would double about every seventy years. There were nearly sixteen doublings of the population in the 1,100 years from 400 to 1500 CE. Double ten sixteen times and see what you get. In theory the population would have grown to 567,000, a mathematical consequence of compound exponential growth at 1 percent per year over 1,100 years. It would never have reached this level because, as proven in 1500, a population in excess of 10,000 was sufficient to exhaust the island's natural resources.

A growing population increased the demand for meat, which eventually led to the natives feasting on the last animal. More people and no animals promoted more intensive tilling of the land, which first had to be cleared of the palms. With fewer palms, erosion increased and, coupled with the pressure to grow more crops, soil fertility declined. Of course the palms did not go to waste as they were needed to support the leading industry on Easter Island: the construction and moving of the Moai, plus of course, canoes. Fish became more important in the diet as the population grew, the animals disappeared, and crop yields fell. Around 1500, the last palm tree was cut down. Bloody intertribal warfare, cannibalism, and starvation marked the demise of a civilization.

On Easter of 1722, the Dutch explorer Jacob Roggeveen rediscovered the island. It presented a great mystery, as the few surviving and utterly impoverished natives had no memory of the tragedy nor did they understand the meaning of the Moai. The gift of Western civilization—infectious disease—ultimately reduced the native population to a remnant of 111 by 1800. In 1888, when the island was annexed by Chile and renamed Rapa Nui, the population had risen to 2,000 (a growth rate considerably in excess of 1 percent!).

## THE MATHEMATICS OF EXTINCTION

Suppose that we depend on a forest for supplying wood for fuel and building material. If the forest grows at 3 percent per year and we remove 2 percent of the forest per year, the resource will last forever (a sustainable resource). The forest also lasts forever if 3 percent is removed per year, but care has to be exercised to ensure that removal does not exceed 3 percent. If consumption exceeds 3 percent as a consequence of a growing population that needs more wood for fuel and shelter, or if a new technology is introduced that consumes a great deal of wood, such as glass- and metal-making, then the forest will eventually be consumed (a nonsustainable resource).

Suppose that a forest consists of 1,000 units of usable wood that increases naturally by 3 percent per year. Figure 1.1 shows what happens to the forest as a resource in terms of units of usable wood when consumption is 3, 3.5, and 4 percent per year. While the forest is a sustainable resource if consumption is limited to 3 percent, in a century the forest will be reduced to 600 and 380 units for consumption rates of 3.5 and 4 percent respectively. One hundred years in the recorded 6,000-year history of humanity is not very long; for a growing minority, it is a single lifetime. But this does

Figure 1.1    **Exhausting a Natural Resource**

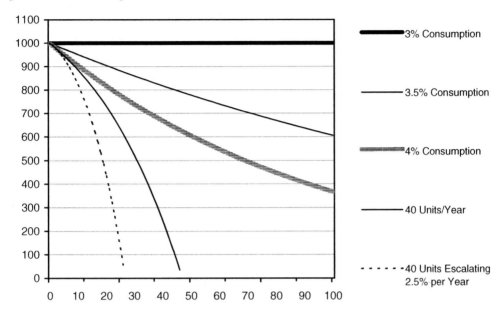

not accurately describe the situation. What is wrong with this projection is that demand declines in absolute terms over time. For example, in the first year the forest gains 30 units and consumption at 4 percent is 40 units, leaving 990 units for the next year. When the forest is down to 800 units, consumption at 4 percent has been reduced from 40 to 32 units.

This is not realistic; there is no reason for demand to decline simply because supply is dwindling. Suppose that consumption remains constant at 40 units with 3 percent growth in forest reserves. Then, as Figure 1.1 shows, the forest is transformed to barren land in 47 years. The final curve is the most realistic. It shows what would happen if consumption climbs at 1 unit per year; 40 units in the first year, 41 units the second, and so on, which is reflective of a growing population. Now the forest is gone in 30 years, a single generation.

Yet, even this projection is not realistic. Consumption, initially growing by 1 unit a year, declines in relative terms over time. For instance, when consumption increases from 40 to 41 units, growth is 2.5 percent; from 50 to 51 units, growth has declined to 2 percent. Another curve could be constructed holding consumption growth at 2.5 percent, based on a starting point of 40 units per year. But the point has already been made: The resource is exhausted within a single generation.

Before the resource is exhausted, other mitigating factors come into play. One is price, a factor not at play on Easter Island. As the forest diminishes in size and consumers and suppliers realize that wood supplies are becoming increasingly scarce, price would increase. The more serious the situation becomes, the higher the price. Higher prices dampen demand and act as an incentive to search for other forests or alternative sources for wood such as coal for energy and plastic for wood products (neither option available to the Easter Islanders).

Price would certainly have caused a change of some sort to deal with the oncoming crisis, but would not have affected the eventual outcome. A very high price for the last Easter Island palm would not have saved a civilization from extinction. The individual who became rich selling the last palm would have to spend his last dime buying the last fish. Easter Island is not the only civilization that collapsed from a shortage of natural resources. It is believed that the fall in agricultural output from a prolonged drought caused the demise of the Mayan civilization in Central America. Ruins of dead civilizations litter the earth, a humbling reminder of their impermanence.

## PROGRESS IS OUR MOST IMPORTANT PRODUCT

About one-third of the earth's population still depends on wood as a primary energy source. Unfortunately, removing forests to clear land for agriculture is often considered a mark of progress. Where cleared land stopped and forests began marked the boundaries of the Roman Empire. Agriculture transformed war-loving hunter-gatherers into law-abiding agrarians. The resuscitation of civilization during the Middle Ages was evidenced by forests and abandoned lands transformed to vineyards and other forms of agricultural enterprise by monks. Removal of forests to support a growing population became too much of a good thing. The first energy crisis occurred early in the Industrial Revolution when wood demand for housing, heating, and the new industries of glass- and metal-making exhausted a natural resource. A crisis turning into a calamity was averted by the discovery of coal in England and forests in North America.

The growth of the United States as a nation can be traced by the clearing of a large portion of the forest covering the eastern half of the nation for farmland. This was a visual sign of progress for pioneers seeking a new life in the Americas. Despite environment protestations to the contrary, clearing forests is still considered a sign of progress. We are intentionally burning down and clearing huge portions of the rain forests in the Amazon and in Southeast Asia for cattle grazing and other forms of agriculture.

Burning wood or biomass faster than it can be replaced by natural growth adds carbon dioxide to the atmosphere. Burning fossil fuels (coal, oil, and natural gas) releases carbon dioxide previously removed from the atmosphere by plant, animal, and marine life millions of years ago. The increasing concentration of carbon dioxide in the atmosphere is blamed on both the continuing clearing of forests and our growing reliance on fossil fuels. At the same time, clearing forests and consuming energy are signs of economic progress to raise living standards. Although there is intense public pressure to reduce carbon dioxide emissions in Europe, Japan, Australia, and New Zealand, over half of the planet's population live in nations in South America and Asia where governments have been active in increasing carbon dioxide emissions in pursuit of economic development. However, in recent years, concerns have been raised on the effect of water and air pollution on the health of the people and efforts are being initiated to curb pollution.

Unlike the unhappy experience of the Easter Islanders, there are countervailing measures being taken to compensate for burning down vast tracts of the world's tropical forests. Tree farms and replanting previously harvested forests ensure a supply of raw materials for lumber and paper-making industries for their long-term sustainability. A number of public service organizations are dedicated to planting trees to combat the rising concentration of carbon dioxide in the atmosphere. An increasing carbon dioxide concentration in the atmosphere itself promotes plant growth that would be a natural countermeasure (an example of a negative feedback system). Yet despite human efforts to the contrary, the world's resource of forests continues to dwindle and the carbon dioxide concentration in the atmosphere continues to climb.

## THE UNREMITTING RISE IN POPULATION

Both energy usage and pollution can be linked directly to population. Indeed, there are groups who advocate population reduction as the primary countermeasure to cut pollution of the land, air, and water. These groups have identified the true culprit of energy exhaustion and environmental pollution, but their suggested means of correcting the problem does not make for comfortable

Figure 1.2 **World Population**

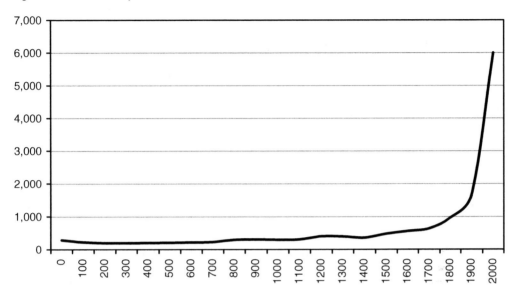

reading. Figure 1.2 shows the world population since the beginning of the Christian era and its phenomenal growth since the Industrial Revolution. [1]

The world's population was remarkably stable up to 1000 CE. The Dark Age of political disorder and economic collapse following the fall of the Roman Empire around 400 CE was instrumental in suppressing population growth. The high death rate for infants and children and the short, dirty, brutish lives of those who survived childhood, coupled with the disintegration of society, prevented runaway population growth. After the Dark Age was over, the population began to grow accompanied by a period of global warming. This continued until the Black Death starting around 1350, which occurred during a period of global cooling. With several recursions over the next hundred years, the Black Death wiped out massive numbers of people in Asia and Europe. More than one-third of Europe's population were victims, with as much as two-thirds in certain areas. It took over a century for the population of Europe to recover to pre-plague levels.

The first billion in the world's population was reached around 1840. The second billion was reached around 1930, only ninety years later, despite the horrendous human losses during the First World War, the Russian Revolution and Civil War, and the Spanish Flu, a pandemic that wiped out 30–40 million lives. This pandemic cost more in human life than the combined efforts of those involved with perpetrating war and revolution and numerically, but not percentagewise, exceeded lives lost to the Black Death. It only took 30 years for the world population to reach its third billion in 1960, despite Stalin's execution of tens of millions of his own people by starvation and firing squad, Hitler's extermination of 12 million Jews and Slavs, plus the deaths of untold millions of military personnel and civilians during the Second World War. The fourth billion was reached fourteen years later in 1974 despite Mao Zedong's failed Great Leap Forward that caused the death of tens of millions from starvation and the genocide perpetuated by the Khmer Rouge in Cambodia, the fifth billion thirteen years later in 1987, and the sixth billion twelve years later in 1999. The seventh billion is projected to occur in 2011.

We should be justifiably proud of the medical advances that have drastically reduced the mortality rate of infant and childhood diseases. No one espouses going back to the days of Queen Anne

(1665–1714), ruler of England from 1702 until her death. Anne had the best medical care that royalty could buy. Yet she had the misfortune of having around six stillbirths plus another twelve who survived birth, but not her. She died at forty-nine without an heir to the throne. As much as we are grateful for advances in treating disease, there are mathematical consequences.

The quickening pace of adding increments of a billion to the population is not an increase in the growth rate but a property of the mathematics of growth. Going from 1 to 2 billion is a 100 percent gain in population, from 2 to 3 billion is a 50 percent gain, from 3 to 4 billion 33 percent, 4 to 5 billion 25 percent, 5 to 6 billion 20 percent, and 6 to 7 billion is 17 percent growth. Eventually only a 10 percent growth in population would be necessary to go from 10 to 11 billion. Thus, each billion increment of the world's population occurs more quickly for a constant population growth rate.

The earth is rapidly getting more crowded, yet there are some who say that we can sustain a much larger population. If every human being were to stand next to one another, how much of the earth would be covered with people? If we place every individual in a 3′×3′ square, enough space sufficient for everyone to stand but not lie down, we can get slightly over 3 million people into a square mile. The area to accommodate 6.8 billion people in 2009 is 2,200 square miles, or a square about 47 miles on a side. Thus, the world's population could fit, standing room only, in Delaware, the nation's second smallest state at just under 2,500 square miles, with a little room to spare.

Demographics affect energy consumption: The larger the number of people, the greater the energy consumption. One way to judge the future population is to calculate the portion of a nation below 15 years of age. A disproportionately high youthful population portends higher than average population growth as this segment reaches the childbearing years. On this basis, future population growth will be centered in the Middle East, Asia (excluding Japan), and South America. On the other hand, Europe, United States, Russia, and Japan have to deal with a growing geriatric generation that has ramifications on future population size and energy consumption.

As Europe and Japan exhibit essentially stagnant population growth, other nations would like to curb their growth. Some years ago, China took draconian efforts to contain its population growth at 1 billion people by restricting families to one child through forced abortions, and financial and even physical forms of punishment, for having more than the authorized number of children. Families restricted to one child preferred boys, which resulted in abortions or abandonment of baby girls. Having a society where males outnumber females may create a serious social problem as large numbers of males find themselves unable to find mates. Despite Herculean efforts to the contrary, the social experiment to contain the nation's population at 1 billion has obviously failed; China's current population is 1.3 billion and climbing.

The rate of world population growth expanded between 1951 and 1964, peaked, and then started a long-term decline, which is projected to be 0.5 percent per year. On a global scale, the average number of children per family has to decline to reduce the population growth rate. But other forces are at work that may effectively cut the increase in population growth, if not the population itself. The fall of communism in 1991, and the subsequent economic turmoil, brought about a decade of a declining birthrate and a shortening of the average life span, resulting in a negative population growth rate in Russia. Diseases such as HIV/AIDS are ravaging the population in sub-Saharan Africa along with social disintegration, civil upheaval, tribal warfare, and, on occasion, holocausts. Some rapidly growing nations such as Bangladesh must be close to, or have already exceeded, their capacity to adequately feed, clothe, and shelter their populations. Similar to Easter Island, Haiti has removed so many trees that the barren land is visible from space as is its boundary with the verdant Dominican Republic. Haitians cannot find sufficient wood to build shelters and burn as

Figure 1.3  **Actual and Projected World Population**

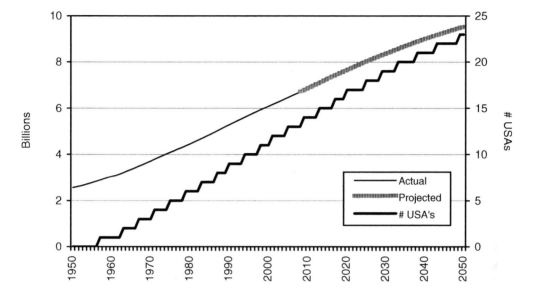

fuel. The removal of the forests has exposed hilltop soil to erosion, which, during the rainy season, has washed down and covered the fertile soil in the valleys, reducing food production. Haiti is on an irreversible course to environmental oblivion, but unlike the Easter Islanders, Haitians are not forced to remain in Haiti and starve: They can flee. Various forms of flu seem to be on the verge of jumping from animals to humans, which could bring on a new Spanish Flu-type pandemic. Modern means of travel make it nearly impossible to isolate or quarantine an outbreak of contagious diseases. Weapons of mass destruction and terrorism are other threats to human survival. Considering all these factors, the projected population of over 9 billion people by 2050, as shown in Figure 1.3, a 30 percent increase from current levels, is not a foregone conclusion.

In one century, we'll be adding the equivalent population of twenty-three United States of Americas (population increments of 300 million). This is a single, though long, lifetime. What will it be like in the succeeding hundred years? Exponential growth, like bacteria overflowing the confines of a Petri dish, is ultimately unsustainable.

## THE CASE OF DOUBLE EXPONENTIAL GROWTH

An oil company executive once observed that the oil industry benefits from two exponential curves: population and per capita energy consumption. Both work together to promote a greater volume of consumption of oil products and, presumably, greater corporate revenues and profits.

To illustrate double exponential growth, suppose that the population is growing at 1 percent per year and per capita energy consumption is growing at 2 percent per year. Further, suppose that the initial total annual consumption of energy for 100 people is 500 barrels of oil, or 5 barrels of oil per person per year. At the end of 25 years, energy consumption would have doubled from 500 barrels to 1,021 barrels for a composite annual growth rate of 2.89 percent. In 100 years energy consumption would be 9,510, nearly 20 times the original amount—the miracle of double exponential growth.

Figure 1.4  **Per Capita Energy Consumption for the World and for China**

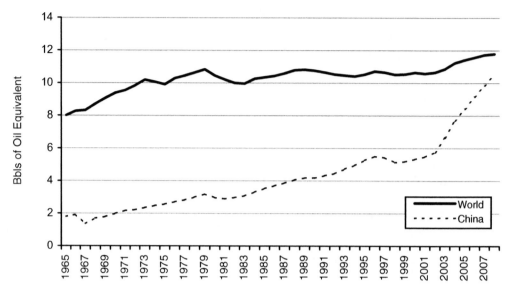

Figure 1.4 shows the per capita consumption of energy for the world and for China from 1965 to 2008. Energy consists of conventional sources of energy (oil, natural gas, coal, nuclear, and hydropower), excluding biomass and alternative energy sources. Energy is expressed in terms of barrels of oil equivalent, which is the equivalent amount of oil that would have to be consumed to release the same amount of energy. A barrel is forty-two gallons, or about three refills of a gasoline tank.

As with China, the world population continues its unremitting climb, with energy consumption rising faster than the population prior to the oil crisis in 1973. High prices in the wake of the crisis slowed energy consumption. The 1973 oil crisis proved that energy consumption is price-sensitive. Per capita energy consumption remained relatively constant until 2002 when it resumed its upward trend primarily caused by the industrialization of China, India, and other nations in Southeast Asia. Much of the steadying of per capita consumption has been caused by a major decline in energy usage in the former Soviet Union after the 1991 fall of communism. Russia has been slowly emerging from its era of economic turmoil. Another factor at work is the decoupling of economic and energy growth in the developed world (United States, Europe, and Japan). Economic activity is less dependent on energy than in the past. Where once 5 percent growth in economic activity was accompanied by a 5 percent growth in energy consumption, now it is 3 percent growth in energy consumption in the United States and even less in Europe. This decoupling of economic and energy growth can be explained by heavy industries, large consumers of energy, moving from the United States and Europe to developing nations in Asia; the rise of the service industry at the expense of manufacturing; and greater energy efficiency in industrial processes, motor vehicles, and home appliances. However, these mitigating factors can no longer compensate for the emergence of India and China as major economic powers. Figure 1.4 shows China, which had significantly lagged in world per capita energy consumption, is rapidly catching up. The double exponential growth curves in China, India, and elsewhere in Asia representing about 40 percent of the world's population have major implications for energy suppliers, consumers, and those responsible for formulating energy policies.

## A LESSON IN FISH

Fish is a finite resource that has the property of being sustainable or nonsustainable, depending on the volume of the catch. If it does not seem possible that resources can disappear in a relatively short time as on Easter Island or in one generation as illustrated in Figure 1.1, ponder the world output of fish. It has been transformed from a sustainable to a nonsustainable resource in one generation. Until this generation, the annual fish catch in the world's oceans was less than the reproduction rate, which maintained the fish population. In one generation—our generation—the population of fish, particularly in open-ocean waters, has been severely diminished.

The Grand Banks off Newfoundland is a series of raised submarine plateaus in relatively shallow waters where the cold southbound Labrador Current interacts with the warm northbound Gulf Stream. It is a living paradise for marine life. When John Cabot discovered the Grand Banks 500 years ago, codfish were so plentiful that they were caught by hanging empty wicker baskets over the ship's side.[2] A century later, English fishing skippers reported cod shoals so thick that it was difficult to row a boat through them. Individual fish were six and seven feet long and weighed as much as 200 pounds. Other signs of abundant life were oysters as large as shoes, children collecting ten- to twenty-pound lobsters with hand rakes during low tide, and rivers choked with salmon, herring, squid, and other sea life. Now the cod are gone and the rivers and streams are quiet, essentially devoid of marine life.

Cod fishing became a victim of modern technology. In 1951, a trawler four times larger than a conventional fishing vessel sailed into the waters of the Grand Banks. Large gantry cranes supported cables, winches, and gear to operate huge nets that were let out and then pulled up a stern ramp to dump the fish straight into an onboard fish processing plant. Automated filleting and fishmeal rendering machines made short work of the catch. The trawler was manned by several crews to allow fishing twenty-four hours a day, seven days a week, for weeks on end. Schools of fish were quickly located with fish-finding sonar, greatly enhancing the vessel's productivity. As time went on trawlers increased in number, size, and technological sophistication until they could tow nets with gaping openings 3,500 feet in circumference that swallowed and hauled in 100–200 tons of fish per hour. The trawlers maintained essentially uninterrupted operations with awaiting tenders to transfer crews and fish. By the 1970s, more than 700 high-tech trawlers were in operation around the world, strip-mining the oceans of marine life.

Though it would be convenient to blame this situation on the greed of capitalist-owned fishing companies, over half these trawlers were from the Soviet Union. Both the Soviet Union and capitalist nations, through government subsidies to build and finance trawlers, were heavy promoters of developing and building ever-larger trawlers. These vessels, equipped with longer and wider nets, greater fish-processing capacity, and more accurate fish finders, were built to bring home large quantities of protein to feed a growing population. The outcome was predictable, or at least it should have been, since the trawlers could scoop up fish far faster than they could reproduce. The cod catch peaked in 1968 at 810,000 tons, three times that of 1951 when the first generation of technically advanced fish trawlers made their appearance on the Grand Banks. To combat the precipitous decline that set in after 1968, Canada unilaterally extended its territorial waters from 12 to 200 miles. While other nations were prohibited from entering these waters, Canadian fishermen took advantage of the situation by adding modern fishing vessels to their fleets. The catch fell to 122,000 tons in 1991, forcing the Canadian government to close the Grand Banks to allow fishing stocks to replenish. This devastated the Canadian fishing industry, which in its heyday employed tens of thousands of people.

Much to everyone's surprise, the codfish population never recouped. Dredge-like trawls, designed to harvest marine life from the bottom of the Grand Banks by scouring an area the size of a footfall field, permanently ruined the habitat for juvenile cod. Without a habitat for juveniles, from whence do the adults come? However, one benefit was that the catch of shrimp and crab, the food for juvenile cod, has improved, providing an alternative, though far smaller, source of revenue for fishermen.

In the twenty-first century, sonar technology can locate schools of fish and fine-mesh fishnets tens of miles long can strip the ocean of all life above the size of minnows. The population for some species of fish has dropped to a point where males are finding it difficult to locate females, or vice versa, in the vast ocean spaces. One example is the catch of North Sea cod that has fallen so precipitously in the early 2000s that scientists feared that there might not be enough mature fish left to maintain the population and called for a moratorium on fishing to allow the cod population to recuperate. But Scottish fishermen reacted to this advice with outrage.

Figure 1.5 shows that world marine production (fish caught on the high seas) peaked in 1989 and then declined for a few years. This peak was thought to be the start of a permanent decline, but world marine production recouped and seemingly stabilized.[3] Leveling off of the fish harvest in open ocean waters was not caused by a rising fish population but by greater numbers of even more efficient fishing trawlers harvesting a diminishing resource. Long lines with thousands of baited hooks stretching for eighty miles and drift nets up to forty miles in length, responsible for the death of countless birds and sea mammals, have got to be the ultimate in open-ocean strip-mining.

The number of larger and more efficient trawlers doubled between 1970 and the early 1990s and has grown since then, yet the total catch remained more or less stable. This suggests that the average catch per vessel fell despite the greater capital investment in capacity and technology. Indeed, tons of catch per registered gross ton of fishing vessels fell from 5.4 tons in 1970 to 3.6 tons in 1992, a one-third decline. Lower productivity does not necessarily mean a smaller return on investment if the price of fish escalates enough to compensate for smaller catches. For many nations, fish is an important part of the diet and governments are not willing to cut off this supply of protein, regardless of the long-term consequences (shades of Easter Island). Another reason why so many governments are reluctant to put effective international controls on fishing is to protect their investment in the form of government subsidies for trawler acquisition and financing. This is what is going on in oil. More money is being spent on wells to tap diminishing reserves in more difficult environments, but profitability can be maintained despite higher capital and operating costs and lower output by a compensating increase in price.

Unlike the Easter Islanders, we have not stood idly by in the face of depleting fish resources in the world's oceans. Many maritime nations have enacted programs to preserve the fish population within their territorial waters by regulating the timing, size, and volume of fish and other marine life that can be caught. As an example, marine biologists survey the egg population of herring in territorial Alaskan waters from the air because the untold billions of herring eggs make the normally dark waters milky white. From their observations they can estimate the herring population and, through a government regulatory agency, mandate the area and timing of the herring harvest. The harvest of herring is controlled on the basis of preserving a resource to ensure its long-term viability rather than depleting a resource in the quest for short-term profits. The volume of the herring harvest is not regulated, only the allowable area and the permitted time for harvesting. Licenses control the number of fishing boats and the nature of the technology being employed. If it is felt that the volume harvested is too great and endangering the population, more stringent restrictions on area and timing and licensing are enacted. If the population of herring is rising, then the restrictions are relaxed.

Regulating fishing in a nation's territorial waters is practiced throughout much of the world. But it is a palliative, not a cure, as fish are free to migrate in and out of territorial waters. Little headway has been made in passing an international convention on open-ocean fishing that would position fishing as a sustaining activity rather than depleting a natural resource. The politically correct-sounding International Convention on Fishing and Conservation of the Living Resources of the High Seas went into force in 1966, but apparently its provisions are either not effective or not effectively enforced to sustain the long-term viability of commercial sea life in international waters.

Those who maintain that nothing can be done to protect open-ocean fish resources should look at the international regulation of the whaling industry. The International Convention for the Regulation of Whaling was proposed in 1946 and came into force in 1948 when the requisite number of nations had ratified it. The Whaling Commission meets annually and determines protected and unprotected species; open and closed seasons and waters; designation of sanctuary areas, size limits, and the maximum catch for each species; and permissible methods, types, and specifications of whaling gear. The commission also controls the methods of measurement and maintains the requisite statistical and biological records, and places tough restrictions on location and season to ensure that the catch does not exceed certain limits. The whale population for various species is monitored to see if any adjustments have to be made to relax or strengthen restrictions on whaling activities.

The international convention on whaling has been responsible for preventing the extinction of various species of whales and also promoting their recovery despite criticism of the Japanese whaling fleet for allegedly violating convention rules. This successful convention not only had a highly desirable environmental impact on sea life, but could also serve as a model for the administration and enforcement of an international convention on open-ocean fishing. However, in all fairness, trying to monitor and control fishing fleets numbering in the millions scattered throughout the world through a system of licenses and quotas would, for all practical purposes, be impossible. The task of the Whaling Commission is made easier by virtue of there being relatively few whaling fleets restricted to only a handful of nations. However, if the world's maritime nations had the collective will to assume the responsibility for monitoring fishing vessels calling on ports within their jurisdiction, or outlawing those practices that essentially strip-mine the ocean of fish, then it might be possible to reverse the further diminishment of a valuable resource.

## FROM HUNTING TO FARMING

Figure 1.5 also shows a successful countermeasure to overexploiting a natural resource. The rising price of fish has created a new industry: fish farming—agricultural enterprises dedicated to raising fish. Fish pens in protected waters in Norway and Canada supply much of the salmon found in the world's marketplace. Decades ago, farmers in the southern United States could not make a living growing and selling grain until they discovered that they could make a living by throwing grain into a pond and selling the catfish. Trout, tilapia, and shrimp are also farmed. Tilapia originated in Africa and was farmed in ponds and rice paddies in Asia for generations; now tilapia is farmed throughout the world. As seen in Figure 1.5, the tonnage of aquaculture production, or fish farming, has grown thirteen-fold in thirty years, providing nearly one-third of total fish consumption.

To be sure, there is opposition to aquaculture, or fish farming, including the potential environmental impact of thousands of tons of waste collected under fish pens, the biological treatments necessary to prevent the spread of disease in crowded fish pens, plus the consequences of fish escaping from an artificial to a natural environment. On the other hand, the human population

Figure 1.5  **Fish Harvest**

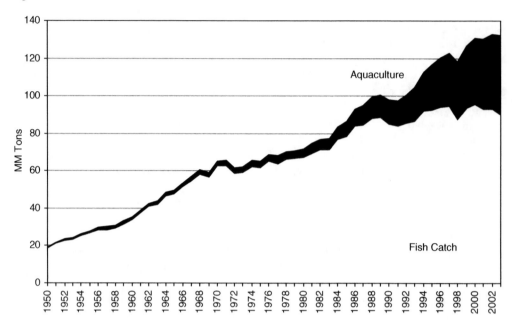

needs to be fed, and providing fish from fish farms rather than depleting the world's open-ocean resources seems to have an inherent advantage that should not be ignored.

## ENERGY DEPLETION

The point of all this is that a trend line indicating that a resource will be exhausted in thirty years need not happen. Unlike fish, which could recuperate in numbers if allowed to, fossil fuels such as coal, oil, and natural gas cannot replenish themselves (ignoring for now speculation about the possible nonorganic origin of natural gas from deep within the earth). With regard to energy, sustainable sources of energy (biofuels, solar, and wind) would be akin to fish farming. The viability of sustainable sources of energy can be assured by a high price on a diminishing source of nonsustainable (fossil) fuel.

We have already set the precedent of having an international convention to preserve a natural resource. International conventions can be successful in preserving natural resources (whales) or unsuccessful (open-ocean fish). As with whales and, perhaps, someday with fish, some form of cooperative action may be necessary to preserve another worldwide resource—energy—if only to prevent the inevitable result of doing nothing: having a planetary-scale Easter Island blowout.

## NOTES

1. Population statistics are from the U.S. Census Bureau Web site, and energy statistics are from the *BP Statistical Review of World Energy* (London: British Petroleum, 2009).

2. Colin Woodard, "A Run on the Banks," *E-Magazine* (March–April 2001).

3. Food and Agricultural Organization of the United Nations (FAO), as listed on the World Resources Institute Web site www.earthtrends.org.

# ELECTRICITY AND THE UTILITY INDUSTRY

The primary fuels are coal, oil, natural gas, nuclear, hydro, biomass, and renewables, but these are not the forms of energy we encounter most often. Other than driving a car and heating a home, the form of energy we are most accustomed to comes from turning on a switch. We use electricity for lighting and running all sorts of electrical appliances and equipment. It is absolutely essential to running a modern economy. Yet, electricity is a secondary form of energy derived from primary fuels. This chapter deals with electricity as a source and use of energy, its origin, the organizational structure of utilities, system operation, and models for determining rates.

## IT TAKES ENERGY TO MAKE ENERGY

Burning a ton of oil releases a certain amount of energy, but burning a ton of coal does not release quite the same amount of energy and burning 1 million cubic feet of natural gas—well, that is hard to compare to a ton of oil or coal. In order to have a common measure for comparison purposes, it is convenient to talk about 1 ton of oil equivalent. This is the amount of energy released by various sources that is equivalent to the amount of energy released by 1 ton of oil. Energy terminology can be quite confusing, but total world primary energy consumption in 2008 can be expressed simply as 11.3 billion tons of oil equivalent.[1] Though this is a large number that taxes one's imagination, it can be brought into perspective by remembering that there are 6.8 billion of us. Thus, total consumption works out to about 1.66 tons of oil equivalent per person per year, or 11.6 barrels of oil equivalent (7 barrels to 1 ton), or 487 gallons (42 gallons in a barrel) of oil equivalent per year, or 1.3 gallons of all primary sources of energy expressed in oil equivalents per person per day. This is an understandable figure and 1.3 gallons of all fuel types per person is not a large number, but again, there are 6.8 billion of us. Moreover, per capita consumption is not equally divided among the world's population—there is an enormous difference between the amount consumed by an American and what everybody else in the world consumes.

As shown in Figure 2.1, the largest single source of energy is oil, which satisfies 31 percent of world demand, followed by coal (26 percent), natural gas (22 percent), biomass (10 percent), hydro (6 percent), nuclear (5 percent), and renewables including geothermal, wind, and solar (less than 1 percent). Of these totals electricity generation consumes all nuclear and hydro, 83 percent of renewable (the remainder is mainly solar thermal heating), 68 percent of coal (the remainder is mainly for steel production), 39 percent of natural gas, and less than 1 percent of oil and biomass.

Most biomass is burned for heat and cooking in the developing world, although a small, but growing portion is being converted to motor vehicle fuels. Oil has far greater value as a motor vehicle fuel than a boiler fuel. However, a portion of the bottom of the barrel—the residue left after refining crude oil and certain waxy crude oils too difficult to refine—are burned as fuel for generating electricity.

Figure 2.1  **World Energy Consumption** (MM Tons of Oil Equivalent)

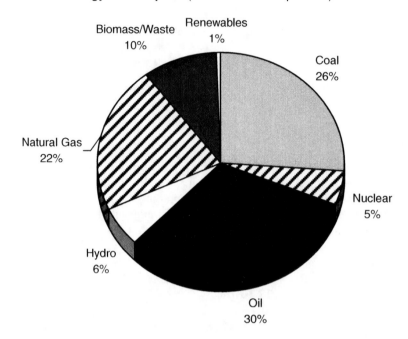

A comparison of the energy output to input for electricity generation shows that the output is about 35 percent of the input. What happened to the remaining 65 percent? The answer is that 65 percent of the energy consumed in generating electricity is thrown away. Most of it is passed to the environment by heating the atmosphere or the water in rivers, lakes, bays, and oceans. Electricity produced by steam, be it fossil or nuclear power, is inherently energy-inefficient. Water is heated to produce steam, steam drives a turbine which in turn drives an electricity generator. The latent heat of vaporization is the heat absorbed to transform water from a liquid to a vapor state, a considerable amount of energy witnessed when heating a pot of water for tea. Steam produced in a boiler is fed to the high-pressure end of a turbine. The efficiency of generating electricity can be enhanced by maximizing the steam pressure differential between the high- and low-pressure ends of a turbine. This is done by increasing the steam pressure entering the high-pressure end of the turbine and reducing the low-pressure end of the turbine to a vacuum by condensing the spent steam to a liquid. The latent heat of vaporization is passed to the water of a river, lake, bay, or ocean via a condenser. Sometimes the warmed condenser water is cooled for recirculation by transferring heat to air in a cooling tower or to a cooling pond. Either way, the latent heat of vaporization contained in the spent steam is lost.

The condensed steam, now in the form of hot water, is pumped back to the boiler where it must reabsorb the latent heat of vaporization to become steam again for another cycle through the turbine. Thus, a typical generator's output of electricity is only about 25–35 percent of the energy input to generate electricity depending on its age and inherent efficiency. Modern high-efficiency steam turbines can operate at around 40 percent, but they can't overcome the inherent loss of the latent heat of vaporization. Another 5–10 percent of the energy content of electricity is lost in transmission and distribution. Heating water in a teakettle using electricity takes three to four times more energy than heating the water directly by flame. Heating is not a good use

Figure 2.2    **Growth in World Electricity Demand** (Terawatt Hours)

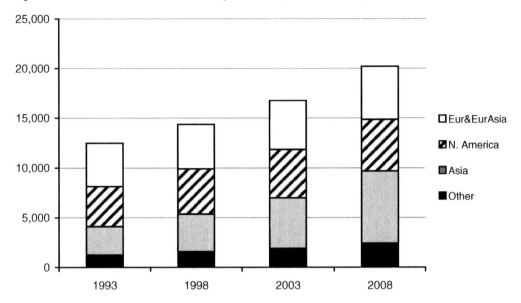

of electricity. A better use is providing lighting and running appliances. Heating a home can be much more efficiently accomplished with heating oil and natural gas, or even coal and firewood, than by electricity.

## ENERGY FOR ELECTRICITY GENERATION

Figure 2.2 shows that the average annual growth in world electricity demand was 3.2 percent per year from 1993 to 2008. Rates of growth on a regional basis vary considerably. The former Soviet Union had a negative growth rate after the fall of communism in 1989, reflecting the economic floundering that plagued this group of nations. The decline in electricity generation reached its nadir in 1998 and has been slowly recuperating since then. Europe and EurAsia, which includes the former Soviet Union, have the smallest growth in electricity consumption at 1.3 percent per year, followed by North America at 1.7 percent per year. Asia has an average 15-year growth rate of 4.1 percent with aggregate growth of other regions (South America, Africa, and the Middle East) at 6.4 percent. These growth rates may not seem high, but they make a difference over time. In 1993, Asia consumed 23 percent of total generated electricity and 36 percent in 2008. As clearly shown in Figure 2.2, Asia has become the largest regional consumer of electricity, led by China and India.

The relative importance of the world's leading electricity-generating nations is shown in Figure 2.3. In 2008, the United States led, generating 21 percent of the world's electricity, followed by a rapidly growing China with 17 percent. Together, these two nations accounted for 38 percent of the world's electricity generation; the top four nations for half; and the dozen nations in Figure 2.3 for 70 percent of world electricity generation.

Electricity demand is slated to grow by 2.5 percent annually to the year 2030. Though this appears to be a modest growth rate, 1,700 gigawatts of capacity will have to be added between 2007 and 2015 and another 2,800 gigawatts between 2015 and 2030 (notice how the magnitude

Figure 2.3   **Leading Nations' Share of Electricity Generation**

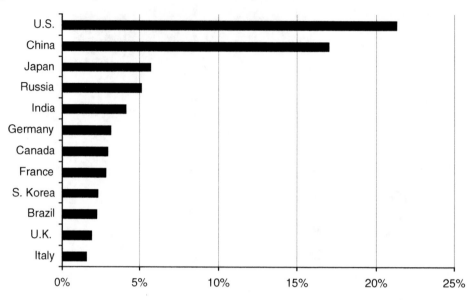

of the expansion has to increase to accommodate a constant growth rate). The total investment for power generation, transmission, and distribution is estimated at $13.6 trillion in 2007 dollars, with Asia having a rapidly growing share. To put a gigawatt, or 1,000 megawatts, or 1 billion watts into perspective, a one-GW plant can supply a city of about 1 million people, or less depending on the industrial load. The largest consumer of electricity, the United States, has a projected growth in electricity demand that is considerably less than 2.5 percent per year. The annual growth in U.S. electricity demand averaged 9 percent in the 1950s, 7.3 percent in the 1960s, 4.2 percent in the 1970s, 3.1 percent in the 1980s, 2.4 percent in the 1990s, 1.1 percent from 2000 to 2007, and is projected to increase 1.0 percent from 2007 to 2030. The reasons for the continual drop-off are structural changes in the economy from manufacturing to service industries, the impact of higher electricity rates, and the imposition of efficiency standards along with improved efficiency of electrical powered devices.[2] It is possible that the projected growth rate could be only 0.83 percent with an outside chance of being only 0.68 percent. This would be achieved primarily through efficiency enhancement, such as the normal replacement of home central air-conditioning units being the most efficient central air conditioning available (ductless inverter-driven mini-split heat pumps) regardless of cost. This logic is carried through for all electricity loads in residential, commercial, and industrial use to arrive at these lower assessments. Needless to say, the needed investment in generating and transmission capacity falls with these lower assessments of growth.[3]

About one-third of humanity is not connected to an electricity grid. Economic development projects are commonly dedicated to bringing electricity to places where much of human effort is spent in the daily drudgery of trekking twenty miles for wood and dung for fuel to heat and cook and manually lifting water from deep wells. While some of the capital spending will expand the electricity grid to those without access to electricity, many will still not be connected by 2030. Even so, trillions of dollars in capital investments to upgrade and expand the global electricity generation and distribution system raises the issues of where these funds are going to come from and, for the developing world, the ability of people to pay electricity rates sufficient to service these enormous capital outlays.

In 2006, only 433 terawatt hours were generated from renewable sources (biomass/waste, wind, solar, geothermal, tide and wave). This is slated to grow to 2,896 terawatt hours in 2030, an impressive nearly seven-fold expansion. But with electricity demand expected to grow from 18,921 terawatt hours to 33,265 terrawatt hours in 2030, the proportion of electricity provided by renewable sources expands from 2 percent to only 9 percent. Coal, which renewable sources are supposed to replace, is expected to increase its share from 41 percent in 2006 to 44 percent in 2030 because of declining shares in natural gas, hydro, and nuclear. Hence, coal will dominate in electricity generation unless a charge is made against carbon emissions that will provide a greater economic incentive for generation facilities powered by nuclear and renewables.

## ENHANCING EFFICIENCY IN ELECTRICITY GENERATION

As mentioned, depending on the age and nature of the electricity-generating plant, typical efficiencies for a utility plant range from 25–35 percent. This can be substantially increased for an industrial plant that consumes both electricity and hot water. The plant can buy electricity from a utility to run the plant and to heat water. Alternatively, a cogeneration plant can be installed on the site that generates electricity required by the plant. The heated water containing the latent heat of vaporization is not thrown away to heat the air or some body of water as with a utility, but consumed internally as a source of hot water. Being able to utilize the latent heat of vaporization and eliminate transmission-line losses by having an on-site cogeneration plant can significantly increase the efficiency of generating electricity. The combined-cycle cogeneration plant has the highest efficiency of all electricity-generating plants. Natural gas first fuels a gas turbine that drives an electricity generator. The hot exhaust gases from the turbine heat water in a boiler for conventional steam generation of electricity. By capturing the heat of vaporization in the condenser water for internal purposes, the resulting efficiency can be between 60 and 65 percent.

Unfortunately, only about 3 percent of U.S. electricity generation is by cogeneration. Cogeneration units are sized to the needs of an industrial plant and, therefore, lack the inherent economies of scale of the much larger-capacity electricity generators of a utility. The economics may favor buying a lot more electricity from a utility to run a plant and heat the water than producing electricity at the plant with a cogeneration unit and utilizing the waste energy as a source of hot water. The irony is that the price of buying electricity from a utility reflects the cost of passing the latent heat of vaporization to the environment. Despite the efficiency of cogeneration plants, most electricity-generating utilities are not keen about losing a customer. Although government policies favor cogeneration plants to enhance energy efficiency, utilities have little incentive to cooperate. Some degree of governmental coercion, or some form of incentive, must be provided to overcome a utility's reluctance to lose a customer to a cogeneration unit.

Some cogeneration plants burn coal to produce steam, which can also be superheated by burning natural gas. The boiler fuel can also be biogas from animal or human wastes, methane from landfills, and agricultural and industrial waste products. Cogeneration plants in the pulp and paper industry consume waste (bark, wood scraps, and the processing residue of papermaking called black liquor) as fuel to generate electricity. Hot water generated from condensing spent steam is consumed internally in the papermaking process. Sugar mills burn waste sugarcane (bagasse) to generate electricity and utilize the hot water from the condenser in the sugar production process. The steel industry burns gases given off from open-hearth steel-making facilities to produce steam for generating electricity to power blast furnace air compressors. If air rather than water captures the latent heat of vaporization from a steam turbine, the heated air can be used for drying agricultural crops and lumber.

## EARLY HISTORY OF ELECTRICITY

Although one might think that the definition of electricity is obvious—it is what turns the light bulb on—the nature of electricity is not that easy to comprehend. Electrical energy that keeps a light bulb shining is similar to X-rays, light, microwaves, and communication signals except that it has a much lower frequency (60 cycles per second in the United States and 50 cycles per second in Europe). Electrical energy is also known as electromagnetic energy, consisting of magnetic and electrostatic fields that move in the vicinity of wires near the speed of light in response to the movement or vibration of electrons.

Matter is made up of atoms, which consist of protons, neutrons, and electrons. Protons have a positive charge and electrons a negative charge. When present in equal numbers, there is no net charge; when imbalanced, there is a charge called static electricity. The nature of matter was not known in 600 BCE when Greeks generated a spark by rubbing amber with fur. The term *electricity* is derived from the Greek word for amber. The discovery in the thirteenth century that lodestones align themselves with the magnetic north pole when free to turn made long sea voyages beyond the sight of land possible, opening up the Age of Exploration. The connection between electricity and magnetism would not be known for another six centuries.[4]

Among the eighteenth-century scientists interested in electricity was Benjamin Franklin, who established the convention of positive and negative charge and the presumed directional flow of electricity. In this, he made an error, scrupulously preserved to this day. His experiment—flying a kite in a lightning storm with a key attached to the end—could have killed him. Lucky for him, a passing bolt of lightning was far enough away to induce only a small current in the kite string that reached the key, causing a spark to jump to Franklin's hand. He concluded that the spark from lightning was the same as a spark from rubbing amber with fur.

The knowledge of electricity advanced one step at a time during the nineteenth century. Charles Coulomb discovered that a charge of electricity weakened with the same inverse square law that Newton had discovered for gravity. For this, his name was attached to a measure of electrical charge, the coulomb. Luigi Galvani, while dissecting a frog, noted that its legs began to twitch. Galvani thought that the cause might have been from lightning in the vicinity. After some experiments, Alessandro Volta decided that two dissimilar metals, the knife and the tray holding the frog, was the actual cause of the twitching. From this he developed the voltaic pile, the forerunner of the battery made of disks of two dissimilar metals such as zinc and copper or silver separated by paper soaked in saltwater. Electricity flowed through the pile when Volta completed the circuit with a copper wire. Although Napoleon honored Volta by making him a count, Volta was more permanently memorialized by having his name attached to a measure of the electromotive force represented by a difference in a given electrical charge, the volt. Galvani was not forgotten and was memorialized in the phrase *galvanic action,* the corrosive interaction of dissimilar metals, and in the verb *galvanize,* to stimulate action as if by electric shock. André-Marie Ampère was one of the first to establish a relationship between magnetism and electricity, inaugurating a new field of study called electromagnetism. As with other discoveries, Hans Oersted simultaneously and independently performed experiments that demonstrated the same relationship. But the honor went to Ampère by having his name attached to a unit of electrical current, the ampere. Oersted was not completely forgotten: the unit of magnetic intensity, the oersted, was named after him. Georg Ohm originated Ohm's Law, which linked electrical potential, a volt, with electrical current, an amp or ampere, passing through a unit of electrical resistance named after him, an ohm.

Michael Faraday, considered one of the greatest experimenters of all time, started out as a bookbinder's assistant who read the books that he was supposed to be binding. He developed an interest in chemistry but was encouraged to switch to electromagnetism, where his repetition of Oersted's experiments led to his discovery of electromagnetic induction. Faraday could induce an electric current by either moving a magnet through a loop of wire or moving a loop of wire over a stationary magnet. From this he developed an electric dynamo, the progenitor of the modern electricity generator. Faraday's experimental work and "lines of force" inspired James Maxwell to mathematically describe the behavior of electricity and magnetism. Faraday postulated that light was a form of electromagnetic wave; a conclusion also reached by Maxwell when he discovered that the speed of electromagnetic waves was close to that of light. Maxwell's equations became the building blocks for Einstein's theories.

## GENERATING ELECTRICITY

An electric current is the flow of electrical charge. When an electric current passes through a conductor such as copper wire, the electrons in the copper are forced to either flow quite slowly in one direction for direct current or vibrate back and forth for alternating current. Electrical energy travels by moving or vibrating the electrons within metallic conductors much as sound waves are propagated by vibrating air molecules. The speed of sound, of the order of 345 meters per second or 770 miles an hour, is not caused by air molecules moving at the speed of sound but by the speed of sound waves propagated by vibrating air molecules. Similarly, electrical energy is not propagated by electrons moving at the speed of light through wires; but by electromagnetic fields traveling close to the speed of light that are associated with the vibration or movement of electrons.

Electricity is a charge measured in coulombs; electrical energy is measured in joules; and electrical power, the flow of energy over time, is measured in watts (one joule per second), a term to honor James Watt for his work in measuring the equivalent horsepower output of a steam engine. As has become customary, if not traditional, the terms *electricity* and *electrical energy* are used interchangeably even though they are technically quite different.

Generators cannot make electricity (technically electrical energy) because electricity is a property of matter. An electricity generator "pumps" an electrical charge back and forth inside a wire sixty times per second, and the electromagnetic fields created around the wire are what is known as electrical energy. Electrical energy flowing through a motor, heater, or light bulb over a period of time becomes electrical power that turns the rotor and warms or lights a room. The electricity industry converts various sources of energy into a single indistinguishable product that is easily distributed for lighting, heating, and running machinery, equipment, and appliances. This is quite unlike the oil industry, which converts a single source of energy into a wide variety of products ranging from motor vehicle fuels to plastics.

To produce electricity, a turbine is rotated to drive an electricity generator. Steam is the most common motive force of rotating a turbine and is produced by burning coal, oil, natural gas, biomass, or from a geothermal or nuclear source. Falling water, tidal currents, river flow, wave action, and wind are other motive forces to rotate a turbine. The only manmade source of electricity not created by rotating a turbine is a solar photoelectric cell that converts sunlight directly into electricity. Our capacity to generate electricity pales into insignificance when compared to nature. Enormous circulating electrical currents surrounding the core create the earth's magnetic field. Lightning occurs when the buildup of static electricity at different cloud levels, or between a cloud and the earth, creates a voltage differential large enough to overcome the resistance of air to conduct electricity. If lightning could be harnessed, it would easily fulfill humanity's dream of unlimited and free electrical energy.

## GENERATING ELECTRICITY COMMERCIALLY

Thomas Edison invented the electric light bulb in 1878 by trial and error. It was the end result of innumerable attempts to find a filament material that could conduct electrical current to the point of incandescence without burning up. Edison was also an astute businessman and founded the first investor-owned utility in 1882. The Pearl Street station lit up lower New York with direct current from electricity generators powered by reciprocating coal-fueled steam engines. He was challenged by George Westinghouse, who backed Nikola Tesla's alternating-current electricity generators. In this contest between two industrial giants, Edison publicly backed the idea of an alternating current electric chair for the state of New York to demonstrate its inherent danger. He won the contest of having an alternating current electric chair, but lost the larger contest as to whether homes and businesses would be fed by direct or alternating current. The problem with direct current was that it could not be distributed over a wide area without significant line losses. In Edison's world, direct current electricity would be distributive in nature with many plants, each serving a small area.

Alternating current was superior to direct current in that it could be transmitted over long distances at a high voltage with relatively small line losses. Alternating current allows for a small number of large centralized generating plants with their inherent economies of scale to serve a wide area via long-distance transmission lines. In 1895 Westinghouse built the first commercial alternating current electricity-generating plant at Niagara Falls, the progenitor for all future electricity-generating plants. Although Niagara Falls used hydropower to turn the generators, Westinghouse also spearheaded the development of the steam turbine, the brainchild of William Rankine. The substitution of the steam turbine for the steam engine increased the thermal efficiency for generating electricity from 5 percent with a reciprocating steam engine ultimately to 35–40 percent for a modern steam turbine.

Generation of electricity (the capital investment plus operating and fuel costs) makes up about one-half of the delivered cost of electricity; the remainder is transmission and distribution costs. Transmission lines, bundles of copper or aluminum wires usually above but sometimes below ground, carry electrical current at several hundred thousand volts from generators to local distribution companies. Transmission makes up 5–15 percent of the delivered cost of electricity to cover capital, operating, and maintenance costs. Electrical energy heats up transmission lines, which expand (lengthen), causing transmission lines to droop noticeably under heavy load. The dissipation of this heat to the environment is known as line losses. In the United States, the average line loss is 7 percent of generated electricity, but actual losses between two points vary with the amount of electrical energy passing through the transmission lines, their design characteristics, the surrounding environmental conditions, and the distance traversed. The remainder of the delivered cost of electricity is local distribution that steps down the voltage through transformers, routes the electricity to individual homes, businesses, and industries, and bills customers, whose payments support the entire financial edifice of the industry.

## SYSTEM OPERATION

Unlike fossil fuels, there is no way to store electricity (batteries are incapable of storing the amount of electricity required to support the operations of a utility). The electricity business is the only one that operates without an inventory. Some maintain that water in back of a dam can be considered stored electricity. Using this logic, a pile of coal sitting outside a generating facility is also stored electricity. But water and coal are not electricity until they provide the motive force to rotate a turbine to drive a generator. Once generated, electrical energy flows at the speed of light between the generator and the consumer when the switch is turned on and stops just as abruptly when the switch is turned off. Unlike oil or natural gas in a pipeline, throttling a valve does not direct the flow of electricity. Electricity follows the path of least resistance. If that path leads to overloading a transmission line and melting the wires, so be it. Although breakers protect transmission lines from overloading, the usual way to decrease the flow of electrical energy through transmission lines from Region A and B is to raise the output of electricity at B and cut the output at A.

During times of low demand, when transmission systems are not limited by capacity constraints, the price of electricity is fairly uniform throughout a region. During times of heavy demand, transmission capacity constraints create local price disparities. For instance, reducing the output at A to prevent overloading the transmission system may involve shutting down a low-cost electricity generator and increasing the output at B, as a substitute source may involve starting up a high-cost electricity generator. This creates a price disparity between points A and B. Another cause of a price disparity between two points is line losses; that is, what goes into a transmission system is not what comes out.

Other than pumped storage plants covered in Chapter 9, there is no way to store large quantities of electricity. The system of generating and transmitting electricity must adjust to variation in demand instantaneously. There is significant variation in demand over the course of a day, when peak daytime demand may be double that of nighttime, over the course of a week, when more electricity is consumed on weekdays than weekends, and over the course of a year, when electricity demand peaks from air conditioning during summer hot spells. In cold climates in areas where electricity heats homes (e.g., eastern Canada), peak demand occurs during the winter. With some exceptions, such as where there is sufficient hydro plant capacity to satisfy peak loads, peaking generators have to be purchased. These are usually combustion turbines (modified jet engines) fueled by natural gas that may run for only a few days or a week or so during an entire year. Amortizing the cost of peaking generators over such a short period of operating time makes for extremely expensive electricity. Yet, if peaking generators are not available, blackouts ensue unless other arrangements have been made to curb demand.

In one such arrangement, operators of office buildings and factories are paid by the utility to disconnect during times of peak seasonal demand and supply themselves with power by operating their emergency backup generators. Another arrangement is for heavy users of electricity to slow operations during times of peak demand and shift some of the load to times of reduced demand. Some plants (e.g., aluminum smelting) have their own electricity-generating capacity. During times of peak demand, it may be more profitable for these plants to curtail production and sell excess electricity to utilities. Other companies pay a lower rate for an interruptible supply of electricity and are willing to be disconnected for a few hours a day during times of peak demand to benefit from lower-cost electricity for the rest of the year. Companies desiring uninterrupted service pay a higher rate to ensure that there is always enough generating capacity available to sustain their operations.

Another way to handle peak demand is to institute demand management. One form of demand management is installing timers on appliances, such as hot-water heaters, so that they operate only during nighttime lulls in electricity demand. The more common form of demand management is time-of-day metering, with electricity rates varying by the hour in response to demand. More costly electricity during times of peak demand creates an incentive for individuals and businesses to reduce their electricity load by turning off their air conditioning for an hour or two when rates (and temperatures) peak. With flat rates that now exist for most consumers, the cost of running an air-conditioning unit is the same regardless of the time of day or night. Consumers are not sensitive to fluctuations in market-priced electricity. Demand management makes them sensitive to the time of day and the day of the week. Running washers and dryers at night and on weekends can significantly reduce electricity bills. The last resort for accommodating peak demand without sufficient generating capacity is controlled rolling blackouts that cover different areas for relatively short periods of time, announced or otherwise, to reduce demand below generating capacity. Failure to take effective action when demand exceeds supply will result in a loss of system control and an unplanned blackout.

System operation is a critical function that controls the output of generators to satisfy demand in real time, where electrical energy flows at the speed of light over the path of least resistance, without the benefit of being able to draw down on inventory. The system operator must deal with imbalances between supply and demand, congestion (overloading transmission lines), and ancillary services. The latter includes power needed to run the system, reserve capacity to meet unexpected demand, backup power plants in case an operating generator fails or a loss of motive force, for example, hydro dams without an adequate water supply, wind turbines when the wind calms, or solar arrays on cloudy days. The system operator is responsible for scheduling (planning the future starting and stopping of generators) and dispatching (real-time starting and stopping). Scheduling and dispatching have to be carefully coordinated to prevent overloading transmission lines while maintaining system stability with continually fluctuating demand. Overloading transmission lines and/or losing system stability are the root causes for blackouts that can spread over large areas of a nation through utility interconnections and last for extended periods of time.

Clearly a cost-effective high-capacity battery would provide an inventory of electricity that could be drawn down during periods of peak demand. This reduces the capacity needed for peak-load generators employed for only days or a few weeks a year. High-capacity batteries would stabilize the system by producing electricity during times of operational difficulties or load imbalances or transmission constraints. The batteries would be recharged at night when there is excess generating capacity to produce cheap electricity. The inventory reserve of cheap electricity can then be expended when electricity is expensive, reducing the average cost of electricity. Technological advances have been made in developing a sodium sulfur battery made of relatively low-cost sulfur, sodium, and ceramics. The battery has to be safeguarded against an accident occurring from its high operating temperature of over 300 degrees Centigrade and the potential for dangerous chemical reactions.[5] Development has been supported by a consortium of Japanese utilities and one U.S. utility, American Electric Power. The batteries can be deployed in distribution grids to improve system reliability, reduce the need for peak-load generators (peak-load shaving), and to store the output from renewable sources (wind, solar) during times of low electricity demand. Other technologies are being explored such as the sodium nickel chloride battery under development in South Africa.

## METHODS OF RATE REGULATION

The century-old approach to electricity was to regulate the industry as a natural monopoly. Multiple transmission and distribution lines from a number of generators, each connected to individual households and businesses to give consumers a choice of provider, would be inordinately expensive. The investment would be much more than having a single wire entering a household or business from a single generator. This would result in high electricity rates to amortize a huge investment in grossly underutilized assets. A natural monopoly comes into being once a decision is made to have only one wire from a single generator connected to each consumer. Once a monopoly is established, a company might be tempted to take advantage of the situation and raise the price of electricity to the point where it would become cheaper to have competitive suppliers with multiple generators and transmission and distribution lines.

There is no inherent impediment to keep monopolists from charging high rates other than their conscience, usually cast aside in the process of becoming a monopolist, and the threat of consumers throwing the switch and doing without. To prevent a natural monopoly from behaving like an actual monopoly, government bodies granting franchises to create natural monopolies also established regulatory agencies to govern rates and oversee business and operating practices. Rates set by regulators cover operating costs and provide a fair rate of return on the monopolists' investments. A fair rate of return takes into consideration the return that can be earned by investing in other businesses of similar risk. A regulated utility serving a franchise area, with rates set to cover costs and provide a return on investment, has little risk compared to a manufacturing company. A manufacturing company must compete against others for the consumer's dollar with little in the way of consumer allegiance if a competitor brings out a better product with a lower price. An adequate return reflecting the inherent risks ensures that a regulated utility can attract sufficient capital to build its asset base to satisfy customer demand. Normally the rate of return for a regulated utility is less than that of a manufacturing company because risks associated with a utility, where rates have to cover costs, are perceived to be less than a manufacturing company having to sell its wares in a competitive marketplace.

Integrated utility companies provide the complete package of generation, transmission, and distribution for a designated area where a single rate covers all costs. Integrated utility companies can obtain high credit ratings if the regulators ensure that rates provide ample cash coverage of interest expenses. A high credit rating results in lower interest rates on debt issued for capital expenditures, which in turn reduces interest expense and, thus, electricity rates. Too high a rate would be reflected in a higher return on investment than warranted for the business risks faced by a regulated utility. If, on the other hand, regulators are too eager to squeeze electricity rates for the benefit of consumers, they are also reducing cash flow coverage of interest expense that can lead to a cut in a utility's credit rating. This results in higher interest rates as investors compensate for the greater perceived risk of default by demanding a higher return. Rates then have to be increased to compensate for the increased interest expense. If the regulators squeeze rates too far for the benefit of consumers, then a utility may not be able to raise the necessary capital to sustain its asset base, making it unable to meet its obligation to provide a reliable and ample supply of electricity to a growing population with higher living-standard expectations.

Too little pressure by regulators results in high electricity rates and a return on the utility's investments above that of a fair return, reflecting its inherent risks. Too much pressure on rates can threaten a utility's operational as well as its financial viability. Regulators must walk a fine line in approving rates, balancing the opposing needs of providing low-cost electricity to the public, and ensuring that a utility has the financial wherewithal to carry out its obligation to the public.

On the surface, regulation of rates based on cost plus a reasonable return appears to be a sound approach for ensuring that a natural monopoly is properly funded, enabling it to provide its intended service at a reasonable cost. However, there are two problems associated with regulation of cost-based rates. The first is the absence of any incentive to be efficient because all operating costs are rolled into the rate base. In fact, there is an incentive to be a little inefficient when rates are being negotiated to obtain a higher rate, then improving efficiency after the rate has been set to enhance profitability. The second is the incentive to overinvest in plant capacity as the return is not only competitive but also more or less guaranteed by the rate-setting mechanism. To combat these drawbacks of cost-based rates, regulators review a utility's operations. Regulators have the power to replace management if operations become too inefficient. With regard to overinvestment, regulators normally insist that a utility clearly demonstrate that new electricity-generating capacity, or any significant capital investment, is needed before approving the expenditure of funds. Despite the best attempts by regulators, who are themselves subject to influence by those being regulated, a lingering suspicion existed that cost-based rates were higher than necessary.

This turned out to be the case when prices fell after the privatization of the British electricity industry. In 1988, concerned over what was perceived to be overpriced electricity from cost-based rates, the British government under Margaret Thatcher announced its intention to privatize the government-owned and -operated electric utility industry. The transformation of a socialized industry to several competing commercial enterprises as part of a national energy policy began in 1990 and was essentially completed by 1999. During this period consumers experienced a 20 percent decrease in retail prices, 34 percent for small industrial customers, and 7–8 percent for medium and large industrial consumers. The overall decline in wholesale electricity prices averaged 2.1 percent per year, demonstrating the ability of market pricing to lower electricity costs to consumers over regulatory cost-based pricing.[6]

In the United States, the roots of deregulation—some prefer to call it liberalization because the electricity utility industry is still highly regulated under deregulation—go back to the 1973 oil crisis. President Nixon's Project Independence was aimed at reducing the nation's dependence on oil and natural gas by switching to other fuels and encouraging energy efficiency and conservation to cut overall energy demand. At that time, oil and natural gas each contributed 20 percent of the fuel consumed in electricity generation. Project Independence sought to cut oil consumption in electricity generation to reduce imports. Though natural gas was indigenous, there was a belief that a natural gas shortage might develop if there were a significant switch from oil to natural gas for generating electricity. Project Independence focused on the development of nuclear power, coal, and renewables for generating electricity.

The electricity-generating industry operated under the Public Utility Holding Act of 1935, a law that had dismantled the pyramid utility holding companies of the 1920s that went bankrupt during the Great Depression of the 1930s. The Act restored the utility business to its original state in which a single corporate entity provided electricity (and natural gas) to a franchise or specified area protected from competition. Within their franchises, utilities were lords and masters of generation, transmission, and distribution, subject, of course, to regulatory oversight. This cozy arrangement ended after the oil crisis. Congress, fearing that utilities would resist adopting new technologies, passed the Public Utility Regulatory Policies Act (PURPA) of 1978. PURPA required state regulatory commissions to establish procedures for qualifying facilities (QFs) that were not utilities to sell electricity made from renewable energy sources, waste, and cogeneration plants run on natural gas to utilities. Cogeneration plants, as noted, have a high thermal efficiency, double that of a conventional plant, because they can utilize waste heat as a source of hot water for industrial or processing purposes. PURPA could be viewed as a form of government coercion in support of cogeneration plants and renewable energy sources.

Utilities were obliged to buy electricity from QFs paying the "avoided" cost, the amount that a utility would have to pay for replacement electricity if it did not buy electricity from the QF. If the avoided cost made it profitable for independent power producers (IPPs) to invest in qualifying electricity-generating facilities whose output had to be purchased by utilities, then so be it. Some states, most notably California, required utilities to buy electricity at a price above avoided cost in order to jump-start new electricity-generating technologies involving solar, wind, and biomass.

The overall effect of PURPA was to raise the price of electricity and, by this narrow definition, could be considered a failure. But PURPA was the first intrusion of independent third parties into the monopoly of electricity generation by inadvertently taking the first step toward liberalization.

PURPA also unintentionally challenged the concept of having a few large nuclear and coal-fired plants supplying a wide area through long-distance transmission lines. These centralized plants were burdened with billions of dollars of cost overruns, resulting in a cost of electricity far higher than originally envisioned. As these plants established the avoided cost, PURPA opened the door to having a more distributive system in which smaller capacity generating plants fueled by renewables and cogeneration plants run on natural gas served a more limited area.

The fear that utilities would exercise their monopoly control over transmission lines to make it difficult for QFs to develop a competitive market for electricity was dealt with in the Energy Policy Act of 1992 and the Federal Energy Regulatory Commission (FERC) Order 888 of 1996, which began the transformation of electricity transmission into a common carrier. These three legislative acts (PURPA, the Energy Policy Act of 1992, and FERC Order 888) established the opportunity for the emergence of wholesale competition in electricity within the regulatory framework governing natural monopolies.

Deregulation/liberalization entails the unbundling of generation, transmission, distribution, and system operation. As an integrated utility, one rate covered all operating and capital costs associated with generating and delivering electricity. Since competition was concentrated in third-party access to electricity generation, and did not cover transmission and distribution, it became necessary to break a single cost into three separate cost components for generation, transmission, and distribution—an accountant's delight to say the least. But shifting the price of generating electricity from cost-based to market price created an immediate problem for integrated utilities. Under the old regulatory regime, cost overruns such as those associated in building nuclear-powered plants were simply rolled into the rate base where higher electricity rates generated the revenue to amortize the cost overrun plus interest.

With third-party access to generation permissible and with IPPs relying on more energy-efficient, lower-capital cost generators run on natural gas (whose price had fallen when the natural gas "bubble" appeared and hung around for two decades after the first energy crisis), market rates for electricity fell below cost-based rates. The market rate of electricity for nuclear power and other large plants plagued with huge cost overruns, when discounted into the future, did not create a book value for these generating assets that was even close to covering their capital costs. This would have necessitated writing down the book value of the assets to their market value, resulting in a diminution and, in some cases, an elimination of shareholders' equity. This difference in asset value between cost-based and market-priced electricity rates was given a name: stranded costs. To save utilities from having their creditworthiness impaired—resulting in lower bond ratings and higher interest rates—an incremental charge was added to electricity rates to cover stranded costs. This increment, charged to all sources of electricity including IPPs, was paid to the affected utilities until their stranded costs were liquidated. The existence of stranded costs was proof positive that rates based on costs were not the most economical way to produce electricity.

## OPERATING MODELS IN AN ERA OF DEREGULATION/ LIBERALIZATION

Where once there had been one model for the electricity business, now there are four. The first model is the traditional vertically integrated monopoly, still operating in many parts of the world, where rates are regulated to cover costs and provide an acceptable rate of return on capital assets. The second model resulted from the PURPA legislation in 1978 that gave IPPs third-party access to utilities. This initial step in liberalizing the industry took the form of a utility entering into a long-term contract to buy the entire output of the IPP generating plant. An IPP was forced to enter into a life-of-asset contract with the utility; otherwise, its investment was at risk. The utility was the IPP's only customer because the IPP did not have open access to transmission lines. Without such access, the IPP could not compete with the utility by entering into a contract with individual customers to supply their electricity needs.

In addition to the United States, this model has been adopted fairly widely in Asia and South America as a means to attract private capital for increasing the generating capacity of state-owned utilities. The creditworthiness for financing the building of the generating plant relies primarily on the nature of the contract between the IPP and the state-owned enterprise, not on the IPP's creditworthiness. Of course potential investors scrutinize the IPP to ensure that it can carry out its operational responsibilities, but security for repayment of debt lies almost exclusively on the sales contract. By issuing what essentially is a self-funding life-of-asset contract to buy the entire output of the IPP's generating plant, a state-owned enterprise does not have to tap external sources of funds or borrow from the government to increase its generating capacity.

The third model gives IPPs access to the transmission system and the ability to enter into contracts with large consumers such as distribution companies and large industrial enterprises and, thereby, compete with the utility. This model was first put into effect in Chile, followed by Argentina, the United Kingdom, and New Zealand. The United States does not have a national policy on how the utility industry is to operate, but the third model was instituted in parts of the United States through utility pools.

In the third model, each generator, whether owned by a utility or an IPP, pays a fee for the use of the transmission system. The fee covers the operating and capital costs of the transmission system, in effect, converting the transmission system into a common carrier in operation, if not in actuality. The rate can be a "postage stamp" rate, which is the same regardless of the distance of transmission, or be based on distance. The latter is preferable because it provides a better means of funding the installation of new or replacement of old transmission capacity. Each generator becomes an independent supplier regardless of its ownership, selling electricity under a variety of contractual arrangements with buyers. Term contracts run for a period of time, fixing the cost of electricity for consumers and the revenue for providers. Term contracts account for the bulk of generated electricity and are arranged directly between the generator owner, either a utility or an IPP, and the consumer, a utility's distribution company or a large industrial consumer, or indirectly through intermediate market makers. The remaining electricity is bought and sold on the spot market. Consumers submit bids on what they are willing to pay for specified amounts of electricity that cover their needs in a specified time frame and providers submit bids for what they are willing to sell the output of particular generating units during the same time frame. These bids can apply to hourly intervals in the day-ahead market and the current spot market, but shorter time frames can be used. A computer program determines the clearing price at which supply meets demand for each hour or specified time frame of the day-ahead market and for the current spot market.

The day-ahead spot market is a contractual arrangement that meets anticipated needs. The spot market handles differences between the planned and actual use of electricity. These differences arise from a buyer not needing all, or needing more, electricity than anticipated, unexpected generator problems that reduce availability of contractual electricity, transmission congestion, and actions necessary to keep the system stable. Day-ahead and spot prices are not determined for an entire region, but at node points (sites of generating capacity) or defined zones. Price disparities between nodes or zones are primarily determined by system transmission capacity constraints, line losses, and differences in generating costs. Price disparities provide useful economic signals for determining the size and location of additional transmission and generating capacity; something entirely missed under cost-based rates.

Obviously, generators have different fixed and variable costs depending on their capital investment, depreciated value, efficiency for converting energy to electricity, type and price of fuel, operating and maintenance costs, and the nature of ownership. Generating plants owned by the U.S. government and by state and municipal authorities operate in a tax-free environment and have access to more favorable financing alternatives than investor-owned utilities and privately-owned generators. Some of these factors affect marginal costs, which play an important role in the rate-setting mechanism. Marginal costs normally reflect the costs of operation including fuel with the investment considered a sunk cost. Rates fixed at the marginal cost generate the minimum revenue necessary to meet the cash operating needs of a utility, but not its capital costs in terms of servicing debt or paying dividends. Continual operation at marginal costs will eventually drive a utility out of business. Marginal cost is like a taxi fare that only covers the costs for the driver, fuel, insurance, and maintenance, with no funds available to pay the cab's financing charges or being accumulated to buy a replacement cab.

Coal, nuclear, and hydro-powered plants have the lowest marginal costs because of their relatively low fuel costs (hydro plants have no fuel costs). Nuclear power and coal-fired plants do not respond well to fluctuating demand because they require considerable time to ramp output up and down. These plants normally supply base-load electricity and enter into term contracts for most of their output. Generators whose output is more easily adjusted (natural gas and hydro) tend to be more exposed to fluctuating demand. Coal and nuclear plants bid at their marginal costs in order to secure employment at night, locking out higher marginal-cost generators fed by natural gas. As demand increases, natural gas generators submit bids for different quantities of electricity at their higher marginal costs that are tallied until demand is satisfied. The wholesale electricity rate is determined by the rate necessary to clear the market; that is, the rate submitted by the last generating plant whose output, when added to all the others, is sufficient to satisfy demand. This rate becomes the single rate paid to all providers, regardless of their bids. Now coal and nuclear generators no longer receive their low bid based on marginal costs that kept them busy all night, but a rate based on the cost of the facility that last cleared the market. This higher wholesale rate provides the additional revenue to repay sunk costs (service debt to the bondholders and dividend payments to the equity investors).

There is a real risk in this business. If too many low-cost base-load plants are built, electricity rates will reflect their marginal costs for longer periods of time during a twenty-four-hour day. As a result, electricity rates may not remain above marginal costs long enough for these plants to recoup their sunk costs (return of and on investment). Moreover, higher-cost units built for transient demand will see their hours of employment and profitability curtailed when there are too many low-cost base-load plants. Independent power producers risk their capital when operating in the third model, which has led to bankruptcies that would have rarely occurred in a fully regulated environment.

The fourth model gives IPP access not just to principal utility customers but also direct access to individual households and small businesses, which are handled by distribution companies under the third model. In the third model, the transmission company becomes a *de facto* common carrier to serve a buyer, the distribution company, which, in turn, supplies thousands or millions of individual consumers. In the fourth model, the distribution company also becomes a *de facto* common carrier and is paid a tariff that covers its operating and capital costs. Individual consumers select a provider (utility or IPP) to supply their needs. An electricity bill then has three components: the contractual arrangement with the provider, a common-carrier charge from the transmission company, and another from the distribution company.

The great advantage of the fourth model is the introduction of demand management. Demand management can only occur if time-of-day automated reading meters are installed in order for rates to reflect what is being paid to providers. This gives individuals and businesses an incentive to reduce electricity usage during hours of peak demand, when the price of electricity is high, by shifting a portion of electricity demand to periods of base demand, when the price is low. In this way part of the load associated with hot water heaters, washers, and clothes dryers can be switched from times of high electricity rates to times of low electricity rates, and consumers receive lower electricity bills by managing their load.

The third and fourth models of direct access to large and small consumers require separate control over transmission independent of generation. In England, it was relatively easy to separate transmission from generation, and transmission from distribution, during privatization of a government-owned industry. The UK government simply organized new corporate entities to serve these three functions as they wished, without much ado other than from those directly involved in managing and operating the proposed companies. Restructuring the electricity utility business is much more complicated in the United States, where generating plants are owned by private and public institutions. Municipal utilities own generating plants along with investor-owned utilities and also the U.S. government, which owns hydro- and nuclear-powered plants under the Tennessee Valley Authority in the east and hydro plants (Hoover, Glen Canyon, Grand Coulee, and others) in the west. The dichotomy of ownership also exists for transmission lines in the United States. Transmission systems within an integrated utility's franchise area are owned by the utility. Interconnecting transmission systems may be owned piecemeal for those portions of the system passing through a utility's franchise area or by a separate corporate entity or the U.S. government. The U.S. government owns transmission lines associated with its generating plants and has also played an active role in providing loans and grants to utilities to build transmission lines to rural America under the Rural Utilities Service (formerly the New Deal Rural Electrification Administration).

In a deregulated system utilities continue to own, operate, and maintain transmission lines, but they cannot have any real or perceived influence or control over their usage. If utilities could influence or exercise control over the transmission system, then the transmission system could be employed to their advantage and to the detriment of IPPs. This would hinder the formation of a wholesale market for electricity in which rates are determined by supply and demand, not by those who have control over access to the transmission system.

In addition to open access to the transmission system, the rate-setting mechanism for wholesale providers of electricity utilities and IPPs cannot allow any single provider to dominate the market. Studies have indicated that market domination might occur if any single participant has more than a 20 percent share of the business. This implies that a market free of manipulation that responds only to underlying shifts in supply and demand must consist of at least a half dozen independent and somewhat equally sized participants. Of course, the more participants there are, the better the market in terms of depth (volume of transactions and the number of parties buying and selling) and freedom from potential manipulation. The mechanism for determining price should be efficient (similar to a stock exchange), liquid (easily transferable obligations to buy or sell electricity), and transparent (transactions displayed and known to all participants). Besides equal access to transmission and the right to compete in order to get the business of distribution companies and major consumers, no cross-subsidies (regulated activities underwriting unregulated activities) can be allowed, and a mechanism for dealing with environmental issues must be instituted that does not interfere with the workings of the marketplace.

Deregulation requires a restructuring of integrated utility companies, separating generation from transmission, if not in ownership, certainly in operation. Historically, the system operator was responsible for the operations of a single integrated utility that owned the generating units, transmission, and distribution systems within its franchise area. The allegiance of a system operator cannot be dedicated to a utility when IPPs are trying to cut deals with the utility's customers. An Independent Systems Operator (ISO) must be established that acts impartially and is not beholden to any provider. The ISO is responsible for scheduling and dispatching (turning generators on and off), for accommodating demand—taking into consideration bilateral sales agreements between buyers (consumers) and sellers (owners of generating units), transmission constraints, and system stability. ISOs in the United States and Canada are responsible for the operation of groups or pools of utilities that cover a number of states and provinces. ISOs also control the system operation of large areas of Australia and China and entire nations such as Argentina, England, France, Mexico, and New Zealand.

The transmission system acts as a separate company under the operational control of the ISO, in effect a common carrier giving no preference to users and charging a regulated tariff that covers operating and capital costs. It would be preferable if the transmission company were truly independent with the general public, financial institutions, utilities, and IPPs owning shares. The present ownership of transmission companies in the United States is split among utilities, corporations, and the U.S. government, with each owning various sections of the national transmission grid system. This arrangement makes decision making on expanding capacity cumbersome. Decision gridlock has not been the cause of limited building of new transmission lines in the United States; rather, the cause is local opposition or BANANAS (building absolutely nothing anywhere near anybody syndrome), which affects many industries. Without building new transmission lines, the United States is consuming the spare capacity of an aging system that can only result in future trouble.

The distribution function of an integrated utility becomes a separate operation in the third and fourth models. While presently owned by utilities, a better alternative for the third and fourth models would be for distribution companies to become independent entities with their own shareholders. In the third model, the utility cannot influence the distribution company's electricity purchases. But there is nothing that precludes a distribution company from entering into a term contract with its owning utility as long as other IPPs have been given equal access to bid for the business. The distribution company charges a regulated tariff that covers its operating and capital costs plus its electricity purchases. At the present time, the regulated rates for distribution companies cover all costs, including the cost of electricity. There really is no incentive for distribution companies to buy from the lowest cost source because the cost of purchasing electricity, no matter what it is, becomes part of the rate base. There has been some movement by regulators to set up an incentive system that rewards distribution companies if they can demonstrate that they have been more successful in seeking the best deal for their customers than other distribution companies. This reward could be in the form of incremental profits based on a portion of the difference between actual purchases and the average purchases by other distribution companies.

Competition in a deregulated, or liberalized, environment is primarily focused on electricity generation—transmission and distribution are still regulated activities essentially free of competition. Ideally, transmission and distribution companies would become separate corporate entities that own the assets rather than the assets being owned by investor- and government-owned utilities. They would charge a regulated rate to cover their operating and financial costs. Under the third model, the rate would also include the cost of electricity because the distribution company is responsible for selecting the electricity provider for its customers. Under the fourth model, the customers must select a provider, thereby reducing the role of the distribution company to that of a conduit or common carrier for direct sales between generator owners (utilities and IPPs) and individuals and businesses. This places the responsibility for purchasing electricity squarely on the shoulders of consumers, not the distribution companies.

For this model to work, consumers need time-of-day meters that automatically communicate electricity use to the utility. This way the utility can charge for electricity by time increments that reflect rates charged by suppliers, which, in turn are influenced by supply and demand. Europe is paving the way in the development of demand management, which has been set up, at least partially, in England and Wales, Scandinavia, and Spain. The Nordic electricity grid (Norway, Sweden, Finland, and Denmark) installed 1 million AMR (automated meter reading) meters in 2005, which number about 8 million meters in 2010. These meters read electricity consumption in five-minute increments and send the information via wireless satellite to providers.

AMRs save money by not having to employ an army of meter readers. Signals from the meter readers keep providers informed of customer usage and whether or not they are receiving service. This allows providers to quickly identify power interruptions and initiate action to restore service. AMRs also benefit providers beyond billing, collections, and customer service. The wealth of information gathered by AMRs can be integrated into asset management, energy procurement, operational control, risk management, and field operations.

Demand management benefits consumers by shifting electricity loads from high- to low-cost periods. Only a portion of the peak day load can be shifted to night, but whatever that portion is, it represents significant savings to the consumer. Demand management also benefits providers. With the shifting of a portion of demand from peak- to low-demand periods, the base load of the utility is increased, with a commensurate reduction in peak demand and the need to invest in peaking generators. Demand management also encourages aggregators to represent groups of consumers. An example of the power of aggregators to lower costs can be seen in some office buildings that aggregate telephone service for all their tenants into one account. The office building enters into a single contract with a communications company. The communications company bills only the office building, which then breaks down the billing to the individual tenants within the building, and receives a fee for this service that represents a portion of the savings. This gives office buildings, as aggregators of phone service, a powerful negotiating presence when dealing with competing communications companies. In the same way, aggregators of electricity representing a group of industrial and commercial users can increase the group's bargaining power with providers in contracting for electricity services. Aggregators could someday represent hundreds or thousands of individual households and small businesses as a single bargaining group.

**Smart Meters/Smart Grids**

A smart meter can tell the occupant of a house or manager of a factory what the cost of electricity is on a real-time basis. Knowing the cost of electricity, an occupant of a house may decide to run a washing machine or dryer at night or a manager may be able to shift some energy-intensive operations to times when electricity rates are lower. A smart grid is much more than a smart meter. A smart grid will be able to integrate a centralized electricity-generating system feeding a transmission system with small combined heat- and electricity-generation plants along with solar panels and wind turbines feeding local distribution systems. Depending on further developments in battery technology, smart grids will control the charging of batteries when demand is low and draw down electricity when demand is high. The smart grid will manage electrical loads during peak times by reducing electricity demand from refrigerators and air-conditioning units in homes and buildings. Batteries and demand planning for load reduction will have a powerful influence on electricity demand by reducing the daily peaks in electricity demand, removing the need to use or invest in peaking generators. A nationwide system of plug-in hybrid electric automobiles can be realized by the smart grid controlling the timing and the electrical load when recharging vehicles. The reliability of transmission and distribution systems can be enhanced by smoothing out the peaks and valleys of electricity demand and by the smart grid being able to take corrective action as problems in load, generation, and distribution begin to emerge. Rather than responding to load changes, a smart grid can actively control loads to prevent blackouts and other service disruptions. The smart grid allows an electricity system to run more efficiently without the same need for spinning or backup turbines to handle unanticipated fluctuations in demand. The smart grid transforms an essentially reactive system to changing loads to a more proactive system of managing loads for increased efficiency, stability, and reliability.[7]

Xcel Energy is installing 50,000 "smart" meters in residences, commercial establishments, and light industries that can remotely watch consumption and adjust consumers' energy use during peak periods. The benefits are operational savings, customer-choice energy management, better grid reliability, greater energy efficiency and conservation options, increased use of renewable energy sources, and support for intelligent-home appliances.[8] Smart meters also require a smart transmission system incorporating an information and communication infrastructure. The "brain" of a smart transmission system can be augmented with the "brawn" capable of delivering the power necessary to fuel plug-in electric hybrids. Progress is being made in developing superconductivity transmission materials where temperatures below a critical temperature present zero resistance to direct current and only minimal resistance to alternating current, virtually eliminating line losses for long-distance transmission. An example of a low-temperature superconductivity material is niobium-titanium alloy that becomes a superconductor at minus 441°F in a liquid helium medium. A "high" temperature superconductivity material is bismuth-based, copper oxide ceramic with a critical temperature of minus 265°F in a liquid nitrogen medium. Another advantage of superconductivity is that a given conductor can carry up to 150 times the amount of power over ambient temperatures. This enhanced flow of power through a superconductivity transmission system allows the widespread adoption of plug-in hybrid electric vehicles. Superconductivity coupled with a smart grid can relieve grid congestion, enhance grid utilization, efficiency and resilience against attack and natural disaster, and anticipate and respond to power surges.[9]

The telecommunications, computer, and Internet industries have adapted well to sophisticated technology with an average lifespan of three years. This may not be possible for an electrical distribution network with an average lifespan of half a century. The utilities are in uncharted waters in determining which devices should be installed on their networks today that will be able to interact with the technology of tomorrow. One way to address this is collaboration among utilities throughout the world to share their challenges, insights, and knowledge base. This way they can begin the process of assisting one another in developing approaches to innovative technology processes and concepts, human resource demands, and regulation.

## UTILITY POOLS

Utility pools predate deregulation. Pools were not set up to challenge the concept of an integrated utility, but as a means of increasing system reliability among independent integrated utilities. In this way, surplus capacity for one utility would be available to meet demand for another utility short on capacity. A *tight pool* is a pooling of utilities with membership restricted to a specific region. Two tight pools, one for New England and one for New York, were formed to share generating capacity among pool members for greater system reliability. New transmission lines were built to interconnect the pool members to allow one utility with surplus electricity-generating capacity to support another facing a shortage. This ability to share capacity enhanced reliability, reducing the risk of blackouts. It also increased the productivity of generating capacity and reduced the need for peaking generators. But the exchange of electricity between utilities required an agreement on a rate for settling accounts, thereby creating a wholesale market between utilities in addition to the retail market between utilities and their customers.

In addition to the New England and the New York pools, three other pools were organized. The PJM pool is an open pool originally organized with utilities in Pennsylvania, New Jersey, and Maryland. The Texas pool is a closed pool limited to utilities in Texas. The California pool is an open pool including utilities in the western part of the United States and Canada. Having pooled their generation and transmission resources and created a wholesale market, it was relatively easy for the pools to admit IPPs when required by PURPA legislation.

Pools had a major impact on the involvement of the Federal Energy Regulatory Commission (FERC) in electricity markets. As independent utilities serving their franchise areas, utilities are exclusively under state or municipal regulation. FERC only has jurisdiction over wholesale buying and selling of electricity between utilities and interstate transmission. Though the Texas pool operating within the state of Texas escaped FERC oversight for interstate transmission, FERC had jurisdiction over wholesale transactions between pool members. For this reason, the spread of pools increased FERC involvement in electricity markets via wholesale deals and interstate transmission to a degree that was not envisioned when FERC was first established.

FERC's limited jurisdictional authority to act was corrected by the Energy Policy Act of 2005, which also abolished the Public Utility Holding Act of 1935. This legislative change better reflected the reality that electricity generation and transmission were no longer a local matter best handled by local regulatory authorities. Electricity generation and transmission had become a regional matter and a growing national matter as a result of the increased tying together of transmission grids and generating stations through pools and utility-to-utility marketing arrangements. Large portions of the nation's electricity grid on either side of the Rockies are integrated, but a large-capacity cross-Rocky Mountain transmission system would have to be built to fully integrate the electricity grid of the nation. This would allow electricity to flow from where it is least needed to where it is most needed across the country. Moreover, there is an increasing flow of electricity both ways across the borders with Mexico and Canada that could result in a continental or international electricity grid.

Two pools deserve mention. One is the highly successful PJM pool, an excellent example of how to organize and run a pool, and the California pool, an excellent example of what not to do. The PJM pool was the world's first electricity power pool, formed by three utilities in 1927 to share their resources. Other utilities joined in 1956, 1965, and 1981, which led to the PJM pool covering most of Pennsylvania, New Jersey, and Maryland. Throughout this period, system operation was handled by one of the member utilities. In 1962 PJM installed an online computer to control generation in real time, and in 1968 set up the Energy Management System to monitor transmission grid operations in real time. The transition to an independent neutral organization began in 1993 and was completed in 1997 with the formation of the PJM Interconnection Association, the nation's first fully functioning ISO approved by FERC.[10]

PJM also became the nation's first fully functioning Regional Transmission Organization (RTO) in 2001 in response to FERC Order 2000. RTOs operate transmission systems on a multistate or regional basis to encourage development of competitive wholesale power markets. PJM Interconnection coordinates the continual buying, selling, and delivery of wholesale electricity throughout its region, balancing the needs of providers and wholesale consumers as well as monitoring market activities to ensure open, fair, and equitable access to all participants. The PJM Energy Market operates much like a stock exchange with market participants establishing a price for electricity through a bidding process that matches supply with demand.

The Energy Market uses location marginal pricing that reflects the value of the electricity at specific locations and time. During times of low demand and no transmission congestion, prices are about the same across the entire grid because providers with the lowest-priced electricity can serve the entire region. During times of transmission congestion that inhibit the free flow of electricity, location marginal price (LMP) differences arise that can be used for planning expansion of transmission and generation capacity. The Energy Market consists of day-ahead and real-time markets. The day-ahead market is a forward market for hourly LMPs based on generation offers, demand bids, and scheduled bilateral transactions. The real-time market is a spot market where real time LMPs are calculated at five-minute intervals, based on grid operating conditions. The spot market complements that portion of the total market not covered by term contracts between buyers and sellers and unforeseen adjustments that have to be made for buying and selling transactions originally made on the day-ahead market.

PJM has expanded from its original base in Pennsylvania, New Jersey, and Maryland to include Virginia, West Virginia, the District of Columbia, a large portion of Ohio, and smaller portions of Indiana, Illinois, Michigan, Kentucky, and Tennessee. It is the world's largest competitive wholesale market, serving a population of 51 million with over 1,000 generating plants with total capacity of 164 GWs, 56,000 miles of transmission lines, and over 500 members and still growing. In addition to creating and serving this market, PJM is also in charge of system reliability including planning for the expansion of transmission and generator capacity. PJM has become a model emulated elsewhere in the world such as in Colombia, where the national pool has been expanded to include utilities in Ecuador and Peru, with plans to bring in utilities in Bolivia, Venezuela, and Brazil.

Another pool started operating in 2009 connecting Kuwait, Saudi Arabia, Bahrain, Qatar, United Arab Emirates, and Oman. The system, which will be fully operational in 2011, is a combination treaty and commercial transaction. Electricity is purchased on term deals for base load, with spare capacity available whose rate is determined by an auction process. System rates are low enough to close out higher-cost facilities not associated with the grid. The grid is capable of shifting electricity to prevent blackouts that had previously plagued local areas, particularly in the peak summer months from air conditioning. The grid utilizes high-voltage, direct current (HVDC) transmission with back-to-back converters. Technological improvements in recent years to direct current transmission have made HVDC transmission cost competitive with less line losses than traditional high-voltage alternating current transmission. HVDC is particularly useful in connecting asynchronous systems such as Saudi Arabia's 60-cycle frequency with the remaining countries that use 50-cycle frequency. HVDC can also be used in undersea transmission, avoiding the much higher line losses of transmitting high-voltage alternating current underwater. HVDC transmission can be built up to 800,000 volts. The Gulf Cooperation Council (GCC) electricity grid is to be a model of cooperation for other projects.

Transmission voltage is measured in hundreds of thousands of volts with the newest transmission lines being 765,000 volts. This allows for more distant transmission of electricity with less line losses. The State Grid Corporation of China, China's largest utility, operates a vast network of power-distribution lines across 26 of China's 32 provinces and regions. The company is building an ultra-high 1 million volt transmission system that will connect Beijing and Shanghai and other eastern cities to dams in southwest China and coal-powered plants in northwest China. The coal-powered plants will have electricity-generating plants at the mouths of mines, eliminating the need to transport coal to utilities located near population centers. Thus pollution abatement in populated areas is accomplished by substituting the transmission of electricity for the movement of coal.[11]

## WHEN DEMAND EXCEEDS SUPPLY

Deregulation assumes that competitive interactions between independent suppliers of electricity (utilities, IPPs) would act in the consumers' best interests by lowering prices through greater efficiency of operations, productivity gains, and investments in capital assets that can generate electricity cheaply. Competition lowers the overall return on investment to a level that sustains the investment process without overly impoverishing or greatly enriching the investor. This assertion only holds true, however, when supply exceeds demand. The devil in free enterprise rears its ugly head whenever demand exceeds supply. When supply exceeds demand, the price of electricity falls to the marginal costs of the last provider needed to clear the market. When demand exceeds supply, there is no real impediment to how high prices rise other than individuals and companies pulling the plug.

The California electricity crisis of 2000 illustrates what can happen when demand exceeds supply. While demand exceeding supply affected not just California but the entire western part of the United States, the peculiar regulatory framework set up in California provided a launch pad for a rocket ride that sent one major public utility company into financial oblivion and reduced others to a precarious state of illiquidity; squandered a state surplus; caused the issuance of bonds to ensure that tomorrow's taxpayers will pay for yesterday's utility costs; created unpaid receivables that will forever remain unpaid; caused financial distress among energy traders and merchants; locked the ratepayers into long-term, high-cost electricity contracts; and set off an avalanche of allegations, investigations, lawsuits, and countersuits to provide guaranteed lifetime employment to a gaggle of lawyers. In short, the California electricity crisis is a classic case study of how not to deregulate the electricity industry.[12]

As background, investor-owned utilities (mainly Pacific Gas and Electric, Southern California Edison, and San Diego Gas and Electric) supplied 72 percent of electricity to California customers; 24 percent was supplied by municipal utilities and the remainder by federal agencies. The investor-owned and municipal utilities had historically operated as vertically integrated monopolies generating, transmitting, and distributing electricity in their franchise areas. The California Public Utilities Commission (CPUC) set the rates for the investor-owned utilities on the basis of covering costs and providing a fair rate of return on vested capital while local authorities regulated the rates for municipal utilities. The CPUC was particularly aggressive in implementing PURPA regulations, opening up third-party access to electricity generation. CPUC forced the investor-owned utilities to enter into contracts at higher rates than what would have applied for conventional sources to justify third-party QF investments in wind farms, biomass- and waste-fueled generators, and cogeneration plants run on natural gas. By 1994, 20 percent of electricity-generation capacity in California was from cogeneration (12 percent) and renewables (8 percent), the highest proportions in the nation. Electricity rates to jump-start renewables, coupled with cost overruns on nuclear power plants, resulted in an average cost of nine cents per kilowatt-hour for California residents in 1998 versus a nationwide average of nearly seven cents per kilowatt-hour. Electricity rates in Hawaii, Alaska, New Jersey, New York, and New England were higher than in California.

In the belief that deregulation (liberalization) would lower retail prices, the CPUC aggressively set out to deregulate the electricity industry to give major customers a choice among competing providers of electricity. The CPUC's *Order Instituting Rulemaking on the Commission's Proposed Policies Governing Restructuring California's Electric Service Industry and Reforming Regulation* (R.94–04–031), commonly referred to as the *Blue Book,* in 1994 started the process of liberalization by first recognizing that existing utilities had stranded costs, such as nuclear power cost overruns, that had to be taken care of before the electricity market could be deregulated. New IPPs with no history of cost overruns could build a plant and offer electricity at rates that would bring financial ruin to existing utilities stuck with stranded costs. The *Blue Book* dealt with stranded costs by creating a rate increment that would be paid by all electricity buyers no matter what the source. The revenue would be directed to the appropriate utility to pay for stranded costs until they were liquidated. There was nothing wrong with this approach other than the CPUC capped retail rates until stranded costs were liquidated. The rationale for capping retail rates was that the CPUC believed that wholesale prices under deregulation would fall. As they fell, a larger portion of the difference between the capped retail price and the wholesale price would be dedicated to repaying stranded costs, hastening the time when stranded costs would be liquidated and the retail price cap removed. However, if wholesale prices rose, a smaller portion would be available for stranded costs, delaying the lifting of the retail cap. The financial strength of the utility would not be affected with capped retail prices and the repayment of stranded costs would offset changes in wholesale prices—as long as wholesale prices did not rise above the retail price cap. Since the unanimous belief was that deregulation would result in an overall lowering of wholesale prices, no one envisioned a situation in which wholesale prices would rise above the retail price cap.

The *Blue Book* was followed by a Memorandum of Understanding that created an independent system operator, the California Independent System Operator (CAISO) with the sole responsibility of managing the electricity grid, and an independent power exchange (PX) with the sole responsibility for managing the spot market in electricity. The only allowable markets were an hourly day-ahead and an hourly spot market with transparent prices and transactions. Whereas deregulation elsewhere called for a tightly integrated structure of managing the grid and overseeing the wholesale trading of electricity, the CPUC made these separate and independent functions with no coordination and limited information flow. This administratively imposed barrier on the interchange of information between CAISO as operator and PX as market maker created inefficiencies that became made-for-order profit opportunities for energy traders and independent merchants. The *Blue Book* and the Memorandum of Understanding set the stage for the passage of Assembly Bill 1890 in 1996, which became effective in 1998. Although the investor-owned utilities still owned generating units, transmission lines, and distribution systems, they could not translate ownership to operational control. Control of transmission would be handled by CAISO and all generated electricity would be sold to the PX. An investor-owned utility supplying its customers would first have to sell its electricity to the PX and then purchase electricity from the PX with CAISO handling the transmission details.

Within the western region, California accounted for 25 percent of electricity consumption. The state was a net importer of electricity during the summer from the increased air-conditioning load and a net exporter to the Pacific Northwest during the winter. Thus, the California utilities were net consumers of electricity when the crisis occurred in the late spring and summer of 2000, purchasing more electricity from the PX than they supplied. In the dubious belief that the only way to create a market with substantial depth to reflect the true value of electricity was to channel all sales through the spot market, the CPUC prohibited investor-owned utilities from entering into term contracts to fix the cost of their purchased electricity. This prohibition was put into effect by mandating the PX as the only conduit for sales and purchases of electricity by the investor-owned utilities. But the PX was limited to buying and selling electricity on the day-ahead and current spot markets. This made it impossible for the investor-owned utilities to enter into term contracts, but municipal utilities could act independently and enter into term contracts with providers because they were not regulated by the CPUC.

The PX operated on a day-ahead basis, accepting bids from each generator to sell its output at some offering price and each investor-owned utility's distribution company or major customer indicating the amount of electricity to be purchased on an hourly basis. Offering-price bids were ranked from the lowest to the highest, and their volumes accumulated until they met demand. The price at which the amount of electricity from the accumulated bids by suppliers equalled the amount of electricity required by purchasers became the hourly market-clearing price for all bids. All sellers received the same market-clearing price even if they had bid less than the clearing price. Sellers who had bid more than the market-clearing price would have no market outlet for their generating units. The underlying rationale for this pricing mechanism was that the risk of bidding too aggressively would result in idle generating units. This fear of idle capacity would encourage bidders of generating capacity to price electricity close to the marginal cost of each generating unit. This rationale held true as long as supply exceeded demand.

A computer system was set up to handle twenty-four separate markets for each hour of the current day and the day-ahead market. Providers basically had to guess at what would be the appropriate bid for each hour and those with multiple generating units would be playing an hourly price-bidding game for each of their units to try to maximize company revenues. Owners of various type plants would bid low on those units that best served base needs to ensure their employment, and higher on those units whose output could be more easily changed to try to capture incremental revenues.

What was not envisioned was how the system would behave if nearly all the generating capacity was needed to satisfy demand. Under these circumstances, owners of generating capacity became emboldened to bid more aggressively for their units that were dedicated to satisfying variable demand. There was less risk of being left with idle capacity because most units had to operate to meet demand. Moreover, the financial loss of being left with an idle unit was less because of the higher clearing price for the operating units. In a tight market with little leeway between system demand and system capacity, meaning few idle generators, a new pricing pattern emerged that was never seen before. It was dubbed the hockey stick pattern. When surplus capacity was plentiful, the price for electricity rose slowly in response to large increments in demand. When surplus capacity became scarce, the price rose sharply in response to small increments in demand. The combination of these two price patterns as demand approached the limits of supply looked like a hockey stick.

Jumps in the spot price were particularly harmful to investor-owned utilities in California who, as net consumers of electricity, were forced to buy and sell exclusively in the spot market. Municipal utilities in California and utilities in other states and provinces of the western region outside the jurisdiction of the CPUC had entered into fixed-rate term contracts for the bulk of their electricity purchases, thereby escaping the financial carnage faced by the California investor-owned utilities. While spikes in spot prices starting in California spread throughout the western region, they had limited impact on the aggregate cost of electricity throughout the system because most electricity needs were filled by fixed-price term contracts. "Throughout the system" was, of course, true everywhere and for everyone except the investor-owned utilities in California whose net electricity purchases were funnelled entirely through the spot market.

Another adverse consequence of prohibiting investor-owned utilities from entering into term contracts affected the construction of new electricity-generating capacity in California. Investors could not reduce their financial risk by entering into term contracts with the investor-owned utilities that made up 72 percent of the market. They could, of course, enter into term contracts with municipal-owned utilities to assure at least partial employment, but that excluded much of the market. Without assurance of employment, investors were generally reluctant to bear the financial risk of building new capacity. On top of this, plants under construction in California faced public hearings, creating inspection hurdles that delayed the start of construction by as much as two or more years compared with other western states.

The separation of responsibilities between the system operator, CAISO, and the PX, as market maker, and the prohibition for these two organizations to coordinate their activities and interchange information, forced CAISO to become a buyer on an immediate spot basis. This was the only way for CAISO to handle mismatches between supply and demand that CAISO was not allowed to communicate to PX. Thus, there came into being two spot markets: one run by PX and the other by CAISO. With limited information transfer between the two, energy traders and merchants had a field day taking advantage of price disparities between these two separate markets. To make gamesmanship a little easier for energy traders to play one market (PX) off the other (CAISO), the computer coding for the CAISO model for determining the price of electricity was in the public domain.

Shortly before the emergence of the crisis in 2000, the three investor-owned utilities were 57 percent reliant on natural gas to run local generating units, 12 percent on nuclear power produced locally, 13 percent on hydropower imported from the Pacific Northwest, 5 percent on imported electricity from coal-burning plants in the Southwest, and the remaining 13 percent renewables (wind, geothermal, biomass, and solar). Growth in natural gas consumption for electricity production was beginning to strain pipeline delivery capacity and the surplus of generating power throughout the western region had been eroded by demand growing faster than supply in the preceding years. A drought in the Northwest forced a reduction in hydro output. This became the precipitating event that led to an overall shortage of capacity to satisfy California electricity demand just as it began to climb toward its seasonal peak in the late spring of 2000.

Before the crisis erupted, the wholesale price in the western region varied between $25–$40 per megawatt-hour, equivalent to $0.025–$0.04 per kilowatt-hour. The average retail price of $0.09 per kilowatt-hour also included distribution and stranded costs pertinent to California. Remembering that retail prices in California were capped and all purchases and sales by the investor-owned utilities had to be transacted through the spot market on the PX, and that they were net buyers of electricity during this time, an intolerable cash-flow squeeze occurred when wholesale prices jumped to $75 per megawatt-hour in early May. This was followed by a decline, then a surge to $175 in mid-May, followed by a decline, then a surge to $300 in early June, a decline, then an all-time record spike of $450 in mid-June, again a decline, then another surge to $350 in late July. At these prices, aluminum smelters and other industrial concerns in the Northwest laid off their workforce in order to sell electricity that was either produced at the facility or had been purchased cheaply on long-term contracts in the spot market. This shutdown of industrial output actually increased the supply of electricity in the western region and contributed to limiting the magnitude of the crisis (the laid-off workers had another view of the situation).

With a tight market in which nearly every generator had to be employed to meet demand, providers, knowing that few of their operating units would remain idle, became extremely aggressive in their bidding. A provider with multiple units could afford to bid high on a couple of units as the probability of ending up with an idle unit was pretty low. Moreover, since the highest bid that cleared the system would apply for all bids, the financial loss of having an idle unit with the rest employed at high rates would be an acceptable outcome. This change of attitude—from fear of idle capacity giving way to unrestrained greed—was reflected in the hockey stick price pattern. To add misery to woe, environmental rights to emit pollution had been issued in California, based on actual nitrous and sulfur oxide emissions in 1993. The intention was for the issuing authority to slowly decrease the availability of such rights. The staged retirement of these rights to emit pollution resulted in a higher price, providing an economic incentive for utilities to build new and cleaner-burning plants or add equipment to existing plants to reduce pollution emissions. This program was successful in gradually reducing pollution emissions by utilities.

But in 2000, with California experiencing rolling blackouts (although these blackouts gained national notoriety, only six occurred, each affecting only a small portion of the population for a relatively short period of time), every plant in California had to be put into operation to generate electricity. This involved reactivating previously mothballed plants with high pollution emissions. These could not be operated without purchasing emission rights. The shortage in emission rights sent their price through the ceiling and added to the cost of generated electricity that could not be recouped from customers. In the midst of the electricity crisis, legal actions were being taken against utilities for not having the necessary pollution rights to cover their emissions. The utilities were faced with an impossible choice: to fulfill their public obligation to supply electricity by breaking the law (not buying the requisite rights to cover total emissions) or obeying the law by buying the requisite rights at extremely high prices and thereby aggravating their cash drain. Though it was possible for them to cut back on their electricity generation to reduce their need for emission rights, this would have caused more chaos in the market, more extended blackouts, higher rates, and charges of manipulating the market. Not only did politicians stand fast on doing nothing to increase the volume of pollution emission rights under these dire circumstances, but they also stood fast in making sure that retail price caps remained intact.

Thus, the investor-owned utilities were drained of all their liquidity by buying high and selling low, leading to the bankruptcy of one and the insolvency of the others. CUPC's insistence on not allowing retail price relief was challenged as a violation of the due-process clause of the Constitution to no avail (the state presumably is not allowed to rob shareholders of their wealth without giving them due process for redress). Electricity providers became increasingly unwilling to accept payment other than cash in advance from utilities rapidly becoming insolvent. Refusing to sell electricity through the PX to investor-owned utilities, the state of California was forced to step in and buy electricity for the investor-owned utilities. Now it was California's turn to buy high and sell low, which quickly squandered its entire surplus. Although California had prohibited utilities from entering into term contracts when wholesale spot prices were low, now California itself entered into term contracts with sellers for large quantities of electricity when wholesale spot prices were at record-breaking highs.

During this entire crisis, retail customers, other than being inconvenienced by an occasional rolling blackout, had no economic incentive to reduce consumption. The only action the state took to reduce demand was to order state office buildings to cut electricity usage and initiate a program to subsidize the introduction of energy-efficient fluorescent light bulbs—hardly a palliative for the ongoing crisis. There was a concerted effort on California's part to ensure that state inspectors did all they could not to unnecessarily delay the completion of electricity-generating plants already under construction. The fact that they did hasten the completion of construction is a bitter commentary on their performance prior to the crisis. The crisis began to cool, along with the weather in the fall of 2000, which reduced the air-conditioning load and the need to import electricity. Eventually, the completion of additional electricity-generating plants in California, and elsewhere in the western region, added enough capacity to restore a surplus and a semblance of order to what really should be a very orderly business.

Having bankrupted one utility and left others stripped of cash, California had to issue bonds to restore the surplus squandered by buying high and selling low. This enabled California taxpayers to foot the bill plus interest over the long term for what they did not have to pay in the short term. And, to complete the picture, the term contracts entered into by California, while attractive when they were inked with record-high wholesale spot prices, became decidedly unattractive when wholesale spot prices fell to pre-crisis levels. The people of California are not only saddled with repaying billions of dollars of bonds to restore the state's liquidity, but also spending more needless billions of dollars for high-priced electricity fixed on term contracts. Not all the purchases of high-priced electricity were paid. The bankruptcy of the PX in January 2001 left those holding PX receivables with something to paper their bathroom walls.

Eventually retail electricity rates were raised substantially, but in a manner that had limited-impact on households consuming less than a baseline amount of electricity. Those who consumed above the baseline amount faced significant step-ups in rates. FERC eventually banned utilities from having to buy and sell all their power through the PX or CAISO, restoring the old world in which utilities could make deals in the forward markets, enter into term deals, and dedicate their generated electricity to supplying their customers. FERC attempts to rectify matters in other areas were resisted by state authorities, who are ultimately responsible for the regulation of utilities under their jurisdiction.

At this point, the California electricity industry is basically under state control. The crisis is past, but its legacy will go on for a long time in terms of repaying bonds, honoring high-priced contracts to buy electricity, rejuvenating financially crippled utilities, dealing with unpaid receivables, plus the accusations and investigations, suits, and countersuits. In 2006 the estimated cost of the California debacle to the state was $70 billion, of which $6.3 billion in settlements had already been made. Sixty different investigations of market manipulation and a host of criminal and civil trials were still in the works. For example, evidence was found of a generating plant that had been shut down to fix a boiler that did not need to be fixed; the only remaining reason was to further restrict supply in order to increase price. E-mails and tapes have been discovered that point to rather unsavory behavior on the part of some energy traders and merchants. But this is only the result of a fatally flawed market design set up by regulators giving suppliers the opportunity to take advantage of a resulting shortage. From the start of the energy debacle, and at all times during the debacle, everything that could have made a bad situation worse was done and everything that could have alleviated a bad situation was not done; truly the worst of all possible worlds.

## THE REAL LESSON OF CALIFORNIA

The real lesson to be learned from the California electricity debacle is that rates become unstable when demand gets too close to supply. When supply is ahead of demand, rates are reduced to marginal costs, which is beneficial to consumers. Deregulation means lower prices only as long as supply exceeds demand. When demand gets too close to supply, rates for electricity—and prices for anything, oil, copper, gold, grain, you name it—do not escalate by a little but by a lot. All commodity traders know about the hockey stick pattern. There is little to moderate prices as buyers attempt to outbid one another for what is perceived to be a commodity in short supply. Escalating panic among buyers is matched by growing greed among sellers. This, of course, is the classic economic signal to increase capacity. The problem is that capacity cannot be added in a fortnight.

The original regulation of electricity—determining rates by covering operating costs and guaranteeing a reasonable rate of return on investment—also guaranteed surplus capacity. Indeed, this has been frequently cited as one of the drawbacks of regulation: with a guaranteed return, the temptation to build excess capacity is overwhelming. This was not limited to the number and size of generating plants, but anything that could be thrown into the rate base. The drawback of letting the market decide electricity rates is that the market does not reward spare capacity, but punishes the company that builds too much capacity by making it difficult or impossible to earn enough revenue to recoup its investment. As a consequence, companies tend to use modest growth rates for projecting demand when deciding on investing in additional capacity as a means to avoid the mistake of building too much capacity. While the market system reduces rates by minimizing the amount of capital invested in excess generating facilities, it also forces supply to be close to demand. This leaves little room for accommodating shocks to the system.

There is also a lesson to be learned from the experience of Colombia. Colombia has hydropower plants that supply a large portion of its needs. It is by far the lowest-cost source of electricity. But droughts can affect hydropower output. To accommodate this potential shock, the electricity-generating authorities of that country have entered into contracts for backup fossil-fueled electricity-generating capacity to be built, but not operated as long as hydropower is available. The operators of these plants are paid regardless of the output for these plants. Electricity rates reflect money spent for idle capacity built just in case it is needed. Some careful attention to this means of establishing spare capacity should be given in market-driven systems to reduce system vulnerability to shocks and avoid the pandemonium that breaks out when demand gets too close to supply.

## NOTES

1. The statistics on energy consumption for the primary sources of energy are from *BP Energy Statistics* (London: British Petroleum, 2009); and the statistics on biomass and renewables and the shares of various energy sources consumed for electricity consumption, electricity consumption, and capital costs are from *World Energy Outlook* (Paris: International Energy Agency, 2008).

2. *Annual Energy Outlook 2009,* Early Release, published by the Energy Information Agency (EIA), Washington, DC, 2008.

3. *Assessment of Achievable Potential from Energy Efficiency and Demand Response Programs in the U.S. (2010–2030),* published by Electric Power Research Institute, Palo Alto, CA, 2009.

4. The Electricity Forum Web site www.electricityforum.com.

5. Electropaedia Web site www.mpoweruk.com/high_temp.htm.

6. Sally Hunt, *Making Competition Work in Electricity* (New York: John Wiley & Sons, 2002), is well worth reading for a more comprehensive view of deregulation.

7. *The Smart Grid, An Introduction,* published by the Office of Electricity Delivery & Energy Reliability of the U.S. Department of Energy Web site www.oe.energy.gov.

8. Xcel Company Web site www.xcelenergy.com.

9. American Superconductor Web site www.amsc.com.

10. PJM Web site www.pjm.com.

11. State Grid of China Web site www.sgcc.com.cn/ywlm/default.shtml.

12. James L. Sweeney, *The California Electricity Crisis* (Stanford, CA: Hoover Press, 2002).

# 3

---

# BIOMASS

Energy is not as it always was. Yesterday's world was entirely dependent on biomass, particularly wood for heating and cooking. Even as late as 1900, biomass satisfied half of energy demand with much of the remainder satisfied by coal. Natural gas was still in its infancy stage as a source of energy for lighting and heating as was hydro for generating electricity. Oil was still primarily a fuel for lighting (kerosene) and the automobile age was just beginning. Nuclear had its beginnings in the Second World War and renewables (solar and wind) in the late twentieth century.

Biomass is generally viewed with disfavor as something associated with abject poverty. Yet, there is now something of a resurgence going on for biomass. As fossil fuel prices increase, biomass promises to play a more active role as a utility fuel, a motor vehicle fuel, and a supplement to natural gas. Biomass will never replace fossil fuels, other than on the margin, nor is there any hope that we can return to a world where biomass played a significant role in satisfying society's energy needs. This chapter examines the past and present roles of biomass and its potential as tomorrow's energy fuel.

## YESTERDAY'S FUEL

Until about 300 or 400 years ago, the world depended nearly exclusively on biomass as a source of energy. The population was low in relation to the number of trees. Nature simply replaced those chopped down for heating and cooking. The environmental impact was minimal because carbon dioxide released by burning wood was absorbed by plant growth that replaced the burnt wood. With no net loss of tree resources, carbon dioxide was recycled, which is described by contemporary proponents of biomass as a closed carbon cycle or a sustainable system. Fossil fuels, on the other hand, release carbon dioxide that was locked away eons ago as partially decayed plants and marine organisms.

Despite the environmental benefits of recycling carbon dioxide and emitting less nitrous and sulfur oxides than coal and oil, pollution—in the form of smoke from burning wood—would have filled the cave, tent, hut, or dwelling before someone devised the chimney. Smoke is a health hazard for the respiratory system and an irritant to the eyes. Early explorers observed that smoke from American Indian fires filled the Los Angeles basin with smog long before the automobile age. Now smoke from burning biomass contributes to the brown cloud overhanging much of southern Asia and to serious health problems in India and elsewhere in Asia where emissions from burning biomass are largely confined within living quarters.

Biomass maintained its dominance as a fuel source up to the advent of the Industrial Revolution. Coal entered the picture first in Britain, followed by the United States and Germany, and then Japan. Even as late as 1850, coal only made up 10 percent of the energy mix and biomass provided 90 percent. By the mid-1870s biomass still contributed twice as much to fulfilling energy needs as coal even though coal had replaced charcoal for producing steel and split wood for fueling railroad locomotives and heating homes. Most "natural" gas piped into homes and businesses was actually manufactured gas from coal. What little energy demand remained after biomass and coal was filled by hydropower (water mills turning shafts that, via belts, powered machinery).

## TODAY'S FUEL

Biomass is still a major source of energy, though often excluded from energy statistics because of the inherent difficulty of gathering reliable data from remote areas where biomass is the principal source of energy. For many, biomass is a noncommercial source of energy freely gathered from the local environment. In recent years, biomass has been gaining ground as a commercial fuel purchased as charcoal for cooking, firewood for heating, and crops grown specifically for their energy content. As noted in Chapter 2, biomass and waste make up 10 percent of total energy consumption—still an impressive amount of energy considering the growth in energy consumption in the last hundred years.

Biomass takes many forms. It is carried on the heads of native women in semi-arid regions of Africa and Asia. Many of these women must trudge ten or twenty miles each day to find limbs of dead trees and dung of camels and other animals. Animal dung must be dried in the open sun before being burned and is a preferred energy source for mud ovens because it burns slowly and evenly and releases a great deal of heat. But the demand for dung from a growing human population is beginning to exceed the supply of droppings from camels and other animals that wander the countryside. Dung burned for fuel also robs the ground of a valuable fertilizer. Introducing an energy-efficient oven would reduce the demand for biomass fuels, but an individual who depends on dung or wood for cooking would most likely not have the financial wherewithal to acquire the latest model. Though treks into the hinterland for wood and dung make for interesting TV documentaries and fascinating photographs in *National Geographic,* the reality is not so attractive. How many of these women would give up the romance of gathering wood and animal droppings for a small kerosene or propane stove to heat their hut and cook their food?

Biomass is organic matter primarily in the form of wood, crop residues, and animal waste, in that order of importance. Biomass as wood is readily available in temperate and tropical regions or, as mentioned, is collected with great personal effort in semi-arid areas. The great advantage of biomass is that it is free, and in temperate and tropical regions, freely available. Wood can be burned directly or be first transformed into charcoal through pyrolysis: the heating of wood in the absence of sufficient oxygen to prevent full combustion. Organic gases and water are evaporated, and leave charcoal, which is nearly pure carbon. Burning the released gases provides the fuel for pyrolysis and for drying fresh wood. Any backyard barbecue hamburger-flipping aficionado can recite the virtues of charcoal over wood: higher heat content, cleaner burning, and conveniently transportable.

Generally speaking, since biomass is "free," it is inefficiently utilized as a residential, or commercial, fuel. For instance, about two-thirds of the energy content of wood is lost when it is transformed into charcoal in developing nations. What does inefficiency mean other than greater personal effort when the wood is freely gathered from the local environment? Most proposals for utilizing biomass in developing nations emphasize energy efficiency to reduce the input of biomass to produce the same output.

Although biomass is estimated to make up 10 percent of all energy consumed, its pattern of consumption varies enormously from nation to nation. The industrialized nations rely on biomass for only about 3 percent of their energy needs. Biomass is burned for heating homes during the winter in New England and other parts of North America and northern Europe. Biomass can be firewood split from logs or bark and edgings residue from a lumber mill. Fireplaces burning split logs provide an attractive background setting in the living rooms of millions of homes. Unfortunately, conventional fireplaces allow most of the heat to escape up the chimney. Some fireplaces may actually increase heating needs by acting as a pump transferring warm air from inside to outside the house. When people depend on biomass to heat their homes, the wood is burned in specially designed space heaters where relatively little heat escapes along with the products of combustion to the outside.

Wood residue is an important source of biomass. As much as 75 percent of a tree becomes residue beginning with the leaves, tree top, branches, and stump left in the forest, to the bark, edgings, and sawdust produced when a log is transformed into lumber, and to the shavings, edgings, and sawdust of making lumber into a finished product. Bark and other wood residue can be used for residential heating, as an industrial fuel by supplying power for lumber mills and other manufacturing activities in the developing world, and for producing electricity in developed nations such as Finland and Germany.

Some sub-Saharan African nations such as Burundi and Rwanda are over 90 percent reliant on energy from biomass while others are 70–80 percent reliant on biomass for their total energy needs, which includes commercial and industrial as well as residential demand. In terms of residential demand, nearly all rural households in Kenya, Tanzania, Mozambique, and Zambia rely on wood, and 90 percent of urban households rely on charcoal for cooking. Heavy biomass users in Asia are Indonesia, the Philippines, Thailand, Myanmar (formerly Burma), Vietnam, Bhutan, Laos, and Cambodia, and in the western hemisphere Guatemala, Honduras, Nicaragua, and Haiti.

Of the world population of 6.8 billion people, an estimated one-third does not have access to electricity. Almost by definition, those without access to electricity depend on biomass. Even with access to electricity, many cannot afford to buy electricity and therefore remain dependent on biomass. With or without access to electricity, it is estimated that 2.4 billion people, or 38 percent of the world population, depend primarily on biomass in the form of wood, agricultural residues, and dung for cooking and heating. Half of these live in India and China, but sub-Saharan Africa has the world's highest per capita dependency on biomass. Not only does heavy reliance on biomass pose health problems, but it also contributes to ecological problems such as deforestation, which is occurring in parts of Africa, India, and elsewhere, in addition to the loss of dung as a fertilizer. As one may surmise, there is a direct link between poverty and dependence on biomass.

## China

About half of China's population relies on biomass in the form of wood and agricultural residues for cooking and heating. Most biomass is consumed in rural areas and provides a little less than 20 percent of China's energy needs. Biomass consumption is expected to remain flat for the foreseeable future, balanced between a rising population and continued migration to urban areas, where commercial fuels are more widely and more efficiently used. Shifting from biomass to commercial fuels is considered beneficial because it reduces local pollution as well as aggregate energy demand.

## India

Nearly 60 percent of the people in India depend on biomass for heating and cooking, with biomass providing about a third of India's total energy consumption. Rural areas of India are almost entirely dependent on biomass, which is leading to widespread deforestation. Of course, where biomass consumption results in deforestation, biomass is no longer a closed carbon cycle or sustainable source of energy. By definition, deforestation means that more carbon dioxide is being released into the atmosphere than is being absorbed by replacement growth.

India has initiated an afforestation program in an area stripped of its indigenous evergreen forests. The aim of the program is to transform what has become wasteland back into forestland. If successful, the forest will reduce soil erosion and increase groundwater. The improved fertility and productivity of the soil will benefit agriculture in the surrounding area while the forest itself will provide employment opportunities and fuel. The goal of the National Forestry Action Program is afforestation of a significant portion of the nation with the local population supplying the labor and the government supplying the material.

**Indonesia**

Many remote and isolated islands of Indonesia and other island nations of Southeast Asia are not well-served by commercial forms of energy. Over 70 percent of the population of Indonesia depends on biomass for heating and cooking, and Indonesia is 30 percent dependent on biomass. Biomass in the form of bark and other residue from lumbering operations provides the steam for running lumber mills. Biomass would be an ideal fuel for micro-electricity-generating plants that could bring the advantages of electricity to isolated islands of Southeast Asia. While the most likely fuel is wood, it could also be bagasse, a residue from processing sugarcane, and rice husks. But such plants face an oftentimes insurmountable hurdle known as financing.

**Brazil**

Brazil is about 20 percent dependent on biomass. Similar to other nations, biomass as wood and charcoal is consumed in Brazil for cooking and heating in rural areas; but over half of biomass is consumed as a commercial or an industrial fuel. Companies in mining, cement, paper and ceramic making, and food processing rely on biomass as a fuel. Another unusual feature of biomass consumption is that most nations use coal to make steel, but Brazil has little in the way of coal reserves suitable for steel production. While Brazil imports some metallurgical coal, most of its charcoal output is dedicated to replacing coal in steel production.

Brazil is not alone in using biomass as a commercial or industrial fuel. Biomass is used in developing nations for smoking fish, curing tobacco, processing food, and drying bricks, lumber, furniture, and ceramics. However, Brazil stands out because of its greater reliance on biomass for commercial and industrial fuels and is unique among nations for its reliance on biomass as a motor vehicle fuel.

**BIOMASS FOR ELECTRICITY GENERATION**

Land dedicated for growing biomass for electricity generation is unused or marginal land unfit for agricultural use, but suitable for fast-growing trees (poplars, willows) and grasses (switchgrass). An example of innovation for biofuels is a newly developed grass (*Miscanthus* x *giganteus*), a hybrid (indicated by the "x" in its name) of an Asian variety related to sugarcane. The plant sprouts each year, requires little water and fertilizer, thrives in untilled fields and cool weather, and grows rapidly to thirteen feet tall. After its leaves drop in the fall, a tall bamboo-like stem can be harvested and burned to generate electricity. It is estimated that if marginal land in Illinois, accounting for

10 percent of the state's area, were dedicated to growing this grass, it could provide half of the state's electricity needs without affecting food output.[1]

The benefits of biofuel for electricity generation are that biomass:

- is plentiful, with large regions of the earth covered by forests and jungles;
- can be increased by planting marginal lands with fast-growing trees and grasses;
- stabilizes the soil and reduces erosion;
- is a renewable and recyclable energy source that does not add to carbon dioxide emissions;
- stores solar energy until needed, then is converted to electricity, whereas solar panels and wind turbines generate electricity, whether needed or not, and then only when the sun is shining and the wind is blowing;
- does not create an ash waste-disposal problem since ash can be spread in the forests or fields to recycle nutrients and not be directed to landfills as is ash from burning coal;
- creates jobs in rural areas.

Some environmentalists are critical of biomass plantations because they deplete nutrients from the soil, promote aesthetic degradation, and increase the loss of biological diversity. While growing biomass as a fuel depletes the soil of nutrients, spreading ash from combustion replenishes the soil with what was removed with the exception of nitrogen. Interspersing nitrogen-fixing plants among the biomass plants can replenish nitrogen rather than relying on nitrogen-based fertilizers made from fossil fuels. On the plus side, biomass plantations can reduce soil erosion and be managed in a way that minimizes their impact on the landscape and on biological life. In fact, there is no reason why biomass plantations cannot make a barren landscape more attractive and encourage biological life. Another argument against biomass as a fuel for making electricity is smoke emissions during combustion. This can be sidestepped by gasifying biomass to feed gas turbines. For this to occur, gasification technology has to be perfected and made cost-effective before it can be adopted for large-scale electricity generation.

Biomass for electricity generation can be forest residues including imperfect commercial trees, noncommercial trees thinned from crowded, unhealthy, or fire-prone forests, dead wood, and branches and other debris from logging operations. Though "free," there is the cost of collecting and shipping a thinly dispersed energy source from remote locations to an electricity-generating plant. More promising from a logistical point of view is collecting bark, edging, and sawdust residues at lumber mills. Lumber mills are generally located closer to population centers and collect logs from a wide area, concentrating wood residues at a few sites making transport to an electricity-generating plant easier and less costly. Furniture manufacturing facilities are also concentrated sources of wood waste. However, some of this waste from lumber mills is already burned to supply power to the lumber mill, and in northern Europe, burned to generate electricity. Waste from paper pulp manufacturing is also burned to power paper pulp plants.

A second source of biomass is the residue of harvesting agricultural crops. These include wheat straw, corn stover (leaves, stalks, and cobs), orchard trimmings, rice straw and husks, and bagasse (sugarcane residue). Sugarcane is harvested and shipped to a sugar-processing plant that concentrates bagasse at a single location, and then burned to supply power to the sugar-processing plant. Other agricultural wastes are generally left in the field and decay to become part of the soil. The high cost for collecting and shipping would make agricultural wastes as commercially unattractive as forest residue. Furthermore, agricultural wastes are seasonal, although they could be combined with wood residues to feed a biomass electricity-generating plant. Total removal of agricultural residues, however, would also have adverse consequences on soil nutrition.

A third source is so-called energy crops grown specifically for fuel. These crops are preferably fast-growing, drought- and pest-resistant, and readily harvestable by mechanical means. Depending on growing conditions, hybrid poplars and willows can be harvested every six to ten years. Trees can be cut and shipped to the utility plant as wood chips, shipped whole and converted to chips at the plant prior to burning, or be burned whole in specially designed boilers. Switchgrass does not require replanting for up to ten years. It is cut, baled, and shipped to a utility plant and ground up prior to burning. However, none of these sources is strictly sustainable in that the fuel burned in tractors and trucks in growing, harvesting, and shipping biomass fuels adds to carbon emissions. Overall carbon emissions would still be lower than burning fossil fuels because of the carbon dioxide absorbed by replacement plant growth.

Another option is to use biomass as a co-fuel in existing coal-burning plants instead of burning it in specialized electricity-generating plants. These facilities would have dedicated storage and material-handling systems for biomass in addition to their existing facilities for handling coal. Biomass would be mixed with coal in proportion to the plant's load factor. The higher the load factor, that is, the closer the plant is operating to its rated capacity, the greater will be the portion of coal given its higher energy content. Technical problems begin to emerge when too much biomass is mixed with coal in a conventional coal-burning plant. For this reason, the typical mix for plants combining biomass and coal is generally less than 10 percent biomass. These technical problems have to be dealt with before higher portions of biomass can be mixed with coal. There are a few specially designed facilities that can burn either 100 percent coal or 100 percent biomass. Again, at high load factors, coal is favored for its higher energy content.

Vegetable oils, used motor vehicle lubricating oils, and paper trash have also been suggested as fuels for electricity-generating plants. Used vegetable oils are not available in the quantities necessary to run an electricity-generating plant and the cost and effort of collecting used vegetable oils from a million and one hamburger franchises would be an inhibiting cost factor. However, there are some imaginative owners of diesel trucks who have discovered that they can stop at friendly fast-food restaurants for a bite of food and then do a favor for the proprietors by disposing of their used vegetable oil free of charge. The concoction of vegetable oil and diesel fuel supposedly burns just as efficiently as pure diesel fuel plus odorizes the exhaust with French fries, fried chicken, or fish.

Because many states prohibit the dumping of used motor vehicle lubricating oils into the environment, used motor vehicle oils are collected for a fee and recycled as rerefined lubricating oil, a higher order of usage than burning it for its heat content. The same is true for paper trash reprocessed and sold as recycled paper and cardboard products.

Biomass energy accounts for less than 1 percent of U.S. electricity generation and 2 percent in Europe, where much of the available biomass is waste from lumbering operations in Finland and Germany. Most existing biomass electricity-generating facilities are small, dedicated to meeting the needs of a local industry or community. Their most important contribution is that they demonstrate the potential for biomass to generate electricity and serve as platforms for improving technology. One such plant in Vermont burns waste wood from nearby logging operations, lumber mill waste, and discarded wood pallets. In addition, there is a low-pressure wood gasifier capable of converting 200 tons per day of wood chips to fuel gas, which is fed directly into the boiler that burns the waste wood. Hot water waste from generating electricity is pipelined to nearby buildings for internal use. Net carbon dioxide emissions, taking into consideration the sustainable growth of biomass, have been cut by over 90 percent compared to burning fossil fuels. Other research activities center on developing more effective technologies to gasify municipal and animal wastes, wood and agricultural wastes, and black liquor waste from papermaking to fuel electricity-generating plants. Gasification eliminates smoke emissions and is an efficient means of delivering biomass to distant electricity-generating plants.[2]

For special circumstances, biomass can economically produce electricity, but the economic viability of large-scale use of biomass to generate electricity remains questionable. Growing, harvesting or collecting, and shipping biomass are costly compared to the alternative of mining and shipping coal, which can be looked upon as concentrated biomass. Biomass electricity-generating facilities built in the United States in response to the oil crisis that were economically sound when oil was $35 per barrel in the early 1980s became financial albatrosses when oil prices fell after 1985. At this point, biomass for large-scale electricity-generating facilities does not appear to be in the cards because biomass is generally more expensive than fossil fuels. This could change if current research and development efforts result in a technological breakthrough that radically changes biomass energy economics or the price of fossil fuels rise to levels that make biomass for electricity generation financially attractive. All the same, for biomass to make any difference in reducing reliance on fossil fuels for electricity generation, its contribution has to double, and then double again, just to show up on the radar screen. At this point, there appears to be relatively subdued interest for significantly expanding the capacity of biomass-generated electricity.

If we take the position that carbon emissions contribute to climatic change, which of itself represents a cost, then one can justify a tax on carbon emissions. A carbon emissions tax placed on burning fossil fuel to generate electricity would make sustainable biomass energy consumption economically attractive because of its 90 percent or so reduction in carbon emissions. If something on its own merits is not economical, then it can be made so by discriminatory taxation. Nevertheless, it would be preferable if technology could make something that is environmentally desirable also economically attractive.

Even without technological breakthroughs, biomass energy is ideal for electricity generation in isolated areas in the temperate and tropical regions, such as the island nations of Southeast Asia and in South America and Africa, that are not connected to electric power grids. Micro-electricity-generating plants could serve the local needs of such communities. Unfortunately, areas already facing deforestation would be worse off if biomass were to become a source of energy for generating electricity unless it were based on sustainable tree plantations. Micro-electricity-generating plants that depended on sustainable sources of biomass fuel would provide basic services, such as lighting, to a village and encourage cottage enterprises to provide basic amenities. This, of course, presumes that the people consider this a desirable outcome. Some indigenous people would rather continue living the way they have for countless generations than adopt the ways of modern society. And who is to say that they are wrong?

## BIOGAS

In the presence of dissolved oxygen, aerobic microorganisms decompose biodegradable organic matter releasing carbon dioxide, water, and heat. However, in the absence of dissolved oxygen, an anaerobic digestion process takes place that releases carbon dioxide and methane, which can be collected as a fuel. Aerobic digestion normally occurs in compost heaps. Anaerobic digestion occurs wherever concentrations of organic matter accumulate in the absence of dissolved oxygen such as the bottom sediments of lakes and ponds, swamps, peat bogs, and in deep layers of landfill sites.

A number of steps involving different microorganisms are necessary to produce biogas. It starts with a hydrolytic process that breaks down complex organic wastes into simpler components. Then fermentation transforms these organic components into short chains of fatty acids plus carbon dioxide and hydrogen. Next the syntrophic process converts the short chains of fatty acids to acetic acid, thereby releasing heat and more carbon dioxide and hydrogen. One type of bacterium converts the acetic acid to methane and carbon dioxide, while another combines hydrogen with carbon dioxide to produce more methane. Still another bacterium reduces any sulfur compounds to hydrogen sulfide, which in turn reacts with any heavy metals that may be present to form insoluble salts. The simple process of decay turns out to be biologically complex.

The resulting biogas from anaerobic decay is approximately two-thirds methane and one-third carbon dioxide and can be made from sewage, animal manure, and other organic matter such as wood chips, household refuse, and industrial organic waste. Biogas production is very slow at ambient temperatures, but it can be sped up by raising the temperature of the organic matter to a specified range. The energy for heating is generated from organic decomposition, and, if necessary, a portion of the biogas production can be siphoned off and burned to further increase the temperature.

Gasification of raw sewage involves an initial screening to remove inorganic objects before being pumped into sedimentation tanks, where the solid organic matter settles as sludge. The sludge is pumped into large anaerobic digester tanks where decomposition takes place at a heightened temperature that hastens the process. In about two months, half the sludge will be converted into gas.[3] The remaining sludge can be dried and used as a fertilizer, burned as a fuel, or dumped into a landfill. The public does not accept sludge from human waste as a desirable fertilizer for the backyard tomato patch and relatively little is burned as a fuel. Most sludge from human sewage is buried in a landfill or dumped at sea.

Biogas is not a high-quality fuel and is usually burned locally in a turbine or fed as a gaseous fuel into a specially adapted internal combustion engine to drive a generator that produces electricity for local consumption. Biogas generating systems are being set up where animal and chicken manure present a disposal problem. In the past, chicken, beef, and pig farms had sufficient land to grow crops for farm animals that were fertilized with their waste. Now runoff from these fields is considered a contaminant of local streams and rivers. Even more importantly, modern chicken, beef, and pig farms are more like factories and buy most, if not all, of their feed. This modern industrial approach to agriculture minimizes the amount of manure that can be spread on fields. Biogas generators are not only a source of energy for running the farm, but also reduce the volume of organic waste by half. What is left can be spread on fields, if permissible, dried and used as fertilizer, burned as a fuel, or disposed of in a landfill.

Carbon dioxide emissions from generating and burning biogas are considered a closed carbon cycle. Human sewage comes from eating plants either as grain, vegetables or fruits, or meat from plant-eating animals. The source of animal waste is plant food fed to the animals. Biogas is not a completely closed carbon cycle because growing and harvesting crops, processing and distributing food, and manufacturing fertilizer require a great deal of energy in the form of gasoline, diesel fuel, and electricity, much of which is generated by burning fossil fuels. Nevertheless, biogas reduces carbon dioxide emissions by substituting for fossil fuels. Europe has taken the lead in producing biogas from organic matter, but biogas contributes less than 0.5 percent to the generation of electricity.

As organic matter decays in a landfill, biogas normally finds its way to the surface and disperses to the atmosphere. If the landfill is covered with a layer of clay to prevent escape to the atmosphere, biogas can be extracted by sinking tubes into the landfill. The biogas can fuel an internal combustion engine or turbine to generate electricity locally. The problem here is that a landfill covered by a layer of clay is probably full and the investment must be justified by the amount of biogas generated from a finite and nonreplenishable source.

In addition to disposing of sludge, disposing of garbage is a major problem for the principal population centers of the world. Ocean dumping and landfills are not desirable ways to dispose of garbage. Ocean dumping off New York City has created a marine dead zone and fish that live nearby have a high incidence of cancer and/or suffer from various grotesque mutations. Landfills near metropolitan areas are usually undesirable although they have a role to play in urban development. Although LaGuardia Airport in New York City is built on top of a landfill, a residential development built on top of a landfill might be a hard sell. Marshes buried under enormous mounds of garbage capped with a layer of soil are becoming less available near populated areas and are negatively perceived by the public. Now landfill sites may be hundreds of miles away from metropolitan areas.

There is an alternative to ocean dumping and transforming picturesque countryside into landfills. Modern garbage disposal starts with people separating recyclables such as paper, cardboard, and items made from plastic, glass, aluminum, tin, and other metals. Recycling reduces the energy intensity of a society because glass and aluminum require 90 percent less energy when made from recycled glass and aluminum than from sand and bauxite. Paper and cardboard made from paper trash and steel made from scrap also require a lot less energy than making paper from trees and steel from iron ore and coal. After removing recyclable waste, what remains can be collected and burned at an electricity-generating plant to produce steam, which can be superheated by burning natural gas to enhance turbine efficiency. The garbage is ultimately reduced to ash, a small fraction of its former volume, which can be buried in a landfill.

Though this may be considered an attractive means of disposing of garbage, it is also costly to build an electricity-generating plant that disposes of garbage. The fuel is not only free, but a charge for garbage collection becomes another source of revenue in addition to generating electricity. Even so, the revenue from selling electricity and collecting garbage may not be sufficient to justify the investment. Burning garbage does not generate nearly the same amount of electricity as burning coal or natural gas. Communities may still find it cheaper to dump the garbage in the ocean or ship it to a distant landfill rather than pay for it to be burned under controlled conditions for generating electricity.

As long as there is no cost associated with dumping garbage into the ocean or in transforming the countryside into landfills, other than shipping and dumping fees, it is economically attractive for municipalities to continue doing business as usual. An environmental degradation tax would internalize the cost of dumping garbage in the ocean or in landfills and make these options more costly. If this were done, then sharp-eyed accountants determining whether to pay the shipping and dumping or landfill fees with an associated environmental degradation tax, versus using a garbage-burning electricity-generation plant without an environmental degradation tax, might have a change of heart. As long as accountants are weighing the relative merits of alternatives strictly in terms of dollars and cents, then internalizing an externality (putting a cost on environment degradation) is a way to sway these individuals to select an environmentally sound way to dispose of garbage. Persuasive arguments and appeals to their better nature mean little when there is a cheaper, though less desirable, alternative. It is unfortunate that accountants make such decisions; but in some ways, this makes it relatively easy to shape their decisions. All that has to be done to make a desirable outcome financially attractive is to ensure that it is the low-cost alternative, which an environmental degradation tax would accomplish. Moreover, the proceeds of the tax can be dedicated to funding the building of environmentally sound garbage-disposal plants whose output of electricity would reduce the need to burn fossil fuels. Such a simple solution to a complex problem seems to escape human attention. Unfortunately, the NIMBY (not in my backyard) syndrome has made it difficult to site plants that produce electric power by burning garbage.

Another drawback has been the discovery that these plants emit mercury and other noxious metal fumes from burning discarded batteries that have found their way into household trash.

Brazil has been a model nation in having a national energy policy aimed at reducing the consumption of fossil fuels and leads the world in utilizing biomass as a motor vehicle fuel. Brazil nearly eliminated fossil-fueled electricity generation by developing its hydropower resources. Its original goal was to have hydropower supply all its electricity needs until a drought caused severe power outages throughout the nation. Faced with the need to find alternative ways to fuel electricity plants, Brazil turned to natural gas. The irony is that Brazil has little in natural gas reserves unless new discoveries are made. Pipelines have been built, or are under consideration, to tap natural gas fields in Bolivia, Argentina, and in remote areas of the Amazon and to import natural gas in a liquefied state. Rather than pursue electricity-generation plants fueled by natural gas, why not plant sustainable tree farms to supply electricity-generating plants? Biomass seems to be a neglected fuel for large-scale generation of electricity. Perhaps Bolivia's nationalization of its natural gas reserves in 2006, a case where Petrobras the national oil company of Brazil stands to lose the most money, will induce Brazil to view biomass in terms of energy security much as we view coal.

The United Nations Development Program (UNDP) is responsible for the implementation of the UN conventions on biological diversity and climate change. The Global Environment Facility (GEF), the financing arm of the UNDP, is funding, along with private corporate support, the development of a biomass integrated gasification/gas turbine (BIG/GT) in Brazil fueled by wood chips from tree plantations. Brazil already leads the world in having huge pine and eucalyptus tree plantations, but these are dedicated to making paper pulp, not generating electricity. BIG/GT transforms wood chips into a clean-burning gas and steam, both of which could be used to generate electricity. BIG/GT can produce electricity at about the same cost of building a hydropower plant, but would create many times the number of jobs in planting and harvesting trees. If proven commercially and technologically feasible, BIG/GT installations can be sized to serve local communities and built wherever there is land fit for growing trees on a sustainable basis to avoid deforestation.

A centralized electricity-generating system requires high-density population centers to financially support the construction of large conventional plants with their long-distance transmission lines that serve the surrounding area. Such systems cannot economically serve remote areas of the Philippines, Indonesia, Malaysia, and Africa, but a distributive electricity-generating system, such as BIG/GT, can be fueled by sustainable tree farms to neutralize carbon dioxide emissions. Yet, micro-electricity biomass-fueled plants capable of serving the needs of about 2 billion people living outside the main power grids have made little progress. Even those villages with biomass-fueled plants for local industrial activities such as lumber mills and food-processing plants are, for the most part, without electricity for light and comfort. The absence of electricity prevents the development of cottage industries that could provide basic amenities. People without electricity are hopelessly locked in poverty because, without electricity, there can be no factories and without factories, there can be no jobs.

One would think that building a micro-electricity-generating plant fueled by freely available biomass in a remote village would be a high-priority item for governments in pursuit of social and economic development, but this is apparently not the case. All one sees is a fairly uniform lack of progress. However, if the BIG/GT technology proves commercially and technologically feasible, distributive BIG/GT installations serving local needs (in conjunction with solar and wind) could contribute to the economic development of large areas of the world that cannot be served by conventional electricity-generating systems.

In the future, it is possible that biomass will be used to produce biopetroleum by utilizing a thermal conversion process that mimics the geological and geothermal processes of nature to produce gas and oils. In what may be the world's first operating biorefinery, turkey and pig slaughterhouse wastes are converted to fertilizer and fuel oil at a thermal conversion processing plant in Carthage, Missouri. The process starts with the grinding of the offal followed by heat and pressure in a first-stage reactor to start the chemical breakdown. A sudden drop in pressure flashes off excess water and minerals. The residue, when dried, produces a high-calcium powdered fertilizer. The remaining concentrated organic soup is heated to 500°F (260°C) and pressurized to 600 pounds per square inch in a second reaction tank. In twenty minutes, the process replicates what happens over millions of years to dead plants and animals buried deep in the earth's sedimentary rock layers by chopping complex molecular chains of hydrogen and carbon into short-chain molecules of oil. Remaining water removed by a centrifuge is laden with nitrogen and amino acids from the slaughterhouse waste and is sold as a potent liquid fertilizer. The fuel oil, superior in quality to crude oil, can be burned directly as fuel for electricity generation or be sold to a conventional refinery for upgrading to high-end petroleum products. At peak production, 500 barrels of high-quality fuel oil are made from 270 tons of turkey offal and 20 tons of pig fat. The same thermal conversion technology can also be adapted to process sewage, old tires, and mixed plastics. It is also energy efficient, consuming only 15 percent of the energy output to power operations. Perhaps someday, towns and cities can build biorefineries at their sewage and organic waste-collection facilities and sell motor vehicle fuels to the public in competition with the oil companies![4]

## BIOFUELS

Biofuels are bioethanol and biodiesel. Ethanol can also be made in an oil refinery by the catalytic hydration of ethylene with sulfuric acid as a catalyst and also from coal gas, but fossil-fuel derived ethanol is used almost exclusively for industrial purposes and only accounts for 5 percent of world ethanol production. "Ethanol" herein will always refer to hydrous bioethanol (around 5 percent water) and anhydrous bioethanol (no more than 1 percent water). Anhydrous bioethanol is the same as 200 proof whisky (ethyl alcohol) except that it is denatured with 2–5 percent gasoline or natural gas liquids to make it unfit for human consumption. Hydrous ethanol can be used as a 100 percent substitute for gasoline, or E-100 (technically E-95, taking denaturing into consideration). Brazilian automobiles that run on E-100 consume hydrous ethanol, which is cheaper than anhydrous ethanol, as the final drying process of removing residual water is not necessary. Gasohol, a mixture of gasoline and ethanol, requires anhydrous ethanol. Unless noted otherwise, ethanol figures exclude alcoholic beverages and ethanol found in consumer products such as cosmetics, paints, ink, and consumed in commercial and industrial processes.[5]

As seen in Figure 3.1, which shows world ethanol production, the United States has overtaken Brazil as the world's largest producer. The two nations account for 89 percent of world production. U.S. production of 9.0 billion gallons in 2008 continues to outpace Brazil as the second largest producer.

The United States relies on corn (maize) to produce ethanol, whereas Brazil relies on sugar. Although the United States is in first place, Brazil has much greater potential to expand sugarcane production than the U.S. has in further converting corn to ethanol. Total ethanol production of 17.3 billion gallons of ethanol is equivalent to 12.1 billion gallons of gasoline on an energy-equivalent basis. Global production of light distillate fuels, primarily made up of gasoline for motor vehicles but also including aviation gasoline and light distillate feedstock, was 26,400,000 barrels per day in 2008, equivalent to 404 billion gallons. Ethanol production in the United

Figure 3.1  **World Ethanol Production** (MM Gallons)

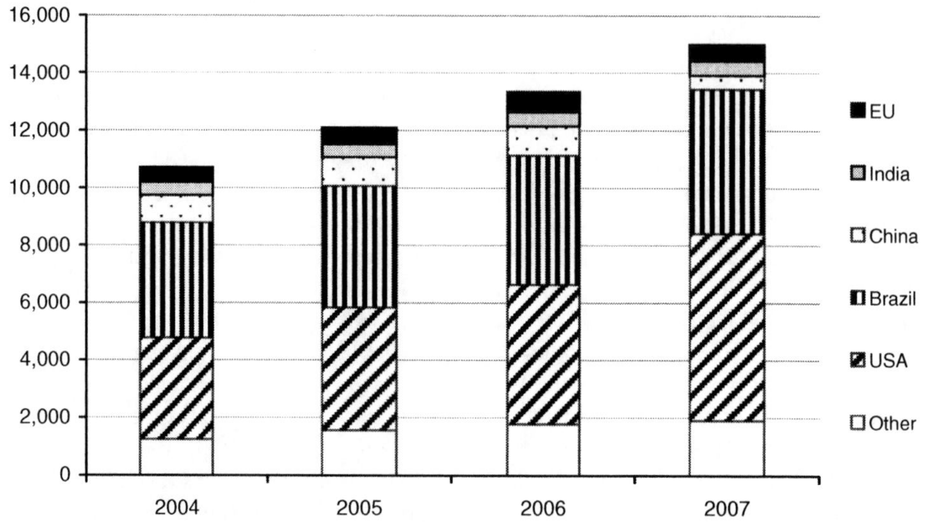

States and Brazil and elsewhere makes up about 5 percent of the global gasoline pool. Although ethanol production capacity is rapidly expanding worldwide, its contribution as a motor vehicle fuel will probably remain below 10 percent for the foreseeable future.

The process for making ethanol was well-established in ancient Egypt when beer was the common beverage for the working people, just as it is today throughout the world where alcohol consumption is allowed. Distillation of wine to raise its alcohol content was discovered by the Chinese around 3000 BCE, reaching its zenith in 200 Proof White Lightning. Interestingly, the distillation process for making whisky was adapted in the earliest days of the oil industry to refine kerosene from crude oil and the same barrel for aging, storing, and shipping whisky became the proverbial 42-gallon barrel of oil.

Ethanol is a renewable transportation fuel that adds carbon dioxide to the Earth's atmosphere to the extent that fossil fuels are consumed in its production and transportation. If ethanol could be produced without the use of fossil fuels, then its contribution is hypothetically zero as the carbon dioxide released during combustion is absorbed by the growth of plant life from which ethanol is derived. Photosynthesis absorbs energy from sunlight to convert carbon dioxide and water to glucose (sugar), the simplest form of carbohydrate, and oxygen:

$$6CO_2 + 6H_2O + Light\ (photosynthesis) \rightarrow C_6H_{12}O_6 + 6O_2$$

The fermentation process decomposes glucose into ethanol and carbon dioxide:

$$C_6H_{12}O_6 \rightarrow 2C_2H_6O + 2CO_2$$

The chemical formula for ethanol is sometimes written as $C_2H_5OH$; either way, ethanol reacts with oxygen during combustion to produce energy that can power an engine along with the waste products of carbon dioxide and water.

$$2C_2H_6O + 6O_2 \rightarrow 4CO_2 + 6H_2O + energy$$

One difference between ethanol and gasoline is that the ethanol molecule contains oxygen, whereas gasoline is a blend of hydrocarbons ranging from $C_5H_{12}$ to $C_{12}H_{26}$. Ethanol is an oxygenate that improves fuel combustion reducing carbon monoxide, unburned hydrocarbons, and particulate emissions in comparison to gasoline. However oxygen in ethanol reacts with atmospheric nitrogen during combustion producing ozone-forming nitrous oxides, the precursor to smog. Ethanol has no sulfur emissions and is a cleaner-burning fuel than gasoline with 13 percent less emissions, even with its higher nitrous oxide emissions. Moreover ethanol, along with biodiesel, is biodegradable if spilled on the ground or leaked from a pipe. Biofuels may be eligible for carbon credits if a cap and trade program is established for carbon dioxide emissions.

Though theoretically carbon-neutral, ethanol is not carbon-neutral because of fossil fuels consumed during planting and harvesting, pesticide and fertilizer production and distribution, and conversion to ethanol and distribution. In the United States, the amount of coal and natural gas in electricity production and the amount of natural gas consumed directly in the conversion process of corn to ethanol, plus the oil consumed in support of agricultural activities and transportation of corn and ethanol is not effective in reducing carbon emissions. Netting ethanol production of the diesel fuel for tractors, trucks, and locomotives to produce and transport bioethanol and the oil consumed in making and shipping pesticides and fertilizers, ethanol does not make a significant contribution to reducing oil imports. At best, ethanol production in the United States is a means to convert fossil fuels (coal, natural gas, and oil) to a gasoline substitute. The major difference between the United States and Brazil is that sugar requires less energy to be converted to ethanol than starch and that bagasse, the residue after extracting sugar juice from sugarcane, is burned to generate electricity for the ethanol conversion process with excess generation supplying the Brazilian electricity grid. But fossil fuel (petrodiesel) is still consumed for agricultural activities and transportation of sugarcane and ethanol. Ethanol production in Brazil is more effective in reducing oil consumption for motor vehicle fuels and greenhouse gas emissions than in the United States, and will become even more so when biodiesel is substituted for petrodiesel for agricultural activities and transportation.

The energy content of 87-octane gasoline is between 18,000 and 19,000 Btu per pound versus 11,500 Btu per pound for ethanol (E-100). On an energy equivalent basis, ethanol requires about 1.5 gallons to be burned to obtain the same energy output as 1 gallon of energy. But ethanol has a higher octane rating of 98–100 compared to 86–94 for gasoline. Higher octane improves engine performance by reducing engine knocks, which occur from premature fuel combustion during acceleration or pulling a heavy load. Higher octane of ethanol results in cleaner and better performing engines improving engine power by about 5 percent. Taking both factors into consideration, an automobile burning E-100 ethanol will get 70 percent of the mileage of one burning gasoline. In other words, a car getting 30 miles per gallon on gasoline would be expected to get 21 miles per gallon on pure ethanol. The reduction in mileage from burning gasohol is directly related to its ethanol content. Besides lower mileage, another drawback of a high percentage of ethanol in gasoline is difficulty in cold-weather starts.

Ethanol requires special conditions for shipping and storage. The existing pipeline and storage infrastructure system for oil products is unsuitable for ethanol because ethanol has an affinity for water. If gasohol is carried in petroleum pipelines and absorbs residual moisture, a phase separation occurs making it virtually impossible to reblend the ethanol with the gasoline. Ethanol is also a solvent that absorbs rust, gums, and other contaminants in piping and storage tanks, making it unfit to be a motor vehicle fuel. Depending on the metallurgy of the pipeline, it is possible for ethanol's electrical conductivity to increase corrosion rates. Ethanol in gasohol can also strip off certain corrosion inhibitor coatings on the interior surface of pipelines and promote stress corrosion cracking. Another problem with moving ethanol in petroleum pipelines is that it is much more difficult to segregate batches of ethanol gasoline blends. Petroleum pipelines operate on the principle of fungible products where what is shipped by a seller may not be what is delivered to a buyer. However, the buyer is assured that what is received has the same specifications of what was purchased. Batches of various blends of gasohol are not fungible because they cannot be easily identified and separated for final delivery to the buyer.

Ethanol and gasohol can be carried in dedicated pipelines built to withstand the technical challenges associated with ethanol. In the United States, the logical ethanol pipeline would run from the Midwest to the Northeast with entry points in Iowa and Illinois to deliver ethanol to markets in Chicago, Philadelphia, and New York City. But the volume has to be large enough to provide a lower-cost alternative than the present practice of transporting ethanol by railroad tank car and by barge down the Mississippi River and its tributaries. Because of the difficulties associated with obtaining the necessary permits and the question of cost effectiveness, the building of such a pipeline is considered improbable.

The current practice in the United States is to load pure ethanol on rail tank cars from ethanol plants to distribution centers in the east where the ethanol is "splashed" into gasoline being pumped into tank trucks for final delivery to retail filling stations. Ethanol is also moved on inland waterway barges down the Mississippi River to terminals for coastal barge movements to east and west coast ports for final delivery by truck to gasoline distribution centers. Ethanol shipments do not require double-hull vessels as do petroleum products. Trucks haul ethanol for short-distance movements within the Midwest. The cost to move ethanol or any liquid within a nation or region is lowest by pipeline, then barge, followed by rail, with truck being a factor of ten times more expensive than rail for long hauls.

The history of the nonalcoholic use of ethanol started with its use for lighting in the nineteenth century. In the 1850s, nearly 90 million gallons of pure ethanol were burned annually as a fuel for lamps. In 1862, an excise tax on alcoholic beverages of $2 per gallon knocked ethanol out of the lighting market for the benefit of other sources such as kerosene, whale oil, and methanol. (The tax authorities were unable to monitor whether ethanol was being drunk or burned in a lamp.)

Early automobile engines ran on a variety of fuels including ethanol, such as Nicholas Otto's first spark-ignition engine and Henry Ford's first automobiles in 1896. With the repeal of the liquor tax in 1906, Ford wanted ethanol to be the fuel of choice for his Model Ts to counter a farming depression. Converting grain to alcohol would create incremental demand for grain, raising its price to improve the living standards of farmers plus boosting rural job opportunities, the same benefits espoused by biofuel aficionados today. The problem facing Ford was the oil industry. The industry was built on kerosene for lighting. At the turn of the century, kerosene faced a dim future with the invention of the electric light bulb. Naphtha, the light end of the refining process, was a waste product often dumped into the nearest stream. The advent of the automobile was the salvation of the oil industry. A new market in gasoline made from the waste product naphtha would be a substitute for a declining market in kerosene.

Cheap gasoline forced Ford to modify the Model T in 1908 to have two fuel tanks—one for ethanol and the other for gasoline. The carburetor was adjustable for either fuel or a mix of the two, the precursor of today's flex-fuel vehicle. Ford and Standard Oil entered into a partnership to distribute corn-based ethanol blended with gasoline. In the 1920s, gasohol represented about 25 percent of Standard Oil's sales in the corn-growing region under the brand Alcogas. But as time went on, gasoline became the motor fuel of choice with ethanol primarily an additive for better engine performance. Prohibition, which lasted from 1919 to 1933, made it illegal for farmers to produce ethanol from the family still for any purpose including being a fuel. Tetraethyl lead took over ethanol's role as an antiknock agent. Nevertheless some bioethanol still found its way into the gasoline stream. With falling corn prices during the 1930s depression, Midwest states sought alternative uses for farm products. Alcolene and Agrol were gasoline blends ranging between 5 percent and 17.5 percent ethanol sold in 2,000 retail outlets from Indiana to South Dakota. Nonetheless, the oil industry in the 1930s lobbied against the blending of alcohol and gasoline as the Depression worsened the financial prospects for oil. Interest in ethanol evaporated after the Second World War as it could not compete against gasoline. But interest revived in the wake of the 1970s oil crisis beginning with Brazil's National Alcohol Program (ProAlcool).

The agricultural feedstock of choice for ethanol is sugar. Sugar is essentially made up of carbohydrates, which the body can easily convert to energy. White refined sugar has virtually no nutritional value while brown sugar, a less refined state of white sugar, retains some vitamins and minerals. Molasses is the residue of the sugar-refining process. Sugar causes tooth decay by metabolizing into an acid that eats away at tooth enamel. It is also a contributor to obesity, diabetes, and perhaps hyperactivity when consumed in excess.

The history of sugar by the evaporation of sugarcane juice can be traced back to 500 BCE in India. From there it spread to the Middle East and China. The Arabs and Berbers introduced Europeans to sugar during the conquest of the Iberian Peninsula in the eighth century. The Crusaders brought sugar back with them on their return to Europe. In the fourteenth century, advances in sugar presses made it economical to grow sugar in southern Spain and Portugal, where it spread to the Canary Islands and the Azores. Spanish and Portuguese explorers and early settlers introduced sugarcane to the Caribbean and Brazil, both perfect environments for growing sugarcane whose low cost undercut supplies from Asia. Market demand for sugar and molasses in Europe and North America provided rich profits for growers, but there was a shortage of labor. Native Americans could not survive the rigors of sugarcane production but Africans could; the economic impetus for the slave trade. Sugarcane rapidly exhausts soil of its nutrients, which was addressed by abandoning nutrient-depleted land and bringing new land into cultivation. Before Castro, Cuba was a major world producer of sugar not only from its favorable growing conditions, but also from the technological leadership displayed by Cuban sugar growers in how to apply fertilizers optimally to prevent soil exhaustion and how to improve the sugar-making process to reduce costs—knowledge that spread throughout the world of sugar.

The discovery of sucrose in sugar beets and the process for making sugar from sugar beets occurred in Europe in the 1700s, but the cost was not competitive with imported sugar made from sugarcane. Napoleon, when cut off from sugar imports by the British blockade, banned sugar imports (interesting timing), which provided the economic impetus for advancing the development of the technology to convert sugar beets to sugar.

Sugarcane is grown in tropical and subtropical regions, while sugar beets are grown in temperate regions of the northern hemisphere. Sugar from sugarcane is cheaper than from sugar beets even though sugar beets have a higher sucrose-yield because of the more complicated process of obtaining sugar from sugar beets. Sugar production is estimated to be 169 million tons in 2007/2008 with a long-term growth rate of 2 percent per year. Over 100 nations grow sugar, of which 78 percent is from sugarcane in tropical areas and the rest from sugar beets in temperate areas. Figure 3.2 shows the world's top ten producers, accounting for 80 percent of world sugar production.

Nearly 70 percent of sugar is consumed locally with the balance traded on the international market. The chart shows that the relationship between production and export for the major sugar exporters. Brazil is the world's largest producer and exporter of sugar. India and Europe export little sugar. Half of SADC (Southern African Development Community) production is from South Africa, and the remainder is from neighboring nations. Thailand, Australia, SADC, and Guatemala

Figure 3.2  **2007/2008 Estimated Sugar Production and Exports** (MM Tons)

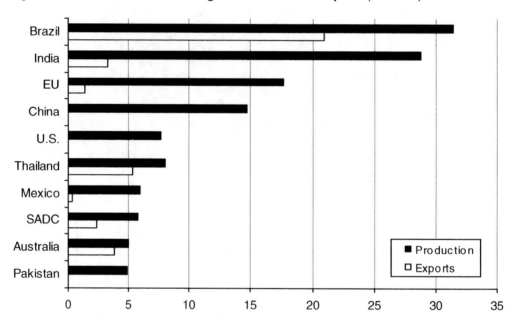

(not among the world's largest producers) are the world's second, third, fourth, and fifth largest exporters accounting, along with Brazil, for 80 percent of the world's exports. The lowest-cost sugar producer is Brazil at $250 per ton of white sugar. Other low-cost producers are SADC, Guatemala, and Australia. India is a medium-cost producer at $370 per ton and China at $440 per ton. Sugar beets in the United Kingdom, United States, and France produce sugar for about $480 per ton. High-cost sugar producers from sugarcane are Cuba at $510 per ton and the United States at $520 per ton. The European Union, the United States, and Japan protect their domestic sugar growers by imposing high tariffs on imports.

**Brazil—The Great Leap Forward for Biofuels**

The development of the ethanol industry in Brazil was not entrepreneurial in nature, but was nurtured by decades of government support programs. In 1975, Brazil imported much of its oil needs, aggravating its negative balance of trade. Brazil also had a social challenge of doing something about the enormous number of idle workers in rural Center-South and North-Northeast regions of Brazil. The solution to both problems was bioethanol. The Brazilian government implemented a program to stimulate ethanol production to reduce reliance on imported oil, to provide job opportunities for large numbers of idle workers, and to convert fallow land to agricultural use. The government provided billions of dollars in low-interest loans for entrepreneurs to finance the construction of ethanol-production plants and the conversion of mostly fallow and unused grazing land to sugarcane plantations.

The government also required Petroleo Brasileiro SA (Petrobras), the state oil company, to purchase ethanol to blend a vehicle fuel with a minimum of 22 percent ethanol (E-22). Petrobras had to refit its gasoline stations to sell gasoline, gasohol, and pure ethanol. A differential tax was placed on motor vehicle fuels to ensure that hydrous ethanol sold initially at a 65 percent discount from the price of gasoline. This, along with tax incentives to purchase automobiles fueled by hydrous ethanol, provided a clear incentive for Brazilians to buy automobiles that ran on E-100. Ethanol consumption grew rapidly from 1983 to 1988 with 90 percent of new car sales being pure ethanol-fueled vehicles. By 1990, over 5 million ethanol-fueled vehicles made up about half of the population of the motor vehicle fleet. The subsidy on ethanol was eventually reduced to 35 percent, making ethanol price competitive with gasoline on an energy-content basis.

The Brazilian automobile industry had to modify engines to burn high concentrations of ethanol in gasoline or pure ethanol by eliminating materials such as aluminum, zinc, brass, and lead whose metal deposits from the use of ethanol would eventually damage an engine. Nonmetallic materials that cannot come in contact with ethanol include natural rubber, polyurethane, cork gasket material, leather, polyvinyl chloride polyamides (PVC), methyl-methacrylate, and certain thermal plastics. Fiberglass reinforced with nonmetallic thermoset was found suitable for storage and piping of ethanol in automobiles. Conventional automobiles can burn gasohol of 10 percent ethanol (E-10) with no modifications. For automobiles to burn between E10 and E25, modifications may have to be made to the fuel injection, pump, pressure device, filter, tank and catalytic converter along with the ignition and evaporative systems, depending on the automobile design. Between E-25 and E-85, further modifications may have to be made to the basic engine design and the intake manifold and exhaust systems. A cold-start system may have to be installed for automobiles to burn E-100.

A ton of sugarcane (2,200 pounds) can produce either 305 pounds of refined sugar or 21 gallons of ethanol. Although Brazilian sugarcane growers are free to sell to either the sugar or ethanol market, whichever is more profitable, Petrobras is required to buy ethanol to ensure that the regulatory minimum content of ethanol in gasoline is satisfied. This creates the market for ethanol. However during the latter part of the 1980s and 1990s, Petrobras discovered offshore oilfields that would eventually make Brazil self-sufficient in oil, reducing the negative trade balance associated with oil imports. Moreover the price of oil fell significantly in the mid-1980s from crisis levels of the late 1970s and early 1980s. The decline in oil imports and oil prices weakened the government's resolve to support biofuels. In 1988, the government permitted the free export of sugar to reduce the amount of subsidies being paid to ethanol producers. As sugarcane growers diverted sugar to the international export market to take advantage of higher prices, the ethanol producers were squeezed between a high price for their raw material input and a low price for their output. In the 1990s, Brazil actually became the world's largest importer of ethanol, but not enough to avert shortages, which resulted in a loss of consumer confidence in pure ethanol-burning automobiles. Brazilians switching from pure ethanol to gasohol-burning automobiles ended the era of pure ethanol automobiles.

In 2000, Brazil deregulated the ethanol market and removed all subsidies, but depending on market conditions, motor vehicle fuels were required to be blended with 20–25 percent ethanol. Brazil stopped importing ethanol and became an exporter. Flex-fuel vehicles were introduced in 2003 that can run on straight ethanol, straight gasoline, or a blend of the two—the same as Henry Ford's early Model Ts. This protects Brazilian drivers from the vicissitudes that had previously plagued pure ethanol-burning vehicles. Currently about 78 percent of new cars made in Brazil are flex-fuel. Filling stations have pumps for gasoline, ethanol, or ethanol-blend (gasohol). Motorists can choose what makes best sense for them, which means that the competitive price of ethanol must be at a 30 percent discount from gasoline to reflect its lower energy content. Drivers can play the arbitrage game as the price of gasoline changes with respect to the price of crude oil and ethanol with respect to the price of sugar. Most distilleries in Brazil are part of sugar mill complexes capable of swinging between 40 and 60 percent ethanol production, allowing their owners to also

Figure 3.3  **Oil Consumption in Brazil** (MM Bpd)

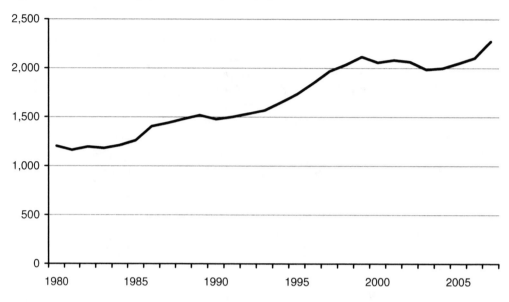

play the arbitrage game. Advocates of bioethanol in the United States point out that it would be necessary to copy the Brazilian model of having most gasoline stations offering both ethanol and gasoline and for auto manufacturers to produce mostly flex-fuel cars before bioethanol can play a significant role as a substitute for gasoline. Figure 3.3 shows oil consumption in Brazil in millions of barrels per day from 1980 to 2008—the conclusion one may reach is that the impact of bioethanol has been to dampen growth in demand, but not demand itself.

Not all oil consumption goes into gasoline; ethanol does not affect the consumption of diesel fuel, jet fuel, lubes, petrochemical feedstocks, and fuel oil. However, ethanol can be substituted for high-octane aviation gasoline to power prop-driven airplanes. One thousand Brazilian crop dusters have logged over 650,000 hours of flight time on pure ethanol. The energy density of ethanol is too low for commercial jet engines, but a blend of biodiesel and jet fuel has been successfully tested.

Bioethanol capacity in Brazil is currently expanding, underwritten by high-priced crude oil. When oil prices decline, as they did in late 2008, so does the incentive to expand ethanol production. On the other hand, since it is highly unlikely that U.S. agriculture can fulfill the goal enunciated by President Bush for American-made ethanol to replace 75 percent of Middle East oil imports, the United States is in position to become a large-scale ethanol importer from Brazil. But this requires the elimination of the U.S. import tariff on ethanol that applies to Brazil. In the meantime, Petrobras is aggressively seeking ethanol outlets in other nations such as Japan, the world's most promising importer, plus China, Sweden, and other nations who view bioethanol as a means to reduce reliance on imported oil.

Though sugar production in Brazil is free of subsidies, there is still a subsidy by the Brazilian government to support a research program to improve sugarcane varieties and fertilizer applications. The success of this research program has more than paid for itself. New varieties have been developed to make sugarcane more resistant to drought and pests while yielding higher sugar content. There are now over 500 commercial varieties of sugarcane, but only 20 are used for 80 percent of sugarcane production. Diversification of varieties is essential for pest and disease control. Rapid replacement of varieties has stemmed highly damaging disease epidemics. Pesticides are also used to control damaging insects plus biological countermeasures, such as parasitoids to control sugarcane beetles and certain fungi to control spittlebugs. In 30 years, the yield of sugar from sugarcane increased from 55 tons per acre in 1975 to over 90 tons per acre in 2003 with a 14.6 percent sugar content, which of itself has increased by 8 percent between 1975 and 2000. As a result of this government investment in research, ethanol yields increased from 242 gallons per acre in the 1970s to 593 gallons per acre in the late 1990s.[6]

The waste products of making sugar from sugarcane are bagasse and vinasse. Bagasse is the sugarcane stalks after the sugar is extracted. Electricity produced by burning bagasse is estimated to be 1,350 megawatts as compared to Brazil's Angra I nuclear power plant of 657 megawatts (a typical large coal or nuclear electricity-generating plant is around 1,000 to 1,200 megawatts). Most of the electricity is consumed internally (1,200 megawatts) for converting sugar to ethanol and the remaining 150 megawatts is sold to electric utilities. This electricity is generated during the dry season when hydropower, the principal source of electricity in Brazil, operates at reduced capacity. It is estimated that replacing current low-pressure steam boilers with more efficient high-pressure boilers and using harvest trash currently left in the fields could substantially increase electricity production from bagasse. Burning bagasse for electricity generation produces little ash and no sulfur. Its nitrous oxide emissions are low as bagasse is burned at relatively low temperatures. Bagasse is also sold as a substitute for burning heavy fuel oil to other processing industries.

Vinasse is a liquid residue from alcohol distillation. Every liter of ethanol produces 10 to 15 liters of vinasse, which contains high levels of organic matter, potassium, calcium, and moderate amounts of nitrogen and phosphorus absorbed by sugarcane. The volume of vinasse, about the same as the entire sewage waste of Brazil, was initially dumped into streams and rivers, resulting in algae blooms and fish kills. With a similar chemical composition to fertilizer, it is now spread on the ground along with another waste product, filtercake, and industrial wastewater. The application of vinasse is optimized for the soil and environmental conditions in order to reduce the amount of fertilizer required for sugarcane cultivation—an example of fertilizer-recycling. The application of vinasse on soil can also be for irrigation, but Brazil is fortunate in having sufficient rainfall to support this water-intensive crop. Irrigation is depleting the water table in many parts of the world, such as in the sugar-growing region in India. Another environmental problem is burning sugarcane fields, which was once a leading cause of air pollution in Brazil. Burning sugarcane prior to harvesting reduces the amount of biomass that a sugarcane cutter has to handle and gets rid of bothersome insects and other pests. Burning is becoming less prevalent with the advance of mechanical harvesting, which is displacing sugercane cutters. Mechanical cutting also increases the amount of biomass waste that can be burned for electricity generation.

Sucrose from sugarcane is normally converted into 83 percent sugar and 17 percent molasses. Molasses is sold at 10–35 percent of the price of sugar, either for direct human consumption or for making rum. By diluting the molasses with water and adding it back into the sugarcane juice stream to produce more ethanol, the sugarcane producer can obtain a near-equivalent price of sugar for molasses. Sugar and ethanol mills operate for 5–6 months during the sugar season in Brazil versus 3–4 months for corn-based ethanol plants in the United States. The longer duration of unused capacity in the United States adds to capital costs per unit of ethanol produced. There is plenty of room to expand bioethanol production in Brazil. Half of Brazil's land mass is Amazon forest and natural forest reserves. The remaining half is shown in Table 3.1. Brazil's sugar industry, once viewed as a remnant of the country's colonial past, now has a prominent place in the future of world energy. About half of the country's 21,000 square miles (nearly 14 million

Table 3.1

**Land Use in Brazil**

|  | Million Acres |
|---|---|
| Pastureland for cattle | 550 |
| Savannah | 225 |
| Urban centers, lakes, other | 185 |
| Cropland (soybeans and other grains) | 105 |
| Permanent crops (oranges, sugarcane, etc) | 37 |
| Reforestation and wood pulp and other wood product farms (pine, eucalyptus) | 12 |

acres) of sugarcane under cultivation is for ethanol. Sugarcane plantations are concentrated in the Center-South region, accounting for 85 percent of the nation's sugarcane production with the remainder in the North-Northeast region. The 336 sugar mills/plantations in Brazil employ an average of 2,000 people at each facility, split about evenly between farming and processing. Total employment for sugar production for both direct consumption and for the production of ethanol is estimated to be 1.8 million.

Many laborers are only employed during the harvest season that extends from November to March. Criticism was directed at plantation towns having less than desirable living conditions; yet for these workers, working for the sugar industry, even on a seasonal basis, is an attractive alternative to stark poverty. A half-million cane workers receive about $1.35 per hour plus a bonus on the amount of sugarcane they cut, which is about double what low-skilled agricultural workers receive and about 50 percent higher than the service sector and 40 percent higher than industrial workers. However, to receive this pay, cane workers are expected to harvest 12 tons of sugarcane per ten-hour day. From 2002–2005, 312 sugarcane and ethanol workers died on the job with nearly 83,000 injuries. As bad as these statistics appear; percentage-wise, they are not as high as those in the transportation, foundry, and refining industries.[7] However, the injury rate is still eight times greater than the rate for laborers in the citrus and grain industries.

Ash clinging in the air after burning sugarcane can result in lung fibrosis among cane workers, a leading cause of occupational death. Currently about 75 percent of sugarcane is harvested by hand, but this is shrinking rapidly with the advance of mechanization. Mechanization not only eliminates the need for burning sugarcane, an environmental benefit that improves air quality, but also increases the quantity of biomass that can be burned for electricity. Despite these criticisms, ethanol has proven to be a way to create jobs for unskilled workers in large areas of Brazil where there was a dearth of employment opportunities. Even with the growing trend to mechanize harvesting of sugarcane, the expansion of sugarcane and ethanol production will still be a source of incremental employment. Brazil has embarked on a program to build 73 new ethanol plants in addition to the existing 335 plants, with another 189 plants under consideration. Another part of this program is to improve the transport infrastructure by building ethanol-carrying pipelines from the sugar-producing regions to ports with substantial terminal storage capacity for the use of larger-sized tankers to promote exports and to bring another 10,000 square miles (close to 7 million acres) under cultivation.

This is a proverbial drop in the bucket compared to 775 million acres of available pastureland and savannah. There is no need to deforest the Amazon jungle to vastly increase the production of sugarcane. Most deforestation of the Amazon is for grazing land and lumber. Much of the

Figure 3.4   **Energy Output/Fossil Fuel Input**

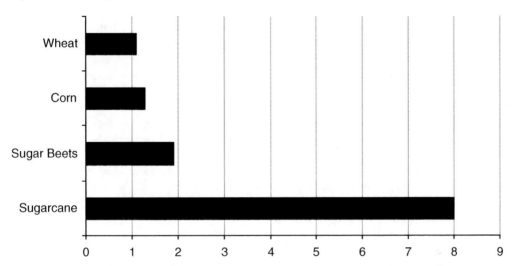

expansion of sugarcane plantations will take place in the Center-South region where sugarcane grows best, but some will also take place in the North-Northeast region despite its lower yields and higher costs. Brazil has high hopes that its low-cost ethanol will replace high-priced gasoline in the world market. Japan and Sweden are expanding the role of ethanol in their gasoline pool to help meet their obligations to cut carbon emissions under the Kyoto Protocol in addition to their concerns over energy security. The United States will most probably not fulfill its ethanol mandate from domestic sources. If Brazil can realize its dreams of becoming the "Saudi Arabia of Ethanol," perhaps ethanol's share of the world's gasoline supply could expand to 8–10 percent or more in 20 years. So confident are Brazilian authorities in the future of ethanol that they have offered to share their technological achievements with other sugar producers in the Caribbean and Latin America.

It is also possible that an ethanol bubble may occur in Brazil if oil prices were to collapse from a falloff in world economic activity from an economic implosion in the United States and/or China as occurred in late 2008. Even so, Brazil is the low-cost producer of ethanol stemming from its development of new sugarcane varieties with higher sugar yields and increased resistance to drought and insects, the use of bagasse as a biofuel, advances in the technology of making ethanol, the optimization of fertilizer application, progressive agricultural management of sugarcane plantations, improvements in harvesting and transportation systems, and efficiently run ethanol plants. For these reasons, it is felt that oil could drop as low as $35 to $40 per barrel and still cover costs for the ethanol producers. Of course, this assertion depends on the price of sugar. A combination of low oil and high sugar prices is a death knell for the ethanol producers.

The ratios of energy output to fossil fuel input for producing ethanol from different crops are shown in Figure 3.4.[8] Output is the energy contained in the ethanol, while input is the energy contained in the fossil fuels consumed in the production of ethanol. Sugarcane produces eight times the energy output compared to energy input. The major reason for this is that biomass (bagasse) is burned to supply electricity for conversion of sugar to ethanol, not fossil fuels (coal and natural gas) as in the United States. The energy output/input for Brazil would be even greater if tractors and trucks employed by the sugar plantations were powered by biodiesel rather than petrodiesel. Corn has a ratio of only 1.3, meaning that 1.3 units of energy in the form of ethanol are obtained from consuming 1 unit of fossil fuel. However this does not mean 1.3 gallons of ethanol equals 1 gallon of oil; rather as previously mentioned, corn-based ethanol can be looked upon as a conversion of fossil fuels (coal, natural gas, oil) to a biofuel that reduces reliance on oil in motor vehicle fuels. As an aside, the energy output/energy input for gasoline is 5, less than 8 for making ethanol from sugar in Brazil, but much better than making ethanol from corn in the United States.

There are two processes for making ethanol from the starch in the kernels of field corn: wet-mill and dry-mill. The wet-mill process produces ethanol plus a variety of food products such as corn sweeteners, corn syrup, corn oil, and gluten feed. Dry-mill plants produce only ethanol and a high-protein animal feed called dried distillers grain and have lower capital and operating costs. Dry-mill plants make up 82 percent of ethanol plants and are more attractive investments for farmer cooperatives, entrepreneurs, and private investors. Wet-mill plants produce higher-valued coproducts that justify their higher capital and operating costs and are mostly owned by large food corporations.

The ethanol production process for corn starts with delivery by truck or rail to an ethanol plant with a storage capacity of 7–10 days. The corn kernels are screened to remove debris such as bits of corn stalks and then ground into coarse flour. Cooking involves preparing hot slurry where the milled corn grain is mixed with water, and the pH of the mixture is adjusted to about 5.8. An alpha-amylase enzyme is added, and the slurry is heated to 180–190 degrees Fahrenheit for 30–45 minutes to reduce its viscosity. Next is primary liquefaction where the slurry is pumped through a pressurized jet cooker at 221°F and held for five minutes and then cooled by an atmospheric or vacuum-flash condenser. This is followed by secondary liquefaction, where the mixture is held for one to two hours at 180–190°F to allow alpha-amylase enzyme to break down the starch into short chain dextrins. After adjusting for pH and temperature a second enzyme, glucoamylase, is added as the mixture is pumped into the fermentation tanks. Now known as mash, the glucoamylase enzyme breaks down the dextrins to form simple sugars.

Once the starch is converted to sugar, the process is the same as making ethanol from juice extracted from sugarcane except for the nature of the residues. Yeast is added to convert sugar to ethanol and carbon dioxide. The fermentation process takes 50–60 hours ending up with a fermented mash of 15 percent ethanol, grain solids, and yeast. Carbon dioxide is captured at some ethanol plants and sold to companies as dry ice for flash freezing and as condensed, pressured gas for carbonating soft drinks. It might one day be pipelined to played-out oil reservoirs as a tertiary means of enhancing recovery, or to greenhouses to enhance plant growth, or to algal farms to produce more biofuels.

The fermented mash is pumped into a multicolumn distillation system where it is heated. The columns take advantage of the differences in the boiling points of ethanol and water to separate hydrous ethanol (95 percent ethanol, 5 percent water) equivalent to 190-proof alcohol. Hydrous ethanol can be consumed directly in pure ethanol-burning automobiles. To produce anhydrous ethanol required in gasohol, hydrous ethanol passes through a molecular sieve that separates water and ethanol molecules yielding 200-proof anhydrous or waterless ethanol. Then a denaturant such as gasoline is added to make the ethanol unfit for human consumption before entering storage normally sized to hold 7–10 days' production.

The difference between using corn and sugar as feedstocks once the corn is reduced to a sugar is in the residues. In Brazil, the waste product of distillation of sugar is vinasse that is applied to sugarcane fields as a form of fertilizer-recycling. In the United States, the stillage in the bottom of the distillation tanks contains the solids and yeast as well as the water that was added during the distillation process. It is passed through centrifuges to separate into thin stillage, a liquid with 5–10 percent solids and wet distillers grain. Some of the thin stillage is routed back to the cook/ slurry tanks as makeup water, reducing the amount of fresh water required to support the ethanol-making process. The rest is sent through a multiple evaporation system to concentrate the stillage into syrup with 25–50 percent solids. The syrup, high in protein and fat content, is mixed with the wet distillers grain from the centrifuges. With the syrup, the wet distillers' grain contains most of the nutritional value of the original corn or other grain feedstock plus the waste residual yeast.

Wet distillers' grain has a limited shelf life, varying between four days to two weeks, and is expensive to transport with its higher water content. Wet distillers' grain, which is 33 percent solid, is sent to dairy farms or cattle feedlots located within 100 miles of the ethanol plant. Dairy cows can be fed rations consisting of up to 43 percent wet distillers' grain, and beef cattle can be fed rations of up to 37 percent wet distillers' grain. The wet distillers' grain can be dried into dry distillers' grain, but the drying process increases energy consumption for older, less efficient plants by as much as 50 percent. Dry distillers' grain has a shelf life of several months, is less costly to transport, and is commonly used as a high-protein ingredient in cattle, swine, poultry, and fish feed. Ruminant feed (dairy cows and cattle) can be up to 40 percent dry distillers' grain and up to 10 percent for nonruminant feed (poultry and swine). Thin stillage, sometimes referred to as sweetwater, from the distillation tanks is evaporated and sold as condensed syrup, or thick stillage, that can be blended or sprayed over distillers dried grains to produce distillers dried grains with solubles. A typical dry mill will produce 2.7 gallons of ethanol, 17.5 pounds of distillers' dried grains, and 17 pounds of carbon dioxide in addition to thin stillage from a bushel of corn. Emerging technologies may increase marketable co-products in the form of germ separation prior to final grinding of the corn kernels and other fermentable products such as lactic acid, acetic acid, glycerol, and others.

In the wet-mill process, the grain is first soaked or "steeped" in water and diluted sulfurous acid for 24–48 hours to separate the components within grain. After steeping, the corn slurry passes through a series of grinders to separate the corn germ from which corn oil is then extracted. Hydroclonic, centrifugal, and screen separators segregate the fiber, gluten, and starch components. The steeping liquor is concentrated to heavy steep water in an evaporator, then co-dried with the fiber component and is sold as corn gluten feed of 21 percent protein to the livestock industry. A portion of the gluten component is further processed for sale as corn gluten meal to poultry breeders with 60 percent protein content and no fiber. The starch can be fermented into ethanol, or dried and sold as cornstarch or processed into corn syrup.

Progress is constantly being made to improve the efficiency and productivity of ethanol production. Between the early 1980s and the early 2000s, there has been a 50 percent decline in energy required to produce ethanol, an increase in production yield of 23 percent from 2.2 gallons per bushel of corn to 2.7 gallons per bushel and a cut in capital costs of 25–30 percent. Earlier plants used azeotropic distillation systems to dehydrate (removal of the last vestiges of water) which proved to be expensive, costly to operate, energy intensive, and hazardous. Today molecular sieves or molsieves are the most popular means to dehydrate ethanol. Molsieves, a bed of ceramic beads, absorb water molecules in vaporized ethanol. Molsieves are lower cost, easier to operate, less energy demanding, and more environmentally friendly compared to azeotropic distillation. Another improvement is energy recycling—the thermal capture of waste energy via heat exchangers for heating purposes. The technology improvements for making enzymes, required for hydrolyzing starches to fermentable sugars, have increased the yield fivefold. The practice of discarding spent yeast and replacing with a new batch, called "pitching," has given way to ethanol plants propagating their own yeast. Ethanol plants that once purchased truckloads of yeast per month now need only a few pounds to start the propagation process. While plant automation has reduced the number of employees required to run an ethanol plant, the remaining workers must have a higher skill level. Automation has improved the efficiency and uniformity of the product, enhancing its quality. The aggregate impact of these improvements has been to cut the cost of producing ethanol from over $2 per gallon to a little over $1 per gallon.

Efforts are underway to further lower production costs, such as high-gravity fermentation. Currently water is added to reduce the solid content to ferment "beer" mash. High-gravity fermentation will allow fermentation to occur at considerably higher levels of solids, thus reducing the amount of water required, which, in turn, reduces the cost of handling and treating water later in the process. A higher concentration of solids results in higher beer yields in a shorter time. The development of yeast that can withstand higher temperatures will increase the alcohol content of beer and reduce energy costs. Presently in a dry-mill process, the entire kernel of corn is processed with corn oil ending up in distillers' dried grains. The development of a quick steeping process will allow dry-millers to separate corn oil prior to processing for sale as a separate and higher-valued product. New strains of corn that can raise the starch content from 33 pounds per bushel to 37 pounds will result in lower unit-processing costs.

Even with these improvements, ethanol plants are still large consumers of energy requiring a combination of electricity and natural gas to run motors and pumps and generate steam for plant operation. With high-cost natural gas, some plants are converting to coal. This consumption of natural gas or coal is a major reason why ethanol from corn is not as effective in replacing fossil fuels as sugar that obtains its power needs from burning bagasse, a biofuel. To counteract this large demand for fossil fuels, a few ethanol plants are planning on using energy supplied by biomass gasification of cattle manure, corn stalks (stover), grasses, and wood chips; fluidized bed reactors to convert biomass into steam; and wind turbines. These projects are under close scrutiny by industry leaders and government program managers to see if they are feasible commercially and are a means for improving the energy output/input relationship to enhance ethanol's capacity to reduce carbon emissions.

Another example of improving the process is a corn-oil extraction technology to make biodiesel. The stillage flow in the evaporation stage of the drying stage is removed when its consistency is that of concentrated syrup and is then heated and sent through an advanced centrifuge to separate the crude corn oil, which is converted to biodiesel. The defatted concentrated stillage residue is dried and sold as defatted dried distillers' grain. This process increases revenues through the manufacture of biodiesel, reduces operating costs and emissions, and recovers up to 75 percent of the corn oil in dried distillers' grain. The traditional ethanol processing plant converts a bushel of corn, weighing about 54 pounds, into about 18 pounds of ethanol, 18 pounds of carbon dioxide, and 18 pounds of dried distillers' grain, which contains about 2 pounds of fat. This corresponds to a corn-to-clean fuel conversion efficiency of about 33 percent, or about 2.8 gallons of clean fuel per bushel of corn. The proposed corn-oil extraction and biodiesel-processing technology converts the fat in dried distillers' grain into a high-grade corn oil that can then be converted into biodiesel on close to a 1:1 volumetric basis. This increases the corn-to-clean fuel conversion efficiency from 33 percent to 36 percent or about 3.0 gallons of clean fuel per bushel of corn. Another proposal is to incorporate a bioreactor to take advantage of the one-third of corn converted to carbon dioxide. The bioreactor will house algae to consume carbon dioxide emissions and give off oxygen and water vapor. If properly cultivated, the algae can double in mass in less than 24 hours and be harvested for conversion into clean fuels. Heating algal biomass with little oxygen (biomass gasification) produces a syngas of carbon monoxide and hydrogen, which can be converted into bioethanol or biodiesel and other products through a catalytic chemical (Fischer-Tropsch) reaction.

This process can also convert defatted dried distillers' grain into liquid fuels to further enhance corn-to-clean fuel conversion ratios.[9]

BP has entered into a partnership with Dupont to develop biofuels based on biobutanol. Both companies believe that biobutanol represents the next significant change in renewable biofuels. Biobutanol has a molecular structure more similar to gasoline than ethanol and is compatible with existing vehicle technology. Biobutanol can be easily added to conventional gasoline because of its low vapor pressure and energy content being closer to that of gasoline than ethanol. It can be blended at higher concentrations than bioethanol for use in standard vehicle engines and is well-suited to current vehicle and engine technologies. Biobutanol is less susceptible to separation in the presence of water than gasohol and can be used in the oil industry's existing distribution infrastructure without modifications in blending facilities, storage tanks, or retail station pumps. Biobutanol is produced from the same agricultural feedstocks as ethanol (i.e., corn, wheat, sugar beet, sorghum, cassava, and sugarcane), and existing ethanol capacity can be cost-effectively retrofitted to biobutanol production with only relatively minor changes in fermentation and distillation. Biobutanol will fit into future developments in cellulosic ethanol from energy crops such as grasses and fast-growing trees and agricultural waste. Emission reduction for biobutanol is on par with ethanol. Biobutanol has the potential to expand the market for biofuels because of its greater compatibility with gasoline and relative ease of distribution.

## The Great Sugar–Corn Debate

Although sugarcane is grown in Florida, Louisiana, Texas, and Hawaii, the climate in the United States is generally too cold for large-scale sugar production, leaving corn as the principal source for ethanol. However, there are definite benefits of utilizing sugar over corn to produce ethanol. Corn is an annual crop requiring plowing, harrowing, and planting whereas sugarcane is replanted every six years. Corn requires heavy applications of fertilizers and pesticides, which require fossil fuels to produce and distribute. Sugarcane takes less in the way of fertilizers, which are recycled, and less in the way of pesticides, which are partly controlled by biological means and by switching sugarcane varieties. Producing ethanol from corn is four times greater in energy consumption to first convert starch to sugar before it can be converted to ethanol. Although both processes consume electricity, electricity is generated from burning bagasse in Brazil whereas electricity generated in the United States is largely from fossil fuels. Brazilian bioethanol makes a much greater contribution to reducing oil demand and greenhouse gas emissions than U.S. ethanol. Brazil's sugar crops can expand without affecting food production, whereas diversion of corn to ethanol in the United States affects food production. All in all, there is not one advantage of using corn over sugar other than ethanol from corn being an effective price-support mechanism.

Corn already has one nonfood use. Polylactide (PLA) is a polymer made from corn for manufacturing a wide variety of everyday items such as clothing, packaging, carpeting, recreational equipment, and food utensils. Products made from PLA offer the environmental benefits of being biodegradable and made from a renewable resource. But making bioethanol from corn is many orders of magnitude greater than PLA. A major argument against corn for ethanol is its impact on the price of food. Corn is chiefly a food for livestock first and humans second. Corn prices were seemingly unaffected by rising ethanol production in 2004 and 2005 but exploded between 2006 and 2008 as ethanol began consuming a quarter and more of the corn crop. Rising corn prices affect the price of soybeans through the corn-soybean complex where corn and soybean oil and meal can be, to some extent, substituted for one another depending on their relative prices. Ethanol spokespeople have retorted to this criticism by maintaining that food prices are more affected by

Table 3.2

**U.S. Ethanol Production and As a Percent of the Corn Crop**

|  | Production (billions gallons) | % of Corn Crop |
|---|---|---|
| 2004 | 4.0 | 14 |
| 2005 | 4.3 | 15 |
| 2006 | 4.9 | 17 |
| 2007 | 6.5 | 23 |
| 2008 | 9.0 | 31 |

oil and other energy costs than by the price of corn since agriculture is a heavy consumer of energy through every stage of production. One pundit remarked that the doubling of corn prices raises the price of a box of corn flakes by about a dime; if true, one wonders what is being purchased when one buys a box of corn flakes!

Corn is generally thought of as corn on the cob for a summer lobster fest. Sweet corn is consumed fresh, frozen, or canned. Sweet corn, as the name suggests, has higher sugar content than commercial or field corn, but its yield in bushels per acre is less. In the United States, most corn is field corn. A kernel of field corn consists of 66 percent starch, 2–4 percent oil, and the remainder mainly cellulosic material. About half of corn production is consumed as livestock feed followed by fuel ethanol now accounting for about one-third of production. High fructose corn syrup consumes about 5 percent of production followed by glucose and dextrose, cornstarch, cereals, and beverage alcohol each with smaller shares of 2 percent or less. Corn grown for seed to plant the following year's crop is a little under 10 percent of production. Exports are in danger of declining as a consequence of higher corn prices and less availability from the increasing diversion of corn to ethanol production. Table 3.2 is constructed on the basis that 1 billion gallons of ethanol production consumes 3.5 percent of the corn crop. This relationship is approximate in that there has been switching from wheat and other crops to corn production that increases the amount of acreage dedicated to ethanol production.

A 30 percent removal of the supply of corn from foodstuffs and animal feed to ethanol production has got to have some impact on food prices. Higher food costs by a combination of high fuel costs and a diversion of corn to ethanol is attracting public criticism. Media criticism is also focusing on the large volume of water consumed to produce corn ethanol, which, in turn, depends on whether corn has to be irrigated and the method of irrigation. Soybean prices have escalated via the corn-soybean complex for those products where corn and soybeans are substitutable. Wheat prices have also spiraled upward, but the blame on rising wheat prices is not corn but adverse weather patterns affecting wheat production in Australia, an important wheat exporter. Another contributing factor is low wheat inventories from consumption exceeding production for seven of eight years between 2001 and 2008. Although technically the blame for high wheat prices cannot be laid at the footstep of corn, nevertheless the finger of blame is pointing towards corn. The critical difference between the United States and Brazil is that the U.S. has limited capacity to bring new land under cultivation to grow more crops. This is not true for South America in general and in particular Brazil. Brazil is a major producer of soybeans, and one would expect that high soybean prices would justify expanding soybean cultivation with increasing production and exports putting pressure on soybean prices, which through the corn-soybean complex would limit the extent of the rise in corn prices.

"No Food for Fuel" is a mantra gaining strength in the public realm, particularly with the enormous escalation of basic food prices in 2007 and 2008. In the case of corn, the United States produces 45 percent of world production followed by China with a 22 percent share. These two nations account for two-thirds of world corn production. The United States is by far the world's largest grain exporter, and aside from a handful of other grain exporters (mainly Canada, Australia, Argentina), most nations are grain importers. This places a great responsibility on the United States as the primary grain supplier of the world. In the case of corn, about 14 percent of world corn production is exported, of which the U.S. accounts for almost 70 percent. Diversion of a significant portion of corn for ethanol production affects the availability of exports leading to upward pressure on the international price of corn and other grains. In response to high grain costs in 2008, China prohibited the making of ethanol from corn, but not sugar, which resulted in cutting ethanol production in half.

Whatever criticism is leveled against ethanol made from corn, most Americans are in favor of biofuels to reduce the nation's oil imports. The people agree with the objective to minimize oil imports from the Middle East. President Bush enunciated the U.S. commitment to biofuels at the Renewable Fuels Association Summit meeting in Washington, D.C., in April 2006:

> Ethanol is good for the whole country . . . We owe it to the American people to be promoting alternative ways to drive their cars so as to make us less dependent on foreign sources of oil. We owe it to the American people to be aggressive in the use of technology so we can diversify away from the hydrocarbon society. That's exactly what we're doing.

To further exemplify America's pro-biofuels stance, the Indianapolis 500, an Americana iconic event, declared the official fuel would be 100 percent (E-100) ethanol.

## The United States Is Following Brazil's Footsteps in a More Complex Way

Biofuels programs require government support. The U.S. biofuel support program was more gradual than Brazil's starting with the U.S. Energy Tax Act of 1978 that officially defined gasohol as a blend of gasoline of at least 10 percent nonfossil fuel ethanol by volume (excluding oil-refinery ethanol). This exempted ethanol from the gasoline excise tax; in effect, providing a direct subsidy for ethanol blended in gasoline. The U.S. Environmental Protection Agency (EPA) became interested in ethanol as an octane booster and volume extender in the 1980s, but this role was ultimately filled by MTBE (methyl tertiary butyl ether), an oxygenate preferred by the oil industry with the banning of tetraethyl lead. Despite the general disinterest in ethanol other than the E-10 gasohol sold in the corn-producing regions of the nation, Congress approved several tax benefit packages along with loan and price guarantees to support ethanol producers and blenders. Nothing came of these incentives when oil prices collapsed in the mid 1980s. The Alternative Motor Fuels Act of 1988 provided credits for automobile manufacturers of building vehicles capable of burning E85, a blend of 85 percent ethanol and 15 percent gasoline. These credits could be applied to meet the requirements of the Corporate Average Fuel Economy (CAFE) standards. This Act had little impact as there were very few fuel retailers offering E85. The Energy Policy Act of 1992 required primarily government-owned automobile fleets to begin purchasing alternative fuel and flex-fuel vehicles capable of burning E85 fuel.

During the 1990s, motorists in the Midwest voluntarily paid a premium for gasohol (E-10) as a means of supporting the local corn growers. The rapid growth of U.S. ethanol production started after 2002, with increasing restrictions being imposed on the use of MTBE as an oxygenate. This movement to ban MTBE as a carcinogen finding its way into drinking water supplies was led by California. MTBE lost 42 percent of its market when New York and Connecticut joined California in banning the product. This provided the opportunity for ethanol to be a substitute for MBTE, but quickly ended with the repeal of the oxygenate requirement for reformulated gas by the Energy Policy Act of 2005. While seemingly negative for ethanol, the Energy Policy Act of 2005 also contained the Renewable Fuel Standard (RFS). The RFS guarantees a market for ethanol by mandating that 4 billion gallons of ethanol be incorporated in gasoline in 2006, an amount nearly met in 2005, to be expanded to 7.5 billion gallons by 2012. The mandate leaves it to the oil companies on how to infuse this amount of ethanol into the gasoline pool, which would result in gasoline containing about 7 percent ethanol by 2012 depending on future gasoline consumption. This is still a far cry from Brazil's success in achieving 20–25 percent ethanol in gasoline, but Brazil consumes a far smaller volume of motor vehicle fuel.

Though ethanol was to be derived from corn, another feature of the Act was providing an incentive for the development of cellulosic ethanol. A crediting procedure was set up whereby cellulosic ethanol has a 2.5 advantage over corn ethanol in terms of meeting minimum ethanol requirements. That is 1,000 gallons of cellulosic ethanol would be treated the same as 2,500 gallons of corn ethanol in fulfilling minimum usage requirements. There is also a mandate for 250 million gallons of cellulosic ethane to be produced and incorporated in gasoline by 2013. Thus the Act both supports corn ethanol and encourages the development of a new technology that will play an increasing role in satisfying the long-term demand for biofuels.

The Energy Independence and Security Act of 2007 passed on December 20, 2007 contains provisions bearing on a number of energy issues. Title I and II are most pertinent to motor vehicle fuels. Title I—Energy Security Through Improved Vehicle Fuel Economy—sets forth the automobile fuel economy average with a goal of achieving 35 miles per gallon for the total fleet of passenger and nonpassenger automobiles manufactured in the United States by 2020 with escalating minimum standards starting in 2011. Between 2021 and 2030, each fleet segment must attain its maximum feasible average fuel economy, not just the overall fleet average. Credits are to be created for fleet segments that exceed compliance minimums and for dual-fueled automobiles (flex-fuel and biodiesel) that are transferable to other fleet segments. Research monies will be made available for developing the electric car and other advanced technologies. The thrust of Title I is to reduce energy demand through greater efficiency. Title II—Energy Security through Increased Production of Biofuels—defined advanced biofuels as ethanol derived from cellulose, hemicellulose or lignin, sugar or starch other than corn starch, waste material and crop residues, biodiesel, biogas including landfill and sewage waste treatment gas, butanol and other alcohols produced from organic matter, and any other fuel derived from biomass including algae, recycled cooking oil, and grease. This section calls for slightly more of a doubling of the 2012 requirement from 7.5 to 15.2 billion gallons, or about 14 percent of the future motor vehicle fuel consumption in 2012 depending on the growth rate, and increases to 36 billion gallons by 2022. On top of this is the advanced biofuel requirement, which covers everything but corn ethanol. This opens up the possibility of making ethanol from sugar and other grains in the United States. While one may look at this as effectively breaking the corn growers' monopoly on ethanol production, there is still plenty of opportunity for the corn growers to produce ethanol—so much so that this Act may open the door to large-scale ethanol imports. The advanced biofuel requirement started in 2009 and grows to 22 billion gallons in 2022, of which a large portion is cellulosic ethanol plus smaller requirements on biodiesel and other advanced biofuels. The amount of advanced biofuels is 22 billion gallons, which when added to the 36 billion gallons of corn ethanol, is a whopping 58 billion gallons. Ethanol production in 2008 of 9 billion gallons is equivalent to about 30 percent of the corn crop. The 15.2 billion gallon goal by 2012 would presumably consume a little over half of the corn crop. Yet as impressive as these goals are, the most they can do is level or marginally decrease gasoline consumption—that is, most biofuels would be consumed meeting incremental gasoline demand even after taking into consideration mandated increased fuel economy of automobiles.

Several conclusions can be drawn from the mandated changes in the Energy Independence and Security Act of 2007:

- The United States automobile manufacturers must respond with flex-fuel vehicles. Conventional vehicles can burn E-10 with no alterations. The existing population of 250 million automobiles is limited to E-10 except for a few E-85 flex-fuel vehicles. In 2009, the ethanol industry made a proposal to raise the ethanol content in gasoline to a maximum of E-15 to meet the requirements of the Act. The proposal raised concerns from automobile manufacturers that their engine warranties will not apply for engines burning more than E-10, and from gasoline distributors whose storage and pumping facilities have not been certified for E-15, and from small-engine manufacturers such as those used for lawnmowers on concerns of poor engine performance.[10] The ultimate solution is for all new automobiles built in the United States to be flex-fuel in order to accommodate the envisioned growth in ethanol consumption.
- Gasoline stations have to be refitted to serve flex-fuel vehicles to make higher content gasohol more available to the public. It is interesting to note that the Energy Act of 2007 prohibits motor vehicle fueling stations franchisers from stopping their franchisees from installing fuel pumps and tanks to serve the public with renewable fuels. For Americans to have a real choice between alternative fuels, it is necessary that higher ethanol content gasohol be available at most of the 200,000 service stations in the nation.
- The required diversion of corn acreage to the production of ethanol has a truly negative impact on food availability and prices. To avoid the scenario of motor vehicle fuels having precedence over food, the United States will have to become a major ethanol importer to meet the minimum renewable energy requirements.
- The logical source of imported ethanol is Brazil. In addition to Brazil, demand for ethanol is sufficient to provide an incentive for the large-scale conversion of sugar to ethanol production in the Caribbean. Sugar plantations and ethanol-processing plants in Colombia and Peru provide farmers an alternative crop to coca plants, the source of cocaine.
- The existence of the $0.54 per gallon tariff set up to protect American-made ethanol has to be eliminated, considering the magnitude of imports. It is amazing that oil is imported free of tariffs from hostile exporters, whereas Brazil, a friendly nation, is faced with a discriminatory tariff that does not apply to the Caribbean, Colombia, Peru, and other Latin American nations.
- The monopoly of the corn growers is broken. There is no way for corn growers to meet mandated demand. Ethanol could be made from U.S.-produced sugar, but the greatest opportunity lies in cellulosic ethanol where the Act guarantees the market for this high-cost source of bioethanol.

Just because Congress dictates a minimum requirement does not mean that the system can produce the necessary output. The Secretaries of Energy and Agriculture have the power to review the status of the program over stated timeframes, and under prescribed conditions, and are allowed to change the minimum biofuels requirements. Tax credits, yet to be promulgated, and grants will be available to support the development for cellulosic biofuels. Grants are also to be given for enhancing engine durability for various blends of biodiesel, optimizing engine design of flex-fuel vehicles, generating biogas for natural gas vehicles, improving the prospects for algal biomass, designing a renewable fuel infrastructure, and establishing bioenergy research centers. An ethanol pipeline feasibility study is to be conducted along with studies on the adequacy of various modes of transport to handle higher volumes of ethanol.

While a number of studies have concluded that ethanol made from sugar in the United States cannot be economically justified, one company is breaking the rule. Pacific West Energy through its subsidiary Gay & Robinson Ag-Energy is developing the first sugarcane-based integrated power and ethanol plant in the United States modeled on the Brazilian sugar success. A 7,500-acre sugar plantation on the island of Kauai is being converted into an energy plantation by constructing a new power plant of about 25 megawatts to burn bagasse and a 12 million gallon per year ethanol plant. The project will operate under state of Hawaii mandates that 10 percent of gasoline sold in the state will be ethanol and that 20 percent of the electricity produced will be from renewable sources. The ethanol mandate creates a market for 45 million gallons per year. Other renewable sources will be considered such as solar, hydroelectric, and municipal waste to take advantage of the mandate for 20 percent of electricity to be from renewable sources. The project is also operating in the favorable commercial environment of Hawaii with the highest gasoline prices and electricity rates in the United States. Another interesting project is a sugar plantation in Peru located in a desert, but which will be irrigated by water flowing from the Andes to the Pacific Ocean. The benefit of low rainfall is year-round harvesting of sugarcane for extremely high yields. Sugarcane cannot be harvested during the rainy season, which lasts for seven or eight months in the Caribbean and Central America. Ethanol will be shipped from a port with a submarine pipeline out to deep water in order to accommodate larger-sized tankers for exporting ethanol.

There are other bioethanol crops such as sugar beets, which have the highest yield of ethanol per acre. In France, sugar beets produce 7,000 liters per hectare (750 gallons per acre); in Brazil, sugarcane produces 5,500 liters per hectare (590 gallons per acre); and in the United States, corn produces 3,000 liters per hectare (320 gallons per acre). Sugar beet production is concentrated in temperate regions of the northern hemisphere and are grown for their sugar content. The root is about one foot long weighing 3–5 pounds and containing 15–20 percent sugar. Sugar beets, while yielding more sugar than sugarcane on a per acre basis, consume more fertilizers and pesticides and are more difficult to harvest as a root than sugarcane as a stalk. Sugar beets cannot be cultivated more than once every three years on the same ground because of pest infestations. Moreover, the process of obtaining sugar from sugar beets is more energy intensive and costly than from sugarcane. Worldwide sugar beet production is declining, and its future role as an ethanol producer is not promising. Incremental ethanol production in Europe is likely to be from wheat and sorghum, not sugar beets. The byproducts of sugar beet ethanol plants are beet pulp and sugar beet molasses, both used as wet or dry livestock feed.

Cassava (tapioca) is another crop that has potential for ethanol production. It is the second most grown crop in Africa, fourth in Southeast Asia, fifth in Latin America and the Caribbean, and seventh in Asia. The highest yields are achieved in Thailand because of less exposure to disease and pests and relatively intensive crop management including irrigation and fertilizers. Cassava has a high tolerance for marginal soils and drought. Thailand and Nigeria place cassava high on the list for their planned ethanol programs. Spain, Germany, France, and Canada are increasing their ethanol production from wheat. Rye and barley are two relatives of wheat more resistant to drier and cooler conditions and can be grown on more acidic soils. They are favored for ethanol feedstocks in Sweden and other parts of northern Europe.

Bioethanol is an internationally traded commodity. In recent years, ethanol production in Europe has been climbing most notably from increases in sugarcane production in Spain and sugar beet and wheat production in France and elsewhere in Europe. The problem with biofuels in Europe is a relative scarcity of cropland. If Europe desires a meaningful infusion of ethanol in its motor vehicle fuels, Europe, now an ethanol exporter, will eventually become a major ethanol importer. Supplies will probably come from Brazil augmented with new supplies from southern Africa, Colombia, Peru, and Central America. The major Asian importers are anticipated to be Japan, China, Korea, and Singapore, which will be primarily supplied by Brazil with smaller contributions from elsewhere in Asia such as Thailand, the Philippines, and southern Africa. Japan is slated to become the world's largest ethanol-importing nation. For the United States that has a mandate to rapidly expand the ethanol content in its gasoline, Brazil, Peru, Colombia, Central America, and perhaps southern Africa would be the major suppliers. It may be necessary to eliminate the import tariff that applies for Brazil, although a portion of Brazilian imports can enter duty-free if the final stage of processing, the removal of residual water, occurs in the Caribbean or Central America. Thus, the nations with the greatest appetite for ethanol imports will be the United States and Japan followed by China and the European Union.

As an internationally traded commodity, bioethanol faces import tariffs and trade restrictions that are more onerous than other energy commodities such as crude oil. One such tax is ad valorem import tariffs. The United States is at a relatively low 2.5 percent of imported value, Brazil and Argentina are at 20 percent, Thailand 30 percent, and India 186 percent. Canada has an import tax of 19 cents per gallon, and the European Union has 87 cents per gallon. The United States' secondary duty of 54 cents per gallon is exempt for bilateral trade agreements such as the U.S.-Israel Free Trade Agreement, the North American Free Trade Agreement, and the more important Central America Free Trade Agreement (CAFTA). CAFTA members are Costa Rica, El Salvador, Guatemala, Honduras, and Nicaragua. CAFTA was expanded by the Central America and Dominican Republic Free Trade Agreement of 2005 (CAFTA-DR) to include the Dominican Republic. For these nations, locally made ethanol enters the United States duty-free. Congress has also created unilateral trade preference programs for ethanol to enter duty-free such as the Caribbean Basin Initiative (CBI) and the Andean Trade Preference Act. CBI nations are Antigua, Aruba, Bahamas, Barbados, Belize, Costa Rica, Dominica, El Salvador, Grenada, Guatemala, Guyana, Haiti, Honduras, British Virgin Islands, Jamaica, Montserrat, Netherlands Antilles, Nicaragua, Panama, Dominican Republic, Saint Kitts and Nevis, Santa Lucia, Saint Vincent and the Grenadines, and Trinidad and Tobago. The Andean Trade Preference Act was enacted in 1991 to combat drug production and trafficking in Bolivia, Colombia, Ecuador, and Peru by offering trade benefits to help these nations develop and strengthen legitimate industries.

Brazilian hydrous ethanol is allowed to flow through CBI countries with no modification other than dehydration up to an annual ceiling representing 7 percent of U.S. fuel ethanol supply without having to pay the U.S. import tariff. In addition, CBI countries may export an additional 35 million gallons into the United States tariff-free if the ethanol is 30 percent derived from local feedstocks plus additional ethanol if at least 50 percent made from local feedstock. The potential market for the 7 percent allowance in 2005 would have been 240 million gallons of imports, but CBI countries fall far short of that target. CAFTA-DR places restrictions on Costa Rica and El Salvador, the primary Central American conduits for Brazilian ethanol. Costa Rica may not export more than 31 million gallons per year and El Salvador 5.2 million gallons per year with annual step-ups of 1.3 million gallons, provided that total exports from these two nations do not make up more than 10 percent of duty-free ethanol in any one year. These trade preference programs are considered gateways to a larger Free Trade Area of the Americas (FTAA) to permit freer access to markets within the western hemisphere and also reflect the intention of Congress to combat poverty and drug trafficking in the Caribbean and in Bolivia, Colombia, Ecuador, and Peru by fostering a

Table 3.3

**Common Crops Associated with Ethanol Production**

| Crop | Annual Yield (gallons/acre) | Greenhouse Gas Savings (% versus petroleum) |
|---|---|---|
| Sugarcane | 570–700 | 87–96 |
| Corn | 330–420 | 10–20 |
| Miscanthus | 780 | 37–73 |
| Poplar | 400–640 | 51–100 |
| Switchgrass | 330–810 | 37–73 |
| Sweet sorghum | 270–750 | No data |

thriving ethanol industry. Ethanol production is currently concentrated in Guatemala, Nicaragua, the Dominican Republic, and Jamaica with smaller production in El Salvador, Costa Rica, and Trinidad and Tobago. Much of this production is locally consumed with the principal exporters to the United States being Costa Rica, El Salvador, Jamaica, and Trinidad and Tobago.

**Cellulosic Ethanol**

Table 3.3 shows the range of ethanol output for common crops that are or may one day be used for ethanol production and the savings in greenhouse gas emissions compared to petroleum products. The figures for sugarcane and corn do not reflect the conversion of bagasse and stover into cellulosic ethanol. The conversion of cellulosic waste along with the sugar or starch would make a considerable improvement in ethanol production. The remaining crops are based solely on cellulosic ethanol production. As can be seen, the output of cellulosic ethanol from biomass is comparable to sugar and starch-based ethanol.

Large-scale commercial production of cellulosic ethanol is not yet possible until further technological advances are made in converting cellulose biomass to ethanol. If these advances are achieved, the potential for making ethanol from cellulose is enormous. The United States has an estimated capacity to produce one billion dry tons of biomass feedstock per year. The sources of cellulosic feedstocks are forest-derived biomass (fire hazard reduction, logging, urban wood, and wood-processing residues), agricultural waste biomass (crop residues, particularly corn stover and wheat straw and processing residues), and special fuel crops grown for their cellulosic content. Bringing into cultivation perennial biomass crops on marginal and idle land has its detractors. Such cultivation could impact cultivated lands by placing constraints on equipment, labor, and transport availability. Removal of large quantities of plant residues such as corn stover and straw from cropland could reduce soil quality, promote erosion, and lead to a loss of soil carbon that might lower crop productivity. Perennial plants for biomass will consume some pesticides and fertilizers, although the degree of application is less than food crops. But the greater demand for pesticides and fertilizers may have an impact on the cost of producing food crops. There is also the question of water availability for perennial biomass croplands that may need irrigation.

On the plus side, perennial plants for biomass fuel would provide a habitat for birds and animals and increase availability for animal feed if protein can be separated from cellulosic biomass in the ethanol-production process. The extensive use of animal manure for biofuels would reduce the pollution of surface and ground water and the cost of disposing of municipal waste. Wildfires would be less menacing if removal of excess plant growth were permitted as a source of biomass fuel. Depending on the assumptions, cellulosic ethanol could contribute between 25 and 60 percent of current gasoline consumption. This would be sufficient to make North America oil independent; that is oil imports from Mexico and Canada to the United States would be sufficient to eliminate imports from elsewhere.

Farmers in Nebraska and the Dakotas participated in the five-year study sponsored by the U.S. Department of Agriculture and the University of Nebraska of planting switchgrass and carefully recording all costs for fuel, fertilizer, and other energy-related costs. The study concluded that cellulosic ethanol production would be 300 gallons per acre, almost the yield of ethanol from cornstarch, and have a 5.4 energy output/energy input. This compares favorably with the 1.3 energy output/ input for corn ethanol, 5 for gasoline from crude oil, and is beaten only by the energy output/input of 8 for sugar ethanol in Brazil.

Cellulosic ethanol technology, based on acids converting (hydrolyzing) cellulose and hemicellulose into simple sugars, has a hundred-year history. The Germans and Russians used cellulosic ethanol technology during wartime to produce alcohol fuels and chemicals from wood. Up to recent times, this process was not economically competitive with low-cost petroleum products because of poor yields, high wastage, and a large volume of unmarketable byproducts. Except for a few plants in Russia, the technology fell into disuse after the Second World War. Interest in this process was rekindled by the oil crisis in the mid 1970s and also by a DuPont article published in *Science* magazine at that time citing 250 chemical products made from petroleum that had previously been made from sugar/ethanol. This spurred university and government laboratories to study the hydrolysis of cellulose using acids or enzymes, led by the Tennessee Valley Authority and Mississippi State University.

Cellulosic biomass would be able to extract ethanol from the complex carbohydrate polymers in the plant cells. The three primary components in cellulosic biomass are cellulose, hemicellulose, and lignin. Cellulose is made up of long chains of glucose molecules with six atoms of carbon per molecule (six-carbon sugar). Hemicellulose consists of a mixture of six- and five-carbon sugars and is easier to break down to sugar than cellulose. Lignin is the "glue" in cell walls that provides the overall rigidity and strength to plant structure. Trees normally have more lignin to allow them to grow taller than other plants. Lignin is very difficult to break down into simpler forms of glucose. Most approaches to cellulosic ethanol call for burning lignin to fuel the process with the potential of selling excess electricity capacity to the grid. Nevertheless, research efforts are underway to convert lignin to ethanol and other useful products because lignin is a significant portion of a plant.

As an approximation, the biomass composition of plants is about 45 percent cellulose (glucose sugar), 25 percent hemicellulose (pentose sugars), 25 percent lignin, and 5 percent other material such as ash, sulfur, potassium. "Black liquor," the residue of the paper-pulping process, is normally burned to power paper mills. Since the paper-making process concentrates the cellulose in paper and the hemicellulose in black liquor, rather than being burned, black liquor has the potential of being a feedstock for ethanol.

The basic steps of making ethanol from cellulosic biomass start with reducing the size of biomass for easier handling and more efficient processing. Agricultural residues would go through a grinding process and wood through a chipping process to achieve a uniform particle size. Dilute sulfuric acid is mixed with the biomass feedstock to cause a chemical reaction (hydrolysis) to break down the complex chains of sugars to simple sugars. The complex hemicellulose sugars are converted to a mix of soluble five-carbon sugars, xylose and arabinose, and soluble six-carbon sugars, mannose and galactose. A small portion of the cellulose is also converted to glucose in this step. Enzymes, which are either grown or purchased, are used to hydrolyze the cellulose fraction of the biomass. Enzymes have to be customized for each type of feedstock. The glucose is then fermented in the traditional manner to make ethanol.

Intense research is being dedicated to finding the right combination of thermal and chemical processes plus the right type of enzymes that can efficiently and economically break down cellulose, hemicellulose, and lignin to simple sugars. Since sugar and starch make up only a small portion of plant matter, successful advances in cellulosic ethanol would permit sugar bagasse and corn stover to become raw materials for ethanol production. Using the whole plant rather than just the sugar juice or the corn kernels nearly doubles ethanol production. The cellulose content of agricultural crops can be increased without affecting the output of the crop—the best example is short and tall varieties of soybeans. If a tall variety of soybean is substituted for a short variety, the soybean crop remains the same, but the amount of cellulosic biomass doubles.

Switchgrass is a favored high-yielding perennial grass that grows well over most of central and eastern United States. Fast-growing trees, normally harvested between three and ten years and replanted for repeat harvests, include poplar and willow in cooler and sycamore and sweetgum in warmer climate and eucalyptus trees now grown in tree farms in Brazil for paper pulp and charcoal. Cellulosic ethanol producing facilities are expensive in terms of capital, but the cost of the feedstock is low (collecting agricultural waste or growing grasses and trees). Most importantly the cost of biomass is fixed, quite unlike corn and sugar whose value as food markedly affects the economics of making ethanol. It is even possible that the cost of a feedstock for cellulosic ethanol production can be negative; that is, the ethanol plant would receive money for consuming a feedstock. One prime example would be disposing of municipal solid waste, currently a costly proposition. Municipalities would be willing to pay a cellulosic ethanol plant processor to get rid of waste. Regardless of the feedstock, the impact of cellulosic ethanol on agricultural crop output would be marginal or none at all.

The most likely candidate for cellulosic ethanol is corn stover, as it is easily available for ethanol plants processing corn kernels. Harvesting stover will require overcoming several challenges. For one thing, corn stover on the ground is contaminated with dirt and rocks. Weather and soil conditions may not allow enough time for field drying, which would be necessary for safe storage. Harvesting corn stover would have to compete with other more valuable crop-harvesting operations. Harvesting would probably be in bales for storage and transport to ethanol plants similar to bales of forage for farm animals. If converting corn stover to ethanol is possible, equipment may be developed that harvests the corn kernels and bales the stover in a single operation. Not all the corn stover can be removed from a field because stover left in the field controls erosion, retains moisture, provides winter forage for animals, and adds nutritional value to the soil. It is felt that only about half of the stover should be removed for ethanol production.

There are a number of companies, including major oil companies, active in cellulosic research. The U.S. Department of Energy has a program to help underwrite the development of biorefineries that would produce cellulosic ethanol along with a variety of bio-based industrial chemicals and products.

## Biodiesel

The first diesel engines invented by Rudolf Diesel ran on a heavy grade of kerosene, but at the Paris Exposition in 1900 the demonstration diesel engine ran on peanut oil. A number of explanations have been put forth including no other fuel was available, or Diesel wanting to demonstrate that the diesel engine could run on a wide variety of fuels, or the French government wanting to promote a potential market for peanuts grown in its African colonies. Regardless of the reason why Diesel used peanut oil at the Paris Exposition, as the years passed, Diesel became a strong advocate for the use of vegetable oils as a fuel as in this 1912 quote:

> The use of vegetable oils for engine fuels may seem insignificant today, but such oil may become, in the course of time, as important as petroleum and coal-tar products of the present time. . . . Motive power can still be produced from the heat of the sun, always available, even when the natural stores of solid and liquid fuels are completely exhausted.[11]

Like 200 proof White Lightning, biodiesel can also be home brewed. "Anyone can make biodiesel in a blender. The recipe calls for some dangerous ingredients such as methanol and lye." After duly providing some safety precautions, "put 200 milliliters of methanol in the blender. Dump in 3.5 grams of lye. Blend." Again precautionary words over not ingesting methanol and the resultant methoxide, "Once you have a successful methoxide reaction, add a liter of vegetable oil and blend for about fifteen minutes. This is the biodiesel reaction, and if the mixing is done correctly you get two nicely defined layers. One is glycerin, the byproduct of the reaction, and one is biodiesel. The glycerin is nontoxic and composted for disposal and the biodiesel can go right into the fuel tank."[12]

The vegetable oil does not have to be "virgin oil," but can be anything such as sausage fat from a pizza restaurant or waste vegetable oil from fast food restaurants—the difference is the amount of lye that has to be added and the smell of the exhaust (some devotees of home brew avoid used vegetable oil from fast food fish restaurants). Methanol and potassium in the lye are entrapped in the glycerin. Heating the glycerin vaporizes the methanol, which can be recovered for recycling by condensing the vapors. Reclaiming potassium is too complicated for the blender operation. The glycerin is not commercial grade, and purifying blender glycerin is much more difficult than making biodiesel. Even if purified, the glycerin cannot be considered commercial grade for making soaps, pharmaceuticals, cosmetics, toothpaste, and other consumer products because blender glycerin cannot be certified as kosher; that is a guarantee that no pork fat has ended up in the blender. Moreover certification for being kosher prohibits the mixing of feedstocks such as different seed oils. With no commercial value, homebrewed glycerin can be disposed by mixing it with hay, wood chips, horse manure, and other ingredients for compost or mixed with alfalfa for goat food.

Biodiesel fuels are oxygenated organic compounds—methyl or ethyl esters—derived from vegetable oil, animal fat, and cooking oil. Oxygen in biodiesel requires stabilization to avoid storage problems. Methyl ester diesel made from vegetable oil and fats mixed with methanol is by far the most common form of biodiesel. In Europe, rapeseed (canola) oil is the most common form of vegetable oil used to make biodiesel, in the United States soybean oil, in Asia palm oil, and in Brazil castor oil. Collectively these fuels are referred to as fatty acid methyl esters (FAME). Biodiesel is produced by first crushing seeds to extract oils followed by a catalytic process called transesterification in which oils (triglycerides) are reacted with an alcohol such as methanol or ethanol into alkyl esters. Fossil-fuel derived methanol is normally used, but Brazil is experimenting with sugarcane-derived ethanol. If successful, this would make biodiesel entirely renewable. Because biodiesel marketed today is made with methanol, emissions and health standards as well as fuel specifications are based on methyl, not ethyl, esters. Glycerin (also called glycerol and sometimes spelled glycerine) and water are byproducts of the reaction and have to be removed along with traces of alcohol, unreacted triglycerides, and catalyst before biodiesel can be sold to the public. Non-kosher glycerin can be used in paints and other commercial products. But some biodiesel producers are finding glycerin an unwanted byproduct and are quietly disposing of it into the nearest stream. Glycerin floats on top of water as gelatinous flotsam, absorbing oxygen and killing fish and marine life. Like an oil spill, it can be traced to its source by those who live downstream.

There is a significant purity problem associated with the glycerin byproduct of biodiesel production. The glycerin produced by transesterification is only about 50 percent pure, containing a significant amount of contaminants such as methanol, soap, and catalyst. The first step of purification is relatively easy by adding hydrochloric acid to the glycerin until its pH is acidic. This splits the soaps into fatty acids and salt. The fatty acids rise to the top of the glycerin and can be removed. The methanol is removed by evaporation. These relatively simple steps will make the glycerin 80–90 percent pure, but it needs to be 99.7 percent pure to be commercially acceptable. This takes a much more sophisticated process of vacuum distillation or ion exchange refining. Vacuum distillation is capital intensive and ion exchange columns, while less capital intensive, generates large volumes of wastewater during regeneration that has to be treated. Even if commercially pure glycerin were produced, there is the matter of price and supply. The total demand for glycerin is about 950,000 tons per year. Large-scale incremental supplies of commercial grade glycerin from biodiesel processing plants would be sufficient to depress prices, making the investment in glycerine purification equipment unprofitable.

The majority of the alkyl esters produced today uses the catalyst-reaction process because it operates at a relatively low temperature (150°F) and pressure (20 psi), has a high conversion rate (98 percent) with no intermediate steps, minimal side reactions, and short reaction time. No exotic materials are needed for plant construction. It is a cost-effective way to produce biodiesel with inputs of 87 percent vegetable oil, 12 percent methanol, and 1 percent catalyst generating outputs of 86 percent methyl ethyl (biodiesel), 9 percent glycerine, 4 percent methanol recapture, and 1 percent fertilizer with no waste![13]

Cetane number is an empirical measure of a diesel fuel's ignition delay measured by the time required for ignition after injection into a compression chamber. Biodiesel has a favorably high cetane number and contains essentially no sulfur and aromatics (benzene, toluene, and xylene), and burns with less particulate (soot), unburned hydrocarbons, and carbon monoxide emissions. Soot may become a major environmental issue. There is scientific speculation that the increased concentration of soot in glacier ice in the northern hemisphere leads to more rapid melting. Soot decreases the reflection of sunlight, increasing the albedo or energy absorption that accelerates glacier meltdown. The primary contributors of soot in the atmosphere are smokestack emissions from burning coal for electricity generation and as an industrial fuel and the exhaust of diesel-fueled motor vehicles. In other words, it may not be just global warming that is melting glaciers but also soot accumulation. Average tailpipe emissions from burning 100 percent biodiesel (B100) is a reduction of 43 percent in carbon monoxide emissions, 56 percent in hydrocarbon emissions, 55 percent in particulates (soot), a 100 percent reduction in sulfur emissions, but a 6 percent increase in nitrous oxide emissions.

Care must be exercised in mixing biodiesel with petrodiesel since its specific gravity of 0.88 is higher than the 0.85 for petroleum diesel. Thus biodiesel should be splashed on top of petroleum diesel to assure proper mixing. B20 is considered a "safe" blend that would not have any meaningful impact over the use of petrodiesel similar to E-10 gasohol in automobiles. B20 minimizes the impact of the higher cost of biodiesel and keeps nitrous oxide increases within 1–4 percent that satisfy legal emission standards for diesel engines. B20 also reduces engine emissions of soot, particulates, hydrocarbons, carbon monoxide, and carbon dioxide by more than 10 percent. B20 keeps the increase in cloud and pour points to manageable levels, which can be controlled through normal cold flow additives. There are also few material compatibility problems with B20 whereas higher-level blends can create problems with rubber seals, gaskets, and hoses unless replaced with biodiesel resistant materials. In short, B20 is a good starting point for new users of biodiesel.

Biodiesel is biodegradable if spilled, making it especially suitable for marine or farm applications. It is safer to transport and store because of its higher flashpoint (over 260 degrees Fahrenheit compared to 125 degrees Fahrenheit for petrodiesel). Biodiesel has better lubricity than petroleum diesel, making it suitable for blending into low and ultralow sulfur diesel, which has poor lubricity. The higher viscosity range of biodiesel helps to reduce barrel-plunger leakage and increases injector efficiency in engines. Its exhaust smell is slightly reminiscent of French fries even without recycled cooking oil. Biodiesel has a heat content of about 121,000 Btu per gallon compared to 135,000 Btu for diesel fuel. Its oxygen content of around 10 percent is higher than petrodiesel, which lowers emissions and enhances combustion efficiency by about 7 percent. Taking the lower energy and higher oxygen content into consideration, B100 has a net 5 percent loss in torque, power, and fuel efficiency compared to petrodiesel; a much better relative performance than E-100 is to gasoline.

Biodiesel has poor oxidative stability. This is also an issue with petrodiesel but not as serious. Oxidative stability refers to the tendency of fuels to react with oxygen at ambient temperatures. These reactions are much slower than those that occur at combustion temperatures and result in varnish deposits and sediments. This becomes a serious problem if storage of biodiesel exceeds six months as is microbial growth, but these are treatable with antioxidants and biocides. Petrodiesel can form sediments, sludge, and slime on the bottom and sides of storage tanks that have not been adequately maintained. Biodiesel, a mild solvent, will dissolve these sediments and carry the dissolved solids to the fuel filters. The fuel filters will catch much of the sediments, but they can become plugged, stopping the flow of fuel. Fuel-injector failure can occur if the dissolved sediments are not filtered out. Thus it is best to start out with B20 until sediments and sludge are gone, but this will call for more frequent changes of fuel filters.

Petrodiesel begins to "cloud" at 20 degrees Fahrenheit where paraffin crystals begin to form, which can clog fuel filters preventing the engine from starting or causing it to stall. At lower temperatures, diesel fuel reaches its pour point, a temperature where it will not pour or flow through fuel lines causing the engine to stop running. Normally, cloud and pour points are about 15–20 degrees Fahrenheit apart. At even lower temperatures, diesel fuel gels with a consistency of petroleum jelly. Biodiesel suffers from all these problems but at higher temperatures. The rule of thumb is that B100 should be stored at temperatures at least 15 degrees Fahrenheit higher than petrodiesel. Biodiesel made from palm oil has worse cold-weather performance than biodiesel made from other vegetable oils. The same winterizing and antigel agents used in petrodiesel can be used in biodiesel fuel. Shipping biodiesel in winter requires tank cars equipped with heaters such as steam coils. Adding kerosene in winter decreases the cloud and pour point temperatures of petro and biodiesel. It might be advisable to burn B20 during the winter and a higher concentration of up to B100 in summer. Having said this, B100 has been successfully used in extremely cold climates such as Yellowstone National Park as long as the vehicles are equipped with suitable diesel fuel winterizing packages.

Both petro and biodiesel fuels oxidize and create sediments in the presence of brass, bronze, copper, lead, tin, and zinc. Suitable metals for both are stainless steel and aluminum. Acceptable storage tank materials include aluminium and steel coated with fluorinated polyethylene and polypropylene and Teflon. Certain types of seals, gaskets, and adhesives including natural and nitrile rubber should be avoided. Most engines built after 1994 have been constructed with gaskets and seals that are biodiesel resistant. Diesel engine warranties are affected by using biodiesel; the impact of biodiesel usage on engine warranties varies greatly among engine manufacturers.

Biodiesel can substitute for home heating oil with no special precautions. However for older

Table 3.4

**Biodiesel Crops**

| Crop | Gallons/acre | % Share |
|------|--------------|---------|
| Oil palm | 635 | 1 |
| Coconut | 287 | — |
| Jatropha | 202 | — |
| Rapeseed/Canola | 127 | 84 |
| Peanut | 113 | — |
| Sunflower | 102 | 13 |
| Safflower | 83 | — |
| Mustard | 61 | — |
| Soybean | 48 | 1 |
| Corn (Maize) | 18 | — |

systems where there may be sludge in the tank, biodiesel should be added along with normal heating oil, such as B20, until the biodiesel has removed the sediments to avoid clogging filters. It is best for heating oil tanks to be inside a house as outdoor temperatures may fall below the pour point. With these precautions, B100 has been successfully substituted for home heating oil. Biodiesel as a fuel or for heating oil is susceptible to microbial growth, which is accelerated by the presence of water. Hence care has to be taken to remove water from fuel tanks, and biocides may be necessary for biodiesel stored for extended periods of time.

**Biodiesel Feedstocks**

There are hundreds of oil-producing plants such as the avocado, almond, sesame, and tobacco seed and a host of nonplant sources including fish oil and animal fats that can be made into biodiesel. Table 3.4 shows crops with the highest yield of oil and the percentage share as a raw material in the production of biodiesel. The skewed percentage share in favor of rapeseed and sunflower oil reflects the fact that most of the world's biodiesel is produced in Europe. Oil palm and soybeans will gain in relative importance as biodiesel is produced in greater quantities in Asia and North America.

The African oil palm is the highest yielding oil-producing plant with production comparable to Brazilian ethanol from sugar. It grows in Africa and Southeast Asia with a stout trunk tree topped with a spray of fronds. Palm trees cover an eighth of the entire land area of Malaysia and even greater area in terms of acreage in nearby Indonesia. The palm is a highly efficient producer of vegetable oil, squeezed from the thick bunches of plum-size bright red fruit. An acre of oil palms yields as much oil as thirteen acres of soybeans and five acres of rapeseed/canola. Palm oil is a major source of cooking oil and an important source of calories for the Asian people rivaled only by sugarcane in terms of calories per acre. Two types of oil are extracted from this plant. The fleshy part of the fruit contains 45–55 percent oil used mainly in the manufacture of cooking oil, soaps, candles, and margarine. The kernel is about 50 percent oil and is used in making ice cream, mayonnaise, baked goods, soaps, and detergents. The pressed pulp after extraction of the oil is an animal feed. Biodiesel from palm oil has a high cloud point, the temperature when wax crystals begin to form, making biodiesel from palm oil less desirable in colder temperatures unless treated.

Palm oil is the principal biodiesel feedstock in Malaysia and Indonesia, the home to 85 percent of the world production of palm oil. Each produces about 17 million tons (Indonesia has recently surpassed Malaysia in palm oil production). The third and fourth leading nations are Thailand and Colombia, each with 2 percent shares. The vast expansion of oil palm plantations for biodiesel production will dramatically increase palm oil production in Southeast Asia, but the palm tree takes eight years to mature before it bears seeds and contributes to the supply of palm oil.

Environmentalists are becoming increasingly concerned over growing evidence that the act of clearing rainforests and even scrubland not only adds to carbon dioxide emissions, but also the replacement biofuel crop is less effective in removing carbon dioxide than the original habitat. The concept of sustainable biofuels is rooted in looking at the whole picture of what was replaced before biofuel crops are cultivated. Palm oil from tree plantations replacing tropical rainforests are not considered sustainable in the sense that the palm tree plantations do not absorb as much carbon dioxide as the rainforests they replaced in addition to the carbon dioxide released when the rainforest was razed. Environmentalists are also concerned about the expansion of oil palm plantations in Borneo threatening the habitat for orangutans.

The United Nations Food and Agricultural Organization estimates that 104,000 square kilometers, the area of the nation of Iceland, is deforested each year on a global basis. Deforestation is caused by lumbering, conversion to agricultural croplands, and forest fires, natural or otherwise. Deforestation does not include conversion of tropical forests to other types of trees such as fruit tree or oil palm plantations or agroforestry operations where trees are replanted after harvesting or lumbering. Thus, the conversion of tropical forests to oil palm plantations is not considered deforestation regardless of their impact on carbon dioxide absorption. Despite growing forest cover from various types of tree plantations in North America, Europe, and China, the world is suffering from net deforestation in which nearly half of the world's removal of forest cover is occurring in Brazil (27 percent) and Indonesia (17 percent) for animal grazing, cultivation of food crops, and lumbering.

Cooking oil is a critical foodstuff among the poor in Asia who raise or grow much of their food and must purchase oil for cooking. The price for cooking oil in Asia, which is primarily palm oil, escalated 70 percent in 2007/2008 caused by a variety of factors. One factor behind the rising price of cooking oil is the rise in food prices in general. Food prices are going up as a consequence of a growing population that is eating more meat relative to grain: one pound of grain for a pound of bread, two pounds of grain for a pound of chicken, four pounds of grain for a pound of pork, and ten pounds of grain for a pound of beef. The shift in diet from less grain to more meat is driving up grain prices and vegetable oils made from grains like corn and soybean oil. This, in turn, affects the price of palm oil. Food prices also rose in 2007/2008 from higher oil prices for transport fuels, a major cost component in agriculture, and record high shipping costs for imported food. Another contributing factor was the conversion of agricultural output to biofuels in the United States and Europe. In response to health concerns associated with transfats (hydrogenated vegetable oils for increased stability), many commercial establishments in the United States turned to palm oil as an alternative to vegetable shortening. All these factors affected the rise in the price of palm oil in 2007/2008; but as with most commodities in general, the price of palm oil collapsed in late 2008/2009.

Malaysian and Indonesian biodiesel processing plants built to consume palm oil stood idle as an economic consequence of high-priced palm oil. It is not high petroleum oil prices that economically support biofuels but the spread in prices between petrofuels as the product and the raw material feedstock, the biorefinery spread. In 2008, the cost of the raw material for making biodiesel exceeded the price that could be obtained from selling biodiesel. This negative biorefinery spread shut down nearly all biodiesel plants.

Coconut is the world's third most-produced vegetable oil after peanuts and soybeans. Its output of biodiesel is comparable to ethanol output of corn. The oil is pressed from the meat of the coconut after it has been husked and dried. The residue is an animal feed. Coconut oil is found in soaps, lubricants, hydraulic fluids, paints, synthetic rubber, margarine, and ice cream. The coconut tree is also a raw material for making twine or rope, mattress padding, mats, rugs, and other products. Coconut trees grow along coastlines of tropical regions. In the Philippines and Papua, New Guinea, there are plans to build biodiesel-processing plants using coconut oil as a feedstock.

Jatropha (Jatropha curcas) is a weed that grows in tropical regions of Africa, South America, India, China, and Southeast Asia. It is thought to have originated in Central America and was introduced into other parts of the world by early explorers. The plant can grow on virtually barren land with little water, needs little fertilizer if cultivated, and produces inedible seeds rich in oil whose biofuel yield per acre beats many biofuel crops. Jatropha needs no fertilizer if the residue after extracting the oil, the inedible seed cake, is placed around the plant (another example of fertilizer-recycling). In Mali, jatropha is grown in long rows as a living fence to keep grazing cattle, repelled by its smell, off crop fields. It can be grown in rows interspersed with agricultural crops or intercropped within fruit groves and tree plantations. The plant prevents soil erosion and can be grown along railways and roads and on land not suitable for agricultural crops—a perfect cash crop for the rural poor, generating income and providing employment opportunities.

Jatropha begins to bear seeds two years after planting, and its yield increases fourfold by the time it is ten years old and maintains this yield throughout the remainder of its 50-year life. It is conceivable that African and Asian oil-importing nations could become biodiesel exporters earning foreign exchange rather than spending their meager hard-currency reserves on petroleum imports. But to do this, biodiesel conversion plants would have to be built. The potential of jatropha is being explored in Bangladesh, Myanmar, Malaysia, Pakistan, Thailand, Laos, Nepal, Sri Lanka, and Vietnam. India is planning large-scale cultivation of one million acres of jatropha on marginal land for biodiesel production. Jatropha is planted along the railroad tracks between Mumbai (Bombay) and New Delhi, and biofuel derived from the jatropha plants supplies about 15–20 percent of the locomotive fuel. India is also looking into other native species such as the mahua and karanji trees as a source of biodiesel. A few Indian villages have converted these inedible oil seeds to biodiesel to power diesel-driven electricity generators that provide power for lights and running water.

Rapeseed in Europe is the same as the canola plant in the United States. Rapeseed is cultivated in more temperate regions of Europe (half in Germany along with France, the Czech Republic, and Poland), and also in Canada and Russia. Rapeseed is the principal feedstock for biodiesel in Europe, and the seed cake after the oil is removed is a high-protein animal feed. Rapeseed is by far the largest source for making biodiesel in the world because most biodiesel production is centered in Europe. Rapeseed needs to be crop-rotated to avoid the spread of plant disease. This, along with soil quality considerations, dampens expansion opportunities for rapeseed. China is looking into rapeseed to meet its biodiesel needs as is Japan. Both nations are also interested in used frying oils for conversion to biodiesel. Australia and New Zealand are eying their plentiful supplies of animal fats as biodiesel feedstock.

Other potential vegetable oils for biodiesel are derived from peanuts, sunflowers, safflowers, and mustard. Peanut oil is used for cooking and in margarine, salad dressing, and shortenings plus in pharmaceuticals, soaps, and lubricants. Peanuts, native to South America, are now widely cultivated in warm climates and sandy soils particularly in Africa. Sunflower, native to the western United States, is cultivated primarily in Europe and Russia and grows in both temperate and tropical regions. Its oil is used for basically the same purposes as peanut oil, and the seed cake after the seed hulls are removed is a high-protein animal feed. Sunflowers supply 13 percent of global biodiesel feedstock. Safflower is a thistle type of herb and is grown mainly for its edible oil-producing seeds. Safflower oil is high in unsaturated fatty acids and is used in salad dressings and cooking oil, margarine, candles, and as a drying oil in paints and varnishes. Safflower is grown in Europe and in North and South America in areas favorable for wheat and barley cultivation. Mustard, a relative of rapeseed, is grown for its vegetable greens and is valued for its seeds, whose oil can be found in lubricants and hair oil. The seed residue is an animal feed, fertilizer, and an organic pesticide. Research is being conducted on its suitability as a biodiesel feedstock including genetic engineering to boost its oil content. Castor bean or castor oil plant (*Ricinus communis*) is a labor-intensive crop that can provide jobs for the unemployed. India is the largest producer and exporter of castor oil followed by China and Brazil. The castor bean contains a poisonous toxin called ricin and is used in food as a preservative, in medicine as a laxative, and in industry in adhesives, brake and hydraulic fluids, paints and lacquers, and other uses. Brazil considers castor oil as its most promising feedstock for biodiesel.

Soybean is a major supplier of protein and is the largest source of seed oil by far, dwarfing the production of all other oil-seed plants. Soybean oil is found in salad oil, margarine, and shortening and is used industrially in paints, printing inks, soap, insecticides, disinfectants, and other products. Though most biodiesel made in the United States is from soybean oil, its global use is minuscule because U.S. biodiesel volume is small compared to Europe's. Soybeans are not considered the best crop for biodiesel production as their output of oil only exceeds corn. Yet soy-diesel is heavily promoted. Its support stems from the enormous acreage of land in the United States dedicated to soybean production and the political clout of various soybean associations. While the relatively low vegetable oil yield of soybeans may be a problem, this is not the determining factor. The determining factor is the cost of soybean oil versus canola oil and other vegetable oils. If soybeans can make a lower cost soy-diesel than biodiesel made from rapeseed then this, in the last analysis, will make soybeans the desired feedstock.

As all these oils are primarily used for cooking, there is a sizable market emerging from waste vegetable oil for biodiesel feedstock, a form of recycling vegetable oils. Waste vegetable oil must be filtered to remove residues and treated for acids produced by high-temperature cooking. But apart from that, used or waste vegetable oils are being converted to biodiesel in many nations led by China, which intends to make biodiesel from processing 40,000 to 60,000 tons of recycled cooking oil a year. Animal fats or tallow from cattle-, pig-, fish-, and chicken-processing plants are being gathered for conversion to biodiesel in the United States, Australia, New Zealand, and elsewhere. Biodiesel facilities are being located near meat-processing plants to take advantage of a low-value feedstock.

Modern agricultural research and development efforts have been responsible for dramatic improvements in crop yields by such means as optimal fertilizer and pesticide applications, plant hybridization, genetic engineering, and greater productivity through mechanization. Corn yields in the United States are up 65 percent since the mid-1970s, oil palm by 200 percent since the 1960s, and soybeans in Brazil up by over 300 percent since 1940. Despite gains in crop yields, there are limits on agricultural output of oilseeds in meeting biofuel demand. Considering both ethanol and biodiesel, for the European Union to obtain 10 percent share of biofuels for transport fuels, over 70 percent of its current agricultural land for growing food crops would have to be dedicated to producing biofuel crops. Obviously, Europe is a huge potential market for biofuel imports if the EU were to switch to biofuels for a significant share of its transport fuel requirements. To meet this same objective of a 10 percent share of biofuels in transport fuels, 35 percent of Canadian agricultural land and 30 percent of U.S. agricultural land would have to be converted to biofuel crops. But on a world basis, only 8 percent, and for Brazil, only 2 percent of its agricultural land would have to be converted to biofuel crops for every 10 percent incremental share of biofuels in transport fuels. Achieving a 10 percent biofuel share of total transport fuel demand would have extreme repercussions on the EU, Canada, and the United States from the point of view of food availability. However the world has an enormous capacity to increase biofuel production such as vastly expanding the uncultivated Brazilian *cerrado* for sugar plantations, palm tree plantations in Southeast Asia, and jatropha plant cultivation on marginal nonagricultural lands throughout Africa and Asia.

Biodiesel can be made from algae, which grow everywhere—oceans, ponds, swimming pools, goldfish bowls. Although these single-celled organisms have the same photosynthetic capacity to convert sunshine into chemical energy as plants, they lack roots, stems, and leaves and the reproductive organs of flowers, seeds, and fruits characteristic of plants. Algae's single-celled structure is extremely efficient in absorbing light and nutrients to reproduce by cell division. Certain types of algae produce oils similar to vegetable oils at 30 to 100 times per acre of pond water greater than the per acre yield of soybeans or corn. Moreover the algae require 99 percent less water than what these biofuel crops absorb in their life cycle, neglecting evaporation of pond water. Oil produced by algae can be converted to biodiesel, and the residue contains carbohydrates and proteins that can be converted to ethanol and a nutritious livestock feed with no waste.

Productivity depends on photosynthesis. The critical aspect of algal ponds is not depth, but surface area and the amount of sunshine. This makes deserts an ideal location as long as there is a ready supply of water to replace that lost by evaporation. The water need not be fresh but can be drawn from saline aquifers, which otherwise have no use. Not only do algae grow vigorously in saline water, but their productivity can be enhanced by building the pond near a coal-burning electricity-generating plant. Stack emissions percolate through the pond water allowing the algae to consume most of the carbon dioxide and nitrous oxides. Carbon dioxide enhances photosynthesis and nitrous oxides act as a fertilizer. Other fertilizers can be animal and human waste. Carbon dioxide, which makes up 13 percent of the stack emissions from a utility plant, is recycled by being absorbed by the algae and released when the biodiesel and bioethanol are burned. The burning of biodiesel and bioethanol made from algae adds little carbon dioxide to the atmosphere as its fossil fuel energy input is quite low. Algal cultivation is a perfect conversion of waste (smokestack emissions, sewage water) into useful products. Algal ponds built around the Salton Sea in the Sonora desert can feed off polluted waters heavily laden with nitrogen and phosphate fertilizers.[14]

The groundwork for producing biodiesel from algae was a nearly twenty-year program (1978 to 1996) conducted by the U.S. Department of Energy's Office of Fuels Development. The peak funding year for the Aquatic Species Program (ASP) was only $2.75 million, yet from this program came the entire framework of identifying the right type of algae and the right conditions for maximum productivity. The conclusion of the program was that the process was not economic. But that was 1996. With current prices of crude oil and with the possibility of selling carbon credits, the economic equation has changed considerably. Moreover, technological progress has been made since the cessation of the ASP to further reduce capital and operating costs and enhance productivity.

Algae-growing ponds are shaped like racetracks where algae, water, and nutrients circulate powered by paddlewheels to keep the algae suspended. Water and nutrients are continually fed to the ponds, and a portion of the pond water is continually drawn off to harvest algae. The ponds are shallow to keep the algae exposed to the maximum degree of sunlight for photosynthesis, and individual raceways can be connected into a single algal factory. The displacement of croplands dedicated to food crops for the production of biofuels is a major concern in the United States. About 450 million acres of land are used for growing crops, much of that for animal feed. Another 580 million acres are grassland pasture and range. Croplands and grazing account for nearly half of the 2.3 billion acres within the United States with only 3 percent, or 66 million acres, considered urban land. It has been estimated that a pond system covering nearly 15,000 square miles or 9.5 million acres would produce enough biofuel to replace petroleum-derived motor vehicle fuels. This is a huge area of ponds that have to be constructed, yet it represents only 2 percent of the 580 million acres of grazing and rangeland. If these ponds were built in deserts, there would be no impact on agriculture or grazing land. The cost would be high, but would be less than what is being spent on acquiring oil from overseas.

Photobioreactors contain the algae within a closed system that drastically reduces the land necessary to grow algae, but adds considerably to capital costs. There is a great deal of biological science involved with photobioreactors to select the right type of algae from thousands of varieties, the correct temperature and pH of the water, and the right mix of carbon dioxide and nutrients. The technological challenges include the design of an effective photobioreactor for high productivity, ease of removing algae, and low capital costs. As with algal ponds, a portion of the algal water in a photobioreactor is removed and run through a centrifuge to remove the algae, which must be dried before being pressed to remove the oil. The residual press cake can be used for a variety of purposes including ethanol production with the remaining residue being a nutritious animal feed. Drying and pressing oil out of algae is a fairly expensive process and more economical processes are being explored.

But the cost cannot be prohibitively high to stop development. Arizona Public Service Company (APS) and its partner GreenFuel Technologies have succeeded in creating biofuels from algae-consuming carbon dioxide and emissions from an electricity-generating power plant. The companies were able to grow algae whose oil yield was 37 times higher than corn and 140 times higher than soybeans on an equivalent area basis. The project is now moving to APS' Four Corners Generation coal power plant in Farmington, New Mexico, with the intent of reducing greenhouse gas emissions to produce alternative fuels. Pipes capture and transport stack emissions to specially designed containers where the algae are grown and then harvested for their lipids, which are transformed into biodiesel, its starches into ethanol, and its protein along with the residue of making biodiesel and ethanol into livestock feed. This marked the first time that algae grown onsite by direct connection to a commercial power plant has been successfully converted to transportation-grade biofuels. The project is being ramped up to test its commercial feasibility.

The annual production capacity for biodiesel in the United States was about 570 million liters in 2004, 24 times smaller than ethanol production capacity. Soybeans account for 80 percent of the feedstock followed by yellow grease. Military vehicles and fleets owned by federal and state agencies and the U.S. Department of Energy make up much of the biodiesel market as required by the Environmental Protection Act of 1992. The U.S. Department of Energy issued a ruling that fleets required to use biodiesel can buy 450 gallons of pure diesel and use it as a blend of at least 20 percent biodiesel (B20) to satisfy 50 percent of their annual alternative fuel vehicle acquisition requirements. In 2002, Minnesota enacted the first state law in the United States requiring that diesel fuel sold in the state be 2 percent (B2) biodiesel. In 2005 this was implemented as a state government mandate, exempting off-road vehicles, railroads, and power stations. The American Jobs Creation Act of 2004 provided a federal excise tax credit for biodiesel consisting of a one-cent credit for each percentage point in a fuel blend made from agricultural products and a 0.5-cent credit for each percentage point of biodiesel made from recycled cooking oils. The tax credit for biodiesel made from soybean oil and other agricultural products is thus $1.00 per gallon for B100 biodiesel. The tax credit took effect in 2005 for a two-year period. The possibility of short-term tax credits not being renewed is a major risk faced by investors for any renewable fuel facility that depends on tax credits for a profitable return.

The growth of biodiesel in Germany has been attributed to the establishment and enforcement of biodiesel quality standards. In like fashion, the American Society of Testing and Materials (ASTM) issued specification D-6751 for diesel fuel. The National Biodiesel Board has established the National Biodiesel Accreditation Commission to develop and implement a voluntary program for accrediting producers and marketers of biodiesel under "BQ-9000, Quality Management System Requirements for the Biodiesel Industry."

In 2008, the number of U.S. biodiesel filling stations was nearly 825 concentrated in the Carolinas, Tennessee, and Texas. However very few of these stations sell B100 (100 percent biodiesel); most sell B5 and B10. In 2004, 25 million gallons of biodiesel were sold, which tripled to 75 million gallons in 2005 and tripled again to 250 million gallons in 2006 and nearly doubled to 450 million gallons in 2007. There were 176 biodiesel plants in 2008 with another 39 under construction that would easily support U.S. consumption of one billion gallons, sufficient to satisfy a national mandate for B2.

The world leader in the production and consumption of biodiesel is the European Union, with approximate production of 4.7 million tons centered in Germany. Diesel fuel plays a more important role than gasoline as a transport fuel in Europe because the EU has a national policy to encourage the use of diesel engines in automobiles. Nevertheless, biodiesel consumption varies widely from country to country. Germany and Austria have made a concerted effort to promote B100, whereas B5 is used almost exclusively in France. Public buses in leading French cities burn a biodiesel blend between B5 and B30. The German Taxi Association requiring taxis to run on biodiesel was a significant spur in the adoption of biodiesel as were automobile manufacturers issuing warranties that applied for automobiles fueled by biodiesel. Some German cities are in the process of converting public buses to biodiesel. Tourist boats and yachts on Lake Constance, Europe's second largest drinking water source, are fueled by B100 to keep the lake free of toxic fuel spills (B100 is biodegradable). In Italy, half of biodiesel production is used as heating oil and the remainder blended as B5 in petroleum diesel.

Two factors have contributed to the EU becoming a world leader in biodiesel production. A reform of the Common Agricultural Policy, a supranational farm policy for EU member countries, established a "set-aside" program to reduce farm surpluses. The program allowed producers of grains, oilseeds, and protein crops to receive direct payments if they removed a specified percentage (up to 10 percent) of their farmland from production. However nonfood crops are permitted on set-aside land. It turned out that farmers were better off growing crops for biofuels than receiving payments for leaving the land idle. The newly expanded EU-25 with accession nations in central and eastern Europe increases the existing 17.3 million acres of set aside lands by another 12 million acres, providing a further impetus to grow biofuel crops.

The other factor for encouraging biodiesel is exemption from a high fuel tax that amounts to 50 percent or more of the retail price of petrodiesel. In 1994, the European Parliament adopted a 90 percent tax exemption for biodiesel and Germany, the largest biodiesel market, has excluded biofuels from taxation altogether. Moreover, some governments have implemented the European Community Scrivener Directive that recommends a certain level of tax relief for investment in biofuel production plants. These actions are necessary to compensate for the cost of biofuels being 2–3 times greater than petroleum fuels. German authorities took the lead in issuing stringent specification standards for biodiesel to win acceptance and confidence of consumers and vehicle manufacturers. The German biodiesel industry worked closely with the automotive industry to persuade the industry to issue the same warranties on diesel engines for biodiesel as for petrodiesel. Moreover, an effort was made to disseminate information and educate the public about biodiesel. In 2002, biodiesel was available at 1,500 filling stations in Germany with the average distance between filling stations selling biodiesel being about 30 kilometers, although there are substantial regional variations.

Brazil deserves special mention as it is one of the two leading ethanol producers in the world and at the forefront of the use of biofuels in automobiles. Nearly all of the world's biodiesel production relies on methanol, but ethanol can be used. While biodiesel made from methanol contains an oil product, biodiesel made from bioethanol would contain none. Trucks and tractors used in growing and harvesting sugarcane and in the transport of ethanol in Brazil run on petrodiesel, but this is about to change. Researchers at the University of Sao Paulo have succeeded in developing a biodiesel formula that uses ethanol instead of methanol, making biodiesel entirely renewable. Petrobras, through its Research Center (Cenpes), has been studying biodiesel production from castor oilseeds and other oleaginous plants for which the company has patented technology. Petrobras is in favor of producing biodiesel from castor oilseed for the following reasons.

- The castor plant is robust and can be planted in several regions of the country (particularly the Northeast) with relatively small demand on soil nutrients and water.
- The crop provides jobs for rural workers and can be grown on marginal agricultural land.
- Plant residue after removing the seeds contributes to soil recovery or can be a source of cellulosic ethanol, or be converted to livestock feed or fertilizer.
- Castor seeds have a high oil content (45–55 percent) and are not edible.
- After the oil is removed, the seed cake can be used as a fertilizer or animal feed, but the latter requires detoxification.
- Castor seed plant leaves can be used to grow silkworms; the flower draws bees for honey production; the stalk can be used for firewood; and the seed's shell is rich in organic fertilizer.

Beginning in 2008, Brazil mandated 2 percent biodiesel in diesel fuel. Petrobras has acquired more than 100 million gallons of biodiesel that satisfied the B2 mandate through the first half of 2008. In 2013, the mandate will be expanded to B5 diesel fuel. Other nations in South and Central America beginning to look into biodiesel are Argentina, Paraguay, Colombia, Nicaragua, Peru, Costa Rica, and Honduras.

Thailand is experimenting with a number of plant oils to replace petrodiesel such as palm coconut, soybean, peanut, sesame, and castor, but it appears that palm oil and used cooking oil are taking the lead. The Thai Navy may convert some of its vessels to run on biodiesel along with vehicles owned by the armed forces and the Energy Ministry. Bangkok Mass Transit Authority may switch to biodiesel to fuel its buses. The government plan for biodiesel calls for consumption of 8.5 million liters per day by 2012 to satisfy a mandatory requirement of B5 in Bangkok. Of this amount 4.8 million liters per day will come from 640,000 hectares of new oil palm plantations, importation of 1.2 million liters per day from neighboring countries, plus 2.5 million liters per day produced from jatropha. Thailand is slated to be an importer of biodiesel and an exporter of ethanol.

China is looking at guang-pi, an oil-bearing tree that can be grown on marginal land; other candidates are other oil seeds, animal fats, and recycled cooking oils. Biodiesel from rapeseed has reportedly been increasing, but China's demand for agricultural products could (or probably should) stand in the way of massive areas of cultivated croplands being used to grow biofuels (China's prohibiting corn from being converted to ethanol in 2008 is a case in point). On the other hand, China possesses enormous areas of marginal land not particularly well-suited for agricultural crops that could be brought into cultivation for biofuel crops. Japan is looking into biodiesel and has a growing number of entrepreneurial businesses being set up to convert used cooking oil from local restaurants and households into biodiesel. Some biodiesel is made from rapeseed grown on idle plots of land or rotated with rice crops. Like China, Japan has enormous demand placed on its land for food production, but marginal land could be dedicated to biofuel crops. South Korea has passed legislation mandating that B3 be sold in the nation. The Philippines is in the process of launching biodiesel made from coconut oil with one company agreeing to make the biodiesel and an oil company agreeing to sell biodiesel at its filling stations. The intention is to mandate B1 throughout the Philippines, which will create demand for 70 million liters. It is anticipated that the concentration of biodiesel will increase with each increment of 1 percent adding another increment of demand for 70 million liters of biodiesel. Papua, New Guinea is looking at its coconut oil production as a possible biodiesel fuel. As mentioned, Indonesia and Malaysia have converted enormous tracts of tropical forests into palm tree plantations. The major difference between Indonesia and Malaysia is that Malaysia is beginning to run out of land for oil palm plantations whereas there are still huge tracts of land suitable for growing oil palms in Indonesia, much of which would involve razing tropical forests. Like Brazil, Australia has enormous tracts of marginal land that can be brought into cultivation. However with its dry climate, care has to be taken as to the choice of crop that grows well in arid climates such as jatropha. Australia is concentrating on used cooking oil and animal fats (tallow) as raw materials as is New Zealand. All in all, Asia is just starting to get its feet wet in the biofuel revolution.

The indigenous peoples of Africa and Asia should take to heart the fact that large inputs of outside capital are not necessary for them to bootstrap themselves into the biofuels age. In the 1930s, the British Institute of Standards in Calcutta examined nonedible oils as potential diesel fuels. In 1940, a textile mill in the state of Andhra Pradesh in India was powered as well as supplying power to the surrounding community with nonedible oils as fuel. This lesson was lost until 1999 when the people of Kagganahalli in the state of Karnataka told Dr. Udupi Shrinivasa, a mechanical engineering professor at the Indian Institute of Science, about the inedible oil from the seeds of the honge tree that had been previously used for lamp oil. Dr. Shrinivasa initiated a project that resulted in a local company converting its diesel electric generators to run on honge oil, sharply reducing energy costs. Now the villagers of Kagganahalli possess electric generators fueled by biodiesel that pump water to irrigate their crops, and the previously dry and desolate village has been transformed into a thriving oasis of agricultural enterprise. He repeated this again with the villagers of Kammeguda in Andhra Pradesh, who now take seeds from the karanji trees to produce biodiesel to power a diesel electric generator for lights and running water. Thus, relatively small capital investments in diesel-driven electricity generators supplied by biodiesel made from local seeds can become the first step in raising living standards and transforming the lives of the most impoverished people in the world. This lesson in "micro-bootstrapping" should be taken to heart—there is no reason why this process has to stop at a few Indian villages.

## Biofuel Risks

No business is without its risks, and biofuels are no exception. Biofuels have historically been more costly than petroleum products requiring various forms of government intervention in the form of subsidies and mandates to keep biofuel companies afloat. One risk is the fickleness of governments to arbitrarily and abruptly change established policies. In the 1980s, the government of Brazil faced increased subsidy payments to support ethanol producers stemming from falling oil prices. Rather than pay more in subsidies, the government, after nurturing and fostering the biofuels revolution, walked away from its energy child. All subsidies to the ethanol producers were ended and sugar growers were permitted to sell into the international market, which had a higher price than the domestic market. Cutting government expenditures and increasing the nation's export earnings benefited the government at the expense of the ethanol producers. Unable to operate profitably, many producers were forced into financial restructuring. Despite ethanol imports, the resulting shortages of E-100 led to a loss of consumer confidence in the availability of pure ethanol. Sales of pure ethanol automobiles plummeted and, in response, the automobile companies concentrated on producing gasohol-burning vehicles. Government policies that brought about the pure ethanol automobile ultimately led to its demise. Interestingly, the advent of the flex-fuel vehicle in recent years gives drivers complete flexibility on the degree of ethanol in motor vehicle fuels, mitigating the risk of another shift in government policy.

One can also conclude from this episode that another major risk for biofuel investments besides the fickleness of government policymakers is the price of oil. Actually this is only half the risk: the other half is the cost of feedstock. The fall in the price of oil in Brazil was also accompanied by a hike in the price of sugar as sugar growers now had the right to sell in the higher-priced international market. The ethanol producers were squeezed by declining revenues (falling oil prices lowered gasoline prices with pure ethanol discounted at 30 percent to compete on an energy-content basis) and by rising costs as the domestic price of sugar increased to the international price. It is not the price of oil that is critical but the spread between the price of oil and the cost of the feedstock. This is the classic refinery margin between the price of refined products (gasoline and diesel) and the cost of crude oil with one major difference. The classic refinery margin dealt with one commodity in two forms: crude oil and refined products where there is a strong price linkage between the two. The biorefinery margin is the price difference between two disparate commodities: crude oil and foodstuffs (sugar, corn, vegetable oils). There is no statistical linkage between the two: they both vary with a mind of their own. From this perspective, the biorefinery margin represents a greater degree of risk than the oil refinery margin.

This risk is still with us. Biodiesel producers in Indonesia and Malaysia suffered from a negative biorefinery margin between the prices of crude oil and palm oil in 2008. As crude oil prices set record highs, one would expect prosperity for the biodiesel producers; but not when palm oil is selling at an even higher price. Caught in this financial vise, with the government unwilling to pay a promised subsidy to keep biodiesel producers financially whole, Indonesian biodiesel production fell by 85 percent in early 2008. While the oil palm plantation owners were making a financial killing, the oil palm biodiesel producers were taking a financial beating. Further investments in biodiesel plants ceased. The general retreat from biodiesel plants was not confined to Indonesia and Malaysia. In 2008 and 2009, ethanol plants in the United States came under financial pressure during times of record high gasoline prices and record high corn prices that drastically reduced the biorefinery spread. This caused some plants to shut down and a few firms to declare bankruptcy. Then in late 2008 and 2009 when both gasoline and corn prices fell, the biorefinery spread did not improve sufficiently to prevent the bankruptcy of a leading ethanol producer.

A mandatory requirement for a certain percentage of bioethanol in gasoline or biodiesel in petrodiesel is not a guarantee that biofuel producers can cover their costs. Mandatory requirements only work when the biorefinery spread between oil prices and feedstock costs cover operating and financial costs of a biofuels plant. If price does not cover costs, there is no point for producers to lock in a loss to fulfill a mandate. Mandatory requirements can only be fulfilled if the government steps forward to make up the difference that keeps biofuel producers whole or mandate a higher price for the biofuel and let the consumer pay the difference. A mandate for a minimum content of biodiesel in petrodiesel in Indonesia or Malaysia had no meaning when there was a negative biorefinery spread between diesel oil and oil palm prices, and the government took no action to keep the biofuel producers financially whole. The result was the same as though there were no mandate; the biodiesel plants were forced to shut down.

Of course, there are means of risk mitigation. Oil refiners have the ability of locking in a spread by taking opposite derivative positions in futures, forwards, and swaps in crude oil and in gasoline and diesel fuel to lock in a spread. This also exists for biofuel producers except that rather than locking in a spread of two forms of the same commodity, biofuel producers must lock in a spread between two disparate commodities: agricultural crops and petroleum. This, of course, makes for a more difficult process for mitigating risk in that the biofuel producers have to be knowledgeable of the market outlook for both petroleum and agricultural crops.

There are other ways to mitigate the risk of a negative biorefinery spread. One is to use feed-stocks not grown for food such as the jatropha and castor bean. Prices for these feedstocks are closely related to their production costs and are relatively fixed, quite unlike the market value of a foodstuff like sugar, corn, rapeseed oil, palm oil, and other vegetable oils. Another way to mitigate risk is the development of cellulosic ethanol. Cellulosic ethanol is made from biomass wastes or cellulosic crops like fast-growing trees and grasses, whose cost is collecting or planting and harvesting, and shipping. These costs are not affected by the price of food. With the cost of cellulosic ethanol feedstock more or less fixed, there is no point in taking a derivatives position to protect against an adverse price change of the raw material feedstock. This simplifies risk mitigation as cellulosic ethanol producers need only worry about the market outlook for oil. If it is possible to separate the protein content from biomass sources of cellulosic ethanol, then food prices become a source of incremental revenue, not a source of incremental cost. The same can be said over the possibility of using algae as a feedstock for biodiesel and bioethanol where the residue is a source of protein for animal feed.

Biofuels and petrofuels are both technologically challenging. In some respects, biofuels are less challenging in that oil exploration and development give way to agricultural pursuits or waste collection. It can be more challenging in that the refining process, particularly for cellulosic etha-nol and algae, has a long way to go before it becomes commercially viable. Cellulosic ethanol and algae are the future of biofuels. With cellulosic ethanol, biofuels can be produced with little impact on food availability consuming raw materials whose cost is independent of food prices and primarily determined by the cost to plant, harvest, and transport biofuels crops or collect and transport biowaste. If cellulosic technology can become commercially viable, there is enough cel-lulosic feedstock in our backyard to make North America independent of oil imports. Cellulosic ethanol has the potential to make corn-based ethanol in the United States and grain-based ethanol in Europe transitional biofuels. Converting food grains to ethanol affects food availability and prices. Perhaps one day, ethanol based on corn and grains will become simply a price-support mechanism; a way to dispose of excess corn and grain when their prices sink too low to provide an adequate income for farmers.

For biodiesel, jatropha and castor beans can fix the cost of raw material to production and shipping and not by their value as a foodstuff. Algae have a great potential for biodiesel and bioethanol production and as livestock feed adding to the food supply. As demonstrated in India, local communities can bootstrap themselves into energy independence relying on low-cost noned-ible oleaginous seeds from weeds and trees for feedstocks. Impoverished oil-importing nations in Africa and Asia have the potential of becoming biodiesel-exporting nations and improving the living standards of their people.

The greatest risk faced by biofuel producers is low oil prices as experienced in late 2008 and early 2009. Dealing in ranges that include variation in the price of feedstocks, ethanol producers in Brazil require a minimum oil price between $35 and $45 per barrel in order to price ethanol to cover costs. The minimum oil price to support ethanol producers in the United States is between $50 and $60 per barrel for them to break even with existing subsidies. Ethanol from grain in the EU requires a minimum crude oil price between $75 and $100, for biodiesel made from vegetable oils the minimum crude price is between $90 and $110, and for cellulosic ethanol a minimum crude price between $100 and $130 is necessary for the existing technology to be commercially feasible.

So what happens when oil prices collapse as they did in late 2008 and early 2009? Ethanol plants in the United States had to shut down, and companies in the ethanol-producing market were in financial straits as were biodiesel plants in Southeast Asia. Low oil prices will destroy the promise of biofuels unless the government mandates that a certain percentage of transportation fuels will be biofuels whereby biofuel producers receive a minimum price to guarantee their financial solvency. This could be in the form of a subsidy by the government or a higher price paid by consumers for motor vehicle fuels. Either way, the public has to pay. They will pay willingly if there is the national will to reduce reliance on petroleum-based transportation fuels; without that will, biofuels may fade from view.

## NOTES

1. For further information about "miscanthus x giganteus," contact Professor Stephen Long, University of Illinois at Urbana-Champaign, 1401 West Green Street, Urbana, Illinois 61801.

2. J. Goldemberg and T.B. Johansson, eds., *Energy as an Instrument for Socio-Economic Development* (New York: United Nations Development Programme, 1995).

3. U.S. Environmental Protection Agency's Web site at www.epa.gov/epaoswer/non-hw/compost/biosolid.pdf); and Zia Haq, "Biomass for Electricity Generation," available online at the U.S. Department of Energy's Web site at www.eia.doe.gov/ oiaf/analysispaper/biomass/.

4. Changing World Technologies Web site www.changingworldtech.com; see also Web sites discovermagazine.com/2006/apr/anything-oil for a description of the process and an environmental assessment at gc.energy.gov/NEPA/nepa_documents/ea/ea1506/FONSI.pdf.

5. *Biofuels: Fuels of the Future* (New York: Energy Intelligence Research, 2008). This study has the complete listing of citations including Renewable Fuels Association Web site www.ethanolrfa.org, Illovo Sugar Ltd www.illovosugar.com, U.S. Department of Agriculture, Alternative Fuels and Advanced Vehicles Data Center of the U.S. Department of Energy www.eere.energy.gov/afdc, Brazilian Automotive Industry Association www.anfavea.com.br, Babcock & Brown–Castle Rock Renewable Fuels www.castlerockethanol.com.

6. *Corn and Soybean Digest* Web site cornandsoybeandigest.com/mag/soybean_ethanols_booming_brazil.

7. Michael Smith and Carlos Caminada, "Ethanol's Deadly Brew," *Bloomberg Markets* (November 2007).

8. Dr. Christoph Berg, "World Fuel Ethanol Analysis and Outlook," Web site www.distill.com/World-Fuel-Ethanol-A&O-2004.html.

9. Green Shift Web site www.gs-cleantech.com/whatwedo.php?mode=2.

10. "Ethanol Industry's 15% Solution Raises Concerns," *New York Times* (May 8, 2009).

11. Greg Pahl, *Biodiesel* (White River Junction, VT: Chelsea Green Publishing, 2005).

12. Lyle Estill, *Biodiesel Power* (Gabriola Island, BC: New Society Publishers, 2005).

13. National Biodiesel Board Web site www.biodiesel.org/pdf_files/fuelfactsheets/Production.PDF.

14. Michael Briggs, "Widescale Biodiesel Production from Algae," 2004, University of New Hampshire Web site www.unh.edu/p2/biodiesel/article_alge.html.

# 4

## COAL

Coal suffers from an incredibly bad image. It has few advocates other than the hundreds of thousands whose livelihoods depend on mining and burning coal by the trainload for generating electricity. No one strikes it rich in coal; that metaphor is reserved for oil. For some, coal brings back an image of coal miners who go in hock to buy a set of tools when they are young and quit decades later with black lung, still in hock to the company store. That might be one of the better images. Another would be the mangled bodies of miners caught in mine mishaps or those trapped by cave-ins awaiting their fate in pitch blackness. Still another would be youngsters harnessed to sleds dragging coal up narrow underground passageways on their hands and knees like pack animals or straddling precariously above fast-moving conveyor belts of coal, picking out the rocks. For still others the image of coal is as a pollutant of the first order that has to be eliminated under any or all circumstances. Nothing short of unconditional surrender can appease these environmental militants.

Yet, at the same time, this biomass fuel from ages past is irreplaceable and absolutely essential to ensure that the lights go on when we flick the switch. World coal consumption, essentially stagnant during the 1990s, surged by 47 percent between 2000 and 2008. Not only is the world consuming more coal, but its share of the energy pie increased from 23.4 percent in 2000 to 29.2 percent in 2008. Coal is becoming more important as a primary source of energy, not less as many people desire. Wishful thinking will not make coal go away, but there are ways to alleviate the worst of its adverse environmental consequences. This chapter reviews the history of coal, its importance in today's economy, and what is being done to overcome its principal drawbacks.

### THE FIRST ENERGY CRISIS

The first energy crisis was associated with living biomass (wood). It was an on-and-off-again crisis that extended over centuries. One of several reasons why the natural growth of forests could not keep up with the axe was glassmaking. Glassmaking has a long history, going back to about 3000–3500 BCE, as a glaze on ceramic objects and nontransparent glass beads. The first true glass vases were made about 1500 BCE in Egypt and Mesopotamia, where the art flourished and spread along the eastern Mediterranean. Glassmaking was a slow, costly process and glass objects were considered as valuable as jewels; Manhattan Island was purchased from the Indians for $24 worth of glass beads, and Cortez was able to exchange glass trinkets for gold!

The blowpipe was invented in Syria around 30 BCE. Using a long thin metal tube to blow hollow glass shapes within a mold greatly increased the variety of glass items and considerably lowered their cost. This technique, still in practice today, spread throughout the Roman Empire and made glass available to the common people. Transparent glass was first made around 100 CE in Alexandria, which became a center of glassmaking expertise, along with the German Rhineland city of Köln (Cologne). During the first golden age of glass, glassmaking became quite sophisticated. For example, glassmakers learned to layer transparent glass of different colors and then cut designs in high relief. All these achievements in glassmaking were lost in the 400s with the fall of the Western Roman Empire.

The so-called Dark Ages take on new meaning with the disappearance of glassmaking, but vestiges of glassmaking remained in Germany, where craftsmen invented the technique for making glass panes around 1000 CE. These were pieced together and joined by lead strips to create transparent or stained glass windows for palaces and churches. The second golden age of glass started in the 1200s when the Crusaders reimported glassmaking technology from the eastern Mediterranean. Centered in the Venetian island of Murano, glassblowers created Cristallo glass, which was nearly colorless, transparent, and blown to extreme thinness in nearly any shape. In the 1400s and 1500s, glassmaking spread to Germany and Bohemia (Czech Republic) and then to England, with each country producing variations in type and design of glass objects. The ubiquitous glass mirror was invented comparatively late, in 1688 in France.[1]

Glass is made from melting a mixture of mostly sand (silicon dioxide) plus limestone (calcium carbonate) and soda ash (sodium carbonate) in a furnace, along with glass waste, at a temperature of around 2,600–2,900°F. Considering what has to be heated to such high temperatures, clearly glassmaking was an energy-intensive process that consumed a lot of wood. As forests were cleared, glassmaking furnaces were moved to keep close to the source of energy rather than moving the source of energy to the furnaces. The first energy crisis began when English manors for the rich and famous were built with wide expanses of glass panes that opened up their interiors to sunlight. Not only did this put a strain on wood resources for making the glass, but also on heating since interior heat passes more easily through a glass pane than a stone wall covered by a heavy wool tapestry.

The growing popularity of glass was not the only villain responsible for deforestation. Part of the blame lies with the increased demand for charcoal used in smelting iron, lead, tin, and copper. Consumption of these metals increased from a growing population, greater economic activity, and an improving standard of living as humanity emerged from the deep sleep of the Dark Ages. Deforestation started around London in 1200 and spread throughout the kingdom. By the 1500s metal ores had to be shipped to Ireland, Scotland, and Wales for smelting, deforesting these regions in turn. One of the economic drivers for the founding of the Jamestown colony in Virginia in 1607 was to take advantage of the New World's ready supply of trees to make glass for export to England. The rapidly escalating price of firewood, the economic consequence of deforestation, provided the necessary incentive to search for an alternative source of energy. The final answer to the energy crisis was not deforesting the living biomass of the New World, but burning the long-dead biomass of the Old World.

## THE ORIGIN AND HISTORY OF COAL

Switching from wood to coal had an environmental consequence. Living plants absorb carbon dioxide from the air, which is released when they decay. For sustainable biomass energy, carbon dioxide is simply recycled between living and dead plant matter and its content in the atmosphere remains unchanged. One way to decrease the amount of carbon dioxide in the atmosphere is to increase the biomass, such as planting trees on treeless land (afforestation), but this is neutralized when living and dead plant matter are once again in balance. The other way is to interrupt the decay process. And this is what happened eons ago when huge quantities of dead plants were quickly submerged in oxygen-starved waters. This delayed onslaught of decay interrupted the natural carbon dioxide cycle.

The partially decayed plants submerged in swamps first became peat. Peat has a high moisture content that is squeezed out if buried by silt of sand, clay, and other minerals from flowing water. Continued burying, either by the land submerging or the ocean rising, added sufficient weight to transform the original deposits of sand and clay to sedimentary rocks and peat to coal. Three to seven feet of compacted plant matter is required to form one foot of coal. Some coal veins are 100 feet thick, which gives one pause to consider how much plant life is incorporated in coal. Most coal was formed 300–400 million years ago during the Devonian and Carboniferous geologic epochs when swamps covered much of the earth and plant life thrived in a higher atmospheric concentration of carbon dioxide. The interruption of plant decay by the formation of massive peat bogs removed huge amounts of carbon dioxide from the atmosphere, clearing the way for a more hospitable environment for animal life. However, some coal is of more recent vintage, laid down 15–100 million years ago, and the newest coal has an estimated age of only 1 million years. When coal is burned we are completing a recycling process interrupted eons ago, or much more recently for those who believe that coal stems from Noah's Flood.

Peat bogs are found in Ireland, England, the Netherlands, Germany, Sweden, Finland, Poland, Russia, Indonesia, and in the United States (the Great Dismal Swamp in North Carolina and Virginia, the Okefenokee Swamp in Georgia, and the Florida Everglades). The high water content has to be removed before peat can be burned as a biomass fuel whose heat content is much lower than coal. Peat is burned in Ireland for heating homes and in Finland for heating homes and generating electricity as a substitute, along with wood waste, for imported fossil fuels. Peat is also mixed with soil to improve its water-holding properties and is a filter material for sewage plants. Once removed, fish can be raised in the resulting pond or, if the peat bog is drained, agricultural crops can be grown, or the peat bog can simply remain fallow. There is always the possibility that these peat bogs may one day become coal beds if buried by hundreds of feet of silt and water.

As in many other areas, the Chinese beat out the Europeans in burning coal. Coal from the Fu-shun mine in northeastern China was consumed for smelting copper and casting coins around 1000 BCE. In 300 BCE the Greek philosopher Theophrastus described how blacksmiths burned a black substance that was quite different from charcoal. From evidence in the form of coal cinders found in archaeological excavations, it is known that Roman forces in England burned coal as a fuel before 400 CE. Although the Romans did not record burning coal, they did record a "pitch-black mineral" that could be carved into trinkets for adorning the human body. That pitch-black mineral was an especially dense type of coal. Like glassmaking, burning coal for heat and blacksmithing and offerings to the gods, plus carving into trinkets for the fashionable of Rome, disappeared along with the Roman Empire. We presume that ever-expanding human knowledge being passed on to following generations has always been ongoing, is ongoing, and will always be ongoing. This, as history clearly shows, is an unwarranted presumption.

The English rediscovered coal in the 1200s during an early episode of deforestation around London, about the same time that the Hopi and Pueblo Indians began burning coal to glaze their ceramic ware in what is now the U.S. Southwest. After the coal gatherers picked up the coal lying on the ground on the banks of the River Tyne near Newcastle, they began chipping away at the exposed seams of coal in the nearby hillsides. Coal mining started when holes became tunnels that bored deep into the thick underground seams of coal. A new profession and a new class of people emerged, ostracized by the rest of society by their origin (displaced peasants) and the widely perceived degrading nature of their work. Coal miners as individuals were at the mercy of the mine owners until they learned to band together for their mutual benefit and protection, giving birth to the modern labor movement.

And there was plenty of incentive for miners to band together as the coal miners bored deeper into the earth. Mining is a very dangerous occupation. Cave-ins can trap the miners. If not immediately snuffed out by the falling rock, they remain trapped, awaiting rescue or dying from asphyxiation or starvation. To combat the peril of cave-ins, miners bonded with huge rats that lived in coal mines by sharing their meals with them. Miners remained alert to the comings and goings of the rats on the theory that rats could sense a cave-in before it occurred, not unlike rats deserting a sinking ship. Perhaps miners' casualty lists best document the perspicacity of rats to sense impending disaster.

In addition to cave-ins, coal miners had to contend with poisonous gases. Mining could release pockets of carbon dioxide or carbon monoxide, odorless and colorless gases of plant decay trapped within the coal seam that quickly killed their victims by asphyxiation. Canaries were the best defense since their chirping meant that they were alive. When they stopped chirping, they were already dead, a dubious warning system at best. A third colorless and odorless gas was methane, also released by mining operations when they exposed pockets of natural gas embedded in the coal seam. Unlike carbon dioxide and monoxide, methane is lighter than air and combustible. As methane accumulates along the ceiling of a mine, it eventually comes in contact with a lighted candle where it either burns or sets off a horrific explosion, depending on its concentration. A new professional, called, euphemistically, a fireman, would wrap his wretched body with wet rags and crawl along the bottom of the mine holding up a stick with a candle at the end, hoping he would discover methane before it was sufficiently concentrated to set off an explosion. Now all he had to do was hug the mine floor while the methane blazed above him.

Coal found in the hills around the River Tyne was moved down to the river and loaded on vessels for shipment to other parts of coastline England, notably London. Access to water provided cheap transportation on ships whereas the overland movement of coal on packhorses was prohibitively expensive. Roads hardly existed and, where they did, deep ruts made them impassable for heavily laden horse-drawn wagons. By 1325, coal became the first internationally traded energy commodity when exported from Newcastle to France and then elsewhere in northern Europe. Thus, coal saved not only the English but also the European forests from devastation. The saying "carrying coals *to* Newcastle" originally referred to something only a simpleton would do since Newcastle was the world's first and largest and most famous coal-exporting port. Six and a half centuries later, coal was carried to Newcastle when Britain began importing coal.

Burning coal made an immediate impression on the people. In 1306, the nobles of England left their country estates to travel to London to serve in Parliament, as was their custom. This time there was something new in the air besides the stench of animal dung, raw sewage, and rotting garbage. The nobles did not like the new pungent aroma spiced with brimstone (sulfur) and succeeded in inducing King Edward I to issue a ban on burning coal. It is one thing for a king to issue a ban, and quite another to enforce it, the classic limit of power faced by parents of teenagers. Regardless of the king's edict, the merchant class of newly emerging metallurgical enterprises had to burn coal because wood was not available in sufficient quantities around London, and what was available was too expensive. Simple economics overruled the king's ban. The fouling of the air of London and other English cities remained for centuries to come. It is hard to imagine that the charming English countryside we know, speckled with quaint towns, cottages, and farms was once, like the eastern United States, nearly one continuous forest.

From the beginning, coal was a matter of dispute between the church, which happened to own the land where the coal was found, the crown, which coveted this natural resource, and the merchant class that transformed coal into a considerable amount of personal wealth. As church, crown, and capital struggled over who would reap the financial benefits, merchant vessels were built to ship coal on the high seas. This, in turn, necessitated building naval vessels to protect the merchant fleet from marauders and pirates. The English also imposed a tax on non-English vessels carrying coal exports, which greatly favored the building and manning of English ships. In this way, coal contributed to making England a sea power and is, therefore, partly responsible for the emergence of England as the world's greatest colonial power. Growth of sea power put more pressure on forests for lumber to build ships and, in particular, trees fit for masts, which eventually would be harvested in English colonies in the New World.

The Black Death did not enhance coal's reputation as its victims turned black while smelling brimstone in the air from burning coal, widely interpreted as to where they might be heading. The Black Death wiped out about one-third of Europeans. The depopulation of London meant less coal had to be burned, improving the quality of its air, and forests regained a toehold in the countryside. The reign of Elizabeth I was marked by increases in population and economic recovery after the Black Death, spurring demand for firewood. She greatly expanded the English Navy to defend the kingdom against the Spanish Armada, increasing the demand for lumber and masts to build warships and charcoal for smelting iron for ship armament. This again put pressure on the kingdom's forests, resulting in widespread deforestation throughout England and another steep rise in the price of firewood.

The adoption of the chimney in London homes in the 1500s allowed for the conversion from wood to coal for heating in the early 1600s, a conversion already completed by industry. While the ability of chimneys to keep the heat inside and channel smoke outside was an advantage for those who dwelt inside, the same could not be said for those who ventured outside. Appalling amounts of acrid smoke eroded and blackened stone in statues and buildings, stunted plant life, affected the health of the population, and made black and dark brown the colors of choice for furnishings and fashion.

London was not the only city that suffered from severe air pollution. During the rapid advance of the Industrial Revolution in the nineteenth century, Manchester became the center of British textile manufacturing and Pittsburgh the center of American steelmaking. The former suffered mightily from coal burned in steam engines to run the textile machines and the latter from coal consumed in making steel. Not all cities suffered equally. Philadelphia and New York were spared at first because of rich anthracite coalfields in eastern Pennsylvania. Anthracite, a hard coal of nearly pure carbon, burns with little smoke. Unfortunately, anthracite reserves were in short supply when coal-burning electricity-generating plants were built at the end of the nineteenth and early twentieth centuries. These plants burned cheaper and more available bituminous coal. New Yorkers staged an early environmental protest against the fouled air that the utility managers could not ignore, so they switched to anthracite coal to appease people while they were awake, but switched back to bituminous while they slept.

We tend to think of air pollution caused by burning coal as a nineteenth-century phenomenon affecting London, Manchester, and Pittsburgh. Yet, only a little over a half-century ago, for four days in early December 1952, a temperature inversion settled over London, trapping a natural white fog so dense that traffic slowed to a crawl and the opera had to be cancelled when the performers could no longer see the conductor. Then coal smoke, also trapped in the temperature inversion, mixed with the fog to produce an unnatural black fog that hugged the ground and cut visibility to less than a foot. Perhaps unbelievably from our vantage point, 4,000 Londoners died from traffic accidents and inhaling sulfur dioxide fumes. Parliament subsequently banned the burning of soft coal in central London, bringing to an end a quaint 700-year-long tradition. In the twenty-first century, Beijing, Shanghai, and other cities in Asia have picked up where London left off. While the results of living in a cloud of polluted air are not as calamitous as in London, nevertheless dwellers in Asian cities suffer from various health impairments.[2]

## Coal and the Industrial Revolution

Coal played an important role in England's emergence as the world's greatest seafaring nation and, subsequently, as the world's leading trading nation and colonial power. It also played an important, if not a pivotal, role in bringing about the Industrial Revolution and England's subsequent emergence as the world's greatest industrial power.

At first coal mines were above the River Tyne and narrow downward shafts dug from the mines to the outside world took care of removing water seepage from rain. As the coal seams bent downward, it was only a matter of time before mining took place under the River Tyne and the North Sea. This opened up a whole new peril for the miners: death by drowning. Even if mining did not breach the river or the sea, water was continually seeping in through the ground, threatening to flood the mines, though not necessarily the miners. For many years the chief way to prevent flooding was to have men haul up buckets of water to the mine surface. As mines went deeper into the earth, a vertical shaft was dug where a continuous chain loop with attached buckets brought water from the bottom of the mine to the surface. Water wheels and windmills powered a few of these continuous chain operations, but most were powered by horses. The capital cost in chain loops, along with their attached buckets and the operating cost of feeding and tending to the horses, encouraged the development of bigger mines employing larger numbers of miners in order to produce the greater quantities of coal needed to cover the higher capital and operating costs. Concentrating coal mining in a smaller number of larger operations meant even deeper mines, perversely exacerbating the problem of water removal.

By the 1690s, Britain's principal industry of providing 80 percent of the world's coal was threatened with a watery extinction. The nation's intellectual resources were focused on solving what seemed to be an overwhelming challenge: how to prevent water from flooding the ever-deeper mines. Denis Papin proposed the idea of having a piston inside a cylinder where water at the bottom of the cylinder would be heated to generate steam under the piston that would drive the piston up. Then the heat would be removed, creating a pressure differential between the top and bottom of the piston as the steam condensed to form a vacuum. Atmospheric pressure on top of the piston would drive the piston down and then the water in the bottom of the cylinder would be reheated to generate steam to drive the piston back up. The up-and-down motion of the piston could power a water pump. Thomas Newcomen, who may or may not have heard of Papin's idea, worked ten years to develop a working engine that did just that.

The Newcomen engine was a piston within a cylinder. Steam from burning coal was fed into the cylinder space below the piston, forcing it up. Then a cold-water spray entered the cylinder space and condensed the steam to create a vacuum and a pressure differential between the top and the bottom of the cylinder. Atmospheric pressure on top of the piston would drive the piston down. Simultaneously, an exhaust gate would open, allowing the water from the spray and condensed steam to drain from the cylinder space. Then the exhaust gate would close and steam would reenter the cylinder space. This continual cycle of feeding steam followed by a spray of water into the bottom of the cylinder kept the piston moving up and down. A crossbeam connected the moving piston to a water pump. Mines could now be emptied of water without horses and chain loops with attached buckets, which by this time had reached their limits of effectiveness. By 1725 Newcomen engines were everywhere and had grown to prodigious size, but the alternate heating and cooling of the lower cylinder walls during each cycle of the piston movement made them extremely energy-inefficient. With coal cheap and plentiful, the Newcomen engine had no technological rival for sixty years. As energy-inefficient as Newcomen engines were, they nevertheless saved the English coal-mining industry from a watery grave and enabled England to maintain its pre-eminence in coal mining for another century.

Thus, coal or, to be more exact, the threat of coal mines filling with water, brought into existence the first industrial fossil-fueled machine that delivered much more power with far greater dependability than wind or water. The fickleness of the wind makes wind power vulnerable and water power is constrained by the capacity of a water wheel to translate falling or moving water into useful power and by the occurrence of droughts. The Newcomen engine had no such limitations.

The building of Newcomen engines required iron and smelting iron consumed charcoal, another contributor to the deforestation of England. The pressure on forests was lifted in 1709 when Abraham Darby, who also advanced the technology of casting pistons and cylinders for Newcomen engines, discovered that coke from coal could substitute for charcoal from wood in smelting iron. It is a bit ironic that coke itself had been discovered some sixty years earlier, in 1642, for brewing beer. London brewers needed a great deal of wood to dry malt. As wood supplies dwindled, they first experimented with coal, but quickly found out that sulfur in coal tainted the malt and, thus, the flavor of the beer. The brewers discovered coke by copying the process of making charcoal from wood, which is essentially baking coal in the absence of oxygen to drive out volatile elements and impurities. Coke is harder than coal, almost pure carbon, and burns at a high temperature without smoke. Malt dried with coke produced a pure, sweet beer.

In 1757 James Watt, an instrument maker for the University of Glasgow, was given an assignment to repair the University's model of the Newcomen engine, which spurred his lifelong interest in steam engines. Watt soon realized that the shortcoming of the Newcomen engine was the energy consumed in reheating the cylinder wall after each injection of cold-water spray. His idea was not to cool the steam in the hot cylinder, but to redirect the steam to another cylinder, or condenser, surrounded by water, where the steam could be condensed without cooling the cylinder wall. Rather than a valve opening to allow a cold spray to condense the steam, a valve opened to allow the expended steam to escape from the cylinder to the condenser. The condensed steam created a vacuum in the bottom of the cylinder, which allowed atmospheric pressure on top of the cylinder to push the piston down. In this way the power cylinder wall would remain hot throughout the operation of the engine, improving its thermal efficiency.

James Watt was assisted by the moral and financial support of Matthew Boulton, a well-known Birmingham manufacturer. After obtaining a patent, the first two steam engines were built in 1776. One pumped water from a coal mine and the other drove air bellows at an iron foundry. The foundry owner, John Wilkenson, invented a new type of lathe to bore cylinders with greater precision, a device that would prove useful for manufacturing steam engines. The final version of the Watt engine came in 1782, when Watt developed the double-acting engine where steam powered the piston in both directions. Steam entering one end of the cylinder drove the piston in one direction, while a valve opening on the other end of the cylinder allowed the spent steam from the previous stroke to exhaust into a condenser. This operation was reversed to drive the piston in the opposite direction. Valves for allowing live steam to enter the cylinder space or spent steam to enter the condenser were opened and shut by the movement of the piston. To further enhance energy efficiency, steam was admitted inside the cylinder only during the first part of the piston stroke, allowing the expansion of the steam to complete the stroke. To further cut heat losses a warm steam jacket surrounded the cylinder and a governor controlled the engine speed. With these enhancements, the Watt steam engine could operate with one-quarter to one-third the energy necessary to operate an equivalent Newcomen engine. Both the Newcomen and Watt engines spurred technological advances in metallurgy to improve metal performance and in manufacturing technology to make cylinders and pistons, lessons not lost on the military for building bigger and better cannons.

Watt's intention was to improve the energy efficiency of the Newcomen engine for pumping water out of mines. Boulton saw Watt's invention as something greater than a more efficient Newcomen engine or a more reliable means of powering his factories than water wheels. Boulton was a visionary who saw the steam engine as a means to harness power for the good of humanity. In Boulton's vision, steam engines would not only drain mines of water but power factories that could be built at any location where coal was nearby. Goods made by machines powered by steam engines would free humans from the curse of drudgery and poverty that had plagued them throughout history.

The world's first industrialized urban center was Manchester, England. The city became the textile center of the world, processing cotton from slave plantations in the United States. Coal was consumed in making iron that went into constructing factory buildings, steam engines, and textile-making machines. Coal also fueled the steam engines that powered the machines and gas given off by heating coal was piped into the factory buildings and burned in lamps to allow round-the-clock operations. All this coal burning smothered Manchester in a thick black blanket of smoke that rivaled pollution in London and, later, Pittsburgh.

The demand for coal from mines near Manchester was so great that narrow shaft seams, which only children could fit into, were brought into use. They had to crawl on their feet and hands dragging heavy sleds of coal behind them like pack animals. Many of these children lived like animals in abandoned portions of mine shafts, separated from their families and daylight. For workers in the Manchester factories, the long hours, the harsh working conditions, the poor pay, the putrid stench of the atmosphere, their appallingly poor health and high death rates, and the breakdown of the family had to be an Orwellian nightmare at its worst, not Boulton's vision at its best. What Freidrich Engels saw in Manchester was recorded in his work *The Condition of the Working Class in England* (1844), which in turn helped Karl Marx shape *The Communist Manifesto* (1848).

## Coal and Railroads

The amount of coal a horse can carry on its back is limited, but its carrying capacity can be improved by having it pull a wagon. The dirt roads of the day, with their deep muddy ruts, were impassable for horses hauling heavy wagonloads of coal. A horse's capacity to move cargo jumps by several orders of magnitude when, instead, it pulls a barge on still water. Canals, not roads, could move large volumes of coal to inland destinations. One of the first canals in Britain moved coal to Manchester from nearby coalfields where horses pulled barges from towpaths alongside the canal. This began the canal-building boom in England where, by the early 1800s, canals were used not only to move coal, but all sorts of raw materials and finished goods to and from cities. Since the nature of the terrain and the availability of water restricted canal construction, wagon ways, where horses were harnessed to cargo-laden carriages riding on wooden rails, complemented canals. Rails made horses more effective in moving coal than pulling loaded wagons on muddy, rutted, dirt roads.

Rails also improved coal-mine productivity. It turned out that getting coal out of the mine was as labor-intensive as mining coal. Often human pack animals were responsible for hauling coal on its journey to the mine surface. One human pack animal would pick up a small wagonload from another human pack animal, tow it a bit, and pass it on to still another human pack animal, then walk back to get the next. Lifetimes were spent hauling coal out of mines and, sometimes, living in mines. Mine operators did what they could to make hauling coal easier, but not strictly for altruistic reasons. Installing rails reduced operating costs by having the same work done by fewer human pack animals, thus improving productivity and, incidentally, profitability. Most rails were made of wood, but a few were made of iron.

Because the use of rails had solved the problem of how to move heavy loads, the concept of the railroad was in place when George Stephenson, the father of railways, put together the elements of iron track with a high-pressure Watt's steam engine on a locomotive platform with flanged iron wheels that pulled flanged iron wheeled carriages. Fittingly, the world's first railroad connected a coal town with a river port twenty-six miles away. The Age of the Railroad began in earnest a few years later, in 1830, when a train on its inaugural run between Liverpool and Manchester hit a top speed of an unbelievable thirty-five miles per hour. By 1845 Britain had 2,200 miles of track, a figure that tripled over the next seven years. While the building of railroads meant relatively cheap and fast transportation between any two points in England, the iron for the rails was not cheap.

## Coal and Steel

The Iron Age began sometime around 2000 BCE, perhaps in the Caucasus region, where iron first replaced bronze. Iron is harder, more durable, and holds a sharper edge longer than bronze. Iron is also the fourth most abundant element, making up 5 percent of the earth's crust. Iron ore is made up of iron oxides plus varying amounts of silicon, sulfur, manganese, and phosphorus. From its start, smelting iron consisted of heating iron ore mixed with charcoal until the iron oxides began reacting with the carbon in the charcoal to release its oxygen content as carbon monoxide or dioxide. Adding crushed seashells or limestone, called flux, removed impurities in the form of slag, which was separated from the heavier molten iron. This left relatively pure iron, intermixed with bits of charcoal and slag that could then be hammered on an anvil by a blacksmith to remove the remaining cinders, slag, and other impurities. The result of the hammering produced wrought (or "worked") iron with a carbon content between 0.02–0.08 percent. This small amount of carbon, absorbed from the charcoal, made the metal both tough and malleable. Wrought iron was the most commonly produced metal throughout the Iron Age.

By the late Middle Ages, European iron makers had developed the blast furnace, a tall chimney-like structure in which combustion was intensified by a blast of air pumped through alternating layers of charcoal, flux, and iron ore. The medieval ironworkers harnessed water wheels to power bellows to force air through the blast furnaces. Centuries later, this would be one of the first tasks for James Watt's steam engines, in addition to pumping water out of coal mines. The blast of air increased the temperature, which allowed the iron to begin absorbing carbon, thereby lowering its melting point. The product of this high-temperature process was cast iron, with between 3–4.5 percent carbon. Cast iron is hard and brittle, liable to shatter under a heavy blow, and cannot be forged (that is, heated and shaped by hammer blows). The molten cast iron was fed through a system of sand troughs, formed into ingots, which reminded people of a sow suckling a litter of piglets, and became known as pig iron. Pig iron was either cast immediately or allowed to cool and shipped to a foundry as ingots, where it was remelted and poured directly into molds to cast stoves, pots, pans, cannons, cannonballs, and church bells.

These early blast furnaces produced cast iron with great efficiency and less cost than wrought iron. However, the process of transforming cast iron to more useful wrought iron by oxidizing excess carbon out of the pig iron was inefficient and costly. More importantly, what was desired was not wrought iron from cast iron, but steel. Steel is iron with carbon content between 0.2–1.5 percent, higher than wrought iron but lower than cast iron. Crucible steel, named after its manufacturing process, was not only very expensive, but the extent of the oxidation of carbon, and therefore the carbon content, could not be controlled. Regardless of its cost, steel was preferred over wrought iron because it was harder and kept a sharp edge longer (the best swords were made of steel) and was preferred over cast iron because it was more malleable and resistant to shock.

Early rails made from wrought iron were soft and had to be replaced every six to eight weeks along busy stretches of track. Steel, in contrast, is perfect for rails because it is harder than wrought iron and more malleable than cast iron. Steel rails, however, were prohibitively expensive. The man of the hour was Henry Bessemer, who was not responding to the needs of the railroad industry, but the military. Bessemer had invented a new artillery shell that had been used in the Crimean War (1853–1856). The army generals complained that the cast iron cannons of the day could not handle Bessemer's more powerful artillery shell. In response Bessemer developed an improved iron-smelting process that involved blasting compressed air through molten pig iron to allow the oxygen in the air to unite with the excess carbon and form carbon dioxide. Ironically, Bessemer's invention, patented in 1855, was similar to the method of refining steel used by the Chinese in the second century BCE.

In 1856 the first Bessemer converter, large and pear-shaped with holes at the bottom for injecting compressed air, was completed. Other individuals contributed to improving the Bessemer converter by adding manganese to get rid of excess oxygen left in the metal by the compressed air and limestone to get rid of any phosphorus in the iron ore, which made steel excessively brittle. Limestone becomes slag after absorbing phosphorus and other impurities and floats at the top of the converter where it is skimmed off before the steel is poured out. Bessemer converters were batch operations to which iron ore, coke, and limestone were added; within a short period of time, molten steel was on the bottom and slag was floating on the top. After removing the slag, the converter was then emptied of its molten steel and then reloaded to make another batch.

The economies of large-scale production utilizing the Bessemer converter transformed undesired wrought-iron rail at $83 per ton in 1867 to desired steel rail at $32 per ton by 1884. It was not long before the Bessemer process had a technological rival: the open-hearth furnace. The open-hearth furnace, while it took longer, could make larger quantities of steel because raw materials were continuously added and slag and steel continually removed. Moreover, steel could be made with more precise technical specifications and scrap steel could be consumed as feedstock along with iron ore, coal, and limestone. Improvements in the chemical composition of steel had increased the life of steel rails and their weight-carrying capacity several fold by 1900, when the open-hearth furnace had largely replaced the Bessemer converter. Another man of the hour, Andrew Carnegie, organizationally shaped the steel industry and, in so doing, reduced the price of steel rail to $14 per ton by the end on the nineteenth century. Carnegie also introduced the I-shaped steel girder for building skyscrapers, a major addition to steel demand once the Otis elevator was perfected.

By 1960, the basic oxygen furnace had, in its turn, replaced the open-hearth furnace. The basic oxygen furnace is essentially a modification of the original Bessemer converter. The first step is feeding iron ore, coke, and limestone into a furnace with air blasted through the mixture to produce molten iron, which is periodically tapped from the bottom of the furnace while the molten slag is periodically removed from the top. The molten iron then goes into the basic oxygen furnace where steel scrap and more limestone are added, along with a blast of oxygen to produce almost pure liquid steel.

In making steel, coking coal supplies carbon to remove the oxygen in the iron ore and heat to melt the iron. Coking, or metallurgical coal, must support the weight of the heavy contents in a furnace yet be sufficiently permeable for gases to rise to the top and molten steel to sink to the bottom of the furnace. Thus, coals are divided into two types: thermal coal fit only for burning and coking coal fit for steelmaking. The liquid and gaseous byproducts in producing coke from metallurgical or coking coal find their way into a host of products such as synthetic rubber, ink, perfume, food and wood preservatives, plastics, varnish, stains, paints, and tars.[3]

The world's largest steel producers are China (501 million tons, over triple its 2001 production), Japan (119 million tons), the United States (91 million tons), Russia (69 million tons), India (55 million tons), South Korea (54 million tons), Germany (46 million tons), Ukraine (37million tons), Brazil (34 million tons), and Italy (31 million tons). The basic oxygen furnace produces 66 percent of the world's crude steel production—about 1,327 million tons in 2008—incidentally consuming 600 million tons of coal. Most of the remaining steel production is made from a more recent innovation, the electric arc furnace.[4] The raw material for electric arc furnaces is scrap. Incidentally, steel is the most recycled commodity on Earth: fourteen million cars in the United States alone are recycled annually. Whereas 1 ton of steel made from raw materials requires, in round terms, 2 tons of iron ore, 1 ton of coal, and a half ton of limestone; 1 ton of recycled steel needs a bit more than 1 ton of scrap. While coal is absent as a raw material in making steel with the electric arc furnace, an electric arc furnace uses a lot of electricity, as one can imagine, which is mainly generated by burning coal augmented by capturing the waste heat of steelmaking. Thus, coal is consumed directly in making steel with the basic oxygen furnace and indirectly in making steel with the electric arc furnace.

Coal played a vital role in shaping the world as we know it today. Coal was needed as a substitute for wood for producing glass and smelting metals after the forests were cut down. Coal became a major export item for England, spurring the development of the English navy. The challenge posed by flooding coal mines frantically called for a solution—the Newcomen engine—the first industrial power-generating machine not dependent on wind or water. The Newcomen engine spurred further advances in metal and toolmaking and led directly to Watt's steam engine. Watt's steam engine powered the Industrial Revolution with coal, steel, and railroads. Coal, then, is at least partly responsible for England becoming a world sea power, a colonial power, and, after the birth of the Industrial Revolution, the world's first and mightiest industrial power. This lasted for over half a century before being challenged by the emergence of rival centers of industrial power in the United States, Germany, and Japan.

## Rise and Fall of King Coal

Though early steam locomotives were fueled by wood, it was not long before they switched to coal. One reason was deforestation; the other was the availability of coal as the most commonly carried commodity. Coal became the sole source of energy for fueling locomotives, which for decades before the automobile age was the sole source of transportation on land other than horses. Robert Fulton invented the first steam-driven riverboat, the *Clermont,* which propelled itself from New York to Albany in 1807. While wood could be burned on riverboats, ocean-going vessels burned coal, a more concentrated form of energy that took up a lot less volume. The famed clipper ships of the waning decades of the nineteenth century marked the final transition from a source of power that was undependable, renewable, and pollution- and cost-free to one that was dependable, nonrenewable, polluting, and not cost-free. Now coal had it all on land and sea. Thomas Edison's first electricity-generating plants were fueled by coal, although hydropower was soon harnessed at Niagara Falls. Coal and hydropower were the principal sources of energy for generating electricity during the first half of the twentieth century.

Coal's share of the energy pie peaked at 60 percent in 1910. Oil, natural gas, and hydropower contributed another 10 percent, and biomass 30 percent. After 1910, things began to change for King Coal. Coal maintained its pre-eminence in passenger transportation until Henry Ford put America, and the world, on gasoline-driven wheels. In 1912, the *Titanic* had 162 coal-fired furnaces fed continuously by 160 stokers working shifts 24/7 shoveling as much as 600 tons of coal per day. This might work well for passenger vessels, but coal-burning warships were constrained in fulfilling their primary mission by the large portion of the crew dedicated to shoveling coal, rather than manning guns, and the amount of space dedicated to holding coal rather than carrying ammunition. Moreover, warships with a heavy cargo of coal moved slowly and their pillars of smoke signaled the enemy as to their whereabouts. Admiral Sir John Fisher, head of the British Navy, spearheaded the transformation from marine boilers powered by coal to oil in the years prior to the First World War. Naysayers scoffed at the idea, but as soon as the obvious advantages of oil over coal were demonstrated in higher speed, greater firepower, and less emissions to betray a vessel's presence, it became a race to dump coal in favor of oil. As ships made the transition from coal to oil, the worldwide network of coal-bunkering stations supplied by coal colliers was converted in tandem to handle oil supplied by tankers (ship's fuel is still referred to as bunkers).

Coal and wood remained the chief sources of energy for cooking until the advent of the electric stove in the 1920s, along with stoves that burned natural gas and liquid propane. About this time, homes began a slow conversion from coal to heating oil and natural gas. Automobiles were taking passengers away from electric trolleys, whose electricity was generated from coal, for inner-city transportation. Intercity railroad passenger train traffic, powered by coal-fueled locomotives, declined as a network of roads sprang into existence. When the fall of King Coal from pre-eminence sped up during and after the Second World War, one individual stood out: John L. Lewis, a former coal miner and president of the United Mine Workers. A contentious personality who had the audacity to defy President Franklin Delano Roosevelt by leading a coal miners' strike during the war, Lewis was instrumental in raising the pay and improving the health and retirement benefits and working conditions for coal miners. As laudable as these well-deserved benefits were, they also increased the price of coal and, in so doing, hastened its demise. Perhaps no better proof of this was Perez Alfonso, a Venezuelan oil minister, who wanted to erect a statue to honor Lewis for boosting the market for Venezuelan oil exports.

The rise in the price of coal from John L. Lewis's success was an added inducement for homeowners to switch from coal, which had to be shoveled into a furnace (from which ashes had to be removed and disposed of) to the much greater convenience of heating oil, propane, and natural gas, which did not require the effort associated with coal. In cooking, the switch was already far advanced from coal to electricity and natural gas and propane.[5] While oil-driven automobiles, buses, and airplanes were diverting people from coal-burning passenger trains, and trucks had taken over local distribution of freight, railroad freight trains still carried the bulk of the nation's intercity freight. Trucks were unable to cut deeply into intercity freight traffic because the road network was relatively undeveloped and better fit for automobiles than trucks. All this changed with the launching of the interstate highway system by President Dwight D. Eisenhower.

A large steam locomotive pulling a loaded freight train burned 1 ton of coal per mile, which required a fulltime fireman to continually shovel coal. Railroads were enormous consumers of coal and railroad executives displayed equally enormous reluctance to abandon steam locomotives when the diesel engine first appeared in the late 1930s. Steam locomotives had become an intimate part of railroading folklore. Distinct in design and operating nuances, they had to be maintained by a dedicated crew that became inseparable from the locomotive, which required a lot of downtime for maintenance and repair.

Railroaders were unwilling to switch from steam to diesel, even though diesel locomotives had inherent advantages. Diesel engines were fuel-efficient because they burned gallons of diesel fuel per mile, not a ton of coal per mile. The diesel engine avoided the inherent energy inefficiency of a steam engine from which the latent heat of vaporization was passed to the atmosphere. In a diesel engine, fuel sprayed into the cylinder space above a piston is ignited by heated compressed air. The expansion of the gases of combustion powers the first downward stroke. After the power stroke, the piston is forced up to expel the exhaust gases, then down to draw in fresh air, then up to compress the air. The heated compressed air ignites another spray of fuel whose expanding gases of combustion powers another downward stroke. Thus, every other downward stroke is a power stroke that, through a crankshaft connected to the other pistons, drives an electricity generator that powers electric motors attached to the engine wheels.

Diesel engines have other advantages as well. They are more reliable because they require less maintenance and repair, both in downtime and cost; less manpower, because no coal has to be shoveled; and less frequent refueling. Steam locomotives of various horsepower have to be built to handle freight trains of different sizes, whereas a number of standard-sized diesel engines can be hooked together to obtain the requisite horsepower. In short, the only reason to keep steam locomotives once diesel engines made their appearance was management's reluctance to change.

The advantages of the diesel engine could no longer be ignored when John L. Lewis's success in improving the lot of coal miners increased the price of coal. The first diesel engines were restricted to moving freight cars around freight yards and were excluded from long intercity runs, the exclusive domain of the steam locomotive. Steam locomotives could persevere as long as all railroad managers agreed to use steam locomotives on intercity freight trains, ensuring equal inefficiency in operations for all. But this holding action could not ignore the competitive threat of a growing volume of trucks gaining access to intercity traffic made possible by the interstate highway system. If any railroad bolted to diesel for hauling intercity freight, then the inherent efficiencies and advantages of diesel locomotion would give that railroad a competitive edge over the others. And that is what happened: one railroad bolted. As soon as one made the switch to diesel for intercity freight trains, it was a race to convert locomotives from coal to oil similar to the race to convert ships from coal to oil. Despite efforts by steam locomotive aficionados and railroad executives to hold the fort, the steam whistle and the chugging locomotive spewing steam, smoke, and at times blazing ashes disappeared within a decade.

Adding to King Coal's woes, electricity-generating plants built after the Second World War were designed to run on oil, natural gas, and nuclear power in addition to coal and hydro. King Coal was no longer king in transportation, electricity generation, heating houses and commercial buildings, and home cooking. By 1965, its share of the energy pie was down to a still respectable 39 percent and declined to 30 percent in 1970 and remained around 25–29 percent until recent years when its share expanded to 30 percent.

## TYPES OF COAL

Aside from peat, a precursor to coal, there are four types of coal. The lowest quality of coal and the largest portion of the world's coal reserves is lignite, a geologically young, soft, brownish-black coal, some of which retains the texture of the original wood. Of all coals, it has the lowest carbon content, 25–35 percent, and the lowest heat content, 4,000–8,300 British thermal units (Btus) per pound. The next step up is sub-bituminous coal, a dull black coal with a carbon content of 35–45 percent and heat content 8,300–13,000 Btus per pound. Both lignite and sub-bituminous coals, known as soft coals, are primarily thermal coals for generating electricity. Some sub-bituminous coals have lower sulfur content than bituminous coal, an environmental advantage.

Next are the hard coals, bituminous and anthracite. Bituminous is superior to soft coal in terms of carbon content, 45–86 percent, and energy content, 10,500–15,500 Btus per pound. Bituminous coal is the most plentiful form of coal in the United States and is used both to generate electricity (thermal coal) and, if it has the right properties, as coking or metallurgical coke for steel production. Anthracite coal has the highest carbon content, 86–98 percent, and a heat content of nearly 15,000 Btus per pound. Anthracite coal was closely associated with home heating because it burned nearly smokeless. As desirable as anthracite is, it is also scarce. In the United States, anthracite is found in only eleven counties in northeastern Pennsylvania and is a largely exhausted resource.

## COAL MINING

Coal mines have historically been subterranean regions where accidents and black lung have taken their toll. Mining coal in the twenty-first century is an activity carried out differently than it was in the past. In developed nations, no gangs of men swing pickaxes to remove the over- and underburden of rock to gain access to the coal, then again to chip out the coal. No gangs of men shovel the rock or coal into small wagons or carts for the trip to the surface. Now the most popular way of removing coal is continuous mining machines with large, rotating, drum-shaped cutting heads studded with carbide-tipped teeth that rip into a seam of coal. Large gathering arms scoop the coal directly into a built-in conveyor for loading into shuttle cars or a conveyor for the trip to the surface. Continuous cutters ripping and grinding their way through coal seams can do in minutes what gangs of miners with pickaxes and shovels took days to accomplish.

The next most popular method for removing is a machine resembling an oversized chain saw that cuts out a section of coal in preparation for blasting to allow for expansion. Holes are then drilled for explosives that blast large chunks of coal loose from the seam. Loaders scoop up the coal into conveyors that fill shuttle cars to haul the coal out through the shaft. For both methods of mining, long rods or roof bolts are driven into the roof of the mine to bind layers of weak strata into a single layer strong enough to support its own weight. If necessary, braces are used for additional support. Wood is favored because it makes a sharp cracking sound if the roof begins to weaken.

An increasingly popular and efficient means of mining introduced into the United States from Europe in the 1950s is longwall mining where a rotating shear moves back and forth in a continuous, smooth motion for several hundred feet across the face or wall of a block of coal. The cut coal drops into a conveyor and is removed from the mine. Some of the rock on top of the coal also collapses, which is then removed to the surface or piled in areas where the coal has been removed. The main supports for the rooms created by longwall mining are pillars of solid coal, which are the last to be mined before a mine is abandoned.

Regardless of the type of mining technology employed, mine shafts for transporting miners and coal either slope down to coal beds that are not too deeply located in the earth or are vertical to reach beds of coal more than 2,000 feet beneath the surface. Huge ventilation fans on the surface pump air through the mineshafts to reduce the amount of coal dust in the air, prevent the accumulation of dangerous gases, and ensure a supply of fresh air for the miners.

In recent decades, surface mining has gained prominence over subterranean mining. In the western part of the United States, 75 percent of the coal produced is obtained from surface mines with coal deposits up to 100 hundred feet thick. Surface mining also occurs in Appalachia. Surface mines produce 60 percent of the coal mined in the United States, while the remaining 40 percent comes from underground coal mines located primarily in Appalachia. Although there are large open-pit mines in other parts of the world, such as Australia and Indonesia, globally speaking about two-thirds of coal comes from underground mines.

A few utility plants are located at the mouths of mines, but most coal is loaded on barges and railroad cars for transport to electricity-generating plants or export ports. In the United States, about 60 percent of the coal mined is moved by railroad to the consumer, often in unit trains of a hundred automatically unloading coal cars, each holding 100 tons of coal, or 10,000 tons of coal in a single trainload. Coal is unloaded by hoppers in the bottom of coal cars that open to drop the coal onto a conveyor belt located below the rails or by a rotating mechanism that empties 100 tons of coal by turning the coal cars upside down as though they were toys. Coal is still a major revenue generator for railroads around the world. Coal in the United States not moved by rail is primarily moved by barge on 25,000 miles of inland waterways. One unconventional way to move coal is to pipeline pulverized coal mixed with water from a coal mine to a power station, where the water is decanted and the pulverized coal is fed directly into a boiler.

After mining, coal is processed to ensure a uniform size and washed to reduce its ash and sulfur content. Washing consists of floating the coal across a tank of water containing magnetite for the correct specific gravity. Heavier rock and other impurities sink to the bottom and are removed as waste. Washing reduces the ash and pyretic sulfur-iron compounds clinging to the surface of the coal, but not the sulfur chemically bonded within the coal. Washing can also reduce carbon dioxide emissions by 5 percent. Magnetite clinging to the coal after washing is separated with a spray of water and recycled. Coal is then shipped by rail or barge to power plants. Some power plants run off a single source of coal while others buy various grades of coal that are mixed together before burning in order to obtain optimal results in heat generation, pollution emissions, and cost control.

Coal-mining operations are highly regulated in the developed world. In the United States, a company must comply with hundreds of laws and thousands of regulations, many of which have to do with the safety and health of the miners and the impact of coal mining on the environment. Legal hurdles may require ten years before a new mine can be developed. A mining company must provide detailed information about how the coal will be mined, the precautions taken to protect the health and safety of the miners, and the mine's impact on the environment. For surface mining, the existing condition of the land must be carefully documented to make sure that reclamation requirements have been successfully fulfilled. Other legal requirements cover archaeological and historical preservation, protection and conservation of endangered species, special provisions to protect fish and wildlife, forest and rangeland, wild and scenic river views, water purity, and noise abatement.

In surface or strip mining, specially designed draglines, wheel excavators, and large shovels strip the overburden to expose the coal seam, which can cover the entire top of an Appalachian mountain. Coal is loaded into huge specially designed trucks by large mechanical shovels for shipment to a coal-burning utility or to awaiting railroad cars or barges. Surface mining has lower operating and capital costs and provides a safer and healthier environment for the workers than underground mining. After the coal is removed, the overburden is replaced and replanted with plant life to restore the land as closely as possible to its original state. Reclaimed land can also be transformed into farmland, recreational areas, or residential or commercial development, as permitted by the regulators.

Critics of surface mining point out the damage done to the landscape when the overburden removed from the top of a mountain or hill is dumped into nearby valleys, called "valley fill." In addition to the destruction of the landscape and vegetation, valley fills become dams creating contaminated ponds of acid runoff from sulfur-bearing rocks and heavy metals such as copper,

Table 4.1

**Employment, Productivity, and Safety**

|  | Employment (2000) | Miners per Million Tons Output | Deaths | Deaths per Million Tons Output |
|---|---|---|---|---|
| Australia | 18 | 76 | 4 | 0.02 |
| United States | 77 | 96 | 38 | 0.05 |
| United Kingdom | 8 | 241 | 4 | 0.05 |
| South Africa | 54 | 298 | 30 | 0.17 |
| Poland | 158 | 1,561 | 28 | 0.28 |
| India | 456 | 2,171 | 100 | 0.48 |
| Russia | 197 | 1,195 | 137 | 0.83 |
| China | 5,000 | 5,501 | 5,786 | 6.36 |

lead, mercury, and arsenic exposed by coal mining. They also object to the dust and noise of strip-mining operations and "fly-rocks" raining down on those unfortunately residing nearby. The scars of surface mining are clear from the air. Residents in West Virginia are split between those who support the economic benefits of surface coal mining and those who want to transform West Virginia into a recreational destination for tourists.[6] Another problem is abandoned underground mines, which eventually fill with water. The water can range from being nearly fit for drinking to containing dangerously high concentrations of acids and metallic compounds that may end up contaminating ground and drinking water.

Of course, the record also shows that there are large established companies mindful of their legal obligations to restore the landscape and protect the environment. There are instances of reclamation carried out so effectively that, with the passage of time, there is no apparent evidence that strip-mining had ever taken place. Aside from corporate ethics, there are sound business reasons for being a responsible corporate citizen such as the desire to remain in business for decades to come. For these companies, the extra costs in protecting the health and safety of the miners and safeguarding the environment generate huge payoffs by allowing them to remain in business over the long haul. Private ownership is a right granted by governments on the basis that the conduct of business is better handled by businesspeople than government bureaucrats. If in reality, or if in the perception of the electorate, the supposed benefits of private ownership are not being achieved, then private ownership itself is threatened.

There has been environmental degradation, but much of this lies with fly-by-night companies that fold without meeting their light-of-day responsibilities. While critics of coal extraction in developed nations abound, the developing nations, most notably China and India, seem to exist on another planet. Coal mining, particularly in the tens of thousands of small mines, violates elemental concerns over health and safety of the workers and the environment. No one in those countries seems to care about spontaneous combustion of coal-mining residues that burn on forever or drinking water and agricultural lands permanently contaminated with poisonous metal compounds.

Employment of coal miners has changed drastically in recent decades as machines have replaced labor. Although there are 7 million coal miners in the world, 5 million are in China and another half million are in India, where the use of picks and shovels is the dominant coal-mining technique. Table 4.1 shows employment, productivity, and safety in terms of the number of miners per million tons of output, the number of miners' deaths, and deaths in terms of a million tons of output for 2000.[7] The table shows the enormous disparity in worker productivity and mortality rates between the developed and developing worlds. More recent data suggest that official coal mining deaths in China may be closer to 4,000, but there is also an element of underreporting from remote areas that suggest that the death rate may be higher than what the statistics show. Note that coal mining in the United Kingdom, where it all began, is now a faint vestige of its former vigor.

Needless to say, the lowest fatality rates occur in nations where there is the strongest commitment to health and safety standards for miners and for workers in general. China has the most abysmal safety record, and that may be a gross understatement. Most casualties are associated with small mines employing women and children, not the large state-owned mines. Methane explosions from lack of proper ventilation and gas monitoring are responsible for half of the deaths. These figures reflect mine mishaps, not deaths from health impairment from mining. A nonfatal occupational risk for miners and for many other industrial workers is loss of hearing. For coal miners, loss of hearing, caused by explosives used to dislodge coal and machinery noise in close quarters, occurs slowly and often without the miner's awareness. With regard to fatal occupational risks, the most common disease is pneumoconiosis, commonly known as black lung disease. Black lung disease has dropped precipitously for mines with ample ventilation to reduce coal dust, but still remains a problem in China and India and other nations where relatively little is invested in protecting the workers' health. China's terrible record in protecting miners extends to the end users. Drying chilies with coal contaminated with arsenic was responsible for thousands of cases of arsenic poisoning. Drying corn with coal contaminated with fluorine caused millions to suffer from dental and skeletal fluorosis.

## COAL IN THE TWENTY-FIRST CENTURY

Coal's retreat in relative standing among other energy sources ended in 2000. Coal is here to stay and is gaining ground in absolute and relative terms. Despite criticisms leveled against coal, it does have virtues that cannot be ignored such as being:

- abundant, frequently reserves are measured in hundreds of years;
- secure, in that coal is available in sufficient quantities without the need for large-scale imports for most coal-consuming nations;
- safe (does not explode like natural gas, but of course mine safety is an issue);
- nonpolluting of water resources as oil spills are (although there are other adverse environmental consequences of mining and burning coal);
- cost-effective, by far the cheapest source of energy.

As seen in Figure 4.1, the volume of coal production leveled out in the 1990s but is heading upward again. The top line is coal mined in physical tons and the bottom line is coal production expressed in terms of the equivalent amount of oil that would have to be burned to match the energy released by burning coal. As the figure shows, close to 2 short tons of coal have to be burned to obtain the same energy release as burning 1 metric ton of oil.[8]

Figure 4.1 also shows the relative contribution that coal makes in satisfying world energy demand for commercial sources, excluding biomass. Since 1981, the percentage of coal's share in satisfying energy needs had been slowly eroding until 2001 when there was a resurgence in coal consumption and in its share of the energy pie. This trend is expected to continue from coal-fired electricity generation capacity being added all over the world but particularly in the United States,

Figure 4.1   **Global Coal Production and Percent Contribution to Global Energy**

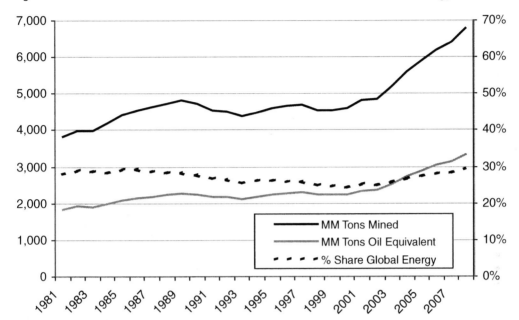

China, and India. However, there has been a sharp decline in ordering new coal-fired electricity-generating capacity in the United States because of the risk of a cap and trade program being imposed by the Obama administration. The global economic recession starting in 2008 also affects utility plans to add capacity. Regardless of the situation in the United States, China and India will remain principal drivers of the world coal business.

Figure 4.2 shows the world's largest consumers and producers of coal in 2008 in terms of millions of tons oil equivalent. China is the world's largest consumer and producer of coal and both exports and imports coal. China suffers from a poorly developed internal logistics system. Movement from inland distributions to coastline population centers relies heavily on China's river systems. Movement of goods and commodities along China's long coastline, where a number of its principal population centers are located, is by water rather than by land. As a substitute for moving commodities along its coastline, China selectively exports and imports. China imports thermal coal to utilities located on its coast from Australia and Indonesia and exports thermal coal to neighboring countries such as North and South Korea and Japan. By becoming a major world steel producer, China has become a major importer of metallurgical or coking coal. The steam locomotive has not entirely gone the way of dinosaurs. China, India, and South Africa still rely on steam locomotives to move coal.

The relative importance of the United States, along with Canada and China, as consumers and producers of coal can be seen by the huge step down to the third largest consumer and producer, India. Thermal and metallurgical or coking coal are two distinct markets. It is possible for a large bulk carrier to move thermal coal from Australia to Europe and return with a cargo of metallurgical coal from the United States or South Africa to Japan. The largest steam and coking coal exporters in 2008 were Australia (252 million tons), Indonesia (203 million tons), Russia (101 million

Figure 4.2    **World's Leading Producers and Consumers of Coal** (MM Tons Oil Equivalent) in 2008

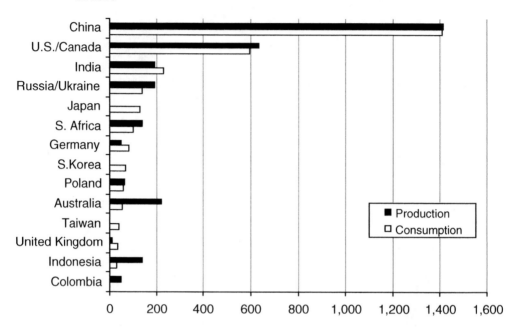

tons), Colombia (74 million tons), United States (74 million tons), South Africa (62 million tons), and China (47 million tons). The largest importers were Japan (186 million tons), South Korea (100 million tons), Taiwan (66 million tons), India (60 million tons), Germany (46 million tons), China (46 million tons), and United Kingdom (44 million tons). Japan, South Korea, and Taiwan view coal as a means of reducing their reliance on Middle East oil. The United Kingdom, once the world's largest exporter of coal, now imports a large share of its coal needs. Both the United Kingdom and Germany have been phasing out the large subsidies paid to keep its domestic coal-producing industry alive in favor of far cheaper imports.

South Africa has abundant coal resources and limited oil resources, and oil-exporting nations were reluctant to trade because of its past apartheid policies. As a consequence, South Africa became a world leader in producing petroleum products (synthetic fuels) and chemicals from coal. The Fischer-Tropsch process, dating back to the 1920s, transforms low-quality coal to high-grade petroleum fuels plus other products.[8] The Germans relied on this technology to make gasoline from its plenteous supplies of coal during the Second World War to compensate for not having indigenous oil resources to run its war machine. These plants were the highest priority targets during Allied bombing of Nazi Germany. The South African plants have been producing 130,000 barrels per day of a mix of 20–30 percent naphtha and 70–80 percent diesel, kerosene, and fuel oil since 1955. About 0.4 tons of coal are consumed for every barrel of oil produced with an overall energy efficiency of 40 percent (60 percent of the energy content of the coal is consumed in transforming coal to liquids). Coal is first gasified to yield a mixture of hydrogen and carbon monoxide, which, after passing through iron or cobalt catalysts, is transformed into methane, synthetic gasoline or diesel fuel, waxes, and alcohols, with water and carbon dioxide as byproducts. Synthetic fuels from coal are higher in quality than those made from oil. For instance, diesel fuel made by the Fischer-Tropsch process has reduced

Figure 4.3  **Known Coal Reserves (Billion Tons) and R/P Ratio** (Years)

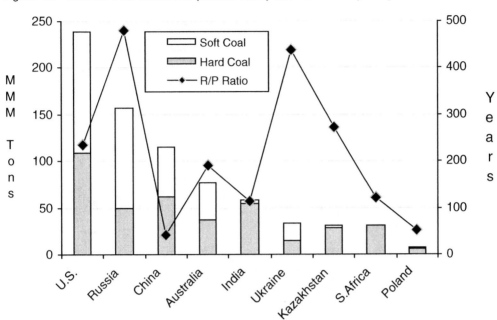

nitrous oxides, hydrocarbons, and carbon monoxide emissions with little or no particulate emissions compared to oil-based diesel fuels.[9]

China is building a coal-to-liquids plant in Inner Mongolia that will produce 20,000 barrels per day of motor vehicle fuel plus other oil products with a planned expansion to 100,000 bpd. The process is a direct liquefaction process transforming coal to a solvent at a high temperature and pressure and then followed by a more complex chemistry to produce 20–30 percent naphtha and 70–80 percent diesel fuel and liquefied petroleum gas. The process is more efficient and uses 0.3–0.4 tons of coal per barrel of oil produced. If successful, other coal-to-liquid plants will be built. One adverse environmental aspect of coal-to-liquid technology is a large emission of carbon dioxide during the production process amounting to about 0.6 tons of carbon dioxide for every barrel of oil.[10]

Unlike oil, where the world's total proven reserves divided by current consumption equal only forty years, over a century (120 years) would be required for current consumption to eat away at proven coal reserves. The reserve to production (R/P) ratio has to be handled gingerly as we have a knack for discovering new reserves. (Theodore Roosevelt estimated that oil reserves would be exhausted in twenty years, given consumption and known reserves in the 1910s.) Moreover, reserves are made up of known reserves plus estimates of probable reserves, and as such are subject to error. Some criticize R/P ratios because they are based on current, not future, consumption and to that extent overestimate the life of existing reserves. On the other hand, they do not take into account future discoveries and so underestimate the life of existing reserves. Unlike oil, there is no active ongoing search for new coal reserves, which means that coal reserves could be substantially upgraded. Figure 4.3 shows the world's largest known coal reserves in terms of size, ranked by how long they will last at the present rate of consumption.

The United States has the world's largest reserves of coal of 238 billion tons with a R/P ratio of 234 years, whereas Russia has 157 billion tons with a R/P of 481 years. The world's largest

Figure 4.4  **U.S. $/Ton Oil, Natural Gas, and Coal Prices** (Constant 2008 $)

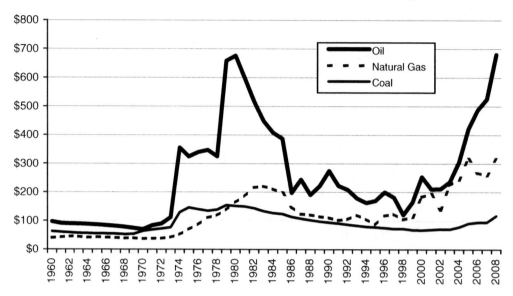

consumer of coal, China, has reserves of 115 billion tons with a R/P of only 41 years. Of course, the nature of the reserves does not reflect the type of coal actually being mined. As previously mentioned, soft coals are lignite and sub-bituminous and hard coals are bituminous and anthracite. Premium bituminous coal for making coking coal for steel production is found in Australia, the United States, Canada, and South Africa. Significant portions of reserves in Russia, Ukraine, and China are soft coals, generally perceived to be greater pollutants than hard coals. But there are exceptions. India has only hard coal, but of poor quality in terms of heat, ash, and sulfur content. Both China and India burn coal with virtually no environmental safeguards. Ash, the residue of burning, is released to the atmosphere in the form of airborne particulates (soot) and sulfur is released as sulfur dioxide gas.

The United States's enormous reserves of coal enhance the nation's energy self-sufficiency. Its reserves can last nearly 250 years at the present rate of production. The coal situation in the United States is quite unlike oil where two-thirds is imported, and the R/P ratio on domestic oil is only twelve years. Some of the imported oil is from volatile and unstable and, at times, distinctly unfriendly nations. Coal does not demand an enormous overseas military presence to ensure security of supply. Moreover, coal has other virtues: it is cheap and its price is much more stable compared to oil and natural gas as shown in Figure 4.4.[11]

A picture is worth a thousand words. Since the oil crisis of 1973, coal prices have been much lower than oil and natural gas (for the most part) and much more stable. But a picture does not include everything. What cannot be seen is that coal is a reliable domestic source of energy not subject to the whims of oil potentates.

The picture for Europe would reflect higher mining costs for coal than in the United States. The picture for Japan would reflect higher shipping costs since all coal must be imported. The picture for China and India would reflect lower mining costs in terms of lack of investment in

Figure 4.5    **Percent Share World Coal Consumption by Nation in 2008**

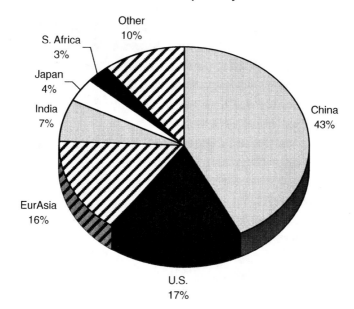

mechanization, near-slave wages for miners, with little spent for personal safeguards for their health and safety and for environmental safeguards to protect the population from pollution. This heavy reliance on low-cost coal affects the competitive position of China and India in world trade since the cost of energy is an element in the price of exported goods.

## ROLE OF COAL AMONG THE MAJOR CONSUMERS

The primary use of coal is in electricity generation followed by steel production. Electricity and cleaner-burning heating oil and natural gas heat homes and cook food in developed nations, but coal (and biomass) are still burned for heating homes and cooking food in China and India. The six leading consumers of coal in 2008 were China, the United States, Europe, Russia and Central Asia (EurAsia), India, Japan, and South Africa as shown in Figure 4.5.

As seen in Figure 4.6, the nations with the greatest dependence on coal (over 50 percent) as an energy source are South Africa, China, Poland, India, and Kazakhstan. In 2000, China's coal consumption temporarily dipped as a result of an order from Beijing to close 50,000 small and inefficient mines for safety and economic reasons. The official data released by China on coal consumption presumed that these mines were closed and no longer producing coal. However, just as King Edward I's ban on burning coal in London was not heeded on the streets of London, it turned out that orders emanating from Beijing were not carried out in the provinces. China, without much in reserves of oil and natural gas, depends on coal as an industrial and residential fuel. Without replacement energy, thousands of small inefficient mines could not be closed, although the official statistics presumed that they were.

The failure of thousands of mines to close when ordered to do so also underscores a critical problem in China; its relentless pursuit of economic development is driving energy consumption through the roof. As much as China desires to diversify its energy sources to reduce the nation's

Figure 4.6  **Percent Dependence of Various Nations on Coal**

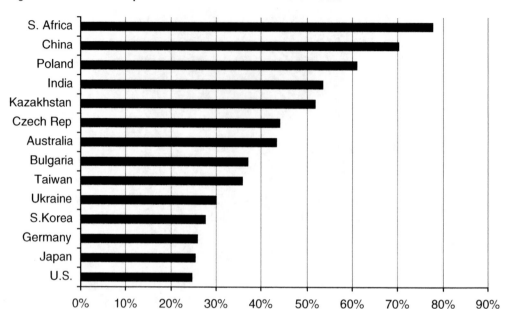

reliance on coal, it cannot cut coal consumption without suffering severe economic dislocation. As long as China's economic locomotive speeds faster and faster, coal will play an increasingly important role. China's building of hydropower dams and nuclear power plants will cut into coal consumption, but it will be years before their construction is completed.

On the surface, India is in a better position than China because it is less dependent on coal, although its dependence has been slowly climbing from its low point in 1999. From another perspective, India is in a worse position than China. China has an enormous trade surplus that is supporting the development of alternative sources of energy to coal (natural gas, hydro and nuclear power). India suffers from a negative trade balance and is less able to finance development of alternative energy sources or the import of energy such as natural gas. Thus, greater coal consumption, and possibly greater biomass consumption, may be the primary solution to India's growing energy needs rather than importing clean energy such as natural gas—unless energy providers are willing to accept rupees rather than dollars (one liquefied natural gas import scheme calls for rupee payments). Until there is a slowing of their economic locomotives, coal consumption in India and China will continue to expand both in volume and relative share of the energy pie.

King Coal was being unceremoniously dumped in the United States until the oil crisis in 1973 when coal's share of the energy pie fell to a low point of 18 percent. Even so, coal consumption in absolute terms was still rising slowly. Consumption accelerated after the oil crisis as coal found a ready market to replace oil as a fuel for electricity generation, rising to 24 percent of the energy pie in 1985. A slowing in the growth of electricity consumption and the collapse in oil prices in 1985 removed the financial incentive for building large coal plants. For environmental and economic reasons, there was a major shift in favor of building lower capital cost and smaller natural gas-burning electricity-generating plants, which better fit growth patterns.

Since 1985 coal's share of the energy pie has been relatively constant, yet coal consumption continued to increase in line with total energy consumption. This is quite remarkable considering that nearly all new electricity-generating plants in the United States in the 1990s and early 2000s were fueled by natural gas. With virtually no coal-burning plants built during these years, the only conclusion one can reach in examining the upward trend in consumption is that existing coal plants were operating at higher average utilization rates. This near-total reliance on natural gas during the almost twenty-year natural gas "bubble" of low natural gas prices burst in 2003 when demand finally outstripped supply. As natural gas prices rose to record levels, utilities took a second look at the idea of constructing coal-fired plants, and began ordering a number of new plants. With the building of these plants, coal's share of the energy pie slowly began to increase. Despite the bad publicity coal receives in the United States, it is still viewed as a national asset, plentiful, cheap, and secure, providing half the nation's electricity. Existing coal-fired electricity-generation plants and new ones being built will keep the coal industry a viable business and ensure the employment of tens of thousands of coal miners for a long time to come even in the face of a costly carbon cap and trade program. It will take decades to replace coal-fired plants with clean-burning alternatives and at a great cost. All that a cap and trade program will do is reduce the future number of coal-fired plants with the consumer bearing a higher cost of electricity.

Europe is one place in the world where coal is in retreat, both in relative and absolute terms. Coal consumption was slowly declining and its share of the energy pie was dropping fast until the oil crisis in 1973. Then coal's share leveled off as coal consumption increased to displace oil in electricity generation. Since 1985, it has been downhill for coal being replaced by nuclear power and natural gas. Nuclear power has been aggressively pursued in Europe, particularly in France. A natural gas pipeline grid has been built connecting the gas fields of Russia, the Netherlands, North Sea, Algeria, and Libya, with customers throughout Europe. Nuclear power and natural gas have largely displaced coal and oil for electricity generation and as an industrial fuel. Moreover, the Europeans are intent on ensuring that the role for coal is not resurrected by relying on wind and natural gas to meet incremental electricity needs. The interruptions of Russian gas supplies in 2006 and 2008/09 as a result of a pricing dispute with the Ukraine have tempered the willingness of Europeans to rely on Russian natural gas and they have inaugurated a program to diversify natural gas supplies.

Coal mining is a heavily subsidized industry in parts of Europe. Given an average import price of $40 per ton range, the average subsidy per ton of coal produced in Germany is estimated to be $144 per ton and $75 in Spain. France has an even higher subsidy rate, but its coal production is small. Subsidizing industry has been losing its allure for the last few decades. The United Kingdom has done away with coal subsidies by closing its most inefficient and heavily subsidized mines and significantly increasing the productivity of those remaining. Moreover, UK coal must compete with other forms of energy after the UK privatized its electricity-generating industry, including imported coal. UK coal production is a shadow of its former self, and German coal production is in a long-term decline. Both nations import a large portion of their coal needs. While European coal production is in a long-term slow decline, it supports steelmaking and still-existent coal-burning electricity-generation plants.

Before the fall of communism in 1989, coal consumption in Russia was fairly steady, although nuclear power and natural gas were eroding coal's share of the energy pie. After 1989, the reduction in coal consumption was primarily caused by the fall in electricity demand that accompanied the collapse of the Russian economy. During the 1990s, oil consumption for electricity generation was sharply curtailed to make room for exports, slowing the decline in the role of coal. Looking into the future, the primary beneficiary for satisfying incremental demand for electricity will be natural gas. The organizational and financial restructuring of coal mines in Russia, the Ukraine, Kazakhstan, and Poland have resulted in the closing of the most inefficient and heavily subsidized mines and enhanced productivity of those remaining. The restructuring has basically stabilized aggregate coal production for these nations.

Japan does not look at coal as a pollutant as much as a means to diversify energy sources to reduce its reliance on oil, most of which comes from the Middle East. Consumption of coal is increasing in recent years as a result of building more coal-fired electricity-generating plants. In addition to thermal coal for generating electricity, Japan, as a major world steel producer, also imports coking or metallurgical coal. As in North America and Europe, coal is burned in an environmentally sound manner in Japan. The role of coal in Japan was stable at around a 17–18 percent share of the energy pie but has recently increased to 25 percent. Coal is having a bit of a revival in Asia, besides China, India, and Japan, as a means of energy diversification. South Korea, Thailand, Malaysia, and the Philippines have built coal-fired electricity-generating plants.

## CASE AGAINST COAL

The case against coal can be put simply, in one word—pollution. Pollution from lower-grade coals, whether soft or hard, is greater than higher-grade coals in terms of the quantities of ash and nitrous and sulfur oxides released during combustion. Also, a greater quantity of lower-grade coals has to be burned for the same release of energy. Airborne, nitrous oxides contribute to smog and sulfur oxide droplets collect on the upper surfaces of clouds, enhancing their reflectivity. This reduces the amount of sunshine reaching the earth and, paradoxically, is a counter-pollution measure to carbon dioxide that reduces the amount of heat that can escape from the atmosphere. Eventually, sulfur and nitrous oxides return to Earth in the form of acid rain, which harms plant and marine life and erodes stone buildings and statues. Mercury, arsenic, selenium, and other heavy metals are also released when coal is burned. Surface mining destroys the landscape and, along with residues from underground mining, affects water supplies.

Abandoned coal mines can catch fire and burn underground. Once on fire, there is little that can be done to stop coal-mine fires other than entering the mine with earth-moving equipment and taking away the source of the fire: the remaining coal in the mine. In 1962, burning trash near the mouth of a mine near Centralia, Pennsylvania, started an underground inferno that has been spreading ever since despite several attempts to extinguish it. The fire is burning at a depth of 300 feet beneath the surface and giving off enough heat to bake the surface, threatening to cremate bodies buried in the local cemetery. There is also venting of poisonous gases and opening up of holes large enough to swallow automobiles. It is thought that the fire will continue for another 250 years in an eight-mile area encompassing 3,700 acres before the fire runs out of fuel. Centralia has been largely abandoned except for a few diehards.[12]

Coal fires are not all the fault of men. Lightning igniting brush fires can cause spontaneous combustion of coal exposed to the atmosphere. Burning Mountain in Australia has been burning for an estimated 6,000 years. Most of the thousands of coal mine fires that threaten towns and roads, poison the air and soil, and worsen global warming are, however, inadvertently started by man. The estimate of the amount of coal burned each year in mine fires in China varies between 20 and 200 million tons per year; the high-end estimate is an appreciable fraction of China's total coal consumption. As bad as China is, India is even worse. Rising surface temperatures and toxic byproducts in the groundwater and soil have turned formerly populated areas into uninhabitable wastelands.

## CLEAN-COAL TECHNOLOGIES

Coal is indispensable in the generation of electricity. A great deal of corporate- and government-sponsored research is dedicated to producing a clean coal, termed an oxymoron by critics. Modern coal-burning utility plants remove 99 percent of the ash produced as residue falling to the bottom of the combustion chamber and by electrostatic precipitators that remove ash from the flue gas. A flue gas desulfurization unit sprays a mixture of limestone and water into flue gas to reduce sulfur oxide emissions by 90–97 percent. Sulfur oxides chemically combine with the limestone to form calcium sulfate, or gypsum.[13] Sulfur emissions have fallen 2–3 percent per year in the United States, despite rising coal consumption, through greater use of scrubbers to remove sulfur and greater reliance on low-sulfur coal.

After mining and washing, coal is transported by train, barge, or truck and piled outside the electricity-generating plant until needed. A conveyor then moves the coal into the plant where it is first crushed and pulverized into a fine powder before being blown by powerful fans into the combustion chamber of a boiler in a conventional plant to be burned at 1,300°C–1,400°C, which transforms water in tubes lining the boiler to high-pressure steam that is fed to a turbine.

In addition to a conventional boiler, a fluidized bed combustion chamber can burn pulverized coal of any quality including coal with a high ash and sulfur content. The pulverized coal is burned suspended in a gas flow with heated particles of limestone at half the temperature (1,500°F) of a conventional coal-fired boiler. At this lower temperature, about 90 percent of the sulfur dioxide can be removed by the limestone absorbing the sulfur dioxide to form calcium sulfate or gypsum without the use of an expensive scrubber. In a conventional plant, water tubes in the combustion chamber generate steam to drive a steam turbine. In a fluidized bed combustion plant, both steam and hot combustion gases drive two types of turbines. Steam from the boiler tubes is fed into a conventional steam turbine. Hot combustion gas, after ash and gypsum have been removed, is fed into a gas turbine. Both the steam and gas turbines power electricity generators. The spent combustion gases from the gas turbine pass through a heat exchanger to further warm condensed water from the steam condenser returning to the combustion chamber. The two advantages to a fluidized bed combustion plant are an enhanced energy efficiency of 45 percent and a reduction of about 40–75 percent in nitrous oxide emissions from the lower temperature of combustion. Fluidized bed combustion chambers normally operate at atmospheric pressure, but one currently being developed would operate at a considerably higher pressure.

The first thermal plants built around 1900 were only 5 percent energy-efficient. The current rate of U.S. efficiency averages around 35 percent, with new plants achieving up to 45 percent, depending on the type of design. The average OECD efficiency is 38 percent, but efficiency in China is only 28 percent. Increasing energy efficiency is a major action item for reducing carbon dioxide emissions because the greater the efficiency, the less coal that has to be burned to generate the same amount of electricity.

Coal gasification is a thermochemical reaction of coal, steam, and oxygen to produce a fuel gas largely made up of carbon monoxide and hydrogen. The integrated coal gasification combined cycle (IGCC) is more complicated than fluidized bed combustion, and in some ways is a step back into history. Manufactured gas, the predecessor of natural gas, was the reduction of coal to a mixture of hydrogen, carbon dioxide, carbon monoxide, and methane that was distributed by pipeline to consumers. Similarly, coal is not burned in coal gasification, but processed to produce combustible products.

The process begins with an air-separation plant that separates oxygen from nitrogen. Coal is milled and dried in preparation for being mixed with oxygen and hot water for gasification. Synthetic gases (syngas), mainly carbon monoxide and hydrogen, are then treated to remove solids (ash) and sulfur. Some of the nitrogen separated out by the air-separation plant is added to the clean syngas prior to burning to control nitrous oxide generation. The syngas is then burned in a combustion chamber to drive a gas turbine and, in turn, an electricity generator. In addition to burning syngas to drive a gas turbine, a steam turbine also runs off steam produced in the gasifier and in cooling the synthetic gas from the gasifier. The spent steam is partly reheated by the exhaust from the gas turbine and fed back into the steam turbine and partly condensed to water to feed the gasifier (the combined cycle part of the IGCC).

The byproducts of an IGCC plant can be hydrogen for the hydrogen economy or a range of motor vehicle fuels. The advantages of IGCC are increased energy efficiency of above 50 percent, less generation of solid waste, lower emissions of sulfur, nitrous oxides, and carbon dioxide, and recovery of chemically pure sulfur. In a conventional coal plant, carbon dioxide emissions are mixed with the intake air, which is 80 percent nitrogen. Carbon dioxide emissions from an IGCC plant are pure carbon dioxide that can be sold or captured. The government-subsidized Wabash River coal gasification plant, in operation since 1971, removes 97 percent of the sulfur, 82 percent of the nitrous oxides, and 50 percent of the mercury from plant emissions. The higher thermal efficiency of an IGCC plant reduces carbon dioxide emissions for the same amount of power output produced by conventional coal-fired plants that operate at a lesser degree of thermal efficiency. These plants cost considerably more than conventional plants and represent a higher level of technological sophistication, along with a greater technical challenge in operation.

Advanced hybrid systems that combine the best of both gasification and combustion technologies are under development. Here the coal is not fully gasified, but partially gasified to run a gas turbine with the residue of gasification also burned to run a steam turbine. Again, higher energy efficiencies with even lower emissions are possible. Ultra-low emissions technology is being funded by the ten-year, $1 billion FuturGen project to build the world's first integrated sequestration and hydrogen-production research power plant. FuturGen employs coal gasification technology integrated with combined cycle electricity generation. FuturGen will be the world's first zero-emissions fossil fuel plant capable of transforming coal to electricity, hydrogen, and carbon dioxide. Hydrogen can fuel pollution-free vehicles using low-cost and abundant coal as the raw material. Electricity can be sold as well as the carbon dioxide byproduct. FuturGen was killed by the Bush Administration in 2007 because of cost overruns, but it was reinstated in 2009 by the Obama Administration.[14]

As with everything else that has to do with this planet, nothing is constant. The concentration of carbon dioxide cycles over the ages peaked at 280 parts per million (ppm). Unfortunately, the start of the Industrial Revolution coincided with a cyclical peak. Since then humanity has added over 100 ppm from burning fossil fuels. The current carbon dioxide concentration of 385 ppm has never occurred before in the known climatic record of the world, which goes back about 400,000 years; thus, there is no precedent for judging its impact.

No practical way exists to capture the 3 tons of carbon dioxide emitted by driving a thirty-mile-per-gallon automobile 10,000 miles.[15] However, a stationary coal-fired power plant does lend itself to capturing and storing its carbon dioxide emissions. A typical large coal-burning power plant of 1,000 megawatts produces about 6 million tons per year of carbon dioxide, equivalent to the emissions of 2 million automobiles. There are about 1,000 of these plants in the world. Flue gas is roughly 15 percent carbon dioxide and the remainder mainly nitrogen and water vapor. Rather than passing the carbon dioxide through a smokestack for disposal in the atmosphere, flue gas passes through an absorption tower containing amines that absorb the carbon dioxide. An associated stripper tower heats the amines, releasing the carbon dioxide and regenerating the amines for another cycle through the absorption tower. The question is on what to do with the carbon dioxide from the stripper tower.

If the power plant sits on top of impermeable caprock below which is a horizontal porous sand formation filled with brine, carbon dioxide can be pumped down a vertical pipeline that reaches the porous formation and is then dispersed via horizontal pipelines running through the formation. The brine formation should be more than 800 meters beneath the surface, where the pressure is sufficient for the injected carbon dioxide to enter into a "super-critical" phase where its density is near that of the brine that it displaces. In addition to the carbon dioxide displacing brine, brine also absorbs some of the carbon dioxide. When carbon dioxide saturates an area of the formation, more horizontal pipelines are necessary to open up new areas. Huge volumes of carbon dioxide can be safely stored in this manner, but the geologic formation has to be about six times larger than a giant oil field to contain the sixty-year lifetime plant output of about 100,000 barrels per day of carbon dioxide condensed to a super-critical phase.

Carbon sequestering means that more coal has to be burned for a given level of power generation to dispose of the carbon dioxide, but it may be possible to also get rid of sulfur dioxide along with the carbon dioxide as a side benefit. The cost of carbon dioxide sequestering is equivalent to a $60 per ton surcharge on coal. This will work its way through the rate structure to the electricity consumer in the form of a rate hike of about two cents per kilowatt hour, or a 20 percent surcharge for consumers paying ten cents per kilowatt hour and more for those paying less. A problem with sequestering carbon dioxide is the relatively low percentage (15 percent) of carbon dioxide in flue gas. Presumably this would have to be separated, which is a very costly process. One idea being explored is burning coal with pure oxygen and then recycling the flue gas back through the combustion chamber to significantly raise the concentration of carbon dioxide in the flue gases for potential separation.

Carbon sequestration is not without its risks. Lake Nyos in Cameroon sits in a volcanic crater where carbon dioxide seeps into the bottom of the lake where it is held in place by the weight of the overlying water. One night in 1986, the lake overturned and released between 100,000 and 300,000 tons of carbon dioxide. Carbon dioxide, heavier than air, poured down two valleys, asphyxiating 1,700 individuals and thousands of livestock. Any geologic formation holding carbon dioxide must act as an effective lock against escape. Carbon dioxide can also be pumped into depleted oil and natural gas fields. Carbon dioxide associated with natural gas production in certain fields in the North Sea and Algeria is separated and sequestered in nearby porous geological formations.

A payback can be generated if carbon dioxide sequestering increases fossil fuel production. Carbon dioxide pumped into methane-rich fractured coal beds displaces the methane, which can then be gathered and sold. Carbon dioxide can also be pumped into older oil reservoirs, where its interaction with residual crude oil eases its migration through the porous reservoir rock to the production wells. One coal-burning plant pipelines its flue gas emissions over 200 miles for tertiary oil recovery.

Not all research is space age. One project is exploring the possibility of adding 10 percent biomass to existing coal-burning plants, which may reduce greenhouse-gas emissions by up to 10 percent. One Japanese utility adds 1 percent biomass in the form of solid municipal sludge to its coal intake, which has improved the performance of the utility.

There are two types of ash: fly ash removed by electrostatic or mechanical precipitation of dust-like particles in the flue gas and ash from the bottom of the combustion chamber. Ash represents a disposal problem; most ends up in landfills. Alternatively, ash from burning coal, gypsum from flue gas desulfurization units, and boiler slag can be made into "cinder" construction blocks, which consume less energy and release less pollution than cement construction blocks. Fly ash added to concrete makes it stronger, more durable, less permeable, and more resistant to chemical attack. Gypsum can be used as a low-grade fertilizer. These waste products can also be used as aggregate or binder in road construction. The Japan Fly Ash Association is dedicated to improving the quality of coal ash, establishing a reliable supply, conducting research for recycling coal ash as an environmental benefit. Research is also being conducted on methods to reduce metals emissions, particularly mercury.

## ELIMINATING COAL NOT SO EASY

Carbon dioxide is the result of a chemical reaction that occurs during combustion. Switching from coal to oil or natural gas only reduces, not eliminates, carbon dioxide emissions. For the United States, further reliance on natural gas would be very costly if demand starts to exceed supply. Switching from coal to oil increases oil imports and U.S. dependence on Middle East oil exporters. Switching to nuclear and hydropower and renewables (wind, solar), and the hydrogen fuel economy would eliminate carbon dioxide emissions entirely, but major impediments have to be overcome. Switching from coal to nuclear power cannot occur unless public opposition to nuclear power is somehow lessened. Switching from coal to hydro is hampered by a lack of suitable sites for damming. Switching from coal to wind and solar, while possible as incremental sources of power, cannot replace coal because generation is dependent on the wind blowing and the sun shining. Switching from coal to hydrogen, while environmentally the best choice—along with solar and wind—is stymied by a less than fully developed and commercially feasible technology.

Much can be done to reduce coal-burning emissions without resorting to clean-coal technologies. Physical washing removes sulfur-iron compounds (pyretic sulfur) on the surface of raw coal, but not sulfur embedded in coal's molecular structure. While coal washing is prevalent in the United States, Europe, Japan, and other developed nations, it is not in China and India, whose high ash and sulfur content coal would benefit most from washing. Although China and India are making headway in washing coal, there are capital constraints in establishing washing facilities, and possibly a shortage of available water in certain areas. A shortage of capital might apply for India, but China, with a large balance-of-payment surplus, does not lack capital. In the past, China lacked the national will to deal with pollution because capital invested in pollution controls could not be dedicated to its economic development. Having said that, China is becoming more concerned over the environmental consequences of its economic policies and is starting to take remedial steps.

Closing small and inefficient mines can improve the environment. Fewer and larger mines ease inspection efforts by government authorities and larger coal volumes more easily justify investments to protect the health and safety of workers and minimize harm to the environment. Using coal and biomass in home cooking and heating is a major source of uncontrolled pollution in Asia. On the surface, greater amounts of coal would have to be burned to switch home cooking from coal to electricity, but burning coal in a few locations provides the means of monitoring and controlling pollution emissions.

The future of coal is certain: It already plays too significant a role in generating electricity to be dismissed out of hand. What is uncertain is what is going to be done to reduce its adverse environmental impact. Two projects may point the way in which the industry may evolve. The Prairie State Energy Campus (PSEC) is a $4 billion joint venture comprising eight public electric utilities and Peabody Coal, the world's largest coal company.[16] The venture is unique in that the participants own both the electricity-generating plant and the coal reserves set aside to service the plant. Coal will be from a mine located adjacent to the plant that will supply 6.4 million tons per year on a continuous basis using the room and pillar technique. The plant is the largest of its kind at 1,600 megawatts compared to the more typical large-sized plants of 1,000–1,200 megawatts and will be capable of serving around 2 million households when completed in 2012. The plant will burn pulverized coal ground to the consistency of talcum powder, which in conjunction with the supercritical steam generating technology, will have an efficiency advantage that will cut the carbon footprint by 15 percent compared to existing plant technology. The plant will be among the cleanest coal-fueled plants in the nation. Coal will be burned at a lower temperature to reduce nitrous oxide emissions, which are further reduced by a selective catalyst-reduction unit that converts a portion of the nitrous oxide emissions to nitrogen and water. Dry and wet electrostatic precipitators will remove 99.9 percent of the particulates in the emissions, and an advanced sulfur dioxide scrubber using limestone and water will remove 98 percent of the sulfur. Mercury will be significantly reduced by the collective action of the selective catalyst reduction unit and the dry and wet electrostatic precipitators. Total emissions are expected to be cut in half compared to existing plants.

The other project is two proposed 629 megawatt IGCC plants to be built by American Electric Power, a major coal-burning utility. In a typical coal-burning utility plant, carbon dioxide is 15 percent of the flue gas whereas in an IGCC plant, the carbon dioxide is a separate gas stream, which allows carbon sequestration to avoid adding carbon dioxide to the atmosphere. American Electric Power is also involved with the technological development of using chilled ammonia that would isolate carbon dioxide from flue gas for sequestration in deep saline aquifers or for tertiary oil recovery. The company is also looking into the use of oxy-coal combustion (burning coal in pure oxygen) as a means of isolating a pure stream of carbon dioxide for sequestration or tertiary oil recovery.[17]

This is one side of the ledger. On the other side, hundreds of coal-burning utility plants are being built in China and India without regard for pollution control. These plants will add particulates and sulfur dioxide to the atmosphere that affect the health of those who breathe the fumes in addition to contributing to acid rain. China and India are trying to adopt clean technologies for generating electricity such as hydro and wind, but the magnitude of their growing demand for electricity is such that they are forced to rely heavily on coal. The problem is that this reliance on coal is on the basis of minimum concern over the environmental impact despite public announcements to the contrary.

To appreciate the magnitude of the problem, North America burns 18.4 percent of the world's coal with essentially no growth rate between 2000 and 2008. Europe including Russia burns 15.8 percent of the world's coal also with no net growth between 2000 and 2008. China alone burns 42.6 percent of the world's coal, greater than North American and Europe including Russia combined, and had a growth rate of 7.9 percent between 2006 and 2007. Adding in India, both nations burned 49.6 percent of the world's coal with growth of 9.2 percent between 2000 and 2008. These two nations represent half of the world's current consumption and are expected to maintain their robust growth rates. China alone is now the world's largest contributor to carbon dioxide emissions. Clearly, leaving these nations out of the successor instrument to the Kyoto Protocol is a major flaw.

## NOTES

1. GlassOnLine Web site from www.glassonline.com/infoserv/history.html.

2. Barbara Freese, *Coal A Human History* (Cambridge, MA: Perseus Publishing, 2003).

3. Joseph S. Spoerl, "A Brief History of Iron and Steel Production," available from author at Saint Anselm College, Manchester, NH.

4. These statistics, as well as statistics on imports and exports and the role of coal in electricity generation, are available from the World Coal Institute at www.worldcoal.org/resources/coal-statistics/coal-steel-statistics/index.php.

5. I remember my father shoveling coal and having to remove and dispose of ashes from a coal furnace before converting to a heating oil furnace in a residential home on Long Island. I also remember my mother cooking on a combination wood- and coal-burning stove before switching to a propane-fueled stove in an upstate farmhouse. And I'm not that old!

6. John McQuaid, "Mining the Mountains," *Smithsonian Magazine* (January 2009), pp. 74–85.

7. The statistics in Table 4.1 are from *Sustainable Entrepreneurship* (December 2001), prepared by the World Coal Institute for the UN Environment Program; the figures are mostly for 2000, but a few are for 1999.

8. Volume data for all figures from *BP Energy Statistics* (London: British Petroleum, 2009). Sasol Corporation Web site www.sasol.com.

9. Clean Alternative Fuels: Fischer-Tropsch Fact Sheet published by the U.S. Environmental Protection Agency.

10. *World Energy Outlook* (Paris: International Energy Agency, 2008).

11. Sources in Figure 4.4 for the price of coal at FOB (free on board, used to specify that product is delivered and placed on board a carrier at a specified point free of charge at the mine mouth) is the U.S. Department of Energy www.eia.doe.gov/emeu/aer/coal.html, for bituminous coal in short tons. Source for the price of oil is *BP Energy Statistics* for $/bbl (dollar cost per barrel) FOB West Texas Intermediate; $/bbl price was multiplied by 7 in order to obtain $/metric ton (cost in dollars per metric ton). Natural gas prices in $/1000 cf were obtained from tonto.eia.doe.gov/dnav/ng/hist/n9190us3a.htm and translated to bbls at 5,610 cf/bbl. The price of coal was multiplied by 1.1 to convert from short tons to metric tons and then by 2 to convert physical tons to tons of oil equivalent to approximate the relationship between oil and coal in terms of equivalent energy released; these figures do not include shipping costs. Adjustments were made to price all three energy sources in 2008 dollars.

12. Kevin Krajick, "Fire in the Hole," *Smithsonian Magazine* (May 2005), p. 54ff.

13. World Coal Institute, London, Web site www.worldcoal.org for clean coal technology.

14. FuturGen is described in the U.S. Department of Fossil Energy Web site www.fe.doe.gov.

15. Robert H. Socolow, "Can We Bury Global Warming?" *Scientific American* (July 2005), p. 33ff.

16. Praire State Energy Campus Web site http://www.prairiestateenergycampus.com/.

17. American Electric Power Web site www.aep.com/citizenship/crreport/energy/generation.aspx.

# 5

# THE STORY OF BIG OIL

When we think of oil, we think of gasoline and diesel fuel for motor vehicles, but the beginning of the oil industry was kerosene for illumination. Kerosene was the foundation of the Rockefeller fortune and marked the birth of Big Oil. Oil provided an alternative fuel for lighting; if oil ran out, it would be back to whale oil, tallow, and vegetable oils. Oil was not indispensable or vital to the running of the economy; now, no oil, no economy. The transition from a preferred fuel for lighting to something without which modern society cannot survive started with Henry Ford putting America on wheels in the early 1900s. The transition was complete by the First World War when military vehicles, tanks, and fighter aircraft fueled by oil played a pivotal role in securing victory for the Allies. Oil had become as important as armaments and ammunition in the conduct of war. During the Second World War, one of the principal targets of the Allies' bombing was the coal plants that produced gasoline to fuel the Wehrmacht. As a depleting resource, oil has moved beyond supporting war efforts to being a cause of war. This chapter looks at the historical development of two of the world's largest oil companies and the role that Big Oil may play in supplying the world with energy products as we proceed "Beyond Petroleum."

## HISTORY OF LIGHTING

Prior to 1800, only torches, lamps, and candles lit the darkness of night. Torches were oil-, pitch-, or resin-impregnated sticks. Lamps—shallow rocks, seashells, or man-made pottery containing a natural fiber wick that burned grease or oil, animal fat, or rendered fat, called tallow—first appeared during the Stone Age. Candles go back to 3000 BCE and were made of tallow until paraffin wax, in use today, made its debut in the nineteenth century. To varying degrees, these modes of illumination produced more smoke than light.

In the early 1800s, the best lamp fuel was whale oil, which became increasingly expensive with the decimation of the whale population. There were plenty of alternatives to whale oil such as vegetable oils (castor, rapeseed, peanut), tallow, turpentine (from pine trees), and a variety of wood and grain alcohols. The most popular lamp fuel was a blend of alcohol and turpentine called camphene. Alcohol was obtained by distillation where vapors from a heated fermented mix of grain, vegetables, or fruits were separated, cooled, and condensed into a liquid. The distilling process for making alcohol for lamp fuel or whiskey was adopted in its entirety by the early oil refiners to separate the constituent parts of crude oil.

Another source of lighting in the 1700s and 1800s was coal gas. Gas emissions (hydrogen, carbon monoxide, carbon dioxide, and methane) produced by baking coal in a closed environment with insufficient air to support combustion were piped to street lamps in cities in Europe and America. Lamplighters lit the street lamps in the evening and extinguished them in the morning.

Coal gas was also piped into factories, buildings, and residences for illumination, but the benefits of coal gas were restricted to urban centers. This experience in piping coal gas to streetlights and buildings would be put to good use when natural gas was discovered in association with oil during the latter part of the 1800s. Nevertheless, despite these advances in lighting, most human activities stopped at sunset.

## HISTORY OF OIL

Asphalt, or tar, was found on the surface in the Caspian Sea, the Middle East, Indonesia, Burma, California (the La Brea tar pit in Los Angeles is a tourist attraction), western Pennsylvania, and elsewhere. Oil was a medicine for various ailments for much of human history. Tar or pitch was mixed with clay as masonry cement in ancient Babylonia, still visible today. The Egyptians used tar as an adhesive in mummification. Romans burned oil as a fumigant to get rid of caterpillar infestations. Cracks between a sailing vessel's wooden planks were sealed with tar to prevent water from seeping through and sinking the vessel. Tar caulked Noah's ark and the bulrush cradle bearing Moses. Oil-soaked soil was burned as a fuel in the tenth century in the Baku region around the Caspian Sea, where Marco Polo also recorded oil seeping from the ground in the fourteenth century. Travelers in Baku in the seventeenth century recorded holes dug into the ground where oil was collected and then transported in wineskins on camels.[1]

Incendiary weapons made of naphtha also have a long history that goes back to the fourth century BCE. Of these the most famous was Greek Fire, which was mechanically projected from flame-throwers installed in the prows of Byzantine ships. Greek Fire was instrumental in turning back two invading fleets against Constantinople in 678 and 718 CE. Similar to modern napalm, it adhered to whatever it struck and could not be extinguished with water. The secret of Greek Fire, thought to be a mixture of naphtha, resins, and sulfur, was passed down from one eastern Roman emperor to the next until it was lost in only about a half century of time, perhaps as a consequence of a less than orderly transfer of power. The Arabs developed a form of Greek Fire to fight Crusader ships and the Chinese developed a similar weapon in the tenth century that was ignited with gunpowder.

In more recent times, Seneca Indians collected oil that seeped from the earth in western Pennsylvania for war paint and caulking canoes. Some of this natural seepage found its way into Oil Creek, giving it an oily sheen long before the discovery of oil. Immigrant settlers in the area dug holes that slowly filled with oil. These small quantities of seep oil, also called rock oil or its Latinized version, petroleum, were sold as medicinal cures for just about everything, first as Seneca Oil, which, when properly pronounced with the accent on the second syllable, became Snake Oil.

As in all human activities, not one, but many individuals made contributions whose aggregate impact was to launch a major industry. In the 1840s, Abraham Gesner, a medical doctor turned geologist, obtained a distilled liquid from coal that he named kerosene from the Greek words for wax and oil. In 1850, he formed the Kerosene Gaslight Company to light houses and streets in Halifax, Nova Scotia. Gesner was convinced that kerosene would one day overtake whale oil if it could be cheaply made.[2] James Young, a Scotsman, patented a process in 1850 for distilling paraffin wax and oil from oil shale and bituminous coal. Paraffin wax was made into candles for the first time and paraffin oil was burned for lighting and heating. By 1862 production of paraffin wax and oil consumed about 3 million tons of oil shale and bituminous coal annually and continued for over half a century before being replaced by distilling crude oil. Distilling oil from oil shale was revived in the United Kingdom during the Second World War to produce petroleum products. It may resume again if crude prices are driven to a point that can economically justify processing vast deposits of oil shale found in parts of the world.

Western Pennsylvania and the Baku region were not the only areas where seep oil was "mined." During the 1850s seep oil from holes dug in the ground in Galicia and Romania was refined for its kerosene content to light lamps. Refining in the United States was more influenced by the activities of Samuel Kier, a whiskey distiller in Pittsburgh, than by Young or Gesner or the refining activities in Europe. In the 1850s Samuel Kier modified a one-barrel still for distilling seep oil in Pittsburgh, Pennsylvania. He later built a five-barrel distilling unit and bought seep oil by the gallon. The experience gained in developing these first tiny commercial refineries was crucial in the development of the American oil-refining industry.

About this time a group of promoters, headed by George Bissell, in search of something to promote, commissioned Benjamin Silliman, a chemistry professor at Yale College, to examine the commercial potential of oil. Silliman's report noted the superior properties of distilled oil to burn brighter and cleaner compared to other illuminating fuels. Bissell also had the intuitive insight to come up with the idea to drill rather than dig for oil. As with so much else, the Chinese had beaten the West by 2,500 years when they succeeded in drilling for oil using a drill bit attached to bamboo poles.[3] Bissell did not know about drilling for oil in China, nor did he know that a well was drilled, not dug, in 1846 in Baku, thirteen years earlier, nor about an oil well drilled in Canada about the time when he thought of the idea. Reinventing the wheel, so common in the past, is less likely in today's world of global communication and information systems. Based on Silliman's report and his insight to drill rather than dig, Bissell put together a group of investors who bought newly minted shares in the Pennsylvania Rock Oil Company.

The oil industry did not spring from nothing—it was an event waiting to happen. It was an accepted fact of the time that anyone who discovered an abundant and cheap source of oil would "strike it rich." In 1859, the event happened, but not before the Pennsylvania Rock Oil investors backing "Colonel" Edwin Drake, a retired railroad conductor (and never a colonel), had given up hope, one by one, on Bissell's idea to drill for oil. The last remaining investor sent a letter notifying Drake that no further funds were forthcoming and to cease operations.

Drake put Bissell's insight into action and modified a derrick device that drilled either for freshwater or for brine for salt manufacture to drill for oil. Drake was first to place a pipe within the drill hole to prevent the ground from closing in and plugging the hole, the forerunner of casing a well, still in practice today. He rigged up a hand-operated water pump to extract oil from the casing within the well if any should appear. As strange as this may sound, his entire approach was ridiculed as Drake's Folly. Anybody with half a brain knew that the only true and tried way of obtaining oil was by digging a hole and extracting the tiny quantities that seeped into the bottom. It seems so strange from our perspective that people who dug for or, in essence, mined liquid oil and drilled for water and salt brine could not make the mental leap to drill for oil.

Besides these technological innovations, Colonel Drake made three strategically important decisions. First, Drake employed William A. Smith (Uncle Billy), who rigged up Drake's contraption so that it would actually work; second, Drake chose to drill in soil saturated with oil; and third, Drake ignored the letter from the last financial backer to cease and desist. He borrowed money to keep the operation going. Despite the fact that he was at the point of financial exhaustion, he doggedly stuck to his guns, a story that would be repeated many times in the development of the oil industry, creating fortunes for some and financial ruin for others. For Drake, it would be a bittersweet combination of both when the "crazy Yankee struck oil." Everyone agrees that the well was sixty-nine feet deep, but there is disagreement on the output of the well, ranging from ten to twenty-five barrels per day and on the price fetched in the market, ranging from $20 to $40 per barrel. Regardless of the actual flow rate and market price, overnight a new industry was born—Drake's claim to fame. For this singular achievement, Drake was to die a pauper, the first of a small, select group of individuals who would not profit from their renowned success.

Immediately, the area around Titusville became a gold rush town typical of the Wild West. A dollar invested in a producing well could yield thousands of dollars in profits. The most despicable and disreputable jostled with the honest and upright to build oil derricks almost on top of each other. The winner of this bonanza would be the individual who had the most wells pumping oil as fast and as furiously as possible. Revenue is price multiplied by volume. Since there is nothing one can do about price, the secret of producing untold wealth was to maximize production before the price fell or the oil field went dry.

Pandemonium reigned. The landscape was disfigured with fallen trees and uprooted vegetation, littered with derricks drilling for or pumping oil, construction gear and equipment tossed hither and yon, with trees, plants, soil, derricks, equipment, and drillers covered in oil. Oil was first stored in pits dug into the ground, soon replaced by wooden, and later, by metal tanks. Barrels originally intended for storing and transporting whiskey were expropriated to get the oil from the pits or tanks to a refinery. The early whiskey turned oil barrels ranged in capacity between thirty and fifty gallons and were standardized at forty-two gallons in the early 1870s. As one might expect, there were insufficient numbers of barrels to carry the oil to market. A barrel boom ensued as cooperage firms employing joiners tried to keep up with the demand. Teamsters moved the barrels of oil on horse-drawn wagons from the oil fields around Titusville to the Allegheny River for loading onto barges that were floated downstream to Pittsburgh, the world's first refining center, thanks to Samuel Kier.[4]

While joiners and teamsters prospered, drillers either made their fortunes or went broke trying. Wells drilled with wild abandon pumping full out soon flooded the market with unwanted oil. Maximizing revenue by maximizing volume works well when supply is less than demand. It is a different story when supply exceeds demand. Oil prices plunged from ten dollars to ten cents per barrel in less than a year, making a barrel more valuable than the oil within. Pumping oil continued unabatedly as prices spiraled downward because individual drillers could still maximize revenue by maximizing production as long as the price of crude oil exceeded the cost of extraction. One driller showing restraint and slowing his rate of production only meant lower revenue for him as others pumped with all their might. Drillers collectively seemed unable to sense the repercussions of what maximizing production today would do to price tomorrow; if they did, there was nothing they could do about it. The oil industry would have to wait for Rockefeller to teach the valuable lesson that practicing restraint today could maximize profits tomorrow.

As boom went bust, overnight fortunes evaporated into a spate of bankruptcies since money was entirely reinvested in drilling rigs, which lost all their value. Collapsing oil prices were not all that brought on the bad times; too many wells operating full out were sucking oil fields dry in no time. Consider the town with the quaint name of Pit Hole, about fifteen miles away from Drake's well in western Pennsylvania. Oil was discovered in what was a sleepy farming "community" of two buildings in January 1865. By September, nine months later, the population had exploded to 12,000–16,000, with a host of hotels and boarding houses to provide shelter and food for one flood tide of those looking for honest work along with another of rank speculators, unscrupulous stock-jobbers, reckless adventurers, and dishonest tricksters.[5] Near-valueless land a few months earlier was selling for over $1 million and interests in producing wells for hundreds of thousands of dollars. Considering the value of a dollar in 1865, these were considerable sums. The post office in Pit Hole became the third busiest in the state after Philadelphia and Pittsburgh. With so many oil wells built with such wild abandon pumping with all their might, the oil field soon went dry. Some oil drillers were bankrupt before their equipment arrived. Aided by two major fires, the city was mostly abandoned in a little over a year. Lumber from the remaining buildings was scavenged for construction elsewhere. Today Pit Hole is a ghost town without buildings.

Gesner was proven right. While oil is now generally under attack by environmentalists, it was oil or, more exactly, kerosene that saved the whales from extinction. In 1846 the whaling fleet numbered 735 vessels and was making a healthy rate of return, especially when the price for whale oil peaked in 1856 at $1.77 per gallon. By 1865 plentiful supplies of kerosene selling for fifty-nine cents a gallon sharply undercut the price of whale oil. The whaling fleet shrunk to thirty-nine vessels by 1876. The price of kerosene kept declining to a little over seven cents per gallon by 1895, when whale oil was selling for forty cents per gallon. With this price differential, there was no incentive to buy whale oil. Kerosene wiped out the whaling industry.[6]

## Enter John D. Rockefeller

Building railroads made a major change in the Oil Regions, which started in Pennsylvania and later spread to Ohio, West Virginia, and Indiana. Oil could now be more cheaply transported to Cleveland by loading barrels on railcars, and later pumping oil into railroad tank cars, than loading barrels onto barges bound for Pittsburgh. The railroads made Cleveland the new world refining center, where John D. Rockefeller, a bookkeeper, happened to reside.

Rockefeller shaped the oil industry more than anybody else. As with many movers and shakers, he started life a nobody. His father, William "Big Bill" Rockefeller, was an itinerant trader taking advantage of price disparities that arose in a world of stationary buyers and sellers who did not know the price of goods over the next hill. Big Bill was a conniver and would play deaf and dumb if it suited his purpose. Considering his business practices, which were at times questionable, and his general behavior toward women, it is strange that he hated tobacco and liquor. It is stranger yet that he ended up marrying a strict Baptist, Eliza Davison, who shared his disdain for liquor but not tobacco (she smoked a corncob pipe). John Davison Rockefeller, their first child, born in 1839, would pick up their mutual aversion to liquor.

The newly wedded couple moved into Bill's cottage where his long-term housekeeper Nancy Brown also lived. Both women gave birth to their first babies about the same time. The Davison family eventually prevailed on Big Bill to send Nancy away. As an itinerant trader, Big Bill was away from home for months at a time. His trading activities had to be fairly successful because he could support one family with his Rockefeller name at one end of his travels and another family under a pseudonym at the other, which he managed to keep secret for many years. He could also finance John D. Rockefeller's first commercial ventures. Big Bill also taught John D. valuable lessons in business such as picking him up as a toddler and then dropping him to the floor with the stern admonition never to trust anyone, not even one's own father![7]

From his earliest days, buying and selling flowed through John D.'s veins. After Big Bill moved his family to Cleveland, Rockefeller enrolled in a commercial school without completing high school. Like his mother, Rockefeller was a strict Baptist and, as a fifteen-year-old, taught Bible class and sang in the choir. He would be an active churchgoer for the rest of his life. At sixteen, Rockefeller was beating the pavement looking for his first job. He eventually found one at a wholesale firm dealing in everything from grain to marble. He was a meticulous bookkeeper and a persistent collector of unpaid invoices. After three months of working from six in the morning to ten at night, the firm thought well enough of Rockefeller to put him on salary.

Even at what was low pay for what he did, Rockefeller showed two seemingly contradictory character traits that would be with him throughout his life: frugality and philanthropy. He was frugal with what he spent on himself and he was frugal in the conduct of business; absolutely nothing went to waste. Yet he was generous with those in need. Rockefeller believed that his ability to make money was a gift from God that was not to be neglected without suffering God's damnation. He must have emblazoned in his mind the parable of the talents where God severely punished the one who did not put his talent to use. Rockefeller also believed that money received was a gift from God and would eventually have to be given back to Him.

Rockefeller seemingly never had an inner personal conflict between being a model family man at all times and a model churchgoer on Sundays, including teaching Sunday School and singing in the choir, with his role as an utterly ruthless businessman for the rest of the week. His approach to business was to unmercifully crush his competition, bringing unChristian-like suffering, misery, and distress to many. In his mind, he viewed his business practices as ultimately beneficial to humanity by bringing order out of disorder and eliminating the waste inherent in untrammeled competition.

Rockefeller carried out his pledge to God that money made as a gift of God would have to be returned. By the time of his death, he had given away much of what he had earned except for a not-so-small kitty to provide for his old age. Of course, much of what remained when he died was given to his only son, John D., Jr., but major beneficiaries were the first college for African-American women, Spelman College in Atlanta, Georgia (which says a lot about the man), the Rockefeller Foundation, Rockefeller University, the founding of the University of Chicago, and the building of Rockefeller Center in New York City during the Great Depression. John D., Jr., would continue returning his father's gift to God by funding the restoration of Versailles and the Rheims Cathedral, creating the Acadia and Grand Teton National Parks, donating land for the construction of the United Nations headquarters in New York, and restoring Colonial Williamsburg.[8]

After Rockefeller served his apprenticeship in a trading firm, he formed the firm Clark and Rockefeller with his friend Maurice Clark with a loan from his father. The firm successfully traded in grain and other commodities. In the early 1860s, with Cleveland hosting twenty refineries, oil began to draw Rockefeller's attention and he visited the Oil Regions. There is a photograph of the early movers and shakers of the oil industry. They stand in a group. Off to the side, distinctly separate from the others, stands a solitary figure in the middle of an empty field. It is not known whether this is Rockefeller, but it is thought that it was Rockefeller because Rockefeller stood alone in creating the oil industry.

Rockefeller was first to recognize the four principal facets of the oil business. One was production, the world of speculative drillers who, collectively, were unable to exercise self-control—a world of boom and bust, depending how supply and demand lined up. The second part of the oil industry was transportation, moving crude from the oil fields to refineries and oil products from the refineries to market. While oil transport first depended on canals and rivers, railroads had taken over much of the transport business by the time Rockefeller arrived on the scene, and railroads did not interest Rockefeller. The third part of the business was oil refining and the fourth, marketing. Refineries were relatively few compared to the number of drillers, and combining refineries under one corporate umbrella was possible, whereas combining drillers under one corporate umbrella was not. By creating a horizontal monopoly, a monopoly that controlled only refining, Rockefeller realized that he could control the entire oil industry. As the sole refiner, he would become the sole buyer of the nation's supply of crude oil and the sole seller to satisfy the nation's thirst for kerosene and lubricating oils.

With financial assistance from Big Bill, Rockefeller formed the firm Andrews, Clark, and Company in 1863 for an investment of $8,000 to get into the refining business. In 1864 he married Laura Spelman, a woman as strong in character and as firm in her religious beliefs as his mother. In 1865, he bought out Clark by carrying out what Clark thought was a bluff and renamed the firm Rockefeller and Andrews. Exercising his God-given penchant for making money, Rockefeller bought and sold oil and the profits rolled in. He brought his brother Will into the firm and opened up the firm's second refinery, the Standard Works. The word *standard* was purposely selected to evoke in the minds of customers the image of a steady and reliable source of oil products made to a consistent standard.

The refineries of the day produced only three products: lubes, or lubricating oils, for machinery; kerosene for lighting; and naphtha. Naphtha is lighter and more volatile than kerosene and could not be used in kerosene lamps without the risk of an explosion. While most refiners dumped naphtha into the nearest stream and burned the heavy end of the barrel for fuel, Rockefeller developed products for the heavy end of the barrel and burned naphtha to fuel his refineries, a sign of his frugality and aversion to waste. It is ironic that what is now considered the most valuable part of a barrel of crude oil, gasoline, which is primarily naphtha, was for four decades a waste product of the refining process. Naphtha would have its day with the coming of the automobile.

People were awed by Rockefeller's rapid ascent to business prominence. His overwhelming impression was one of power. His blank eyes revealed nothing, yet his eyes seemed to penetrate and read the minds of others. He knew everything going on in the oil business as if God had given him special powers to see "around the corner." Seeing around the corner was a special knack that Rockefeller had for posting paid observers who reported to him all that was happening in the oil patch. Rockefeller was secretive in nature and devised a code for internal communications within Standard Oil. His contracts contained secrecy clauses that voided the contracts if their contents were revealed. With or without God's help, Rockefeller knew everything happening around him and those around him knew nothing about what Rockefeller was doing and, more importantly, what he was up to.

Other than providing his family with the accoutrements of success, and giving to charities and to deserving individuals in need, Rockefeller plowed every penny the company earned back into oil. He believed and practiced frugality to an extreme. He knew that a penny saved a million times over was a lot of money that could also be plowed back into the firm. In addition to generating cash, he also knew how to tap bankers' money and borrowed heavily to finance the expansion of his business. In 1867 Rockefeller and Andrews became Rockefeller, Andrews, and Flagler, and by 1869 the three partners employed 900 workers producing 1,500 barrels per day of oil products. With 10 percent of the global refining capacity, they were the world's largest refinery operators. This implies a total global refinery capacity of 15,000 barrels per day, which is about one-tenth to one-twentieth the capacity of a typical modern refinery.

Rockefeller was a trust maker compared to Theodore Roosevelt, a trust buster. In Rockefeller's mind, a trust had real benefits. It deals directly with the one principal fault of the free market, a lack of stability marked by boom and bust. When supply is short of demand, prices shoot up, bringing on a boom, encouraging overenthusiasm for increasing productive capacity. This lasts until there is an excess of productive capacity, which transforms a shortage into a glut, causing prices to collapse. The ensuing bust lasts until demand catches up with supply, fueling the next boom.

A trust brings stability to an industry in chaos. A trust would never overindulge in building excess productive capacity to bring on a bust because the decision to expand productive capacity is in the hands of a single individual, or a small group of individuals acting as a cartel. A trust, as the sole buyer, would be able to purchase supplies and raw materials at the lowest cost, which means lower prices for consumers. Focusing on oil, a trust would have large-capacity refineries whose inherent economies of scale would further lower costs, which could never be achieved with many independent producers, each operating a small refinery. An oil trust would set prices for its products at levels that ensured the industry's profitability. Steady profits would be able to pay for an adequate supply of oil at a fair price, which, in turn, would provide job security for work- ers, ensure sound bank loans and a flow of dividends for shareholders. In essence, Rockefeller wanted to set up a system that outlawed the business cycle along with its layoffs, bankruptcies, stock-market plunges, and banking crises.

After taking over a market by wiping out the competition, Rockefeller did not take advantage of being the sole supplier and set an exorbitant price, as one might expect. Rather, he set a price where he could make a profit, but not a profit high enough to tempt new entrants into building a refinery. Rockefeller could maintain a monopoly by not being too greedy. Too high a price would only invite a new competitor to build a refinery, which Rockefeller would then have to crush by lowering prices below the competitor's costs, forcing the sale of the refinery to Rockefeller. Even so, some individuals were not above building a refinery just to force Rockefeller to buy it.

In 1870 the company was renamed the Standard Oil Company, with Rockefeller, now thirty- one years old, having the largest share (29 percent) of the company's stock. By 1879, in less than a decade, the Standard Oil Company owned 90 percent of the nation's refining capacity, having removed most, though not all, of its 250 original competitors by one of the following methods:

- Rockefeller's God-given talent for making money when others failed.
- Rockefeller's penchant for secrecy, preventing others from knowing what he was up to, but through "his men" knowing everything going on in the industry. For instance, railroads had to tell Rockefeller the details of shipments by his competitors including the volume, destina- tion, and shipping rate. Corporate intelligence was a major weapon in Rockefeller's business arsenal for vanquishing his foes.
- Rockefeller's realization of the inherent economies of scale of large refineries before anyone else. Rockefeller had the best-operated, most efficient, and the largest refineries, making him the low-cost producer. He concentrated his refining at three plants, which at one time represented 75 percent of global refinery capacity. His refining costs were half those of his competitors. Being the low-cost producer was a major card to hold in the corporate game of King of the Hill since Rockefeller could lower his price to a point where his competitors were losing their shirts while he was not. Rockefeller was not above buying a refinery from an independent and closing it, then adding capacity to one of his refineries to replace the scrapped capacity, benefiting from further gains in economies of scale.
- Rockefeller, as the largest refinery operator, was able, through the efforts of Henry Flagler, to get the railroads to offer a secret rebate for Rockefeller's business.[9] Railroads, as common carriers, were at least morally, though not legally, bound to charge the same rates for everyone. With the cost of shipping crude oil about the same as its value, shipping was an important component in determining profitability. As the industry's largest shipper and also the owner of a fleet of railroad tank cars, Rockefeller took advantage of the intense competition among three railroads to negotiate a secret rebate. This rebate cut Rockefeller's shipping cost by nearly half. Then, on top of this, he negotiated a drawback, a kickback, of the shipping rates charged to his competitors. Rockefeller's competitors had to pay not only twice the shipping rate he did, but, to add insult to injury, part of what they paid to the railroads also flowed to Rockefeller through the innocuous-sounding South Improvement Company.
- Rockefeller was the first to sell his products in Europe and Asia. From the beginning, a large portion of U.S. kerosene production was exported and Rockefeller made Standard Oil the first multinational oil company and the United States the world's largest oil exporter. With widely dispersed markets throughout the United States and the world, Standard Oil was the only company so positioned that profits in one area subsidized losses in another. This was a

great advantage for Rockefeller when it came time to give a competitor a "good sweating." Rockefeller could bring any competitor to heel, domestically or internationally, through discriminatory price-cutting without suffering an overall loss.

- Rockefeller was not above sabotaging a competitor's refinery if that was necessary to bring the competitor under his control. He practiced corporate espionage by paying employees of competitors to spy for him. He was also a master at corporate deceit. One time, Rockefeller purchased a refinery on the condition that the seller would not reveal the purchase. The ex-owner continued to operate the refinery as an "independent" and combined with other independent refinery operators in order to better combat Rockefeller's ruthless takeover of the refining business. The sellers learned too late that they were now within the firm grip of Rockefeller's octopus.

- Rockefeller knew how to handle bankers and was always able to cajole, when he could not convince, bankers to finance his acquisitions. The bankers were willing lenders because Rockefeller never defaulted on one penny of his borrowings, a valuable piece of business advice from his father.

Rockefeller achieved his high-water mark of over 90 percent control of the refining industry in the late 1870s. The lines on his face began to reveal the never-ending stress of working strenuously by day and worrying mightily by night. Even though Rockefeller seemingly held all the cards, it was not a simple matter for him to achieve his objective of total control over the refining industry. The American independents were just as determined to escape from Rockefeller's grasp, survive, and come back to fight again as Rockefeller was to subdue them. The American independents were absolutely determined and dedicated to not ending up as Rockefeller's property just as, a few years later, the Russian independents would be equally determined and dedicated to not ending up as Nobel and Rothschild property.

To combat Rockefeller's control over the railroads and his favorable shipping rates, the independents started building a pipeline to connect the Oil Regions with the east coast market. Rockefeller put every legal impediment in their way that his lawyers could devise. He bought land through which the pipeline would pass with the intent to deny permission for its construction. The independents, utterly determined to defeat Rockefeller, would change the pipeline path around Rockefeller's land. Then Rockefeller convinced the railroads not to sell the right-of-way for the pipeline to cross their tracks. Unable to cross a railroad track, the pipeline ended on one side of the track and started on the other side. Oil from the pipeline had to be loaded on wagons to cross the railroad tracks and then be put back into the pipeline. When this failed to stop the flow of oil, Rockefeller had the railroads park a train across track crossings to disrupt transfer operations.

Despite this towering wall of opposition, the independents managed to complete the pipeline. Pumping oil through a pipeline is far cheaper than shipping by railroad. For one thing, railroad tank cars had to be taken back empty for another shipment—an expense not relevant to a pipeline. Another voided cost of a pipeline was the cost of moving a locomotive and tank cars along with the oil. Moreover the capital cost of a pipeline is less than a railroad. The completion of the pipeline meant that Rockefeller had not only lost his strategic advantage over the independents, but that he now suffered from a strategic disadvantage. Once the independents could reach the east coast market cheaper than Rockefeller, Rockefeller did an about-face and became a pipeline builder. He eventually built 13,000 miles of pipelines connecting the Oil Regions with the east coast markets and took over nearly 90 percent of pipeline traffic, amply demonstrating what it was like to cross his path.

Rockefeller also manufactured kerosene lamps and sold them at cost to induce people to switch to kerosene. He pioneered in making lamps and stoves safer to lower the death rate of several thousand per year from kerosene fires and explosions. The hazardous nature of kerosene increased when unscrupulous refiners spiked their kerosene with more volatile naphtha rather than throw it away. Consumers could count on Rockefeller's "standard" kerosene product to be free of such dangerous adulteration. To expand his market beyond kerosene, Rockefeller spearheaded the development of other oil products including asphalt for road construction, special lubricants for railroad locomotives, and ingredients for paint, paint remover, and chewing gum. By creating products for the lower end of the barrel, he could burn the upper end, naphtha, as fuel to run his refineries while his competitors burned the lower end for fuel and were forced to dispose of the naphtha as waste. He made sure that Standard Oil stayed with the business it knew best: oil. Having established a horizontal monopoly in refining that stabilized the price of oil, he then strove for a vertical monopoly by acquiring oil-producing properties. By 1879, Standard Oil's oil fields from Pennsylvania to Indiana pumped one-third of the nation's oil. This was also the year that Thomas Edison invented the electric light bulb, the start of a slow death for the kerosene lamp.

When Rockefeller got into oil production, he discovered that natural gas associated with oil production was flared or vented to the atmosphere. Because of his aversion to waste, Rockefeller started plowing his oil profits into developing a natural gas industry. Natural gas could supply streetlights, buildings, and factories as a substitute for coal gas if there were a means to get natural gas from the oil wells to towns and cities already served with coal-gas pipelines. Standard Oil was active in building natural gas pipelines and obtaining municipal franchises to supply communities with natural gas, which was cleaner burning, cheaper, and had a higher heat content than coal gas. Sometimes he had to pay a bribe to get a municipal franchise, and sometimes he resorted to corporate trickery. One municipality decided to split a franchise between two independent firms so that consumers could benefit from competition. Although the two companies that won the split franchise seemed to be rivals, in reality both were subsidiaries of Standard Oil.

Is there anything that can be said in favor of the way Rockefeller conducted business? Actually there was one—when a competitor was crushed and had no choice but to sell to Standard Oil, Rockefeller would offer either cash or shares in Standard Oil, recommending the latter. Frequently sellers, after being beaten by Rockefeller into abject submission, took the cash just to avoid further entanglement with him. This was indeed unfortunate because the value of the stock would, in time, vastly exceed the value of cash.

Ida Tarbell, a journalist-author of a series of magazine articles starting in 1902 in *McClure's Magazine* entitled "The History of the Standard Oil Company," exposed the company's nefarious business practices. These articles turned public opinion against Rockefeller and fueled Theodore Roosevelt's aversion to monopolies. Ida was a perfect person to write such a series of articles. Her father was a joiner, or barrelmaker, who profited in the early days of oil by being the first to make wooden tanks for storing oil, rather than pits dug in the ground. He built a house for his family by scavenging lumber from an abandoned hotel in Pit Hole. His days of prosperity ended abruptly with the advent of metal tanks. Throughout his life, he was a strong advocate of American independents. He was allied with one that was eventually crushed by Standard Oil, a fate shared by Rockefeller's brother Frank.

By 1882 Standard Oil, a conglomerate of subsidiaries created by Rockefeller's numerous acquisitions, was becoming difficult to control. Rockefeller reorganized the company as the Standard Oil Trust, whereby control of forty-one companies was vested in nine trustees including Rockefeller, who operated out of Standard Oil's New York City office at 26 Broadway. As the years went by, Rockefeller controlled less of the company's operations and spent more time grooming his successors plus time in court fending off victims seeking restitution and at hearings fending off government inquiries into his business practices. Rockefeller was moving into the public spotlight, and the public did not like what they saw. Rockefeller's business practices did not fit the picture of America as a land of opportunity for pioneers and family owned businesses. Forcing competitors to sell against their wishes, even if the price were fair, was not considered a fair business practice.

Rockefeller's business practices, while not technically illegal at the time, inspired legislation that made them illegal. The Interstate Commerce Act of 1887 required railroads, as common carriers, to charge the same rates for all customers and outlawed secret rebates and kickbacks and established the first federal regulatory watchdog agency, the Interstate Commerce Commission. In 1890 Congress passed the Sherman Antitrust Act, which banned trusts and combinations that restrained trade and sought to control pricing through conspiratorial means. In 1892 the Ohio Supreme Court ordered the local Standard Oil company to leave the Standard Oil Trust, but Rockefeller instead dissolved the Trust and set up a new corporate holding company, Standard Oil of New Jersey (New Jersey was selected for its lax corporate laws). Standard Oil Trust as a legal entity lasted only ten years, but its name would last forever. Independently of Standard Oil, Rockefeller also got involved in investments in mining iron and copper ores and banking, which, in the Rockefeller tradition, all made money. The banking investment turned out to be a predecessor bank to Chase Manhattan, which was eventually run by his grandson, David Rockefeller.

With all these successful achievements in business, Rockefeller had one more favor from God awaiting him: Theodore Roosevelt. Rockefeller the trust maker fought Roosevelt the trust buster for years before Roosevelt won in 1911 with the Supreme Court decision that forced Standard Oil to dissolve itself into thirty-four separate and distinct companies. Rockefeller, rather than holding shares in Standard Oil, now held the equivalent number of shares in thirty-four companies including what would become Exxon (Standard Oil of New Jersey), Mobil (Standard Oil of New York), Amoco (Standard Oil of Indiana), Sohio (Standard Oil of Ohio), Chevron (Standard Oil of California), ARCO (Atlantic Refining), Conoco (Continental Oil), Marathon (Ohio Oil), Pennzoil (South Penn Oil), and twenty-five others.

Before the divestiture, and with Rockefeller exerting less control, Standard Oil was becoming bureaucratic and lethargic, the twin banes of large successful organizations. After the breakup and an initial period of cooperation among the sister companies, each went their separate ways, opening up and exploiting new markets that Rockefeller had not envisioned. The net impact of splitting up Standard Oil was to invigorate the company with a host of new managements and multiply the stock value of Rockefeller's original holdings in Standard Oil many times over. Rockefeller, fully retired after the Standard Oil breakup, became far wealthier than when he was actively engaged in business. Rockefeller died in 1937 at age ninety-eight, two years shy of his goal and, by all accounts, well-pleased with the course of his life. He had given away all but $26 million of his money, although a nice chunk of change was in his son's hands. Whether God was actually pleased with him is unknown.

**Enter Marcus Samuel**

The story of the transition of a small trading house in seashells to a major oil company known as Shell Oil serves as a counterpoint to the story of Standard Oil. It has more twists and turns and impinges more on the affairs of other oil companies, which, one day, would become part of Big Oil. The story begins with Marcus Samuel, the father of two sons, who would found Shell. The elder Marcus, a British Jew, purchased seashells and other objects from sailors who frequented the London waterfront. The shells were cleaned, polished, and, attached to boxes, sold in seaside towns and curio shops. By the 1860s, the elder Marcus began to branch out into general merchandise purchased as it landed on the dockside in London. Marcus saw the end of an era of shipping when a vessel left London with goods without any clear idea of what the goods would be sold for until the vessel arrived in Asia, where the proceeds would purchase Asian goods whose value was unknown until the vessel docked in London. Trading was a real gamble in terms of commercial risk: buying goods with no idea of what they would fetch if they survived the hazards of being carried aboard a vessel at sea. The opening of the Suez Canal, which shortened the voyage time between London and Asia, and the start of a regular mail service, which allowed buyers and sellers to communicate with each other, reduced the extent of operating in the dark although traders still had to contend with price changes during the weeks or months between buying and selling goods.

The elder Marcus's volume of business began to blossom as the British Empire expanded, first into India and then to British enclaves in Singapore, Hong Kong, Shanghai, and other Asian ports such as Bangkok, and finally the opening up of trade with Japan. Rather than buy and resell goods as they arrived in London, Marcus started working through agents in Bangkok, Singapore, and elsewhere to secure imports paid for by exports of British manufactured goods. The elder Marcus set up a trading house and conducted business through letters that took weeks to exchange, never visiting his agents. The agents learned to trust Marcus because he kept his word even if market conditions changed. This was a bit unusual in a world where reneging on deals was fairly common, particularly during times of financial distress when banks closed and trading houses collapsed. In 1870 the elder Marcus died, and the eldest son Joseph took charge of the family business, while the two younger sons, Marcus and Samuel, inherited only their father's reputation for sticking by his word.[10]

After spending some time at the family business, the younger Marcus—at twenty years of age—set out on his first voyage to Asia in 1873. Marcus discovered a famine while visiting his father's agent in India and surplus rice while visiting his father's agent in Bangkok. Marcus put together his first international deal with rice merchants and ship owners to relieve the famine in India, a deal both humanitarian and profitable. He returned home in 1874, shortly before his mother's death and, on his second voyage in 1877, made the acquaintance of the great trading families in Asia. At that time trade was either between Asia and Europe via the newly opened Suez Canal or within the borders of a nation. Marcus sold goods he acquired—not in England, as was expected—but to other Asian nations, "at the least possible distance." Strange as this must sound from a modern perspective, Marcus is credited with the start of intraregional trade among Asian nations as opposed to trade being confined within a nation's borders or with England.

Marcus reached Japan just as it was opening its borders to trade and established an office to import English textile machines in exchange for Japanese wares such as rare seashells, china, and silk. As the years progressed, the two brothers, operating from their office in London, built up a substantial trading house working through trusted employees and third-party agents in Asia. By the 1880s they owned the largest foreign concern in Japan and were involved with all types of cargo including Japanese coal exports for fueling steamships and kerosene imports in tin containers, called case-oil, from the Black Sea port of Batum.

At that time Standard Oil was a leading force in the case-oil market, but it was not alone. The Russian czar permitted the development of Caucasus oil in 1873 by awarding a concession to the Nobel brothers, Robert and Ludwig; a third brother, Alfred, was the inventor of dynamite and originator of the Nobel Prizes. The two Nobel brothers developed the oil resources of the landlocked Caspian Sea, located in the Baku region of modern Azerbaijan. As in Titusville, oil seeped to the surface and was "mined" for centuries before the two Nobel brothers began drilling for it. Although we tend to think of the oil industry as strictly American, the Nobel brothers made several important contributions to drilling and refining oil and in shipping oil by pipeline and tanker. The Nobels led the effort to make Baku a major world supplier with Caspian oil, which at the beginning of the twentieth century accounted for over half of the world's supply of oil (11.5 million tons versus U.S. production of 9.1 million tons).

To get kerosene to Europe, the case-oil was shipped in barges from a Caspian Sea refinery through the Volga River and canal system, then transferred to the Russian railroad for transport to a Baltic Sea port, and then by water to Europe. The Nobels had high shipping costs and, once their case-oil arrived in Europe they faced Standard Oil. Rockefeller moved into Europe early on, first moving kerosene in barrels to Europe on general cargo vessels and later in bulk on the world's first tankers. These early tankers proved to be dangerous. Fires and explosions often cut their lives short, a weak point that Marcus would eventually exploit.

The Nobels had learned a valuable lesson from Rockefeller's successful control of the railroads, which assured him a monopoly over American oil. The Nobels' version was to gain virtual control over water transportation up the Volga River. To beat this monopoly, the independent Russian producers started to build a railroad from Baku to Batum, on the Black Sea. If completed, Caucasus oil would be shipped by rail from Baku to Batum and then by tanker through the Black and Mediterranean seas to Europe. The oil would arrive in Europe cheaper than the Nobels transporting it to Europe via the Volga River and the Russian railway system to a Baltic port. This would place the Russian independents at a competitive advantage with the Nobel brothers in Europe. The Nobels, just as ruthless as Rockefeller, lowered the price of Russian oil and starved the Russian independents of the funds necessary to complete the railroad. Confident that they had crushed the Russian independents, the Nobels had inadvertently opened up the opportunity for the Paris Rothschilds to enter the oil game by financing the completion of the railroad. The Rothschilds extracted an exclusive purchasing arrangement from the Russian independents as a price for financing the railroad. With a secure source of oil, the Rothschilds built a refinery at Batum and began to market kerosene in Europe in competition with the Nobels and Rockefeller.

The Nobels were in deep trouble because transporting oil by canal and railroad to the Baltic via the Volga River was more expensive than by rail to the Black Sea and then by tanker to Europe. Like Rockefeller, the Nobels were not easily beaten. They built a pipeline from the Caspian Sea to the Black Sea, using their brother's dynamite to clear the way. Now it was the Rothschilds' and the Russian independents' turn to "sweat" as it was cheaper to pipeline oil to the Black Sea than to transport by railroad. Having lost their strategic advantage, the Rothschilds were in a weak bargaining position, locked in third place after Standard Oil and the Nobels in the race to supply kerosene to Europe.

In 1885 a London ship broker, Fred Lane, "Shady" Lane to his critics, was the London representative of the Paris Rothschilds. Lane approached Marcus with the idea of selling Rothschilds' kerosene in Asia. The Rothschilds were eager to diversify their market to counter their competitive disadvantage in Europe. But no matter where the Rothschilds attempted to sell kerosene in Europe, Standard Oil would step in, lower the price, and chase them away. Another approach was needed and that was to establish the Rothschilds in Asia, and over the following years Lane and Marcus hatched a strategy to do just that.

First, the relatively expensive transportation of case-oil, including the cost of tin containers, would be replaced by bulk transport in newly built tankers from Batum to Asia via the Suez Canal. Storage depots would be built in the principal ports in Asia to receive bulk oil shipments. The storage depots, where possible, would be connected to railroads or roads for bulk transport in railroad tank cars or horse-drawn wagons to inland destinations. To assure the success of the venture, the Rothschilds entered into a low-priced long-term supply contract for kerosene. As attractive as this sounded, it had one serious drawback. Bulk shipments of kerosene in tankers were not allowed to transit the Suez Canal because of their poor safety record. If Marcus could build tankers to a higher standard of safety and receive permission to transit the Suez Canal, then the Rothschilds would have a strategic advantage over Standard Oil.

The project faced enormous obstacles. The first obstacle was financing the tankers. Marcus became an alderman of the city of London, which, in addition to his being a successful business-man, would aid in garnering the necessary financing for the tankers, whose ultimate use was to be kept a secret from those providing the financing. The Rothschilds could not put up the financing as that would compromise the secrecy of the project. The second obstacle was that the Rothschilds had a hidden agenda—they intended to use the contract with Marcus as a means for putting together a more attractive deal to amalgamate their interests with Standard Oil. This made the Rothschilds an unreliable partner, although Marcus did not know it. The third obstacle was the Suez Canal Authority, who had no idea what tanker standards should be imposed to permit safe transits. Marcus was building tankers whose standards might or might not satisfy the Suez Canal Authority. The fourth obstacle was building storage terminals in Asia, for which Marcus had no experience, just as he had no experience with building tankers. The fifth obstacle was that Marcus, while a successful trader, had no background either in oil or in leading such a Herculean business enterprise, although he must have had the Rothschilds' confidence that he could successfully take on Standard Oil. The sixth obstacle was keeping Standard Oil from learning the entirety of the plan, in which case the project would face its full fury. The seventh obstacle was the two brothers themselves who continually bickered with one another because they had different personalities, different approaches to business, and, most importantly, different perceptions of risk. The eighth obstacle was that the financial stake was of such a magnitude that, if it failed, Marcus would be disgraced. The ninth obstacle was that Marcus preferred to act through inexperienced blood rela-tives, two nephews in particular, rather than through those with experience, although operating through his nephews might have been necessary in Marcus's mind to preserve secrecy.

The tankers under construction for Marcus incorporated the lessons learned from fires and ex-plosions on existing tankers. Kerosene would not be carried in the bow section of the ship, which would protect the cargo in case of a collision. Tanks were added to contain the thermal expansion of the cargo when the vessels passed through warm tropical waters. The individual cargo tanks were of limited capacity and airtight to enhance safety and would be thoroughly cleaned after discharging their cargo to prevent evaporating residues from forming an explosive gas mixture. The tankers would be registered with Lloyds Register's highest classification rating.

Two young nephews of the Samuel brothers were put in charge of building storage facilities in Asia, but they had no experience in acquiring property rights and building storage tanks. Port authorities opposed bulk storage facilities for oil products because they were considered potentially unsafe. Local business interests were against constructing storage tanks since change of a nature they did not understand could best be addressed by resisting it. The nephews were bombarded with micromanagement cables from their uncles that ran from close scrutiny of their expense accounts to attending to other aspects of the firm's trading activities. Their uncles' advice on building stor-age facilities was anything but helpful.

Owners of existing tankers who had been denied permission to pass through the Suez Canal were not keen to see a new class of tankers built that could. This would make their vessels obso-lete, at least from the point of view of trading between Europe and Asia. Members of the Russian imperial family, who were large shareholders of a Black Sea fleet of tankers, were in a position to have the Russian government petition the Suez Canal Authority to deny permission to Marcus's new tankers. Other petitioners included tanker owners and tin-plate manufacturers of cases for holding oil, whose business would be threatened by bulk shipments of kerosene, plus a host of companies, many of which were not engaged in the case-oil trade or shipping. Standard Oil's name did not appear among those opposing Marcus's application. It would have been utterly out of character for Standard Oil to be absent from such proceedings, but for whatever reason Standard Oil preferred to pull the legal strings through other parties and remain hidden behind lawyer-client privilege.

In the end, the Suez Canal Authority concluded that tanker transits would add to canal revenue and accepted Lloyd's highest classification rating as adequate criteria for safe passage. Despite all odds, including near-continuous interference from their uncles, the two young nephews succeeded in having storage tanks built in Bangkok and Singapore and were making progress in building tanks in Hong Kong and Kobe when, in 1892, the first tanker, the *Murex,* named after a seashell, passed through the Suez Canal with a cargo of Rothschild kerosene. The vessel unloaded its 4,000 tons of cargo at Bangkok and Singapore (actually at Freshwater Island, outside the jurisdiction of the Singapore port authority, which had denied permission to build an oil storage facility within Singapore). Ten more vessels were launched in 1893, creating a fleet of eleven vessels, all named after seashells as a tribute to the elder Marcus. By the end of 1895, sixty-nine Suez Canal tanker transits were made, of which all but four were tankers either owned or chartered by the Samuels. In 1906, Marcus shipped 90 percent of the 2 million tons of oil that passed through the Suez Canal. Marcus and the Rothschilds had beaten Standard Oil at its own game, a singular achievement, which by any measure must rank as a commercial miracle.

In 1892, after being told by a doctor that he was dying from cancer, Marcus organized the Tank Syndicate to carry on the tanker business after his death. The Tank Syndicate included family and friends such as merchants responsible for local distribution and individuals who had supplied storage tank facilities. The syndicate members were also responsible for garnering return cargoes for the tankers, which the Samuels sold in Europe. Trading transactions were done on the basis of a joint account for the syndicate members, all of whom became quite rich. When the doctor was proven wrong, the Tank Syndicate was reorganized as The Shell Transport and Trading Company in 1897.

All this was built on a house of cards. The Rothschilds were negotiating with Standard Oil and the Nobel brothers to form a world cartel, thus ending the intermittent price wars between the oligarchs. Standard Oil, sensing the importance of Marcus to the Rothschilds, opened negotiations to make Marcus part of Standard Oil. Marcus turned down a generous offer because he did not want to see a British firm become American or lose the Shell trademark and his identity as a businessman. In the game of King of the Hill, only one is left standing at the top, the primary reason why proposals for amalgamation among the Oil Kings failed. With the failure to come to terms with Standard Oil, Marcus was back skating on thin ice without a truly secure source of oil.

As fortune would have it, a company by the name of Royal Dutch in the Dutch East Indies produced oil, but was unable to transport and market its production. Royal Dutch was none of the things its name might imply. Its chief claim to fame was being the first oil company on record that relied on a government (the Dutch authorities in Dutch East Indies) to protect its oil holdings from insurgents. Royal Dutch had borrowed money to finance kerosene held in storage just as the price of kerosene crashed from Marcus's bulk-oil shipments and Standard Oil's campaign to chase American independents out of the Asian market. Royal Dutch approached Marcus about buying its Sumatra refinery output, but Marcus proved to be a tough negotiator, perhaps too tough. A subsequent rise in oil prices saved Royal Dutch and Marcus lost his first opportunity to obtain a secure source of oil and take over a company that perfectly complemented his own. In the end, Royal Dutch would take over Shell on its terms.

In 1895, the cards turned on Marcus. Standard Oil, the Rothschilds, the Nobels, and the Russian independent producers reached a price agreement. The oligarchs controlled the entire world supply of oil except for that of the American independents. As oil prices stiffened, Marcus had to cut the shipping rate on his fleet to stay in business, although selling return cargoes of general merchandise carried on Shell tankers made up for the losses in shipping oil. As things were becoming more difficult for Marcus, fortune smiled and the Shell fleet profited from the Sino-Japanese war because different elements within Shell supplied both China and Japan. Shell would come out a winner no matter who won. Marcus represented that portion of Shell allied with Japan. Marcus was able to take commercial advantage of Japan's winning the war by becoming a merchant banker and floating the first Japanese sterling loan in London in 1896. Now a merchant banker, Marcus's star continued to ascend with his election as sheriff of London, which placed him in the direct line of succession to the highest civic office in Britain, lord mayor of London. With his newfound wealth, Marcus purchased a 500-acre estate bordering on the parsonage of Bearsted, marking the high point of his career when he was only forty-three years old.

The contract with the Rothschilds was half over and an alternative source of oil would have to be arranged if the contract were not renewed. As luck would have it, a Dutch East Indies mining engineer with an oil concession in Borneo showed up at Marcus's door in 1896. By this time Mark, the younger of the two nephews, was carrying quite a load. He was responsible for building tank storage facilities and inland distribution points, identifying new agents to handle distribution, ensuring proper discharge and cargo handling of the Shell tankers, and tending to a myriad of instructions from London on the firm's trading business plus continuing to explain every item on his personal expense account. He also covered his uncles' mistakes, such as how to get the kerosene from the company's tanks to users. Users could not accept bulk shipments; they bought kerosene in a tin. The uncles had not taken this last crucial step in the supply chain into consideration, thinking that the buyers would supply their own tins; they did not. The only tins were the blue Standard Oil tins, which had other uses that did not include buying Shell kerosene.

This, too, became Mark's responsibility. He was building storage facilities with no previous experience; now, with no previous experience, he had to build a factory for making Shell red tins that competed with the Standard Oil blue tins. Once the factory was set up, Mark was selected to do something else for which he had no experience: operate an oil field in Borneo. His preparation was a crash course consisting of a three-week visit to Baku, cut short to two weeks to hasten his return to Singapore. Mark's training proved inadequate for drilling for oil in the fever-ridden, rain-drenched, mosquito-infested, inaccessible jungle in Borneo at the Black Spot, a place where the soil was saturated with oil. Mark faced severe challenges in acquiring and getting the necessary equipment and workers to the site. Once on site, the equipment would break down and parts were difficult to obtain while tropical diseases decimated the workforce.

In retrospect, it would have been better for Marcus to make a deal with Royal Dutch, when it was having financial difficulties, to transport and market their refined oil rather than develop an oil field and build a refinery. Royal Dutch, with its headquarters in The Hague, Netherlands, had a successful oil concession in the Dutch East Indies and was knowledgeable about exploration, production, and refining. Royal Dutch was a perfect complement to Marcus: one company rich in exploration, production, and refining and poor in distribution and marketing, the other rich in distribution and marketing and poor in exploration, production, and refining. Marcus was betting on Borneo crude taking the place of Royal Dutch, but Borneo crude was not fit for making kerosene. It was more useful as a fuel oil substitute for coal to power factories and ships.

In 1898, Standard Oil decided to get control over oil production in the Dutch East Indies. To do so, Standard Oil let out a false rumor that its intent in taking control over Dutch oil producers was to stop production and replace Dutch oil with Standard Oil's American oil. The next step would be to get rid of the Russian oil coming in on Shell tankers and have the Asian market for itself. The rumor worked as shares in Dutch East Indies oil companies plummeted, and Royal Dutch and Shell were again talking to one another. Since the original talks, Royal Dutch had not been sitting idle, depending on Shell for marketing and distribution. Henri Deterding, a bookkeeper who by now was a rising star in Royal Dutch, strongly advocated Royal Dutch having its own marketing department, if only to be able to play a tougher hand in the cat-and-mouse negotiations with Marcus. A cooperative arrangement between the two companies, signed in 1898, while flawed because agents of both companies continued to compete against one another, did prevent Standard Oil from carrying out its plans to bring the entire Asian market into its embracing tentacles.

That same year Marcus scored a publicity coup. The British warship *Victorious* went aground in the Suez Canal, much to the embarrassment of the British Navy. All attempts to free the vessel failed until Marcus showed up with the Shell-owned *Pectan,* the most powerful tug in the world. The tug freed the *Victorious* and Marcus deliberately did not submit a salvage claim, which he was entitled to, and in return received a knighthood from Queen Victoria. Not one to let a knighthood stand in the way of a commercial deal, and with Borneo oil being too heavy to make kerosene but perfectly fit for burning as ships' fuel instead of coal, Marcus used the *Victorious* incident to establish a relationship with the British Navy. This was the opening shot of what would become nearly a fifteen-year campaign to induce the British Navy to shift from burning coal to oil, something that Marcus had already done with his tankers.

Marcus found strong support in a young naval officer who would one day be Lord Fisher, head of the British Navy. Coal smoke revealed the presence of a warship and oil burned with relatively little smoke. With higher energy content, oil consumption would be less than coal, allowing warships to travel further without refueling. Refueling time would be considerably shortened since coal was carried on board in bags, whereas oil could be much more rapidly pumped aboard a vessel. Oil removed the necessity for stokers to shovel coal into the ship's boilers, reducing crew size. Converting space for holding coal to carrying ammunition increased the ship's battle endurance. However, to Fisher, the most important advantage of oil over coal was the greater speed that the British Navy had to have in order to stand up against the emerging German navy.

Marcus and Fisher, however, could not overcome the principal argument against converting to oil—coal was a domestic fuel whereas oil had to be imported from foreign sources. Thus, oil was less reliable and less secure than coal, a critical matter for warships. Although Shell had refueling stations for oil in the Pacific, they had none in the Atlantic. The lack of sufficient coverage to supply fuel oil was an obstacle to convincing ship owners and admirals to switch from coal to oil. Until this chicken-and-egg conundrum was resolved, the British Navy and ship owners who traded worldwide could not convert to oil. Nevertheless, ship owners trading within a region adequately covered by fuel oil bunkering stations could switch from coal to oil.

The fortunes of Shell and Royal Dutch oscillated like a pendulum on an overwound clock. In 1897, troubles hit Royal Dutch when its wells went dry. Royal Dutch then purchased Russian oil for sale through its marketing outlets in direct competition with Shell. A price war with Shell would have ended with the demise of Royal Dutch, but Marcus chose not to do so because he felt that the Asian market would grow to accommodate both companies. This was quite unusual thinking at a time when oil magnates did not hesitate to crush one another at the first opportunity. Unusual or not, this marked Marcus's second failure to acquire Royal Dutch.

In 1898, it was Shell's turn to face a sharp decline in its Borneo production. Shell's people in Borneo tried to keep the matter a secret from its competitors, but an agent in Singapore got wind of it and kept Standard Oil better informed of the situation than was Shell's London office.

Declining production was just one of the worries on Marcus's shoulders. In addition to running a major oil company he was trading goods that still included seashells, operating a merchant banking house for floating Japanese bonds in England, and participating in an active civic and social life. Marcus had little time to spend on the upcoming renewal of the Rothschild contract. He had to demonstrate that Shell, through its producing properties in Borneo, could live without the Rothschilds' contract in order to be able to renew the contract on favorable terms. Borneo crude would generate significant savings in shipping costs for Shell, but, perversely, would leave Shell tankers bereft of cargoes.

Marcus had to carry out this critical renegotiation in a business environment of continually shifting alliances among Standard Oil, the Rothschilds, the Nobels, and the Russian and American independents. One grouping of these companies would gang up against the others in one part of the world and another group would do the same somewhere else. Alliances came and went like liaisons in a brothel. How quickly the alliances could shift was clear when, in late 1899, Standard Oil broke its agreement with the Nobels and started a price war in Europe to get rid (again) of the American independents. The Nobels, caught by surprise and with a large inventory of high-priced kerosene, decided to join forces with the Rothschilds and the Russian independents to push Standard Oil out of Europe. Then, Standard Oil decided to join the very group set up to ostracize it to exert a more formidable force against the American independents in Europe. The American independents could not compete against an alliance of Standard Oil, the Nobels, the Rothschilds, and the Russian independents. Shell was now in danger if this alliance were expanded to include Asia.

In response to this threat, Marcus started discussions with Dutch East Indies producing companies to secure an alternative source of oil, excluding Royal Dutch, which was still selling Russian oil in Asia in direct competition with Shell. In the midst of the Boer War, which strained relations between England and Holland, Marcus was able to strengthen his position with the Dutch independents in the East Indies, who found getting in bed with a British firm infinitely more tolerable than getting in bed with Standard Oil. Unfortunately, Marcus let an opportunity to fix long-term contracts with the Dutch independents, who resented Royal Dutch selling Russian oil in Asia in competition with their own, slip through his fingers.

Meanwhile, Royal Dutch had obtained a new concession and was among the first to hire geologists to assist in identifying sites for exploratory drilling. The world was rapidly running out of sites where the surface soil was saturated with seep oil. Marcus was against hiring geologists because he thought that they were better able to tell where oil could not be found rather than where it could be found. He failed to realize that negative information, if true, is valued intelligence. Despite his failed attempts to secure a long-term supply of oil, he was still making money, particularly when ship rates rose to replenish the British army during the Boer War. With shipping rates and oil prices escalating, Marcus, against his brother's objections, took long positions in kerosene to cover the period until Borneo would be producing kerosene in sufficient quantities to meet Shell's needs. Marcus had placed two bets: one on kerosene prices continuing to rise and another on Borneo producing kerosene in sufficient quantities to take the place of the Rothschild kerosene. He built more tankers (two, each at 9,000 tons, were the world's largest tankers at that time), expanded his storage facilities, and filled them with high-priced kerosene. He would lose both bets.

The year 1900 started well for Marcus. He reported record profits to his shareholders and called for a stock split to permit more shareholders to buy shares. He renewed his contract with the Rothschilds but without the exclusive right to sell Rothschild oil in Asia. Marcus was not worried because the Rothschilds, without tankers, would not be able to sell their oil in Asia, an impediment that they would eventually find their way around. Only a few months later, Marcus's world began to collapse. It started with falling coal prices, which diminished the market for fuel oil as oil-fired ships reverted to coal. Then freight rates collapsed. Then the Russian economy slumped, further reducing demand for fuel oil. With less demand for fuel oil to run Russian factories, the Russian independents began producing more kerosene, creating a glut at Batum. As kerosene prices fell at Batum, Standard Oil dropped its prices, and the rest of the world followed suit. This left Marcus with a huge inventory of high-priced kerosene plus a slew of term contracts to continue buying kerosene at even higher prices. To make matters worse, the Boxer Rebellion broke out in China in 1900, and Shell's property was looted including 60,000 tons of kerosene along with the steel in the storage tanks. Troubles next spread to India, where Shell had more storage than all its competitors combined, also filled to the brim with high-priced kerosene. Shell competed against cheap kerosene from the Russian independents, the Nobels, Royal Dutch, and a new competitor, Burmah Oil.

Burma was the last place where oil was discovered by drilling into oil-saturated soil. Since Burma and India were British colonies, Burma could export oil to India without paying the import fees associated with oil from foreign sources such as the Dutch East Indies and Russia. The situation in China and India left Marcus's newly expanded fleet without cargoes at a time of low freight rates. To top this off, the Borneo oil field was producing a fraction of what was expected and the refinery built to process Borneo crude suffered severe operating problems.

Motorcars were just beginning to appear in England. With only a few thousand registrations, Marcus saw automobiles as another business opportunity, as did other oil magnates. Up to this time, naphtha produced from refineries was either burned or in some way discarded. Automobiles would be an ideal market for selling a waste product. Gasoline in England was already being sold in blue Standard Oil tins when Marcus began dreaming of bright red Shell tins. He had made the opening moves to sell gasoline in London by leasing storage space, overlooking the fact that gasoline was not a permitted cargo for transiting the Suez Canal in bulk tankers. Not yet having obtained permission from the Suez Canal Authority to use the canal, Marcus shipped a cargo of gasoline from his Borneo refinery around the Cape of Good Hope, a dangerous undertaking. Standard Oil was fully prepared for the arrival of Shell's first shipment of gasoline to England. It had forced every agent and distributor in Britain to enter into a contract not to sell any brand but Standard Oil. This knocked Shell out of the gasoline market in England. Then the carnivorous Standard Oil purchased a U.S. west coast fuel oil producer for the sole purpose of exporting fuel oil to Asia and put the final squeeze on Marcus. Caught in the Standard Oil juggernaut in England and Asia, "discussions" began between the two firms.

Meanwhile, Royal Dutch, which at times bordered on bankruptcy, aided by advice from geologists was now on the comeback trail with discoveries of new oil fields in the Dutch East Indies. Deterding, now president of Royal Dutch, had done all that he could in the past to prevent an amalgamation between Royal Dutch and Shell. Marcus had lost his strongest supporter at Royal Dutch with the death of Deterding's predecessor and now faced an individual who relished taking full advantage of Royal Dutch's ascendancy over an ailing Shell. Whereas in the past Marcus was absolutely determined that Shell would not play second fiddle to Royal Dutch, now the tables had turned and Deterding was just as adamant that Royal Dutch would not play second fiddle to Shell. To add insult to injury, Royal Dutch geologists discovered oil in the same location in Borneo where Shell, without geologists (at Marcus's insistence), had failed. Just as prospects for Marcus were almost pitch-black, a new twist entered his life.

## Spindletop

Patillo Higgens left his hometown of Beaumont as a one-armed young man who could fight better than most Texans with two. He returned in the middle 1880s as a Baptist churchgoer and Sunday school instructor and made a living in real estate and timberland. He took his class to picnic on a large mound that rose fifteen feet above the flat prairie and covered thousands of acres. He punched a cane into the ground and lit the escaping gas to amuse the children. Higgens was intrigued by the sour smell, the square boxes that held blue, green, and yellow waters for bathing or drinking or passing livestock through to rid them of the mange, and St. Elmo's lights that hovered over the mound at night. These were signs of something, but it was not until he paid a visit to the Oil Regions in Pennsylvania and elsewhere (trying to figure out how to get into the brick-making business) that he figured out the source of these mysterious signs.[11]

Without funds, he convinced others to purchase land on what would eventually be called Spindletop after a nearby town, and tried to keep himself in the picture. In 1892, Higgens formed a company called Gladys City to corral investors in what he saw as a future oil company (the stock certificates featured the portrait of a local young girl named Gladys, along with imaginary oil wells, tanks, and refineries). Higgens was convinced that oil would be discovered if a well were drilled to 1,000 feet, but time was against him. He had purchased options on some land parcels and was having difficulty raising the necessary funds.

Spindletop made life tough for drillers with its quicksand, gas pockets, and loose conglomerate. The first hole was drilled to a little over 400 feet before being abandoned by the driller. Higgens persisted. A second driller made it to 350 feet before Spindletop put a stop to his attempts to uncover its secrets. To beef up support for drilling a third well, Higgens got a Texas state geologist's opinion about Spindletop. He did opine: petroleum means rock oil and with no rocks in Spindletop, no oil. This is what Higgens did not want to hear. The geologist, utterly convinced of his findings, sent a letter to the local newspaper to warn the good people of Beaumont not to waste their money looking for oil. This letter convinced the local townspeople of what they already suspected: Higgens was losing his mind from sniffing the sour gas fumes coming from Spindletop. As a last act of desperation, Higgens advertised for investors. He received only one response from a Captain Lucas.

Lucas was looking for sulfur, not oil, and had a theory about finding sulfur in salt domes. After listening to Higgens, it was an easy leap of faith to think that oil might also be found in salt domes. Higgens, short on cash, arranged for Lucas to obtain a lease on all of his Gladys City landholdings, for which Higgins ended up with a 10 percent share. Higgens was reduced to acting as an agent on commission for the company he had founded. Lucas brought in a rotary rig, not the traditional cable-tool rig used by the previous two drillers. Spindletop proved to be too much for Lucas's rig. Lucas ran out of money after drilling two dry holes. Now with four dry holes, and unable to raise funds locally, Lucas sought help from Standard Oil. After examining the property, Standard Oil's expert geologist opined that no one would ever find oil at Spindletop, as did another geologist employed by the federal government.

Lucas then made contact with a team—Galey, a driller, and Guffey, a promoter—with close ties with the Mellons. Guffey demanded that Lucas get rights to all the land on Spindletop before doing any drilling and that Higgens be kept in the dark to keep their involvement a secret. With Mellon money backing Guffey, Lucas was able to get leases on 15,000 acres, except for what would turn out to be a critical omission, the many small tracts that ran across the top of Spindletop, which included the thirty-three-acre lot owned by Lucas. The new partnership left Lucas with a relatively small share, greatly diminishing Higgens's 10 percent residual interest as well.

Galey visited the property and drove a stake into the ground. Had he driven the stake fifty feet away, the well would have missed its target. Galey arranged for the Hamill brothers, who had their own rotary rig, to drill the well. When the Hamills hit the same quicksand that had stopped the other drillers, they found that using drilling fluid spiked with mud, obtained by driving a herd of cattle around a slush pit, would seal the sidewalls and keep the quicksand from filling up the well bore. This was the first use of drilling mud, now universally used in drilling. When they reached a point where the mud would not seal up the sidewalls, the Hamills devised a means of inserting a pipe casing that supported the walls of the well, allowing drilling to proceed. At about 650 feet, the Hamills ran into gas pockets that made the circulating mud boil and flow up rather than down the drill pipe. The Hamills overcame this problem, along with others, when the drill struck the salt dome caprock at 880 feet.

The night of January 9, 1901, turned out to be the last great show of St. Elmo's fire, ghostly blue flames usually associated with an electrical discharge, ever seen on Spindletop. The next morning, while the Hamills were lowering drill pipe into the now 1,200-foot-deep drill hole, mud suddenly started to spurt high above the derrick. The crew ran for their lives as six tons of drill pipe blasted from the hole destroying the derrick. This was followed shortly thereafter by a cannon shot of gas followed by a one hundred-foot-high, 100,000-barrels-per-day geyser of oil, clearly visible from Beaumont and everywhere else within a twelve-mile radius, accompanied by a stupendous roar. Higgins found out about the oil geyser that afternoon when he rode into town. A few days later the Hamills would be the first to devise a way to cap an oil gusher, the local pronunciation of *geyser*.

Pandemonium reigned in Beaumont as in Pit Hole. In the months that followed, Beaumont grew from 9,000 to 50,000 inhabitants with six special trains running between Beaumont and Houston daily. Those who did not go back to Houston could share the same hotel room with twenty other people. The bars and brothels never closed. Stock manipulators and scoundrels sold leases that either did not exist or turned out to be far from Spindletop, even far into the Gulf of Mexico. Stocks in companies without clear title to the land or without a promise to do anything were traded daily in an improvised stock exchange. It did not matter if the title to the land or a lease was bogus or compromised if it could be sold at a higher price. Fortunes were made on dubious securities and leases. Eventually lawyers would make even more money settling litigation over whom, exactly, possessed title to producing wells. Higgens was lost in all the pandemonium surrounding Spindle-top. Like Drake, he would die without fame or fortune, but at least not quite a pauper.

After the discovery of Spindletop, Guffey lined up financial support from the Mellons. The Mellons, while primarily bankers, had previous experience in the oil patch. In 1889, the Mellons owned an oil field in Pennsylvania and had decided to fight rather than become Standard Oil property. In 1892, they succeeded in getting a contract with a French company to refine their oil. Immediately the Pennsylvania Railroad hiked its shipping rates to prohibitive levels, and the Reading Railroad refused to carry Mellon oil. When the Mellons attempted to build a pipeline to the east coast, hired thugs of the Pennsylvania Railroad fought the pipe layers by day and ripped up laid pipe by night. The Mellons were forced to sell out to Standard Oil, but they did make a handsome $2.5 million for their troubles. (It was not Rockefeller's price that people objected to necessarily but his forcing the sale against the sellers' wishes.)

There was one thing Texans, and the Texas legislature, was bent on doing: keeping Standard Oil out of Texas. They succeeded by passing antitrust legislation that made it virtually impossible for Standard Oil to establish a toehold in Texas. Spindletop gave birth to Gulf Oil, the successor company to Guffey Petroleum Company and Texaco, the successor to the Texas Fuel Oil Company. Moreover, the spate of oil exploration in the rest of Texas set off by Spindletop would create Sun Oil and Humble Oil, named after a town. Humble Oil would eventually become Standard Oil's entry into Texas oil fields when it acquired a half interest in the firm in 1917. Eventually, Humble Oil, the most misnamed company imaginable, would be absorbed into Exxon. Oil flowing from Spindletop, which would account for half the nation's production, broke the Standard Oil monopoly in America. Spindletop oil, heavy and better fit for burning as a fuel than for making kerosene, was immediately recognized as a replacement for coal.

## Spindletop and Shell

The Mellons, back in the oil business by financially backing Guffey, wanted the oil sold to anyone but Standard Oil. Marcus realized that Spindletop crude was unfit for kerosene production, but was an ideal fuel oil. With Spindletop crude, Marcus could fulfill Fisher's dream of fuel oil being available in both hemispheres to supply the British Navy. In June of 1901, Marcus agreed to buy half of Guffey's production for twenty-one years at about twenty-five cents per barrel, plus a 50 percent share of the profit in the net sales of the oil with a minimum takeoff of 100,000 tons per year. This was the second major transaction for Marcus in 1901; the first was the sale of the company's seashell business to a relative.

In the game of oil, the positions of the chairs had again shifted. Standard Oil now saw Shell not as a competitor about to be crushed, but as a means of getting its hands on Spindletop oil. Rather than wiping out Shell, the objective now was to make Shell part of the Standard Oil family. Deterding knew that any alliance between Standard Oil and Shell would spell trouble for Royal Dutch, so Deterding entered the unholy alliance and the three companies divided the non-Russian world oil market among themselves. They actually reached an agreement on divvying up the world market by oil products, of which there were then five: kerosene, the mainstay of the business, lubricating oils, the emerging markets in gasoline, fuel oil, and what was called solar oil, a substitute for coal for manufactured gas to light municipal street lamps and buildings. There was also agreement on which geographic areas each firm would operate.

In the midst of these critical discussions in late 1901, Marcus took time out for the pomp and ceremony of becoming lord mayor of London. While Marcus was being showered with honors, the Rothschilds were attempting to unite themselves with the Nobels and the Russian independents into a single marketing entity to counter any Standard Oil-Shell-Royal Dutch combine. In early 1902, talks between Standard Oil, Shell, and Royal Dutch collapsed, despite their marked progress in carving up the world market. The cause of the failure was the same for the failure of every proposed amalgamation: the name of the game is King of the Hill, not Kings of the Hill. No one could agree on which oil company would head the combine other than their own.

The pleasantries exchanged during negotiations between Standard Oil, Shell, and Royal Dutch gave way to open commercial warfare. This rekindled negotiations between Deterding and Marcus, which led to the signing of the British-Dutch Agreement in mid-1902. After the signing, the Rothschilds wanted to join the two, which Marcus opposed and Deterding supported. In the end, Deterding won and the British-Dutch Agreement was amended to become the Asiatic Agreement, marking the birth of the Asiatic Petroleum Company. Because the agreement called for all three companies to participate in a joint venture for refining and marketing oil products in Asia, the Rothschilds had finally found a way around Marcus to market oil in Asia. The Rothschilds, as in the past, saw the agreement as a means to improve their negotiating strength with Standard Oil. Marcus saw the Asiatic Agreement as something temporary to keep Standard Oil at bay. Deterding saw the agreement as something permanent, leading to the final ascendancy of Royal Dutch over Shell. This was virtually assured when Marcus allowed Deterding to be in charge of Asiatic Petroleum's operations.

The gods turned against Marcus. The *Hannibal*, a British warship put on trials to test out Marcus's idea of burning oil, was enveloped in black smoke when the fuel was shifted from coal to oil. The experiment was a total failure because the wrong atomizers had been installed. This would delay the conversion of the British Navy from coal to oil for another ten years, much to the chagrin of Marcus and Fisher. The Port Arthur refinery built to process Spindletop oil was having serious operating problems, but this was nothing compared to the news that the production of the hodgepodge of oil wells at Spindletop, one nearly on top of the other, had gone into a sudden decline, particularly those owned by Guffey. A young nephew of the Mellons surveyed the scene and concluded that the refinery was unworkable, the oil was gone, and their investment was wasted. The only way to recoup the Mellon investment in Spindletop was to create a totally new integrated oil company with a massive capital infusion. Rockefeller came out of partial retirement to tell the Mellons personally, with some degree of relish, that there was no way Standard Oil would assist them.

Colonel Guffey was set aside and new management installed to allow the Mellons to reorganize Guffey Petroleum into what would become Gulf Oil. Honoring the Shell contract was impossible, not because oil production at Spindletop had essentially ceased, but that the price of oil was above twenty-five cents per barrel. The Mellons could not buy oil on the open market to honor the contract without taking an enormous financial loss. Unwilling to absorb such losses, the Shell contract was unilaterally canceled and Andrew Mellon inveigled Marcus to substitute a much less onerous contract, which in the end was also not honored. Shell's tankers, built to carry Spindletop oil, were converted to cattle carriers.

Some think that Marcus should have sued the Mellons and saved Shell through litigation. This would not have been as easy as one might expect because the terms in the contract left something to be desired if exposed to the scrutiny of a court of law. Others thought that Marcus might have been thinking of the long-term implications of not suing the Mellons, perhaps hoping for a potentially profitable collaboration between Gulf and Shell in the future. The implication of future collaboration might have been a keen insight on the part of Marcus, but the short-term effect was disastrous.

If this was not bad enough, Marcus received word that Deterding was unhappy with the Asiatic Agreement and that adjustments would have to be made to the agreement, adjustments of a type that would not benefit Marcus. Although his investiture as lord mayor of London, with its pomp and ceremonies, was a great honor for Marcus,[12] the time consumed prevented his meeting with the representatives of the Rothschilds and the Nobels to deal with yet another problem in Germany where Shell was facing the full fury of Standard Oil. This placing of civic responsibilities ahead of business was to cost Marcus dearly.

In early 1903, Lane submitted a letter of resignation stating that he was unable to continue as a director of a company as poorly managed as Shell. He complained of Marcus's attention being diverted from the oil business to trading merchandise, running a merchant bank, participating in civic activities, placing inexperienced nephews in charge of major projects, and relying on a brother's opinion rather than a more formal approach to planning before making critical business decisions. Indeed, the head count in Shell's London office, the heart and soul of a major world oil enterprise, was just under fifty including clerks, typists, bookkeepers, and messengers.

Things were going from bad to worse with Deterding running Asiatic Petroleum. Deterding limited Shell's profits to freight paid for its tankers and rentals on its storage facilities. Money made in marketing and distributing kerosene in Asia ended up in the Royal Dutch accounts. By the sleight of hand of a very experienced and adept bookkeeper, Shell suffered declining profits while those of Royal Dutch rose. Moreover, Asiatic Petroleum was extremely late in issuing its financial reports, without which Shell could not issue its final financial statements. This proved to be something else that depressed the value of Shell shares. Deterding had placed Marcus in a desperate strait, having wrecked Shell's profits and the value of its shares. Exhausted from his year as lord mayor of London and disillusioned with those about him, Marcus was at the point of giving up, something Deterding had been striving for since taking charge of Asiatic Petroleum.

Before Shell fell under Royal Dutch rule, Marcus was given a last-minute reprieve in the form of a financial shot in the arm from the profits made by the Shell fleet's support of Japan in the 1904 Russo-Japanese War. This proved to be the incendiary that ignited the 1905 Russian Revolution when revolting oil workers set fire to the Baku oil installations, a dress rehearsal for 1917 and a training ground for Stalin. The pathetically slow progress of the coal-fueled Russian fleet as it sailed from the Baltic to its destruction off Japan provided impetus for the British Navy to switch to oil. When the British Navy did switch, Shell was no longer an independent company.

The emergence of the automobile age in the United States made gasoline a mainstay for Standard Oil and kerosene a byproduct. Standard Oil dumped its excess American kerosene in Europe and formed a joint marketing effort with the Rothschilds (Shell's partner in Asiatic Petroleum), and the Nobels to keep kerosene prices low. Shell, whose mainstay was still kerosene, had to face this combine alone. Everyone was losing money by selling kerosene in Europe, but Shell did not have the financial wherewithal to outlast the others. Like wolves gathering for the final kill, Shell was forced to sell six of its best tankers at a tremendous loss to recoup its investment in Germany. By 1906, beaten in Europe by Standard Oil and beaten in Asia by Deterding, Marcus had no choice but to appeal to Deterding for an amalgamation of the two companies.

Marcus went to Deterding's office. Deterding gave Marcus his first and final offer. If Marcus left without accepting the offer on the spot, the offer was dead and so was Shell. The offer was the formation of a holding company called Royal Dutch-Shell Group, of which Royal Dutch would own 60 percent and Shell 40 percent. Although Marcus was nominally in control of the holding company, the King of the Hill was definitely Deterding. To further ensure Royal Dutch dominance, Deterding had Royal Dutch buy 25 percent of Shell's shares at thirty shillings per share when the price of the stock three years' previous had been three pounds. Deterding considered this a very generous offer under the circumstances, which it may have been. Maybe it was Deterding's way of thanking Marcus for passing up several opportunities to take over Royal Dutch and become King of the Hill himself.

Two new operating companies were formed, one British and one Dutch. The British company controlled transportation and storage, and the Dutch company production and refining. Royal Dutch and Shell were then emptied of all assets and became holding companies in which each party held a 60–40 percent share in the two operating companies. Asiatic Petroleum continued to market products in Asia with two-thirds shareholding of this company reallocated 60 percent to Royal Dutch and 40 percent to Shell; the remaining third stayed in the hands of the Rothschilds. In 1907, when the Group was formally established, Marcus, though personally rich, considered himself an abject failure.

As with so much of his life, there was a new twist. Deterding, contrary to all the rules of the game, did not leave Marcus out in the cold. Deterding decided to operate out of Shell's London office and not out of Royal Dutch's Hague office. With Marcus sitting in the same office, Deterding found that he could be more effective if he kept Marcus informed of the latest developments and conferred with Marcus before making any major policy decisions. This consultative arrangement between Deterding and Marcus worked to their mutual advantage, and this unique method of managing a large firm survived the two individuals. After Deterding retired from Shell, all major decisions had to receive a favorable ruling from two committees—one representing Royal Dutch and the other Shell. The committees were made up of personnel with long-standing records of achievement who, rather than retire to a golf course in Scotland, met on a regular basis to confer on important matters and make recommendations based on their extensive experience. This consultative and collegial method of decision making, unique in the corporate world, has been adopted by the principal operating companies within the Royal Dutch-Shell Group.

Deterding, though a Dutchman, saw a greater commercial advantage if the newly formed Group was associated more closely with Britain than Holland to take advantage of operating within the British Empire. In 1910 the British Navy finally switched to fuel oil, which was a great boon to the Shell Group. However the Group was considered non-British because its sources of oil did not lie within the British Empire, and a Dutch company owned 60 percent. Shell still benefited by selling fuel oil obtained from foreign sources to qualified British companies, which, in turn, supplied the British Navy. Even though Deterding was "on top," Marcus was not idle. He turned his attention to Egypt, and, following up on rumors, insisted that the Group explore for oil because if found (and it was found) the Shell Group would have a source of oil on British colonial soil. This would permit the Shell Group to sell fuel oil directly to the British Navy. Deterding was no slacker either. He acquired oil properties in California that were later expanded to Oklahoma, allowing the Shell Group to confront Standard Oil on its home turf, plus getting involved with oil fields in Mexico and Venezuela. In 1912, with Lane in the middle, the Rothschilds exchanged their Russian holdings for stock in Royal Dutch-Shell, thereby becoming one of its largest shareholders. In light of what was to occur only a few years later, this exchange of oil properties in Russia for shareholding interests in Royal Dutch-Shell proved to be a most astute move because diversification mitigated the financial risk of having all one's eggs in a single basket.

Winston Churchill, as first lord of the admiralty, agreed with Fisher on converting warships from coal to oil, with one major reservation. Churchill believed that the British Navy should not rely exclusively on contracts from suppliers, but that the government should have its own oil fields to guarantee a supply of fuel for the navy. Marcus attempted to convince Churchill that the Shell Group, along with Standard Oil, could supply the British Navy in any location throughout the world. Marcus argued that the navy would be better served building storage facilities, not buying oil fields. Despite Marcus's pleas, the British government went ahead with Churchill's plan and purchased a 51 percent interest in Anglo-Persian Oil Company, an offshoot of Burmah Oil, in 1914, weeks before the start of the First World War.[13]

Anglo-Persian Company was originally formed in 1908 when another oil explorer with the drive of Colonel Drake, ignoring a letter to cease looking for oil, found oil. A 130-mile pipeline, the first in the Middle East, was laid between the oil field and a refinery built in Abadan. Having only one outlet to the marketplace, through the Shell Group, Anglo-Persian Oil was in a weak bargaining position and vulnerable to a Shell Group takeover. Moreover, it was in a weak financial condition. The company wanted an investment by the British government to gain a major new client, the British Navy, and planned to expand its refinery with the proceeds to become the largest in the world, diversify its markets, and serve those markets with its own tanker fleet. By owning an oil field, Churchill felt that he would not be at the mercy of oil companies with regard to price and supply. The British government did not interfere with the running of Anglo-Persian Oil, and its members on the board of directors made sure that the company's operations did not conflict with the government's strategic objectives.

At the start of the war, the Shell Group chartered its entire fleet of over seventy tankers to the British Admiralty at prewar rates as a show of support for Britain. As a consequence, the company had to charter in other tankers at up to four times these rates to meet its needs. The Dutch side of the company transferred as much of their operations to London as possible. Marcus converted his mansion into a military hospital, and his two sons and two sons-in-law served in the military. Only one survived.

The Shell Group became the sole supplier of aviation fuel and the principal source of motor vehicle fuel to the British Expeditionary Force. The toluene in the explosive TNT (trinitrotoluene) came from processing coal. Though crude oil normally contains only trace amounts of toluene, Shell's Borneo crude was unusually rich in toluene (10 percent). To process Borneo crude for its toluene content, the Shell Group's refinery in Rotterdam was dismantled and "smuggled" to England. In addition to having the Shell Group invest in National War Loans, Marcus spearheaded the conversion of general cargo vessels into tankers and had others fitted with double bottoms for supplying fuel to the expeditionary forces in Europe. He was also active in introducing diesel propulsion to replace oil-fueled steam propulsion plants. In 1916, when it was clear that Romania would fall to German forces, Marcus and Deterding authorized company personnel to destroy the Shell Group's Romanian oil assets without any promise of restitution by the British government. Ironically, Shell Group gasoline was distributed in Britain before the war under a contract with British Petroleum, at that time a German-owned marketing company. British Petroleum shares were seized by the British government and turned over to the Anglo-Persian Oil Company, marking the official birth of BP.

The British government was the first government to have majority ownership of an oil company but chose not to run it. The first government that actually ran an oil company was the Soviet Union after it expropriated the oil-producing properties of the Nobels, the Shell Group, and the Russian independents after the Russian civil war. But the Nobels did not leave empty-handed because Exxon bought their oil rights in Russia in 1920, on the remote chance that the Whites would win the Russian civil war. Although the Nobels received money for their oil properties, they were out of the oil business. The Rothschilds' loss could have been disastrous, aside from their one-third ownership of Asiatic Petroleum, had they not exchanged their Russian oil-producing properties for shares in Royal Dutch-Shell. The Russian independents were lucky to escape with their lives. Now the Soviet Union was in the oil business and depended on oil exports to build communism, in much the same way that Russian oil rebuilt the Russian economy after the fall of communism in 1991.

In 1920, despite all that Marcus had done in support of the British war effort during the First World War, the public rose against him and accused him of greed in the face of rising petrol prices. Only a decade earlier the darling of London society, Marcus was now a pariah, accused of siphoning money out of everyone's pocket. It was his turn to endure the vituperation heaped on Rockefeller. Marcus's appeal to the harsh law of supply and demand for establishing the price for oil to clear the market did not endear him with the public. This display of public ill will might have played a role in his retiring as chairman and board member. In 1925 he became Lord Bearsted (Deterding was knighted in 1921 in recognition of his war services), and two years later both Marcus and his wife died within twenty-four hours of one another.

### Emergence of Oil as a Strategically Vital Commodity

Winston Churchill was the first government official to sense the strategic importance of oil. Oil had its beginnings in lighting, but kerosene lamps were giving way to electric light bulbs. Automobiles were toys for the rich at the beginning of the twentieth century, but when Henry Ford began to mass-produce Model Ts, the era of the horse and wagon ended. During the years prior to the First World War, oil was becoming an integral part of national economies without anyone taking notice, but during the war, when success in combat depended on a steady and reliable flow of oil to fuel military vehicles, tanks, and fighter planes, it was noticed. National survival placed a whole new emphasis on the importance of oil. Oil was no longer a consumer item but a means to ensure military success; a commodity of national security importance.

The Second World War only reinforced the lessons learned in the First. Oil followed only armaments and ammunition in importance for winning a war. Hitler, cognizant of Germany's lack of raw materials and energy, except for coal, built facilities in Germany that made gasoline from coal. Gasoline fueled the aircraft and tanks essential for the success of the blitzkrieg: a rapid deployment of armies to envelop an enemy before resistance could be organized. The Nazi army quickly invaded Romania to seize its oil fields. Hitler's thrust into the Soviet Union and Rommel's invasion of North Africa were to meet at the Baku oil fields, placing Middle East and Soviet oil under Axis control. Fortunately for the Allies, both suffered from severed supply lines. Hitler's army's replenishment lifeline was cut at Stalingrad as was Rommel's gasoline lifeline to North Africa. Likewise, in the Battle of the Atlantic, Hitler tried to cut the British lifeline of troops, armaments, ammunition, and oil flowing from the United States with submarine U-boats. Germany's capacity to wage modern warfare ended when the Allies finally won air supremacy and bombed Hitler's coal-to-gasoline production plants.

The war in the Pacific was likewise heavily influenced by oil and by attempts to interrupt its flow. In the months prior to Pearl Harbor, the United States imposed an embargo of scrap steel and oil to Japan as a sign of its disapproval of Japan's invasion of China. With the United States supplying 80 percent of Japanese oil, the embargo forced Japan to set its sights on the Dutch East Indies oil fields. The Japanese knew that the supply line of oil from the Dutch East Indies to Japan was long and vulnerable to naval interruption. Only one navy was powerful enough to interrupt Japan's oil lifeline; the oil embargo made Pearl Harbor inevitable. Severing the lifeline of raw materials and oil to Japan from its conquered territories in Southeast Asia was a major goal of the war in the Pacific.

**Era of the Seven Sisters**

For over a half-century, between the First World War and the oil crisis of 1973, the world oil business was conducted largely through the seven sisters: Exxon, Shell, British Petroleum (BP), Gulf, Texaco, Mobil, and Chevron, each ranking among the world's largest companies. Exxon, Mobil, and Chevron were the leftovers of the Standard Oil Trust breakup. Gulf and Texaco were the products of keeping Standard Oil out of Texas (Exxon eventually became a major player in Texas through its subsidiary, Humble Oil). BP, Churchill's brainchild, branched out far from its original purpose. Since the 1973 oil crisis, the seven sisters have been reduced to four: Exxon and Mobil have recombined, Chevron purchased Gulf Oil and combined with Texaco, and BP, while it did not combine with any of the other seven sisters, absorbed three leftovers of the Standard Oil breakup, Sohio, Amoco, and Arco. Apparently, the earlier conflicts that had plagued attempts to amalgamate had been overcome. As the decades passed, top executives with no links to the founders or their immediate successors, stepped aside to let others head the amalgamations, their hurt feelings assuaged by generous bonuses and retirement packages.

The seven sisters were fully integrated multinational companies that controlled every facet of the oil business. Upstream activities included exploring and developing oil fields. Downstream activities included refining crude oil and distributing refined products by pipelines, tankers, and tank trucks to gas stations and industrial, commercial, and residential end users. The oil companies felt that they owned an oil field, even if it were located in a foreign nation under a concession agreement. Every aspect of the oil business from exploring, drilling, production, refining, distribution, and marketing was not only controlled but the assets in oil fields, pipelines, tankers, refineries, storage facilities, tank trucks, and filling stations were owned by the oil companies. Price and production volumes were set with the oil companies sitting on one side of the table and oil producers on the other, with a generally one-way dialog between the two. This world collapsed in 1973, a pivotal year in the oil industry.[14]

The seven sisters both competed and cooperated. They competed with one another over market share and cooperated with one another in exploring and developing oil-producing properties. Oil industry leaders had to learn to deal with this dichotomy, but in a way they were groomed to both cooperate and compete from the beginning. An individual I know was starting to climb the corporate ladder as drilling manager in an isolated part of South America. Over the hill was another individual in charge of drilling for a competing oil company. When a drill bit broke in the middle of nowhere, the individual could order a replacement from the home office but it would have taken weeks to receive it, which would have caused him to miss the scheduled completion date. Alternatively, he could walk over the hill and borrow one from his competitor. The competitor's drilling manager was more than willing to cooperate because he knew that he now also had a ready source of replacement parts across the hill that would allow him to complete his drilling program on time. Because the performance of both men would be judged in terms of the time and cost required to complete their respective drilling programs, both advanced their careers by walking over the hill when they needed spare parts.

Costly and risky oil exploration and development programs are often carried out by a syndicate of oil companies. The potentially enormous losses associated with exploration and oil-field development can be spread over the participating companies in a syndicate without having a single oil company bear the entire risk of loss. The risk of loss has not been reduced, but the extent of loss a single company must bear is limited to its share of the syndicate. But to some degree, the risk of loss is reduced since cooperation allows oil companies to share particular skill sets and technological expertise with others. Thus, not every company has to be an expert in every facet of exploration and development. In a well-structured syndicate, companies assume responsibility for specific functions they are particularly adept at fulfilling. Nevertheless, each participant keeps a wary eye on the others to ensure that no one takes advantage of a situation as Deterding did with Marcus.

## Opening Up the Middle East

The opening up of the Middle East is synonymous with the rise of Calouste Gulbenkian. His father and uncle were petty merchants who rose to the position of being responsible for collecting revenues for the Sultan's privy purse in Mesopotamia. This gave them the opportunity to found a merchant bank to finance transactions between Constantinople and Baghdad.[15] As a reward for Gulbenkian's father's service to the Sublime Porte, he was given the governorship of Trebizond, where he became involved with kerosene imports from Baku on behalf of the Turkish government. Through contacts developed with the Baku oil exporters as a representative of the Turkish Crown, he enriched himself greatly as a private merchant handling kerosene imports into the Ottoman Empire.

His son Calouste was educated in Britain. As a young man in the 1890s, Gulbenkian was sent to the Caucasus to learn about oil, which began his lifelong interest in oil. He wrote a book about his experiences, including an assessment of the Baku oil industry, which attracted the attention of the Turkish Crown. Gulbenkian was commissioned to do a report on oil prospects in Mesopotamia (now Iraq). The book was a compilation of existing sources plus observations from railroad engineers who had been in Mesopotamia, a place Gulbenkian was never to visit. The book whetted the Sultan's appetite and induced him to transfer enormous land holdings from the government to the Crown for his personal aggrandisement should oil be discovered.

Fleeing Turkey with his family during the Armenian massacres of 1896, Gulbenkian appeared on the world stage of oil as the London representative of Mantachoff, a leading Armenian Russian oil magnate. Gulbenkian worked with Frederick Lane, who he considered the father of the British oil industry, to bring Russian oil interests into the Royal Dutch-Shell Group. Gulbenkian's experience led him to believe in the importance of pooling oil resources, production, and marketing to achieve price stability, an idea shared by others responsible for creating the oil industry. Unlike his father, Gulbenkian had no interest in the business aspects of oil. He saw himself as a creative architect of oil business arrangements. His failure to seize upon an early opportunity to get involved with an oil concession in Persia, which became the basis for the Anglo-Persian Oil Company, led him to adopt his lifelong business obsession—never give up an oil concession!

In 1908, an oil strike in Persia whetted Gulbenkian's interest in Mesopotamia. Gulbenkian convinced Deterding to open a Constantinople office with Gulbenkian in charge, although he also continued to be a financial advisor to the Turkish embassies in Paris and London and to the Turkish government. However, others shared Gulbenkian's intuitive insight. The Germans were eager to build a railroad to Baghdad that would give them oil rights for about thirteen miles on both sides of the track. The Anglo-Persian Oil Company saw Mesopotamia as an area with great oil potential. The Ottoman-American Development Corporation also had its eye on Mesopotamia. The British government, alarmed over growing German influence in Turkey, needed someone known to European oil interests who spoke the language, had the contacts and knowledge of the oil industry, plus possessed the business acumen, skills, and foresight to represent their interests in the Near East. Gulbenkian possessed all these traits and was in the right place at the right time; if he had not existed, the British government would have had to invent him.

In 1910, in addition to his other activities with Shell and the Turkish government, Gulbenkian became an adviser to British financial interests when they formed the National Bank of Turkey in order to make loans within the Ottoman Empire. Working under the auspices of the National Bank of Turkey, Gulbenkian formed the Turkish Petroleum Company in 1912; Deutsche Bank held 25 percent of the stock, Gulbenkian 40 percent, and the National Bank of Turkey 35 percent. To entice Shell into the deal, Gulbenkian gave Shell a 25 percent interest, reducing his to 15 percent. Neither the National Bank of Turkey nor the Turkish Petroleum Company had any Turkish investors.

When Anglo-Persian Oil pursued an oil concession in Mesopotamia, Gulbenkian rearranged the shareholding in the Turkish Petroleum Company to include Anglo-Persian Oil. (Gulbenkian believed that it is better to embrace rather than fight a potential competitor.) The ownership of the Turkish Petroleum Company was now split: Anglo-Persian Oil had a 47.5 percent share, Deutsche Bank a 25 percent share, Shell 22.5 percent, and Gulbenkian 5 percent, with the Turkish National Bank no longer sitting at the shareholders' table. In 1914, just before the outbreak of the First World War, the Ottoman government wrote a letter to the British and German ambassadors in Constantinople acknowledging that the Turkish Petroleum Company had an oil concession in the provinces around Baghdad and Basra.

After the War, Britain and France proceeded to carve up the Middle East as spoils of war, excluding the United States because it had not officially declared war on Turkey. The British government agreed with Gulbenkian's assertion that the concession granted to the Turkish Petroleum Company by the Ottoman government was still valid, even though the Ottoman Empire no longer existed. The British government wanted to turn Deutsche Bank's quarter share over to Anglo-Persian Oil. To avoid giving too much power to Anglo-Persian Oil, Gulbenkian inveigled the French government to take over the German quarter share interest in the Turkish Petroleum Company as a war prize. In 1922 the U.S. government, concerned over a possible shortage of crude oil, negotiated an interest in the Turkish Petroleum Company in the name of the Near East Development Corporation (again with Gulbenkian's support, based on his practice of embracing potential rivals rather than fighting them). The corporation did not specifically name any U.S. oil companies, but was eventually represented by six; these were reduced to two, Exxon and Mobil. After deliberations with Gulbenkian's involvement, the Turkish Petroleum Company was evenly split among the Near East Development Corporation, the French government, Shell, and Anglo-Persian, which accepted a halving of its share for a 10 percent overriding royalty. The new reorganization still contained Gulbenkian's 5 percent share. This would become a bone of contention from this point forward between Mr. Five Per Cent and his partners, even though there was not a single drop of known oil reserves. Without any activity in oil production and marketing, the oilmen, working out of luxury hotel suites, saw no value in Gulbenkian's creative architectural corporate designs. Gulbenkian noted this lack of gratitude by remarking that "oil friends are slippery"!

In 1925, the new nation of Iraq signed an agreement with the Turkish Petroleum Company, to be renamed the Iraq Petroleum Company, whereby the government of Iraq would receive a royalty on any oil produced, if any were discovered, until 2000. At some point in the discussions, the government of Iraq was promised 20 percent participation, but the participation was excluded from the final agreement. This would be a bitter source of contention between the Iraq Petroleum Company, owned by the oil companies, and the host government of Iraq for nearly half a century.

All this maneuvering was merely an academic exercise because the Iraq Petroleum Company was a scrap of paper until the 1927 discovery of one of the world's largest oil fields. Gulbenkian now insisted that the concession granted by the Ottoman Empire was not restricted to Iraq, but included all the lands under the former empire. Gulbenkian took a map and drew a red line over what he thought was the former Ottoman Empire, which included all of the Middle East (Turkey, Jordan, Syria, Iraq, and Saudi Arabia) except Kuwait and Iran. Although the Ottoman Empire did control the religious centers along the Red Sea (what was to become Saudi Arabia), its control over the vast emptiness of deserts inhabited by nomads was nominal, to say the least. No one, including Gulbenkian, foresaw the implications of having what was to become Saudi Arabia within the Red Line Agreement. Signed in 1928, the Red Line Agreement stipulated that no oil field within the red line could be developed unless there was equal participation by the companies owning the Iraq Petroleum Company, which, of course, included Gulbenkian's 5 percent share.

As the only oil company with operating experience in producing Middle East oil, BP initially handled Iraqi oil production. Exxon and Mobil soon became more actively involved as did Compagnie Francaise de Petroles (CFP), a national oil company organized by the French government in 1924, modeled after BP, to handle its share of the Iraq Petroleum Company. The world of oil now had three governments involved with oil: the British government's half interest in an independently run BP with a concession in Iran and Iraq, the French government's wholly owned interest in an independently run CFP, with a concession in Iraq, and the Soviet Union, which exercised absolute control over its oil resources.

In addition to opening up the Middle East and playing second fiddle to Frederick Lane in bringing in Russian oil interests to the newly formed Shell Group, Gulbenkian brought Shell into the Turkish Petroleum Company and helped raise money for Shell as an intermediary with New York investment bankers. He also arranged contracts for Shell to supply the French and Italian governments with petroleum products during the war. In 1918 he orchestrated the Shell takeover of Mexican Eagle Oil Company, the start of Shell's activities in Mexico. To further cement his relationship with Shell, Gulbenkian arranged for his son, Nubar, to become the personal assistant to Deterding. It was rumored at the time that Nubar might be in line to succeed Deterding, but his son's career with Shell ended abruptly some years later when Gulbenkian yanked him away to become his personal assistant.

Gulbenkian was asked to act on behalf of British investors with an oil concession in Venezuela called, appropriately, Venezuela Oil Concessions (VOC). Gulbenkian brought this investment opportunity to Deterding's attention, which ended up with Shell owning two-thirds of VOC and Gulbenkian and other shareholders, including Venezuelans, with the remaining third. Deterding believed that any investment made by Shell was to be controlled and run in the best interests of Shell. Deterding practiced what he preached. As majority and controlling owner, Shell was in a position to determine the price of oil exported from Venezuela. It was in Shell's financial interests to set a low price for the exported oil, but not in the financial interests of the minority VOC shareholders. Gulbenkian's failure to reach an agreement with Deterding on his behalf and the behalf of other minority shareholders eventually led to a breach between the two.

After the Second World War, Exxon and Mobil, the two remaining U.S. shareholders in the Iraq Petroleum Company, took on the decades-old task of squeezing out Gulbenkian's 5 percent share. During these discussions, Walter C. Teagle (Exxon's president) referred to Gulbenkian as an oil merchant, to which Gulbenkian angrily responded that he was a business architect, not an oil merchant, a perfect description of his role in oil. Gulbenkian once pointed to a strange-looking ship in a harbor and asked what it was and had to be told that the ship was a tanker that might be carrying his oil! While oilmen had a jaundiced view of Gulbenkian, Gulbenkian's view of oilmen as cats in the night—"by their sound no one can tell if they're fighting or making love!"—was equally negative.

Finally Gulbenkian was informed that the 1928 Red Line Agreement was void because it violated American antitrust legislation, an interesting tactic on the part of oil companies, which were occasionally threatened by Congress for violating the same legislation. For Gulbenkian's alleged violation, Exxon and Mobil stated that they were no longer bound by the 1928 Agreement. The revised 1948 Agreement left Exxon and Mobil free to develop Saudi Arabian oil reserves on their own. Between 1948 and 1954, Gulbenkian negotiated a replacement for the Red Line Agreement from his various hotel suites. The 1954 agreement not only reaffirmed his 5 percent interest in the Iraq Petroleum Company, but he was also reimbursed for previous unpaid receivables.

Gulbenkian's annual succession of seventeen- and eighteen-year-old mistresses ended with his death in 1955 at the age of eighty-six. After his death, he bequeathed the bulk of his wealth and future revenue to a foundation based in Lisbon. In the end, the oilmen won. Gulbenkian's 5 percent share was wiped out with the nationalization of the Iraq Oil Company in the 1970s; but so too were theirs. Nevertheless, the Gulbenkian Foundation has continued to prosper, with income from his shareholdings in a Middle East oil company and other investments.

## Early Attempts at Oil Price Controls

Rockefeller, of course, was the first to attempt to control prices, and he pretty much succeeded when he achieved 90 percent control over the U.S. refinery industry. His idea of an acceptable price for kerosene was the price that would not encourage outsiders to build refineries. Too high a price would only create more problems for Rockefeller by providing an incentive for others to get into the refining business. This idea is still alive. OPEC realizes that an oil price that is too high financially underwrites the development of high-cost non-OPEC oil fields that will eventually erode OPEC's market share.

The first to attempt to bring order to the oil industry on a global scale was the oil power brokers of the day, Teagle, of Exxon (a distant relative of Maurice Clark, Rockefeller's first partner) and Deterding, of Shell. In 1922 they stood together, along with others, to present a united front in dealing with oil sales by the Soviet Union, which they viewed as buying back stolen property.

While the two power brokers were shaking hands and expressing mutual dismay over Soviet duplicity in expropriating oil properties without compensation, Deterding secretly purchased a large quantity of Soviet oil at less than the agreed price with Exxon, which he promptly dumped in the Far East. Subsequent attempts by Teagle and Deterding to restore some semblance of order sometimes worked and sometimes did not, but in 1927 Deterding abandoned any further pretext of cooperating with Exxon over the matter of Soviet oil. This time the reason was not related to oil, but to his second marriage to a White Russian. Cross-accusations between Teagle and Deterding eventually induced Deterding to start what turned out to be a disastrous price war. The Soviets thought that they had succeeded in creating chaos in the world oil patch by successfully playing one oil company off another, perhaps bringing back memories of the Nobels and the Rothschilds. Soviet satisfaction over spreading confusion in the capitalistic world of oil stemmed not so much from their conspiratorial plans, or Deterding's ill-fated venture into a price war, but from a world flooded with crude from the Soviet Union, Mexico, and Venezuela.

The 1920s started with a feeling that oil would be in short supply, so the U.S. government forced Exxon and Mobil to get involved with Middle East oil through its interest in the Turkish Petroleum Company. By the late 1920s, and continuing on through the global depression of the 1930s, the world was awash in oil. Something had to be done. Oil companies had made massive investments on the basis of a certain projected price of crude oil; as crude prices sank, so did the return on these investments. In 1928, in a Scottish castle, Deterding held a social affair that happened to include Teagle from Exxon and Mellon from Gulf Oil and other oil magnates, including the head of BP. This social affair led to a pooling arrangement to control price through cooperation in production and in sharing incremental demand among the cartel of supposedly competing oil companies. The reference price would be American oil in the U.S. Gulf, with adjustments to take into account freight from the U.S. Gulf.

Once this system was set up, other oil companies joined. If a participating oil company purchased oil in the Middle East and sold it in France, the selling price would not be the FOB price in the Middle East plus freight from the Middle East to France, but the price of oil in the U.S. Gulf plus freight from the U.S. Gulf to France. This system stabilized the price at a healthy level for the oil companies as long as others joined, which they did. With a mechanism in place for allocating incremental production to meet growing demand among the participating oil companies, the global oil business, with the exception of Soviet oil, was under the control of a cartel of oil companies. Of course, for those U.S. oil companies involved in this arrangement to fix pricing and production was in direct violation of the Sherman Antitrust Act. The Rockefeller dream of world control over oil, for the most part, had finally come true, but not with domination vested in the hands of an individual, but a small group of executives who, in the aggregate, controlled most of the world oil. The success of this agreement hinged on all the individuals continuing to cooperate, something rarely seen in the world of oil.

In 1930, only two years after the system was set up, price stability was threatened by yet another mammoth oil discovery. Like Drake and Higgens, an old wildcatter, Dad Joiner, persisted where others had given up. Joiner did not drill on land that had promising geologic characteristics but on land owned by promising widows who might invest in Joiner's ventures. Joiner must have had a way with the widows for they were all financially disappointed with Joiner's ventures; except for one, on whose east Texas farm in Kilgore Joiner brought in a gusher. Joiner had proved the oil geologists wrong and Kilgore became another Pit Hole and Spindletop all rolled into one, with oil derricks almost on top of one another pumping with all their might. This strike would lead to the discovery of other oil fields in east Texas much larger than anyone imagined. Unfortunately, Joiner was in financial straits from his past ventures with widows and could not hold onto his holdings.

Forced to sell out to H.L. Hunt, who made billions on Joiner's and other east Texas properties, Joiner was to die as poor as Drake and Higgens.

The east Texas oil boom, coming at the time of the Great Depression, created a glut and oil prices collapsed locally to ten cents a barrel. Teagle and Deterding were powerless because they did not control the east Texas oil fields. The Texas "independents" demanded federal and state intervention. The state governments of Texas and Oklahoma obliged and declared martial law on the basis that the independents were squandering a valuable natural resource, particularly at ten cents a barrel. Using conservation to justify the states' actions, and the local militia to enforce their will, oil production was stopped. Then the Texas Railroad Commission was authorized to set up a rationing system to control production. Although individual producers cheated whenever they could, the Texas Railroad Commission eventually got the upper hand over the producers and was able to ration production of individual wells and prices rose. This government action to protect and conserve a natural resource, which today would be viewed as environmentally desirable, served the interests of the global oil cartel as well. Thus, capitalism and conservation joined hands with a common objective, but different goals. Deterding's pooling arrangement and the Texas Railroad Commission's rationing of production stabilized the world price of oil and both were valuable lessons for OPEC when it gained control over oil prices and production in the 1970s.

## Enter Saudi Arabia and Kuwait

With the price of oil reestablished by controlling east Texas production, the last thing the oil companies wanted was another east Texas discovery. Another oil rogue, New Zealander Frank Holmes, believed that oil was waiting to be discovered in Arabia. Gulbenkian's Red Line Agreement prohibited exploration in Arabia without the joint cooperation of the signatories. Socal, the name of Chevron at that time, was not a signatory of the Red Line Agreement, and for $50,000 bought Holmes's concession in Bahrain, an island nation off of Saudi Arabia, and in 1931 struck oil. While Bahrain would never become a major oil producer, it indicated that Holmes might be right about Arabia.

In 1927, the desert king Ibn Saud subdued his rivals along the Red Sea coastline and named his new kingdom after his clan. In 1930, desperate for money, King Saud inveigled Socal to buy a concession in Saudi Arabia. The major oil companies, bound by the Red Line Agreement and in no mood to discover more oil, passed up the opportunity to make a deal with King Saud. Socal did some exploration, which turned out to be promising; but short on capital in the event that oil were discovered, the company teamed up with Texaco, another nonsignatory to the Red Line Agreement. Texaco bought a half share of Socal's interests in Bahrain and Saudi Arabia. Eventually oil was discovered in Saudi Arabia, and in 1939 King Saud opened up a valve and oil began to flow into an awaiting tanker. The king was so pleased that he increased Socal's and Texaco's concession to an area as large as Texas, Louisiana, Oklahoma, and New Mexico combined.

Frank Holmes was also involved with opening up Kuwait, which was also outside of the Red Line Agreement. Eventually BP and Gulf set up a joint venture after a fair degree of behind-the-scenes maneuvering by the British and U.S. governments. In 1938 oil was discovered. Although Frank Holmes was instrumental in opening up oil exploration in Bahrain, Saudi Arabia, and Kuwait, all successful finds, he made no fortune from the enormous wealth that he was instrumental in creating for the oil companies and producers. Originating and transforming a good idea to reality does not necessarily translate into personal wealth. This is the lesson of Drake, Higgens, Joiner, and Holmes; something else was needed.

## Exit the Key Players

Hitler inadvertently took down three leading oil company executives. The first to fall was Deterding, who was showing signs of mental imbalance (megalomania) as his management style became increasingly dictatorial. In his memoirs, composed in 1934 in the midst of the Great Depression, when tens of millions of idle workers were desperately seeking work, he wrote that all idlers should be shot on sight. Upset over the loss of Shell properties in Russia after the revolution, Deterding's position against communism hardened with his second marriage to a White Russian and his third to a German. Deterding became a Nazi sympathizer because of their determination to rip communism out root and branch. Deterding would not be the only industrialist, statesman, monarchist, or church leader to support the Nazis for this reason. The board of directors removed Deterding from his position in 1936 by forcing him to retire, and he died six months before the war started. Shell's penchant for collegiality and corroboration in the decision-making process might be partly in reaction to Deterding's last years of rule.

The second to fall was Rieber, the head of Texaco. In 1937 Rieber diverted Texaco tankers taking oil to Belgium to support Franco in Spain, and in 1940 he got around a British oil embargo against Germany by shipping oil to Germany from neutral ports. Unable to take money out of Germany, Rieber worked out a barter agreement whereby he accepted German-built tankers in exchange for oil. Rieber was forced to resign in 1940 in the wake of a British intelligence revelation that a Texaco employee was sending information to Germany about American war preparations.

The third to fall was Teagle, who had entered into an agreement before the rise of Hitler with I.G. Farben, a German chemical company. Farben was to research and develop synthetic rubber for Exxon in exchange for Exxon's patents for tetraethyl lead, a vital ingredient in aviation fuel. Teagle was unable to see the military implications of this arrangement even after Hitler's rise to power and after the Japanese had overrun the rubber plantations in Southeast Asia. Teagle refused to break what he considered first and foremost a business deal, which remained in force until revelations by the U.S. Justice Department led to his resignation in 1942.

All three were counterpoints to Marcus Samuel, who put civic duties and patriotism above business. Deterding, Teagle, and Rieber put business above all else. Buy for a little less here, sell for a little more there, was their key to success. Business plans were to fit the immutable laws of supply and demand. The name of the game is making money. Politicians come and go and have little use other than passing laws and establishing regulations that protect business interests or guarantee their success. Governments rise and fall, but business remains forever; it is the great constant.

## Shareholders and Stakeholders

The modern corporation is based on the premise that its mission is maximizing shareholder wealth. One way to do this is to spawn new products and expand market reach to millions of individuals as Rockefeller did. Another way to maximize shareholder wealth is to widen the spread between the price received for a product and its cost of production, also a Rockefeller practice. While maximizing wealth for a corporation's shareholders is what the game is all about, there are other constituencies, or stakeholders, affected by the operation of a private corporation. For instance, an oil company has some degree of latitude concerning where profits are assigned. Profits can be shifted between upstream activities (crude oil production) or downstream activities (refining and marketing) through internal transfer prices. If an oil company has its oil fields, refineries, distribution system, and market within the borders of a single nation, such as the United States, it does not matter how profit is assigned internally when a company consolidates its financial statements and tax returns. The federal government collects the same in income taxes regardless of how internal transfer prices are set, although internal transfer prices can affect state income taxes. When an oil company is buying crude oil from one nation, processing it in a second, and selling in a third, the internal assignment of profits through transfer pricing can heavily influence taxes and royalties paid by oil companies to host governments. This in turn affects the well-being of the people of oil-exporting nations, who are, in every sense of the word, stakeholders in a company that is exploiting their nation's natural resources.

Deterding noted the importance of the triangle linking the mutual interests of an oil company with the people and with the host government in which all three should benefit from developing a nation's oil resources.[16] Although Shell operated in Mexico, the government and the people felt they were getting a raw deal from the oil companies and, in 1938, nationalized the industry. The oil companies struck back by refusing to buy Mexican oil until they received restitution, which Pemex, the newly formed national oil company of Mexico, was forced to pay in order to gain access to foreign markets. Now two nations directly controlled their oil resources: the Soviet Union and Mexico. Yet the oil companies did not learn the essential lesson of Mexico—a one-sided relationship in which an oil company exploited the oil resources of a nation with limited benefit to the people or the government was not in the best long-term interests of the oil company. No one viewed Mexico as a harbinger of more to come when new oil discoveries in Venezuela diverted oil company attention from Mexico.

## Development of Saudi Arabia's Oil Fields

Saudi Arabia was the answer to Washington's worry, one that had first bothered Theodore Roosevelt and would come back now and then to haunt government energy policymakers: The world was going to run out of oil. Socal and Texaco operated in Saudi Arabia under the corporate umbrella of Aramco, the Arabian-American Oil Company. Socal and Texaco advanced the idea during the early years of the Second World War of the U.S. government setting up a Petroleum Reserve Corporation to buy a controlling interest in Aramco and constructing a refinery in the Persian Gulf. The idea was well received by Franklin D. Roosevelt, who, like Churchill, was attracted by the idea of government ownership of a foreign oil field. However, the oil companies abruptly broke off negotiations in 1943. Only in hindsight can one see the timing between the success of Rommel in North Africa and the proposal for the Petroleum Reserve Corporation and Rommel's defeat in 1943 with the proposal's demise. Obviously, oil company investments in the Middle East would be in danger if Rommel succeeded in his master plan to link his army in North Africa with Hitler's in Baku. Oil companies generally oppose government intervention in their operations unless, of course, such intervention promotes their agenda.

The U.S. government then proposed constructing a thousand-mile pipeline to carry Saudi crude to the Mediterranean and the oil companies would guarantee a 20 percent interest in the oil fields as a naval reserve. The Trans-Arabian Pipeline (Tapline) pipeline was completed, without U.S. government involvement, in 1950 when Saudi crude was loaded on a tanker in Sidon, Lebanon. The pipeline, passing through Saudi Arabia, Syria, and Lebanon, was shut down in 1975 during a time of turmoil in Lebanon. However, the pipeline's capability of carrying oil cheaply to Europe when in operation meant a great deal to Socal and Texaco.

Having achieved such success in Saudi Arabia, Socal and Texaco passed up an opportunity to become dominant players in the oil business by not wanting to challenge the other major oil companies. They felt that involvement of the other major oil companies was necessary for access to oil markets, capital to develop Saudi oil resources, and garnering diplomatic support if there were an unfriendly successor to King Saud. Admitting Exxon and Mobil and excluding the other signatory oil companies violated the Red Line Agreement. Using American antitrust legislation as a lame excuse, Exxon and Mobil walked away from the Red Line Agreement and joined Aramco, thereby locking BP, Shell, and CFP out of Saudi Arabia.

Aramco proved to be a model for a company operating in a host nation. Its employees had their own town and concentrated on the business of finding, developing, and operating the oil fields and building and running refineries, pipelines, and terminals. By any measure, Aramco was considered a "good corporate citizen." Aramco permitted the United States to have two allies diametrically opposed to one another. The state department dealt directly with Israel and, when necessary, used Aramco as a go-between in its dealings with Saudi Arabia. In the twenty-first century the company is known as Saudi Aramco, with 54,000 employees of whom 86 percent are Saudis. The company prides itself on its ability to manage Saudi energy resources and contribute to the nation's development.

*Shoes Begin to Fall*

It is one matter when foreign producers supply 10 percent of the world's oil, which can easily be replaced by other sources. This keeps the producers in a weak bargaining position as they learned in Mexico. It is another matter when their share grows to 30–40 percent, which no longer can be replaced; then their bargaining position is not quite so weak. The oil companies failed to realize the growing bargaining strength of the oil producers that accompanied the growing world dependence on foreign oil. The next shoe to fall after the Mexican nationalization of its oil industry came in 1948, when Venezuela passed a law for a 50:50 sharing of profits, an idea of Juan Pablo Perez Alfonso, the Venezuelan oil minister and chief architect of OPEC. The idea was not total anathema to the oil companies if sharing profits meant forestalling nationalization as had occurred in Mexico (better to have half than none). Moreover, the oil companies had the power to define profitability by how they allocated profits through internal transfer pricing.

King Saud, whose huge family's lifestyle had become incredibly expensive, joined the fray and demanded a share of the profits. Aramco turned to the U.S. government for support, and the government, fearing a communist takeover in the Middle East, agreed to have the Aramco partners treat the additional payments to Saudi Arabia as a foreign income tax. This was a great boon to the Aramco partners because this meant, under rules on double taxation, that taxes paid to the U.S. government would decrease one dollar for every extra dollar in taxes paid to Saudi Arabia. In other words, the U.S. government, hence U.S. taxpayers, was subsidizing the extra cost of oil. Such a ruling could not be restricted to some oil companies, equal treatment demanded that this apply for all. The upshot of this ruling was that it became more profitable for oil companies to develop oil properties overseas than domestically. The oil companies could shift a part of what they were paying foreign suppliers in the form of taxes to reduce their U.S. taxes, something that would not apply to a U.S. source of supply. Another tax bonanza for the oil companies was applying the oil depletion allowance to foreign as well as domestic sources of oil. These two tax rulings placed oil companies in a quasi tax-free environment at that time, which is not true today.

*Next Shoe to Fall*

BP, still half-owned by the British government, had expanded into activities far beyond those envisioned by Churchill. While its principal source of oil was still Iran, BP had a major position in Iraq and Kuwait and had developed a worldwide marketing network served by its fleet of tankers. In 1951, a new Iranian leader appeared on the scene, Mohammad Mossadegh, who called for nationalization of Iranian oil fields after BP's refusal to adopt a deal similar to that between Aramco and Saudi Arabia. The Iranian prime minister, who opposed Mossadegh, stated that he would not allow Iran to repudiate its concession with BP. That remark caused his assassination, opening the way for Mossadegh to become prime minister and nationalize BP's oil fields. The Labor Party, then in power in Britain, was hardly in a position to enforce this legacy of colonialism. With no help from the British government, BP took legal action, not in Iran, but in every nation where a cargo of Iranian oil landed. This lasted two years. By then the civil unrest that resulted from the loss of revenue led to a coup, encouraged by the CIA, which reinstated the son of a previous shah. In 1954 an agreement was hammered out whereby the National Iranian Oil Company, formed by Mossadegh, would remain owner of the oil fields along with the Abadan refinery. However, the oil would be sold through a consortium in which BP had a 40 percent share, Shell 14 percent, with the rest divided among CFP and the five remaining American sisters. In other words, the seven sisters, eight counting CFP, had total market control over Iranian oil production. The agreement taught the oil companies their first lesson—ownership of an oil field is not nearly as critical as access to its oil.

Later on, five smaller U.S. oil companies inveigled a 5 percent share. Among these were Getty Oil and Tidewater, both owned by Jean Paul Getty. Getty was the son of a lawyer who struck it rich in oil in Oklahoma. The son was just as talented, if not more, as his father. Getty became a billionaire, partly as a result of his flying with an oil geologist over the Neutral Zone between Saudi Arabia and Kuwait. The Kuwait side of the Neutral Zone was already producing oil. The geologist noted from the air that a certain sector of the Neutral Zone in Saudi Arabia had geologic features similar to that of the oil-producing sector in Kuwait. Getty immediately started negotiating with Ibn Saud for a concession. Drilling revealed a huge oil field, big enough to make Getty a billionaire and for the geologist to be reimbursed for his travel expenses.

Besides Getty there was Hunt, another billionaire not given to sharing with those responsible for his wealth (Dad Joiner comes to mind), and Armand Hammer. Hammer had received a medical degree but did not practice medicine, as his father had, who had befriended Lenin. Hammer took advantage of his father's relationship with Lenin to make commercial deals in the Soviet Union, including setting up a pencil factory and purchasing Russian art treasures for pennies on the dollar. Hammer, at an age when many contemplate retiring, got interested in oil and eventually took over a small oil company called Occidental Petroleum. By dint of his determination and driving force, Hammer transformed Occidental Petroleum into an international oil company with the discovery of three major oil fields in Libya. Hammer would play a pivotal role in the oil crisis of 1973.

Another thorn in the side of the seven sisters was Enrico Mattei, head of the Italian State Oil Company, who was able to prick the seven sisters by negotiating an independent concession with the Iranian National Oil Company (NIOC) in 1957 and making a private deal with Khrushchev for cheap Soviet oil, much as Deterding before him had done. The seven sisters then had to contend with CFP's discovery of oil in Algeria. New discoveries of supply remained ahead of rapidly growing demand. Despite the best efforts of the seven sisters to keep production matched with demand to sustain prices, there was a glut of oil on the market and oil prices remained cheap. Unbeknownst to the Iranian government, the oil companies in the consortium that purchased the output of the NIOC made a secret side-agreement to reduce Iranian sales in order to avoid a global glut of oil. Neither the shah nor the NIOC knew about this agreement, which effectively made Iran a swing producer to maintain world oil prices.

This perhaps marked the zenith of oil company power. The oil companies had reinstated their position

Table 5.1

**Shareholders' Ownership Percentage**

|  | Iran Consortium | Iraq IPC | Saudi Arabia Aramco | Kuwait KOC | Abu Dhabi Petroleum |
|---|---|---|---|---|---|
| BP | 40 | 23.750 | — | 50 | 23.750 |
| Shell | 14 | 23.750 | — | — | 23.750 |
| Exxon | 7 | 11.875 | 30 | — | 11.875 |
| Mobil | 7 | 11.875 | 10 | — | 11.875 |
| Gulf | 7 | — | — | 50 | — |
| Texaco | 7 | — | 30 | — | — |
| Socal | 7 | — | 30 | — | — |
| CFP | 6 | 23.750 | — | — | 23.750 |
| Others | 5 | — | — | — | — |

in Iran even though their properties had been nationalized by preventing access to the world market, the same stratagem used in Mexico. Mossadegh's political demise served as a warning to other interlopers. Notwithstanding the success of Hunt, Getty, Hammer, and Mattei, there were limited opportunities for third parties to reach the market unless they went through one or more of the seven sisters. The seven sisters exerted the power of Rockefeller's horizontal monopoly on a global scale. Table 5.1 lists the shareholders of the various Middle East oil concessions in play up to the eve of the 1973 oil crisis.

Nasser's 1956 takeover of the Suez Canal did not affect the oil companies as much as it created fortunes for tanker owners. Because it took longer to get the oil around South Africa, Humble Oil, the Texas subsidiary of Exxon, took advantage of the temporary shortage of oil in Europe and raised crude prices by thirty-five cents per barrel. This incurred the wrath of Congress, which from a contemporary perspective appears ludicrous when price changes of thirty-five cents per barrel are hardly noticed. Of course, thirty-five cents per barrel of oil when it cost around $2 per barrel was a large percentage change. What this showed was a major consuming government's keen interest in keeping a lid on oil prices; in fact, one might conclude that consuming governments depended on oil companies to keep a lid on oil prices. Keeping communists out of the oil-producing nations and keeping oil prices low for consumers were the reasons why the U.S. government never seriously pursued antitrust actions against the American oil majors, which clearly violated the Sherman Antitrust Act when they cooperated with competitors to fix prices and limit production. The British government took a far more pragmatic view of the situation and did not share the U.S. government's vexation when oil companies attempted to stabilize something as critical to the world economy as oil.

**Birth of OPEC**

By the late 1950s cheap Soviet crude was cutting into the seven sisters' markets in Italy, India, and Japan. The seven sisters had to lower their prices in these nations to maintain their market presence, which, of course, meant lower profit margins. In 1959, Exxon resolved that it must cut posted prices to oil producers to preserve its profit margin. When the other oil companies followed suit, the Arab oil producers organized the first meeting of the Arab Petroleum Congress, the fruit of private talks between the oil ministers of Venezuela and Saudi Arabia. A second round of Exxon-inspired cuts provoked a stronger surge of unity among the oil producers. Another meeting in 1960 of the oil ministers of Saudi Arabia, Iran, Iraq, Kuwait, and Venezuela gave birth to the Organization of Petroleum Exporting Countries (OPEC). The purpose of OPEC was not to raise oil prices but to prevent further reductions in posted prices. The original unity of purpose was gone by the second OPEC meeting in 1961, when a rough and tumble battle broke out among OPEC members as each sought to garner a larger export volume at the expense of others. OPEC was behaving no differently than the earliest oil drillers in Pit Hole; it was every man for himself.

By no measure could OPEC be considered a success during the 1960s. There was little coordination among the members and politics kept getting in the way of negotiations. Meanwhile, new sources were coming onstream, such as Nigeria, putting more pressure on OPEC's approach to maximizing revenue by maximizing production, another reminder of Pit Hole. In 1965, OPEC failed at an attempt to gain control over future increases in production just as it failed to gain control over current production. The seven sisters meanwhile were trying to restrain production to prevent further declines in oil prices. The irony is that in only ten years, OPEC would take over the oil companies' role of restraining production to control prices. The role reversal would not be complete as the OPEC idea of price in the 1970s would be radically different than that of the oil companies in the 1960s.

The 1967 Six-Day War between Israel and Egypt sparked the first Arab boycott. The war was over before the boycott had any effect, which was doomed anyway when Venezuela and Iran refused to join. The formation of the Organization of Arab Petroleum Exporting Countries (OAPEC) within OPEC in 1970 did not succeed in strengthening the resolve of OPEC to bring order to the oil market. Order, of course, meant maximizing the respective production volume of each member to maximize revenue. Oil company attempts to rein in production to maintain prices, which varied for each member of OPEC, irritated the oil producers who now had to contend with new oil production from Qatar, Dubai, Oman, and Abu Dhabi.

In 1970, the Alyeska Pipeline Company was formed to handle the 1968 oil discovery by Arco (then Atlantic Richfield) in Prudhoe Bay on the north slope of Alaska. Compared to the Middle East exporters, this is expensive oil. Arco, short on crude, viewed the development of the North Slope field as vital to its survival. Two other major participants were Exxon and BP, the latter having acquired Sohio to gain greater access to the U.S. market. These two companies, with more cheap Middle East oil than they wanted, did not need expensive North Slope oil. At first the environmentalists were successful in blocking the building of an 800-mile pipeline to Valdez. Congress set an interesting precedent by overriding environmental concerns in the wake of the 1973 oil crisis and authorized the construction of the pipeline. Alaskan oil began flowing in 1977.

Another source of high-cost oil was the 1969 discovery of the Ekofisk oil field in the Norwegian sector of the North Sea by Phillips Petroleum. This was followed a year later by the BP discovery of the Forties field north of Aberdeen and the following year by the Shell and Exxon discoveries of the Brent field off the Shetland Islands. The involvement of Exxon, BP, and Shell in oil fields far more costly to develop than buying Middle East crude, intentionally or unintentionally, could be interpreted as manifesting their concern over the rising dependence on Middle East oil.

The 1973 oil crisis was not caused by a shortage of oil. Indeed, the greatest worry right up to the eve of the crisis was how to keep new production from flooding the market and further weakening oil prices. The producers were worried about anything that would shrink their export volumes. The shah of Iran wanted to increase export volumes in order to expand Iran's military power and develop its economy, and saw his role as a guarantor of stability of the Middle East, for which he had received President Richard Nixon's blessing.

## 1973 Oil Crisis

Figure 5.1 shows the growth of world oil consumption from the beginning of the oil age and OPEC production since 1960.[17]

Figure 5.1  **Growth in World Oil Consumption and OPEC Production** (MM Tpy)

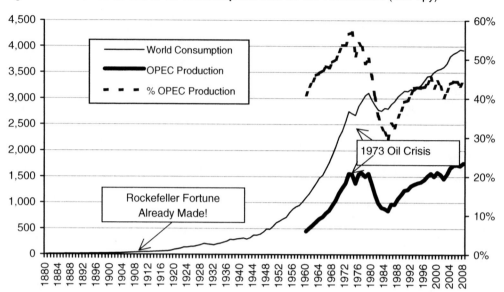

From the birth of the automobile age around 1900, oil consumption began to double about every decade. Even the Great Depression did not dampen growth in oil consumption, but the age of oil did not begin in earnest until after the Second World War, when successive doublings really started to kick in (one penny doubled is two pennies, two pennies doubled is four, doubled again eight, doubled again sixteen, doubled again thirty-two). The slopes of the curves for both world oil consumption and OPEC production appear about the same from 1960 to 1973, which implies that nearly all incremental oil demand was coming from the OPEC nations. A closer examination reveals that in 1960 OPEC was supplying 38 percent of world oil consumption, 47 percent in 1965, and 56 percent in 1973, meaning that OPEC exports were growing faster than world oil demand. Much of this rapid growth in consumption was in Europe and Japan, both recovering from the War. While oil consumption growth in the United States was more subdued, nevertheless the U.S. was heavily responsible for growth in OPEC demand as it made the transition from being the world's largest oil exporter to the world's largest oil importer, as shown in Figure 5.2.

The early 1970s was a period of rapidly rising U.S. oil imports, of which a greater portion was coming from the Middle East. The oil crisis halted growth in U.S. consumption, and twenty years were to pass before U.S. consumption would surpass its 1978 peak. Middle East exports around 2000 were just about back to where they were in the late 1970s. Though the United States is criticized as the energy hog of the world, its share of the oil pie has been much worse in the past. The U.S. portion of world oil consumption was 42 percent in 1960, which declined to 23 percent by 2008. Obviously, incremental growth in oil consumption has been concentrated elsewhere.

The high point of oil company ascendancy over national powers was the BP-inspired embargo against Mossadegh that led to his fall from power in 1953 and brought Iran to heel. Between then and the 1973 oil crisis, there was a shift from a buyers' to a sellers' market that occurred without public fanfare. The question raised by Figure 5.2 is—why did it take so long? Another way of putting it, from the consumers' perspective, would be that the oil companies should be congratulated because they had kept oil prices low for as long as they did. Yet, there had to be an

Figure 5.2  **U.S. Oil Consumption, Production, and Imports** (000 Bpd)

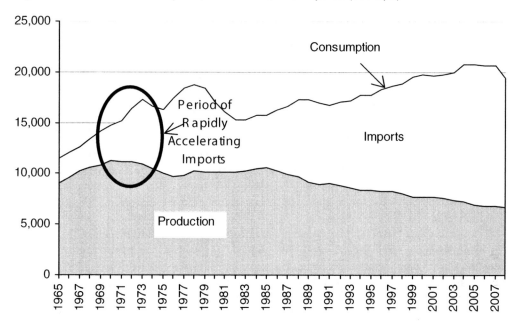

underlying unease with respect to the state of the oil market. Why else would major oil companies start searching for oil in such high-cost areas as the North Slope and the North Sea?

The underlying shift from a buyers' to a sellers' market needed a precipitating event to make it manifest. Actually, it was a series of events that started with Colonel Gadhafi's successful military coup in Libya in 1969. At this time, Libya was supplying about one-quarter of Europe's needs with high-quality and low-sulfur crude. Moreover, Libya is located on the right side of the Suez Canal from the point of view of European oil buyers. The Canal was closed in 1956, then reopened in 1957 when Nasser nationalized it, then closed again in 1967 during the Israeli-Arab War and not reopened until 1975. Libya received no premium for its oil, considering its quality and nearness to market. Gadhafi was not to be cowed by the major oil companies' resistance to any price change. In 1970, Gadhafi struck at the weakest link in the supply chain: the independents, particularly those dependent on Libyan crude. Of these, the most dependent was Occidental Petroleum. Gadhafi chose his target wisely.

Hammer pleaded with the majors to sell him replacement oil at the same price he was paying for Libyan oil. In their shortsightedness, they offered Hammer higher-priced oil. Facing a disastrous interruption to supply, Occidental gave in to Gadhafi's new price and tax demands, which were relatively modest from today's perspective. Flushed with victory, Gadhafi went after the majors. To everyone's surprise, the majors did not embargo Libyan crude and replace it from other sources as they had with Mexico and Iran. Instead, they capitulated to Gadhafi's demands, a stiff price to pay for not coming to Hammer's aid. The producers now sensed that a fundamental change had taken place in the market. The world was shifting from a buyers' to a sellers' market.

As a consequence of Gadhafi's success, a hastily convened OPEC meeting in Caracas in late 1970 agreed to higher minimum taxes and higher posted prices that, when announced, only made Gadhafi leapfrog with even greater demands, followed by Venezuela. This infuriated the shah because this challenged his leadership. To shore up the resistance of the independents to further

OPEC demands, the majors agreed that appropriately priced replacement oil would be provided to the independents to prevent them from caving in to producer demands. It was too late.

With U.S. government support, the oil companies attempted to get the oil producers to agree to common terms and to moderate their demands, that is, to get control over Gadhafi. A meeting was held in Tehran in 1971 attended by delegates from the oil-producing nations, the oil companies, and the U.S. State Department. The shah insisted that Libya and Venezuela not attend. The majors hoped that the presence of the State Department would aid in their negotiations, but it proved to be a weak straw. The State Department wanted to avoid a confrontation between the oil companies and producers because it depended on Iran and Saudi Arabia to act as regional police to suppress communist-inspired radicals. The State Department and the oil majors were not on the same page. Similarly, government representatives of several European nations and Japan proved equally inept at influencing the outcome. Without strong government backing, and considering the importance of OPEC oil in the general scheme of things, the oil companies made no new demands and shifted their approach from confrontation to a call for moderation. It was now a matter of damage control.

The capitulation of the oil companies to the oil producers was the final piece of evidence that convinced the oil producers that the market had shifted in their favor. One top oil executive publicly quipped that the buyers' market was over. The agreed price increase in February of 1971 was an extra thirty cents per barrel on top of the posted price, escalating to fifty cents per barrel in 1975. This price adjustment held for the Gulf producers; now a meeting was necessary with Libya. A separate Tripoli agreement, signed six weeks after the Tehran agreement, called for a higher price without Libya providing a similar guarantee on future prices. The shah was infuriated by Gadhafi's leapfrogging over what he had agreed to.

Whereas the 1960s were years of worry over looming oil gluts, the early 1970s were years of a growing concern over a potential shortage, a reversal of the change in perception that occurred between the early and late 1920s. This change in sentiment spurred the oil producers to increase their demands for part ownership of their natural resources in the two-year hiatus between the Tehran agreement and the oil crisis of 1973. The oil producers felt that the original concessions granted to oil companies belonged to a bygone age of colonialism and imperialism. They wanted to move into the modern era and control their national resources through joint ownership rather than merely collecting taxes on their exports. The producers favored joint ownership with the oil companies over nationalization because nationalization removed the oil companies' incentive for making money in the upstream, or production, side of the business. By limiting their profits to the downstream side of refining and marketing, oil companies would only be interested in buying crude at the cheapest price and the producers would be back to undercutting one another as the only way to attract an oil company's attention.

Joint ownership turned out to be an idle thought. The British withdrawal of their military presence from the Middle East in 1971 created a power vacuum that allowed Iran to seize some small islands near the Strait of Hormuz. Gadhafi used Iranian aggression as an excuse to nationalize all of BP's holdings in Libya, along with Bunker Hunt's concession, and then 51 percent of the remaining concessions, including Hammer's. Algeria and Iraq joined in the frenzy of nationalizing oil assets. In early 1973 the shah announced his intention not to have the NIOC renew its operating agreement with the oil companies when it expired in 1979, and to transform NIOC from a domestic oil producer into a major global oil company.

By making separate deals with oil companies, the oil producers were fast learning how to play one of the seven sisters off another just as effectively as the seven sisters used to play one producer off another. The oil companies were beside themselves as their oil fields and physical assets were transferred from their books unto the books of the oil producers. They were at loggerheads over a common approach that would minimize their loss of power and enable them to obtain restitution. Their appeals to the U.S. government for help were interpreted as a sign of weakness. Then the independent oil companies broke ranks with the seven sisters and began a bidding war to assure their oil supplies, another sign of weakness. The imposing facade of oil company power was exposed for what it was: an imposing facade.

With governments standing helplessly aside, the oil companies prepared to meet with the OPEC producers in Vienna in October 1973. The meeting took place just as Syria and Egypt invaded Israel, hardly an auspicious omen. The meeting broke down when the oil producers demanded a price hike to $5 per barrel. The oil companies played a weak hand and tried to refer the matter to their respective governments before making a formal reply. Oil companies had never appealed to their governments for permission before, so why now unless they were in desperate straits? Shortly after, in mid-October, King Faisal delivered an ultimatum to Nixon: immediate cessation of U.S. military aid to Israel or face an embargo. The ultimatum arrived just as the U.S. Senate had overwhelmingly voted to send reinforcements to Israel.

Events were now entirely out of the hands of the oil companies and consuming nations. In quick response to continued U.S. military support of Israel, the members of OPEC meeting in Kuwait unilaterally raised the price of a barrel of oil from $3 to $5, accompanied by a 5 percent cutback in production. The oil weapon, mentioned in the past, was now taken out of its sheath for the first time. The production cut was intended to sway the United States not to continue supporting Israel. Then, three days later Saudi Arabia announced a 10 percent cutback in production plus an embargo of oil to the United States and the Netherlands. This embargo had to be carried out by the oil companies themselves, even though a majority of them were U.S. companies. Of course, Saudi Arabia could not stop the oil companies from supplying oil to the Netherlands and the United States from other sources. Nevertheless, the embargo created a hiatus in oil moving into the United States, resulting in long lines at gasoline stations in November only a month later. The irony was that on October 21, when the embargo went into effect, Israel agreed to a ceasefire. But the Humpty Dumpy of the old world could not be put back together again. The oil companies made fruitless attempts to regain control over market prices. The first oil shock reached its apogee in December, when independents panicked over oil supplies and Iran conducted an auction with the highest bid coming in at $17 per barrel.

One argument advanced for raising oil prices by the oil producers was the fact that European governments collected more in taxes on a barrel of crude than what they received for selling a finite and depleting resource (this relationship still holds). Another was that when oil displaced coal, it proved that oil was underpriced with respect to coal. Hence, it was in the long-term interests of energy consumers to reinstate coal as a source of energy, which could be accomplished, according to the shah, if crude were priced at $11.65 per barrel, the price necessary to make oil products from coal and shale oil at that time. The benefit to consumers was that a higher price of oil would cut oil consumption and postpone the time when the world would run out of oil.

The shah was absolutely right. If the oil crisis had not happened, there presumably would have been three more doublings between 1973 and 2003. World oil consumption was 2,750 million tons in 1973; three doublings is a projected consumption of 11,000 million tons compared to the 3,682 million tons consumed in 2003. An oil crisis was inevitable at some point because there was no way for production in 2003 to triple to accommodate a continued doubling of consumption every decade.

As the shah was justifying why oil prices had to be increased, an oil auction held in Nigeria fetched a whopping $23 per barrel, although the winner did not show up to take delivery. At the

Figure 5.3  **History of Crude Oil Prices** ($/Bbl)

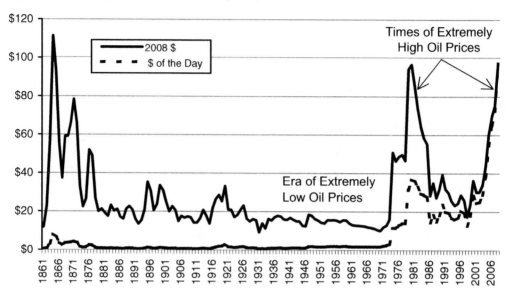

end of 1973, with an OPEC meeting to determine the appropriate price for a barrel of oil, the shah of Iran unilaterally announced a price of $11.65 per barrel, much to the chagrin of the other producers.[18] Even though the shah would be accused of moderation in a sea of immoderation, his price still represented a doubling of the then-posted price and a quadrupling of the posted price only a few months earlier. He accompanied his announcement of the new price with the warning that Western living styles would have to change and everyone would have to learn to work harder. The world no longer had to face a cartel of oil companies but a cartel of oil-producing states. The greatest transfer of wealth in history was about to occur.

**First Time of High Oil Prices**

Figure 5.3 shows the history of oil prices in constant dollars and dollars of the day. Dollars of the day are actual prices of oil paid at points in time. Constant dollars reflect the purchasing power of 2008 dollars. Crude prices expressed in constant 2008 dollars are higher than in current dollars, reflecting the loss of purchasing power from inflation (in 1980/81, crude prices were about $36 per barrel in dollars of the day whereas in constant 2008 dollars, prices are nearly $100 per barrel).[19]

Although the peak price in 2008 was $147 per barrel, the average annual price shown in Figure 5.3 was $97 per barrel. In terms of constant 2008 dollars, the highest annual average price occurred in 1864, when prices expressed in constant 2008 dollars averaged $110 per barrel. This explains a lot about Pit Hole. With Rockefeller in control by 1880, oil prices in terms of 2008 dollars averaged $21 per barrel, and varied between $13–$35 per barrel until 1910. From 1910–1930 the average was $19 per barrel with about the same range. Thus, oil prices were fairly stable for a half century. The Great Depression of the 1930s saw average prices decline to $15 per barrel, ranging between $9–$18 per barrel, again in 2008 dollars. The 1940s and 1950s were a continuation of depression prices, averaging $15 per barrel with a narrow range between $12–$18 per barrel. This is another thirty years of essentially constant prices that were close to those of the Depression. The 1960s up to 1972 was the absolutely worst period for oil producers, with an average price of $13 per barrel, ranging between $10–$14 per barrel. It is ironic that the oil producers were facing the lowest prices in the history of oil while export volumes were virtually exploding. As long as exploding export volumes stayed ahead of exploding import volumes, the oil companies could maintain the upper hand. As soon as exploding import volumes got ahead of exploding export volumes, which happened when Saudi Arabia imposed its embargo, all hell broke loose.

After the 1973 price hikes, the shah now had the means to make Iran the military powerhouse of the Middle East, transform its economy to that of a modern state and make NIOC a global oil powerhouse. Rather than giving him the means to pursue his grandiose dreams, all he got for his financial bonanza was exile (he went on a vacation from which he never returned in early 1979). The Iranian Revolution, which broke out in 1978 as national strikes, ended in 1979 with the ascendancy of Khomeini, a cleric with a decidedly anti-Western bent. The Iranian Revolution marked the second oil shock when the cessation of Iranian crude exports of over 5 million barrels per day (bpd) caused oil prices to climb precipitously to $37 per barrel on an average annual basis, prices that would not be seen again until 2004, in terms of dollars of the day but not until 2008 in constant dollars.

The cessation of Iranian production and the accompanying panic buying and hoarding brought about a reoccurrence of long lines of automobiles at gasoline filling stations. As Khomeini was finding his way around Tehran, Saddam Hussein staged a coup and made himself dictator of Iraq. Two years later, in 1981, Saddam cast his eye on Khomeini's army, whose weapons were no longer being supplied by the United States, and whose officers, commissioned by the shah, had been purged and replaced by loyal, but untrained, revolutionaries. Saddam decided that Khomeini's army, unlike the shah's, was no match for Iraq's army, newly equipped by the Soviet Union, and he invaded Iraq.[20]

While the Iranians and Iraqis were waging war and Saudi Arabians were having problems digesting their newfound wealth, changes in the world of energy were at work that would come back to haunt the oil producers. Among these was a worldwide economic decline that reduced overall energy demand. High oil prices instigated a desperate search for alternative sources to oil, leading to a resurgence of coal, an accelerated pace in building nuclear power plants, a greater reliance on natural gas and anything else not called oil, including wood-burning electricity-generating plants. There were great gains in energy efficiency where cooling a refrigerator, heating a home, running an automobile, truck, locomotive, marine, or jet engine could be achieved with significantly less energy. Conservation of energy took the form of keeping indoor temperatures higher in summer and lower in winter, driving the family car fewer miles, and recycling energy-intensive products such as glass, aluminum, and paper. Companies set up energy managers to scrutinize every aspect of energy use in order to identify ways to reduce consumption.

In addition to slashing demand, high-priced oil caused an explosion in non-OPEC crude supplies, best exemplified in the North Slope of Alaska and in the North Sea. The North Slope of Alaska is an inhospitable place to develop and operate an oil field and necessitated the construction of an 800-mile-long pipeline to the port of Valdez over mountain ranges and tundra. North Slope production peaked at 2 million bpd a few years after the pipeline started operating in 1977. The North Sea was an even greater challenge with its hundred-knot gales and hundred-foot seas. Floating oil-drilling platforms explored for oil in waters a thousand feet deep. "Oceanscrapers," structures higher than the Empire State Building, were built on land, floated out to sea, and flooded (carefully) to come to rest on the bottom as production platforms. North Sea oil started with 45,000 bpd of output in 1974 and grew to over 500,000 bpd in 1975, to 1 million bpd in 1977, to 2 million bpd in 1979, to 3 million bpd in 1983, eventually peaking at 6 million bpd in the mid-1990s. Every barrel from the North Slope and North Sea was one barrel less from the Middle East.

Oil exporters dictated prices after the 1973 oil crisis, but continually changing prices implied that OPEC could not control the price as well as the oil companies had. When oil prices fluctuate widely, no one knows, including the oil producers, what will be tomorrow's price. This provides speculative opportunities for traders who try to outwit or outguess oil producers. All they needed was a place where they could place their bets. Once the traders started placing bets, buyers and sellers of oil had an opportunity to hedge their investments against adverse price changes.

Future and forward contracts of commodities with wide price swings were already traded, providing buyers with a means to hedge against the risk of a rising price and sellers a means to hedge against the risk of a falling price. The first futures were traded in grain in the nineteenth century. Grain growers could then short the futures market and lock in their revenue whereas bakers could buy futures and lock in their costs. Futures then spread to other agricultural products and industrial metals to stabilize prices, provide a means of hedging against price swings, and function as chips in a gambling casino for speculators whose buying and selling add depth to the market. There was no reason to have a futures contract in gold, interest, and currency exchange rates when these were essentially fixed by government fiat. As governments lost control over gold prices, interest and currency exchange rates during the 1970s, future contracts were developed to help buyers and sellers deal with the risk of price and rate volatility.

When oil companies controlled oil prices within a narrow range, there was no point in having futures. When they lost control over pricing, and with oil prices gyrating widely from a combination of oil producer greed, political instability, and Middle East conflicts, it was only a matter of time before someone would create a futures contract in oil. The New York Mercantile Exchange (NYMEX), with a long history in butter, cheese, and eggs, and later potatoes, needed a new trading commodity to keep its doors open. In the early 1980s, NYMEX started trading futures in heating oil, then gasoline, and finally crude oil. First attracting primarily speculators, soon oil companies as buyers and oil producers as sellers started trading. The development of a cash and futures market, with contracts that could be settled in monetary or physical terms and with market crudes expanding from West Texas Intermediate to a variety of specific crudes in the Middle East, West Africa, and the North Sea eventually eroded the oil producers' control over price. Since the early-1980s, the primary determinant of oil prices has been the relationship between supply and demand. The oil producers (OPEC) attempt to influence price by cutting back or expanding production, and in this indirect way affect the price of oil. But they no longer dictate price as they had in the years immediately following the 1973 oil crisis.

## End of High Oil Prices

With consumers doing everything they could to reduce oil consumption, and with every OPEC and non-OPEC producer operating full out, taking advantage of the price bonanza to maximize revenue, it was becoming increasingly difficult to maintain price. There had to be a swing producer to maintain a balance between supply and demand to keep prices high and, as Figure 5.4 clearly shows, the swing producer was Saudi Arabia.

Saudi Arabia's production was initially boosted as replacement crude during the Iranian Revolution in 1978 and 1979 and during the early years of the Iran-Iraq war. After production in Iran and Iraq was restored, Saudi Arabia had to cut back sharply to maintain price. Those holding huge inventories in anticipation of further price increases had a change of heart when some semblance of order was restored and prices began to decline. Liquidating excess inventories caused OPEC

Figure 5.4   **Saudi Arabia Oil Production, Exports, and Consumption** (000 Bpd) **1965–1990**

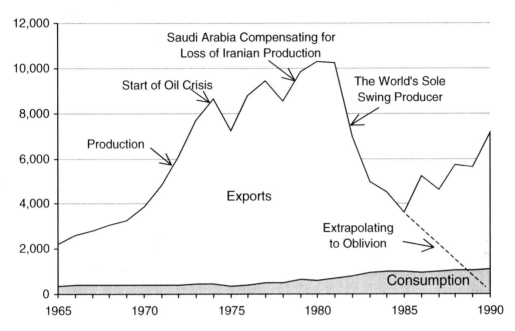

oil demand to slump just as panic buying and hoarding caused it to jump. With OPEC members producing full out, Saudi Arabia had to cut production again to keep prices from eroding further. Saudi Arabia was now playing the same historical role played by the United States when the Texas Railroad Commission had the authority to control oil production to maintain oil prices. The United States ceased being a swing producer in 1971 when the Commission authorized 100 percent production for all wells under its jurisdiction.

From the perspective of 1985, with cessation of exports just over the horizon, Saudi Arabia was at the end of the line of playing the role of swing producer. Something had to be done. In 1985 Saudi Arabia unsheathed the oil weapon, not against the consuming nations but against its fellow OPEC members. Saudi Arabia opened the oil spigot and flooded the market with oil, causing oil prices to collapse below $10 per barrel threatening to financially wipe out OPEC. Saudi Arabia then forced its fellow producers to sit around a table and come to an agreement on production quotas and a mechanism for sharing production cutbacks whereby Saudi Arabia would cease to be the sole swing producer. The cartel would now act as a cartel.

**Era of Moderate Oil Prices**

Thus began the era of moderate oil prices, shown in Figure 5.3. Immediately world and U.S. consumption began to increase (see Figures 5.1 and 5.2) along with OPEC (Figure 5.1) and Saudi Arabia (Figure 5.4) production. What happened to energy conservation and efficiency? By the mid-1980s, most of the mechanisms to achieve energy conservation and efficiency were already in place. Energy conservation and efficiency are noble undertakings; wasting a nonreplenishable resource cannot be justified. But the dark side of energy conservation is that it only works when prices are high. If energy conservation and efficiency succeed in decreasing demand to the point where prices fall, then it becomes a different ball game. Suppose an individual buys a fuel-efficient car when the price of gasoline is high. The individual is using less gasoline. If repeated over millions of individuals, reduced consumption may be sufficient for the price of gasoline to fall. Once gasoline is cheaper, there is a temptation to take an additional vacation trip, perhaps as a reward for having a fuel-efficient automobile, which increases gasoline consumption.

A house has been insulated, and the temperature is lowered to use less heating oil in winter to cut heating oil consumption. If repeated in millions of homes, the cut in consumption may be sufficient to cause the price of heating oil to decline. When this occurs, the temptation is to increase the indoor temperature for greater comfort, causing heating oil consumption to rise. Fuel-efficient jet engines cut jet fuel consumption. If the airline industry converts to fuel-efficient jet aircraft, reduced consumption eventually cuts the price of jet fuel. Suppose that fuel-efficient jet aircraft are underemployed from a lack of passenger traffic. As jet fuel prices fall, the temptation is to use the savings in jet fuel to underwrite a cut in the price of passenger tickets to attract more business. Cheaper tickets encourage more flights, increasing jet fuel consumption. Fresh fruits can be flown to Europe and the United States from New Zealand and Chile as jet fuel prices decline, which causes jet fuel demand to climb. Thus, if conservation and efficiency succeed in cutting demand to the point where energy prices decline, then cheaper energy will restore consumption, closing the gap between current usage and what energy consumption was before conservation and efficiency measures were put into effect. This phenomenon is clearly seen in Figures 5.1, 5.2, and 5.4. Ultimately, conservation and efficiency are self-defeating, which does not mean that energy conservation and efficiency should be discarded. It has to be recognized that high prices have to be sustained in order to maintain the benefits of conservation and efficiency.[21]

## Second Time for High Oil Prices

The second time for high oil prices was from 2007 to late 2008 with the all-time record price of $147 per barrel set in 2008. The pseudo-economic growth fueled by enormous debt acquisition by U.S. consumers resulted in higher crude oil growth rates in both the United States and Asia, particularly China as Manufacturer of the World. Spare capacity for the OPEC producers fell to about 1–2 million barrels per day, a far cry from the late 1970s/early 1980s when Saudi Arabia could make up for the cessation of exports from Iran of nearly 6 million barrels per day and still have capacity to spare. A low level of spare capacity is just another way of saying that demand is getting too close to supply, which can cause huge jumps in price as described in Chapter 2 with regard to electricity rates in California. Another contributing factor was the enormous investing of hedge funds in commodities, particularly oil. It was felt, though not proven, that their enthusiastic if not blind buying of near-term futures affected the cash price of a range of commodities of which oil was but one. Some commentators felt that the subsequent collapse of oil prices to $32 per barrel in late December 2008 was aided and abetted by hedge funds liquidating their positions. But this is a difficult point to prove as the sharp retreat of world economies dampened oil demand, which of itself would cause prices to fall. Speculators do not control the direction of the market, at least not for long. Oil prices were going up because demand was getting too close to supply. Oil prices were going down because demand was weakening as economies slumped. The net impact of the speculators may have been to exaggerate price change movements whether up or down by acquiring or liquidating massive positions in futures. Some maintain that buying and selling in the futures market do not affect cash prices. However, there is a physical connection between cash prices and futures if the two trade with a difference sufficient for a person or company to purchase oil, place it in storage for future delivery, and sell the oil when the futures contract matures. When the difference in the cash and futures price pays for the interest of borrowing money to buy the oil and for the storage costs and yields a profit when the position is unwound or liquidated, then the supply of oil is reduced by the amount of oil tied up in these transactions. A reduction in supply affects cash prices. If acquiring or liquidating huge volumes of short-term derivatives affect cash prices, then financial derivatives whose purpose is to hedge price risk may of themselves, through the actions of speculators, add to price volatility, and in this sense contribute to the very risk they are supposed to mitigate.

### It's Not Oil Prices Anymore, It's Oil Security

The British pulled out of the Middle East in 1971, leaving a power vacuum that contributed to the unfolding of events that led to the 1973 oil crisis. Before the 1973 oil crisis, U.S. military presence was limited to providing military weapons and advice to Saudi Arabia and Iran either for cash or as part of a military aid package. After the oil crisis, the U.S. military presence and involvement ballooned. It started under President Carter in 1979 when forces loyal to Khomeini held U.S. embassy personnel hostage for 444 days, a situation worsened by a failed rescue mission. The U.S. Navy was charged with keeping the Arabian Gulf sea lanes open during the long Iran-Iraq War from 1981–1989. Failing to vanquish Iran, and desperate for money to repay loans for military equipment, mainly from the Soviet Union, Saddam cast his eye south to another neighboring state, Kuwait. Furious that Kuwait had refused to cancel Iraq's debts as he had requested and short on funds, the temptation to take over Kuwait's enormous oil fields proved more than he could resist.

The United States led the coalition forces in the first Gulf war of 1990–1991. The retreating Iraqi forces set fire to Kuwait's oil fields, creating an environmental disaster in their wake. U.S. military presence in the Middle East remained strong between the first and second Gulf wars. In 2003, it was Iraq's turn to be devastated. Now, with occupying troops in Iraq, the United States is a de facto OPEC member. President George Bush's policy of transforming Iraq to an island of democracy in a sea of autocracy, led by a stable government capable of keeping the terrorist elements at bay, now has to succeed under President Obama. There is no alternative. If this policy fails and terrorists seize control of Iraq, there will be no oil security anywhere in the Middle East.

When examining the current situation in the Middle East, one should consider the lasting benefits of the oil producers finally receiving just compensation for their oil exports. Although living standards have increased in Kuwait and the smaller Gulf producers, can the same be said of Iraq, Iran, Nigeria, and Venezuela? Wars and corruption have taken their toll. Figure 5.5 is the per capita gross domestic product (GDP) of Saudi Arabia and Venezuela, the founding nations of OPEC, and Japan, a leading oil importer, indexed at 100 in 1972. Admittedly, this may not be the best way to determine whether the population has benefited from higher oil prices, but it is at least an indication of the pace of internal development of a nation's capacity to produce goods and services.[22]

The chart shows that per capita GDP contracted in Japan immediately following the price hikes in 1973, then resumed its upward course despite the high price of oil. Ironically, the Japanese benefited from the oil crisis even though they import all their energy needs. In the early 1970s the Japanese were producing higher-quality, more fuel-efficient automobiles than the mediocre gas guzzlers being sold at that time in the United States. In the wake of the oil crisis, the Japanese succeeded in capturing a significant share of the U.S. automobile market, which they managed to keep after Detroit began producing higher-quality automobiles with better gas mileage. Per capita GDP for other nations in Asia, particularly the Industrial Tigers, which include South Korea, Taiwan, Singapore, and Hong Kong, would show an even more dramatic rise.

For the oil exporters, Saudi Arabia and Venezuela, per capita GDP expanded in the years immedi-

Figure 5.5  **Per Capita GDP in Japan, Saudi Arabia, and Venezuela Since the 1973 Oil Crisis**

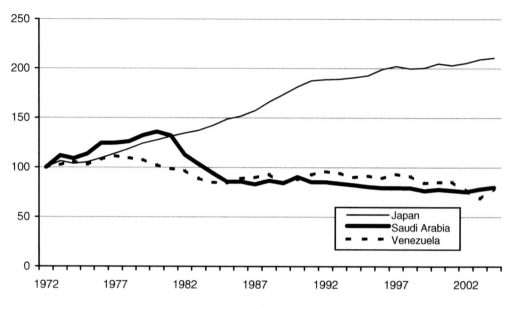

ately following the 1973 oil crisis, particularly for the former. However, these gains began to evaporate during the era of high oil prices and continued to erode during the era of moderate oil prices. What is surprising is that the decline in per capita GDP has fallen below 100. This implies that these nations are producing fewer goods and services now on a per capita basis than they were before the oil crisis. However, this does not necessarily mean a lower standard of living because per capita GDP may not entirely reflect the portion of petroleum revenue that is distributed to the people in the form of social, educational, and medical services. The falling per capita GDP does imply an increasing dependence on oil revenue to sustain living standards. This can be blamed on an understandable, though not a constructive, attitude that people in oil-exporting nations should not have to work. Perhaps the oil producers should heed the shah's advice that Westerners should learn to work harder.

Another contributing factor for the declining per capita GDP in Venezuela and Saudi Arabia is their booming populations. The population of Venezuela has more than doubled, from 11 million in 1972 to 26 million in 2008, while the population of Saudi Arabia has more than tripled, from 6.6 million in 1972 to nearly 28 million in 2008. GDP would have to double for Venezuela or triple for Saudi Arabia simply to keep per capita GDP constant. Part of Venezuela's decline in per capita GDP in the early 2000s was a consequence of civil unrest. Perez Alfonso, principal architect of OPEC and Venezuelan oil minister in the 1970s, wrote that oil was the "devil's excrement" and would eventually ruin Venezuela. Maybe he will be proven right. Venezuela, Iran, Nigeria, Mexico, Russia, and perhaps other oil exporters need high-priced per barrel oil to fulfil the social promises that they've made to their people. Political instability in these nations may occur if there were a prolonged period of low oil prices.

## OIL AND DIPLOMACY

Oilmen, most of whom have engineering backgrounds, often end up playing a diplomatic role to protect their investments in foreign nations. An excellent example before the 1973 oil crisis occurred when Great Britain imposed a trade embargo against the then-existing nation of Rhodesia (now Zimbabwe). South Africa deemed such an embargo illegal for the oil companies operating in South Africa. No matter what BP and Shell did, as British companies operating in South Africa, they were breaking someone's law. If they continued to trade with Rhodesia, they violated British law. If they stopped trading, they violated South African law. During this period of apartheid, Shell was despised by the general public for dealing with South Africa and, perversely, reprimanded by the South African government for its practice of hiring, training, and giving blacks positions of responsibility and authority in violation of apartheid. As a result, Shell found itself breaking the law in both Britain or South Africa and, simultaneously, being criticized by outsiders for having investments in South Africa, and by insiders (the South African government) for not upholding the spirit of apartheid.[23]

Another time when oil companies found themselves on the proverbial horns of a political dilemma was during the Yom Kippur War in 1973, when U.S. oil companies had to enforce an embargo of Saudi crude to America. The challenges of oil companies operating in foreign nations remain no less daunting. Helping Russia to reopen its oil resources has put oil companies at loggerheads with the government over its practice of unilaterally changing tax laws and terms of contractual agreements, with no means of judicial appeal, and restrictions on the rights of minority shareholders in Russian corporations. Oil company executives and Russian government officials have had to work together to come to some sort of compromise that affects Russian laws on taxation, the nature of contracts, and judicial appeal, and the rights of minority shareholders before major investments could be made. The laying of pipelines in the Caspian Sea region brings oil companies in contact with governments hostile to one another through which the pipelines must pass. Tariff structures, security measures, and ways for resolving disputes have to be just as carefully planned as selecting the pipeline route and engineering its construction. Resolving the conflicting interests of different peoples and governments to determine a fair share of the benefits of oil exports for the people and their governments, along with the participating oil companies, still poses enormous challenges.

## OIL AND ENVIRONMENTALISTS

In more recent times, oil executives have had to learn to deal with environmental groups that have learned ways to pursue their agendas other than public communication media and demonstrations. Shell's plans to dispose of an abandoned North Sea oil platform were changed by environmental groups lobbying for a government ruling that resulted in a different and far more costly means of disposal. In addition to being active in sponsoring environmental laws, environmental groups have learned to gain their objectives through loan covenants, conditions that have to be satisfied before funds can be advanced. In response to environmental group lobbying, the World Bank imposed environmental conditions as loan covenants that affected the construction of two pipeline projects; one for moving oil from an oil field in Chad to a port in Cameroon and the other for moving oil in Ecuador from an oil field in the Amazon over the Andes to an exporting port. These loan covenants ensured that a portion of the oil revenues would be paid directly to indigenous peoples, along with changes in pipeline routing to deal with environmental concerns. Both the government oil companies and those building and operating the pipelines had to agree to comply with these loan covenants to obtain World Bank financing.

The environmentalists point to oil as being primarily responsible for pollution, along with coal. Pollution-emission regulations, a concept that no one can really oppose, can pose significant operational challenges for the oil companies. Yet these seemingly insurmountable barriers to their continued existence are surmountable. The oil companies have learned to cope, if not thrive, in this changing business environment. The "Beyond Petroleum" of BP, which must sound sacrilegious to the ears of oilmen of yore, is recognition that oil companies must operate in an environmentally friendly way and consider issues beyond their focus on oil.

Of course, this world of environmental concern exists mostly in North America, Europe, Japan, Australia, and New Zealand. The rest of the world is more interested in making economic progress without any overdue sensitivity over adverse environmental consequences, as epitomized by the nonreaction of most Asian nations to a brown cloud of pollution that hangs above a large portion of the continent. Nevertheless, oil companies must respond to environmental challenges in the quality of their product and in the nature of their operations or face a daunting public relations challenge.

## ROLE OF OIL COMPANIES AFTER THE OIL CRISIS

Although the oil companies were literally thrown out of producing nations after the oil crisis, there has been a return to the situation that existed prior to the oil crisis. Oil companies are, to widely varying degrees, involved with oil production with nearly all the producers that had previously nationalized their oil fields and facilities. The major difference is that the accounting entries for oil reserves in OPEC nations have been obliterated from oil companies' books. These were always fictional because the oil fields were located outside the nations of domicile of the oil companies. The oil companies never had any legal recourse to protect their property rights against actions taken by host governments. This makes ownership a spurious claim, to say the least.

National oil companies operate under encumbrances that Big Oil does not have. National oil companies are limited in their activities to exploiting a nation's wealth of oil and natural gas and, by government fiat, do not and cannot look outside the box. Most national companies are not run as government bodies even though they are wholly owned by their respective governments. Normally, they operate as quasi-independent oil companies. While some have managed their nations' energy resources and infrastructures quite well, others have a less than sterling record. Some oil-exporting nations are looking at privatization, at least in part, as an alternative to a nationalized oil company or to introduce a taste of competition to reinvigorate a moribund organization. Lest we forget, *privatization* would not be a word had it not been for the failure of government-owned companies to deliver goods and services that they were set up to provide.

While national oil companies do not worry about making a profit or surviving in an extremely competitive world, their financial life is not one of idle comfort. National oil companies are the chief revenue generators for many oil-producing nations and they have to fight over every dollar with their exclusive shareholders, their national governments. National oil companies sometimes come up short in the struggle over whether a dollar of revenue should be spent supporting a social program, funding a government expenditure, or being plowed back into the oil infrastructure. Some national oil companies are short on funds needed to maintain oil productivity, others lack technical expertise to expand their oil infrastructure or have limited access to markets. Having chased the oil companies out with a broom, oil companies are back under a variety of contractual arrangements to assist national oil companies with capital infusions, technical expertise, and market access. Since these are the same functions oil companies provided before their oil reserves and properties were nationalized, the circle has been closed.

Oil companies have learned that what counts is not who owns the oil fields but who has access to the oil. Access is provided under a variety of joint venture and production-sharing agreements with the producers. These agreements would not be necessary if the national oil companies could fully replicate the oil companies' contributions in capital, technology, and market access. Having said that, some oil producers have been successful in becoming more integrated by acquiring refineries and service stations in consuming nations and tankers to ship their oil. Kuwait purchased Gulf Oil's refinery and distribution system in northern Europe. Venezuela purchased refineries offshore and in the United States and owns a chain of gas stations in the United States. Both nations have tanker fleets to transport a portion of their oil exports. These investments assure Kuwait and Venezuela of outlets for their oil exports and secure transportation. These moves by producing nations to become integrated oil companies have not diminished the role for the major oil companies and hundreds of independents in the global oil business. Just as Marcus Samuel remarked, there is room for both Shell and Royal Dutch to succeed in an expanding Asian oil market (although he may have lived to regret that remark), so too is there room for government and privately owned oil companies to succeed in an expanding world oil market.

## A Changing World

The world of the twenty-first century is different for the oil companies, but in one respect it is easier: they need not worry about pricing. That is no longer in their hands, or not nearly as much in the hands of the oil producers as they would like; that role has been taken over by the immutable laws of supply and demand. Moreover, they are no longer concerned about ownership of oil in foreign lands as long as they have access to that oil. Before the oil crisis, the goal of the oil companies was to reduce costs, that being the price of crude oil. The irony is that profits are not based on costs but on the spread between the price of oil products and the cost of crude oil. It does not matter what the cost of oil is as long as the margin can be maintained. In addition, an oil company can enter into a variety of contracts and financial derivatives such as swaps, futures, and forwards to hedge against the risk of an adverse change in oil prices.

One can expand this concept to the environmental cost of doing business. It does not matter what incremental costs are placed on an oil company's operations to safeguard the environment as long as every oil company is bearing the same cost. Then it becomes just another cost of doing business, such as the cost of crude oil or the obligation to pay taxes, all of which are simply passed on to consumers in the form of higher prices. Ultimately, it is the consumer who pays for higher-priced crude, increased environmental costs, and additional tax burdens. As long as these are approximately equally borne by all oil companies and can be passed on to consumers, why should the oil companies care? All they have to focus on is maintaining their margins, which in the last analysis means covering their costs. Furthermore, they really do not have to be overly concerned about security of supply. Before the 1973 oil crisis, it was not a significant concern and, since the crisis, the responsibility has been assumed by the taxpayers who foot the bill for an American and Allied military presence in the Middle East.

## Are Oil Companies' Margins All That Great?

Some politicians accuse oil companies of making unconscionable profits. Oil companies do make a lot of money in the tens of billions of dollars. In Figure 5.6, the retail margin of six cents per gallon is mainly for gas station operators, which are normally not owned by the oil company. The profit has to be embedded in the 26 cents per gallon for refining and marketing.[24] For oil-producing companies, excluding refiners, profits are also made for producing crude. The normally accepted estimate for after tax profits is ten cents per gallon or less.[25] The other interesting fact is that oil companies are major contributors to federal and state tax receipts as shown in the

Figure 5.6    **Cost Factors of a U.S. Gallon of Regular Gasoline in 2008**

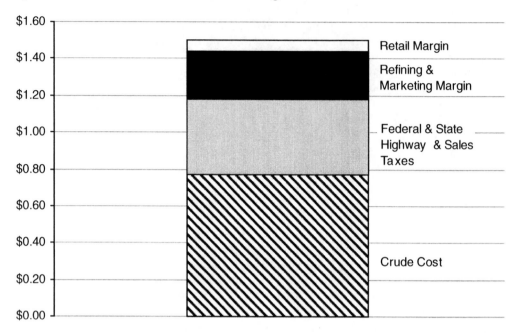

highway and sales taxes paid on every gallon of gasoline, taxes on profits, and payments to the government for oil leases. Governments make far more in revenue on a gallon of gasoline than do oil companies.

Figure 5.7 shows the comparison between European and American prices. Europeans pay between 2–3 times what Americans pay for gasoline, and motor vehicle fuel taxes are an important source of revenue for European governments.[26] This is the primary reason why Europeans prefer fuel-efficient, smaller-sized automobiles and are more sensitive about their driving habits. European oil consumption in 2008 was about the same as in the early 1990s.

European governments still make far more in tax revenue from selling a gallon of gasoline or diesel fuel than the oil producers get for selling a gallon of a depleting natural resource; one of the justifications of the price hikes in 1973. As a point of comparison, mineral waters sell at a substantial premium to gasoline. When one compares the effort to explore, develop, refine, distribute, and market one gallon of gasoline with the cost of bottling one gallon of mineral water plus taking into consideration the amount paid to governments in the form of sales and highway taxes and paid to the producing nations for the crude, the oil industry has got to be one of the most efficiently run operations on Earth. We get far more on the ten cents per gallon we pay the oil companies than the dollar or more we pay the oil producers.

**Future Role of Oil Companies**

Most oil companies specialize in some facet of the oil business. They have neither the capital nor the technical expertise nor the desire to explore energy alternatives outside the oil box. Big Oil is a relatively small group of publicly traded corporations that play a paramount role in finding and

Figure 5.7    **Average Annual Price of Gasoline Europe vs. U.S. ($/Gallon)**

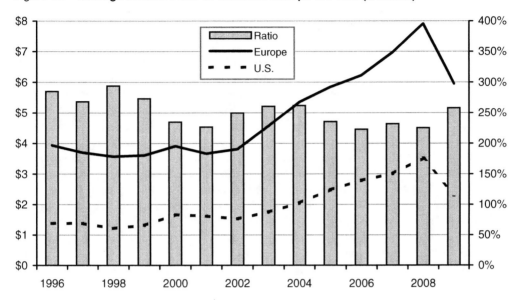

developing large oil fields and in refining and marketing oil. Unlike smaller oil companies, they have an eye on the future of energy with or without oil. Big Oil is aware that the energy business goes beyond getting crude out of the ground and gasoline into a tank. They realize that the era of oil may draw to a close much as the era of biomass in the nineteenth century and the era of coal in the twentieth. This is not to say that oil will disappear any more than biomass and coal have disappeared. The major oil companies are investing in the development of alternative fuels. If not enthusiastic endorsers of developing alternative energy technologies, they are certainly cognizant of their own well-being. Oil is but one facet of the energy industry, and if the role of oil changes Big Oil wants to be part of that change. This is the only way they can ensure their survival as major players in the energy game.

Big Oil's ability to adjust to a changing business environment has been amply demonstrated. They have survived the greatest assault imaginable on their privileged position by losing control over vast oil resources once considered their own. They have also lost the ability to determine the price of oil. Such losses could have led to their demise, yet they are prospering more now than ever before. Once unceremoniously thrown out of oil-producing nations, they have since been invited back by the national oil companies that had taken over their oil fields and distribution and refining assets.

There are some who say that oil is too important to be left in the hands of businesspeople bent on making a buck. Oil should be in the hands of a benign government body that knows best how to serve the wide interests of the people rather than the narrow interests of the shareholders. As alluring as this sounds, the privatization of the ex-Soviet oil industry revealed the outmoded technology, managerial ineptness, and the disregard for the environment of a government-owned and -operated oil company.

Unfortunately, profit has a bad name. For many, all profit means is the right of unscrupulous individuals or companies to gouge the public when the opportunity arises, as was exercised by certain energy traders and merchants who supplied electricity to California during the 2000 energy crisis. Allegations have been made of certain supplying companies holding back on generating electricity to create an artificial shortage that hiked electricity rates. In fairness, the California state regulatory body that established a flawed energy policy and provided poor oversight must bear some of the blame. Nevertheless, this crisis—along with the exposure of executive compensation for certain companies of hundreds of millions at the expense of corporate liquidity and stakeholder value—reinforced the public's generally negative image of corporate executives as profit-gouging, irresponsible, selfish, self-serving gluttons. These accusations arose again in 2008/09 when executives of top financial houses paid themselves aggregate bonuses of billions of dollars for creating what turned out to be pseudo-profits,

Profit means that revenue covers costs. No one can seriously argue against the concept of a public or private undertaking covering its costs; that is, having enough money in the bank to pay its bills. The only objection that can be raised against profits is the degree of coverage. As has been shown, profits made by oil companies expressed in cents per gallon are quite modest in comparison to what consuming governments receive in the form of taxes and what producing governments receive in the form of revenue. The key question is whether we are getting value for what the oil companies charge for their services. By focusing on making money, oil companies have been able to bridge the gap between consumers and suppliers, acting as a neutral third party serving the widely divergent interests of both.

The oil companies' possession of engineering technology, capital resources, and market access cannot be duplicated. If we interpret profits as some excess over costs, which by any measure cannot be considered excessive, then the oil companies should continue to play their historical role of a neutral buffer between consumers and suppliers. If we believe what they report in their annual reports, major oil companies view themselves as energy companies with a particular focus on oil, with that focus subject to change as conditions warrant. If tar deposits in Canada and Venezuela and oil shale deposits around the world become technologically and economically feasible, the oil companies will be there. If another fuel replaces gasoline as the fuel of choice, the oil companies will be part of the transition. Their survival as major global companies hinges on their ability to adapt to changing times. As this chapter readily shows, they have proven their adaptability in the past, and there is every reason to expect that they will do so in the future.

## NOTES

1. Mir Yusif Mir-Babayev, "Azerbaijan's Oil History: A Chronology Leading up to the Soviet Era," *Azerbaijan International* 10 (Summer 2002), Web site www.azer.com.

2. "Abraham Gesner: Lighting up the Nineteenth Century, 1797–1864," Volume IV, *Pathfinders: Canadian Tributes,* Canada Heirloom Series of Canada's Digital Collections, Web site collections.ic.gc.ca/heirloom_series.

3. "The History of the Oil Industry: Oil Through the Ages, 347 BC to 1859," Web site www.sjgs.com/history.html.

4. Early Petroleum History Web site little-mountain.com/oilwell/.

5. J.T. Henry, *The Early and Later History of Petroleum* (New York: Augustus M. Kelley Publishers, 1970). First published in 1878 by Jas. B. Rodgers Co., Philadelphia.

6. James S. Robbins, "How Capitalism Saved the Whales," Web site www.alts.net/ns1625/gesner.html.

7. Unless otherwise noted, the primary source for the life of John D. Rockefeller is Grant Segall's, *John D. Rockefeller: Anointed with Oil* (New York: Oxford University Press, 2001).

8. John D. Rockefeller, Jr.'s philanthropic works are described in the June 2004 issue of the *Smithsonian Magazine,* Dorie McCullough Lawson, "Who Wants to Be a Billionaire?"

9. Rockefeller considered Flagler the brains behind Standard Oil. After 1885, and while still a director of Standard Oil, Flagler became a prominent Florida developer in St. Augustine, Palm Beach, and Miami. He also organized the Florida East Coast Railroad, which ran the length of the state from Jacksonville to Miami. He extended the railroad to Key West, which was considered an engineering feat of the day (see www.flagler.org).

10. Unless otherwise noted, the primary source for the life of Marcus Samuel is Robert D.Q. Henriques' *Bearsted: A Biography of Marcus Samuel, First Viscount Bearsted and Founder of "Shell" Transport and Trading Co.* (New York: Viking Press, 1960).

11. James A. Clark and Michel T. Halbouty, *Spindletop* (Houston, TX: Gulf Publishing, 2004). First published in 1952 by Random House.

12. As Lord Mayor, Marcus did what he could to counter pogroms in Romania and Russia, warning the Russian ambassador that continued violence against the Jews would lead to the undoing of the czar.

13. As mentioned previously in the text, Burmah Oil had the unique status of being, in the eyes of the government, the only true British oil company. This mantle was taken over by BP when it became involved with North Sea oil. Burmah Oil would eventually be without oil-producing properties when the Burmese oil fields were exhausted. As a result of speculative investments, Burmah Oil went bankrupt in 1974 and its 20 percent holding in BP was taken over by the Bank of England.

14. Unless otherwise noted, the primary source on the oil business up to the 1973 oil crisis is Anthony Sampson, *The Seven Sisters: The Great Oil Companies and the World They Made* (New York: Viking Press, 1975).

15. Ralph Hewins, *Mr. Five Percent: The Story of Calouste Gulbenkian* (New York: Rinehart & Co., 1958); Nubar Gulbenkian, *Portrait in Oil: An Autobiography of Nubar Gulbenkian* (New York: Simon and Schuster, 1965).

16. Stephen Howarth, *A Century in Oil: The "Shell" Transport and Trading Company, 1897–1997* (London: Weidenfeld & Nicolson, 1997).

17. The statistics reported in Figure 5.1 can be found in *BP Energy Statistics* (London: British Petroleum, 2009).

18. A detailed chronology of events prepared by National Public Radio (NPR), "Gas & Oil Prices: A Chronology," is available at www.npr.org/news/specials/oil/gasprices.chronology.html.

19. *BP Energy Statistics* (London: British Petroleum, 2009).

20. The primary source for the post-1975 history is Daniel Yergin's, *The Prize: The Epic Quest for Oil, Money, and Power* (New York: Simon & Schuster, 1991).

21. Herbert Inhaber, *Why Energy Conservation Fails* (Westport, CT: Quorum Books, 2002).

22. International Monetary Fund, *International Financial Statistics Yearbook* (Washington, DC, 2008); International Monetary Fund, *World Economic Outlook, A Survey by the Staff of the International Monetary Fund* (Washington, DC, 2008).

23. Stephen Howarth, *A Century in Oil: The "Shell" Transport and Trading Company, 1897–1997* (London: Weidenfeld & Nicolson, 1997).

24. California Energy Commission at Web site www.energy.ca.gov.

25. The average oil profit per gallon for 2007 was reported as 10 cents per gallon by the Oxford Club Investment, Web site www.investmentu.com/IUEL/2007/20070323.html, and the Associated Business Press quoted the first quarter of 2008 Exxon's earnings being described as four cents per gallon of gasoline and diesel, down from eight cents per gallon from the previous year's first quarter as listed on Web site www.wmi.org/bassfish/bassboard/other_topics/ message.html?message_id=298879. In the first edition of this book, I estimated that the Shell Group made 8.5 cents per gallon and Amerada Hess made 6.6 cents per gallon on its oil sales in 2003. Ten cents per gallon is a fair estimate in good years for the oil companies, while 5–10 cents per gallon is a fair estimate of overall profitability for more typical years.

26. U.S. Energy Information Agency, Web site www.eia.doe.gov/emeu/international/gas1.html.

# 6

OIL

This chapter describes the journey oil takes from deep in the earth until it reaches consumers in a wide range of products from plastics to motor vehicle fuels to fertilizers and pesticides. The sojourn starts with exploration and the development of oil wells onshore and offshore, the refining and transportation of oil products, and the use of enhanced recovery methods to get the most out of oil fields. The adequacy of oil reserves to continue to fuel our economy, the potential of nonconventional oil sources, and alternative motor vehicle fuel substitutes are covered. The chapter ends with a discussion of the geopolitical aspects of oil with a call to internalize an externality called oil security.

## THE EARTH AS AN OIL MANUFACTURER

Terra firma it is not; the daily chronicle of earthquakes and volcanoes attests otherwise. The earth, with a radius of less than 4,000 miles, has a core with a radius of about 2,000 miles made up mostly of an alloy of nickel and iron. The center of the core is solid with a liquid outer portion. Enormous currents of electricity flow around the core generating the earth's magnetic field, which protects the earth from harmful radiation from the sun and from space. If stripped of the mantle and crust, the core would shine as brightly as the sun, heated by the weight of the overburden and radioactive decay. Between the core and the outer crust is a nearly 2,000-mile-thick mantle of semiliquid rock and metals called magma. Magma is less dense than the core of pure metal, but denser than the crust, which is made largely of rock. Magma is a viscous fluid with upward convection flows of hotter magma from near the core balanced by downward flows of cooler magma from near the crust. There may be an internal structure to magma consisting of gigantic plumes hundreds of miles high. The upper 50- to 150-mile portion of the mantle is called the asthenosphere, which has a chemical composition closer to that of the crust than the underlying magma.

Literally floating on top of the asthenosphere is a relatively thin, brittle crust made up of mainly less dense stone mixed with metals called the lithosphere. The lithosphere is only between four to seven miles deep beneath the oceans and up to sixty miles deep beneath mountain ranges. Its average depth of nearly twenty miles is only 0.5 percent of the earth's radius. Oceanic crust is mostly relatively heavy basalt while the continental crust is mostly relatively light granite. The crust is broken into major segments called tectonic plates including the Eurasian, North and South American, African, Pacific, Antarctic, Australian, Arabian, and Indian plates. There are also smaller plates such as the Philippine plate, the Juan de Fuca plate (off west coast Canada and United States), the Caribbean plate, the Cocos plate (west of Central America), the Nazca plate (west of South America), and the Scotia plate (between the Antarctic and South American plates). These plates separate, collide, or slip by one another in response to underlying flows of magma in the asthenosphere.

We recognize the continents and oceans as major geological features, but so too is the mid-ocean ridge, largely unseen except where it protrudes above the ocean in Iceland and the Azores. Made of two mountain chains separated by a rift valley, the mid-ocean ridge can be up to two miles in height above the ocean floor and as much as 1,000 miles wide. The ridge is 35,000 miles in length and encircles the world like the stitching on a baseball. Tectonic plates along the mid-ocean ridge are separating about as fast as a fingernail grows with new crust formed by upwelling magma from volcanoes and fumaroles. The East African rift marks a plate separation that may one day be a new body of water like the Red Sea; other rifts include Lake Baikal, Rio Grande, and Rhine Graben.

Subduction occurs when two plates collide and one overrides the other, forcing the lower plate back into the mantle to become new magma. Subduction zones are located at ocean trenches such as the Chilean trench and the Marianas trench in Indonesia and are marked by volcanoes. If two tectonic plates collide, but neither is massive enough to cause the other to submerge, a mountain chain may emerge (e.g., the Caucasus and Himalayas). The collision between two plates in the Middle East was not sufficient to create a mountain range or a subduction zone, but folds in the rock capable of trapping the earth's greatest concentration of oil and natural gas. A fault is created when plates slip by one another laterally such as the San Andreas fault in California. Faults and folded rock are critical in the formation of oil reservoirs.[1]

The original theory of the origin of oil in the Western world was that it came from dead animal matter, but a cemetery, where bodies decay and turn to dust, is not a future oil field. For the earth to manufacture a fossil fuel, the decaying process must be interrupted either by dead plant and animal matter falling into oxygen-starved waters or rapid burial. It was once thought that oil came from dinosaurs, the symbol of Sinclair Oil. This theory has been discredited because the earth could not possibly have sustained a population of dinosaurs, even over millions of years, large enough to create so much oil even if one ignores the special circumstances that must accompany death for dinosaurs to become a fossil fuel. In the twenty-first century the accepted theory postulates that ocean plankton, algae, and other forms of simple marine life die and sink into oxygen-starved waters that prevent further decay. Sediments from rivers mix with the partially decayed matter to form an organically rich concoction. Continued burying by more layers of sediment squeezes out the water, and when buried by a mile or more of new sediment over millions of years, the original sediment is transformed to sedimentary rock and the organic matter to oil.

Based on this hypothesis, a favorite place to explore for oil is near river mouths such as the Mississippi and Niger rivers, where shifting deltas and rising and falling sea levels over millions of years have created widespread oil and gas deposits at various ocean depths. Geologists look for what appear to be buried river mouths in sedimentary rock for likely places to drill. A location where oil and natural gas may be in the making is the Bosporus, where Mediterranean water enters the Black Sea. Dead and dying marine organisms sink to the bottom and mix with the sediments in oxygen-starved waters. If buried by a mile or more of overburden during the next many millions of years (a scenario that requires the Black Sea to drop by more than a mile or the land around the Black Sea to rise by more than a mile, or some combination of the two), then the sediment will be transformed to rock and the entrapped organic matter to oil. Then a new budding oil field can await discovery by a petroleum geologist yet to be born eons from now.

The crust has three general types of rocks. Upwelling magma, when cooled, becomes igneous (fire-formed) rock such as granite and basalt. Deeply buried igneous or sedimentary rocks, subject to enormous heat and pressure, can be transformed into metamorphic rocks such as marble and slate. From a Western petroleum geologist's point of view, the presence of igneous and metamorphic basement rock underlying sedimentary rock is good reason to stop drilling because oil and gas are found only in sedimentary rocks.

Two of the three types of sedimentary rocks are created by erosion, which would level the earth were it not for emergence of new mountain chains from colliding tectonic plates (the Himalayas are still rising as the Indian plate continues to plow into the Eurasian plate). Wind, rain, and flowing water are the principal agents of erosion. When water seeps into cracks and crevices of rock and freezes, it expands, fracturing the rock and making it more vulnerable to erosion. The debris of erosion suspended in flowing water is another powerful force of erosion that can cut deep gorges into solid rock. When carbon dioxide in the atmosphere mixes with water, it forms dilute carbonic acid that eats away at limestone and forms underground caverns. Finally, the debris of erosion, as gravel, sand, and clay, is deposited in river deltas. Other sources of sediment are shells of dying plankton deposited on the ocean floor and the precipitation of dissolved calcium carbonate from evaporating seawater in shallow lagoons. Under sufficient pressure from overburden, and with calcium carbonate and silica acting as cementing agents, gravel is transformed into a conglomerate, sand to sandstone, clay to shale, lime mud to a gray to black limestone, and microscopic seashells to white limestone called chalk, such as the White Cliffs of Dover. The most common form of sedimentary rock is shale and the most common form of petroleum reservoir rock is sandstone.

The compressive force of plate movements near subduction zones creates folds in hot, plastic sedimentary rocks. An upward fold is called a syncline and a downward fold is called an anticline. Anticlines are shaped like an upside down or inverted bowl and faults (breaks in sedimentary rock layers caused by tectonic plate slippage) of nonpermeable rock (or caprock) form traps to prevent oil and gas from completing their migratory journey to the earth's surface. If they are not trapped, natural gas and the lighter components in oil evaporate as they migrate toward the earth's surface, finally emerging as a viscous crude or thick tar called seep oil.

Different types of sedimentary rock layered one on top of the other are on display at the Grand Canyon, each with a unique geological origin. A typical cross-section of the earth contains a mile of sedimentary rock with about 100 layers of various types of sedimentary rocks underlain by a basement of igneous or metamorphic rock. Sedimentary rock layers on the ocean floor are only about one-half mile thick on average, with the thinnest at the mid-ocean ridge, becoming thicker as the ocean floor approaches the continental shelf. The thickest sediments (about ten miles in depth) are located on continental shelves, but can also be found inland. Colorado is one such place where sedimentary rocks were formed when that area of the world was covered by a shallow sea. Glaciers can strip basement rock of their sedimentary rock cover as occurred in eastern Canada and New York's Central Park. Drilling for oil in Central Park would be useless: no sedimentary rock, no oil. Even with the earth covered by a mile of sedimentary rock, the presence of sedimentary rock does not mean the presence of oil. The secret to success in oil drilling is identifying traps overlain with nonpermeable caprock and underlain by sedimentary rock whose pores, or spaces between the grains, are saturated with oil and natural gas.

Sedimentary rocks buried deep in the earth were originally made from debris from eroding mountains or the deposition of shells from marine life. These rocks may one day be uplifted by colliding tectonic plates and again become mountains vulnerable to erosion. The rough jagged peaks of the Alps, Rockies, Andes, and Himalayas are geologically new compared to the far older rounded Urals and Appalachians. As new and old mountains erode, their sediments are deposited in river deltas, which if buried by a mile of overburden, become new sedimentary rock, which over time may be thrust up again as a recycled mountain range. The Himalayas are such a range where, three to five miles above sea level, marine fossils can be found in sedimentary rock.

## FORMATION OF OIL

Dead organic matter must lie in either stagnant, oxygen-free waters at the bottom of the sea until buried or be buried quickly after death and achieve a concentration of 1–3 percent by weight to become a future oil reservoir, although this concentration can be as high as 10 percent. The next step is burying the organically rich sediment deep enough to generate the temperature and pressure necessary to transform organic matter to oil. With 7,000 feet of overburden, the pressure is sufficient to raise the sediment's temperature to 150°F, the minimum to produce a heavy and generally undesirable grade of crude oil. Preferred light crudes are produced as one approaches 18,000 feet and 300°F. Beyond 18,000 feet, the temperature and pressure are sufficient to transform oil to graphite (carbon) and natural gas. The oil window is 7,000–18,000 feet below the surface of the earth, meaning that sediments at river mouths must be buried between 1.5–3.5 miles of debris to produce oil by either the ocean bottom sinking or the surrounding land mass rising or a combination of both. The properties of the oil depend on the type of organism, its concentration, depth of burial, and the nature of the surrounding sediment. Oil properties vary from one field to another and no two oil fields have exactly the same properties. Commercial grades of crude are really a mix of oil from different oil fields in the same region that have similar properties. A few are from different oil fields with dissimilar properties such as Urals, a specified mix of light sweet crude from western Siberia and heavy sour crude from the Ural region of Russia.

Once formed in source rock, oil and natural gas, being lighter than water, begin to migrate laterally and vertically through migratory rock. Oil and gas pass through the pore space within the sedimentary rock structure and through fractures in rock layers. This migration may extend as far as 200 miles from source rock. The rate of migration depends on the porosity and permeability of the migratory rock. Porosity is a measure of the spaces (pores) within the rock that can be filled with fluids (oil, gas, and water), and permeability is a measure of the ease with which a fluid can pass from one pore to the next. Both are critical in determining the flow of hydrocarbons (and water) into a well; generally speaking, the greater the porosity, the greater the permeability. Oil and gas migration continues until interrupted by an intervening rock formation shaped like an inverted bowl or a fault made of a well-cemented rock with no spaces between the grains. Once migrating oil and gas are trapped in reservoir rock, natural gas, the lightest, rises to the top of the reservoir and forms a gas cap; saltwater, the heaviest, sinks to the bottom, leaving oil in the middle. In some reservoirs, a small concentration of natural gas may remain mixed with crude oil without forming a gas cap; in still others, there is no associated natural gas. The subsurface water that makes up the water table is fresh, produced by rain percolating through the soil; but the water beneath the water table is more or less as saline as ocean water.

Contrary to a popular conception that originated with the dawn of the oil age, an oil reservoir does not consist of a void space filled with a pool of oil; rather, it is migratory rock turned reservoir rock, saturated with oil and gas that is prevented from continuing its journey to the earth's surface. The geometry of a trap is one determinant of the size of an oil field; the larger the dome or fault of caprock and the greater the distance from the top of the trap to the spill point (where oil and gas can flow around the caprock and continue migrating to the surface), the larger the size of the potential oil field. Other determinants are porosity, which determines the quantity of oil and gas contained in the reservoir rock, its permeability, which determines the flow of the oil and gas to a well and its potential recoverability, and, of course, the concentration of oil and natural gas in the reservoir rock. Sandstone has the largest pores for the greatest porosity and permeability, followed by limestone, and then shale, which have the smallest pores. Most reservoir rocks are sandstone and limestone, but even here tight sands and dense limestone have low degrees of porosity and permeability.

Salt domes are another mechanism that can trap oil. Salt can be deposited hundreds or thousands of feet deep when ocean water in shallow lagoons, which were periodically connected and disconnected from the ocean, evaporates to form salt pans. These accumulations of salt pans, which can reach depths of thousands of feet, are then buried by a mile or more of overburden. The less dense salt does not begin to flow through the overburden until the overburden has reached a depth where the lighter density salt can exert sufficient thrust to begin flowing through weak spots in what has now become a mile or more of rock. The plug of salt works its way toward the surface, fracturing rock layers along the way and forming potential traps for oil. The top layer of the salt plug becomes a dome of nonpermeable gypsum, limestone, dolomite, or other rock residue left after salt has been leeched out by subsurface waters. Salt dome caprock can be 100–1,000 feet thick and a salt plug can be from one-half to six miles across and extend as much as four miles below the surface. There are hundreds of salt domes in the Gulf of Mexico and the coastal plains of Texas, Louisiana, and Mississippi; most do not trap oil. Spindletop, an exception—with oil trapped below its salt dome of dolomite—was drained after only one year of unrestrained production. It became a new site for oil production when, twenty years later, oil was found trapped in fractured rock along its flanks.

The amount of partially decayed organic or biotic matter that would have to be contained in ocean sediment to create all the known reserves of oil and natural gas might strain one's imagination. In the 1950s Russian petroleum geologists proposed an alternative theory for the origin of oil, but it was and generally still is discredited by Western geologists. The theory was revived in the 1990s when an oil well named Eugene Island 330 suddenly began producing more oil. The well had originally begun production in 1972, and peaked at 15,000 barrels per day. By 1989, production had declined to 4,000 barrels per day. Then, suddenly, production rose to 13,000 barrels per day and estimates of its reserves were revised upward from 60 to 400 million barrels. The well was located near a huge towerlike structure with deep fissures and fractures and the new oil was from an earlier geological age. Seismic evidence seemed to suggest that the new oil was flowing up from one of the deep fissures.

The inorganic or abiotic origin of oil theorizes that there are vast deposits of natural gas in the earth's mantle. Natural gas penetrates the crust and is transformed into crude oil as it rises toward the surface with its properties determined by surrounding rock. As it ascends to the surface, the oil picks up organic matter in the sedimentary rock, which, according to those who support the abiotic theory of oil's origin, explains the presence of organic matter in oil. If natural gas rises close to a volcano, it is transformed into carbon dioxide and steam, gases commonly emitted by volcanoes. The presence of helium in oil and gas, but not in sedimentary rock or organic matter, is put forth as further evidence of an inorganic origin from within the earth's mantle. The most compelling argument against the abiotic origin made by Western petroleum geologists is that they have successfully discovered oil and natural gas on the basis of a biotic or organic origin. Coincidentally, this is the same argument advanced by Russian petroleum geologists who have discovered oil in the base rock beneath sedimentary rock on the assumption that oil has an abiotic origin.

If the abiotic explanation is true, as some earth scientists maintain, then oil and gas may become sustainable forms of energy if the earth produces oil and gas as fast as we consume them. This would have an enormous impact on energy policy if oil and gas were being replenished by the earth or if oil and gas reserves are underestimated by a factor of 100 as suggested by some advocates of an abiotic origin.[2] However, even if the abiotic origin of oil is true, we can still run out of oil in a relatively short time if the rate of production significantly lags the rate of consumption.

## OIL EXPLORATION AND PRODUCTION

In the early years of oil, drillers imagined that they were drilling for a pool or an underground river of oil using oil seeps as a guide for where to drill. Such exploration was successful if the surface oil came from an oil reservoir directly beneath the seep. Many seeps offered little reward to the driller as they merely marked the spot where the migratory rock breeched the earth's surface. Drilling straight down missed oil embedded in a layer of migratory rock slanted at an angle to the surface. Since the first oil was found near a creek, early oil drillers followed creek beds, thinking that oil flowed beneath running water. Once oil was discovered, production wells were placed as close as possible to one another to ensure commercial success. Spacing wells more widely apart increased the chance of drilling a dry hole beyond the perimeter of an oil reservoir. This practice—having the greatest possible concentration of wells furiously pumping oil—rapidly exhausted an oil reservoir and another search for seep oil began. Once sites marked by seep oil were exhausted, and the creek theory debunked, oil drillers turned to geologists for advice on prospective sites. Geologists examined the land for hints of the presence of three necessary conditions for oil: (1) source rock to generate petroleum, (2) migratory rock through which petroleum moves toward the earth's surface, and (3) reservoir rock where there is an impediment preventing further migration. Whether sedimentary rock is source, migratory, or reservoir rock is a matter of circumstance.

Early geologists became geophysicists when they started using gravity meters and magnetometers to search for oil. A gravity meter is sensitive to the density of rocks below the surface. A mile of sedimentary rocks on top of basement rock is dense compared to a salt dome or a layer of porous reef or lighter rocks, which are detectable as anomalies or variations in gravity. Gravity meters were particularly useful in discovering salt domes in Louisiana and Texas during the early 1900s and in the 1948 discovery of Ghawar, the world's largest oil field, in Saudi Arabia. Magnetometers, because they are sensitive to anomalies or variations in the earth's magnetic field generated by magnetite in basement rock, are useful for estimating the thickness of overlying sedimentary rock. Both gravity and magnetic anomalies may indicate an anticline or fault that holds an oil reservoir.

Seismic analysis measures the time interval between creating a sound burst and the return of its echo from a subsurface geological structure embedded within sedimentary rock capable of reflecting sound. Seismic analysis is very useful in identifying potential traps. Dynamite was first exploded in shot holes dug through the surface soil to solid rock. The shot holes were laid out in geometric patterns to get a better idea of the subsurface structures. Later, explosive cord was used in a trench about one foot deep or suspended in air. Nowadays, seismic work on land may utilize a specially-rigged truck that lowers a pad to sustain most of its weight. Hydraulic motors in the truck vibrate the ground, creating sound waves whose echoes can be analyzed for subsurface structures.

Seismic surveys on land are often conducted in difficult, inaccessible, inhospitable, and often unhealthy terrain such as jungles, deserts, mountains, or tundra. Seismic surveys are easier to conduct at sea. An array of pressurized air guns towed by a seismic boat is fired and the returning echoes are recorded by hydrophones, also under tow. The geometry of the array of air guns, their size, and sequence of firing are arranged to obtain a high signal-to-noise ratio of any returning echoes to more easily identify subsurface structures. Though the first successful use of a seismic survey occurred in 1928 when an oil field in Oklahoma was discovered, seismic analysis did not reach its full potential until after the Second World War with the advent of computers capable of processing the enormous volume of data contained on a digital magnetic tape.

The first seismic pictures were two-dimensional (2-D) vertical views of what was beneath the ground. While this was valuable information in itself, a better picture of the size of a potential oil field would emerge if its horizontal dimensions were known. This could be obtained by taking a series of 2-D seismics; but by the 1980s, computer-processing speed, data storage capacity, and software programs had advanced to the point of being able to digest and analyze the mountain of seismic data necessary to obtain a three-dimensional (3-D) view of a subsurface structure. A 3-D seismic on land involves parallel receiver cables with shot points laid out perpendicular to the receiver cables. At sea a vessel, or several vessels sailing in parallel formation, towing several lines of air guns and hydrophone receivers collects the requisite data. Once processed, an underwater subsurface structure can be rotated on a computer screen in order to assess its shape in terms of length, width, and depth from any angle. Though 3-D seismics are costly, they are also cost-effective because they lower the probability of drilling unsuccessful exploratory oil wells, reduce the need for development wells to determine the size of an oil field, and make it possible to plan the placement of production wells to effectively drain a reservoir. Three-D seismics can identify natural gas reservoirs by the unique sound reflections of natural gas in rock. Four-D seismics are a series of 3-D seismics taken over time to assess the remaining reserves of a producing field.

## Drilling Rights

The United States and Canada are unique in permitting individuals and companies to own both the surface and the subsurface rights of land. All other nations consider subsurface minerals the property of the state regardless of who owns the surface land. In the United States and Canada, surface rights to build a house or farm the land can be separated from the subsurface rights to explore and develop mineral finds. If separated, a lease agreement has to be reached between the owners of the surface and subsurface rights with regard to access to the land, the conditions for exploration and the development of any discovered minerals, including oil and gas. Lease agreements usually contain a bonus payment on signing and a royalty payment to be paid to the owner of the surface rights if minerals, including oil and gas, are found and stipulate a time limit for the start of exploration. If exploration has not started by the time established in the lease, the lease becomes null and void and the subsurface mineral rights revert to the owner of the surface rights. Leases can also be farmed out to third parties who conduct exploration, and working interests can be sold to third parties to raise funds to develop an oil or mineral find.

Large portions of the United States and Canada are not owned by individuals, but by the federal governments. In the United States, the federal government holds auctions for mineral rights on its land holdings and offshore waters. Rights to drill on blocks on the continental shelf, whose depth is within the capability of offshore drilling rigs, are offered periodically in a closed-bid auction. The highest bidder has a five- or ten-year period, depending on the depth of the water, to begin exploration or the mineral rights revert back to the federal government. The U.S. government receives a one-sixth royalty if oil is found. Canada has different rules that vary among the provinces. In addition, if oil is discovered on land, there are government regulations on the spacing of production wells to avoid overproduction, the fruit of the bitter lessons learned from the early exhaustion of oil fields in western Pennsylvania, Spindletop, and elsewhere. Of course, providing a long-term optimal return on a costly investment is also a strong guiding force for oil field managers in determining the spacing between producing wells.

For the rest of the world, governments own the mineral rights regardless of who owns the surface land. Oil companies normally enter into individual or collective contracts with governments or their national oil companies for the three phases of oil and gas operations: exploration, development, and production. The type of contract most commonly used before the oil crisis in 1973 was an exclusive concession granted to an oil company for a defined geographic area. The oil company bore all risks and costs and the host government received some combination of bonuses, taxes, and royalties if oil and natural gas were discovered. Since the oil crisis, the most common form of contract has been the production-sharing contract that was first written in Indonesia in

1966. Again, the oil company bears all risks and costs. The oil company explores for oil, and, if it is successful, develops the oil field for production. A large share of the initial oil and gas revenue is dedicated to the recovery of exploration and development costs. After these costs, with a stated rate of return, have been recouped, the oil company and the host government, usually through its national oil company, share the remaining revenue. Some contracts have the host government's national oil company bear a portion of the costs and risks of exploration and the responsibilities of development. Service contracts are payments to oil companies for services rendered in exploration, development, or production, with the profits of production residing solely with the host government. However, a host government may provide incentives to the oil company for meeting certain goals, and, from this perspective, the oil company shares in the profits. Of course, some national oil companies prefer to go it alone without assistance from Western oil companies.

## Drilling Equipment

There are three types of wells: exploratory or wildcat wells, appraisal or development wells, and production wells. Wildcat wells are drilled a significant distance from known oil fields in search of new oil. This is the pure gambling aspect of oil. Less risky exploratory wells are drilled near existing oil fields to see if they extend in one direction or another. If oil is discovered, then the development phase of an oil field begins with the drilling of appraisal, or step-out, wells to measure the extent of an oil field and determine the number and placement of production wells. Appraisal wells are normally abandoned after an oil field has been evaluated. Drilling onshore or offshore is similar, with the major difference being the nature of the drilling rig and in having from several hundred feet to two miles of drill pipe between the rig and the well bore.

Cable-tool rigs have a long history for drilling for freshwater or brine, which was evaporated for its salt content. By the time of "Colonel" Drake, the founding father of the oil industry, a cable-tool rig was a four-legged wooden tower, called a derrick, between seventy-two and eighty-seven feet high. A steam engine drove a wooden walking beam mounted on a Samson post that created an up-and-down motion. A chisel-pointed steel cylinder, or bit, about four feet in length, attached by a cable or rope to the walking beam, pulverized the rock at the bottom of the well. Every three to eight feet, the bit was raised and a bailer lowered into the well to remove the rock chips. Drake was the first to use a cable-tool rig to drill, not for freshwater or brine, but for oil. He was also the first to install a casing of large diameter pipe in the well to keep water from filling the well and to prevent the sides of the well from caving in, a practice still in use today.

The advantage of the cable-tool rig was its simplicity of design and operation, requiring only two or three men (a driller, a tool dresser, and maybe a helper). The disadvantage was that it was slow, averaging about twenty-five feet per day depending on the type of rock. While rotary drilling bits had been used to drill for water as far back as the early 1820s, the cable-tool rig was exclusively used to drill for oil after Drake's discovery. Captain Lucas, developer of Spindletop, is credited with the first use of a rotary rig for oil exploration, where cable-tool rigs could not drill to the desired depth in the soft, sandy soil. The Hamill brothers, employed by Lucas, were major innovators in rotary rig operations. The rig employed at Spindletop, while primitive by contemporary standards, possessed the essential elements of a modern rotary rig. Early rotaries required five or more people to operate and were much more efficient in drilling a hole than a cable-tool rig.

The modern tricone rotary drilling bit, exclusively in use today, is capable of drilling hundreds or a few thousand feet per day depending on the type of rig and the nature of the rock. A rotary drilling bit is a fixed attachment at the end of a drill string, rotated by rotating the entire drill string. The invention of the tricone rotary drilling bit in 1908 by Howard Hughes, Sr., founder of

Hughes Tool Company, with its greater productivity should have spelled the instant death of the cable-tool rig, but it did not. Drilling with a rotary drilling bit requires more costly equipment and a larger and more knowledgeable crew, making it more expensive and complex to operate. Despite its higher productivity, as late as 1950, half of the drilling rigs in the United States were still cable-tool rigs. Desperately in need of replacement after being idle during the Great Depression of the 1930s, and worn out by operating without spare parts during the Second World War, cable-tool rigs quickly passed from the scene by a massive conversion to rotaries. This greatly benefited Hughes Tool and the son of its founder, Howard Hughes, Jr., the infamous billionaire Hollywood movie producer, aircraft designer, mining mogul, casino owner, front for a government secret mission to raise a sunken Soviet submarine, tax evader, and ladies' man, who died a bitter and mentally disturbed recluse in 1976. The lesson with Hughes is that one does not have to discover oil to become an oil billionaire. Maybe there is another lesson. . . .

When drilling on land, the ground is first prepared to support a rig and a cellar is dug into the ground in preparation for the conductor casing. For shallow wells of up to 3,000 feet, the rig can be mounted on the back of a truck. For deeper wells, the rig is broken down into segments, transported by truck, and reassembled at the site. The deeper the well, the stronger the rig has to be to support and pull out the drill string. Drilling a well starts with drilling, called spudding, a hole twenty to one hundred feet deep to cement in a conductor casing of up to twenty inches in diameter. The conductor casing stabilizes the top of the well and provides an anchorage for the blowout preventer, which, as the name suggests, is a sure-fire way to seal a well against a blowout of natural gas and oil.

A cable passing through the topmost crown block of a rig is connected to a kelly (a very strong four- or six-sided molybdenum steel pipe forty or fifty-four feet in length) by a swivel. The sides of the kelly are gripped by a rotary table turned by electric motors powered by diesel engines of 1,000–3,000 horsepower. Attached to the kelly is drill pipe in lengths from eighteen to forty-five feet, but most commonly thirty feet. Every thirty feet, drilling is stopped to add another length of drill pipe below the kelly. The outer diameter of drill pipe varies between three and six inches. Drill pipe nearest the bit is heaviest in gauge to provide additional weight to control drilling and prevent the drill string from kinking and breaking.

The tricone drill bit is a solid fixed cone at the bottom of the drill pipe with three counter-rotating sets of teeth of steel, or high-grade tungsten carbide steel, or industrial diamonds, depending on the type of rock and the speed of drilling. The well bore is larger in diameter than the drill pipe to allow the drill pipe to rotate and slide up and down in the well. The drill string, driven by the kelly, rotates fifty to one hundred turns per minute, enabling the teeth of the drill bit to pulverize the underlying rock. The teeth on the drill bit wear out after 40–60 hours of use on average, but can last as long as 200 hours, depending on the type of rock and the type of teeth. The success of the tricone drill bit was that it lasted much longer than previous bits, sharply reducing the number of trips that had to be taken to replace the drill bit. The increased drilling productivity allowed Hughes to charge a premium price for his bits and, thereby, amass a large fortune.

*Tripping out* refers to the process of pulling the drill string and unscrewing each length of pipe for stacking in the derrick. For an offshore drilling rig that is floating on mile-deep water and drilling a well two miles into the earth's crust, tripping out requires pulling up and disconnecting three miles of drill pipe. For deeper waters and wells of greater depth, this may mean up to eight miles of pipe, a length at the current limits of drilling technology. After a new bit is attached, the reverse process of *tripping in*, or connecting from three to eight miles of pipe, is performed, so that during an entire trip six to sixteen miles of pipe must be handled. Taking a trip is dirty, tough, and dangerous work; no wonder the workers are called roughnecks. Drilling is a twenty-four-hour, seven-day (24–7) operation requiring three shifts of workers working eight-hour shifts, or two shifts of workers working twelve-hour shifts plus spare shifts to give the workers time off.

Drilling mud, which carries away the debris of pulverized rock from the bottom of the well, is forced down the center of the drill pipe and passes through the middle of the tricone bit. The mixture of mud and pulverized rock is forced to flow up the annulus, the space between the drill pipe and the walls of the drill hole or well bore. Separators on the surface remove rock chips so that the mud can be recycled. Drilling mud, first introduced by the Hamill brothers when they drove cows through a mud pit at Spindletop, is now a science. Mud consists of a mixture of clay, weighting material, and chemicals mixed with water or diesel oil. Bentonite clay remains suspended in water for a long time after agitation and adding barite or galena controls drilling mud's viscosity and weight. Viscosity affects how fast the mud can pass through the tricone bit and the weight of the mud, along with the weight of the drill pipe, must exceed the pressure of oil, gas, or water in the well to prevent a blowout. Depending on the circumstances, it may be necessary to add bactericides, defoamers, emulsifiers, flocculants, filtrate reducers, foaming agents, or a compound to control alkalinity. When drilling through soft or porous rock, rising mud can penetrate the surrounding rock to strengthen the sides of the well and form a seal, preventing subsurface fluids from flowing into the well.

Nothing about drilling is easy. One of the many challenges facing a driller is the possibility that the drill string might bend and bind itself to the well wall or break as a result of metal embrittlement, which occurs when hydrogen sulfide enters a well. Nothing is more risky. Safe operations to reduce the risk of an accident are of paramount importance. An unexpected release of high-pressure gas into the well, whose expansion in the mud lowers its density, may lead to a blowout. A blowout can shoot drill pipe out of a well like cannon shot, wrecking a rig and killing or maiming the drillers. If a blowout is about to occur, pipe rams and other means within the blowout preventer seal the well. Drillers are sensitive to the dangers that threaten drilling by relying both on instrument readings and sight, sound, and smell for warnings of potential trouble.

In the case of the United States, only 22 percent of exploratory wells were successful in 1973, but this increased to 71 percent in 2008, primarily as the result of improvements in computer software, processing speeds, and storage capacity for 3-D seismic analysis.[3] However, these exploratory wells were not true wildcat wells in that most of them were drilled in the vicinity of known fields. True wildcat wells, drilled far from any known source of oil, have much lower success ratios.

Seventy-eight percent of development wells were successfully completed in 1973, and this improved to 92 percent in 2008. Failure in drilling production wells can be caused by the well hole missing the oil reservoir (3-D seismic pictures can reduce the chances of this happening) or by twisting, binding, or breaking of the drill string, shattering of the drilling bit, or the damage incurred when a tool is dropped down the well. When the drill string or drilling bit breaks, various methods of fishing out the broken pipe or bit have been devised, including the use of powerful magnets and explosives. If these fail, the well may have to be abandoned. In 1973, the average rig drilled wells whose total depth amounted to 22 miles each year. If the average depth per well is two miles, then this is equivalent to drilling eleven wells a year. In 2008, the total average depth per rig was 35 miles, and on the basis of two miles per well, 17.5 wells a year, a 60 percent increase in productivity. Land rig activity has remained flat in the United States as oil exploration moves into more promising areas overseas and into offshore waters.

## Directional Drilling

One would think that a drill string made up of thirty-foot lengths of steel pipe would be rigid, but this is not at all true when the drill string is measured in miles. It is rather flexible, sometimes described as being similar to spaghetti, and, like a rubber band, actually twists several times when being rotated before the bit begins to turn. Drilling a vertical hole requires constant attention. The bit, turning clockwise, tends to introduce a clockwise corkscrew pattern to what one would suppose would be a straight hole. Moreover, nonhorizontal layers of hard rock can cause a deviation or drift from the vertical. Drift measurements are necessary every several hundred feet of drilling, or when a bit is being changed, to verify the vertical direction of a well hole.

Wells on land are drilled vertically, and a producing oil field is served by many individual wells. Historically, the only slanted wells were those that tapped a neighbor's oil field! The idea of horizontal drilling was patented in 1891, but for drilling teeth, not oil. The first true horizontal well was drilled in 1939. In the 1970s, control over direction was still poor but markedly improved in the 1980s by the development of the steerable downhole motor. It was not until the 1990s that horizontal drilling came into its own when the decade started with 1,000 horizontal wells and ended with twenty times as many. To a casual observer drill pipe is rigid, but it can actually flex when strung together for thousands of feet. In contemplating horizontal wells, it should be kept in mind that the drill pipe does not rotate; it is mud forced to flow through the drill pipe that actually powers the drilling. Normally the mud motor that drives the drill bit is fixed vertically so that the well is drilled straight down, but it can be bent via a joint that can cause the drill pipe to depart from the vertical. The drill pipe can be curved until it becomes horizontal. A Measure While Drilling (MWD) device equipped with an accelerometer and magnetometer placed just above the mud motor lets the driller know the direction and angle of inclination and its precise location in relation to 3-D seismic imaging of potential oil or gas bearing geological structures. The MWD can also be equipped with Logging While Drilling devices such as gamma ray detectors and instruments to measure resistivity and conductivity and other variables. These technological advances allow the driller to stay within oil or gas-bearing zones in real time without having to pull out the drill pipe and run a wireline-based logging tool down the hole to evaluate the well's progress.

Horizontal drilling can be used to enhance recovery after production from a vertical well is nearing exhaustion. Reentry is made in the vertical well to attach a whipstock at a preset depth. A special bit at the end of the drill pipe is deflected by the whipstock to cut a hole through the metal casing and out the side of the well. From this window, a MWD mud motor passes through the original drill pipe and starts drilling a curved path that eventually becomes horizontal.

Horizontal drilling is necessary from offshore platforms where multiple platforms with vertical wells would be prohibitively expensive. Thus, a single platform with vertical wells that turn horizontal can cover a much wider area that vertical wells alone. Horizontal wells are employed in low-porosity rock formations such as dense shale or limestone to extract the low volume of gas, which cannot be commercially tapped by vertical wells. Once the horizontal well is drilled, "fracks" (fissures caused by fracturing the rock with high pressure water) allow gas to escape into the wellbore. This technique is also being used to extract coal bed methane from coal seams too deep to mine. Despite being more costly to drill, horizontal wells take advantage of oil and gas fields being wider than they are thick. A horizontal well can drain a much larger area of an oil or gas formation and be cost effective by reducing the total number of wells that have to be drilled to tap an oil or gas field. Horizontal wells are two to three times more costly to drill, but they can be up to twenty times more productive in extracting oil or gas than vertical wells. The longest reach of a horizontal well is 35,000 feet (6.6 miles) from an onshore production rig in the United Kingdom tapping the offshore Wytch Farm oil field.

Historically, one horizontal well was drilled from a single vertical well with the vertical wells being quite close to one another on a small plot of land or from an offshore production platform. It is now possible to have multiple horizontal wells branching from a single vertical well with other branches emanating from these branches called multilateral branching. Multilateral branching allows for more effective drainage of pockets of gas or oil reservoirs, and may one day cover an area tens of miles from a single production platform in several or all directions. Horizontal wells are better for environmentally sensitive areas, such as northern Alaska, since they can tap a wider area with fewer staging pads and roads whose simpler infrastructure would reduce the risk of environmental damage.

Recently developed techniques include a rotary steerable drill string that rotates for faster well completion than a mud motor. Another technique is a highly specialized type of mud motor with kick pads that orient the drill bit to the right angle rather than relying on a bent mud motor. Another innovation is substituting flexible coiled tubing that can be continuously unreeled from a giant spool up to 4,000 feet in length for a rigid drill string. The tubing is made of special alloys to allow it to be reeled on a giant spool like electrical cable, yet be strong enough to maintain its shape within an oil well. Coiled tubing allows for uninterrupted drilling, reduces the equipment footprint at the drill site, and lets the production well wander, or snake, horizontally from one gas or oil formation to another.

Taking the lead from oil companies, horizontal drilling is now being used to lay underground water and gas pipelines and communication cables without opening a trench. Horizontal drilling is being used to remediate land under airport runways and industrial plants to clean up spilled jet fuel and chemicals without disturbing the operations of the runway or the industrial enterprise and to introduce microbes for bioremediation of toxic soil. Horizontal drilling can be used to place leak-detection censors or install gas- or liquid-collection systems beneath solid or hazardous waste landfills, dewater hillsides to prevent mudslides from endangering housing developments or stabilize mine waste dumps, and convey fluids between vertical wells and treatment facilities.[4]

## Offshore Drilling Rigs

Seventy percent of the earth's surface is covered by water, a tempting prospect for oilmen when the promise of discovering large onshore oil fields dimmed. In the 1890s a slanted well was drilled onshore to tap an offshore oil deposit, and oil rigs were built on wharves extending out to waters thirty feet deep in the Santa Barbara channel. In 1910, a gas well was completed one mile from shore in Lake Erie. In 1937 a grounded barge in shallow waters off Louisiana was the first submersible drilling rig, which does not mean that operations were conducted underwater. The submerged barge formed a barrier to keep the water out and exposed the bottom for drilling as though it were on land.

The birth of the modern offshore drilling industry occurred after the Second World War. The Depression of the 1930s dampened demand for developing new oil fields and the War dedicated the nation's resources to the production of ammunition and armaments, making it necessary for onshore oil fields to be worked with old equipment. Steel was not available for building rigs, for manufacturing spare parts, or for producing consumer goods and automobiles. The end of the war also marked the end of postponing the good life. Americans proceeded to build homes, manufacture consumer goods to fill the homes, and build roads and manufacture automobiles to fill the roads. The postwar demand for oil exploded, but the chance of discovering major or giant new fields onshore was not overly bright because much of the land surface had already been explored. The gently sloping Gulf of Mexico and its relatively shallow waters, bordered by onshore oil fields, provided a promising new area for exploration.

In very shallow waters, submersible drilling barges were sunk to rest on the bottom and keep water away from the well for drilling to proceed as though it were on dry land, a practice still in use. Floating drilling barges were and still are used in waters up to about twenty feet in depth. The drilling platform is mounted in the center of the barge and the drill pipe runs through a moon pool, a hole in the bottom of the barge surrounded by a cylinder that keeps water from flooding the barge. Kerr-McGee was among the first companies to convert excess barges and landing craft built during the Second World War to floating offshore rigs and was a technological innovator in developing a new industry. In 1947, the first offshore production rig was built on steel pilings driven into the sea floor by a pile-driver that repeatedly drops a heavy weight on a piling. The rig was in waters eighteen feet deep, twelve miles off the coast of Louisiana.

Legislation was passed in 1953 that granted state control over mineral rights in coastal waters and past that point to the federal government. Sales of leases are an important source of revenue for states that permit offshore drilling (Louisiana and Texas) and the federal government. Most states have banned offshore drilling in their coastal waters or new exploratory activity if offshore operations already exist (California). States have also succeeded in prohibiting exploration in offshore waters outside their jurisdiction such as the Hudson River canyon, where some believe an oil field may exist. In 1998 President Clinton signed an executive order extending a moratorium on leasing oil-drilling sites on the outer continental shelf until 2012. This moratorium includes nearly all the coastlines of California, Washington, Oregon, the Aleutian Islands, New England, the north and mid-Atlantic, and the eastern Gulf of Mexico, which includes an extensive area off the coast of southwest Florida. The Middle East is not the only place where oil companies face geopolitical risk.

In 1954, a submersible called "Mr. Charlie" was built. It consisted of a lower barge with a moon pool on which cylindrical columns were built to support a drilling platform. The barge was sunk in waters up to forty feet deep by flooding the lower barge, leaving the drilling platform above the water surface. When the well was completed, water was pumped out to refloat the barge for towing to a new location. "Mr. Charlie" drilled hundreds of wells before retiring in 1986 and was a springboard in the development of offshore drilling technology. For deeper waters, jack-up rigs were developed. These consisted of three legs and an upper and lower hollow hull. In transit, the lower and upper hulls are together with the legs sticking up in the air. At the drill site, the lower hull is flooded and the legs are jacked down until the lower hull is firmly on the ocean floor. For hard ocean bottoms, cylinders built on the legs, rather than a lower hull, support the rig. With the lower hull or cylinders firmly on the bottom, the jack-up rig continues to jack down the legs, raising the upper hull with the drilling platform off the surface of the water until it is 100 feet above the ocean surface. The drilling platform must be high enough above the water surface to prevent waves from striking and possibly capsizing the rig. The first jack-ups were used in waters up to 80 feet deep and are now capable of operating in waters up to 400 feet deep. In order for the drilling platform to be 100 feet above the water surface, the legs have to be 500 feet long. When being towed to a new site, the jacked-up legs stick up 500 feet into the air (equivalent to a thirty-story building), presenting a rather ungainly sight with transits limited to fair weather.

Drilling in deeper waters required another major step in technological development, which began with the government-sponsored Project Mohole (1958–1966), which envisioned drilling a well 25,000 feet deep in 15,000 feet of water. The purpose of the project was not to advance offshore drilling, but to enhance the understanding of the earth's geology by drilling through the crust in a place where it was thin enough to obtain a sample of the earth's mantle. While the project itself was never completed, it helped advance the technology of deep-water drilling. Five holes, one 600 feet deep, were drilled in 11,700 feet of water through a moon pool in the bottom of the drilling vessel. A system of swivel-mounted propellers was invented that imitated the method lobstermen use to keep their boats on station while retrieving lobster pots. The system was a precursor of computer-controlled dynamic positioning.[5]

Drill ships and semisubmersibles are employed for deep-water drilling. A semisubmersible is a floating drilling platform mounted on top of a set of columns connected to large pontoons. The pontoons are empty when in transit, then flooded when on-station to lower the rig to a semisubmerged state with the pontoons thirty to fifty feet below the ocean surface. When in a semisubmerged condition with the drilling platform above the surface, the rig is quite stable even in stormy seas such as in the North Sea, where waves may strike the drilling platform. An anchor system was sufficient to keep the first generation of semisubmersibles on-station for drilling in water up to 2,000 feet deep. Modern ultra-deep fifth-generation semisubmersibles drill in waters up to 10,000 feet deep, and are kept on-station by a dynamic positioning system. Either sound impulses from transmitters located on the ocean floor or global positioning navigational satellites keep track of the rig's position and computer-controlled thruster engines maintain the rig on-station.

Drill ships have a drilling rig mounted at the center of the ship where the drill pipe passes through a moon pool. Depending on the depth of water, a drill ship remains on-station utilizing either an anchoring system or dynamic positioning. While top-of-the-line drill ships can also drill in waters 10,000 feet deep, drill ships lack the inherent stability of semisubmersibles. The vertical motion of a drill ship from wave motion would place an enormous strain on the drill string. A motion-compensated crown block keeps the drill string steady even though the ship is not. The *Discoverer Enterprise,* built by Transocean, can drill in water up to 10,000 feet deep, with well depths (combined horizontal and vertical length) of 35,000 feet, a figure not that far from the overall goal of the Mohole Project. At its extreme limits of operational capability, the drilling rig is rotating over eight miles of drill pipe. To reduce the number of connections that have to be made when making a sixteen-mile trip, this drill ship uses 135-foot pipe lengths rather than the more conventional 90-foot lengths usually used for offshore drilling.[6]

Similar to drilling on land, offshore drilling starts with a 100- to 250-foot, 30-inch diameter conductor pipe to which the blowout preventer is bolted. Remotely operated vehicles (ROVs) do the necessary work at the bottom of the ocean with lighting systems, television cameras, and remotely operated "arms" and "wrists" doing work at pressures that would crush a human body. A flexible, metal hollow tube called the marine riser connects the drilling rig with the borehole. Transponders and underwater television identify the location of the borehole and a jet-assist device at the bottom of the marine riser lets the driller guide the riser into the borehole. The drill string passes through the marine riser forming a closed system for circulating drilling mud. Once set up, drilling progresses much as it does on land, except for longer drill pipes and the additional risks of drilling at sea. Crew safety takes on a greater sense of urgency because the crew on an offshore drilling rig has limited means of escape if the rig catches fire, explodes, or capsizes during a storm. An additional risk is drilling into a large pocket of natural gas, which, if released in massive quantities, surrounds the rig and causes a loss of buoyancy that may result in its capsizing or sinking.

Drilling offshore wells requires a crew that varies with the size of the operation, but basically consists of a driller, who oversees operations, plus an assortment of derrickmen, motormen, diesel-engine operators, pump operators, mud men, and crane operators, plus roughnecks and roustabouts. Roughnecks handle connecting and disconnecting drill pipe and roustabouts handle supplies, including bringing drill pipe onboard the rig. Others are employed in maintenance and repair of machinery and equipment, keeping the rig on-station, and maintaining a livable environment. Schedules vary, but basically there are four crews, two aboard the rig working twelve-hour shifts and two on shore waiting their turn. The length of their stays onboard the rig depends on the rig's location: the more remote the location, the longer the stay. Crew transfers can be accomplished either by fast boats for rigs relatively close to shore, or by helicopters.

The growing number of offshore-drilling rigs capable of drilling in ever deeper waters is an indication of the growing challenge of finding new oil fields; an indication that we may be running out of places to look for oil. The world fleet of offshore rigs totaled 586 in mid-2000s, of which 383 were jack-up rigs, 160 were semisubmersibles, 36 were drill ships, and 7 were submersibles. Of the 383 jack-up rigs, 174 are capable of drilling in waters over 300 feet in depth. The 160 semisubmersibles have gone through five generations of technological advancement; none of the first generation rigs remain. Eighty-four of the second generation, thirty-six of the third, twenty-eight of the fourth, and twelve of the fifth-generation rigs are still in operation. High-end semisubmersibles and drill ships, used for drilling exploration and development wells, can cost up to $350 million each. Depending on the operational capacity of the rigs and the state of the market, the rate to employ a semisubmersible or drill ship can range from $30,000 to over $200,000 per day. Although a rule of thumb is that each million-dollar increment in construction cost increases the daily rate for employment by $1,000 per day, wildly fluctuating rates are not so much in tune with what it costs to build a rig as much as in fluctuations in the underlying demand with respect to supply. Net demand for jack-up and semisubmersible rigs in mid-2000s, in terms of numbers, was about the same as in 1990. But newer rigs have greater operational capabilities and higher productivity than older rigs, thus masking rising demand. Generally speaking, jack-ups are employed in the more shallow waters of the Gulf of Mexico, South America, and the Middle East. Semisubmersibles are employed in the North Sea, and along with drill ships, in deeper waters of the Gulf of Mexico and offshore Brazil.

Of these areas, the North Sea is by far the most challenging, where drilling proceeds 24–7 in freezing weather with frequent, strong, and long-lasting storms. These rigs have to be capable of operating in hundred-knot winds and hundred-foot waves. However, rigs operating in the relatively calm waters of the Gulf of Mexico must be able to withstand hurricane force winds and waves. Petrobras, the state oil company of Brazil, has introduced many technological developments and was the first company to successfully drill in water more than 8,000 feet deep. This record was broken in 2003 when a Transocean drill ship operated at a record depth of 10,000 feet in the Gulf of Mexico. Transocean, the world's largest offshore drilling rig company, also held the record for the deepest subsea completion in waters of nearly 7,600 feet. The company's most recent delivery is an ultradeep semisubmersible ultimately capable of drilling in 10,000 feet of water with a drilling depth of 30,000 feet, a total of 7.6 miles of drill pipe. Petrobras and Transocean frequently swap new world offshore drilling records. New and exploitable oil fields have been discovered offshore Nigeria, Angola, Brazil, and in the Gulf of Mexico, dwarfing onshore exploratory efforts.

Once an oil field has been discovered and appraised, a permanent offshore production platform is installed. In shallower waters, a production platform is built on steel piles. For deeper water (hundreds of feet), a bottom-supported steel structure with hollow chambers to hold water is constructed on its side on land. Upon completion, the structure is placed on a barge and towed to the site. The barge is then partially flooded to launch the structure, which initially floats horizontally on the surface. By flooding designated chambers, the structure is slowly brought to an upright position; further flooding sets the structure on the sea bottom. Steel piles that pass through the structure's jacket are driven into the sea bottom. Once the structure is fixed to the sea bottom, equipment modules are loaded and assembled on the production platform.

Pile drivers cannot operate in the thousand-foot ocean depths of the North Sea. The first production platforms were gravity-based platforms built on land with massive steel and concrete bottoms with steel and concrete legs connected to a platform that extended above the ocean surface. The structures, ranking among the tallest on Earth, were built on their side, maneuvered onboard a barge, and towed to deep water. Near the site, the barge was partially flooded to offload the platform, which was then partially flooded to an upright position. After being towed to its final site, other hollow chambers in the base were flooded to allow the platform to sink vertically until its massive base penetrated deep into the ocean bottom. The remaining hollow cylinders connecting the base with the platform could be used for more seawater ballast, for storage of the diesel fuel needed for its operation or crude oil. Gravity-based platforms were extremely expensive and are no longer built.

Nowadays, the tension-leg buoyant platform is used for producing oil and natural gas in deep waters. The platform floats above an offshore field; hollow steel tubes called tendons connect the floating production platform with heavy weights on the sea floor. These tendons are under tension and pull the platform down into the water to prevent it from rising and falling with waves and tides. Tension production platforms are very stable and have been successfully employed in the Gulf of Mexico and elsewhere in waters thousands of feet deep. Although tension production platforms are built to survive extreme weather, in 2005 Hurricane Katrina proved too much for one of them and turned it upside down. Like offshore exploratory rigs, production rigs operate 24–7.

Deep-sea production platforms are usually connected to a shoreside terminal by underwater pipelines, except in isolated regions of the North Sea, the offshore waters of Canada (Hibernia), West Africa, and Brazil, where shuttle tankers move oil from storage tanks within the production platform to a terminal. Besides isolation, another reason for not pipelining oil to a shore location is security of supply in locations where terminal operations are threatened by civil disturbances. When an oil field is exhausted, a production platform becomes obsolete and has to be removed and disposed of at considerable cost. In 1995, the environmental group Greenpeace aroused sufficient public opposition to Shell Oil's plan to move an obsolete production platform to deep water for sinking that Shell had to opt for the far more expensive method of towing the platform to a shoreside facility for dismantling.

A Floating Production, Storage, and Offshore Loading vessel (FPSO), often a conversion of an older but still seaworthy large crude carrier, has a production platform incorporated on the vessel's hull above an installed moon pool. The vessel provides storage for the oil and has an offloading arm for pumping crude from its tanks to shuttle tankers for transport to shoreside terminals. The advantage of a FPSO over a fixed production platform is that it is far less costly to build and install and its storage capacity eliminates the need for an underwater pipeline. The FPSO, because it relies on an anchoring system to remain on station, cannot serve deep oil fields that require dynamic positioning. FPSOs can, however, exploit offshore oil fields that are too small to economically justify building a fixed production platform and laying a pipeline to shore. Once an oil field is exhausted, a FPSO sails to another oil field, avoiding the cost of dismantling a fixed platform and building a new one.

### Evaluating a Well

Completing a production well, whether on- or offshore, is more costly than drilling an exploration or appraisal well. A careful evaluation of various logs obtained during the course of drilling an exploratory or appraisal well has to be completed prior to making a decision on whether to drill a production well. The lithographic, or sample, log records the nature of the coarser samples of rock chips separated from the drilling mud as to the type of rock, texture, grain size, porosity, microfossil content, and oil stains. Oil stains are examined in ultraviolet light to assess their nature and quality. The drilling-time log records the rate of penetration through subsurface rocks; a change in the rate of penetration indicates a change in the type of rock. The mud log records the chemical analysis of drilling mud for traces of subsurface gas and oil at various depths. The wireline well log, first introduced by Conrad Schlumberger in France during the 1920s, was, as with Hughes Tool, the basis for another oil fortune not directly related to owning oil-producing properties. The wireline well log was obtained by removing the drill string and inserting a sonde, a torpedo-shaped device laden with instruments. The first instrument was an electrical log to measure the resistance of the rocks to electricity. Changes in resistance indicate the degree of saturation of water, oil, and gas. Later additions included a natural gamma ray log to read the background radioactivity of rocks in the well. Since shale is the only sedimentary rock that emits radiation from radioactive potassium, the gamma ray log identifies the presence of shale rock or the degree of shale in mixed rock. A gamma-emitting radioactive source in the sonde creates a density or gamma-gamma log from returning gamma rays to measure porosity. The neutron porosity log records the results of bombarding rock adjacent to the well bore with neutrons. The intensity of returning neutrons from collisions indicates the presence of hydrogen, which is found in oil, gas, and water. The comparative results of the neutron porosity and gamma-gamma density logs identify the presence of natural gas. The caliper log measures the diameter of the well bore, which can widen when soft rocks slough off from the upward flow of mud in the annulus. This information is needed to calculate the amount of cement needed to case the well. The acoustic velocity, or sonic, log measures the speed of sound through a rock layer, which, for a known type of rock, indicates its porosity and the presence of fractures. The dip log measures the orientation of rock layers, or slant, from the horizontal.

Originally the sonde, with its various sensors, required pulling the drill string and removing the drill bit; since 1980, it is located just above the drill bit to provide real-time log analysis. Results of these logs are interpreted at each increment of depth by experts as to the likely productivity of the well; a key factor in deciding whether to complete a production well. If the experts decide to abandon a well, its conductor casing is pulled for salvage and the well is cemented at appropriate levels to prevent saltwater and oil seepage from rising and polluting surface waters.

**Completing a Well**

After the decision has been made to complete a well, the process starts with preparing a well for casing. Casing stabilizes a well, preventing the sides from caving in and protecting freshwater aquifers near the surface that might be polluted with oil, gas, and saltwater. If the casing is to be installed in a single operation after the well is completed, drill pipe is lowered with a used bit to circulate mud and remove any remaining cuttings from the bottom of the well. Wall scratchers remove mud from the sides of the well. Casing is thin-walled steel pipe, usually in thirty-foot lengths sized to fit inside the well bore. After the well is prepared for casing, casing pipe is screwed together and lowered into the well. A guide shoe guides the casing down the well and centralizers position the casing string in the center of the well. A float collar near the bottom of the casing string acts as a check valve to prevent mud in the well from flowing up the casing pipe. After the casing is in place, Portland cement is mixed with additives to control its density and the timing required for the cement to set. Cement is pumped down the center of the casing through the float collar, forcing its way through the bottom plug out of the casing pipe and up the annulus between the outer casing wall and the well bore. Then a top plug is added and mud is pumped down the casing, which forces the remaining cement in the casing into the annulus. The driller has to ensure that an adequate amount of cement is injected into the annulus to complete the cementing of the casing string. When the top plug meets the bottom plug cementing is complete and the wiper plugs, guide shoe, and cement at the bottom of the well are drilled out and the mud is removed from the casing pipe.

A variation of this method is to case a well in segments. After the well is drilled, the lowest section of the casing is cemented first, then a plug is installed at the top of the casing. More casing is added with holes drilled in the coupling with the installed casing to force cement out of the bottom to fill the annulus. The plug is removed and the process is repeated until the entire casing is installed. Some wells have three or four concentric casing strings installed in segments as the well is being drilled, with the largest diameter casing installed at the top of the well. After the casing is installed, the well is drilled deeper and another, narrower casing is added. This process continues until the narrowest casing string is added at the bottom of the well.

If the well ends in a producing zone, the bottom of the well is opened and filled with gravel. Smaller diameter liner pipe is run down the casing to the bottom of the well. Then the casing pipe is perforated, and fractures are created in the rock and in any impregnated mud to ease the flow of oil and gas to the perforated casing wall and then into the liner pipe. Perforation was first accomplished in 1932 using a bullet gun, a device lowered to the bottom of the well that fires bullets similar to ball bearings in all directions. The bullet gun is still in use and has been successfully employed in horizontal wells. Bullets are reduced to fine particles after firing. Shaped charges are also used, along with hydraulic injection of large volumes of diesel oil, nitrogen foam, water, or water with acid under high pressure for limestone reservoirs (the acid contains an inhibitor to prevent corrosion of the steel casing and tubing). Working over a well, which must be done several times over its lifetime, includes not only fixing mechanical problems and cleaning out the bottom of the well, but also taking measures to enhance the permeability of the surrounding rock.

The annulus between the liner pipe and the inner casing wall is sealed to prevent oil and gas from coming in contact with the casing pipe, which would corrode and weaken the casing. If the well passes through several producing zones, each has its own tubing and packing to ensure that the output of each zone is segregated in order to identify the output of each zone. Normally, a well will not have more than three producing zones. Shaped charges, or firing bullets, perforate the casing and fracture the surrounding rock at each producing zone. Seals are installed to ensure that oil and gas enter the liner pipe, not the casing pipe.

A "Christmas tree," normally made from a single block of metal, is mounted on top of the casing with a master valve that can shut off a well under emergency conditions. Other valves control the pressure and flow from each producing liner pipe or tubing string within the well with associated gauges that measure the tubing pressure. A new well usually has sufficient reservoir pressure to cause the oil to flow naturally from the top of the liner pipe or tubing string. If the reservoir pressure declines to a point at which oil no longer flows from the well, the most common form of lifting device is the sucker rod pump. A motor powered by electricity or natural gas from the well drives a walking beam mounted on a Samson post to obtain a vertical up-and-down motion to drive a pump. On the downward stroke, a ball unseats from a seal, letting oil flow into the pump. On the upward stroke, the ball seats and forces the oil up while the space below the pump fills up with more oil. The pumping rate has to be less than the fill rate for the pump to operate properly. A gas lock can form in the pump if natural gas is present. A sucker rod pump may have to be used in natural gas fields that release a lot of water. A gas lift system, which injects some of the natural gas produced by the well into the annulus between the tubing and the casing, can be installed for wells producing a mixture of saltwater, oil, and gas. Gas lift valves installed along the tubing string allow the gas to enter the tubing. The expanding bubbles in the liquid force the mixture of water, oil, and natural gas up the tubing. Gas lift systems are simple and inexpensive to operate, but are only effective for relatively shallow wells. Alternatively, an electrically or hydraulically driven submersible pump can be installed at the bottom of a well.

**Moving the Oil to the Well**

The primary force that causes oil and gas to flow through pores in the reservoir rock toward the bottom of the well is the pressure differential between the oil and gas within the reservoir rock and the pressure at the bottom of a well. The driving force in the reservoir can be provided by dissolved natural gas in the oil or by a natural gas cap on top of the oil that expands as oil is removed from a reservoir. Natural gas cannot maintain the same initial reservoir pressure as it expands, which causes oil production to decline with time. Subsurface water entering an oil reservoir from its bottom or sides as a primary driving force can maintain nearly constant reservoir pressure and oil production. An oil well goes "dry" when natural gas or water reaches the bottom of the well. Gravity can also be an effective drive mechanism for wells drilled into the bottom of steeply inclined reservoirs. Most oil reservoirs have more than one of these four primary driving forces.

Natural gas reservoirs are either driven by expanding gas or by water. Natural gas wells do not go dry in the sense that oil does, but their pressure may decline to somewhere between 700–1,000 psi, the lowest pressure acceptable for a gas pipeline. A compressor can extend the life of a gas well. If production from an oil well falls below 10 barrels per day, it is known as a stripper well. Stripper wells number about half a million in the United States, with many producing as little as 2 or 3 barrels per day. They are kept in production or reactivated if shut-in as long as revenue exceeds the costs of operation and reactivation.

**Maintaining Reservoir Pressure**

The recovery factor—the portion of the oil and gas removed from a reservoir—depends on the driving force. The recovery factor is lowest for oil reservoirs driven by natural gas in solution with the oil or by gravity, higher if driven by a natural gas cap, and higher yet if driven by water. The overall average recovery factor for oil fields is only about one-third (natural gas fields have higher recovery factors). Thus, when a well that relies on the natural drive of the reservoir goes "dry," about two-thirds of the oil is still in the ground.

Secondary methods to maintain reservoir pressure and promote oil recovery normally involve injecting water or natural gas. Injection wells, either specifically drilled or converted from abandoned producing wells, are placed to enhance the flow of oil in the direction of the producing wells. Water injection is the most common method for maintaining the pressure of an oil reservoir and is an environmentally acceptable way of getting rid of any brine produced by the well to avoid contaminating the freshwater table. If brine cannot be pumped into subsurface rock below the freshwater table, it must be disposed of in an acceptable manner. Brine may be placed in open tanks to let evaporation get rid of most of the water before disposal.

Depending on the type of reservoir rock, an alkaline chemical such as sodium hydroxide is mixed with the injected water to enhance recovery. Injected water must be compatible with the type of reservoir rock to ensure that a potential chemical reaction does not decrease its permeability. Pores in the reservoir rock can be plugged by injecting suspended solids in the water or by slimes feeding on injected bacteria and organic matter. Natural gas from an oil well, called associated natural gas, is normally sold, but for isolated wells far from natural gas pipelines, it is often reinjected into the oil field to maintain reservoir pressure. However, natural gas is not as effective as water in enhancing oil recovery.

Secondary methods can raise recovery to 40 percent on average from the one-third average recovery of primary methods. To reach 50 percent, tertiary or enhanced recovery methods must be employed. The price of oil plays a critical role in determining whether more costly tertiary recovery methods should be employed. Thermal recovery is utilized when the remaining oil is heavy and viscous. "Huff and puff" burns crude oil at the surface of the well to produce steam that is injected down a well. The well is shut in to allow steam to heat up the surrounding crude to reduce its viscosity, enhancing its flow through the rock. Then the well is put back into operation to extract the heated crude. Steam flooding is a continuous process in which injected steam maintains pressure on previously injected condensed steam to drive heated crude toward the producing wells. Placement of the steam injection wells is critical to ensure that the oil flows in the right direction. Thermal recovery is effective as long as crude production exceeds the amount burned to produce steam.

A fireflood is setting subsurface oil on fire and keeping it burning by forcing large quantities of air down an injection well, with or without water to create steam. The heat reduces the viscosity of the crude while increasing the pressure within the reservoir rock to enhance the flow of oil toward the producing wells. The amount of air has to be limited to avoid burning all the oil in the reservoir. Firefloods cannot be used if there is any appreciable sulfur in the oil because of the formation of sulfuric acid that eats away the liner pipe. Though simple in concept, firefloods are difficult in practice.

A chemical flood involves inserting detergent into injected water to form tiny droplets of oil to aid in their migration to a producing well. As long as water is not present, miscible floods of natural gas liquids such as butane and propane act as solvents and wash the oil out of the reservoir rock. This is one of the most effective tertiary methods of oil recovery, but it is very expensive unless the butane and propane can be recovered for recycling. Carbon dioxide floods involve either carbon dioxide as a gas or dissolved in water. Soluble in oil, carbon dioxide promotes migration to the producing wells by increasing the volume of oil and reducing its viscosity. Injected carbon dioxide can be separated from the oil at the surface of the producing well for recycling. This is not sequestration of carbon dioxide as it returns to the surface dissolved in the oil. Carbon dioxide is brought to the well in a liquefied state in tanks or is piped in from wells that produce large amounts of carbon dioxide or as a waste byproduct from nearby power, chemical, and fertilizer plants.

Tertiary recovery methods do not always succeed and require high-priced crude oil to justify their cost, but they do reduce the need to find new oil fields. With tertiary recovery, about half of the oil can be removed from an oil reservoir on average, although, as with any average, there are higher and lower recovery factors. Nevertheless, tertiary recovery methods still leave about half of the oil entrapped within the pores of reservoir rock after an oil field has gone "dry."

## GETTING THE OIL TO A REFINERY

Most wells produce a mixture of oil and saltwater with or without associated natural gas. The output from a well enters a gas oil cylinder-shaped separator where natural gas, if present, rises to the top and water sinks to the bottom, leaving oil in between the two. A heater or demulsifier may be necessary to break down an emulsion of oil and water. A certain retention time is necessary to allow the two to separate. Natural gas, if present, is diverted to a natural gas pipeline gathering system. Once separated from water, oil is pumped to a staging area that serves a number of wells and then through collecting pipelines to larger capacity pipelines that eventually connect to refineries or oil export terminals.

Pipelines provide the lowest cost means of moving crude oil and oil products on land. Crude oil pipelines are not built unless there are sufficient reserves to guarantee pipeline throughput and provide an adequate financial return. Technological advances made in building the "Big Inch," a twenty-four-inch pipeline, and the "Little Inch," a twenty-inch pipeline from the U.S. Gulf region to the northeast during the Second World War set off an explosion in pipeline construction. Modern trunk lines are up to forty-eight inches in diameter and have a throughput capacity of 1–2 million barrels per day, depending on pumping capacity. Additives to make oil more "slippery" by reducing the friction or turbulence at the boundary layer between the oil and steel pipe can improve pipeline throughput capacity. The speed of oil in a pipeline is not very impressive, about that of a fast walk, but over twenty-four hours a pipeline with a diameter of four feet can move a lot of oil. The pipeline industry in the United States and Canada is regulated as a common carrier. Tariffs are set to limit earnings on investment with assurances that all shippers have equal access and pay the same base rate.

Oil pipelines are like blood vessels in a living being, with the United States having hundreds of thousands of miles of gathering and collecting pipelines connecting countless producing wells to refineries. Most offshore oil fields such as those in the Gulf of Mexico and the North Sea are connected to land by underwater pipelines, although more remote fields use shuttle tankers. The Louisiana Offshore Oil Port (LOOP), located about twenty miles off the Mississippi River mouth in deep water, is a system of three single buoy moorings that serves large crude carriers carrying oil from the world's exporting oil nations. A discharging crude carrier pumps cargo from its tanks through a hose to the floating buoy. The floating buoy is connected via an underwater pipeline to an offshore marine pumping station. The pumping station moves the crude to onshore salt caverns for storage and connection to other crude oil pipeline systems that serve two-thirds of U.S. refinery capacity from the Gulf Coast to as far north as Chicago and as far east as the Middle Atlantic states. Russia also has an extensive crude oil pipeline system to handle domestic distribution and exports to Europe. Crude oil pipelines have been built to ship landlocked Caspian crude to Black Sea ports, and a major pipeline has been built to ship Caspian crude to a Mediterranean port in Turkey. Major projects under consideration involve pipelining Siberian oil to China and Japan and Russian oil to Murmansk, a year-round ice-free Arctic port, for export to Europe and the United States.

In addition to crude oil pipelines, product pipelines take the output from refineries to oil distribution terminals near population centers. Large product pipelines move refined products from the U.S. Gulf Coast refineries to the Atlantic and northeast markets and from Russian refineries to markets in Europe. Tank trucks complete the movement from storage tanks at pipeline distribution terminals to wholesalers and retailers. In a few nations, railroads still move crude and oil products where the volume is insufficient to justify building a pipeline.

## Tankers and Barges

Water transport is an even lower-cost alternative than pipelines because the "highway" is free, although investments have to be made in ports, terminals, and ships. Tankers and barges move about half of the oil produced either as crude from exporting terminals to refineries or as refined oil products from refineries to distribution terminals and customers. All the OPEC producers export oil by tanker, although pipelines can shorten the tanker voyage. The first Middle East export pipelines, now inoperative, carried Saudi crude to ports in Lebanon and Syria, eliminating the tanker movement from the Arabian Gulf to the Mediterranean via the Suez Canal. A portion of Iraqi crude is pipelined to a Mediterranean port in Turkey and some Saudi crude is pipelined to a Red Sea port for transfer to tankers for transit to the southern terminal of the Sumed pipeline that parallels the Suez Canal. Oil is shipped in tankers from the northern terminal of the Sumed pipeline in the Mediterranean to ports in southern and northern Europe. The Sumed pipeline allows the use of very large tankers that cannot transit the Suez Canal fully loaded to move Middle East crude to Europe. However, in about ten years' time, the Suez Canal will be widened and deepened enough to accommodate most of the world's largest tankers fully loaded.

Refineries on or near the coastline distribute oil products locally by small tankers and barges. Barges distribute the output of Rotterdam refineries up the Rhine River into central Europe and along the northern European seaboard and from refineries in the U.S. Gulf up the Mississippi River and along the Atlantic seaboard. Product carriers move cargoes from export-refining centers in the Caribbean, Mediterranean (southern Italy), Middle East, Singapore, India, and Korea to nearby and far-off markets. Price differentials arise between regions when production and distribution do not exactly match demand. Traders take advantage of price differentials once they exceed shipping costs to arrange a shipment from a low-priced to a high-priced market. Arbitrage trading completes the balancing of global refinery supply with global consumer demand.

Standard Oil was the first company to export oil. The initial shipments of kerosene from the United States to Europe were carried in barrels on general cargo sailing vessels, some of which were lost at sea when leaking fumes came in contact with an open flame in the ship's galley. The first tanker, the *Gluckauf*, built in Germany in 1886, was compartmentalized into several cargo tanks whose outer tank surface was the hull itself, now called a single-hull tanker. The vessel's deadweight ton (dwt) capacity was 3,000 tons. As a rough rule, the cargo capacity of a tanker is about 95 percent of its deadweight. Shell Trading was a major impetus in building larger and safer tankers in the early part of the twentieth century to ship Black Sea kerosene to Asia through the Suez Canal. By the end of the Second World War, the standard tanker, which had been built in large numbers for the war effort, was 16,000 dwt. As world oil movements increased in volume in the postwar era, tankers grew in carrying capacity to take advantage of their inherent economies of scale. The same size crew is required regardless of the size of the ship and the cost of building a vessel does not rise proportionately with its carrying capacity. Thus, the larger the tanker, the less its operating and capital costs in terms of cents per ton-mile of transported cargo. Though there was talk of mammoth tankers of 750,000 and 1 million dwt in the early 1970s, the 1973 oil crisis cut short the development of these behemoths. Indeed, the fall in oil exports after the 1973 crisis brought on the most devastating and long-lasting tanker depression in history.

Very few tankers over 500,000 dwt were built (the largest are just over 550,000 dwt) as they proved to be too unwieldy to serve most of the world's terminals and ended their days as storage vessels. Water depth in ports, channels and alongside terminals, terminal storage capacity, cargo availability, and the annual throughput volume determine the optimally sized tanker for each trade. The largest tankers, called Very Large Crude Carriers (Vlccs), range between 200,000–350,000 dwt. Tankers above 350,000 are known as Ultra Large Crude Carriers (Ulccs). These vessels, which number a little over 500, dominate Middle East exports. Seventy percent of Middle East cargoes are destined for Asia, 30 percent are headed around South Africa primarily to North America, and the rest to northern Europe. This is the opposite of the split in cargo destinations in the early 1970s, when these tankers made their debut, and reflects the growing importance of Asia for Middle East exports. While these vessels were originally built to serve Middle East crude exports exclusively, nowadays Middle East exports provide about 70 percent of Vlcc employment. The remaining 30 percent hauls primarily West African crude to the United States and Europe and as backhaul cargoes to Asia. Other backhaul cargoes to Asia are North Sea crude, fuel oil from Europe and the U.S. Gulf, and orimulsion (a mixture of 70 percent bitumen and 30 percent water, which is burned as a substitute for coal) from Venezuela. A few Vlccs move Saudi crude from the Red Sea pipeline terminal to the southern Sumed pipeline terminal and from the northern Sumed terminal to northern Europe.

The next size category, Suezmax tankers between 120,000–200,000 dwt, number about 300 vessels, and are primarily employed handling crude exports from West and North Africa and the North and Black Seas. Tankers smaller than Suezmaxes have more diverse trading patterns. Yet, despite there being about 4,500 tankers above 20,000 dwt, the 500 Vlccs, which represent a bit over 10 percent of the world fleet in number, make up over 40 percent in carrying capacity. Clean or refined oil products are usually transported in carriers of less than 50,000 dwt, although naphtha shipments between the Middle East and Japan are carried in product carriers as large as 100,000 dwt. Clean products tankers are smaller than crude carriers, reflecting terminal capacity and water-depth restrictions and lower throughput volume of clean products versus crude oil trades. They are also more sophisticated than crude carriers, with coated tanks and segregated cargo-handling systems to ensure cargo integrity. There are thousands of tankers and barges below 20,000 dwt, but these vessels are normally involved with intraregional distribution of oil products, not interregional trading.

## Oil Spills

Although larger-sized tankers reduce the number of tankers needed to transport oil, and, hence, the number of collisions, the environmental consequences of large tankers breaking up in open or offshore waters is worsened considerably by the greater quantity of oil that can be spilled. Tankers sinking far out at sea barely get mentioned in the press, but an oil spill that reaches land is another matter. Two of the first large oil spills were the *Torrey Canyon* in the English Channel in 1967 and the grounding of the *Amoco Cadiz* on the French coast in 1978. This sharpened environmental opposition to tankers, which came to a head in the 1989 *Exxon Valdez* spill in Alaska. Although only 15 percent of the vessel's cargo entered the environment (the rest was safely offloaded on barges), it was enough to foul nearly a thousand miles of pristine coastline. The uproar over this spill was responsible for the passage of the U.S. Oil Pollution Act of 1990, which greatly increased the limits of liability associated with oil spills and required a gradual phase-in of double-hull tankers calling on U.S. ports. This was followed by amendments to an international convention that required double-hull construction for all tankers delivered after July 1996, along with a mandatory phaseout schedule of single-hull tankers based on age.

Double-hull tankers have a space between two hulls, where the inner hull is the exterior surface of the cargo tanks. Thus a grounding, or a collision, must be of sufficient force to pierce both hulls before oil can be spilled into the environment. The space between the outer and inner hulls holds ballast water to maintain a tanker's stability when it is empty and returning to a load port, and is empty when the tanker is carrying a cargo. In single-hull tankers, ballast water had to be carried in the cargo tanks. Although these tanks were cleaned prior to taking on ballast water, there was still some contamination of ballast water from oily residues. Ballast water in double hull tankers is free of oil pollution. However, this does not prevent the migration of sea life from one part of the world to another when ballast water is pumped overboard at the load port.

The sinking of the *Erika* in 1999 polluted the French shoreline and the sinking of the *Prestige* in 2002 polluted the Spanish and Portuguese shorelines with fuel oil. The lighter ends of crude oil tend to evaporate when released, somewhat reducing environmental damage. Fuel oil is the residue of the refining process after the lighter end products have been removed. This makes fuel oil a worse pollutant than crude oil. The environmental damage wrought by these two spills reinforced public determination for "oil-spill-proof" tankers. Like the unilateral action taken by the United States after the *Exxon Valdez* incident, the European Union unilaterally shortened the phase-in of double-hull standards in European waters without bothering to obtain international approval or cooperation.

No one makes money in an oil spill other than those involved in cleanup operations and in handling lawsuits stemming from real or perceived damage. Certainly tanker owners and oil companies do not profit from an oil spill. The 1989 *Exxon Valdez* spill has cost Exxon $2.1 billion in clean-up costs, $0.3 billion in compensation payments, $0.9 billion in fines and a potential for another $2.5 billion in punitive damages under appeal, which was ultimately reduced to $0.5 billion plus twenty years of legal fees.[7]

Tanker owners and oil companies have taken positive and costly steps to ensure the safe delivery of cargo. The record for tanker spills has improved markedly since the 1970s, with less crude spilled in absolute (total tons) and in relative terms (percentage of oil carried). But this record of achievement, never accepted in the public's mind as a manifestation of good intentions, evaporated as soon as the first drop of fuel oil from the *Erika* and the *Prestige* reached the shoreline.

Most people take great solace in the double hull being the magic cure for tanker spills. Actually, spills are the result of human error, the root cause of collisions whether they be groundings, floundering on reefs, shoals, and rocks, poor tanker vessel design, shoddiness of construction, lack of thoroughness in tanker inspections, and in not maintaining a vessel fit for service at sea. It is true that double-hull construction prevents oil spills from low-energy collisions or groundings where only the outer hull is breached. This is not true for high-energy collisions or groundings where both hulls are breached. The *Exxon Valdez,* a single-hull tanker, floundered on an underwater rock that breached its single hull. The crude cargo, being less dense than water, kept the vessel afloat, permitting barges to come alongside and remove 85 percent of the cargo. Had the vessel been double hulled, the floundering would most probably have breeched both hulls. Water entering the space between the two hulls could have sunk the vessel, making it much more difficult to offload the cargo, and perhaps resulting in greater oil spillage. Try selling that concept to members of Congress reacting to public outrage!

## Refining

There are approximately 40,000 oil fields in the world, which means there are 40,000 grades of crude oil because no two crude oils from different oil fields are exactly the same. However, oil from different oil fields in the same geographic region, with more or less common characteristics, share the same gathering and collecting systems that blend the slight differences into a common commercial oil such as West Texas Intermediate, Brent Blend, and so forth. Each commercial grade of crude oil has unique properties that determine its value with respect to others.

American Petroleum Institute (API) degree ratings measure the density of crude oil. Light crudes have a lower density than heavy crudes. Condensates, extra-light forms of crude oil found in natural gas fields, have API ratings as high as 65 degrees. Medium crudes are 22–30 degrees and heavy viscous crudes vary between 7–22 degrees. Sweet crudes are under 0.5 percent sulfur and sour crudes are over 1 percent sulfur, with intermediate crudes between the two.[8] Crude oils are also classed as naphthenic or paraffinic. Naphthenic crudes are more highly valued because they produce more naphtha, the principal ingredient in gasoline and the principal driver of the entire oil industry. Paraffinic crudes are waxy, an undesirable trait. Some extra-heavy waxy crudes are unfit for refining and are burned directly as fuel. Waxy crudes require heating coils in the cargo tanks to keep the oil warm enough to be pumped in cold weather. There have been a few instances of heating coils failing during cold weather transits, resulting in the cargo congealing into one enormous ship-shaped candle.

The most highly valued crudes are naphthenic, light, sweet crude such as West Texas Intermediate. The output product slate of a refinery using light sweet crude is skewed to gasoline and other valuable light-end products. Arab Light is a paraffinic light sour crude oil, less desirable and less light than West Texas Intermediate. Heavy crude has an output product slate skewed to gasoil and fuel oil such as Duri, an Indonesian heavy sweet crude and Bachaquero 17, a Venezuelan heavy sour crude. The output product slate of a particular crude oil depends on the design of the refinery and its mode of operation. Some refineries are rather simple in design and restricted to light sweet crudes. Others are designed to run on a single type of crude oil with little ability to vary the output. If the output is too great for one product and not enough of another, the refinery operator may export one and import the other to balance supply and demand rather than change the refinery product slate. Often the residues of simpler refineries, called straight run, are sold to more sophisticated refineries capable of cracking straight run into more valuable clean products. More sophisticated refineries, so-called merchant refineries, can take a variety of crudes and process them with different modes of operation for different product slates. A mathematical modeling technique called linear programming selects the type of crude based on delivered cost, the output slate based on product prices, and the refinery mode of operation that maximizes profitability.

There is no such thing as a generic or plain vanilla oil product. Each oil product has several grades, each with a specific slate of characteristics or requirements to meet the demands of different markets. Motor gasoline has different specifications or limitations on octane rating, vapor pressure, sulfur, lead, phosphorus, gum, and corrosive impurities in addition to volatility standards (the degree of evaporation at specified temperatures). Specifications of gasoline sold in Europe are different than those in the United States. The U.S. gasoline market is fragmented, where California, for instance, has different specifications for gasoline than other states.

Jet fuels have specifications on acidity, aromatics, olefins, sulfur and mercaptans (a malodorous form of organic sulfur), flash point, gravity, vapor pressure, freezing point, viscosity, combustion and corrosion properties, and thermal stability. Although the same as jet fuel, kerosene for lighting and heating has, as one might expect, fewer and less demanding specifications. Gasoil for home heating and diesel fuel have standards that vary in terms of flash, pour, and cloud points, carbon, ash, viscosity, specific gravity, cetane (analogous to octane) rating, sulfur, and corrosive impurities. Diesel fuels have another set of specifications, depending on the type of diesel engine. Even heavy fuel oil, the bottom of the barrel, the residue of the refining process, has various specifications with regard to flash and pour points, water, sediment, sulfur, ash content, and viscosity, depending on its end use, that is, whether it is to be burned in industrial plants or as bunkers for marine engines.

Refining is a bit of a misnomer since refining suggests purification. Refining is not so much purifying crude oil, but transforming it into different products by separating, altering, and blending various hydrocarbon molecules. The refinery process starts with preheating crude oil and adding chemicals and water. The mixture sits in a desalting unit where gravity separates the oil and water, washing out inorganic salts and trace metals that can corrode refining equipment and poison catalysts. Atmospheric distillation first heats crude oil above 720°F, and the resulting vapors enter a distillation column or fractionating tower stacked with perforated trays. Hydrocarbon vapors rise and condense to a liquid on the trays and are transformed back into a vapor by heat exchange with other upwelling hot vapors. The vaporized hydrocarbons rise to a higher tray, condense, and are turned back to a vapor and rise again. Eventually a particular hydrocarbon vapor reaches a tray where it condenses to a liquid, but cannot collect enough energy from passing hydrocarbons to change back to a vapor. This continuous exchange of heat between liquid and vapor allows hydrocarbon molecules of a similar nature to collect on the same tray. The sorted liquid hydrocarbons are drawn off through outlets placed at different heights on the distillation column. The lightest hydrocarbons with the lowest boiling points or temperatures of condensation are drawn off at the top of the fractionating tower and the heaviest hydrocarbons with the highest boiling points or temperatures of condensation at the bottom.

Starting at the top of the fractionating tower, methane in the oil escapes without condensing and is collected and used in the refining process. Flaring of unwanted gases, while common in the past, now means a loss of revenue. The lightest hydrocarbons of butane, propane, and ethane condense below 90°F. A refinery does not just produce simple butane and propane, but also more complex forms such as butylene and propylene. To provide a brief taste of the complexity of the refining process, an alkylation unit with either a sulfuric or hydrofluoric acid catalyst (a catalyst promotes a chemical reaction without being part of it) can transform butylene to alkylate, a high-octane ingredient for motor gasoline or aviation fuel, plus other light end byproducts, butane and isobutane.

Light end products of the refining process can become part of the gasoline pool or end up as petrochemical feedstock to create the wonderful world of plastics. Walk around a house and look at all the objects made from plastic. One would be surprised at the extent of plastic in automobiles or the use of plastic in medical facilities (tubing and plastic bags for intravenous feeding and a host of other uses, blood sample vials, gowns for patients and medical personnel, bedding, gloves, and even body parts). This amazing world of plastics comes from the light ends of the distillation process that are feedstock for steam crackers that produce ethylene plus a whole array of other petrochemicals such as propylene, butadiene, butylene, benzene, toluene, xylene, and raffinate. Ethylene can be changed into other petrochemicals such as polyethylene, ethylene oxide, dichloride, and others to become plastic packaging, trash bags, plastic containers, antifreeze, flooring, paints, adhesives, polyester for textiles, and upholstery for furniture. Propylene goes through its intermediary transformations to end up as polyurethane foams, polyester resins, protective coatings, film, and adhesive for plywood. Butadiene ends up in tires, rubber goods, nylon, and high-impact plastic products. Benzene becomes polystyrene, which is found in insulation and disposable dinnerware, while other forms of benzene become detergents, fiberglass, herbicides, and pesticides. Toluene and xylene can end up in the motor gasoline pool or in paints, coatings, and in polyurethane and polyester products, depending on their respective value in the gasoline pool or as paints and plastics.

The next level down in a fractionating tower produces light naphthas that condense between 90°F–175°F and become part of the gasoline pool. Heavy naphthas condense between 175°F–350°F and are fed into a catalytic reformer to produce a mix of reformate for high-octane gasoline and BTX (benzene, toluene, xylene). The mix of reformate and BTX from a catalytic reformer can be varied according to their respective prices in the gasoline pool or as petrochemicals. The butane and isobutene byproducts of naphtha reforming are sold or used elsewhere in the refining process and the hydrogen byproduct is consumed in a refinery's hydrotreating and hydrocracking units.

Kerosene condenses between 350°F–450°F and can be sold as kerosene or jet fuel with or without a run through a hydrotreater. A hydrotreater uses hydrogen from the naphtha reformer and a catalyst to purify kerosene and gasoil to improve combustion performance and remove sulfur. Sulfur comes out as hydrogen sulfide and is then reduced to pure sulfur for sale to industrial users and fertilizer manufacturers. Light gasoil condenses between 450°F–650°F and is sold as heating oil and diesel fuel. Heavy gasoil condenses between 650°F–720°F. Catalytic cracking splits the long hydrocarbon chains of heavy gasoil into shorter chains by breaking carbon-carbon bonds with a special silicon dust catalyst. The resulting free carbon sticks to the silicon dust, which inhibits its effectiveness until it is burned away in a regenerator. The output of the cat cracker is primarily naphtha and gasoil; the mix is adjustable to make more gasoline during the summer or more heating oil during the winter. Heavy cycle oil produced by the cat cracker is either recycled or becomes part of the residual fuel pool.

In addition to catalytic cracking, hydrocracking is another method used to break long hydrocar-

Table 6.1

**Historical Development of Refining Processes**

|  | Process | Purpose | By-Product |
|---|---|---|---|
| 1862 | Atmospheric distillation | Produce kerosene | Naphtha, tar |
| 1870 | Vacuum distillation | Lubricants | Asphalt, resids |
| 1913 | Thermal cracking | Gasoline | Resids |
| 1916 | Sweetening | Reduce sulfur | Sulfur |
| 1930 | Thermal reforming | Improve octane | Resids |
| 1932 | Hydrogenation | Remove sulfur | Sulfur |
| 1932 | Coking | Gasoline base stocks | Coke |
| 1933 | Solvent extraction | Improve lubes | Aromatics |
| 1935 | Solvent dewaxing | Improve pour point | Waxes |
| 1935 | Catalytic polymerization | Improve gasoline yield and octane | Petrochemical feedstocks |
| 1937 | Catalytic cracking | Improve gasoline octane | Petrochemical feedstocks |
| 1939 | Visbreaking | Reduce viscosity | Distillates, tar |
| 1940 | Isomerization | Alkylate feedstock | Naphtha |
| 1942 | Fluid catalytic cracking | Improve gasoline yield and octane | Petrochemical feedstocks |
| 1950 | Deasphalting | Increase cracking feedstock | Asphalt |
| 1952 | Catalytic reforming | Upgrade low-quality naphtha | Aromatics |
| 1954 | Hydrodesulfurization | Remove sulfur | Sulfur |
| 1956 | Inhibitor sweetening | Remove mercaptans | Disulfides |
| 1957 | Catalytic isomerization | Convert to high octane molecules | Alkylation feedstocks |
| 1960 | Hydrocracking | Improve quality and reduce sulfur | Alkylation feedstocks |
| 1974 | Catalytic dewaxing | Improve pour point | Waxes |
| 1975 | Residual hydrocracking | Increase gasoline yield from resids | Heavy resids |

bon chains into shorter chains of more valuable naphtha, jet fuel, and light gasoil. Hydrocracking employs high temperatures (650°F–800°F) and hydrogen from the naphtha reformer under high pressure (1,500–4,000 psi) in the presence of a catalyst to split hydrocarbon chains. Refiners prefer to consume hydrogen byproduct from naphtha reformers rather than purchase it or strip it from methane. Refinery operators have a long history of the safe production and distribution of hydrogen within a refinery, which may come in handy someday if society begins the slow shift to a hydrogen economy.

What is left at the bottom of the distillation column is called atmospheric (or atmos) or straight run resid. Simpler designed refineries that cannot further process straight run resid normally sell it to more sophisticated refineries that can. Vacuum distillation heats straight run to nearly 1,100°F, then injects a blast of steam in a vacuum to create light and heavy vacuum gasoil. The heavy vacuum gasoil can be fed to a cat cracker to further break down the hydrocarbon chains into lighter end products. What is left is called flasher bottoms, a heavy fuel oil burned as an industrial and utility fuel, as bunkers for marine engines, or made into lubricating oils. Viscosity breakers, or visbreakers, also break up long molecular chains of hydrocarbons to recover more gasoline and gasoil from resids. Cokers crack heavy refinery streams into light products, leaving nearly solid carbon, called petroleum coke, which looks like charcoal briquettes and is burned like coal. Petroleum coke and asphalt are the very bottom of the bottom of the barrel. Considering the nature of asphalt and petroleum coke, one can conclude that refinery operators have learned to squeeze the last light hydrocarbon molecule out of crude oil. All this did not happen overnight. Table 6.1 shows the historical development of refinery processes (note how many are associated with increasing gasoline yield).[9]

## OIL RESERVES

Oil resources are the totality of oil in the ground. Half of this is irretrievable, even with the most costly recovery methods. Oil that is retrievable is called reserves. Reserves of an oil and gas field are not known with certainty until the last well is dry. Reserves are an estimate of the amount of oil and gas that can be removed from a reservoir under current oil prices employing current extraction technology, not the amount of oil resources actually in the ground. Thus, an improvement in the price of oil that can support more costly recovery methods, or an advance in oil-extraction technology, can change the amount of proven reserves. Oil resources are fixed by what is in the ground whereas reserves are a variable dependent on oil prices and extraction technologies. Proven oil reserves can be considered working inventory but not an inventory that appears on the balance sheets of oil companies. Proven oil reserves are reported as a footnote in an annual report. The reported book value of a share of oil company stock based on its balance sheet does not include the value of the company's proven reserves. Proven reserves are, however, acceptable as collateral for bank loans.

Proven reserves are reserves that can be calculated with reasonable accuracy based on field production and the results of appraisal or development wells that measure the potential size of an oil field. The calculation of proven reserves is based on the volume of the pay zone, the porosity and permeability of the reservoir, the degree of oil saturation, and the recovery factor. Porosity is obtained from well logs or cores and oil saturation from a resistivity well log. The recovery factor is estimated by the reservoir drive, nature of the oil, and permeability of the reservoir rock. Another method of estimating proven reserves is based on the decline curve, the falloff in production over time. The materials balance method is another mathematical approach that correlates the volume of oil, water, and gas produced with the change in reservoir pressure.

Proven reserves are either developed (within reach of existing wells) or undeveloped (new wells would have to be drilled to access the oil). Probable and possible reserves are calculated in a fashion similar to proven reserves, but their lower classification reflects the greater degree of uncertainty associated with the underlying data. Rule 4.10(a) of Regulation S-X under the U.S. Securities Act of 1933 was promulgated to protect investors from being fleeced by unscrupulous speculators selling east Texas oil properties. The required methodology for calculating proven reserves is based on actual production. In 2004 the U.S. Securities and Exchange Commission (SEC) ordered Shell Oil to remove over 4 billion barrels of oil, equivalent to 20 percent of its reserves, from proven reserves because Shell had not followed the prescribed methodology. Shell had categorized certain deep-water reserves as proven based on the results of exploratory wells and 3-D seismic analysis of their reservoir structures. Shell retorted that the SEC was using a dated methodology applicable to onshore reservoirs, not deep-water offshore reservoirs. The SEC response was that its rules are clear—an assessment of proven reserves must be based on actual production from existing wells using an analytical approach that can substantiate at least a 90 percent chance of recoverability. Without following the SEC script for determining reserves, this portion of Shell's reserves could not be considered proven, but could be considered probable if a 50 percent chance of recoverability could be demonstrated or, lacking that, the reserves could be considered possible. Thus, while Shell's total proven, probable, and possible reserves remained unchanged, the portion considered proven took a significant hit.

More ominous was the *Petroleum Intelligence Weekly* (*PIW*) report in January 2006 that Kuwait's assessment of proven reserves of 99 billion barrels, representing 10 percent of known world reserves, might be overstated by as much as four times. If true, then Kuwait's proven reserves are only 25 billion barrels. *PIW* estimated that proven and unproven reserves may total 48 billion

Table 6.2

**Write-up of OPEC Reserves**

| Nation | Year | Write-up of Reserves Billion Barrels |
|---|---|---|
| Kuwait | 1983 | 25.7 |
| Venezuela | 1985 | 26.5 |
| Iran | 1986 | 33.9 |
| Iraq | 1986–87 | 35.0 |
| United Arab Emirates | 1986 | 64.2 |
| Saudi Arabia | 1988 | 85.4 |

barrels, about half the official estimate. If true, writing off 5–7.5 percent of the world's known petroleum reserves in one blow cannot be lightly dismissed.

**Are We on a Slippery Slope?**

Indonesia, the United Kingdom, and the United States have three things in common—they were once exporters, their production has already peaked (down 3.2 million bpd [barrels per day] from their aggregate production of 12.5 million bpd in 1997), and are now oil importers. Nations whose oil production is less in 2008 than in 2000 include Argentina, Australia, Brunei, Colombia, Denmark, Egypt, Indonesia, Mexico, Nigeria, Norway, Oman, Romania, Syria, the United Kingdom, the United States, Venezuela, Vietnam, and Yemen. In some cases, the fault is not finding sufficient replacement oil and in others mismanagement of oil resources. Indonesia is the first OPEC nation to become a net oil importer and is no longer a member. However, Indonesia is still a net energy exporter as it continues to exploit its vast natural gas and coal resources.

The United States, once the world's largest oil exporter, is now the world's largest oil importer. Despite discoveries of oil in the North Slope of Alaska and in the Gulf of Mexico, oil production in the United States has been in a slow decline from exhaustion of Lower 48 oil fields and the decades-long prohibition of exploration in the Arctic National Wildlife Reserve and in offshore waters other than Louisiana and Texas. The prohibition of oil drilling in offshore Florida waters was strongly supported by yacht owners who did not want their ocean vistas ruined by the drilling rigs that provide oil for their fuel-guzzling yachts—an obvious disconnect between desire and reality. Those who own gas-guzzling SUVs for their daily trips to the shopping mall, yet oppose anything the oil industry proposes, are guilty of the same disconnect.

World oil reserves are 1,258 billion barrels (1.258 trillion barrels), a figure that includes 270.5 billion barrels of OPEC write-ups, shown in Table 6.2.[10] These write-ups are held in suspicion as they were not accompanied by new discoveries. While it is true that existing reserves could have been recalculated to the higher totals, it is also true that during this time, OPEC was setting production quotas based on proven reserves. A warranted or unwarranted write-up of proven reserves would have resulted in a higher oil production quota and higher revenue.

Table 6.3 lists the world's largest oil fields. The cumulative percentage is based on the adjusted proven reserves of a little over 900 billion barrels, net of the write-ups in Table 6.2. The Ghawar field represents 7 percent of the world's proven resources. The total of the Ghawar and the Greater Burgan fields represent 10 percent of the world's proven reserves, and so forth.[11]

These eighteen supergiant fields account for one-third of the world's known proven reserves in

Table 6.3

**World's Largest Oil Fields**

| Ultimate Recovery Oil Millions Bbls | Country | Field Name | Discovery Year | Cumulative Percentage |
|---|---|---|---|---|
| 66,058 | Saudi Arabia | Ghawar | 1948 | 7 |
| 31,795 | Kuwait | Greater Burgan | 1938 | 10 |
| 22,000 | Iraq | Rumaila North & South | 1953 | 13 |
| 21,145 | Saudi Arabia | Safaniya | 1951 | 15 |
| 17,223 | Abu Dhabi | Zakum | 1964 | 17 |
| 17,000 | Iraq | Kirkuk | 1927 | 19 |
| 16,820 | Saudi Arabia | Manifa | 1957 | 20 |
| 13,390 | Venezuela | Tia Juana | 1928 | 22 |
| 13,350 | Iran | Ahwaz | 1958 | 23 |
| 13,010 | USA-Alaska | Prudhoe Bay | 1967 | 25 |
| 13,000 | Kazakhstan | Kashagan | 2000 | 26 |
| 12,631 | Iran | Marun | 1964 | 27 |
| 12,237 | Saudi Arabia | Zuluf | 1965 | 29 |
| 12,000 | Iraq | Majnoon | 1977 | 30 |
| 11,800 | Iran | Gachsaran | 1928 | 31 |
| 10,276 | Abu Dhabi | Murban Bab | 1954 | 32 |
| 10,265 | Saudi Arabia | Abqaiq | 1940 | 33 |
| 10,000 | Iran | Fereidoon | 1960 | 34 |

40,000 oil fields. Two-thirds of these were discovered in and prior to 1960, nearly half a century ago. All but three are in the Middle East. OPEC, which is made up of Middle East nations plus Algeria, Libya, Angola, Nigeria, Ecuador, and Venezuela, possesses 76 percent of the world's oil reserves and produces nearly 45 percent of the world's oil. Asia consumes 30 percent of world oil production, North America 27 percent, and EurAsia (Europe plus Former Soviet Union) 24 percent. Asia, North America and Europe are dependent on imports, but Asia is far more dependent on Middle East imports than North America or Europe. The location of major world oil reserves and major oil consumers illustrates with great clarity the geopolitics of oil—the world is utterly incapable of extricating itself from reliance on OPEC oil. But the United States could become independent of Middle East (not OPEC) oil if it had the will to do so.

In 1956 M. King Hubbert, a geophysicist with a background in exploration for Shell Oil, postulated that U.S. oil production would peak in the early 1970s based on an assessment of discoverable oil (known oil reserves plus that yet-to-be discovered). Scorned by his contemporaries, he turned out to be basically right. Hubbert was off a bit on the actual timing of the peak in production because, since he made his original prediction, more oil was discovered in Alaska and in the Gulf of Mexico than he anticipated. But he was not off by much.

Modern-day followers of Hubbert assess the quantity of ultimately discoverable oil and compare that to cumulative production on a global scale. Oil production peaks when cumulative production has consumed half of the ultimately discoverable reserves. Ultimately discoverable reserves consist of known reserves, including enhanced production from played-out fields through secondary and tertiary recovery methods, and an assessment of what has not yet been discovered. When on the downhill slope of a bell-shaped curve, exploration and extraction become more expensive as fewer and smaller oil fields are discovered in more remote areas and more costly methods have to be employed to maintain production in aging oil fields. Furthermore, oil becomes more viscous as a field ages, a fact that increases refining costs.

When applying Hubbert's thinking on a global scale, one still has to deal with the challenge of assessing ultimately discoverable oil. As with discoveries in Alaska and the Gulf of Mexico, any discovery that increases the assessment on ultimately discoverable oil postpones the peaking of production. Right now the favorite assessment for ultimately discoverable oil is between 2–3 trillion barrels. The lower estimate comes from followers of Hubbert,[12] while the higher estimate is from the U.S. Geological Survey.[13]

If we take the lower estimate of ultimately discoverable and recoverable oil of 2 trillion barrels and assume that 1 trillion barrels have already been consumed, we are either peaking now or shortly will be. If the higher estimate of 3 trillion barrels is valid, then we have some breathing room. The higher estimate places us 0.5 trillion barrels away from peaking if we have already consumed 1 trillion barrels. At consumption levels of 80 million barrels per day, we will consume the 0.5 trillion barrels separating us from peak production in seventeen-and-one-half years. If consumption grows by 1 million barrels per day, which is less than historical growth, peaking occurs in sixteen years. At an annual growth of 1.5 percent per year, peaking occurs in fifteen years. Whether peaking occurs at fifteen or twenty years is not critical; what is critical is that, even if peaking occurs in twenty years, we will end this century with no oil. Many of us will be dead by then, but what of our progeny?

The times of trouble do not begin when the oil is gone, but after production has peaked. This is not a prescription for cheap oil, but expensive oil. Oil-extraction costs are already rising as we explore in more inhospitable and remote locations for oil. The historical survey of water-depth capacity and level of sophistication of offshore-drilling rigs attests vividly to the increasing challenge of finding new oil fields. Higher-priced oil slows or depresses economic activity in industrialized nations and sends developing nations with little indigenous supplies of oil and a perennial negative trade balance into an economic tailspin. Every unsuccessful exploratory well decreases the overall chance of finding another supergiant oil field. Huge finds are necessary to increase reserves in a world of rising consumption. Decreasing oil reserves after peak production will create greater stress among nations in an ever more evanescent search for security of supply. We may be at the beginning of the times of trouble with our military involvement in the Middle East, which started in the 1980s during the Iran-Iraq War to keep the sea lanes open, then escalated sharply in 1990 with protecting Kuwait and escalated sharply again with the invasion of Iraq in 2003. Figure 6.1 shows the historical record for discovering giant oil fields of greater than 500 million barrels. Clearly the peak of discovery has passed. Prior to 1968, the problem faced by oil executives was how to control production to maintain price in the face of mounting discoveries. Since 1968, with the exception of two or three years, discoveries have not kept up with consumption by a significant margin. Current estimates are that discoveries compensate for only one third of consumption; a sure-fire prescription for running out of oil.

In 1980, remaining proven oil reserves were about 670 billion barrels, compared to the current estimate of 1.2 trillion barrels. One may wonder how reserves can be getting larger if the rate of discovery of new fields lags behind consumption. Part of the answer is that Figure 6.1 only measures large finds of over 500 million barrels; smaller fields are not being counted. Part of the answer also lies in the fact that proven reserves of a new field, once established, may not always be written down as it is being depleted. Proven reserves of major OPEC exporting nations with no discoveries of note remain the same year after year despite significant production. This cannot be, but any write-down would reduce their production quotas. Reserves should take into consideration both new discoveries and the depletion of existing reserves and write-ups of existing reserves. The U.S. Geological Survey evaluated the growth of petroleum reserves between 1996 and 2003.[14] During this eight-year period (including 2003), oil reserves increased 240 billion barrels of which

Figure 6.1    **Number of Giant Oil Field Discoveries**

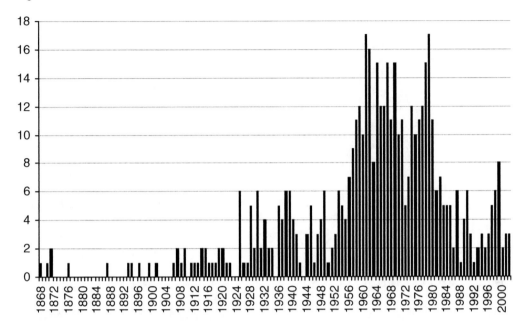

69 billion barrels were new discoveries and 171 billion barrels were write-ups of existing oil reserves. Sub-Saharan Africa was the largest source of new discoveries (20 billion barrels) followed by the Middle East and North Africa (14 billion barrels). In terms of write-ups of existing reserves, nearly half (83 billion barrels) occurred in the Middle East and North Africa. During these eight years, total consumption was 197 billion barrels, less than the additions to reserves. Indeed, the ratio of proven reserves to annual production has been in a slight uptrend since 1980 of 40 years, or 30 years if the write-ups in Table 6.2 are removed. Taking the figures at their face value, additions to reserves mainly in the form of increases to existing reserves are keeping slightly ahead of consumption. This would suggest that we are not yet at peak oil. The problem is that reserves of older fields not being adjusted to reflect production result in an overstatement of reserves.

Since the beginning of the oil age, predictions of the world running out of oil have been made, and all have been proven wrong. In 1879, the U.S. Geological Survey was formed in response to a fear of an oil shortage. In 1882 the Institute of Mining Engineers estimated that there were 95 million barrels left, an amount that would be exhausted in four years at the then-present consumption rate of 25 million barrels per year. In the early 1900s, Theodore Roosevelt opined that there were about twenty years of reserves left and hearings were held in Washington on the adequacy of supply. In 1919, the *Scientific American* warned that there were only twenty years of oil left in the ground and made a plea for automobile engines to be designed for greater energy efficiency (déjà vu?). In 1920, the U.S. Geological Survey estimated that U.S. reserves were only 6.7 billion barrels, including what was known and remaining to be discovered (current U.S. reserves are 30 billion barrels after eighty-odd years of production).[15] In the 1920s, the U.S. government, worried over the adequacy of oil supplies, secured an interest in the Turkish Petroleum Company and had to almost coerce reluctant U.S. oil companies to get involved with Middle East oil.

All these forecasts have been proven wrong, but that does not mean that the current spate of dire forecasts is necessarily wrong. The big difference between past and present forecasts is a lack of large oil discoveries. A forty-year hiatus in discovering supergiant fields should not be ignored. If oil cannot be replenished as fast as it is being consumed, then it is a wasting asset. It is not a question of whether, but when, we run out of oil. Yet, all this hand-wringing is based on proven reserves. There is something unsettling about considering only proven reserves, which is a variable based on current oil prices and current extraction technology. Increase price or improve extraction technology, and proven reserves will increase from the reclassification of probable reserves to proven and, perhaps, possible reserves upgraded to probable. Oil reserve statistics are also subject to manipulation for political or commercial reasons. Perhaps some OPEC nations exaggerated their reserves to get a higher production quota. Perhaps others do not want the world to know the true amount of their reserves in order to sustain oil prices. A particular geographic area may be a very strong candidate for harboring enormous oil reserves, but exploration might be postponed on the theory that what may be in the ground will be worth more if discovered tomorrow than if discovered today.

Probable and possible reserves and unconventional sources of oil could make a difference. As things stand, unless the world experiences the thrill of a discovery of supergiant fields with some degree of regularity, it is clear that the frequency of discovering major oil finds is dropping, the size of newly discovered oil fields is falling, the cost of extraction is increasing, the overall quality of oil from aging fields is dropping—all signs that oil is peaking. Having said that, top oil company executives maintain that there is plenty of oil to be discovered beneath the ground, but the problem is above the ground. Above-ground challenges include not being able to negotiate a reasonable deal with national oil companies, not being permitted to drill as in offshore waters of the continental United States or Alaska, and reneging of contracts and unilateral changes in contractual arrangements as in Venezuela and Russia.

## Was 2004 a Watershed Year?

Two prominent government projections published in 2004 indicated that a doubling to a near tripling of Middle East oil exports by 2025 and 2030 would be necessary to keep up with world growth in demand.[16] A review of the Middle East oil producers rapidly leads to the conclusion that Saudi Arabia is the mainstay of incremental exports. The presumption that Saudi Arabia has the spare capacity to export whatever is required is now being questioned. The reservoir pressure in Ghawar, the world's largest oil field and responsible for 60 percent of Saudi output, is maintained by pumping in seawater. Over time seawater mixes with crude oil, with an increasing concentration of seawater in oil coming from producing wells. The end of Ghawar will be marked when mostly saltwater comes out of its oil wells.[17] While Saudi Arabia vociferously denies the rumor that Ghawar is showing signs of aging by an increasing presence of seawater, other supergiant oil fields in Russia, Mexico, Venezuela, the United States, and Indonesia are showing indisputable signs of aging.

While once Saudi Arabia was capable of ramping up its production when another OPEC member such as Nigeria and Venezuela stopped exporting oil, this is no longer possible other than for short disruptions. Events in 2004 indicated that Saudi Arabia was not capable of pumping sufficient quantities of light to medium sweet grades of crude to satisfy demand by the world's refinery operators. Although Saudi Arabia was able to pump heavy sour grades in large quantities, there was insuffiient capacity of the world's refineries to refine this crude, causing a record price spread between these two grades plus a sharp rise in sweet crude prices.

The world was up against two constraints in 2004: the capacity of the oil producers to meet demand for light sweet crude and the capacity of the oil refiners to process heavy sour crude.

The decline in OPEC's theoretical maximum production capacity from 39 million bpd in 1979 to 32 million bpd in 2004 has to be treated as another warning that the Middle East cannot be considered an infinite source of oil.[18] The matter is worse when viewed in terms of spare capacity. In both 1979 and 2004, OPEC production was 31 million bpd. This implies a spare capacity of 8 million bpd in 1979 and only 1 million bpd in 2004. There is little margin for OPEC as a group to satisfy world demand if a single major OPEC nation ceases to export for other than a short period of time. The runup in prices in 2008 demonstrated just how narrow the gap between supply and demand had become.

Some people look to Russia as a potential safety valve for augmenting global spare capacity. Russia has large oil and natural gas reserves but has proven to be a difficult place to invest. Russia has made life difficult for both domestic and foreign oil companies by unilaterally redefining tax liabilities and changing contractual obligations. Changing the rules of the game does not make Russia a safe place to invest. Nor is Russia a dependable exporter. In 2006 and again in 2009, Russia interrupted natural gas shipments to the Ukraine over a price dispute that also interrupted natural gas flows to Europe in the midst of the winter heating season. Having Russia fill the shoes of the Middle East, even if physically possible, would not be an effective way to deal with geopolitical risk.

The United States was once the world's swing producer when oil production was controlled by the Texas Railroad Commission. The Texas Railroad Commission curtailed production to maintain price in order not to waste a natural resource. Of course, maintaining price was also in the interests of Big Oil, but not necessarily for conservation purposes. In 1971, the Texas Railroad Commission authorized 100 percent production for all wells under its jurisdiction, thus ending the days of the United States being a swing producer. Since the oil crisis of 1973, the mantle of swing producer has been worn by Saudi Arabia. Saudi Arabia, by all accounts, has been a fairly responsible swing producer, seeking a price that was not too low to support its social programs in medical care, housing, and education for its rapidly growing population as well as providing funds to build a value-added infrastructure of refineries and petrochemical plants. Saudi Arabia also realizes that too high a price dampens world economic activity, subsidizes the development of high-cost oil fields elsewhere, and promotes alternative sources of energy. This is the lesson Saudi Arabia learned to its disadvantage during the late 1970s and early 1980s.

OPEC maintains what it deems an acceptable range of oil prices by raising production quotas when oil prices are too high and lowering them when prices are too low. Since most oil producers within OPEC operate at or near their maximum sustainable rates, the nation with the greatest capacity to increase production and the strongest will to reduce production is Saudi Arabia. In 2004, Saudi Arabia made several announcements of its intention to increase production to dampen oil prices. Increased Saudi production did not cool oil prices as expected. Contrary to the naysayers who maintained that Saudi Arabia was bluffing, tanker rates soared, proof of higher Saudi export volumes. However, prices did not react as much as Saudi Arabia desired. What this showed was the lack of sufficient spare capacity in Saudi Arabia to keep oil prices from getting out of control. Proof positive that there was no longer sufficient spare capacity in the world to control prices occurred in 2008 when prices soared to $147 per barrel.

The primary source for incremental oil demand that taxes OPEC's capacity to produce oil from 2004 to 2008 was China, which rose in rank to become the world's first or second largest consumer of a number of commodities such as copper, tin, zinc, platinum, steel and iron ore, aluminum, lead, nickel, driving up prices for all these commodities to record levels. Capital goods exports from Europe and Japan for machinery and electricity-generating equipment surged in response to China's rapid industrialization. All this collapsed in 2008 in the wake of a series of bursting bubbles beginning with the U.S. housing market. Thus the $147 per barrel price in oil lost nearly

80 percent of its value in six months time not from an economic retreat caused by high energy prices as in the late 1970s and early 1980s, but from a global bursting of a series of financial bubbles that sent the world economies into a tailspin.

Even with moderate oil prices in 2009, oil remains in a very precarious state. This can be seen in the Baku-Tbilisi-Ceyhan (BTC) Oil Pipeline, built by British Petroleum, which came onstream in 2005. Its fully rated capacity of 1 million bpd of Caspian crude will be exported from the Turkish port of Ceyhan. This may seem like a lot of oil by any measure, but is it? This crude is needed as replacement of declining North Sea oil production, which in 2008 was down 2 million bpd since 2000. Thus, this new source of crude does nothing but half fill the gap of declining North Sea oil and in no way contributes to satisfying incremental growth in global oil consumption.

China is well aware of its inability to expand its domestic oil production in significant volumes, yet it is unwilling to reduce its growth in oil demand by sacrificing economic development. This leaves the nation vulnerable because it relies on the Middle East as a major and growing source of oil. In order to reduce its reliance on Middle East oil, China has been actively pursuing diversification of oil supplies by encouraging Russia to build an oil pipeline to ship Siberian oil to China, by investing or buying oil properties in Indonesia, Europe, and Canada, and by taking an active role in the development of oil projects in other nations such as a major oil export project in Sudan. With China shopping for oil in the Atlantic basin, it is sure to come in conflict with the United States over an increasingly scarce and vital commodity.

Events in 2004 raised the question of whether refinery capacity in the United States was adequate. The well-publicized fact that no grassroots refinery has been built in the United States since 1976 ignores that there was excess U.S. refinery capacity between the mid-1970s and mid-1990s, which provided little in the way of an economic incentive to build new refineries. However, there was an ongoing program of upgrading and debottlenecking existing facilities that increased refinery throughput capacity, called refinery creep. Luckily for the United States, its refiners invested in facilities to handle heavy grades of crude oils that remained in plentiful supply during times of limited spare-producing capacity. Moreover, the switch by Europeans from gasoline- to diesel-driven automobiles freed up gasoline refining capacity to help meet growing U.S. gasoline import needs. Once this spare capacity is consumed, presumably more refineries will have to be built; if not in the United States then somewhere in the Atlantic basin, and if not there, then in the Middle East, which will only increase our reliance on Middle East oil.

One might think that high oil prices would be a strong incentive for building refinery capacity, but that is not how the system works. It is the spread between the price of oil products and the cost of crude oil that determines refinery profitability. A high price of crude oil does not automatically translate to high refinery profits unless the spread widens. Even a widening price spread between crude and refined oil products may not be sufficient to induce refinery construction. A refinery operator who is making a great deal of money on a refinery with a cost base of $200 million may not have the financial wherewithal to construct an equivalent-sized refinery that would cost $2 billion unless the spread widens further.

Of course, none of this need happen. This logjam of constraints has been broken by a severe economic contraction caused by a global financial meltdown. When a global economic recovery takes place, these constraints will reappear. The current economic malaise has given the world a reprieve in time to perhaps discovering a supergiant oil field or two. One potential area is the South China Sea, where territorial claims by six littoral nations have inhibited exploration. Another potential area for discovery of a supergiant oil field is, surprisingly, Iraq, which is largely unexplored. In late 2009, Iraq signed a deal with oil companies that will greatly increase its crude oil production. Another potential area of discovery is offshore Cuba, which may contain a 10 billion barrel oil field, an unproven estimate until wells are drilled to confirm its existence. Russia,

Vietnam, and China have made deals with Cuba to explore not far from offshore U.S. waters, but they appear reluctant to begin operations. Perhaps it's related to Cuba not paying foreign operators for existing Cuban production and then buying out their ownership interests for a small fraction of what was owed to them. It would be ironic that the masters of expropriation are wary of having their investments expropriated! Another unexplored potentially large oil field resides within the United States in the Bakken formation in western North and South Dakota, eastern Montana, and Canada. The U.S. Geological Survey estimates that a potential oil field of 3–4.3 billion barrels may exist in this formation, a 25-fold increase from its earlier 1995 estimate. The step-up in an unproven estimate is based on new geological models designed to evaluate the potential of the Bakken formation, advances in drilling and production techniques that make extraction of oil from this formation possible, and the results of early drilling activity.[19] As with Cuba, these estimates are not included in proven reserves until "proven."

## SYNTHETIC CRUDE

Synthetic crude, or syncrude, is a nonconventional source of oil that must be processed to produce an acceptable grade of crude oil before it can be fed into conventional refineries. Major nonconventional sources of synthetic crude are bitumen deposits in Canada, Venezuela, and Russia, plus oil shale found in various parts of the world. Bitumen is a thick, sticky form of crude oil, sometimes called extra-heavy oil, with the consistency of molasses; too viscous to flow in a pipeline unless mixed with light petroleum liquid. Bitumen also has high sulfur and metals content that complicates upgrading to a syncrude fit for a conventional refinery. These undesirable traits are offset by huge deposits of bitumen, as shown in Figure 6.2. With the exception of a small portion of heavy crude in Venezuela's proven oil reserves, these deposits are not included in official oil reserve figures.

In Canada, huge volumes of oil migrated horizontally and vertically through more than seventy miles of rock without entrapment by anticlines or faults. As the seep oil emerged on the surface, it mixed with sand and some clay and became a feast for microorganisms that transformed the oil into bitumen. It is estimated that the bacteria consumed between two and three times the present volume of bitumen, an incredible amount of oil when one considers that Canadian tar sands (now called oil sands) hold about 2.5 trillion barrels of bitumen. This implies that the original source rock generated 5 to 7.5 trillion barrels, compared to 2 or 3 trillion barrels of ultimately discoverable global oil reserves, including all that has been consumed since Drake first discovered oil in 1859. That is a whole lot of ocean plankton, algae, and other forms of simple marine life to die and settle in oxygen-starved sediment in a single province of Canada.

As a recoverable resource using present technology, Canadian oil sand is equivalent to 175 billion barrels of crude oil, somewhat less than the 264 billion barrels of proven oil reserves in Saudi Arabia. This estimate is based on a price of crude oil high enough to financially justify the necessary capital investment. In 2009, older syncrude plants required about $30 per barrel to sustain their operation, newer and more costly plants $60 per barrel, and even more costly grassroot investments $80–$90 per barrel. Technological advances could considerably raise the estimated amount of proven oil reserves since the estimate of 175 billion barrels of recoverable oil is based on surface mining. The Athabasca deposit in Alberta is the world's largest oil sand deposit, containing about two-thirds of Canadian bitumen resources. Oil sand with about 12 percent bitumen by weight is mined similar to the way coal is surface-mined. The overburden is removed and stockpiled for reclamation after strip-mining operations cease. However during mining operations, the land surface is scarred as in strip-mining coal. Giant

Figure 6.2  **World Heavy Oil and Bitumen Resources** (Billion Bls)

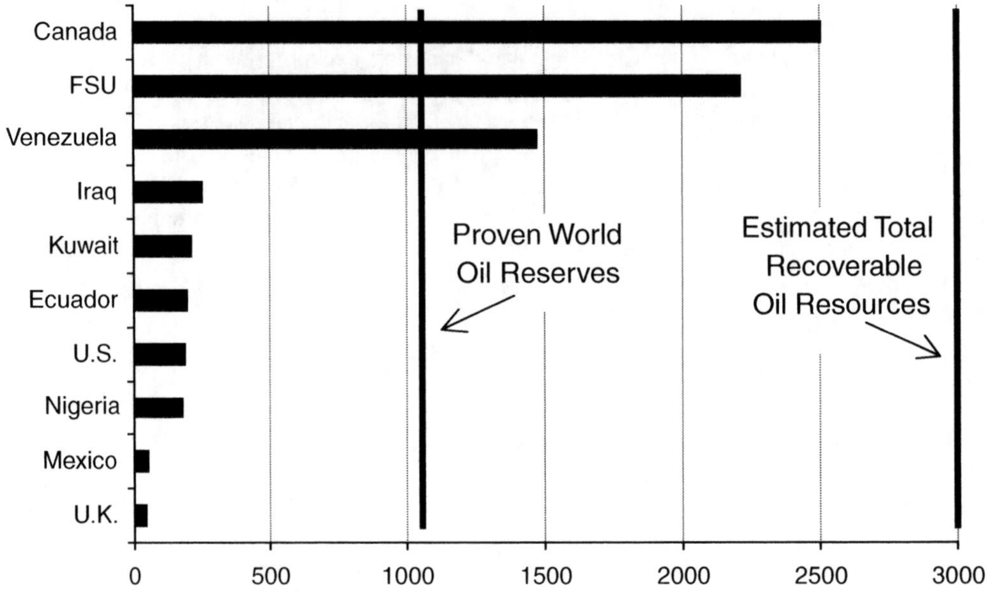

mining shovels working 24–7 fill huge trucks with 360–380 tons of oil sand for transport to an upgrading plant.[20]

The first step is an extraction plant where the oil sand is crushed and mixed with hot water. It is then sent to a large separation vessel where sand falls to the bottom and bitumen, trapped in tiny air bubbles, rises to the top of the water as froth. The froth is skimmed off, mixed with a solvent, and spun in a centrifuge to remove the remaining water and sand. Water and sand residue, called tailings, are placed in a settling pond where any remaining bitumen is skimmed off the surface. Sand is mixed with water and returned to the mine site by pipeline to fill in mined-out areas, and the water is separated and pumped to a settling pond for recycling. This method minimizes undesirable environmental consequences and recovers over 90 percent of the bitumen in the sand. For deeper deposits of oil sands, wells are drilled and high-pressure steam is injected into the well to soften up the surrounding bitumen. Bitumen flows into the well and is then pumped to the surface. When production slows, a cycle of "huff and puff" softens up another batch of bitumen. This method recovers a relatively small portion of the bitumen and also releases a poisonous gas, hydrogen sulphide, which requires environmental safeguards to prevent its escape to the atmosphere.

After the bitumen is extracted, it is ready for upgrading, which converts it into synthetic, or processed, crude with a density and viscosity similar to conventional crude oils. Upgrading involves removing carbon and sulfur and adding hydrogen. Coking removes carbon atoms from the large, carbon-rich hydrocarbon chains, breaking them up into shorter chains. Hydrotreating removes sulfur, which is sold to fertilizer manufacturers. Hydrocracking adds hydrogen to hydrocarbon chains to increase the yield of light-end products when the syncrude is refined in a conventional refinery. The processed syncrude is mixed with condensate, a very light oil associated with natural gas production, for pipelining to a refinery.

The process for making syncrude requires a lot of natural gas as a source of hydrogen for hydrocracking and hydrotreating and to heat water for extracting the bitumen from the sand. A great deal of water is used for separating the bitumen from the sand and in pumping the spent sand back to the mine site. While water can be recycled up to seventeen times, the residue is a black foul liquid collected in tailing ponds. Care has to be exercised that this liquid does not escape to the environment. Thus, the enormous reserves of bitumen are ultimately dependent on the availability of water, a naturally replenishable resource up to a point, and natural gas, a wasting resource. Without a pipeline to ship local supplies of natural gas to market, syncrude production creates value for stranded gas. With a pipeline that can ship natural gas to markets in Canada and the United States, the issue then becomes whether to consume natural gas locally for syncrude production, where its value is determined by the price of crude oil, or to sell it as commercial pipeline natural gas to the Lower 48. In terms of the environment, natural gas consumed in producing syncrude and treating the oil sand, plus the energy consumed in mining and transporting bitumen to the syncrude plant, multiply carbon emissions of gasoline made from syncrude over crude oil by three times. The Obama administration is not a proponent of gasoline from syncrude because of this marked increase in its carbon footprint. Syncrude production in Canada was 800,000 bpd in 2003, increased to 1,200,000 bpd in 2008, and is expected to reach 3,300,000 bpd in 2020 taking into consideration reduction in expansion plans from low crude oil prices in early 2009.

Alberta's 175 billion of proven reserves are surface oil sands that can be stripped-mined. But five times that amount lies out of reach of strip mining, about equal to the entire oil reserves of the Middle East. Little of this resource is being tapped by the "huff and puff" method of forcing down steam which loosens up the bitumen allowing it to be pumped to the surface via wells. To improve the efficacy of recovery of deep oil sands deposits, various proposals have been made such as drilling a hole and igniting the oil sands to heat up its surroundings allowing the heated crude to flow to the surface via wells. Another idea is pumping down a solvent that absorbs the crude in the oil sands. The mixture of solvent and crude is separated at the surface for recycling of the solvent. Still another idea is to force hot high pressure air into the oil sands that heats the crude so that it can flow to the surface. It is possible that this method may partially refine the crude by the time it emerges at the surface, avoiding or reducing the need for synthetic crude treatment. While not proven solutions, a technology will have to be developed to tap below-surface deposits of oil sands if they are to play a significant role in satisfying North American oil needs.

Bitumen deposits in Venezuela are located in the Orinoco region and lie on the surface. Unlike Canada, the bitumen is not intermingled with the soil. Bitumen mixed with 30 percent water and other chemicals is sold as a coal substitute called Orimulsion. Bitumen for syncrude manufacture is mixed with naphtha to reduce its viscosity for pipelining to a syncrude plant. There the naphtha is recovered and pipelined back to the bitumen deposit for recycling. The costs of getting bitumen to a syncrude plant and preparing it for processing are far less in Venezuela than in Canada.

Venezuela entered into four grassroots joint ventures with foreign oil companies. But these plants were taken over by Venezuela without due compensation to the investors. Having scared off further foreign investment by oil companies, Venezuela began courting China and Iran as potential investors in new syncrude production facilities, but neither nation seems anxious to consummate a deal.

Syncrude may not be a significant substitute for conventional crude oil, considering its capital and natural gas requirements, but it could be effective in reducing U.S. reliance on Middle East crude oil imports. Middle East oil exports to North America have been relatively flat at 2.4 million bpd (some Middle East crude is exported to east coast Canadian refineries whose output is both consumed domestically and exported to the United States). A tripling of current Canadian syncrude production of 1.2 million bpd would make the United States essentially independent of Mideast crude. It is possible that syncrude plants could be built in Venezuela, although one may argue over the geopolitical risk associated with substituting syncrude from Venezuela for crude from the Middle East. Venezuela's attitude toward the United States could change if Venezuela viewed a large step-up in syncrude production as a means of creating and sustaining a "Greater Venezuela." Whether President Obama can improve U.S. relations with Venezuela remains to be seen, but Venezuela, hurt by falling revenues in early 2009 and apparently unable to entice China or Iran to invest, has put out feelers for oil companies to enter into joint ventures to build syncrude plants. But this would first require resolution of problems associated with Venezuela's past treatment of oil company investments.

Syncrude can also be made from oil shale. Like so many things, "oil shale" is a misnomer. The oil in the rock is not oil, but an organic material called kerogen that has not been heated to the requisite temperature to become oil. Hence, the process of making oil from oil shale involves the application of heat to complete the process. Nor is it necessary for the rock to be shale, it can be any kind of rock that contains kerogen, although normally it is a relatively hard rock called *mari*. About 72 percent of the world's oil shale resources are in the United States. Most of this lies in a 16,000-square-mile area, mostly in Colorado, with extensions into eastern Utah and southern Wyoming, called the Green River formation. The Green River formation is estimated to have as much as 2 trillion equivalent barrels of oil. Other nations with oil shale resources are China, Brazil, and Morocco, each with 5 percent of world reserves, Jordan, with 4 percent, and the remaining 9 percent in Australia, Thailand, Israel, Ukraine, and Estonia. Estonia burns oil shale for power generation.[21]

Oil shale has to be mined, transported, crushed, and heated to a high temperature (450°C) in the presence of hydrogen to produce a low-quality crude oil. The process requires a great deal of water, a commodity in short supply in the western United States, plus natural gas as a source of energy to heat the oil shale and as a source for hydrogen. The crushed rock residue takes up more volume than the original rock, presenting a significant disposal problem in the scenic Rockies. The United States invested a great deal of money during the oil crisis in the 1970s to commercially develop oil shale, but to no avail. As promising as oil shale may appear, in a practical sense, mining of shale does not offer a viable solution to a shortfall in conventional oil production.

This negative outlook may change. Shell Oil's Mahogany Project in northwest Colorado took a different approach to oil shale. Rather than mining the oil shale and then extracting the oil, electric heating elements were embedded between 1,000 and 2,000 feet below the surface to heat the shale rock *in situ* to 650 to 750° F. Over time, this produces a hydrocarbon mix of about one-third natural gas and two-thirds light high-grade oil, which can be retrieved by traditional drilling methods. The high-grade oil can easily be refined to gasoline, jet fuel, and diesel oil. The process is energy-efficient; that is, the energy derived from the projects exceeds the energy consumed in heating the shale, but, of course, is not as energy-efficient as simply drilling for oil. Denser oil shale formations may be capable of producing up to a billion barrels of oil per square mile. If these estimates of oil shale resources are accurate, and if this method proves to be commercially feasible, the Green River Formation will have 2–4 percent more oil reserves than Saudi Arabia.

## CHALLENGE OF OIL: THE AUTOMOBILE

Oil is the fuel of choice for automobiles, trucks, buses, railroad locomotives, aircraft, and ships. Ship's bunkers are the waste or residue of the refining process. Trucks, buses, and railroads consume diesel fuel and airlines jet fuel. For the most part, automobiles run on gasoline, although Europe has succeeded in inducing a switch from gasoline- to diesel-fueled automobiles through tax incentives. Figure 6.3 shows the percentage distribution of the world population of automobiles (SUVs, vans, and pickups included only for the United States as light trucks).[22]

Figure 6.3    **Percentage Distribution of 747 MM Automobiles** (2007)

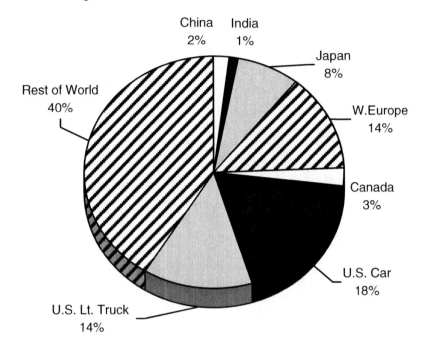

Henry Ford pioneered the motor vehicle industry in the United States in the early 1900s. Even as late as 1950, 76 percent of the world's motor vehicles of 53 million were registered in the United States. In 2007, the U.S. population of motor vehicles consisted of 135 million automobiles plus another 101 million minivans, vans, pickup trucks, and SUVs designated as light trucks, a large portion of which are used for personal travel. The initial rapid growth in the population of motor vehicles after the Second World War was concentrated first in Europe (1960–1985), then Japan (1970–1985), afterward in the emerging economies of the Industrial Tigers (Korea, Taiwan, Singapore, and Hong Kong), from there to South America and eastern Europe, and now India and China.

Table 6.4 shows the number of automobiles owned per 1,000 people. The U.S. automobile figures includes SUVs, pickups, and vans, which exaggerates the number of automobiles per thousand people in the sense that pickups and vans are also used for commercial purposes.

The greatest potential growth in automobile ownership is in China and India. If the number of automobiles in India and China were to increase to 100 per thousand people, the population of automobiles for a combined human population of 2.5 billion in 2009 would be 250 million automobiles less the current population of about 20 million, for a jump of 230 million automobiles, or 30 percent on top of a present population of 747 million. Light distillates consumption is 26.4 million barrels per day. Suppose that 80 percent of this is gasoline for motor vehicles or 21.1 million bpd. An increase of 30 percent in automobiles would increase global gasoline consumption

Table 6.4

**Automobiles per One Thousand Population (2007)**

| | |
|---|---|
| United States | 785 |
| Canada | 583 |
| U.K. | 514 |
| Germany | 500 |
| France | 474 |
| Japan | 452 |
| China | 10 |
| India | 8 |

to 27.5 million bpd; 6.4 million bpd in incremental gasoline demand would require incremental refinery consumption to handle 21 million bpd of crude assuming 30 percent of refinery output is gasoline. (Thirty percent is the global refinery conversion rate of gasoline from crude oil.) This is equivalent to adding two Saudi Arabias. Even if this were physically possible, there would be huge oil price increases reflecting supply shortages and much wider refinery margins to justify building enormous additions to refinery capacity. Clearly the progress of China, and to a lesser extent India, into the automobile age will place China and the United States at loggerheads over a vital commodity; another reason to exit the Middle East.

**Vehicles That Use Alternative Fuels**

One way to attack oil demand for motor vehicles is to find an alternative to gasoline. The U.S. Department of Energy defines alternative fuels as substantially nonpetroleum methods that enhance energy security and the environment. The list includes methanol and ethanol fuels of at least 70 percent alcohol, compressed or liquefied natural gas, liquefied petroleum gas (LPG), hydrogen, coal-derived liquid fuels, biofuels, and electricity, including solar power. All are currently more costly than gasoline and diesel oil and, more importantly, lack an infrastructure for serving customers. As Table 6.5 shows, the energy content of alternative fuels is lower than gasoline and diesel oil, which means that motor vehicles that use alternative fuels will get lower mileage (miles per gallon) than those running on gasoline and diesel fuel.[23]

The antigasoline public sentiment is "fueled" by the desire to improve air quality and the concern over oil security. California suffers from the worst polluted air in the nation, and the state energy authorities are acutely aware of declining California and Alaska oil production and its impact on oil security. The state leads the nation in initiating legislation to promote the demise of the conventional gasoline engine. Many states look to California as a model for motor vehicle pollution legislation.

Ethanol and biodiesel, both biomass fuels, were discussed in Chapter 3. Gasohol (E10) is now fairly available in the United States and is no longer limited to the Midwest corn-growing region. There are 1,413 refueling sites offering E85 principally located in Minnesota, Illinois, Indiana, Iowa, and Missouri. There are 651 biodiesel sites, but not all these sell B100; B20 is a more commonly available. Leading states are North and South Carolina, Tennessee, and Texas.

Methanol is an alcohol fuel made from natural gas, but it can also be produced from coal and biomass. The primary methanol fuel is M85 (85 percent methanol and 15 percent unleaded gasoline). In order to use methanol as a fuel, engine parts made of magnesium, copper, lead, zinc, and aluminum must be replaced to prevent corrosion. Methanol cannot be handled in the same

Table 6.5

**Energy Content of Motor Vehicle Fuels**

| Fuel | Btu/Gallon |
|---|---|
| Diesel | 129,000 |
| Gasoline | 111,400 |
| E85(3) | 105,545 |
| Propane | 84,000 |
| Ethanol (E100) | 75,000 |
| Methanol (M100) | 65,350 |
| Liquid hydrogen | 34,000 |
| CNG at 3,000psi | 29,000 |
| Hydrogen at 3,000psi | 9,667 |

distribution system as petroleum products, and the necessity of building a new distribution system limits methanol's potential use as an automobile fuel. There are no commercial outlets in the United States selling methanol, and there is little point to change to methanol from an environmental point of view because emissions from M85 are not significantly lower than those from gasoline.

Interest in natural gas (mostly methane) as an alternative fuel stems from its clean-burning qualities and its availability through a well-developed pipeline distribution system. But engines must be modified in order to accommodate natural gas, which is stored in tanks either as compressed (CNG) or liquefied (LNG) natural gas. CNG-fueled vehicles require compression stations either at distribution centers or homes served by natural gas. Natural gas distribution companies commonly use CNG-fueled vehicles. Major American car manufacturers have models that run on CNG exclusively or are bifueled to run on either CNG or gasoline. Most CNG-fueled vehicles are restricted to fleet buyers such as natural gas producers or distributors who have ready access to the fuel. LNG-fueled vehicles must have some way of keeping natural gas in a liquefied state unless their tanks can withstand the pressure created when the liquid gasifies. There are thirty-five sites where LNG can be purchased, of which twenty-nine are in California. CNG is sold at 790 sites, of which 189 are in California followed by 89 in New York and 60 in Utah. The run-up in natural gas prices and the growing need to import natural gas are inhibiting factors for a significant conversion of automobiles from gasoline to natural gas.

LPG is propane or butane alone or as a mix. LPG is a byproduct of natural gas processing and petroleum refining. As a vehicle fuel in the United States, LPG is mainly propane and has been in use for over sixty years. Propane is gaseous at normal temperatures and must be pressurized to remain in a liquid state. Emissions from the combustion of propane, however, are significantly lower than those produced by gasoline and diesel fuel, making propane the fuel of choice for forklift trucks and other vehicles that must operate in closed spaces such as warehouses and terminals. There are a few fleets of municipal taxis, school buses, and police cars of propane-fueled vehicles, with 2,200 refueling sites nationwide, of which 525 are in Texas and 206 in California. However, large-scale switching from gasoline to LPG is not possible because the quantity of LPG is fixed by refinery operations and domestic production of natural gas.

Electricity can run a vehicle via a battery or a fuel cell. Batteries store electricity, while a fuel cell generates electricity. The cost and weight of batteries have discouraged their use in the past, but progress has been made for battery-powered vehicles to become technologically and economically feasible. Nissan produces two automobiles that run on electricity for sale in California. GM is planning to offer an electric car around 2012. Some electricity-generating companies are thinking about refueling electric automobiles overnight in garages without running special cables to a house. However, it would be advisable to have time-sensitive meters that charge lower rates during times of least demand such as overnight and on weekends. There are 435 commercial electricity "refueling" sites in the United States with 370 in California. A large number of battery-powered vehicles would have significant repercussions on electricity generation, transmission, and distribution capacity and on the economics of running an electric utility.

The assertion that electric vehicles are pollution-free is true only if viewed in isolation. Electricity stored in motor vehicle batteries is not pollution-free if it is generated from burning fossil fuels. Nor is the electric vehicle energy-efficient when the inefficiencies of electricity generation and transmission are taken into account. From this viewpoint, electric vehicles are neither pollution-free nor energy-efficient. However, if the electricity to power an electric vehicle comes from wind or solar energy (including solar-powered cars) or from hydro or nuclear, then the argument that electric vehicles are pollution-free is valid.

Vehicles fueled by hydrogen are another possibility. Its chief advantage is that the only combustion emission is water; it is the preferred fuel for a fuel cell for the same reason. Hydrogen-fueled vehicles and fuel cells are discussed under Hydrogen Economy in Chapter 10; but for now the prognosis for large numbers of automobiles fueled by hydrogen, either for direct combustion in a conventional engine or feedstock for a fuel cell, is quite dim.

Despite intense government and private efforts to support the technological development of vehicles run by alternative fuels, including the development of fuel cells, over the past thirty-five years (all of this started in the aftermath of the 1973 oil crisis), most of the world's fleet of automobiles and trucks is still powered by gasoline and diesel fuel. In the United States, the total population of automobiles, vans, pickups, SUVs is 236 million. Vehicles fueled by LPG (including forklifts) number 174,000; CNG-fueled vehicles nearly 118,000; LNG-fueled vehicles 2,700; E85 fueled vehicles 246,000; electric vehicles 51,000; and 119 hydrogen-fueled vehicles. Counting forklifts as motor vehicles and assuming E85 fueled vehicles never run on gasoline, both unwarranted assumptions, the total population of alternative-fueled vehicles is only 0.25 percent of the entire motor vehicle population. Or put another way, 99.75 percent of the motor vehicle population runs on oil.

It is possible that long-term oil consumption could be affected by technological breakthroughs that bring the cost of alternative fuels closer to that of gasoline and diesel fuel. The other way is for the price of gasoline to rise to a level that can support alternative fuels, which occurred in 2008 when gasoline approached $4 per gallon. But this didn't last long. Although not a challenge to crude oil yet, the conversion of natural gas to motor vehicle fuels (discussed in Chapter 7), could eventually have some impact on crude oil demand as a motor vehicle fuel, but not in the near future.

One thing is certain; the lack of significant progress for motor vehicles fueled by alternative means is not being hampered by the automobile industry. Automobile manufacturers share the general public sentiment that the conventional gasoline engine is becoming archaic and needs to be replaced. Carmakers are not wedded to the oil industry, but they are wedded to a technology that works and a fuel that is readily available. Until there is an alternative fuel that works and is readily available, oil will remain the preferred fuel. There will be no easy divorce from oil.

**Enhancing Engine Efficiency**

There has been substantial private and governmental support to enhance engine efficiency. Increased efficiency has two benefits: better mileage with less pollution. Doubling mileage cuts both fuel consumption and pollution emissions in half.

The U.S. Department of Energy, through the National Renewable Energy Laboratory, has funded development costs for hybrid electric vehicles (HEVs) with high fuel economy and low emissions. GM and Ford have begun to offer hybrid vehicles, although Honda and Toyota have had models available for a number of years (another testament to the decline of American leadership in technology).

An HEV obtains higher mileage by converting the energy lost during deceleration to electrical energy that can be stored in a battery. HEVs can be designed in a series or parallel configuration. In a series configuration, the primary engine drives a generator that powers electric motors to drive the vehicle and charge the battery. The vehicle is driven solely by the electric motors. HEVs now on the market have a parallel configuration in which the car is driven directly by a gasoline-fueled engine augmented by electric motors. The electric motors are run by electricity stored in a battery that supplements the power from the gasoline engine, and cut in when the car needs extra power. The nickel metal hydride or possibly the lithium-ion battery is recharged during deceleration, when regenerative braking captures the energy normally passed to the environment as waste heat, and also during normal motor operation if a charge is necessary. The electric hybrid can also be charged by plugging into a conventional electricity outlet. This is the forerunner to an all-electric car.

Supplemental acceleration using electric motors means that automobiles can be built with gasoline or diesel engines of lower horsepower, which consume less fuel. Fuel efficiency is further enhanced by "cutting out" the firing of a cylinder at cruising speed when on level ground. In addition, an HEV has less weight because its engine components are made from lighter-weight aluminum, magnesium, and plastic. The vehicle's body, also made of lightweight aluminum, is aerodynamically designed to reduce wind resistance. Depending on the style of HEV, mileage can range from thirty to more than sixty miles per gallon. An HEV's mileage performance, compared to that of a conventional automobile, is more impressive in stop-and-go traffic than in steady highway driving. HEVs' engine emissions meet California's stringent ultra-low vehicle emission standards. The most striking aspect of HEVs is that their sales jumped when gasoline prices spiked during the summer of 2004 and again in 2008, sending SUV sales into a slump. Moreover, HEV sales slump and SUV sales jump when oil prices are low. This lesson is vital in coming to terms with the future when oil becomes a more scarce and expensive resource.

## INTERNALIZING AN EXTERNALITY

The government supports the oil industry by ensuring security of supply. This is not a subsidy to the oil companies because oil companies are not in the business of military interventions. Government participation in the civilian economy is common. The automobile industry would have been truncated (to say the least) if town, county, state, and federal governments did not build roads. It would be just as unfair for automobile companies to be responsible for building roads as it would be for oil companies to ensure oil security. The big difference is in the method of payment. The cost of building and maintaining roads falls on the user in the form of a highway tax, whereas the cost of oil security falls on the taxpayer as a government expenditure. It is high time that those who benefit from oil bear the full cost of oil through an oil security tax.

The United States consumes 7 million bpd of gasoil as both heating oil and diesel fuel for equipment, machinery, motor vehicles (mostly trucks), and locomotives. The advantage of trucks over railroads is their flexibility—they can go anywhere there is a road. The advantage of railroads is their inherent efficiency—a train crew of only three members can haul several hundred containers or truck trailers on flatbed railcars, a number that would require an equal number of truck drivers. Aside from this labor savings, railroads with steel wheels on steel tracks are far more energy-efficient than trucks with rubber wheels on concrete or asphalt roads. An optimal blend of both modes of transport is intermodal transport (piggyback) of combining trucks for

Figure 6.4  **Average Miles Driven per Year for Passenger Cars**

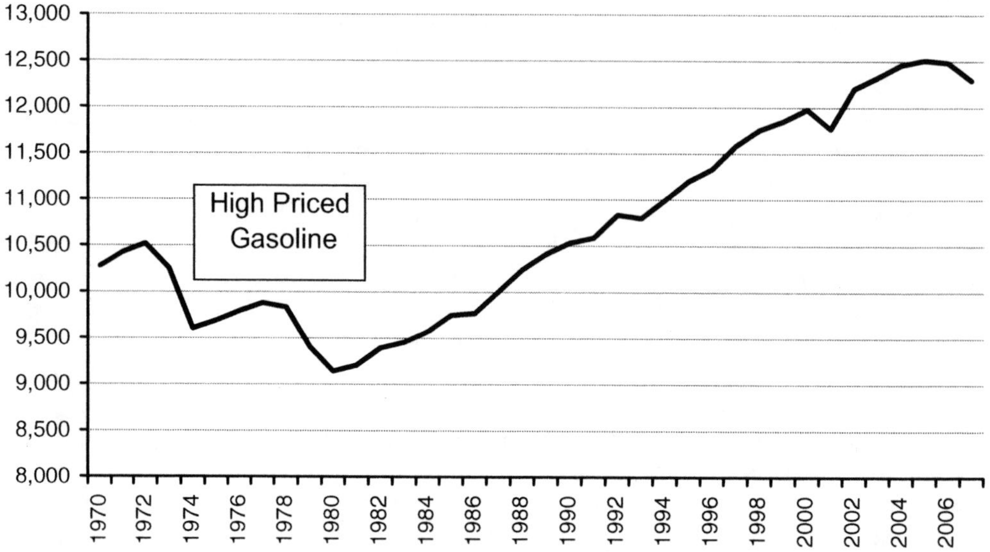

short-distance delivery with rail for long-distance hauling. A higher price for diesel fuel would provide an economic incentive to get some of the trucks off the road and their payloads on a train. This would reduce oil consumption and highway congestion.

In addition, the United States consumes about 10 million bpd of gasoline for automobiles. This amounts to 420 million gallons per day (42 gallons in a barrel) or 150 billion gallons per year. A $1 tax on each gallon of gasoline will support $150 billion in annual war expenditures in the Middle East. It would probably take a few dollars per gallon tax to internalize the external cost of military activity in the Middle East. Such a high price on gasoline affects both mileage driven and type of automobile purchased. It also supports the development of alternative fuels. All these would help to extricate the United States from dependence on Middle East crude. Figure 6.4 shows the impact of gasoline prices on the average number of miles driven by U.S. automobiles.

In round terms, the average miles driven per year fell about 10 percent during the era of high-priced gasoline during the late 1970s and early 1980s. People were not deprived of the driving experience, they just thought more carefully about how they drove their cars. Carpooling, taking the bus or train to work, not visiting the shopping mall every day, letting the kids take the bus from school rather than picking them up, and shortening the distance traveled for family vacations can have a significant impact on the number of miles driven in a year. In addition to driving less, people were incentivized to buy fuel-efficient Toyotas and other Japanese cars at the expense of gas-guzzling American made automobiles. All this happened again in recent years when gas prices briefly passed $4 per gallon. Figure 6.5 shows the relationship between motor vehicle-miles and gasoline since 1984. Motor vehicle-miles reflect an aggregate measure of miles driven per vehicle and the population of vehicles prices, both growing throughout most of this period.[24]

Low gasoline prices do not affect aggregate motor vehicle-miles. But the long-term trend in motor vehicle-miles was broken before gasoline prices spiked at $4 per gallon in 2008. As shown more clearly in Figure 6.6, the long-term trend changed in the fall of 2005 when gasoline prices approached $3 per gallon.

Figure 6.5    **12-Month Moving Average Billion Vehicle-Miles versus Gasoline Prices**
(1984–2009)

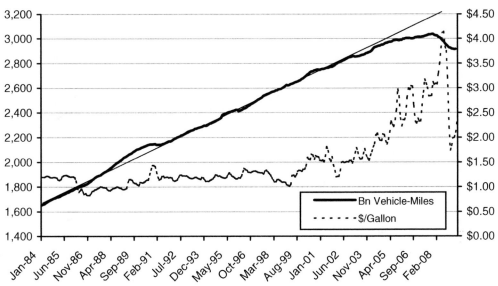

Thus, it appears that $3 per gallon gasoline can suppress driving activity. At higher prices between $3 and 4 per gallon, people not only drove less, but switched from gas-guzzling SUVs to hybrids. It has been observed that sales for SUVs increase and sales for hybrids decrease whenever gasoline prices fall below $3 per gallon. Notice that the peak price of $4 per gallon occurred after the downturn in motor vehicle-miles. Thus, the actual fall-off in motor vehicle-miles was more the result of the economy collapsing from the global financial meltdown than from high gasoline prices.

Suppose that $3–4 per gallon gasoline is sufficient to cut mileage driven per year and encourage the switch from SUVs to fuel-efficient hybrids to reduce gasoline consumption by 10 percent. A 10 percent savings on 10 million bpd of gasoline consumed by automobiles is one million bpd of gasoline, which requires about 2.5 million bpd of crude oil assuming 40 percent weighted average output of gasoline between U.S. and European refineries. (The United States depends on European refineries to fill some of its gasoline needs.) Two-and-a-half million bpd savings in crude imports would have to be apportioned between Europe and the United States, depending on which refineries were affected. Nevertheless, 2.5 million bpd is close to what the United States and Canada import from the Middle East. A gasoline tax that brings the price of gasoline between $3–4 per gallon can, in time, drastically reduce the demand for Middle East oil. Parenthetically, 1.5 million bpd of West African crude is exported to Asia. Diverting a portion of this to the United States would decrease our Arabian Gulf imports commensurately, hastening the day when we can eliminate the need to meddle militarily in the Middle East.

Of course some time has to pass to allow energy-efficient automobiles to replace gasoline-hogs. But with incremental crude from oil sands production in Canada and greater imports from regions in the Atlantic basin showing promise of higher oil production such as Brazil and West

Figure 6.6    **12-Month Moving Average Billion Vehicle-Miles versus Gasoline Prices**
(2000–2009)

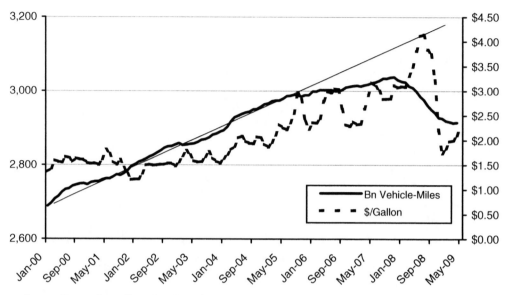

*Source:* For retail gasoline prices http://www.eia.gov/emeu/petro.html. For vehicle distance billion miles
U.S. Department of Transportation, Federal Highway Administration at http://www.fhwa.dot.gov/ohim/
tvtw/tvtpage.cfm

Africa, and allowing more bioethanol to enter the United States by eliminating the discriminatory
tax against Brazilian ethanol, we are within reach of eliminating Middle East imports to North
America altogether in a few years. Figure 6.7 shows that the United States accounts for relatively
little of Arabian Gulf exports. We have been on the line since the late 1970s to defend the interests of the oil-importing world for trillions of taxpayer dollars with nearly five thousand dead
and countless others without limbs and suffering from the consequences of wounds, physical and
mental, for the rest of their lives. Yet the true beneficiaries have barely paid a dime for our effort.
When will we learn?

## IS THIS POLITICALLY ACCEPTABLE?

Of course reducing our dependence on oil from the Middle East by hiking gasoline prices is not
politically acceptable, but what relevance is that? If we do nothing, we will be doing our part
to ensure that the world remains dangerously close to supply not being able to satisfy demand.
The problem with being on the razor's edge is that one can easily fall off. In the world of oil, an
extended supply disruption in Nigeria or Venezuela or Iran, or any number of other possibilities
can reduce the oil supply below demand. Once this happens, there is no upper limit on oil prices.
This is what was experienced in 2008 when oil peaked at $147 per barrel with forecasts at that
time of $200 per barrel up to $300 per barrel. Supply hardly was able to meet demand. While
some blamed hedge funds and speculators for loading up on oil futures for high oil prices, the
general consensus is that this only exaggerated the underlying price movement. The real reason
why prices were strong was a lack of spare capacity. Six months later in early 2009, oil was in the

Figure 6.7   **Arabian Gulf Oil Exports and U.S. Imports from the Arabian Gulf** (MM Bpd)

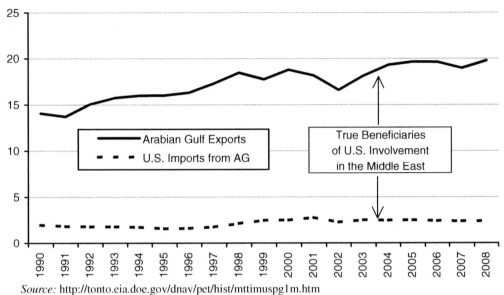

*Source:* http://tonto.eia.doe.gov/dnav/pet/hist/mttimuspg1m.htm

low-$30s with forecasts of $30 per barrel down to $20 per barrel. From this low point, oil prices increased to $70–$80 per barrel by late 2009. So much for forecasts and those who depend on price forecasts to establish government energy policies! Unlike the oil crisis in the 1970s when a sharp decline in economic activity from high-energy prices reduced demand to eventually cause prices to fall, this time it was a global financial meltdown stemming from the subprime mortgage fiasco. What we should learn from the high oil prices in 2008 is that a gasoline price of $3–4 per gallon appears sufficient to persuade U.S. drivers to drive less and buy fuel-efficient automobiles. This in turn will eventually allow us to extricate ourselves from the Middle East saving billions, if not trillions, of dollars and many lives, increasing the availability of oil for the rest of the world, and in so doing, easing the strain on global oil supplies.

Stated in the most simplistic way, we have a choice of paying $3–4 per gallon or paying $3–4 per gallon. The choice is only differentiated by when and where the money flows: to the U.S. government to ease the budget deficit or to the coffers of the oil exporters. Either way, there will be an economic incentive for the development of alternative fuels, but it may be too late to save the economy if we continue to procrastinate. The time to wean our dependence on oil imports in favor of alternative fuels was yesterday, but nothing can be done about that. The time is now before the next crisis strikes.

We had our first warning in the 1970s oil crisis that life will not be the same, and we managed to do nothing in the subsequent four decades to deal with a highly explosive situation. Matters are not getting better, and each subsequent oil crisis will bring even higher prices that will last longer. It is about time that we do something to at least reduce the growth in demand and our dependence on Middle East oil and become more serious about developing alternative motor vehicle fuels. The old saw that alternative fuels cannot be developed because of our enormous vested interest in the infrastructure of oil-production facilities, refineries, and associated processing plants, pipelines, ships, storage tanks, and distribution facilities is not going to carry much weight when that infrastructure goes dry.

## NOTES

1. The primary sources of information are: Charles F. Conaway, *The Petroleum Industry: A Nontechnical Guide* (Tulsa, OK: PennWell Books, 1999); Norman J. Hyne, *Nontechnical Guide to Petroleum Geology, Exploration, Drilling, and Production* (Tulsa, OK: PennWell Books, 2001); Robert O. Anderson, *Fundamentals of the Petroleum Industry* (Norman, OK: University of Oklahoma Press, 1984).

2. Aspects of the abiogenic gas debate can be found in J.F. Kenney, Vladimir A. Kutcherov, Nikolai A. Bendeliani, and Vladimir A. Alekseev, "The Evolution of Multicomponent Systems at High Pressures: VI. The Thermodynamic Stability of the Hydrogen–Carbon System: The Genesis of Hydrocarbons and the Origin of Petroleum," *Proceedings of the National Academy of Sciences*, 99, 17 (August 2002), pp. 10,976–10,981; and at the American Association of Petroleum Geologists Web site at www.aapg.org/explorer/2002/11nov/ abiogenic. cfmg.

3. *Monthly Energy Review* (Section 5), (Washington, DC: Energy Information Administration).

4. *How Oil and Gas Wells Are Drilled Horizontally,* Web site energyindustryphotos.com/ how_oil_ and_gas_wells_are_drilled.htm, *Horizontal Drilling* Web site www.horizontaldrilling.org; *A Fresh Angle on Drilling* Geotimes Web site www.geotimes.org/mar04/feature_horizdrill.html; Baker Hughes (Baker Oil Tools) Web site www.bakerhughes.com for the latest achievements in horizontal, multi-lateral, and coil tubing drilling; Shell Oil snake well drilling Web site realenergy.shell.us.

5. Mohole Project Web site www.nas.edu/history/mohole.

6. Transocean Company Web site www. deepwater.com.

7. Exxon Valdez Oil Spill Case Review as of 2/27/2008 published in Mining Exploration News Web site paguntaka.org/2008/02/27/exxon-valdez-oil-spill-case-1989-review; and CBS News item Exxon Valdez Twenty Years Later, Web site www.cbsnews.com/stories/2009/02/02/eveningnews/main4769329.shtml.

8. *Oil Literacy* (New York: Poten & Partners, 1988).

9. *OSHA Technical Manual,* Chapter 2, Section IV (Washington, DC: U.S. Department of Labor, 1999) Web site www.osha-slc.gov.

10. *BP Energy Statistics* (London: British Petroleum, 2009).

11. Michel T. Halbouty, ed., *Giant Oil and Gas Fields of the Decade (1990–1999)* (Tulsa, OK: American Association of Petroleum Geologists, 2003).

12. "Deepwater Oil Discovery Rate May Have Peaked, Production Peak May Follow in Ten Years," *Oil & Gas Journal* (July 26, 2004), one of a six-part series on Hubbert Revisited, Tulsa, OK; the Association for the Study of Peak Oil and Gas Web site www.asponews.org and www.peakoilnet; lecture by C.J. Campbell, "Peak Oil," Web site www.geologie.tu-clausthal.de/ Campbell/lecture.html; *The Wolf at the Door: Beginner's Guide to Oil Depletion,* Web site www. wolfatthedoor.org.uk; "Future World Oil Supplies," Web site www. dieoff.org; Hubbert Peak of Oil Production Web sitewww. hubbertpeak.com.

13. U.S. Geological Survey, *World Petroleum Assessment 2000* (Washington, DC, 2000).

14. An Evaluation of the USGS World Petroleum Assessment 2000-Supporting Data (Open-File Report 2007–1021; Reston, VA, U.S Geological Survey, 2007).

15. Bill Kovarik, *The Oil Reserve Fallacy: Proven Reserves Are Not a Measure of Future Supply,* Web site www.radford.edu/~wkovarik/oil/oilreservehistory.html.

16. The *International Energy Outlook 2004* (Washington, DC: Energy Information Administration, 2004) calls for a 200 percent increase in OPEC exports by 2025, whereas the *World Energy Outlook* (Paris: International Energy Agency, 2004) calls for a 270 percent increase.

17. Matthew R. Simmons, *Twilight in the Desert: The Coming Saudi Oil Shock and the World Economy* (Hoboken, NJ: Wiley, 2006).

18. "OPEC Adds Less than Meets the Eye," *Petroleum Intelligence Weekly* (June 28, 2004).

19. U.S. Geological Survey Web site www.usgs.gov/newsroom/article.asp?ID=1911.

20. Petroleum Communication Foundation, *Canada's Oil Sands and Heavy Oil* (Calgary, Alberta, Canada: 2000) Web site www.centreforenergy.com.

21. Julie Cart, "U.S. Backs Squeezing Oil from a Stone," *Los Angeles Times* (November 30, 2004); World Energy Council Web site www.worldenergy.org.

22. Data for Figures 6.3 and 6.4 taken from *Transportation Energy Data Book* (Washington, DC: U.S. Department of Energy, 2008).

23. National Alternative Fuels Data Center (U.S. Department of Energy) Web site www.afdc. doe. gov.

24. Data for Figures 6.5 and 6.6 for the moving 12-month total vehicle-distance travelled in billion miles are from U.S. Federal Highway Administration of the DOT Web site www.fhwa.dot.gov/ohim/tvtw/tvtpage.cfm, and gasoline prices are from the U.S. Department of Energy Web site www.eia.doe.gov/emeu/mer/petro.html.

# 7

## NATURAL GAS

With reserves to production ratio of natural gas 50 percent larger than oil and with plenty of potential for expansion, the "oil and gas industry" may one day be dubbed the "gas and oil industry." This chapter covers the history of natural gas from its beginning as a manufactured gas made from coal. It is the most regulated of fossil fuels because only one natural gas pipeline can be connected to a house, just as a house can have only one electrical cable. Like electricity, natural gas is in the midst of deregulation (liberalization). How natural gas travels from the earth to consumption point is discussed, along with the growth of the international trade in natural gas and the possibility of developing nonconventional sources of methane.

### BACKGROUND

Natural gas is made up of primarily methane, a carbon atom surrounded by four hydrogen atoms. It is the cleanest-burning fossil fuel with only water and carbon dioxide as products of combustion. Carbon monoxide emissions, if any, are caused by insufficient oxygen to support combustion. Nitrous oxides stem from nitrogen in the air reacting with the heat of a flame. Natural gas produces far less nitrous oxides than oil and coal, which contain nitrogen within their molecular structures. Burning natural gas produces virtually no sulfur oxides and no particulate or metallic emissions. A greater ratio of hydrogen to carbon atoms releases less carbon dioxide per unit of energy than coal and oil. Moreover, cogeneration plants fueled by natural gas have a higher thermal efficiency than coal and oil, further lowering carbon dioxide emissions for the same output of electricity.

Natural gas fields have about double the reservoir recovery (70–80 percent) than oil (30–40 percent), which lessens the need to continually find new gas fields. Unlike oil, natural gas requires relatively little processing to become "pipeline-quality." On the minus side, natural gas has always been a logistical challenge. In the beginning decades of the oil age, much of the natural gas produced in association with crude oil was flared (burned) or vented to the atmosphere. The primitive state of pipeline technology restricted natural gas to the local market. Large amounts of natural gas associated with oil production were available with the development of oil and gas discoveries in the U.S. Southwest. With no nearby markets to consume the gas and no means to get the gas to distant markets, vast quantities of natural gas associated with crude oil production were vented to the atmosphere. This waste of a "free" energy source and the waning of natural gas fields in Appalachia provided a strong incentive to improve pipeline technology to connect suppliers with consumers over long distances in a safe, reliable, and cost-effective manner.

Another drawback is that leaking natural gas can asphyxiate the occupants of a building or trigger a fire or an explosion that can level a building or, on occasion, a city block. Fires fueled by broken gas mains in the aftermath of earthquakes, such as occurred in San Francisco in 1906 and Kobe, Japan, in 1995, exacerbated the damage and suffering. Unlike liquid petroleum products, consumers have no way of storing natural gas. Natural gas delivery systems must be designed to handle extreme vagaries in demand.

Most pipelines are largely confined to a single nation or region, such as North America, where they connect producers and consumers in Canada, the United States, and Mexico. The United States alone has 300,000 miles of transmission pipelines and about 1 million miles each of gathering and distribution pipelines. Russia has a well-developed natural gas pipeline system to serve its domestic needs and exports large volumes to the European pipeline grid. The grid crosses national borders, much as pipelines cross state borders in the United States, connecting European consumers to gas fields in Russia, the Netherlands, the North Sea, and Algeria via two undersea trans-Mediterranean pipelines. One pipeline from Algeria crosses Morocco and the Mediterranean Sea to Spain (near Gibraltar) and the other crosses Tunisia, the Mediterranean, Sicily, and the Strait of Messina to mainland Italy. Another undersea trans-Meditteranean natural gas pipeline connects Libya and Sicily.

There are limits to pipeline transmission that leave enormous reserves of stranded gas beyond the reach of consumers. With limited domestic consumption, natural gas associated with oil production in the Middle East, Southeast Asia, and West Africa is either flared or vented to the atmosphere or reinjected into oil fields. Flaring and venting are a horrendous waste of energy, equivalent to burning money in this world of high-energy prices. Reinjection maintains the pressure of oil fields and preserves a valuable energy resource. In recent decades a new method of shipping natural gas in a liquefied state aboard highly specialized tankers has emerged. Liquefied natural gas (LNG) export plants, coupled with specialized import terminals and LNG carriers, have monetized these reserves of stranded gas by making them available to consumers. Since LNG cargoes can be shipped from exporting terminals in North and West Africa, Latin America, the Middle East, Southeast Asia, and Australia to receiving terminals in the United States, Europe, and Asia, natural gas is in the beginning stages of being transformed from a regional to a globally traded commodity like oil. Furthermore, technological progress has been made in converting natural gas to liquid motor vehicle fuels, giving natural gas access to the same delivery system that serves petroleum.

A long-standing and complex relationship exists between natural gas and electricity as the proliferation of electric and gas utilities suggests. Gas both supplies fuel to generate electricity and competes with electricity to supply consumers with a means to cook, heat water and living spaces, and run appliances. Both became federally regulated commodities in the 1930s as a result of interstate transmission. Later on, natural gas regulation was expanded to include natural gas suppliers of regulated interstate transmission pipelines. This experiment in total regulation of an industry turned into a bureaucratic quagmire with internal contradictions and undesired consequences plaguing the regulators. The final solution to the problems induced by regulation was deregulation of natural gas production, transmission, and distribution, beginning in the late 1970s. Again, the link between electricity and natural gas can be seen in the parallel deregulation of electricity generation, transmission, and distribution. While the breakdown of the monopoly status of natural gas and electricity is quite advanced in the United States and the United Kingdom, it is still an ongoing process. Deregulation (liberalization) is actively being pursued elsewhere in the world.

Natural gas as an energy source looks extremely promising for the coming decades and has a number of advantages working in its favor. However, natural gas, like oil, will eventually become another depleting resource, a fact that the world will eventually have to contend with. Some say that day, while admittedly further away than that for oil, may not be that far in the future.

## EARLY HISTORY OF COAL GAS

The beginning of the natural gas industry was not natural gas from the first oil wells in western Pennsylvania, but manufactured gas from coal—a case of a synthetic or manufactured fuel preceding the natural fuel. In 1609, a Belgian physician and chemist reduced sixty-two pounds of coal to one pound of ash and speculated about what had happened to the missing sixty-one pounds, the first published account of coal gas. While burning coal in the presence of air reduces it to ash, heating coal in a closed environment, without a fresh supply of air, produces coke, tar, and gas. Coke, primarily carbon, is burned as a fuel or consumed in steel production. Coal tar was originally a waste product, dumped willy-nilly in streams, rivers, ponds, and on land adjacent to manufactured gas plants. "Free" coal tar, as a potential raw material for useful products, became the cornerstone of the chemical industry by first being transformed to creosote, tar, pitch, wood preservatives, mothballs, and carbon black. Later on the chemical industry learned to extract benzene, toluene, and xylene, which can be used as gasoline components or feedstock for the petrochemical industry. Other products included phenol and polynuclear aromatic hydrocarbons found in synthetic fibers, epoxies, resins, dyes, plastics, disinfectants, germicides, fungicides, pesticides, and pharmaceuticals. Unfortunately, a large amount of the early coal tar was not processed. When natural gas replaced manufactured gas, the thousands of abandoned manufactured gas plants became classified as hazardous and toxic waste dumpsites whose cost of cleanup is under the Superfund Program of the U.S. Environmental Protection Agency (an example of the consumer not paying the full cost for a service).

The purpose of manufactured gas plants was not to make coke or coal tar, but coal gas, a mixture of hydrogen, carbon monoxide, carbon dioxide, and methane. The heat content of coal gas, made up partially of noncombustible carbon dioxide, is half that of natural gas. The first demonstration of coal gas as an energy source occurred in 1683 when an English clergyman stored coal gas in an ox bladder; when he was ready to use it, he pricked the bladder and lit the outgoing gas. The first demonstration of coal gas as a means of illumination occurred a century later, in 1785, when a professor of natural philosophy lit his classroom by burning coal gas in a lamp. In 1801, a French engineer used coal gas to light and heat a Parisian hotel. William Murdoch, an engineer working for Boulton and Watt, the manufacturer of James Watt's steam engines, produced coal gas that passed through seventy feet of copper and tin pipe to light a room in his house in 1792 and, in 1802, to light a foundry. He experimented with various types of coal heated to different temperatures for varying lengths of time, which led to the first major commercial use of coal gas: to light the Manchester cotton mills for round-the-clock operation. For his pioneering work, Murdoch was called the father of the gas industry.[1]

Other advances included purifying coal gas by passing it through limewater and devising meters to measure its usage. Friedrich Albrecht Winzer, a German entrepreneur, proposed the first centralized gas works where gas would be made in large quantities and pipelined to customers for lighting and heating. Germany was not ready for the idea, so he anglicized his name to Fredrick Albert Winsor and sold the concept to the Prince of Wales, a fellow German of the house of Hanover, who had gaslights installed for celebrating King George III's birthday in 1805. In 1812 the Westminster Gas Light and Coke Company was chartered by Parliament, and by 1815 the company was supplying London from a centralized coal gas producing plant via twenty-six miles of gas mains of the same three-quarters-inch pipe used to make rifle barrels. This placed England in the forefront of a new industry and a font of technological know-how for the introduction of gas lighting in Europe and America.

Two sons of Charles Peale, a well-known portrait painter of Revolutionary War heroes (including fourteen of George Washington), played important roles in what would lead to the formation of the Gas Light Company of Baltimore in 1816. In 1817, the company received a franchise from Baltimore to provide gas lighting. Progress was slow, and only two miles of gas mains were supplying 3,000 private and 100 public lamps by 1833. The company's activities spread into manufacturing and repair of gas meters, along with producing chandeliers, pipes, and fittings in order to be able to sell coal gas for illumination. The spread of manufactured gas in major cities for lighting was not particularly rapid, beginning with Baltimore in 1817, New York City in 1825 (the Great White Way of Broadway was first lit with gas, not electricity), Philadelphia in 1836 (the first municipal-owned gas works), Cincinnati, St. Louis, and Chicago in the 1840s, San Francisco in 1854, Kansas City and Los Angeles in 1867, and Minneapolis and Seattle in the 1870s. The advantage of coal gas was easy shipment of coal to manufactured gas-producing plants strategically located in the center of their markets. This minimized the cost of laying pipes causing coal gas plants to proliferate. The slow adoption of manufactured gas for lighting was its cost, which ranged between $2.50–$3.50 per thousand cubic feet (Mcf). In twenty-first-century dollars, this would be equivalent to about $60 per Mcf compared to $6.80 per Mcf for the average price of natural gas delivered to residential consumers during the 1990s and $11.85 from 2000–2008.

Consumers have a choice of oil companies when buying liquid petroleum products, the hallmark of a competitive market. Manufactured gas began as a natural monopoly because laying multiple gas mains to give consumers a choice of supplier was not deemed cost-effective. Moreover, manufactured gas companies required municipal assistance, support, and cooperation to get into business including a franchise to be sole supplier, permits to lay gas mains under city streets, and a contract to light city streets. All these were necessary for a manufactured gas company to assure potential investors of sufficient revenue for a satisfactory return on their investment. Once the gas mains were laid for city lighting, it was a relatively simple matter to connect to residences and businesses. While municipal authorities recognized that a single company could provide gas at a lower cost than two competing companies with twice the investment in facilities and pipelines, they also recognized that a single company, once ensconced in a market as a natural monopoly, would not be cheaper. Thus, a franchise that granted a monopoly also specified municipal oversight on entry, expansion, exit, safety, and rates to protect the public interest.

Local or municipal regulation worked well with manufactured gas providers whose plant and distribution system were within the legal jurisdiction of a municipality. Things changed when natural gas began to displace manufactured gas because natural gas fields were normally outside of a municipality's legal jurisdiction. This complicated regulation for the municipalities, a problem that was solved when state governments replaced municipal regulation. Since a natural gas field generally served several municipalities, the natural gas industry opted for statewide rather than municipal regulation, a situation that promised greater consistency of rules and rates and reduced the number of regulators to be dealt with (or influenced).

## HISTORY OF NATURAL GAS

Sacred fires in Persia and elsewhere were natural gas seeps that may have been ignited by lightning. The temple of Delphi was built around a "burning spring." Around 400 BCE the Chinese discovered natural gas bubbling through brine, which they separated and burned to distill salt. Around 200 CE the Chinese learned to tap natural gas deposits and route the gas through bamboo pipes to distill salt from seawater and cook food. The earliest reference to natural gas in the United States was in the 1600s when explorers noted certain Indian tribes burning gaseous emissions from the earth. In 1821, a more organized approach to capturing escaping or seep gas started in Fredonia, New

York, when a gunsmith piped seep gas to nearby buildings for lighting. In 1827, another source of naturally occurring seep gas was harnessed to supply a lighthouse on Lake Erie. In 1840, the first industrial use of natural gas occurred in Pennsylvania, where gas was burned to heat brine to distill salt, the same thing the Chinese had done more than two millennia earlier.

While natural gas provided the lift for Drake's well, for the most part, natural gas found along with oil was vented to the atmosphere. Drilling for oil and discovering natural gas was equivalent to a dry hole. Natural gas was normally out of reach of municipalities and was unable to compete with manufactured gas protected by municipal franchises. In 1872 the Rochester Natural Gas Light Company was formed to provide natural gas to Rochester, New York, from a field twenty-five miles away. Pipes made of two- to eight-foot segments of hollowed-out Canadian white pine logs reflected the primitive state of pipeline technology. The problems associated with a rotting and leaking wooden pipeline eventually led to the company's demise. In the same year a five-and-a-half-mile, two-inch-wide wrought-iron pipeline was successfully constructed to carry waste gas from oil wells near Titusville to 250 townspeople.

But cast- and wrought-iron pipelines were plagued by breaks and leaking connections held together by screws. Before the day of compressors, transmission distance was limited by gas well pressure. In 1870, Pittsburgh became the first city to start consuming natural gas as a substitute for manufactured gas from coal to clean up its smoke-laden atmosphere. The Natural Gas Act, passed in 1885 by the Pennsylvania legislature, permitted natural gas to compete with manufactured gas. This proved to be the driving wedge that enabled natural gas to penetrate the manufactured coal gas business and resulted in the formation of Peoples Natural Gas, which by 1887 was serving 35,000 households in Pittsburgh. Another Pittsburgh natural gas distributor, Chartiers Valley Gas, was the first company to telescope pipe from an initial eight to ten and finally twelve inches in diameter to reduce gas pressure before it entered a home, business, or industrial plant. By this time, screws had given way to threaded pipe to hold pipe segments together. Dresser and Company, formed in 1880, specialized in pipe couplings, and in 1887 received a patent for a leak-proof coupling that incorporated a rubber ring in the pipe joints; an invention that would dominate the market until the 1920s.

George Westinghouse, inventor of the compressed-air railroad brake, became interested in natural gas and decided to drill for natural gas. He selected, of all places, his backyard and, lo and behold, he struck natural gas as one might expect for the rich to get richer. He became one of the largest gas distributors in Pittsburgh, and relied on the natural gas produced from one hundred wells in and around Pittsburgh, including his backyard. Westinghouse was well-versed in the dangers associated with natural gas such as gas users not turning off their gas appliances (lamps, stoves, heaters) when natural gas pipelines were shut down for repair of breaks and leaks. When pipeline service was restored, a nearly odorless and colorless gas seeped into homes and shops, threatening to kill those within from asphyxiation, fire, or explosion. Westinghouse put his experience with compressed air to good use and originated a number of patents for enclosing main gas lines in residential areas with a conducting pipe to contain gas leaks, introducing pressure regulators to reduce gas pressure before it entered residences and commercial establishments, and cutoff values to prevent any further flow of gas once gas pressure fell below a set point.

These improvements made Pittsburgh the center of the natural gas industry by the late 1880s, with 500 miles of pipeline to transport natural gas from surrounding wells to the city and another 230 miles of pipeline within the city limits. Andrew Carnegie, the steel magnate, promoted the use of natural gas in steelmaking. Natural gas became the fuel of choice not only for steel mills, but also glassmaking plants, breweries, businesses, homes, and a crematorium. Hundreds of natural gas companies were formed to sell gas to municipalities in Pennsylvania, West Virginia, Ohio, and

Indiana with a local supply of natural gas. Some of these gas fields were rapidly depleted, forcing a switch back to manufactured gas. Early customers were simply charged a monthly rate for a hookup without a means to measure the amount of gas consumed. When meters were eventually installed, a new business sprang up: renting "gas dogs" to greet meter readers on their days of visitation.

John D. Rockefeller entered the natural gas business in 1881. True to form, through mergers with existing pipeline companies and expanding their business activities once they were under his control, Standard Oil established a major market presence in the gas-producing states in Appalachia. Rockefeller's success at monopolization led to the passage of the Hepburn Act in 1906, which was intended to give the Interstate Commerce Commission (ICC) regulatory authority over interstate natural gas pipelines, even though very few existed at the time. In the end, the Hepburn Act exempted natural gas and water pipelines from regulatory oversight, but growing concern over Rockefeller's hold on the oil industry led to the U.S. Department of Justice filing suit under the Sherman Antitrust Act against Standard Oil. Curiously, in the Standard Oil breakup in 1911, the company's natural gas properties and activities remained intact within Standard Oil of New Jersey, enabling the company to maintain its standing as a major natural gas player in the Midwest and Northeast and, eventually, the Southwest.

**The Battle Over Lighting**

Manufactured gas commanded the market for lighting in urban areas while kerosene continued to be used in rural areas and towns not hooked up to manufactured gas. Though vulnerable to penetration by natural gas, coal gas was given a new lease on life by the discovery of a technique for making "water gas" by injecting steam into anthracite coal or coke heated to incandescence. This produced a flammable mixture of hydrogen and carbon monoxide that was sprayed with atomized oil (a new market for oil) to increase its heat content to match that of coal gas. Less costly to make than coal gas, water gas had 75 percent of the manufactured gas market by 1900.

Although water gas could temporarily hold natural gas at bay, a new competitive threat entered the lighting business, affecting both manufactured and natural gas: electricity. In 1880, Edison rigged Broadway for illumination by electricity and lost no time attacking gas lighting for its odors, leaks, fires, explosions, and transport in "sewer pipes," ignoring, of course, the risk of electric shock, electrocution, and fires from exposed wires. In 1882, the Pearl Street generating station provided electricity to 1,284 lamps within one mile of the plant. Edison used existing gas statutes for permission to install electric wiring under streets and set up a system to supply electricity that mirrored gas as closely as possible to make it easier for customers to switch. The gas-distribution companies knew that electricity would replace gas for lighting and responded with a two-pronged program to meet the new competitive threat. The first was to shift the emphasis of gas from lighting to cooking and heating, and the second was to pursue corporate consolidation to strengthen their position.

As the availability of electricity spread throughout the nation, it did not take long for managers of consolidated gas companies to see the virtue of expanding their merger activities to include electricity-generating firms ("if you can't beat the enemy, embrace him"). The coke byproduct from coal gas production could be burned to make electricity, and mergers would result in major savings in corporate overhead. The first merger occurred in Boston in 1887, setting the example for the creation of innumerable gas and electric or electric and gas utility companies across the nation. Consolidating gas companies and merging with electricity-generating companies into independent gas and electric utilities further evolved into the public holding company, which owned controlling interests in independent electric and gas companies.

The first public holding company was formed by Henry L. Doherty, who started out as an office boy and rose to chief engineer of a natural gas company. Noticing that poorly designed gas stoves were a drag on natural gas sales, Doherty increased gas sales by working with stove manufacturers to improve their product. He switched to marketing, where he was an instant success because of his ability to motivate and lead salespeople, initiating all sorts of promotional activities, and setting high standards of customer service. Doherty then established his own company to provide advice on the reorganization, management, and financing of public utility companies. He began to attract investor interest and in 1910 formed Cities Service Company, the first public holding company. As the name suggested, the company was to serve cities across the nation with gas and electricity and, by 1913, Cities Service controlled fifty utilities in fourteen states.

Cities Service was a model for a much larger public utility empire created by Samuel Insull, who started out as the English representative of a U.S. bank handling Thomas Edison's interests in London. He ended up working directly for Edison as his private secretary by day and learned the electricity-generating business at the Pearl Street plant by night. He eventually rose to third place in the newly formed General Electric, a merger involving Edison Electric, then to chief executive of Chicago Edison, and finally to chairman of Peoples Gas in Chicago, where he managed a corporate turnaround. This string of successes led to the 1912 founding of Middle West Utilities and later to Insull Utility Investments, both holding companies for electric and gas utilities. By 1926 Insull's utility empire encompassed 6,000 communities across thirty-two states, and by 1930 it had grown to 4 million customers controlling 12 percent of the nation's electricity-generating and gas-distribution capacity.

The War Industries Board encouraged the formation of nationwide industrial organizations to carry out its mandate to coordinate the nation's industrial activities during the First World War. Natural gas suppliers responded by combining several predecessor organizations into the American Gas Association (AGA) in 1918 to centralize the exchange of information, set industry-wide standards, and encourage cooperation and coordination among its members. The AGA also represented the industry viewpoint to the public at Congressional hearings and before natural gas regulatory bodies. The complete conversion of natural gas from lighting to cooking and heating took place at this time, symbolized by natural gas being sold in units of energy (British thermal units) rather than units of illumination (candlepower).

## Long-Distance Transmission

The discovery of huge natural gas fields in the Southwest, the Panhandle Field in northern Texas in 1918, followed by the Hugoton gas fields in the Kansas, Oklahoma, and Texas border areas in 1922, changed the nature of the gas business. Both fields covered over 1.6 million acres and accounted for much of the nation's reserves. Exploiting oil found in these fields resulted in venting enormous quantities of associated natural gas to the atmosphere. The discovery of natural gas fields in the Southwest occurred just as natural gas fields in Appalachia were beginning to wane. The promise of commercial reward to be gained by substituting "free" Southwest gas for valuable Appalachian gas spurred R&D efforts in long-distance pipeline transmission resulting in thin-walled, high tensile strength, large diameter, seamless pipe segments joined together by electric arc welding, gas compressors for moving large volumes of natural gas at high pressures, and in ditch digging and filling machinery for laying pipe. An indication of the progress in gas transmission can be seen in pipeline diameters and design working pressures. In the 1920s and 1930s, large transmission pipelines were between twenty and twenty-six inches in diameter and could sustain up to 500 pounds working pressure; in the 1940s, diameters were up to thirty inches, and working pressure was up to 800 pounds; by the 1960s, up to thirty-six inches in diameter and 1,000 pounds; in the 1970s, diameters up to forty-two inches and 1,260 pounds; and after 1980, pipelines were fifty-six inches in diameter and working pressure up to 2,000 pounds.

Manufactured coal gas companies financed many of the first long-distance pipelines built in the 1920s for mixing cheap natural gas into water gas to raise its heat content. The first long-distance pipeline was 250 miles long and made of twenty-inch diameter pipe built by Cities Service in 1927/28 to connect the Panhandle field with Kansas City. This was quickly followed by Standard Oil of New Jersey's 350-mile, twenty-two-inch line from the Texas-New Mexico border to Denver. In 1929, natural gas was pipelined 300 miles from the San Joaquin Valley to San Francisco, the first metropolitan area to switch from manufactured to natural gas. These pipelines carried a considerable amount of gas that had to find a "home," spawning an intense marketing effort to induce consumers to buy gas-powered appliances such as space and water heaters, stoves, and clothes dryers. Individual burners for manufactured gas had to be adjusted to handle the higher heat content of natural gas, no small effort when a city had hundreds of thousands of individual burners. In 1930, the industry accepted a standard and distinctive mercaptan odorant to detect escaping gas.

A consortium of companies controlled by Doherty, Insull, and Standard Oil of New Jersey built the first 1,000-mile pipeline (actually 980 miles) from north Texas to Chicago, called the Chicago Line. The twenty-four-inch diameter pipeline, started in 1930 and completed one year later, primarily served Insull's Chicago area utilities. The pipeline transmitted a sufficient volume of attractively priced gas to eventually convert Chicago from manufactured to natural gas. The three principal partners to varying degrees owned and controlled the natural gas fields and the pipeline transmission and distribution systems. A similar arrangement was behind the Northern Natural Gas 1,110-mile, twenty-six-inch pipeline from the Hugoton gas field to Omaha, then continuing on to Minnesota. Essentially the same power trust, but with different shareholdings and minority participants, controlled both pipelines. With no competition between the two pipeline systems in their respective "territories," and the same partners owning the natural gas fields, the pipeline transmission and distribution systems, consumers were at the mercy of a natural monopoly whose operations were far beyond the purview of state regulatory authorities.

The Panhandle Eastern pipeline was intended to introduce competition in the "territories." The power trusts then in existence employed various legal shenanigans to stop the building of the pipeline, including putting pressure on financial institutions not to fund the project. While ultimately unsuccessful, the trusts did succeed in drawing public attention to their power to thwart competition. Yet, it was in the public interest to build more long-distance gas pipelines to reduce the wasteful practice of venting natural gas to the atmosphere. As seen in Figure 7.1, venting amounted to over half of natural gas production in the Southwest.

An average of a little under 400 billion cubic feet were vented to the atmosphere per year for the eleven years shown in Figure 7.1; perhaps in no small way contributing to the buildup of methane, a greenhouse gas, in the atmosphere. To understand what this waste means in terms of oil, a cubic foot of natural gas contains 1,026 Btu, whereas a barrel of crude oil contains 5.8 million Btu. One Btu is the amount of energy to increase the temperature of one pound of water by 1°F; it is a small measure of energy equivalent to burning a blue-tip kitchen match. One barrel of oil is energy-equivalent to 5,653 cubic feet of natural gas, or one barrel of oil per day for one year is energy-equivalent to 2.063 million cubic feet of natural gas. Thus, 1 trillion cubic feet of gas per year is energy-equivalent to 484,648 barrels of oil per day or, in round numbers, 0.5 million barrels per day. The waste of, say, 0.4 trillion cubic feet of gas per year vented to the atmosphere was energy-equivalent to throwing away about 200,000 barrels of crude oil per day for a year, at a time when energy consumption was a minuscule fraction of current levels.

Figure 7.1  **Consumption versus Waste of Natural Gas** (Billion Cubic Feet)

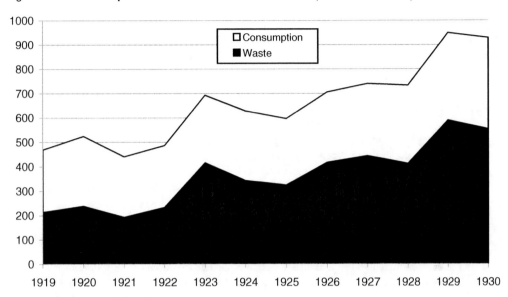

This waste was primarily natural gas associated with oil production. A lower oil production rate would result in less waste. Unfortunately, the common-law principal applicable to the ownership of underground hydrocarbons is the rule of capture, which simply states that whoever draws the oil out of the ground owns the oil (assuming vertical wells!). If three individuals or companies own the land and mineral rights over an oil reservoir, and only one drills wells on his or her property and, over time, drains the entire reservoir dry, the other two have no claim on the revenue or profits of the driller. The rule of capture forces everyone whose land lies over an oil reservoir to drill as many wells as possible and to pump as hard as possible to get their "rightful" share. Under these conditions, natural gas associated with oil production had no way to go but up into the atmosphere.

**Federal Regulation**

The construction of long-distance natural gas pipelines came to an abrupt end with the Great Depression of the 1930s, when only three pipelines of less than 300 miles in length were built. Existing natural gas pipelines and electric utilities operated far below capacity and many could no longer produce enough revenue to support their operating and capital costs. Insull Utility Investments, the darling of the Roaring Twenties, had issued bonds galore to finance the takeover of many of the nation's utilities at stock prices inflated by investor enthusiasm and overvalued assets. The Great Depression wrung the last drop of excess out of the stocks in Insull's empire and the discovery of accounting irregularities hastened its demise in 1932, incurring the wrath of shareholders, bondholders, the Federal Power Commission (FPC), and Franklin Delano Roosevelt.

While criticism of the monopolistic corporate structure of public utilities was voiced before the 1929 stock market crash, the collapse of Insull's house of cards led to a 1935 ninety-six-volume FPC report assailing the electricity and natural gas industries. With regard to natural gas, the report focused on the waste of venting natural gas to the atmosphere, the monopolistic control by the same corporate entities over natural gas production, transmission, and distribution, and reckless financial manipulation. The report pointed out the practice common among natural gas and electricity-generating companies of inflating book values to increase the rate base for pricing electricity, and their unrelenting pressure to influence state regulators to get higher rates and protect their "territories." The report noted only four companies, one being Standard Oil of New Jersey, controlled 60 percent of natural gas pipelines in terms of mileage and a like amount of the nation's natural gas production. With natural gas in interstate trade passing through thirty-four states serving 7 million customers, the report concluded that it was high time for the public utility industry to come under public scrutiny.

The passage of the Public Utility Holding Act of 1935 dismantled the pyramid utility holding companies. The public utility business would henceforth be organized into single, locally managed entities providing electricity and gas and serving a specific area. Although electricity and gas operations were still allowed under one corporate umbrella, they were housed in separate organizations. The Act essentially put the utility business back to where it was before Doherty and Insull started building their pyramids.

In 1937, an explosion in a Texas high school from natural gas leaking into the basement killed nearly 300 students and teachers. Although it was industry practice to put an odorant in natural gas to detect accumulation of gas in a closed space, the particular source of natural gas for the high school did not have an odorant. Perched on top of the wreckage was part of a blackboard with the intact inscription: "Oil and natural gas are East Texas' greatest mineral blessings. Without them this school would not be here, and none of us would be here learning our lessons." This tragedy hastened the passage of the Natural Gas Act of 1938, which empowered the FPC to regulate interstate natural gas pipelines. Viewed as an extension of its 1930 mandate to regulate the interstate transmission of electricity, the Act gave the FPC authority to approve natural gas pipeline rates based on a just and reasonable return, to require regulated pipeline companies to submit extensive documentation on operational and financial matters, and to order actions to be taken on a variety of matters if deemed necessary.

No interstate pipeline could be constructed without a Federal Certificate of Public Convenience and Necessity. To obtain this certificate, the promoting company or companies had to have a twenty or so year contract for an adequate supply of natural gas, must demonstrate a sound and proven ability to attract the necessary financing, and propose a rate based on a just and reasonable return on its investment. Moreover, the granting of the certificate had to take into consideration the impact of the proposed pipeline on other natural gas suppliers serving the intended market. The wording of this last point would prove to be a regulatory sticking point for certifying natural gas pipelines intended for areas without existing natural gas services. As bizarre as this sounds, the inability to measure the impact of a natural gas pipeline in a market not already served by natural gas pipelines would end up being an effective way for opponents of natural gas to obstruct the building of natural gas pipelines.

Before the passage of the Act, the owning corporations decided who had access to the pipeline and what rates would be charged. After the passage of the Act, interstate pipelines would be common carriers charging the same FPC-approved rates to all users without restrictions to access. The certificate, once granted, was a franchise for a natural gas pipeline company to exclusively serve a specified market. Thus, the concept of the franchise survived, but who determined the franchise had changed. Before the passage of the Act, corporations set up an exclusive "territory" where only the members of the cartel had access to the market. After the passage of the Act, the regulators would determine the "territory" where a pipeline transmission company had an exclusive franchise. The franchise was protected from competition by government fiat rather than corporate connivance. Having a chief executive with an "in" with the FPC regulators could be a natural gas pipeline's greatest asset.

Curiously, the Act did not grant the right of eminent domain to pipeline companies for building natural gas pipelines. Coal-carrying railroads, coal-mining companies, and manufactured gas producers would be able to obstruct the building of natural gas pipelines by taking advantage of the lack of a right of eminent domain and the requirement to evaluate the impact of a pipeline on other natural gas providers serving an area that had none. Standard Oil of New Jersey's response to this massive government intrusion into the natural gas business was to distribute shares in its natural gas and pipeline subsidiaries to its stockholders and abandon the natural gas business.

**The War Years**

The Second World War significantly boosted demand for natural gas to fuel factories and armament plants. This stimulated the building of new pipelines to tap Southwest gas to replace declining production in Appalachia. Despite wartime needs, a proposal to build a natural gas pipeline from the Southwest to New York was thwarted by coal-mining companies, railroads, and manufactured gas producers. As an alternative, a newly organized company, Tennessee Gas and Transmission, made a proposal to build a pipeline from Louisiana to Tennessee. The application failed because the company could not demonstrate how the pipeline would affect other natural gas suppliers in an area that had none! Attempts to correct this legislative imbroglio were bitterly opposed by railroads, coal companies, and manufactured coal gas producers.

When reason finally prevailed and appropriate legislative changes were made to modify this obstructive requirement, the railroads, coal mining, and manufactured gas companies were granted the right to intervene directly in natural gas pipeline certification hearings. Having lost one means to obstruct the building of natural gas pipelines, they were awarded another. The saga for granting the Certificate of Public Convenience and Necessity to build the Tennessee Gas pipeline involved political intrigue right on up to the office of the President along with major changes in the source of natural gas, changes in the financing, changes in the corporate structure of the company, and changes in its ownership. Appeals were made to the War Production Board to support the pipeline application in order to alleviate the growing shortage of natural gas in Appalachia, which was critical to fueling wartime industries. Perhaps the exigency of military industrial enterprises running out of natural gas or perhaps the rare triumph of reason over vested interests finally prevailed, and the FPC granted the required certification for building this twenty-four-inch pipeline.

**Opening Up the Northeast**

Manufactured gas companies, along with the coal-mining industry and the coal-carrying railroads, were intent on maintaining their last market bastion in the Northeast, the population center of the nation. All they had to do was obstruct the building of any natural gas pipeline. The Tennessee Gas pipeline extended the market reach of Southwest gas to Appalachia but not to the Northeast.

During the Second World War, tankers transported oil from the U.S. Gulf to the Northeast as the first step in shipping oil to Europe in support of the war effort. The eastern seaboard cities refused to turn off their lights at night, and the silhouetted tankers passing against their skylines became easy targets for U-Boats. As a countermeasure, the U.S. government built two oil pipelines, the Big Inch (twenty-four-inch) and the Little Inch (twenty-inch), from Texas to Pennsylvania and New Jersey. After the war, the oil companies reverted to tanker shipments and the pipelines, now under the Surplus Property Administration, were put up for sale. Congressmen representing the coal-producing states joined the railroads, coal companies, and manufactured gas producers to prevent the sale of these pipelines to a natural gas pipeline company. Proponents of natural gas pointed to the prospect of the continuing waste of venting natural gas to the atmosphere in the Southwest if these oil pipelines were not converted to natural gas. Opponents pointed to the millions of tons of coal that would be displaced to the detriment of the coal-mining industry and the transporting railroads if these oil pipelines were converted.

The winning bid at the first auction was Tennessee Gas, which obtained a one-year lease to pipeline natural gas to Ohio, with the promise that it would not to try to move gas into the Northeast. This converted the oil pipelines to gas transmission. At the expiration of the lease in 1947, a second auction was held and another fledging company, Texas Eastern, won with a bid of $143 million, about equal to the government's cost of construction. Later that year, a bill granting eminent domain to the natural gas pipeline industry quietly slipped through Congress. Philadelphia was the first northeastern city to convert to natural gas in 1948, and within a decade its manufactured gas industry was gone. The FPC then approved the building of the Transcontinental pipeline from Texas to New York City. Begun in 1949, the thirty-inch, 1,000-mile pipeline, including the "Costliest Inch" connection under Manhattan to five receiving gas utilities in New York City and Long Island, was completed in 1951.

The conversion of New York City and Long Island from manufactured to natural gas made New England the last bastion of manufactured gas in the United States. Progress, once underway, was hard to stop. A two-year dispute between Texas Eastern and Tennessee Gas before the FPC ended up with Texas Eastern being the supplier to Algonquin pipeline to provide service to Connecticut, Rhode Island, and eastern Massachusetts, including Boston. A subsidiary of Tennessee Gas was given permission to pipeline gas from a connection in Buffalo through upstate New York to western Massachusetts. Natural gas flowing into New England in 1953 marked the end of a century of domination by manufactured gas producers.

## Last Stop Before Total Regulation

The Natural Gas Act of 1938 split the natural gas business into three entities: the unregulated natural gas producers, interstate pipelines regulated by the FPC, and local distribution companies (LDCs) regulated by state or municipal authorities. In the 1940s, Panhandle Eastern attempted to sell gas directly to a Detroit utility, bypassing the LDC. The irate LDC decided not to object, but to build a competitive pipeline to cut out Panhandle Eastern. Now it was Panhandle Eastern's turn to object to the granting of a certificate for building a competing pipeline. Despite legal maneuvering, Panhandle Eastern lost the case. The alternative pipeline had contracted with Phillips Petroleum for its entire gas supply. The pipeline fell behind schedule in 1950, forcing a renegotiation of the contract. Phillips exercised its monopolistic hold over the pipeline's gas supply by hiking the price by 60 percent, raising the hackles of those in Congress representing the pipeline's consumers. The upshot was the "Phillips Decision" by the U.S. Supreme Court that brought natural gas producers selling gas to interstate pipelines under regulatory control.

Now the FPC had jurisdiction not only over 157 interstate gas pipeline companies but also over tens of thousands of independent producers. While arriving at a just and reasonable tariff for pipelines was a regulatory possibility (because pipeline projects were relatively few in number with well-documented costs), now the FPC had to deal with tens of thousands of independent producers who owned hundreds of thousands of individual wells each with its unique cost structure. What is a fair and reasonable price for natural gas coming from a deep well, drilled at great expense with high operating costs, and drawing gas from a reservoir with a short life versus the fair and reasonable price for gas coming from a shallow well with low operating costs tapping a field that will last for decades? Pricing gas on a well-by-well basis proved impossible and the FPC resorted to the "fair field" method to regulate natural gas prices in interstate trade, which was challenged and overturned in a 1955 court decision. In 1960 the FPC, facing a monumental backlog of applications for price increases by independent natural gas producers selling gas to interstate pipelines, decided to establish common prices for five geographic areas. In 1965, five years later, the FPC published its first area price; another five years were to pass before the second area price was published.

The never-ending regulatory wrangling prevented price increases for natural gas sold to interstate pipelines. The availability of cheap surplus gas in the Southwest encouraged the building of interstate pipelines. California began to suffer from a decline in local supplies of natural gas and interstate pipelines were built to its border for transfer to intrastate pipelines (California prohibits the building of interstate pipelines within its borders). Another large natural gas market was tapped by building an interstate pipeline to Florida. The new gas pipelines absorbed excess production in the Southwest, eliminating the wasteful practice of venting, but the continued building of interstate pipelines began to outstrip supply. Ignoring the lessons of Economics 101, the FPC set a regulated price for natural gas in interstate commerce at a level that encouraged consumption but discouraged investment in developing new gas fields. With a price set too low, proven reserves started to decline after 1970 and an impending natural gas shortage was looming when the oil crisis struck in 1973.

**Unraveling Natural Gas Regulation**

The 1973 oil crisis sent oil prices spiraling, which, in turn, caused the prices of all forms of energy to rise sharply, with the exception of regulated interstate natural gas. Though prices for regulated interstate gas remained unchanged, prices for unregulated intrastate natural gas jumped. Natural gas producers sold all they could to intrastate pipelines and reduced the volume sold to interstate pipelines to the absolute minimum contractual amounts. Natural gas shortages amounting to 1 trillion cubic feet in the Midwest and Northeast started in 1973 and continued to worsen. They became particularly severe during a long and cold winter in 1976–1977, reaching a peak shortfall of 3.8 trillion cubic feet with New York State declaring a state of emergency.

The FPC was at its wit's end trying to cope with the deteriorating situation, with its primary focus more on how to prevent an owner of an existing regulated well from enjoying a windfall profit than solving the natural gas shortage. Cracks in the regulatory facade started to occur in 1975 when the FPC allowed LDCs to make direct contract with producers to buy gas at higher than regulated prices. Interstate pipeline owners opposed this scheme because it threatened their merchant status, which allowed them to be the sole buyers and sellers of natural gas carried by their pipelines. The interstate pipeline owners initiated an advance payment program to natural gas producers that was essentially a five-year interest-free loan to encourage exploration, but this was abrogated by the FPC. Finally, the FPC abandoned area pricing and set a nationwide price for regulated gas 50 percent below intrastate gas prices. When this failed to stimulate exploration, the FPC announced a price menu that authorized higher prices for "new" gas and lower prices for "old" gas.

The Iranian Revolution of 1979–1980 worsened the natural gas situation with another spike in oil prices. The Synthetic Fuels Corporation, formed under Carter's Energy Security Act of 1978, was to make America energy independent. With vast deposits of coal, the most promising solution was a return to manufactured, or synthetic, gas made from coal. The Fischer-Tropsch process employed in Europe and South Africa produced nearly pure methane from coal without the adverse environmental consequences of the bygone era of manufactured gas. All but one of the proposed synfuel projects failed for a variety of environmental, commercial, and legal reasons. The one that succeeded came onstream in 1984, with four interstate pipelines companies forced to buy its output of synthetic gas made from coal at a resounding $6.75 per million Btu, nearly fifteen times the price of wellhead "old" gas when the project was conceived.

The second response to increasing natural gas supplies without increasing the price of old gas was to exploit the huge natural gas reserves found along with oil at Prudhoe Bay in Alaska. Three proposals were offered to tap this gas. One was a 2,500-mile, forty-eight-inch pipeline from Prudhoe Bay, along the coast of the Beaufort Sea, into Canada to the Mackenzie River Delta, also a source of natural gas. The pipeline would then proceed south along the Mackenzie River to pipeline connections in Alberta for delivery of the natural gas to customers in the Midwest and California. Environmentalists successfully opposed this project on the basis of potential damage to the Arctic National Wildlife Refuge. Although this project failed, two pipelines built in anticipation of its approval now carry Alberta gas to the Midwest and California.

A second proposal was to build a parallel natural gas pipeline to the existing crude oil pipeline that carried Prudhoe Bay oil to Valdez for shipment in tankers to U.S. markets. The natural gas would be liquefied at Valdez and shipped in LNG carriers to California. President Carter did not favor this project and preferred a third proposal: building a 1,600-mile pipeline from Prudhoe Bay parallel to the crude oil pipeline and then south parallel to the Alcan Highway through Canada, reentering the United States in Montana. Financing problems plagued the project until it was shelved in 1982.

The third response to increase natural gas supply was LNG imports. LNG production already existed in the United States since 1969 with Phillips Petroleum and Marathon Oil exporting LNG from Cook Inlet in Alaska to Japan. Anticipating natural gas shortages, Distrigas, a subsidiary of Cabot Corporation at the time and now part of the Suez LNG, built a terminal near Boston to receive LNG from Algeria to satisfy peak winter demand. An early proposal to import LNG from the Soviet Union failed for political reasons. In 1969, before the oil crisis and also anticipating natural gas shortages, El Paso Natural Gas organized a major LNG project with Sonatrach, the Algerian state-owned oil and gas company. Sonatrach would receive an export price for LNG that reflected the then low value for natural gas in the United States. El Paso built a fleet of nine LNG carriers and contracted with three east coast gas companies to receive the gas at specially built LNG terminals along the eastern seaboard. Panhandle Eastern entered into a similar agreement for Algerian LNG deliveries at a terminal built at Lake Charles, Louisiana, to feed Trunkline, a pipeline subsidiary that was running low on natural gas. (If a pipeline is running out of gas supplies and LNG can be delivered to either end of the pipeline, why have LNG fill the pipeline?)

The El Paso project survived only the first shipments when Sonatrach unilaterally repriced LNG to fit market realities, giving El Paso the opportunity to walk away from the deal. The Trunkline failure took a bit longer because its deal with Sonatrach had tied the price of LNG to fuel oil. Whereas El Paso walked away from the project when Sonatrach repriced LNG, here Trunkline customers did the walking. The price they had to pay was a blended price of relatively cheap interstate gas and expensive LNG. Faced with opportunities to buy lower-priced gas from other sources, one Trunkline customer after another took their business elsewhere. As its customer base eroded, the rising portion of expensive Algerian gas in Trunkline's pipeline increased the price of the blended gas, encouraging others to walk. From 1982–1984, customer defection halved pipeline volume forcing Trunkline to walk away from the Sonatrach contract. Sonatrach successfully sued Panhandle Eastern for partial restitution.

All in all, natural gas regulation was a bitter lesson for the regulators, who seemed to forget the lessons of Economics 101. By pricing gas too low starting in the late 1960s, the regulators encouraged growth in demand while simultaneously discouraging growth in supply. Their reaction to the energy crisis—proposing esoteric solutions such as synfuels, developing isolated reserves, and using LNG rather than raising the price of old gas—simply exacerbated the situation.

## The Road to Deregulation

The 1976 Carter campaign for the presidency pledged the "moral equivalent of war" on the ongoing energy crisis. Following through on his campaign pledge, Carter created the Department of Energy as part of the National Energy Act of 1978, which was preceded by Congress reorganizing the harassed Federal Power Commission as the Federal Energy Regulatory Commission (FERC). The Natural Gas Policy Act of 1978 permitted FERC to price natural gas that came into production in and after 1978 into nine categories with subcategories depending on well depth, source, and other factors, until 1985 when all post-1978 gas would be deregulated. Old gas in production prior to 1978 would be indefinitely regulated with three price tiers. The significantly higher-priced new gas flowing into the system had "unexpected" Economics 101 consequences—it provided an incentive for consumers to reduce demand by switching to other sources of energy and taking steps to conserve energy, at the same time providing an incentive for producers to expand supply. New gas prices dropped when controls were lifted in 1985 because the gas shortage of too little supply chasing too much demand had been transformed to a gas "bubble" of too much supply chasing too little demand. The word bubble was intentionally used to describe what FERC thought would be a transient state of oversupply, but "transient" was a situation that lasted for nearly two decades. Natural gas prices fell to the point where synthetic gas, Alaskan gas, and LNG were far from being economically viable. The fall in natural gas prices as a result of letting the market work its magic (higher prices spurring exploration to expand supply and conservation and energy-switching to dampen demand) made it easy for Congress to pass the Natural Gas Wellhead Decontrol Act of 1989 abrogating price controls on all wellhead gas.

Unfortunately, the pipeline companies had arranged for twenty-year, back-to-back, take-or-pay, fixed-price contracts between electric utilities and natural gas suppliers at the prevailing high natural gas prices of the late 1970s. The growing presence of lower-priced gas during the first half of the 1980s placed a great deal of pressure on utilities to break their high-priced gas contracts. FERC bent to their demands and, through various rulings, allowed utilities to walk away from these contracts and buy natural gas directly from producers at lower prices and pay a fee to the pipeline companies for transmission services. This started the transformation of natural gas-transmission companies from merchants to transporters, the first step in breaking a monopoly in which a consumer had no choice but to buy from the transmission company.

Once the utilities were allowed to break their contracts with pipeline companies, the pipeline companies were stuck with the other side of the take-or-pay contracts to buy natural gas at high prices. Faced with multi-billion dollar liabilities, in 1987 FERC issued Order 500, the first step toward breaking take-or-pay contracts with natural gas producers, allowing pipeline companies to set up a system of pipeline transmission credits against producers' take-or-pay claims. While not an entirely satisfactory resolution of the matter, Order 500 turned out to be the precursor to a series of orders that ended up with Order 636 in 1992, which mandated the final solution to the national gas regulatory problem: deregulation.

To its credit, regulation either fostered or, at least, did not prevent the building of hundreds of thousands of miles of interstate gas pipelines linking natural gas producers to consumers throughout the nation. Under the sanction of the FPC, natural gas pipeline merchants acquired natural gas, transmitted the gas through their pipelines, and sold the gas in their respective franchised territories. The pipeline merchants generally made more money buying and selling gas than transmitting it. This system ended with Order 636. The whole natural gas system was unbundled into three distinct activities: natural gas producers, pipeline transmitters, and the end-use buyers—either LDCs or major consumers such as utilities or industrial plants.

Order 636 restricted the service offered by interstate pipeline companies to transmission of natural gas at a regulated rate that provided a just and reasonable return on their investments. LDCs and major consumers would be responsible for arranging their own supplies by contracting with natural gas producers to cover their needs. This created a marketing opportunity for companies to acquire natural gas production or represent the interest of natural gas producers and sell to end users. The pipeline transmission carriers were reduced to contract carriers and were obligated to set up Electronic Bulletin Boards in order for buyers and sellers to keep track of gas flows and pipeline allocations.

In 1983, 95 percent of all interstate commerce gas was purchased by the pipeline companies from natural gas producers and sold to LDCs and major consumers. By 1987 the pipeline companies arranged for the buying and selling of less than half of the gas going through their pipelines, and by 1994, they were fully converted to common carriers. Thus ended the world of the pipeline companies where they dealt with producers for a supply of gas and then marketed the gas to LDCs and large end users. Now the pipeline company was no longer a gas merchant but a common contract carrier like a railroad. Marketing firms were the intermediaries between natural gas producers and LDCs and large end users. However, pipeline carriers were free to set up marketing organizations to compete with independent marketers in arranging and brokering deals between natural gas buyers and sellers. By 1993 the marketing arms of pipeline companies had more than a 40 percent share of the market, but they had to operate independently of the pipeline transmission organization; any collusion between the two, or less than arm's-length transactions, were subject to heavy fines.

This process of unbundling of services is not complete. LDCs buy natural gas from producers and pay a toll to an interstate natural gas pipeline as a common carrier at a rate determined to provide a reasonable return and supply the gas to their customers. This principle can be expanded to include customers of the LDCs, in theory down to individual households, who can arrange for their natural gas needs directly with producers, pay the interstate pipeline company one toll for the use of its transmission system, and then pay another toll to the LDC for the use of its distribution system at a rate that represents a fair return.

## FROM SOURCE TO CONSUMER

Natural gas comes from the well as a mixture of hydrocarbons. For instance, Southwest natural gas has average proportions of 88 percent methane, 5 percent ethane, 2 percent propane, 1 percent butane, plus heavier hydrocarbons and impurities. A methane molecule is one carbon atom and four hydrogen atoms; ethane is two carbon atoms and six hydrogen atoms; propane has three carbon atoms and eight hydrogen; butane, four carbon and ten hydrogen. Heavier hydrocarbons of pentane (with five carbon atoms and twelve hydrogen atoms), hexane (with five carbon atoms and fourteen hydrogen), and heptane (seven carbon atoms and sixteen hydrogen) are in a gaseous state when in a natural gas reservoir, but "fall out," or condense, to a liquid called condensates when brought to the surface. Condensates are separated from natural gas and sold separately to refiners. Ethane is fairly expensive to separate with its low liquefying temperature, and normally remains in the natural gas stream. Propane and butane are more easily separated by fractionation, or a cooling of the natural gas, and are sold separately as liquefied petroleum gases (LPG). Impurities such as hydrogen sulfide, carbon dioxide, nitrogen, and water have to be removed. "Pipeline-quality" natural gas is primarily methane with some ethane, cleaned of impurities and stripped of condensates and petroleum gas liquids, with a heat content of 1,000–1,050 Btus per cubic foot at standard atmospheric conditions.[2]

The cleaning and stripping functions are performed in the pipeline-gathering system connecting the producing wells with transmission pipelines; the last step is raising the pressure of natural gas to transmission system pressure. Transmission pipelines typically are twenty-four- to thirty-six-inch diameter operating between 600 and 1,200 psi pressure, although there are wider diameter pipelines operating at higher pressures. Compressor stations are located about every seventy miles and the speed of the gas varies between fifteen and thirty miles per hour, depending on the gas pressure, compressor capacity, and pipeline diameter. Monitoring devices and shutoff values are strategically placed about every five to twenty miles to deal with potential pipeline ruptures and routine pipe maintenance. Both the inner and outer pipe surfaces are coated to protect against corrosion. The inner surface is kept clean by running a "pig" through the pipeline for routine maintenance; a "smart pig" can also transmit data on the internal condition of the pipeline. There are also routine maintenance inspections of the external condition of pipelines to detect leaks and other potential problems.

Storage facilities are available along a pipeline. In the Gulf region, natural gas is stored under pressure in salt caverns where the salt has been leached out. In other areas of the nation, abandoned or played-out natural gas reservoirs are used for storage. Natural gas is reinjected into these reservoirs under pressure during times of weak demand and lower prices to be withdrawn during times of strong demand and higher prices. Before deregulation, natural gas was stored during the summer and drawn out during the winter. Since deregulation, natural gas in storage is recycled several times a year in response to changing prices, not necessarily related to times of peak demand. The 300,000 miles of transmission pipelines have an inherent storage capacity that can be increased by increasing the gas pressure. Metering is a vital operation as gas enters and leaves the gas transmission system and associated storage facilities for both accurate paying of suppliers, charging of customers, and system control.

Gas planning for a transmission company depends on long- and short-term forecasting models. Long-term forecasts determine investments in order for the pipeline system to meet future demand. Short-term forecasts ensure that the volume of gas can accommodate current demand. Nominations are made one to two days in advance to ensure that enough gas enters the system upstream to match demand downstream without exceeding pipeline capacity. Scheduling acceptances of gas from thousands of suppliers and deliveries of gas to thousands of consumers, each with their specific needs and different contractual arrangements, is both complex and crucial to the smooth operation of the system. A system of allocation cuts based on a previously arranged and agreed-on priority ranking is activated when nominations exceed the limits of pipeline capacity.

In today's deregulated climate, natural gas can be drawn from storage or obtained directly from natural gas producers or from other interstate transmission companies via hubs. Hubs connect various interstate pipelines in a common system whereby natural gas consumers connected into one interstate pipeline can obtain supplies from natural gas suppliers hooked into other interstate pipelines. There are about a dozen major hubs in the United States, the most important being Henry Hub in Louisiana, where a multitude of pipelines connect natural gas suppliers and interstate pipelines into what amounts to one huge common system. Hubs not only allow for common distribution, but also common pricing. The Henry Hub is the most important distribution and pricing hub in the United States; its price is the base price for the nation. Other hubs are generally priced at the

Henry Hub price plus transmission costs with local market-related variations. As an example, three interstate pipelines serve New York City. Through local interconnections, major gas purchasers can bargain for natural gas from suppliers in three different Southwest natural gas regions. These continual negotiations for the best price create a pricing hub in New York City, where price does not vary much regardless of which transmission company is actually supplying the gas. If a gap in price does appear among the transmission companies, then consumers' continual quest for the cheapest source of natural gas tends to close the gap. Another pricing hub is in Boston, where gas from two interstate pipelines from the Southwest and two pipelines from the western and eastern provinces of Canada are interconnected, providing major customers with the opportunity to buy gas for the best price from suppliers in four different natural gas-producing regions. The search by large consumers for the best price ends up with a more or less common price in Boston, regardless of the source. Natural gas prices in New York and Boston are not the same. The New York basis price reflects the price in Henry Hub plus transmission costs. The presence of Canadian producers in the Boston market affects the basis price of Boston gas and its relationship with the New York basis price and the price in Henry Hub. It is possible for Canadian gas to penetrate the New York market by reversing the Algonquin pipeline between New York and Boston. Deregulation has introduced a dynamic in the natural gas business that was lacking under regulation.

The simple days when gas producers sold to interstate pipeline companies which then sold to LDCs selling to residential, commercial, industrial, and electricity-generating customers at a regulated price based on costs are gone. Natural gas suppliers are no longer regulated. Pipeline transmission companies have lost their status as natural monopolies. No longer merchants, they have become common carriers with regulated long-term transmission rates. Life is now more complex for customers because they must examine many options such as buying direct from gas producers via independent marketing firms, the marketing arms of transmission companies, from storage providers, or from other gas transmission pipelines and their natural gas suppliers via hubs.

While natural gas consumers are doing their best to buy at the lowest cost, natural gas producers are doing their best to sell at the highest price. Producers look at the basis price at every hub that they have access to and net the basis price of the transmission cost to obtain the netback value for their gas and then sell to the pricing hub with the highest netback value. The enormous number of individual transactions among buyers seeking the lowest delivered cost and sellers seeking the highest netback price, in a market where no individual dominates and where buy-and-sell transactions are simplified, transferable, and transparent, leads to commoditization. Natural gas prices are set by market conditions that reflect supply and demand, not regulated cost plus pricing. The regulators' role is to ensure that no one tries to manipulate the price, reduce the transparency of transactions, or in any way attempts to control the market. In a commodity market, where the providers are all selling at the same approximate price, differentiation among natural gas providers becomes one of value-added services. A buyer selects a provider based not only on price, but also on reliability, dependability, and behind-the-meter services. Behind-the-meter services can include maintenance and repair of natural gas equipment owned by the buyer or advice on how to utilize natural gas more efficiently. In the future, companies may provide a bundled service in which gas is combined with other utility services such as electricity and water, or even communication, to woo customers away from competitors.

Deregulation has not made life easy for transmission companies because increasing revenue means attracting more customers by, perhaps, cutting rates on spare capacity, reducing operating expenses and capital commitments, and providing value-added services behind the meter. Nor is life easier for the consumer. With natural gas prices fluctuating widely and long-term contracts becoming less available, there is a greater exposure to adverse price fluctuations in the spot and short-term markets. Independent gas marketers can also be at great risk if their buy-and-sell commitments do not match up either in volume or time duration, which exposes them to the potential of huge financial losses from an adverse change in natural gas prices.

The risk of adverse price changes generates a need for risk mitigation among natural gas suppliers, consumers, and marketers. Banks and other financial institutions provide an active over-the-counter market for swaps tailored to meet the particular needs of suppliers and consumers. A swap protects a supplier from a low price and consumers from a high price that can threaten their financial well-being. NYMEX is the nation's leading center for buying and selling natural gas futures contracts. In addition to traditional hedging, the public trading of natural gas futures contracts opens up the opportunity for individuals (including hedgers turned gamblers) to speculate on the future price of natural gas, which is why the futures volume far exceeds the physical volume. Speculators add depth to the market by accepting the risk that hedgers are trying to shed. However, not all risks can be mitigated by financial instruments such as volume risk (a customer uses more or less than the nominated amount), counterparty risk (one of the parties to a transaction does not honor its commitment), execution risk (a transaction is not properly concluded), regulatory risk (the possibility of a change in the rules after a transaction has been signed), operational risk (system failure), and basis risk (the possibility of the price at a hub such as Boston moving differently than expected from the price used to hedge a risk such as Henry Hub).

The demarcation point between transmission and distribution is the citygate where regulators reduce the gas pressure; scrubbers and filters remove any remaining traces of contaminants and water vapor, and mercaptan is added as an odorant to detect gas leaks. The nation's million-mile distribution system is made up of two- to twenty-four-inch pipe with pressures from 60 psi down to one-quarter psi (above atmospheric) for natural gas entering a home or business, and higher for industrial and electricity-generating customers. Though distribution pipe had traditionally been made of steel, nowadays plastic or PVC is used for its flexibility, resistance to corrosion, and lower cost.

To ensure an adequate supply of natural gas, LDCs contract with the transmission companies for pipeline volume capacity that meets peak demand. The rate charged to LDCs is the regulated rate that ensures a fair and reasonable return on the interstate pipeline investment. However, during times of less than peak demand, LDCs are free to sell their spare transmission capacity to third parties. While these rates are generally less than what the LDCs are paying, the revenue so earned reduces LDC transmission costs. This creates a market for interstate pipeline capacity that generally disappears during times of peak demand. But if a LDC finds itself in a position with spare capacity during times of peak demand, it can sell this spare capacity at either the market rate or a maximum rate imposed by government regulations.

In addition to the marketing of spare transmission capacity, another opportunity has opened up to address nomination imbalances. Major customers of transmission pipelines (LDCs, utilities, industrial plants) must address an imbalance between their nominated and actual usage of more than 10 percent either way or face a monetary penalty. Rather than face a monetary penalty, customers can contact a marketing outfit that specializes in finding other users with the opposite imbalance.

The unbundling of services has created a plethora of marketing opportunities and commercial dealings that has commodized natural gas, natural gas transmission and storage capacity, nomination imbalances, and risk mitigation. The buying and selling of natural gas has become just like any other commodity such as grain or metals. Yet, there is still a great deal of regulation in the natural gas industry. FERC establishes services to be provided by interstate pipelines, determines rates based on a fair and reasonable return, and approves construction of new interstate pipelines. LDCs

Table 7.1

**World Natural Gas Consumption in Trillion Cubic Feet** (Tcf)

|  | # Tcf | % World Total |
|---|---|---|
| North America | 29.0 | 27 |
| Europe | 20.3 | 19 |
| FSU | 20.0 | 19 |
| Asia | 17.1 | 16 |
| Middle East | 11.5 | 11 |
| South America | 5.0 | 5 |
| Africa | 3.4 | 3 |

are regulated by the states and, in some cases, municipalities, where no two state or municipal regulators issue the same set of regulations for conducting business, determining rate structures, approving construction of new facilities, and addressing complaints by users.

Rates charged by LDCs are based on covering operating and capital costs including the purchase of natural gas. Consistent with interstate transmission companies, a fair and reasonable return for LDCs is based on determining the appropriate rate of return that induces shareholders to invest in plant and equipment consistent with the inherent risk of the business and the opportunity to invest elsewhere. A balancing account keeps track of the difference between required and actual revenue, which eventually leads to upward or downward rate adjustments. Rates also reflect customer categories to take into account the peculiarities associated with each. The capital and service requirements for hundreds of thousands of residential and commercial customers in a local distribution system are quite different than those for a few industrial and utility customers.

Various states are experimenting with unbundling LDC services, but progress is slow. It is possible that regulation may not be deregulated but transformed to incentive regulation, which gives the regulated LDC an opportunity to profit from exceptional performance. One form of incentive regulation is performance-based regulation in which the LDC's cost of procuring gas for residential customers is compared to an index value for other LDCs. If the cost is lower than the index value, then the LDC shareholders and ratepayers benefit by splitting the savings. If higher, the incremental cost is again split and the shareholders suffer along with ratepayers. Incentive regulation can take the form of benchmarking with adjustments for both inflation and productivity gains. If productivity gains exceed the impact of inflation, then both shareholders and ratepayers share the benefit; if not, both suffer. Another alternative is rate caps, a method whereby shareholders either suffer or benefit from actual rates being above or below the cap. Incentive regulation provides an opportunity for LDCs to enhance their profitability by becoming more astute in gas purchases and more eager to pursue productivity gains.

## NATURAL GAS AS A FUEL

Natural gas provides nearly 24 percent of world energy demand excluding biofuels. The consuming regions of natural gas in Table 7.1 are ranked in terms of trillion cubic feet (tcf) per year.[3] Consumption of 1 tcf per year is roughly equivalent to 0.5 million barrels of oil per day. North America and Europe account for 46 percent of world consumption. Whereas the United States is at the brink of becoming an importer of natural gas, Russia has long been a major exporter to Europe.

Under communism, natural gas in the Soviet Union was free, obviating the need for meters and thermostats. Torridly hot rooms were cooled by a blast of frigid Arctic air through an opened window. Since the fall of communism, meters and thermostats have been installed and natural gas usage is now charged to stop this wasteful practice, freeing up supplies for hard-currency exports. However, gas sold within Russia is only a fraction of the value received from European importers. The conflict between Russia and the Ukraine that took place in 2006 and 2009 was exactly on this point.

The categories of use for any energy source are transportation, residential, commercial, industrial, and electricity generation. Natural gas as a vehicle fuel is extremely clean-burning, emitting a small fraction of the precursors to ozone formation (organic gases and nitrous oxides) and carbon monoxide compared to oil-based motor fuels. Moreover, there are no particulates (soot), virtually no sulfur oxides, and less carbon dioxide emissions. The most difficult hurdle for natural gas to overcome to be an acceptable motor vehicle fuel is the logistics of refueling. For this reason, very little natural gas is actually consumed in transportation with most compressed natural gas-fueled vehicles owned by natural gas pipeline and distribution companies.

Using projected 2010 figures for the United States, about 20 percent of consumption is consumed by over 60 million residential customers for space and water heating, cooking, clothes drying, pool heating, and gas fireplaces. Residential demand peaks during winter months, accounting for as much as 70 percent of annual gas consumption, which of itself can vary greatly between cold and mild winters. Residential customers pay the highest rates for natural gas because they support a distribution system connected to each individual home capable of handling peak winter needs. Moreover, residential customers consume the greatest volume of natural gas when natural gas prices are high, which, of course, are high because of increased residential demand (the chicken-and-egg syndrome). Five million commercial customers use about 15 percent of total demand, paying the second highest price for natural gas. The commercial sector consists of restaurants, motels and hotels, retail establishments, hospitals and healthcare facilities, and office and government buildings. Though their natural gas usage is similar to that of residential customers, there is less of a swing in demand between summer and winter from space cooling fueled by natural gas. In addition to the weather, consumption in the commercial sector is sensitive to general business activity.

The industrial sector is the largest consumer at about 35 percent of total demand, with over 200,000 customers. Natural gas supplies the energy needs of a host of manufacturing industries plus waste treatment, incineration, drying and dehumidification processes, and is a feedstock for the fertilizer, chemical, and petrochemical industries. Natural gas prices directly affect food prices because natural gas is a raw material for making ammonia-based nitrogen fertilizers and is used for drying crops, pumping irrigation water, and processing food. While seasonal variations are less than those of residential and commercial users, the industrial sector experiences significant fluctuations in demand from changes in economic activity. Moreover, one-third of industrial users can switch to propane and fuel oil if natural gas prices get out of line with these alternative fuels. The industrial sector ranks third in what is paid for natural gas, while plants that generate electricity pay the lowest price. This sector consists of only 5,700 customers that account for nearly 30 percent of total demand. Electricity generation was the fastest growing market segment, with approximately 5,000 natural gas-fueled electricity-generating plants, not counting the cogeneration units run by commercial and industrial customers, until cheap natural gas went away with the natural gas bubble in 2000. Up until the bursting of the bubble, nearly all incremental electricity-generating capacity was fueled by natural gas. Since then, coal has been in the ascendancy, although many natural gas plants are still being built. Natural gas usage in electricity generation is affected by seasonal factors, changes in economic activity, and the relative cost of electricity generated from natural gas compared to coal, oil, and nuclear and hydropower. Some dual-fueled electricity-generating plants can easily switch between natural gas and fuel oil, depending on their relative costs. On a global scale, the residential sector consumes 17 percent of natural gas, commercial sector 6 percent, industrial sector 43 percent, and transportation sector 1 percent. The remaining share is the electricity-generating sector, whose share of 33 percent is expected to grow in the future at the expense of the other sectors.[4]

Natural gas in electricity generation employs a variety of technologies including conventional steam generators, combustion turbines, and combined-cycle plants. Natural gas burned in a steam generator is similar in context to burning coal or oil to produce steam that passes through a turbine that drives an electricity generator. Efficiency is about 35–40 percent for new plants and about 25–35 percent for older plants, regardless of the fuel. Most of the remaining energy passes to the environment as the latent heat of vaporization (the heat consumed for water to change to steam). Combustion turbines are basically modified jet engines attached to turbines to generate electricity for peak shaving. Peak shaving occurs for relatively short periods of time such as air-conditioning demand during a heat wave. Combustion turbines are best for peak shaving because their low capital cost minimizes a utility's investment in equipment that is run only for short periods of time. However, combustion turbines have a high operating cost since a large portion of the energy input is released to the environment as turbine exhaust.

A combined-cycle plant directs the escaping exhaust gases from a combustion turbine through a steam generator to drive an electricity-generating turbine. A combined-cycle plant can increase thermal efficiency up to 50 percent, higher than that of an oil- or coal-fired steam-generating plant, by the inclusion of a combustion turbine. A combined-cycle plant has lower capital costs than coal or nuclear plants, shorter construction times, greater operational flexibility, and is the preferred choice for smaller capacity plants. With a higher fuel cost, natural gas plants of various generating capacities are built to meet the variable needs of electricity-generating utilities, leaving base-load generation to large coal and nuclear plants. Hydro plants would be ideal for base-load generation since the fuel cost (water) is free. But it is difficult to ramp coal and nuclear plants up and down—they are best employed for base-load demand. Hydro plants, on the other hand, can be easily ramped up or down by changing the amount of water flowing through the turbine. In nations where hydro is a principal source of power, hydro satisfies both base and variable needs whereas in other nations such as the United States, hydro and natural gas plants primarily satisfy variable needs. As a general rule, natural gas plants satisfy variable needs because of higher fuel costs and the relative ease to respond to changing electricity demand.

Many companies need large quantities of hot water and have historically purchased electricity for both power and for heating water. These companies are increasingly installing cogeneration plants that do not necessarily have to be fueled by natural gas. When fueled by natural gas, a cogeneration plant is a combined-cycle plant with both a combustion turbine and a steam turbine to produce electricity, with none of the line losses associated with offsite electricity generation. Moreover, water containing the latent heat of vaporization from the steam turbine condenser can be substituted for the hot water that had previously been heated with electricity. Being able to utilize the "free" hot water raises the overall efficiency of cogenerating plants to 60 percent or higher.

For global electricity generation, the natural gas share as an energy source grew from 13 percent in 1971 to 20 percent in 2005 and is expected to increase to 22 percent in 2010 and continue to increase to 25 percent in 2030, outpacing growth in electricity and essentially making up for the falloff in the share of electricity generated by nuclear energy. Coal is expected to maintain its share, meaning of course, that consumption will follow growth in electricity demand.

## THE EUROPEAN VERSION OF DEREGULATION

Europe never had a regulatory regime similar to that of the United States. European nations carried out their respective energy policies through "championed" energy companies. Championed energy companies had the support of their respective governments to dominate a nation's electricity or natural gas business. Governments exercised control over these companies by either having seats on the board of directors and/or approving the appointment of top executives. This comfortable relationship resulted in European governments being assured of a secure supply delivered in a dependable and reliable manner, in championed companies that operated profitably in a secure business environment, and in consumers who paid a high price for energy.

The first European leader to react against high-priced energy was Prime Minister Thatcher, who cut subsidies to coal companies, privatized national energy companies, and started the process of major consumers having direct access to energy providers to negotiate electricity and natural gas supplies. The ability to choose suppliers introduced competition to what had previously been a natural monopoly. Thus, the two paths taken by the United States and the United Kingdom were basically parallel and arrived at the same destination. For the United States, the path was deregulation of a regulated industry; for the United Kingdom, the path was cutting the umbilical cord to subsidized energy companies, privatizing previously nationalized companies, and giving major consumers third-party access to natural gas and electricity-transmission systems in order to be able to select suppliers. Both paths led to the introduction of a competitive marketplace where buyers can negotiate with suppliers to lower electricity and natural gas costs.

Although the unbundling of the UK natural gas and electricity markets in the late 1990s is very similar to what happened in the United States, it stands apart from Europe. European nations have been reluctant to liberalize their energy markets and give buyers the ability to negotiate with suppliers. While high-cost energy was widely recognized as a deterrent to European economic growth in the mid-1980s, the first EU directives for liberalizing electricity and natural gas did not appear until the latter half of the 1990s. These directives established a time frame for specified percentages of natural gas and electricity that had to be satisfied in a competitive marketplace. In 2003, another EU directive was issued to accelerate the process of liberalization. Independent transmission and distribution system operators were to be created to separate services formerly provided by integrated transmission and distribution companies, with a target year of 2007 for the unbundling of the gas and electricity markets.

With regard to natural gas, the objectives were to give major consumers access to gas-transmission networks with the ability to negotiate firm or interruptible, short- or long-term service contracts not only with gas suppliers, but also with operators of gas storage facilities and LNG terminals. Natural gas charges were to reflect actual costs, thereby avoiding cross-subsidies, and capacity allocation was to be transparent and nondiscriminatory. Interconnecting pipeline hubs and pricing hubs were to be established to give buyers access to various suppliers so they could negotiate price and terms. Yet in the 2000s, despite some liberalization, competition in Europe is limited in scope with gas prices still linked primarily to oil prices, which thwarts price competition, and transactions being more opaque than transparent. Existing long-term take-or-pay contracts between customers and integrated energy companies impede the pace of unbundling as do high transmission costs. Liberalization is not heartily endorsed by national governments; in particular, Germany, the powerhouse of Europe, sees no need to unbundle the services of its championed integrated energy companies. These companies have worked well in the past, providing security of supply, which to the German government is more important than cost.

Yet for competition to be effective, the number of natural gas supply sources must be increased, a market for physical and financial trading of natural gas has to be developed, the link between gas and oil pricing has to be severed, new entrants must be permitted in the energy business, and governments have to become more supportive of liberalization and less willing to shield their championed companies from competition. This foot-dragging by European nations is at variance with the EU energy bureaucrats in Brussels. In 2005, the EU warned a number of nations within the European Union that they will be brought before the European Court of Justice and face stiff fines unless they open up their energy markets.

Spain and Italy have taken steps to adopt an infrastructure of freedom of choice for consumers, with less progress being made in Austria, Ireland, Sweden, Belgium, and the Netherlands, and still less in Denmark, France, and Germany. A lack of uniformity of approach to the problem of dealing with supply, transmission, storage, and liquefied natural gas (LNG) terminals in a common natural gas pipeline grid among the various nations of Europe is the focus of the Gas Transmission Europe, an association of forty-five European companies in thirty countries. This organization not only deals with proposals concerning the hardware of interconnections between pipelines, storage facilities, and LNG terminals for improved network access, but also in the software of internal controls, gas flow and transaction information systems, nomination procedures, and other operational matters.[5]

Even with unbundling, natural gas prices may remain high if the primary sources of natural gas (the North Sea, the Netherlands, Russia, and Algeria) form a common front against lower prices. Natural gas buyers with access to LNG terminals may be able to break this common front were it to occur. LNG suppliers in Latin America, West Africa, and the Middle East are less controllable than traditional European gas suppliers. For instance, they may be tempted to get rid of excess production by selling low-priced cargoes into Europe. With third-party access to LNG terminals, a surfeit of LNG cargoes may exert sufficient commercial pressure on the traditional suppliers to break any common front and create a truly competitive market.

## LPG: PRELUDE TO LNG

Liquefied petroleum gases (LPG) are primarily propane and butane. LPG is formed as a byproduct of oil refining and is stripped out of a natural gas stream by a fractionating unit. In the 1910s light-end gases from a barrel of crude were kept in a liquid state under pressure and fueled early automobiles, then blowtorches for metal cutting, and, in 1927, gas stoves. Butane was one of the propulsion fuels for dirigibles until the market for butane-fueled dirigibles crashed in 1937 with the *Hindenburg*. An entrepreneur began selling unwanted bottles of butane as fuel for gas stoves in Brazil. All went well until he ran out of dirigible fuel. To replace the butane, he began to import cylinders of pressurized butane on the decks of cargo liners, thus marking the humble beginning of the international trade of LPG.[6]

A 1927 court decision made the fractionating process available to industry, which opened the door for the development of the LPG business. With an increased availability of supply came the opportunity to develop a new market. The industry grew slowly, with bobtail trucks delivering pressurized propane in a liquid state to refill cylinders that fueled stoves, water heaters, clothes dryers, and space heaters in rural areas and towns not served by natural gas pipelines. LPG was also used for crop drying. Propane was a preferred fuel for bakeries and glassmaking facilities and other commercial and industrial enterprises that required a greater degree of control over temperature and flame characteristics. Cleaner-burning propane became a motor fuel of choice over gasoline for forklift trucks and other vehicles that operated in semiclosed environments such as terminals and warehouses. Butane eventually found a home as fuel for cigarette lighters and taxicabs. LPG became a gasoline blending stock and a feedstock for steam crackers to make ethylene, the precursor to plastics, and other petrochemicals. Railroad tank cars were the primary means of moving LPG over long distances until they were replaced by pipelines in the late 1960s.

Wells drilled into a salt dome at Mont Belvieu in Texas leached out the salt to form a cavern to store LPG. This would eventually become the nation's principal storage hub and central marketplace for LPG, with extensive gas liquids pipeline connections to major suppliers and buyers in the Gulf Coast, Midwest, and Northeast. Another storage hub in Kansas served the upper Midwest via pipeline. LPG was carried in pressurized tanks mounted on vessels and barges along the eastern seaboard and the Mississippi River. In 1971 President Nixon put price controls on oil, which happened to include LPG. Not surprisingly, this encouraged the consumption of LPG because of its lower cost compared to other fuels.

In the United States, refinery-produced LPG is generally consumed internally for gasoline blending or pipelined as feedstock to an associated petrochemical plant. The commercial market for LPG was primarily supplied by stripping gas liquids from natural gas. In contrast, LPG development in Europe was based on refinery operations and rail-car imports from the Soviet Union because there were no indigenous supplies of natural gas until the late 1970s, when the North Sea natural gas fields came onstream. LPG consumption was primarily propane in the north and butane in the south because propane vaporized more easily in warm climates. In the 1970s, Italy promoted the use of butane as a motor vehicle fuel. Small shipments in pressurized tanks installed on vessels carried LPG from refineries in Rotterdam to destinations in northern Europe and from refineries in Italy, Libya, and Algeria to southern Europe and the eastern Mediterranean.

In Japan, the LPG market grew out of the desires of Japanese housewives and restaurant owners to cook with propane rather than kerosene. Switching from kerosene to propane was a sign of a rising standard of living. Japan also encouraged the use of butane-fueled taxicabs. Unlike the United States and Europe, Japan had to import much of its LPG aside from that produced as a byproduct in domestic refineries. Shipping LPG at sea was costly because LPG was carried in cargo tanks built to withstand the pressure necessary to keep LPG liquid at ambient temperatures. The weight of the steel in the cargo tanks was about the same as the weight of the cargo, restricting the cargo-carrying capacity of the vessel.

To counter high shipping costs, Japanese shipyards developed and began building fully refrigerated LPG carriers in the 1960s. The temperature of the cargo was reduced to keep LPG liquid at atmospheric pressure (–43°C for propane and–1°C for butane). The cargo tanks had to withstand a lower-temperature cargo and had to be insulated to minimize heat transfer from the outside environment. An onboard cargo refrigeration unit kept the cargo at the requisite temperature to prevent pressure buildup in the cargo tanks. Fully refrigerated cargoes made it possible to use a simpler design for the cargo tanks, which could be built to conform to the shape of the hull, because they did not have to satisfy the structural requirements of a pressurized cargo. This allowed an order of magnitude increase in the carrying capacity from several thousand cubic meters to 30,000–50,000 cubic meters. Parenthetically, with a specific gravity of about 0.6, a cubic meter of LPG weighs about 0.6 metric tons, compared to close to 1 metric ton for a cubic meter of crude oil. A fully loaded LPG carrier transports less cargo weight-wise than a crude carrier of an equivalent cargo volume. The first large-sized LPG carriers were employed shipping LPG between Kuwait and Japan. By 1970, the Japanese LPG carrier fleet numbered a dozen vessels with the largest being 72,000 cubic meters.

The United States was primed for large-scale imports with adequate storage at Mont Belvieu, inland pipeline connections (the Little Inch was converted from natural gas to gas liquids), and LPG terminals, originally built for export in the U.S. Gulf, with importing terminals in the Northeast.

All that was missing was an LPG shortage, the appearance of a major new export source, and a means of transport. All the missing elements fell into place following the oil crisis of 1973. Shortages in natural gas stemming from the consequences of government price regulations of natural gas in interstate commerce reduced the domestic supply of LPG. Fractionating plants built in the Middle East and Europe to strip out gas liquids from natural gas greatly increased the overseas supply. Transport was available as more shipyards began building large-sized, fully refrigerated LPG carriers.

While all the elements fell in place for the United States to become a major LPG importer, large-scale imports never quite got off the ground. The appearance of new supplies of natural gas, along with deregulation of "new" gas, increased the domestic availability of LPG. LPG demand slackened when oil (and LPG) price controls were partially lifted, and finally dismantled, by President Reagan in 1981. Increased availability, coupled with a decline in demand from higher prices, reduced the need for large-scale imports. Without the U.S. import market developing to any significant degree, the enormous capacity of new LPG export plants in Saudi Arabia and elsewhere in the Middle East and in Europe created a glut. There is nothing like a glut to present an opportunity for entrepreneurs to develop a market, as had already happened with the glut created by discoveries of huge reserves of natural gas in the U.S. Southwest.

The international price for LPG swung between a premium or a discount from the price of crude oil on an energy-equivalent basis and thus was more volatile than oil. These price swings reflected the success or failure of entrepreneurs in finding a home for the new supplies of LPG. Those who bought a cargo of Middle East LPG and loaded it on a ship without a firm commitment from someone to buy the cargo when delivered in the United States or Europe were at the mercy of a fickle market while the vessel was at sea. Millions of dollars could be made or lost during a single voyage, depending on whether the buyer was on the right or wrong side of a price swing. Some of the founding firms instrumental in developing the international LPG market were merged or liquidated when they eventually found themselves on the wrong side. The same thing happened to independent LPG carrier owners when more vessels were delivered from shipyards than there were cargoes to fill the vessels. Lining up long-term deals between suppliers and buyers, along with the ships to carry the cargoes, would drastically reduce the degree of commercial risk; but long-term deals were not always available, and, when they were available, they were not always to the liking of either the buyer or the seller.

While Western firms were enjoying a financial bonanza or going bust, the Japanese LPG players just kept rolling along in a secure business environment, the result of how business is conducted in Japan. Of course, steady growth in propane consumption as a substitute for kerosene and as a substitute for naphtha for steam crackers to produce petrochemicals would provide an element of stability anywhere. But the Japanese are particularly adept at calming the financial waters. In the case of LPG, they developed a fully integrated logistics supply chain consisting of long-term contracts arranged with Middle East exporters, vessels to move the cargoes, terminals to unload the vessels, storage facilities to store the cargoes, and cylinder bottles to distribute LPG to consumers. The Ministry of International Trade and Industry (MITI) coordinated activities with the cooperation of an industry made up of a relatively few participants who respected each other's "territories." MITI was also in a position to dictate the amount of LPG to be consumed by the petrochemical industry, which smoothed out any bumps and wrinkles in the supply chain. LPG carriers received a "regulated" rate to cover costs and ensure an adequate return on vested funds over the life of the vessel. The modest return on investment reflected little risk of unemployment for vessels built to serve a single trade for the duration of their physical lives. This investment philosophy was shared by the other elements of the supply chain. The price of LPG sold in Japan took into consideration the cost of acquiring the LPG, and the capital and operating costs of transmission (by ship, not pipeline), storage, and local distribution. The Japanese people, accustomed to paying a high price for energy, did not object to this arrangement. There was no political advantage for a Japanese government body that guided an industry to curry the favor of the electorate by underpricing a fuel. Government guidance of energy policy in Japan proved to be superior to the regulatory experience in the United States, where energy policies seem to be a series of "fits and starts" that eventually have to be scrapped. Managing LPG imports on a systems, or supply chain, basis would turn out to be the prelude to LNG imports.

The history of LPG consumption is a series of developing markets that started at a point in time and reached maturity at another. The U.S. market began in earnest in 1950 and reached maturity around 1975; for Europe the growth stage spanned 1960 to around 1980, for Japan from 1965 to 1985, and for Korea from 1980 to the late 1990s. In the early 2000s, China entered the growth phase of a new LPG market, with India slated to be next. Although the rate of growth in aggregate LPG consumption is somewhat constant, its center of activity travels around the world as one market begins to be developed and another matures. Thus, what appears to be a stable business growing at a modest rate to outsiders is, in reality, a continual opening up of new opportunities by insiders including entrepreneurs, marketers, traders, and suppliers. The LPG business, like so much of the energy business, is a challenge for those who like to be on the cusp of change where money can be made by correctly assessing its twists and turns.

In 2000, the United States was the world's leading LPG consumer at 51 million tons annually and was essentially self-sufficient, importing and exporting only about 1 million tons annually. The second-largest consumer was Europe at 31 million tons, exporting 7 million tons from the North Sea to the Mediterranean and Brazil and importing 15 million tons from Algeria, Venezuela, and the Middle East. While simultaneous importing and exporting may not make immediate sense, LPG is made of two distinct products, propane and butane, each of which can be long or short on a regional basis. Furthermore, it may pay to export from one location and import into another, rather than ship directly between the two, to take advantage of price disparities. The third-largest consumer was Japan, at 19 million tons, of which 15 million tons were imported primarily from the Middle East and the remainder produced in domestic refineries. Saudi Arabia was by far the world's largest LPG-exporting nation, followed by Algeria, Abu Dhabi, Kuwait, and Norway.

In the mid-2000s the fastest growing importers were China, followed by Korea, both having negligible consumption in 1980. Korea consumed about 7 million tons in 2000 and China over 13 million tons, each importing about 5 million tons mainly from the Middle East. While Korea is reaching maturity, China is far from maturity and India is just beginning to move into the growth stage. In a way, Korea, China, and India mimic Japan. Burning propane for cooking is a status symbol and indicates a rising standard of living. In Japan, propane displaced kerosene, while in Korea propane displaced charcoal briquettes, and in China propane is displacing coal and biofuels (charcoal, wood, and agricultural waste such as straw and animal dung). The next market to be developed is India, where coal and biofuels also dominate home cooking.

Substituting LPG for coal and biofuels is a big step toward a cleaner environment because it does not emit air particulate (smoke), carbon monoxide, nitrous oxides, and, in the case of coal, sulfur oxides and metal (arsenic and mercury) emissions. However, a high price for oil becomes a high price for LPG. For millions of the world's poor, high-priced LPG means continued cooking with coal and biofuels, ingesting the pollution along with the food.

Natural gas liquids in international trade in the mid-2000s required an LPG carrier fleet of a hundred large carriers over 60,000 cubic meters (most between 70,000–80,000 cubic meters) and another seventy vessels between 40,000–60,000 cubic meters. There are also more than sixty

Table 7.2

**International Natural Gas Pipeline Movements in Billion Cubic Meters** (Bcm)

| Importer | Domestic Consumption | Pipeline Imports | Supplier | Percent of Importer's Consumption |
|---|---|---|---|---|
| Europe* | 576 | 154 | Russia | 27 |
| United States** | 657 | 89 | Canada | 14 |
| Europe* | 576 | 46 | Algeria and Libya*** | 8 |

* Europe, excluding the Russian Federation.
** Net of U.S. exports to Canada.
*** Via trans-Mediterranean pipelines to Spain and Italy.

semirefrigerated LPG carriers between 10,000–20,000 cubic meters in size, used more for local distribution than long-haul trading, in which the cargoes are cooled, but not enough for the gas to remain liquid at atmospheric pressure. LPG carriers can also carry liquid cargoes of ammonia, butadiene, and vinyl chloride monomer (VCM). Another twenty ethylene carriers carry liquefied ethylene at a much lower temperature than LPG, but not low enough to carry LNG. While ethylene carriers can carry LPG as backup when no ethylene cargoes are available, they make their real money carrying ethylene cargoes that cannot be carried by LPG carriers.

## LIQUEFIED NATURAL GAS

As mentioned repeatedly in this text, natural gas is constrained by logistics. The development of long-distance pipeline transmission was crucial to natural gas becoming a commercial energy resource. Pipelines are fixed installations connecting a specific set of suppliers with a specific set of consumers and are an inflexible mode of transmission. Most pipelines are within a single nation because political considerations enter the picture when pipelines cross national borders. A proposed pipeline from Iran to India that would cross Pakistan was, for many years, considered impossible because of the rivalry and bitter feelings between Pakistan and India. However, in the 2000s progress was made in advancing this proposal in response to Pakistan's own need for energy and the potential earnings from transit fees. A pipeline connection between Turkey and Greece, long-time bitter foes, has been completed. Another example of long-time foes cementing better relationships through energy is a pipeline supplying Egyptian gas to Israel.

A major pipeline project nearing final approval is the Nabucco pipeline project that will ultimately transport 31 bcm per year of Caspian natural gas in a 3,300 kilometer, 56 inch pipeline stretching from the Caspian region across Turkey, Bulgaria, Romania, Hungary, and Austria where it will connect into the European pipeline distribution system. If approved as expected, construction will start in 2010 and the pipeline will be completed in 2013. When in full operation, Nabucco pipeline will give Europe a major alternative source of natural gas that does not involve the Russian natural gas pipeline system. Table 7.2 shows that there is a healthy international natural gas pipeline trade.[7]

Total world reserves are 185 trillion cubic meters (tcm) in 2008, up from 110 tcm in 1988 and 148 tcm in 1998. With world consumption at 3.0 trillion cubic meters in 2008, the reserve-to-consumption ratio is sixty years as compared to forty years for oil. Forty-one percent of natural gas reserves are in the Middle East, of which 16 percent of world's reserves are in Iran and 14 percent in Qatar. Russia possesses 23 percent of world reserves. These three nations account for 53 percent of world's reserves; all other nations pale in comparison (for instance, the United States accounts for only 4 percent of the world's reserves).

Reserves can be misleading. For instance, proven reserves in Alaska exclude potentially vast gas fields in the North Slope that have not been sufficiently assessed to classify them as proven. With the exception of Russia and the United States, much of the world's natural gas reserves would be stranded if pipelines were the only means of transmission. Construction of long-distance undersea pipelines to connect remote fields in Iran, Qatar, Nigeria, Venezuela, Indonesia, and Malaysia with industrially developed nations, with pumping stations every 50–100 miles, is prohibitively expensive. Even Australia's natural gas fields in the northwest part of the nation are too remote from the principal cities in the southeast for economic pipeline transport. The natural gas reserves for these nations remained stranded with no commercial value until a new means of transmission was devised.

Compressed natural gas (2,000–4,000 psi) can be transported in specially built tanks. The problem is the cost of building large-capacity cargo tanks that can withstand this magnitude of pressure with a cargo still four times greater in volume than in a liquefied state. However, there are special circumstances in which compressed natural gas carriers are feasible such as small natural gas fields in remote areas of the Amazon River, where reserves are not sufficient to justify building a long-distance pipeline or a liquefaction plant or for natural gas delivery to Caribbean islands whose consumption is far too small to sustain an LNG import terminal.

Just as liquefied gas liquids (propane and butane) are refrigerated for transport as a liquid at ambient pressure, so too can natural gas. As a liquid, natural gas takes up 600 times less volume than at ambient conditions with a specific gravity a little less than LPG. The problem is that natural gas is a liquid at atmospheric pressure at a much colder temperature of −161°C (−258°F). This imposes severe constraints on tank design and insulation to prevent the cargo from coming in contact with the hull. Conventional steel in ship hulls, if exposed to the cold temperature of LNG, is subject to instantaneous cracking, known as brittle fracture. A huge tank 50 feet wide and 90 feet wide containing 2.3 million gallons of molasses split apart from brittle fracture on a cold January day in 1919 in Boston; it is memorialized as the Great Molasses Flood. A few mass-produced Liberty freighters during the Second World War sunk while transiting the cold Atlantic waters when their hulls split open from brittle fracture. A belt of steel welded around succeeding vessels resulted in no further losses from this cause. Better-quality steel can prevent brittle fracture at freezing temperatures but not from the cold of liquefied natural gas.

A much greater technological challenge in tank design and insulation than LPG carriers had to be faced before natural gas could be transported as a liquid. The success of independent research efforts in the 1950s led to the first LNG delivery in 1964 from a liquefaction plant in Algeria to a regasification terminal on an island in the Thames River. From this time forward, Algeria would remain a major force in the LNG business, expanding its export capacity in 1973, 1978, 1980, and 1981. Small-scale LNG plants were built to export LNG from Alaska (Cook Inlet) to Japan in 1969 and from Libya to Europe in 1970. Brunei was the first large-scale LNG export project to serve Japan, starting in 1972, and was followed by other large-scale LNG export projects in Indonesia and Abu Dhabi in 1977, Malaysia in 1983 (a second in 1994), Australia in 1989, Qatar in 1997 (a second in 1999), Trinidad and Nigeria in 1999, Oman in 2000, and Egypt in 2005. Many of these nations are currently expanding their LNG-production capacity. The relative importance of LNG-importing nations in the mid-2000s can be ranked by the number of receiving terminals, with Japan in first place with twenty-six, Europe with thirteen, Korea with six, the United States with four (now undergoing rapid expansion), Taiwan with two, and Puerto Rico with one.[8]

In the wake of the energy crisis in the 1970s, Japan adopted an energy policy of diversifying its energy sources to reduce its dependence on Middle East crude oil. The first generation of large-scale LNG projects were long-term contractual arrangements of twenty or more years for the entire output of a liquefaction plant dedicated to a small group of Japanese utilities. LNG carriers were assigned to a project for their entire serviceable lives. As such, the first LNG export projects were as inflexible as long-distance pipelines and were organized similarly to LPG projects as totally integrated supply chains.

The price of LNG sold in Japan was based on the delivered cost of crude oil. Low crude oil prices during the latter part of the 1980s and much of the 1990s kept a lid on LNG prices and, consequently, on the value of stranded gas. New LNG projects were few and far between until the passing of the natural gas bubble in the United States. This was the dawn of a new day for LNG projects because it was perceived that the United States might become a major LNG importer, spurring new LNG projects in Egypt, Qatar, Nigeria, Oman, and Trinidad. But this time building new or expanding existing LNG export plants was not in response to an energy policy to diversify energy sources, as in Japan and later Korea and Taiwan, but to the commercial opportunities associated with the prospect of large-scale LNG imports into the United States. Ironically, as with LPG, the United States has not yet become a large-scale LNG importer. One reason is that natural gas production has increased, reducing the need for imports. The other is that natural gas prices are less in the United States than in Europe and Asia, abrogating the commercial incentive to import large volumes of LNG. Alternative LNG markets are being developed in Europe as a means to reduce dependence on Russia gas pipeline imports and in Asia to meet the burgeoning demand for energy.

The LNG business is unique in several aspects. One is the sheer size of the investment. Unlike oil, coal, and other commodity businesses that start small and become large through accretion, LNG starts out as a large multi-billion-dollar project. LNG projects are rivaled in size, complexity, and capital requirements only by nuclear power plants. But unlike a nuclear power plant connected to a local electricity grid, an LNG project involves two sovereign powers—the nation with stranded gas reserves and the nation in need of natural gas. Though an LNG project is like a long-distance pipeline, which requires that suppliers and consumers be lined up before the pipeline can be built, an LNG Sales and Purchase Agreement (SPA) is more akin to a commercial agreement between two sovereign powers. One is the nation with the gas supply, whose interests are pursued by its national energy company, and the other is the nation with an energy policy that calls for greater consumption of natural gas, whose interests are pursued by its receiving utilities. In both cases, a sovereign power has made a policy decision to either export or import LNG and has delegated oversight to a national energy company or the receiving utilities.

The SPA establishes the commercial link between the buyer (the receiving utilities) and the seller (the national energy company), laying the foundation for the financial structure of the project. Laying the foundation for the physical structure is the engineering, procurement, and construction (EPC) contract. The EPC contract selects a consortium of companies with the requisite skill sets in project management and technical expertise to design the plant, procure the necessary equipment, build a liquefaction plant in a rather remote part of the world, and put it in operation. Shipping contracts have to be arranged, with the delivery of ships timed to the startup and the step-ups in liquefaction plant output. It can take as long as four years for a multi-train liquefaction plant to reach its full capacity.

For Japan, and later Korea and Taiwan, it was not a simple matter of building a receiving terminal with sufficient storage capacity and berths to off-load the LNG carriers, along with a regasification plant to convert LNG back to a gas. These nations had to create a market for natural gas. The first customers were electricity-generating plants located near the receiving facilities. Eventually an entire natural gas pipeline distribution infrastructure, replete with customers, had to be organized, designed, and built for natural gas to become an important contributor to a nation's energy supply. Getting approvals for the requisite permits to build a natural gas pipeline grid would have been impossible if the government had not endorsed the LNG project.

The LNG supply chain consists of three major segments. The first segment is the upstream end of natural gas fields with their wells and gathering system. A gas-treatment facility removes undesirable elements (nitrogen, carbon dioxide, hydrogen sulfide, sulfur, and water) and separates gas liquids and condensates from the natural gas stream. These, along with any sulfur, are sold to third parties to provide additional revenue. A pipeline delivers the treated natural gas from the gas fields to the second segment, the downstream end, which consists of the liquefaction plant and the LNG carriers. After the last remaining contaminants are removed, a mixed refrigeration process cools methane to its liquefaction temperature using various refrigerants, starting with propane and switching to butane, pentane, ethane, methane, and finally nitrogen. Terminal storage capacity at the liquefaction plant is about two shiploads of cargo plus berthing facilities and a sufficiently sized fleet of LNG carriers to ship the desired throughput from the loading to the receiving terminals. The third segment is the market end of the supply chain, which is made up of the receiving and storage facilities and the regasification plant at the importing nation to warm and feed LNG into a natural gas pipeline distribution system. The receiving facilities must have sufficient storage for unloading a vessel plus extra storage to ensure sufficient quantities for transient and seasonal fluctuations in demand and delays in vessel arrivals. The regasification plant must be connected to a natural gas-distribution pipeline grid with sufficient customers to consume the LNG.

## Organizing and Financing the LNG Supply Chain

The three segments of the LNG supply chain can have different organizational structures. The simplest is to have the same participants throughout the supply chain. This "seamless" structure avoids the need for negotiating transfer price and sales conditions as natural gas or LNG passes through each segment of the chain. But this form of organization can lead to management by committee in which representatives of each segment of the supply chain vote on critical matters for a particular segment. This can have undesirable repercussions if the representatives are not well versed in the technical aspects of each segment. Moreover, funding of the project may be in jeopardy if a participant in one segment does not desire or does not have sufficiently deep pockets to fund its share of the entire project.

The second alternative with regard to ownership is the upstream and downstream segments of the project (natural gas fields and the liquefaction plant) being a separate profit center that sells LNG either free on board (FOB) at the loading terminal or delivered at the receiving terminal, where the price of the LNG includes cargo, insurance, and freight (CIF). The profit for the upstream and downstream portions of an LNG supply chain is the revenue from selling LNG less all operating and capital costs, the acquisition cost of the natural gas, taxes, and royalties. A floor price for the LNG may be incorporated in the SPA to ensure a positive cash flow and a minimum value for the natural gas. The third alternative is using the liquefaction plant as a cost center that simply receives a toll for services rendered that covers its operating and capital costs. These last two alternatives can have different participants with different shares within each segment of the LNG supply chain. Segmented ownership arrangements among the participants can create interface problems in transfer pricing and risk sharing. A conflict-resolution mechanism should be established to resolve potentially contentious issues as, or preferably before, they arise. Splitting the ownership of the various supply chain segments has the advantage of having participants who are interested in dedicating their financial and technical resources to a particular segment.

An LNG project can be entirely funded by equity. The return on equity is determined by the cash flow (revenue less operating costs, taxes, royalties, and acquisition costs). The advantage of equity funding is that the participants are not beholden to outside financial institutions. The disadvantage is that the participants must have deep pockets. The dedication of funds to a single multi-billion-dollar project may preclude becoming involved in other LNG projects. At the other extreme, an LNG project can be financed entirely by debt. The debt may be supplied by the sovereign nation that borrows on the basis of its creditworthiness or provides a sovereign guarantee. Revenue is funneled into a special account from which debt service charges are drawn off first and what remains pays for operating costs, royalties, and taxes; whatever is left determines the value of the natural gas.

The proceeds of an LNG project from a government's perspective are its receipts of royalties and taxes and what the national oil company, normally wholly owned by the government, earns on its natural gas sales to the LNG project plus the return on its investment in the project. The split in government payments in the form of royalties and taxes on profits is critical for LNG project participants in the event of a drop in LNG prices. Royalty payments remain fixed and independent of the price of LNG. Taxes on profits, on the other hand, decline as the price of LNG falls. The risk of a negative cash flow can be better dealt with by favoring taxes over royalties. The cost of mitigating this risk is that more money will be paid to the government when LNG prices are high.

A popular form of raising capital is project financing. Here the LNG supply chain is set up to be self-financing, with debt holders looking only to the financial wherewithal of the project itself, not the project sponsors, for interest and debt repayment. Debt issued by an LNG supply chain project is initially limited recourse debt—the sponsors assume full liability for funds advanced only during construction. Once the plant operates at its defined specifications, the debt becomes nonrecourse and the project sponsors assume no liability for debt service obligations; debt repayment relies exclusively on the financial performance of the project.

Project financing is usually equity and debt whose mix is determined by a cash flow analysis that takes into account the value of crude oil and other determinants on the price for LNG, the operating costs of the liquefaction plant and the upstream natural gas field, the acquisition cost of the natural gas, the LNG carriers (if part of the project), royalties and taxes, and debt-servicing requirements. Project financing exposes the LNG supply chain to the scrutiny of third parties when they exercise due diligence prior to making a commitment. Sponsors and host governments are more likely to agree to an organizational and legal structure imposed by a third party because of the benefit of external sourcing of capital. In this sense, project financing has been a healthy influence because it discourages a sponsor from insisting on conditions that would not only be detrimental to others, but would also jeopardize the external funding of the project.

Project financing removes the necessity for the sponsors to have sufficient internal funds to finance the entire project by equity alone. By reducing funding requirements, the sponsors are free to participate in other LNG projects, spreading their risk and expanding their presence in the LNG business. Project financing also allows the importing nation to participate directly in an LNG supply chain by purchasing a meaningful portion of the debt. These benefits of project financing have to be balanced by the costs of satisfying third-party due diligence requirements, managing lender-project relationships, and arranging creditor agreements with various financial institutions.

Underwriters for project financing face the challenge of making an internationally oriented

LNG project attractive to prospective buyers of the underlying debt. In packaging the securities, underwriters must deal with the sovereign risk of the host country (e.g., a Middle East nation), a variety of contractual arrangements with several receiving utilities from one or more nations (e.g., Europe), vessel chartering agreements involving a number of legal jurisdictions (e.g., Korea as shipbuilder, London as center of operations, Bermuda as shipowner, Liberia as ship registry), and multiple equity participants incorporated in different nations with unequal shares in various segments of an LNG project. Financial institutions funding LNG projects include pension funds seeking long-term maturities, and commercial banks and private investors interested in short- and medium-term maturities. Another source of debt funding is low-interest credits issued by governments to finance exports.

Depending on the distance between the liquefaction plant and the receiving facility, LNG carriers may account for 25–40 percent of the total investment in an LNG project, the same general magnitude of investment as the liquefaction plant. The remaining investment is primarily the development of the natural gas fields. The regasification system is usually the responsibility of the receiving utility, but for Japan, Korea, and Taiwan, a natural gas pipeline distribution system also had to be built. The development of the natural gas fields, the construction of the liquefaction plant, the building of the ships, and the receiving terminal, including the regasification plant and a natural gas distribution system with a sufficient number of consumers to absorb the LNG imports, have to be coordinated on a fairly tight schedule for all the elements of an LNG project to fall into place in a synchronous fashion. As large and as complex as LNG projects are, a number have been completed and the LNG trade has blossomed. As a point of reference, in 2008 the total volume of the international trade by pipeline of natural gas is 587 bcm compared to 226 bcm of LNG.

The world's largest suppliers of LNG are Qatar (18 percent), Malaysia (13 percent), Indonesia (12 percent), Algeria (10 percent), Nigeria and Australia (9 percent each), Trinidad (8 percent) with smaller shares from Egypt, Oman, Brunei, and UAE (United Arab Emirates). Japan, South Korea, and Taiwan consume 62 percent of the world's LNG and absorb nearly the entire output of LNG export plants in Brunei, Indonesia, and Malaysia, plus much of the output of LNG export plants in Australia, Qatar, Oman, and UAE. Europe receives 24 percent of the world movement of LNG with Spain and France being the primary importers, most of which comes from Algeria, Nigeria, and Egypt. Over 40 percent of Trinidad's LNG production is shipped to the United States, almost 30 percent to Europe with the remainder mainly to Mexico and the Caribbean, and a little to Asia. Unlike most LNG plants whose production is largely fixed by contractual arrangements, Trinidad is more oriented to commercial sales and the destructions of LNG can vary greatly from year to year. Much of the remainder of U.S. LNG imports is from Egypt, Nigeria, and Algeria. The United States is also a minor exporter of LNG from Alaska (Cook Inlet) to Japan. Between 2007 and 2012, LNG production capacity is expected to grow by nearly 60 percent with the largest incremental gain in Qatar, which is projected to supply 25 percent of world LNG production with other major capacity additions in Australia, Russia, and Indonesia.

Despite best intentions, LNG projects, if not organized properly, can fail. The El Paso and Trunkline projects are prime examples with another in India. The largely completed $3 billion Dabhol project foundered with a change in the local government in 2001. The winners of an election campaigned on a platform that the Enron-sponsored project was rife with political corruption and lacked competitive bidding and transparency. They opposed a local state government contract to purchase nearly all the electricity produced from the imported LNG at a price that consumers could not afford. The project was abandoned as a result of the election. Negotiations began for the possible purchase of the largely completed plant with the intent to bring it into operation in a manner that would have both government and popular support. The plant was eventually purchased by

Ratnagiri Gas and Power and was expecting its first shipment of LNG in early 2009. The terminal will run at 20–30 percent of its 5 million ton capacity until a breakwater is completed in 2011. [9]

## LNG Carriers

LNG carriers can be owned by the project for delivered sales where the price at the receiving terminal includes insurance and freight or they can be owned by the buyer for purchase at the loading terminal for free on board sales. Alternatively, the vessels do not have to be owned by either the buyer or seller but can be chartered from third parties (independent shipowners, energy companies, or financial institutions) under a variety of arrangements. Charters shift the responsibility for raising capital to finance the vessels from the LNG project to the vessel owners.

LNG carriers are classified by their containment systems: spherical or membrane. In the spherical containment system, a thick aluminum spherical shell covered by insulation and an outer steel shell is supported by a freestanding skirt that accommodates expansion or contraction of the cargo tank. Propagation of a crack, should any occur, is very slow, with little chance of leakage. While there is no need for a full secondary barrier, a partial barrier prevents any LNG leakage from coming in contact with the hull. The spherical tanks limit sloshing of the cargo when at sea for improved ship stability, but their protrusion above the main deck affects visibility from the bridge. The principal disadvantage of spherical tanks is the inefficient utilization of space within a ship's hull. Spherical tanks are also used for storage at loading and receiving terminals.

The alternative containment system is the membrane design in which the cargo tanks conform to the shape of the ship's hull, increasing a vessel's cargo-carrying capacity. Rather than thick aluminum, the membrane is a thin primary barrier covering insulation installed on the inner hull surface of the ship. This considerably reduces the weight of the metal in an LNG tank. Membrane tanks are not self-supporting, but an integral part of the ship's hull that directly bears the weight of the cargo. The structure holding the insulation material must be strong enough to transfer the weight of the cargo to the inner hull, be an effective insulator in its own right, and prevent any liquid gas from coming in contact with the ship's hull.

The membrane for the Gaz Transport system is made of a special stainless steel alloy called invar of 36 percent nickel with a very low coefficient of thermal expansion, eliminating the need for expansion joints. Both the primary and secondary insulation consists of a layer of thin (0.7mm) invar membrane covering plywood boxes filled with perlite, a naturally occurring insulating material made from volcanic glass. The primary and secondary insulation provides 100 percent redundancy. The membrane for Technigaz system is thin (1.2mm), low-carbon corrugated stainless steel with a relatively high coefficient of thermal expansion. The corrugation is designed to accommodate expansion and contraction of the metal caused by temperature changes. Earlier LNG carriers of this design used balsa wood as insulation material. Now two layers of reinforced polyurethane panels, separated by a secondary membrane made of a thin sheet of aluminum between two layers of glass cloth, form the primary and secondary insulation. The latest membrane system (CS1) combines the Gaz Transport and Techigas technologies with a membrane of invar and insulation of reinforced polyurethane panels.

The membrane design requires less material, but construction is more labor-intensive. Spherical tanks require more material, but their construction is more automated. Thus, the comparative cost of LNG carriers of the spherical or membrane design depends on shipyard labor costs. An LNG carrier of spherical tank design costs less in Japan than membrane design because labor costs are high; the opposite prevails in Korea, where labor costs are lower.

The first generation of LNG carriers built in the 1970s was 75,000 cubic meters, but these

Figure 7.2    **Number of Existing and Newbuilding LNG Carriers**

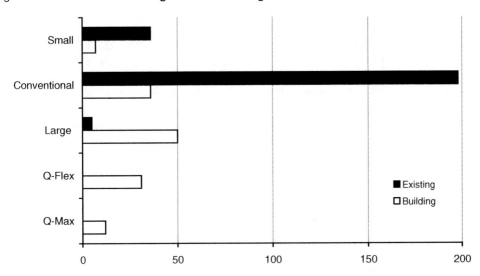

were quickly followed by what turned out to be a standard size of 125,000 cubic meters. The 1980s was not an active time for new LNG projects with little demand for new LNG carriers, but vessels built in the 1990s were typically 135,000 cubic meters (cbm). The anticipated growth in LNG imports in the 2000s spurred new building orders that will significantly expand the carrying capacity of the fleet. In mid-2007, the existing fleet consisted of 239 vessels dominated by the conventional-sized vessel of between 120,000 and 150,000 cbm. As seen in Figure 7.2, there were 136 vessels on order in 2007 spread over five size categories, but concentrated in the large size category of 150,000–180,000 cbm along with the Qatar Gas Transport orders for Q-Flex vessels of 200,000–220,000 cbm and Q-Max vessels of 266,000 cbm.[10] Whereas 55 percent of the existing fleet was built with the membrane design, 80 percent of the fleet under construction incorporates this design. Shipyards capable of building LNG carriers are in Korea, Japan, Spain, France, and China (a newcomer), with an aggregate capacity of delivering over forty LNG carriers a year of which Korea accounts for half.

Heat passing through the insulation can warm the cargo and increase the pressure within the cargo tank. Unlike LPG cargoes where a refrigeration plant keeps the cargo cool enough to remain liquid at atmospheric pressure, an LNG cargo is kept liquefied by boil-off, which removes the heat transmitted through the insulation into the cargo. The better the insulation, the less the boil-off; typical boil-off rates for modern vessels are about 0.15 percent of the cargo volume per day. While nearly all merchant vessels have diesel engine propulsion plants that burn heavy fuel oil, existing LNG carriers have dual fuel steam turbine propulsion systems that burn either heavy fuel oil or LNG boil-off, which typically provides 60 percent of the fuel requirements. This avoids wasting boil-off by flaring or venting to the atmosphere. Not all the LNG cargo on a vessel is discharged at the receiving terminal. A heel or small amount of LNG is left in the cargo tanks to keep the tanks cold via boil-off on the ballast voyage to the loading port. This eliminates the necessity of cooling the cargo tanks before loading the next cargo and minimizes stress from repeated thermal cycling. The ship is charged for the boil-off burned for ship propulsion on an energy-equivalent basis with heavy fuel oil.

Of the ships on order, only 40 percent are steam turbine with the remainder somewhat split between diesel engines with reliquefaction units to keep boil-off as part of the cargo and the rest dual fuel diesel-electric engines that burn boil-off or heavy fuel oil. The choice of engine is the result of an economic analysis of benefits and costs. The benefit of diesel engines with a reliquefaction unit is discharging a larger cargo of LNG and having smaller bunker costs from using only heavy fuel cargo; the cost is the necessity of having a reliquefaction unit on board the vessel. The benefit of dual fuel diesel-electric engines that burn either boil-off or heavy fuel oil is not having a reliquefaction unit on board; the cost is a smaller cargo to be discharged and higher bunker costs. The Q-Flex vessels can trade commercial cargoes of Qatar LNG cargoes to existing terminals large enough to accommodate these vessels. The Q-Max vessels are built for long-term contracts where the receiving terminals will be built specifically to handle these larger sized vessels. Both vessel types have significant shipping cost savings of the order of 20–30 percent from the economies of scale of larger-sized vessels and the fuel economy inherent in diesel engines compared to steam turbines.

The LNG cargo is pumped into LNG storage tanks at the receiving terminal. LNG has to be warmed to a gaseous state before entering natural gas pipelines for distribution to consumers. The most common way to heat LNG is to pass it through a seawater heat exchanger where the seawater is cooled and the LNG warmed to about 5°C (41°F). A gas-fired vaporizer is available if needed. A few Japanese import terminals tap the "waste cold" of LNG to cool brine or Freon for freezing food and for chemical and industrial processes that require cooling water.

## LNG Pricing

Pricing LNG in Japan is formula-based on the blended cost of crude oil imports (Japan Customs Cleared Crude) on an energy-equivalent basis, later adopted by South Korea and Taiwan. Thus the natural-gas exporting nation received for its natural gas a price that reflected the blended cost of crude delivered in Japan less the operating and capital costs associated with the natural gas gathering system, the liquefaction plant, and the LNG carriers (regasification facilities are owned by the receiving nation's gas utility). A minimum floor on the LNG price, if incorporated in the SAP contract, assured the exporting nation of a minimum price for its gas exports and the debt providers of a positive cash flow. The price relationship between LNG and crude oil is tempered to partially protect LNG importers from oil price shocks. Pricing of LNG imported into Europe is based on a formula reflecting the prices of European pipeline gas from natural gas fields, Brent crude, high- and low-sulfur fuel oil, and coal. The pricing of LNG imported into the United States is based on the price of natural gas at Henry Hub as indicated by near-term futures trading of natural gas contracts on the New York Mercantile Exchange (NYMEX).

The early LNG projects were based on fixed-quantity, twenty-or-more-year contracts between importers and exporters. Beginning in the latter part of the 1990s, spot LNG cargoes began to appear. These cargoes were the result of liquefaction plants producing more LNG than their nominal nameplate capacity (from conservative design features), improved productivity, and debottlenecking (the removal of constraints that restrict production). The first liquefaction plants were eventually able to produce 25 percent more than their indicated design capacity at a time of retrenchment in Asian economic activity, particularly in South Korea, which could not absorb its contractual volumes. Now there were cargoes without a home. The third element was the availability of laid-up LNG carriers from the failed El Paso and Trunkline projects plus a few built on speculation. The fourth element that caused the emergence of a spot trade in LNG was sufficient market demand in Europe and the United States to absorb these cargoes.

Since then other factors have come into play, transforming the LNG business from fixed

Figure 7.3  **U.S. Average Natural Gas Wellhead Price** ($/MMBtu)

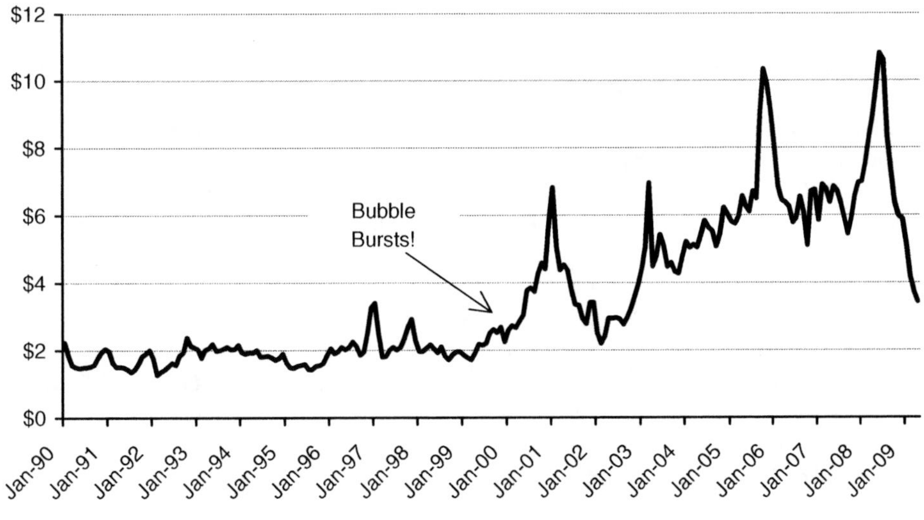

*Source:* http://tonto.eia.doe.gov/dnav/ng/hist/n9190us3a.htm

long-term contracts based on the price of oil to a more commercially oriented business like oil and coal where the market realities of supply and demand play an important role in determining price. One was the continual decline in the cost of LNG carriers. In 1995, the cost of building a large LNG carrier was three times that of a large crude oil carrier ($280 million). Since an LNG carrier can only transport about one-third as much energy as a large crude carrier of the same cargo volume, LNG shipping costs were nine times higher than crude oil on a Btu basis. By the 2000s, the shipbuilding cost had fallen to $150–$160 million, or a 50–60 percent premium over large crude carriers, knocking down the premium on an energy basis to about five times. Lower shipyard costs were partially caused by moving down the learning curve where repetition tends to iron out or eliminate problems that were previously encountered. Gains in shipyard productivity from automation also contributed to lower shipbuilding costs. Whereas only a few shipyards were capable of building LNG carriers in the 1970s, in the 2000s there were a dozen. Increased competition to keep building berths busy narrows shipyard profit margins and provides an incentive to further improve shipbuilding technology. Lower shipyard prices, combined with the economies of scale of larger-sized LNG carriers, have reduced shipping costs.

Greater output and improved system design of liquefaction trains built in the 2000s have resulted in a one-third reduction in capital and operating costs for liquefying natural gas. Two or three engineering, procurement, and construction (EPC) consortia capable of undertaking a massive and complex LNG project in the 1970s increased to about five in the 2000s. Energy companies with the requisite project-management skills, technical expertise, and the financial wherewithal to organize LNG supply-chain projects have grown from three or four in the 1970s to about ten in the 2000s. Project funding has become more sophisticated and innovative with project managers and financial underwriters well-versed on how to structure LNG projects in order to make their underlying debt attractive to potential investors. Greater reliance on debt in the financial structure of LNG projects reduces capital costs. Although all these factors have lowered the delivered cost of LNG, there has also been a concomitant rise in natural gas prices, illustrated in Figure 7.3.

The average wellhead price of natural gas was about $2 per million Btu in the 1990s and tripled in the early 2000s. The significant rise in natural gas prices, coupled with a significant fall in the cost of producing and shipping LNG, has made LNG projects commercially attractive without the need for fixed long-term contractual arrangements to cover the entire output. Contemporary LNG sponsors are not so much interested in protecting against the commercial risk of an LNG project as in taking advantage of commercial opportunities. LNG project sponsors look to a mix of long-term commitments to cover the minimum financial requirements with a portion of total capacity dedicated to short-term deals to enhance profitability. The willingness of LNG sponsors to accept commercial risk and the desire of buyers not to have to commit to twenty-year, take-or-pay-contracts have encouraged the emergence of spot and short-term markets.

LNG buyers, no longer contractually chained to a single supplier for twenty years at a fixed formula-based price, can now select their LNG providers on a variety of short- and medium-term deals, creating a diversified portfolio of LNG purchases at prices that reflect market realities. The possibilities of commercial opportunities have led to the construction or expansion of liquefaction facilities in Australia, Algeria, Angola, Egypt, Equatorial Guinea, Indonesia, Malaysia, Nigeria, Oman, Peru, Qatar, Russia, Trinidad, and Yemen. Nonproducing LNG nations seriously contemplating monetizing their stranded gas by building LNG liquefaction plants include Iran, Venezuela, and Bolivia.

**The Future of LNG**

The LNG market with the greatest potential of growth is the United States. The U.S. government recognizes the need to build LNG terminals to avert a potential shortage of natural gas. Various projections call for the United States to be importing from 12–20 percent of its natural gas needs as LNG by 2025. U.S. reserves have been in a general decline reaching a low point of 4.65 trillion cubic meters in 1998, but have subsequently been rising to 6.7 trillion cubic meters in 2008 for a reserve to production ratio of 11.6 years. U.S. natural gas production and reserves have been increasing largely from nonconventional gas sources since 2005, delaying the incursion of the anticipated large-scale imports of LNG. Nevertheless, the industry has been gearing up for large-scale imports by building LNG terminals.

Until 2004, there were only four receiving terminals (Lake Charles in Louisiana, Elba Island in Georgia, Cove Point in Maryland, and Everett, Massachusetts). The first three were built in response to the energy crisis in the 1970s and were idle. The terminal in Everett has been active, receiving seasonal deliveries of LNG to meet peak winter demand in New England. As a consequence of the anticipation of large-scale LNG imports, the three receiving terminals were reactivated and another four terminals had been built by 2009 (Gulf of Mexico, Offshore Boston, Freeport, Texas, and Sabine, Louisiana) plus two in Mexico (Altamira and Baja California).There are another 28 LNG projects that have been approved of which 7 are under construction. Unless there is a major shift in near-term LNG prospects, it is problematic whether the approved projects not under construction will be built.

The LNG terminal on the Mexican Atlantic coast (Altamira) will supply Mexico with natural gas which will back out U.S. exports to Mexico to increase U.S. domestic supply. The LNG terminal in Baja California sidesteps the regulatory hassle of siting an LNG receiving facility in California. LNG can enter California via Mexico as pipeline natural gas or electricity generated from natural gas. Natural gas from the LNG terminal in eastern Canada can be shipped via an underutilized pipeline carrying eastern Canadian gas into New England.

Building LNG terminals in Mexico and eastern Canada reflect the difficulty of siting LNG terminals in the United States. Licenses are required from the Department of Transportation, the

Coast Guard, and the Maritime Administration, along with permissions from the Research and Special Programs Administration, which enforces deepwater-port pipeline regulations, and the Department of the Interior for pipeline right-of-way. The Fish and Wildlife Service is concerned with the ramifications of an LNG receiving terminal on endangered species; the Minerals Management Service with potential hazards and underwater artifacts of archeological interest; and the Environmental Protection Agency with carrying out the provisions of the Clean Air Act. The Department of Energy must issue an import certificate and the FERC must issue a Certificate of Public Convenience and Necessity. Other Federal agencies involved are the Department of Defense, the Department of State, the Department of Commerce, the National Oceanic and Atmospheric Administration, the Bureau of Oceans, the Army Corps of Engineers, and the Advisory Council on Historic Preservation. Besides these, various state bodies involved with coastal zone management, pollution control, wildlife and fisheries, and historical preservation present their own hurdles for building a receiving terminal. Most importantly, an LNG receiving terminal cannot be built without a permit from the municipality within which the receiving terminal would be located. For this to occur, the local population must be in support of an LNG facility built in their midst.[11]

Proposed terminals in California and the Northeast have to combat the "not in my backyard" or "Nimby" syndrome represented by local citizens who can exert sufficient political clout to stop a municipality from issuing a permit. Where once "Nimby" was concerned with the sight and smells and sounds of having an industrial plant in one's backyard, now there are concerns over potential terrorist actions against an LNG facility. Resolution of these issues not only determines the future volume of LNG trade, but also the prospects of owners who have ordered LNG carriers on speculation without any commitment for employment by either an LNG supplier or buyer.

An innovative approach to bypass "Nimby" occurred in 2005 when an LNG terminal of a radically different design was inaugurated for service. A normal LNG terminal is located in a port with a storage facility and a regasification unit for transforming LNG to natural gas as needed. The Gulf Gateway Deepwater Port, located 116 miles off Louisiana, is a floating buoy connected to an already existing and underutilized natural gas pipeline. Located outside municipal and state jurisdictions, approvals are federal only. Specially constructed LNG carriers with built-in regasification units tie up to the buoy for about five days to regasify their cargoes prior to discharge into the natural gas pipeline. The pipeline is connected to several transmission pipeline systems that can contract for the natural gas. Without associated storage facilities, the regasified natural gas must enter a pipeline transmission system directly from the ship, which can cause operational problems with other natural gas suppliers. This, of course, can be corrected if access can be gained to a storage facility or an accommodation can be worked out with the suppliers. The additional cost of $25 million per vessel for an installed regasification unit and the extended discharge time increases shipping costs in relationship to direct discharge to a U.S. Gulf LNG terminal. But it is an alternative way to import LNG when it is not possible to build an onshore LNG terminal.

Another development to move LNG terminals out of ports into offshore waters is the proposed building of a gravity-based terminal that will be sunk about ten miles offshore from Venice, Italy. The terminal is to be built in a graving dock in Spain, and, when completed, the graving dock will be flooded to float the terminal. Then the terminal will be towed to offshore Venice, and, when onsite, the terminal is sunk by filling its empty ballast tanks with water. Later, heavier material will be added to permanently ballast the terminal. LNG carriers will off-load their cargoes into the terminal's storage tanks. LNG will be regasified at the terminal and pipelined to onshore natural gas connections. The development of such terminals can bring LNG directly into populated areas where it is needed, bypassing local opposition to building LNG terminals and storage tanks within the confines of populated areas.

Imports of LNG into the United States were expected to grow rapidly from 0.6 trillion cubic feet in 2005 to 2.1 trillion cubic feet in 2015. However, actual imports are trailing this projection because of climbing domestic gas production. Having the world's lowest priced natural gas, some thought has been given to converting a newly constructed and idle import LNG terminal to an export terminal by adding an LNG liquefaction plant. However by the time the permitting process is completed, the U.S. will probably be importing large quantities of LNG, which would defeat the purpose of such a project. While the United States' appetite for LNG imports is temporarily waning, this is not true for the rest of the world. The United Kingdom is facing declining production and reserves of its North Sea oil and gas finds. The Interconnecter, a natural gas pipeline between the United Kingdom and Europe, was built for two-way flow, exporting gas to Europe during the summer and importing gas during the winter. One might expect that the Interconnecter will be flowing in one direction from Europe to the U.K. as output from North Sea gas fields dwindles, but this may not happen. A pipeline is being built to connect the United Kingdom with a Norwegian gas field, LNG terminals in the United Kingdom are being expanded to handle a higher throughput, and depleted natural gas fields are being converted to storage facilities as in the United States. How these developments play out will determine the future direction of flow through the Interconnecter.

Italy, Spain, and France are expanding their LNG terminals as Europe becomes more committed to natural gas to meet its carbon dioxide emission obligations under the Kyoto Protocol. The interruption of Russian gas supplies to Europe in 2009 as a result of a dispute between Russia and the Ukraine over pricing, the second such occurrence (the first occurred in 2006), is a clear warning to Europe not to become too reliant on the Russian Bear for its natural gas supplies. The expansion of European LNG terminals will allow imports of LNG from the Atlantic basin and the Middle East to supplement natural gas supplies. It is anticipated that LNG imports may grow by several orders of magnitude as Europe reduces its reliance on Russian natural gas for energy security reasons.

China has a huge thirst for energy, including LNG imports and, through its balance-of-trade surplus, has the capital to invest in LNG terminals and build a natural gas infrastructure. India is another nation with an enormous thirst for energy, but that nation is stymied by balance-of-trade deficits and relatively limited capital reserves. Nevertheless, a number of companies are investigating the possibility of LNG projects in India with at least one company expressing a willingness to accept payment in Indian rupees rather than U.S. dollars. The enormous expansion of LNG-producing capacity may turn out to be necessary to satisfy energy security concerns in Europe and energy needs in Asia, even if U.S. LNG imports fail to meet expectations.

LNG terminals in Japan serve regional needs with no interregional pipelines. Yet the natural gas price is essentially the same throughout Japan because the price of LNG imported into each region refers to the same pricing formula on a delivered basis. Without price differentials, there is no economic justification to build interregional pipelines in Japan. With this thought in mind, LNG terminals will have a major impact on basis pricing of natural gas in the United States. For instance, there is a newly built LNG terminal in New England. The LNG export plant in Trinidad, or possibly one built in Venezuela, has nearly the same shipping distance to the U.S. Gulf as to the U.S. Northeast. Thus, it is conceivable for LNG to enter both regions at the same delivered price. If sufficient volumes were imported at both locations, the price differential between the two regions would shrink, raising havoc with tolls for the pipelines connecting the U.S. Gulf with the Northeast.

An LNG plant in Nigeria has about the same shipping distance to the U.S. Gulf, the U.S. Northeast, and Europe. This permits arbitrage trading that would tend to equalize natural gas prices in all three regions. If price differentials were large enough to absorb the extra shipping costs, LNG cargoes from Trinidad or Venezuela (if an LNG plant were built there) could also be sold in Europe and LNG cargoes from Murmansk (if an LNG plant were built) could also be sold in the United States. Moreover, LNG terminals in the Middle East with excess capacity could sell cargoes west or east (Atlantic or Pacific basins), depending on netback values. The upshot of spot trading of sufficient volumes of LNG cargoes is that the price of natural gas in Europe and the United States and Asia might not be materially different, making natural gas a globally traded commodity similar to oil.

The price of natural gas may remain closely tied to oil on an energy-equivalent basis. The price of LNG in Japan, Korea, and Taiwan is directly tied to oil. The price of LNG imported into Europe is partly tied to the price of Brent crude and fuel oil. The price of natural gas in the United States was only weakly related to oil prices during the 1990s when natural gas was in surplus. With the passing of the natural gas bubble, a closer relationship between natural gas and crude oil prices on an energy-equivalent basis has been established. Thus, spot trading in LNG may not only equalize the price of natural gas on a global basis but also maintain parity between the price of natural gas and crude oil. This has significant ramifications for natural gas consumers if crude oil supply cannot keep up with demand, resulting in another spiking of oil prices.

## Gas to Liquids (GTL) Technology

Reservoirs of stranded gas too remote for access by pipeline, and lacking sufficient reserves to support an LNG export project, can be made accessible to the market through gas to liquids (GTL) technology. Combining methane with air at high temperatures produces a mixture of carbon monoxide and hydrogen, which, via the Fischer-Tropsch process, in the presence of iron or cobalt catalysts, can create long hydrocarbon chains. These are then broken down to produce a combination of naphtha, kerosene, diesel fuel, lubricating oil, and wax.[12] The Fischer-Tropsch process is very versatile as it can also create liquid hydrocarbon fuels from coal and biofuels (wood and other plant life).

Diesel fuel produced by the GTL process is very clean-burning with significantly less nitrous oxide and particulate emissions and virtually no sulfur oxide emissions. Shell Oil has been in the forefront of GTL development and has been producing over 14,000 bpd of liquid petroleum products from its Bintula plant in Malaysia for a number of years. Qatar has been actively seeking joint venture partners to build GTL plants. The Oryx GTL plant, a joint venture between Qatar and Sasol of South Africa, began operations in 2006. The plant consumes 330 million cubic feet of natural gas per day, producing 34,000 bpd of petroleum products (24,000 bpd of diesel fuel, 9,000 bpd of naphtha, and 1,000 bpd of LPG). Shell, utilizing its experience from the Bintula plant, is building the Pearl GTL plant in a joint venture with Qatar. The plant is anticipated to be completed in 2010 and will produce 140,000 bpd of naphtha, kerosene, diesel fuel, lubricating oils, and paraffin plus 120,000 bpd of natural gas liquids and ethane stripped from the 1.6 million cubic feet per day of natural gas feedstock. Chevron, utilizing its experience in a GTL project with Sasol, is building a 34,000 bpd GTL plant in Escravos, Nigeria, in partnership with the Nigerian National Oil Company, to be completed in 2010. There are plans for this plant to be expanded to 120,000 bpd within ten years of completion. Russia is looking into GTL production for isolated gas fields in Siberia and to capture the value lost by gas flaring. A proposal has been made to build barge-mounted GTL plants to reach isolated gas fields located near water in Southeast Asia and elsewhere.

Selling GTL petroleum products is a virtually unlimited market from the perspective of natural gas producers, whereas LNG is ultimately limited by the throughput capacity of LNG receiving terminals. One drawback to GTL production is the cost of the GTL plant, which could be reduced with further technological advances and by economies of scale in building larger-sized plants much as the cost of building LNG liquefaction plants has fallen over time. Another drawback is that the GTL process is about twice as thermally inefficient as an LNG liquefaction plant. This means that a lot more of the original energy content of natural gas is lost when natural gas is converted to petroleum products than to LNG. In addition, the Fischer-Tropsch process produces a great deal of carbon dioxide as a waste product (the process has been dubbed a carbon dioxide production plant by critics). While the petroleum products made by the Fischer-Tropsch process are cleaner-burning than those made from crude oil, the carbon footprint is larger when emissions from the production process are taken into account. The carbon footprint would be smaller if the GTL plant were consuming natural gas that would otherwise be flared. Earlier projections of the contribution of GTL as a source of motor vehicle fuels may not materialize from a combination of higher capital costs for building a GTL plant, the thermal inefficiency of the process, and a larger perceived growth in LNG exports to Europe and Asia. This reduces the need for gas-exporting nations to diversify their exports by transforming natural gas to oil products and may be behind the cancellation of a proposed GTL project involving Exxon-Mobil and Qatar.

## NONCONVENTIONAL GAS

Nonconventional gas refers to natural gas whose production requires special stimulation and drilling techniques to release the gas trapped in reservoirs. The principal sources of nonconventional gas are coalbed methane and tight gas shale and sand formations. It is difficult to estimate the reserves of nonconventional gas because of the nature of their geological structures and the ultimate recovery of gas from these reservoirs. At this time, the global estimate is over 900 tcm as compared to conventional global natural gas reserves of 177 tcm. Although reserves of nonconventional gas dwarf conventional sources, actual recovery may be only 10–15 percent because of the difficulty of removing gas embedded in coal seams and impermeable rock. Nonconventional gas fields are concentrated with 25 percent in the United States and Canada and 15 percent each in China, India, and the former Soviet Union. Nonconventional gas is a rapidly growing source of gas in the United States and to a lesser extent in Canada.

While not considered nonconventional, sour gas reserves are plentiful, amounting to 40 percent of global and 60 percent of Middle East gas reserves. Sour gas is natural gas with a significant content of either hydrogen sulfide or carbon dioxide or both. The presence of either gas poses a number of technical challenges as these gases must be separated from natural gas and disposed in an acceptable manner. Hydrogen sulfide is normally converted to sulfur and sold to industrial enterprises. However, sour gas containing hydrogen sulphide requires special alloys for the steel pipe used in natural gas production to prevent corrosion. There is no effective and economical way of disposing of carbon dioxide. The 1.3 tcm Natuna gas field in Indonesia, Southeast Asia's largest gas field, has a carbon dioxide concentration of over 70 percent. Disposal of this amount of carbon dioxide has prevented the development of this field for over two decades. However, there are a few examples of successful sequestration of gas fields with high carbon dioxide content. One such gas field in Norway and another in Algeria have successfully separated and injected the carbon dioxide content into nearby depleted gas fields, providing useful data and experience on carbon sequestration. But there is a cost that has to be taken into account of separating carbon dioxide from natural gas and in compressing, transporting, and injecting the carbon dioxide into underground formations.

## Methane from Coal

Methane found with coal has been responsible for the death of many miners. Coal bed methane (CBM) is "mining" coal beds not for their coal, but for their methane. CBM works best for mines that are too deep for mining (below 3,000 feet) with fractured methane-rich coal beds that are submerged in water. Water surrounding the coal absorbs and retains methane as long as the water is under pressure. Methane has a low solubility in water and readily comes out of solution when the water pressure is dropped.

A well is drilled to the coal seam to allow the water to rise to the surface, where it is capped and kept under pressure. From time to time water is pumped out of the well to lower its pressure. The released methane is collected and diverted to a gathering system that serves a number of wells. The gathering system is connected to a natural gas pipeline. After the release of methane, pumping stops and the well is capped to increase its internal pressure. Once the concentration of methane is restored, the well is pumped again to lower the pressure and release the methane. The principal region for CBM wells in the United States is the San Juan basin encompassing the Four Corners region (northwestern New Mexico, northeastern Arizona, southwestern Colorado and southeastern Utah), Powder River Basin (southeastern Montana and northeastern Wyoming), and other basins and regions such as Appalachia. CBM already contributes about 10 percent of the nonassociated natural gas production in the United States, 5 percent of Canada's gas production, 7 percent of Australia's gas production with Indonesia, India, and China in the early stages of developing CBM production. CBM is expected to continue growing rapidly, particularly with the rise in natural gas prices.

Environmentalists object to the pristine Western wilderness being crisscrossed with gathering pipelines and its quiet disturbed by the noise of equipment pumping water out of wells and compressors moving gas in pipelines. Much of the water from CBM wells is saline and can damage agricultural and natural plant life. Saline water is kept in ponds, but some can seep into the surface groundwater. Reinjecting saline water into the CBM well avoids the risk of surface water contamination, but at the present time, relatively little is reinjected.[13] Enhanced coal-bed methane involves injection of carbon dioxide into the coal bed. Fractures in a coal bed can absorb twice as much carbon dioxide as methane. The carbon dioxide remains trapped in the coal bed displacing the methane. This has the double benefit of sequestering carbon dioxide while enhancing methane production. Between 0.1 and 0.2 tons of methane can be recovered for every ton of injected carbon dioxide. Experimentation of enhanced CBM is being undertaken in the United States, China, Japan, and Poland. Sequestering carbon dioxide in coal beds would require separating carbon dioxide from flue gases and pipelining it from an electricity-generating plant to a CBM site, which, as one might expect, would be quite costly at this time.

## Methane from Tight Shale

Vertical drilling for conventional sources of oil and gas sometimes penetrated thick layers of shale rock hundreds of meters thick. This rock could not be economically exploited because of its low permeability. In recent years, technological advances have been made to tap this resource. Horizontal drilling can collect natural gas in shale if there are vertical fractures in the rock for the gas to flow into the well bore. "Hydraulic fracturing" or "hydrofracing" has been developed to increase the productivity of a horizontal well by increasing the number of fractures in a well bore. To do this, a portion of the well bore is sealed off and water or gel is injected under very high pressure (3,500 psi) to fracture the rock and expand existing fractures. Tons of sand or other "propant" is pumped down the well and into the pressurized portion of the hole to force millions of grains of sand into the fractures. If enough sand grains are trapped in the fractures, the fractures will remain propped open when the pressure is reduced. This increases the permeability of the rock, which allows a greater flow of gas into the well bore. This technique was first applied in the Barnett shale formation in north central Texas. Other promising formations under development are Marcellus shale in West Virginia, eastern Ohio, western Pennsylvania, and southern New York; Haynesville shale in northwestern Louisiana and eastern Texas; and Fayetteville shale in Arkansas. Thirty-five percent of the estimated global shale-gas reserves of 450 tcm are in North America with an equal sharing in the Asia-Pacific region and 15 percent in the Middle East. The United States is the only large-scale producer of shale gas, accounting for nearly 5 percent of total gas production, but shale gas is under development at the Horn River basin in northeastern British Columbia.

## Methane from Tight Sands

Tight gas sands are sandstone with a low permeability, and extracting methane is similar to that of tight shale formations. Tight sand formations are found mainly in the Rocky Mountain region but also in the Gulf coast, midcontinent, and northeast regions. World tight gas sand recoverable reserves are about 200 tcm, of which about 40 percent is in North America, 25 percent in Asia-Pacific with other deposits in former Soviet Union, Middle East, and Africa. The United States and Canada have been leaders in tight gas sands development. In 2006, 40 percent of new gas wells were in tight gas sands formations, accounting for nearly 30 percent of natural gas production. By 2009, nonconventional gas production was equal to conventional gas production, raising the issue of whether the descriptive term "nonconventional gas" was appropriate. However wells in tight shale and sands have a relatively short life, and drilling activity must be continuous to sustain production. But their high cost and short lives require a high price for natural gas. A fall-off in the price of natural gas, such as the one that occurred in late 2008/09, will have deleterious effects on natural gas production from nonconventional sources, leading to a greater dependence on imported LNG.

## Methane Hydrates

Methane hydrates are essentially natural gas molecules trapped in a lattice of ice whose structure is maintained in a low-temperature and moderate-to-high-pressure environment. Methane hydrates look like ice crystals. An ice ball of methane hydrates looks like those carefully sculpted by Calvin in the "Calvin and Hobbs" comic strip to throw at Suzie. The only difference is that the methane hydrate ice ball can be ignited. One cubic meter of methane hydrates contain 160 cubic meters of embedded natural gas. Methane hydrates are found beneath large portions of the world's permafrost as well as in offshore sediments. They are thought to have been formed by migrating natural gas or seep gas that came in contact with cold seawater at sufficient depths to form hydrates or by the decay of marine life in bottom sediments. Cold and pressure keep the methane entrapped in the ice lattice but it is released if warmed or the pressure reduced. Some climatologists fear that global warming of the tundra regions could release methane now entrapped as methane hydrates in the permafrost. This would lead to runaway global warming because methane is twenty times more effective than carbon dioxide in reflecting back infrared radiation from the earth. The challenge is how to "mine" methane hydrates considering their inherent instability.[14]

Methane hydrates are not limited to the arctic regions. Large deposits of methane hydrates have been found in coastal regions around Japan, both coasts of the United States, Central and South

America, and elsewhere. The known world reserves of natural gas are over 6,500 tcf, while the worldwide estimate of methane in methane hydrates is over 100 times greater at 700,000 tcf. For the United States, the estimate is 200,000 tcf versus natural gas reserves of 238 tcf, over 800 times larger. There is an awful lot of methane locked up in methane hydrates, and such a potential cannot be ignored. Research efforts are being conducted in Japan, Canada, Korea, the United States, China, and India to better understand the nature of methane hydrate deposits as a first step toward dealing with the technological challenge of how to mine them.

It is thought that ships lost in the Bermuda Triangle may have actually been caught in a gigantic bubble of methane released from methane hydrates and floundered from a loss of buoyancy. Aircraft passing through a cloud of methane-enriched air might suffer from a loss of power by methane displacing oxygen or from an explosion or fire from methane coming in contact with the hot engine exhaust. As an aside, brine pools with an extreme concentration of salt have been found in certain areas of the ocean. These pools are also rich sources of methane surrounded by colonies of mussels, which have formed a symbiotic relationship with methane-metabolizing bacteria that live on their gills. Methane-metabolizing bacteria have also been found living symbiotically with worms in methane hydrate deposits at the bottom of the Gulf of Mexico. Methane hydrate deposits and brine pools are fairly recent discoveries as is methane in the atmosphere of Saturn's moon, Titan, which appears to have lakes of LNG. These newly discovered sources of methane show that we live in an amazing world in an equally amazing universe.

## NOTES

1. Primary sources for the history of coal gas are Christopher J. Castaneda, *Invisible Fuel* (New York: Twayne Publisher, 1999); and Arlon R. Tussing and Bob Tippee, *The Natural Gas Industry* (Tulsa, OK: PennWell Books, 1995).

2. Bob Shively and John Ferrare, *Understanding Today's Natural Gas Business* (San Francisco: Enerdynamics, 2004).

3. *BP Energy Statistics* (London: British Petroleum, 2009).

4. *International Energy Outlook* (Washington, DC: Energy Information Administration, U.S. Department of Energy, 2008).

5. International Energy Agency, *World Energy Outlook* (Paris, 2008).

6. Colin Shelley, *The Story of LPG* (New York: Poten & Partners, 2003).

7. *BP Energy Statistics* (London: British Petroleum, 2009).

8. Michael Tusiani and Gordon Shearer, *LNG: A Nontechnical Guide* (Tulsa, OK: PennWell Books, 2007).

9. Minority Staff Report U.S. House of Representatives Committee of Government Reform, *Background on Enron's Dabhol Power Project* (February 22, 2002), Web site www.democrats.reform.house.gov/ Documents/ 20040830150742–77212.pdf. See also Yahoo Financial News Web site uk.biz.yahoo.com/ 26022009/323/india-s-dabhol-first-lng-cargo-shell.html.

10. Two-Stroke Propulsion Trends in LNG Carriers (Copenhagen: MAN Diesel A/S, 2007), Web site www.manbw.com/files/news/filesof8074/5510–0035–00-lo.pdf.

11. *LNG in North America Markets* from a Citigroup Smith Barney report of August 27, 2004.

12. An animated explanation of a GTL project is available on the Shell Oil Web site www.shell.com/ home/content/shellgasandpower-en/products_and_services/what_is_gtl/gas_to_liquid/whatisgtl_0112_1532. html.

13. National Energy Technology Laboratory, *Integrated Process of Coalbed Brine and Methane Disposal*, Web site www.netl.doe.gov; Environmental Protection Agency, *Coal Mine Methane Use in Brine Water Treatment*, Web site www.epa.gov.

14. National Methane Hydrate Program of the National Energy Technology Laboratory Web site www.netl. doe.gov, and the National Research Council's *Charting the Future of Methane Hydrate Research* (Washington, DC: 2004).

# 8

## NUCLEAR AND HYDROPOWER

Oftentimes nuclear and hydro are linked together in energy statistics. Of course, they are quite different: nuclear power is generally viewed as dangerous while hydro is viewed as benign. This really is not quite true for either. Despite Three Mile Island and Chernobyl, the safety record for nuclear power speaks for itself: There have been over 13,000 reactor-years of safe commercial plant operation, coupled with an equivalent span of safe operation for nuclear-powered warships. The worst accident by far was Chernobyl, a case of an unsafe reactor design unsafely operated. Hydropower has its opponents, and dam failures are not unknown phenomena. This chapter covers the principal aspects of nuclear and hydropower as energy sources.

### BACKGROUND

Nuclear power is the outgrowth of the nuclear weapons program to transform the world's most destructive weapon to peaceful uses. The 1953 launching of the Atoms for Peace program foretold a world where commercial nuclear energy would be clean, abundant, safe, and too cheap to even meter! Nuclear power is clean, because it does not generate emissions that contribute to global warming, but dirty because the spent fuel must somehow be disposed. Three Mile Island buried the myth that nuclear power was inherently safe, and Chernobyl showed how dangerous it could be. And cheap it is not, with cost overruns in the billions.

Despite predictions of a phase-out of nuclear power plants and general pessimism over the prospects for nuclear power as an energy source, 42 nuclear power plants are under construction (11 in China, 8 in Russia, 6 in India, 5 in South Korea, 2 each in Canada, Slovakia, and Japan, and 1 each in Argentina, Finland, France, Iran, Pakistan, and the United States).[1] There are some who believe that we may be at the dawn of a new age in nuclear power. One cannot cavalierly dismiss the fact that nuclear power is free of greenhouse gas emissions. Table 8.1 shows the EPA's estimates on the pounds of emissions to produce one megawatt-hour of electrical power; nuclear power leaves no carbon footprint. Emissions avoided by the U.S. nuclear industry in 2007 alone have been estimated to be 1 million tons of sulfur dioxide, 3 million tons of nitrogen oxides, and 693 million tons of carbon dioxide.[2]

Electricity rates are directly and significantly affected by fluctuations in energy costs of coal and natural gas, which are influenced by the cost of crude oil, but nuclear power is relatively insensitive to fuel costs. Though fuel assemblies have to be replaced over the life of a nuclear plant, fluctuations in the cost of uranium have a relatively minor impact on the price of electricity produced by a nuclear plant.

Nuclear power in the United States is criticized for being heavily subsidized. Table 8.2 shows

Table 8.1

**Average Pounds of Emissions to Produce One Megawatt-Hour of Electricity**

|  | Coal | Oil | Natural Gas | Nuclear |
|---|---|---|---|---|
| Carbon Dioxide | 2,249 | 1,672 | 1,135 | 0 |
| Sulfur Dioxide | 13 | 12 | 0.1 | 0 |
| Nitrogen Oxides | 6 | 4 | 1.7 | 0 |

Table 8.2

**Subsidies of Electricity Production**

|  | Net Generation (million megawatt hours) | Subsidies (million $) | Subsidies $/ Megawatt-Hour |
|---|---|---|---|
| Natural Gas & Petroleum Liquids | 919 | $227 | $0.25 |
| Coal | 1,946 | $854 | $0.44 |
| Hydroelectric | 258 | $174 | $0.67 |
| Biomass | 40 | $36 | $0.89 |
| Geothermal | 15 | $14 | $0.92 |
| Nuclear | 794 | $1,267 | $1.59 |
| Wind | 31 | $724 | $23.37 |
| Solar | 1 | $174 | $24.34 |
| Clean coal | 72 | $2,156 | $29.81 |

that all sources of electricity are subsidized and that nuclear power is far less subsidized than wind, solar, and clean coal.[3]

The promise of standardized "cookie-cutter" plants, built the way Ford manufactured Model Ts, would eliminate the enormous cost overruns associated with the one-of-a-kind nuclear plants that dominated past construction in the United States. Advancements in nuclear power technology, coupled with series production of a standard plant design, built as modules in a central manufacturing facility and shipped to a plant site, would make the cost of electricity from nuclear plants quite attractive compared to fossil fuel plants. The economics further favor nuclear power plants as fossil fuel prices continue to rise or a cap and trade program for carbon emissions or a tax on carbon are enacted. What has to be accomplished before any renaissance of nuclear power becomes possible is assuring the public that the human errors and circumstances responsible for the Three Mile Island incident and the Chernobyl catastrophe cannot happen again.

Human error played a major role in both the Three Mile Island incident and the Chernobyl catastrophe. Yet, nearly all of the radioactive release of the Three Mile Island incident was kept within its containment system, as it was designed to do. Soviet nuclear power plants do not have containment systems built to withstand the pressure generated from a ruptured reactor system, but are housed in buildings without an internal structure to withstand pressure. Nor did the Soviet Union select a safe plant design. Whereas most reactors shut down when the water moderator in the core boils away (an example of a negative feedback system), the same phenomenon with the Soviet graphite-moderated reactor led to a runaway power surge (an example of a positive feedback system).

In the United States where there is a higher per capita consumption of electricity, a typical large-sized nuclear power and coal-fired plants with an output of 1,000 megawatts, or 1 gigawatt can supply the needs of 600,000 people depending on the degree of industrial activity. On a global scale where per capita consumption of electricity is considerably less as in Asia, a 1 gigawatt plant can serve the needs of 2 million people. For purposes of discussion, it is assumed that a 1 gigawatt plant can supply the electricity needs of one million people.

Base-load needs are most commonly handled by large nuclear and coal-fired plants. A 1-gigawatt coal-fired power plant releases about 6 million tons of carbon dioxide each year, plus potentially a large quantity of sulfur dioxides into the environment depending on the sulfur content of the coal and the effectiveness of the plant's scrubbers (if any). There is also pollution in the form of soot unless removed by precipitators, nitrous oxides, plus health-affecting emissions of mercury, cadmium, and arsenic. A nuclear plant of the same size consumes about 25 tons of enriched uranium (3.5–5 percent of the isotope U235) per year, which requires over 200 tons of uranium oxide concentrate produced by mining 25,000–100,000 tons of ore depending on the uranium concentration. The annual waste from a nuclear power plant is less than 30 tons of spent fuel, a highly radioactive and toxic waste. If reprocessed (chopped up and dissolved in acid to recover fissionable material for recycling), spent fuel can be reduced to about 1 ton of waste. Though even more dangerous and toxic than spent fuel, such relatively small quantities should be effectively managed for transport and permanent storage, or at least so it was thought.

Uranium is as common as tin and is mined both on the surface and underground. Half of the world's uranium ore production is in Canada and Australia, followed by Kazakhstan, Niger, Russia, Namibia, Uzbekistan, and the United States. The ore is first finely ground, then leached with sulfuric acid to remove uranium in the form of uranium oxide, called "yellow cake," which is then transformed to uranium fluoride gas. Both the gaseous diffusion and high-speed centrifuge processes take advantage of the fact that U235 is slightly lighter than U238. These processes create two streams of uranium fluoride gas: one enriched with U235 and the other depleted of U235. Starting with a concentration of 0.7 percent U235, the enriched stream has a concentration of about 3.5–5 percent, depending on the type of reactor, and the depleted stream is nearly pure U238. The depleted stream is 1.7 times denser than lead and can be used for reactor shielding and armor-piercing shells. Although most is stockpiled, some has been drawn down in recent years to mix with highly enriched uranium released from the Russian and U.S. weapons programs for transformation to reactor fuel.

Enriched uranium fluoride is converted to uranium oxide, pressed into small cylindrical ceramic pellets, and inserted into thin tubes of zirconium alloy or stainless steel to form fuel rods. These are then sealed and assembled into reactor fuel assemblies and placed in the core of the nuclear reactor. The core of a 1,000-megawatt or 1-gigawatt reactor contains about 75 tons of enriched uranium. The presence of a moderator such as water or graphite slows down the neutrons sufficiently for the U235 isotope to fission (or split) in a chain reaction that produces heat to transform water to steam. From that point on, the generation of electricity is the same as in a fossil-fueled plant.

Uranium reserves for conventional reactors can last over a century. Reserves can be extended by a factor of 100 or more by reprocessing spent fuel to reuse the plutonium generated by the fission process, by breeder reactors designed to create their own fuel, and by utilizing thorium, which becomes fissionable when transformed to U233 in a nuclear reactor. Taking into consideration uranium life extension through reprocessing, breeding, and transforming thorium to fissionable material, some view nuclear energy as a virtually inexhaustible source of energy.

## PHYSICS OF A NUCLEAR REACTOR

U235 fissions or splits into fission byproducts such as barium and krypton, releasing about 2.5 prompt or fast neutrons and other products. The fission byproducts also decay, releasing delayed (or slow) neutrons. Both prompt and delayed neutrons are necessary to maintain criticality (a constant rate of fission). Slowing down fast neutrons in a moderator such as graphite or water is necessary for the neutrons to be absorbed by fissionable material in a conventional reactor. The exception is fast breeder reactors that depend only on prompt or fast neutrons to maintain criticality. The total mass of fission byproducts is less than the original U235 atom, and the heat released is equivalent to the loss of mass multiplied by the square of the speed of light (Einstein's famous $E = mc^2$).

From the perspective of converting matter to energy, a nuclear bomb and a nuclear reactor are similar. But a nuclear bomb is designed to have a runaway reaction, whereas a nuclear reactor is designed to prevent a runaway reaction. A nuclear bomb concentrates over 90 percent fissionable material for a single explosive event. A nuclear reactor disperses a low concentration (3.5–5 percent) of fissionable material within a fuel assembly, along with channels for coolant to pass through and to insert neutron-absorbing control rods. It is impossible for a nuclear reactor to sustain a nuclear explosion, but it is possible for the core to meltdown from a loss of coolant and release radioactivity.

A reactor is shut down when control rods are fully inserted. To operate a reactor, control rods are pulled out until a critical mass is formed where a self-sustaining chain reaction can occur (a constant number of fissions over time). The power output of the reactor is increased by pulling the control rods out further to increase the fission rate. A reactor control system scrams (or shuts down) the reactor by rapid insertion of control rods if system performance does not fit a tight set of specifications. Heat is generated within a reactor by the transfer of kinetic energy from fission byproducts to molecules in the fuel rod and then to molecules in the coolant and by slowing down of neutrons in the moderator. With exceptions, coolant is normally water flowing through channels within the assemblies of fuel rods and control rods. Nearly all fission products are locked in the fuel rod to ensure that the water coolant has a low degree of radioactivity. The water not only transfers heat from the reactor to the steam generators to drive the electricity generators, but, with exceptions, also serves as a moderator to slow down the neutrons.[4]

## NUCLEAR INCIDENTS AND ACCIDENTS

A nuclear incident occurs when released radioactivity is contained; that is, prevented from escaping to the outside environment with no resulting loss of life and with minimal impact on the health of those exposed to radiation. Nuclear accidents involve radioactivity escaping to the outside environment with or without injuries or deaths. The history of nuclear accidents starts in 1952 with a partial meltdown of a reactor's core at Chalk River near Ottawa, Canada, when four control rods were accidentally removed. The resulting radioactive release was contained in millions of gallons of water and no injuries resulted. In 1957, Windscale Pile No. 1 north of Liverpool, England, sustained a fire in a graphite-moderated reactor and spewed radiation over a 200-square-mile area. In the same year, an explosion of radioactive wastes at a Soviet nuclear weapons factory in the South Ural Mountains forced the evacuation of over 10,000 people from the contaminated area. In 1976, a failure of safety systems during a fire nearly caused a reactor meltdown near Greifswald in former East Germany. Of all nuclear accidents, two stand out: Three Mile Island and Chernobyl.

### Three Mile Island Incident

The Three Mile Island incident in March 28, 1979, was preceded by the release of the movie *China Syndrome* on March 16, 1979, a case of Hollywood prescience or fiction preceding fact. *China*

*Syndrome* was about a nuclear plant with internal problems that, if unattended, could have led to a core meltdown, which would then burrow its way toward China. The film dealt with management's decision to ignore and cover up the plant's problems.

The Three Mile Island incident proved that nuclear power plants were not immune to accidents, despite claims to the contrary. In this case a malfunction of the secondary cooling circuit caused the temperature in the primary coolant to rise, shutting down the reactor as expected. What was not expected was the failure of a relief valve to close and stop the primary coolant from draining away. The relief valve indicator on the instrumentation panel showed the valve as being closed, making it difficult for the operators to diagnose the true cause of the problem. As a result, the coolant continued to drain away until the core was uncovered. Without coolant, the residual decay heat in the reactor core raised the temperature within the core and led to a partial core meltdown.

Although the instrumentation panel failed to show that the relief valve was still open, the blame for the accident was eventually assigned to inadequate emergency-response training on the part of the operators. In other words, despite faulty indication of the relief valve, the operators should have identified the true cause of the problem and taken proper action before it was too late. The containment system performed as it was designed to do—nearly all the released radioactivity was prevented from escaping to the outside environment. Contrary to the *China Syndrome* plot, management did not hide the plant's problems from the public and the core did not melt through the earth.

There were minor health impacts and no injuries from the Three Mile Island incident. Even though the nuclear power industry took remedial steps to improve training and operations to make reactors even more safe and reliable, the Three Mile Island incident dealt a deathblow to the U.S. nuclear power industry. The incident halted all further orders of nuclear power plants in the United States and the cancellation of over forty orders for plants not yet started. Most plants under construction were completed, although a few were converted to fossil fuel plants. The public concern over nuclear safety generated by this incident was sufficient to prevent the Shoreham plant on Long Island from becoming operational when it was completed in 1984. A study showed that if a more serious incident than that of Three Mile Island were to occur at the Shoreham plant, the few bridges and tunnels connecting Long Island with the mainland would preclude any large-scale evacuation. For this reason, the plant was dismantled in 1992.

## Chernobyl

In one respect, the two events were similar: Both involved human error. At Chernobyl, a runaway reactor occurred during a test, ironically one associated with reactor safety—how long could turbines supply power when cut off from reactor power? What made Chernobyl so much worse than Three Mile Island was the nature of its reactor design, actions taken by operators to defeat safety features, and the absence of a containment system (the reactor housing was not built to contain a pressure buildup from a rupture of the reactor or its piping). In conducting the test, the automatic reactor trip mechanisms were disabled and the emergency core cooling system was shut off. With its valves locked shut, none of the operators knew who had the keys! Having disabled the reactor's safety features, the two principal operators started "doing their own thing" without communicating to each other what they were doing.

The reactor design made a bad situation worse. The Soviet reactor used graphite as a moderator and water as a coolant. Graphite has several undesirable features as a moderator. At too high a temperature, graphite can burn or react violently with steam to generate hydrogen and carbon monoxide, both combustible gases. In a U.S. reactor, water, as both moderator and coolant, shuts down the reactor when water boils in the core. Void spaces in boiling water reduce the number of neutrons being slowed down to keep the reactor critical (negative feedback). In the Soviet reactor, the creation of void spaces in boiling water allowed a larger number of neutrons to reach the graphite moderator, increasing the fission rate (positive feedback). From a low power condition, the operators retracted more control rods than recommended and the reactor went supercritical, generating enough heat to turn the coolant to steam, which further increased the number of fissions. The resulting power surge ruptured the fuel elements and blew off the reactor cover plate. The graphite moderator burst into flames when air gained access to the core, and the resulting blast, along with the escaping steam, ruptured the roof of the building housing the reactor. Large chunks of the reactor core and graphite moderator were scattered outside the building, releasing far more radioactivity than the nuclear bombs dropped on Hiroshima and Nagasaki.

Death quickly followed for those in contact with the radioactive debris or caught in the radioactive cloud close by the plant. A group of people standing on a bridge not far away died from the exposure to radioactivity from gazing in wonderment at the strange lights given off by the reactor. About 200,000 people living within a thirty-kilometer radius of the plant had to be resettled, and increasing the exclusion zone a few years later required resettling another 200,000. Those caught in the radioactive cloud that reached to eastern Europe and Scandinavia now suffer from a higher incidence of cancer and birth defects. Although Russian inspectors monitor food for radioactivity from farms, they miss large quantities of contaminated berries and mushrooms gathered by individuals from forests that "all but glow in the dark." Many believe that the actual death toll far exceeds the official death count of a few hundred. Even so, this does not include the shortening of life from a higher incidence of cancer and the large number of babies born with serious birth defects.

Since the Chernobyl accident, Russian reactors have been retrofitted with modifications to overcome the deficiencies in the original design. Moreover, there has been significant collaboration between Russian and Western nuclear engineers to advance safety in nuclear reactor design and operation. The hurried Chernobyl reactor entombment is showing signs of deterioration, which will have to be revisited in order to ensure that the large amounts of radioactive material still entrapped in the building do not escape to the environment. Nevertheless, the legacy of these two events will live on. The Three Mile Island incident cast a pall over the U.S. nuclear power program and the Chernobyl nuclear catastrophe had far-ranging global implications.

The most recent nuclear incident occurred in 1999 in Tokaimura, Japan, in a uranium-reprocessing nuclear fuel plant. Workers inadvertently mixed spent uranium in solution in a container large enough to create a critical mass. Although there was no explosion, the liquid went critical, giving off large amounts of radioactivity. As the liquid solution boiled, void spaces stopped the chain reaction (lack of a moderator to slow down the neutrons). When cooled, the solution became critical again. This lasted for twenty hours before a neutron absorber could be added to the tank to keep its contents subcritical. Twenty-seven people were exposed to very high levels of radioactivity and two died, and more than 600 others were exposed to less dangerous levels of radiation.

Actually, Japan does relatively little fuel reprocessing; much of its spent fuel is shipped to the United Kingdom and France. Fissionable material from reprocessing is returned to Japan as a mixed oxide fuel for fabricating new fuel elements. Three years after this incident, in 2002, a scandal broke out when it was learned that Japanese utility management hid the fact that there were cracks in nuclear power plant piping (shades of *China Syndrome*). All nuclear power plants in Japan were shut down for inspection and repair, if necessary. No reactor incident came of this, but there was a justifiable loss of confidence in management, raising doubts about Japan's future reliance on nuclear power.

## Weapons Proliferation

The chain reaction transforms some of the U238 in the reactor core to various plutonium isotopes. What is of concern is fissionable plutonium 239 that remains in the spent fuel when about 75 percent of the U235 has been consumed. A typical light-water reactor breeds about 8 kilograms of plutonium 239 per month of operation, although one-third undergoes fission, supplying more power to the reactor. A fast breeder reactor is designed to create more plutonium 239 from irradiating uranium 238 than the fissionable material consumed. A fast breeder reactor depends only on prompt or fast neutrons, not delayed or slow neutrons, to maintain a chain reaction, requiring a greater degree of technological sophistication for reactor control. Fast breeder reactors can extend uranium reserves forever, at least from the perspective of human existence. Three fast breeder reactors exist and two more are being built in India and Russia.

The possibility of nuclear weapons made from plutonium 239 extracted from spent fuel has been of concern to the world community for many years. With regard to weapons proliferation, only fifteen kilograms of plutonium 239 can make a crude nuclear weapon and more sophisticated varieties require less, which represents about two or three months of reactor operation. Plutonium 239 can be separated chemically from spent fuel after it is ground up and dissolved in acid. The International Atomic Energy Agency (IAEA) was set up to ensure that nuclear materials at reactor sites and at enrichment and reprocessing facilities are not diverted to nuclear weapons manufacture. The potential, real or otherwise, for diversion of plutonium 239 from spent fuel from a reactor in Iran and another in North Korea for nuclear weapons is unsettling the world community.

In recent years, a new weapon of mass destruction has arisen for the terrorists' arsenal. It consists of a metal container filled with highly radioactive spent fuel ground to fine particles surrounded by conventional explosive. When detonated, the explosion vaporizes and disperses the particles as an aerosol, spreading lethal amounts of radioactivity over a wide area. Only a few micrograms of ingested or inhaled plutonium 239 are fatal. The knowledge that terrorists have seriously considered flying an airliner into a nuclear power plant is another disincentive for building nuclear power plants. Containment systems, with walls typically four feet thick made of steel-reinforced concrete, are designed to sustain the accidental crash of a jet liner. However, intentionally ramming a jet liner at full speed into a reactor may be another matter.

## Disposal of Spent Fuel

About one-third of the fuel assemblies are removed from nuclear reactors each year as spent fuel and replaced with fresh fuel. Spent fuel still contains about 96 percent of its original uranium, although its fissionable U235 content has been reduced to less than 1 percent. Highly radioactive spent fuel gives off heat and is normally stored in a spent fuel pool at the reactor site; the water shields the environment from radiation and absorbs the heat. This has to be considered temporary storage, however, because the radioactivity will persist for thousands of years, far beyond the life of the plant.

Spent fuel can either be sent to permanent storage or reprocessed. Reprocessing plants, located in Europe, Russia, and Japan, separate the uranium and plutonium. Recovered uranium is converted back to uranium fluoride and re-enriched with U235. Plutonium can be blended with enriched uranium to produce a mixed oxide fuel. About thirty European reactors can be loaded with 20–50 percent mixed oxide fuel, and Japan plans to have one-third of its reactors capable of using mixed oxide fuel. This recycling of spent fuel greatly reduces the demand for uranium and the volume of spent fuel. After recycling, the remaining 3 percent of highly radioactive wastes is mixed in liquefied Pyrex glass, which contains neutron-absorbing boron, and poured into steel canisters. One ton of reprocessed waste is embedded in 5 tons of glass.

The problem is now where to store the canisters. Final disposition sites for these canisters have not been built, but geological formations made of granite, volcanic tuff, salt, or shale are being examined. One proposal is to drop the boron impregnated glass canisters into ocean trenches for "natural" disposal. The glass prevents any escape of radioactive material into the environment. The canisters are adequately shielded with five to seven miles of ocean water. If the ocean trench is also a subduction zone, over millions of years the canisters will be dragged into the earth's mantle, melted, and dispersed. It is possible that the waste could return to the earth's surface in volcanic lava in some tens or hundreds of millions of years; but by that time, its radioactivity will be gone.

Public objections to dumping nuclear toxic waste in ocean trenches have ruled out what may be a very practical solution to nuclear waste. Yet, there is a precedent. About 2 billion years ago, at a place called Oklo in Gabon, West Africa, six "nuclear reactors" operated naturally within a rich vein of uranium ore that went critical after being saturated with water. The water acted as a moderator and the "reactors" remained critical, producing heat and radioactive fission byproducts before running out of fuel about a half million years ago. The radioactive residue, which totals over 5 tons of fission products and 1.5 tons of plutonium, has all decayed into harmless nonradioactive isotopes. It has also been theorized that another natural reactor exists in the earth's core, maintaining its high temperature and keeping its outer layer liquid to induce the enormous flow of electricity responsible for the earth's magnetic field.

The problem with land storage is that the radioactivity will persist for many thousands of years, far exceeding recorded history. Any water seepage into the storage area could become contaminated and affect the surrounding water table. Sweden, Finland, and Germany are in the process of developing permanent storage facilities. The most publicized proposed permanent storage site is Yucca Mountain in Nevada. The U.S. Congress approved this site in 2002 after $4 billion and twenty years of study. It was to be licensed by the Nuclear Regulatory Commission after it had examined the suitability of Yucca Mountain's geology, hydrology, biology, and climate. The factors favoring Yucca Mountain were its remote location with regard to population centers, its dry climate, and the deep depth of the underlying water table. An unexpected source of opposition was the state of Nevada, which had second thoughts about becoming the nation's sole nuclear waste depository (dumpsite). The state filed a lawsuit against the U.S. Department of Energy for using public rail transport to ship spent fuel to the site. This suit became moot when in 2009, the Obama administration cut off further funding that supported studying the feasibility of Yucca Mountain as a national depository for nuclear waste. Consequently several utilities have filed suit as a result of this decision since the Federal government agreed to provide a permanent storage facility as a precondition for building nuclear reactor plants. As of now, spent fuel is kept in cooled water at nuclear plant sites.

## COMMERCIAL REACTORS

The first reactor was a small boiling water reactor (BWR) built for a nuclear submarine, a project spearheaded by Admiral Hyman Rickover in 1954. The first commercial reactor was a pressurized water reactor (PWR) built in 1957. Others were to follow, but these early reactors were really prototypes built to gain expertise to build larger plants. A BWR feeds steam directly from the reactor to the turbines that drive the generators. This introduces a low level of radioactivity to the steam turbines, condensers, and associated piping. A PWR operates under higher pressure; a heat

Figure 8.1   **Growth in Nuclear Power in Terms of Displaced Fossil Fuels** (MM Bpd)

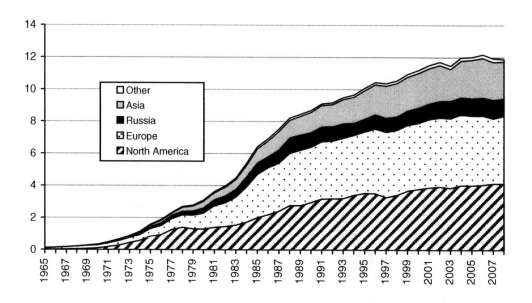

exchanger between the reactor coolant and water in a steam generator precludes any reactor coolant from entering the steam generator, turbine, and associated equipment. The higher temperatures possible with a PWR design make it more thermally efficient than a BWR. Most reactors in the United States are BWRs built by General Electric and PWRs built by Westinghouse that use light or normal water as a moderator.

Figure 8.1 shows the historical growth in nuclear power in terms of the amount of fossil fuel that would have been burned to generate the equivalent amount of electricity, assuming a thermal efficiency of 38 percent for converting fossil fuel to electricity. Generating electricity equivalent to burning 12 million barrels per day of fossil fuel is a significant reduction in carbon dioxide emissions. On a global scale, fossil fuel plants (mainly coal but also natural gas and a smaller amount of oil) emitted 11.4 billion tons of carbon dioxide in 2006 making up 41 percent of carbon dioxide emissions. Because of the growth in coal-fired plants, power plants are projected to contribute 45 percent of carbon emissions by 2030.[5] This trend cannot be reversed unless there is a resurgence in nuclear power augmented by wind and solar.

The upward sweep in nuclear power output for North America shown in Figure 8.1 did not result from building more nuclear plants. The reorganization of the electricity industry from a regulated cost-plus regime to a more liberalized competitive business environment was chiefly responsible for the higher nuclear power output. Under a cost-plus regulatory regime, there was no incentive to get more out of a nuclear power plant than what was convenient. In a liberalized competitive environment, as in the United Kingdom and the United States (and spreading elsewhere), the profit motive residing within deregulation (or liberalization) improved capacity utilization. In the case of the United States, nuclear power plant utilization increased from 65 percent in 1980 to 90 percent in 1990, from the result of better scheduling of maintenance and refueling to reduce downtime and relying more on nuclear power to take advantage of its low variable cost.

In 2009, there were 436 operating reactors: 42 under construction and 110 in the planning stage with proposals for a whopping 272 reactors with 77 in China, 20–25 each in Russia, Ukraine,

Figure 8.2   **World Population of Commercial Nuclear Reactors**

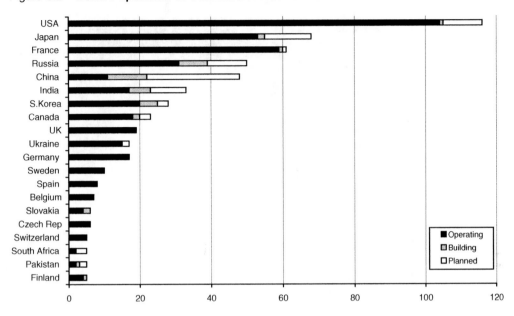

the United States, and South Africa, 15 in India, and 10 in Italy, and 1–2 in a number of other nations. Figure 8.2 shows the number of existing nuclear reactors plus those under construction or in the planning stage.[6]

Nuclear reactors are found in thirty nations, with half in the United States, Japan, and France. Of the 436 reactors, 260 are PWRs and 92 are BWRs. There are also twenty-six gas-cooled reactors, nineteen pressurized heavy-water reactors (popular in Canada), seventeen light-water graphite reactors (found only in FSU), and three fast breeder reactors in Japan, France, and Russia. The U.K.-designed gas-cooled reactor has a graphite moderator and carbon dioxide coolant. Carbon dioxide circulates through the core, where it is heated before passing through steam generator tubes contained within the concrete-and-steel pressure vessel. Steam from the generator passes through the pressure vessel to steam turbines that drive electricity generators. The Canadian-designed heavy-water reactors use natural, not enriched, uranium as fuel, but require a more efficient heavy water moderator where some water molecules have a deuterium atom (one proton and one neutron in the nucleus) rather than a hydrogen atom (one proton in the nucleus). Thus, there is a cost trade-off whether to enrich the fuel with U235 or enrich the moderator with deuterium.

France is a world leader in nuclear power, generating 77 percent of its electricity needs plus exporting electricity to other nations. Lithuania's single reactor is sufficient to cover 71 percent of its electricity needs. Slovakia (4 operating reactors) and Belgium (7 operating reactors) generate over half their electricity demand from nuclear power. Figure 8.3 shows the nations with the highest percentage of electricity generated by nuclear power.

India has six times more thorium than uranium and is independently advancing nuclear technology to take advantage of its ample thorium supplies. India has inaugurated a three-stage reactor program of building a pressurized heavy-water reactor to produce plutonium. In the second stage, plutonium will be the fissionable fuel for a fast breeder reactor to breed uranium 233 from thorium. In the third stage, uranium 233 will be the fissionable fuel for an advanced heavy-water reactor.

Figure 8.3  **World's Largest Nuclear Producers** (Percent of Total Electricity Output)

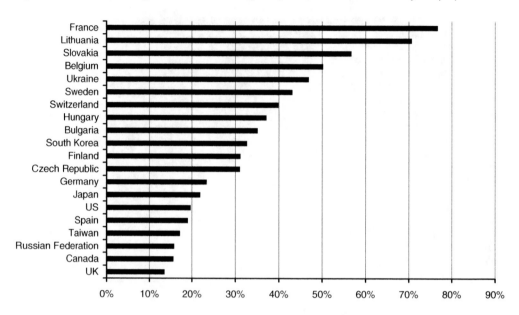

Advances in nuclear technology have not been curtailed by Chernobyl. Members of Generation IV International Forum (GIF), organized in 2001, include Argentina, Brazil, Canada, China, Euratom, France, Japan, South Korea, Russia, South Africa, Switzerland, United Kingdom, and the United States. The objective of the GIF is to obtain a standardized design for various types of nuclear reactors to expedite licensing and reduce capital costs and construction time. The intended design is to be simple and rugged, have a long life, be easy to operate, and less vulnerable to operator errors and circumstances that could lead to a nuclear accident. Technologies under consideration include a gas-cooled fast reactor, lead-cooled fast reactor (an adaptation of Russian submarine reactors), sodium-cooled fast reactor, supercritical water-cooled reactor, and the very high temperature reactor.[7]

### European Pressurized (Evolutionary Power) Reactor

France has been a leader in nuclear power and is still a leader in the post-Chernobyl world. The major differences between nuclear power in the United States and in France are public attitudes towards nuclear power and the organization of nuclear power activities.[8] After the oil crisis of 1973, France did not have the requisite coal and natural gas reserves of the United States to rely on for electricity generation. The French people accepted the government decision to pursue nuclear power because of their respect for and trust in their civil servants and government officials, many of whom were scientists and engineers by training. Moreover, the organization of the nuclear power industry was placed under government oversight for every facet of its activities. The government was responsible for selecting a reactor design, which comes in three sizes (1,450, 1,300, and 900 megawatts of electricity). The "cookie-cutter" approach by limiting reactors to three varieties of a single design reduces manufacturing and construction costs of nuclear components and facilities and simplifies the process of licensing and permitting. Efficiencies gained from progressing down the learning curve of permitting, building, and licensing multiple units of essentially identical plants reduce scheduling delays, cost overruns, and capital costs. All nuclear electricity-generating facilities and reprocessing plants are in government-owned companies. The government is responsible for dealing with nuclear wastes. Government ownership reduces the risk premium that would have to be paid by publicly owned nuclear facilities for financing nuclear plants. Government control ensures a simpler regulatory regime and positive guidance over the future role of nuclear power in satisfying the nation's electricity needs.

In the United States, the Three Mile Island reactor nuclear incident in 1979 brought an abrupt end to nuclear power construction, already plagued with cost overruns and construction scheduling delays by each utility essentially building one-of-a-kind nuclear facilities. Nuclear power plants in the United States satisfy base-load needs, which means that they operate close to full capacity at all times. French reactors supply power for both base and variable needs. Some contend that the continual cycling of power output affects safety from potential power surges and stressing of internal components.

The third-generation European Pressurized Reactor is called the Evolutionary Power Reactor (EPR) manufactured by a joint venture between the French companies Areva and Electricité de France and the German company Siemens. Two EPRs are currently under construction in Finland and France, and both are scheduled for completion in 2012. The EPR reactor has been scaled up to an output of 1,650 megawatts (1.65 gigawatts) using a 5 percent enriched uranium oxide fuel or a 50 percent mixed uranium plutonium oxide fuel. In addition to enhanced output, the major improvement incorporated in the EPR is safety. The nuclear power plant foundation is built to withstand the largest potential earthquake, and four independent emergency cooling systems provide ample redundancy. In addition to a leak-tight containment system surrounding the reactor, an extra or secondary containment and cooling area has been built under the reactor base to handle the potential accident of a molten core penetrating the bottom of the primary reactor containment. The outer containment has a two-layer concrete wall, each layer 2.6 meters thick, designed to withstand impact by aircraft and the internal pressures from a reactor accident. These safety enhancements increase the cost of the EPR, but the economy of scale associated with its greater output can still reduce the cost of electricity by 10 percent from existing plants. In common with building the first of anything, the Finnish EPR is suffering from cost overruns and scheduling delays. But the learning curve associated with series production guarantees that cost overruns and scheduling delays would be experienced to a far lesser degree with follow-on orders such as the two ordered by China's Guangdong Nuclear Power Company. As seen by China's orders, the EPR is being marketed throughout the world.

## Pebble Bed Reactor

The concept of the pebble bed reactor is not new. It was proposed at the dawn of the nuclear age in 1943 when the Manhattan Project team led by Enrico Fermi sustained the first nuclear chain reaction in a pile of uranium blocks at the University of Chicago. Farrington Daniels, a chemist, who joined the effort a short time later, proposed the harnessing of nuclear power for cheap, clean electricity using a reactor containing enriched uranium "pebbles"—a term borrowed from chemistry—cooled by helium transferring energy to a turbine driving an electricity generator. Under President Eisenhower's "atoms for peace" program, the newly created General Atomics division of General Dynamics assembled forty top nuclear scientists in 1956 to brainstorm reactor designs. Edward Teller, godfather of the H-bomb, argued that reactors must be inherently safe and advocated that the only acceptable design being one where every control rod could be pulled out without causing a meltdown. But Admiral Hyman Rickover's competing idea of building a water-cooled and moderated pressurized reactor with control rods to power submarines prevailed over a gaseous pebble bed reactor that satisfied Teller's criterion. Rickover's proposed design was adopted by the utility industry until the partial meltdown at Three Mile Island in 1979, and the reactor explosion at Chernobyl in 1986 essentially brought nuclear reactor construction to an abrupt halt other than for warships.[9]

The pebble bed reactor idea did not entirely die with Rickover's decision. Rudolf Schulten, a German physicist, picked up on the pebble bed idea and spearheaded the building of a 15 megawatt demonstration reactor known as the AVR (Arbeitsgemeinschaft Versuchsreaktor) at the Julich Research Center in West Germany. The reactor was online in 1966 and ran for over twenty years before being decommissioned in 1988 because of the Chernobyl disaster plus certain operational problems that occurred at that time. The AVR was originally intended to breed uranium-233 from the much more abundant thorium-232, but the pebbles of the AVR contained the fuel so well that the transmuted fuels could not be economically extracted. The background radiation given off by the AVR was only one-fifth of that which would have been given off by a conventional reactor. Following this, a 300 megawatt thorium fueled pebble bed reactor was built in 1985 and operated for three years with over 16,000 hours of operations. It too was decommissioned as a result of the Chernobyl disaster, along with the consequences of a jammed pebble in a feeder tube that released radiation.

Although there were research activities in the United States and the Netherlands on pebble bed reactors, the baton of actual development passed to South Africa. In the mid-1990s, the national utility company, Eskom, petitioned to build a pebble bed reactor both for domestic use and for export. Opposition from the environmental group EarthAfrica effectively killed the ultimate objective of the program to build 20–30 165 megawatt pebble plants, each holding 450,000 pebbles to produce an aggregate output between 4 and 5 gigawatts of electricity. Though the South African development program for pebble bed reactors is still active, the baton of leadership has been handed over to China. The prototype pebble bed reactor HTR-10 fueled by 27,000 pebbles achieved initial criticality at Tsinghua University in 2003 under the leadership of Qian Jihui, a scientist. Based on the continuing successful operation of this prototype, two 250 megawatt pebble bed reactors are scheduled to begin construction in 2009 at the Shidaowan plant (Huaneng Power International) in Shandong Province for completion in 2013. These plants will produce electricity for the national grid and for cracking steam to produce hydrogen for fuel-cell powered motor vehicles. While China's massive expansion of nuclear energy will be primarily traditional pressurized water reactors, a small portion of the nuclear energy will be satisfied by pebble bed reactors. If successful in a commercial environment, pebble bed reactors are intended to fulfill a larger share of nuclear energy production.

A pebble is a tennis ball sized micro-reactor made primarily of graphite with a diameter of 60 millimeters. The outer 5 millimeters of the pebble is pure graphite. Within this graphite shell is a graphite matrix containing 10,000–15,000 microspheres of coated particles within which is the uranium fuel. The coated microspheres consist of an outer shell of pyrolytic carbon, then a barrier shell of silicon carbide, then inner shells of pyrolytic carbon and a porous carbon buffer. Within these shells in the center of the microsphere is the enriched uranium-235 or some combination of thorium and plutonium with unenriched uranium, or MOX (a mixture of uranium and plutonium) from reprocessing conventional nuclear fuel assemblies or decommissioned nuclear weapons. Any release of radioactivity from a coated particle would be extremely small.

The primary safety feature of a pebble bed reactor is its low fuel density with a power density only one-thirtieth of that of a pressurized water reactor. The reactor is inherently safe when there is a total loss of coolant—no core meltdown occurs as in a pressurized water reactor. A loss of coolant causes the pebbles to heat up to a maximum temperature of 1,600 degrees Centigrade, well below that of the 2,000 degrees Centigrade needed to melt the ceramic coating surrounding each bit of fissionable fuel. As the pebbles heat up, the frequency of fissions drops which lowers the power output of the reactor to a level where more heat escapes through the reactor wall than is produced by nuclear reactions. The reactor cannot crack, explode, melt, or spew hazardous materials—it simply remains at an "idle" temperature with the pebbles intact and undamaged. Known as passive nuclear safety, the reactor's low fuel density allows more heat to escape than is generated in the absence of coolant rather than having to depend on an active nuclear safety feature such as inserting control rods. The pebble bed reactor is inherently safer than traditional reactors. It is impossible to have a runaway reaction as occurred at Chernobyl by a sudden withdrawal of the control rods that caused the reactor to go supercritical or to have a partial core meltdown as occurred at Three Mile Island by a loss of coolant.

In order to ensure this inherent safety, the output capacity of pebble reactors is kept relatively small between 100 and 250 megawatts versus 1,650 megawatts for the EPR. Six or seven pebble reactors would be built at a single site for the same power output of an EPR. These increments in reactor capacity can be added at a central facility in response to growing demand obviating the building of a large facility that must operate at partial power until demand grows to utilize its full capacity. Alternatively, pebble reactors can be built at diverse locations for a more distributive form of electricity-generating system reducing transmission costs. The modular design of pebble reactors allows for mass production at a central location for shipment by truck or rail to the facility site. Modular construction of a single design at a central site can significantly lower construction costs and safety certification costs.

Criticality is achieved by loading several hundred thousand pebbles in a reactor. Helium, an inert gas, is heated by passing through the spherical pebbles to a temperature of 500° C (932° F) at a pressure of 1,323 pounds per square inch (psi). The helium can be directly fed into turbines that drive generators to produce electricity, but this exposes the turbines to low levels of radioactivity. An indirect system eliminates this problem by exchanging heat from the reactor helium with helium fed to the generators, but this adds to costs. Helium, being less dense than steam, requires larger-sized turbines. The energy output of the reactor is controlled by the flow of helium coolant passing through the pebbles. The higher temperature and lower pressure of a HTGR (high-temperature gas reactor) results in greater thermal efficiency (nearly 50 percent) than conventional reactors. As with conventional turbines, energy exchange is a function of the pressure drop across the turbine, which can be maximized by cooling the exhaust helium with air. It is possible that the hot helium exhaust from the turbines can be used as a source of energy to heat water via a heat exchanger and generate more electricity or be a source of hot water for industrial purposes. The cooled exhaust helium is then pressurized by compressors for recycling through the reactor. The lower operational pressure reduces the cost of protecting against pressure breaks and hydrogen embrittlement of the reactor vessel and components. Redundant safety systems found in conventional nuclear reactors are not required, and the core is far less radioactive. However, water and air must be kept isolated from the pebbles in the reactor as their presence with hot graphite would lead to a hazardous condition. The containment building must be capable of resisting aircraft crashes and earthquakes.

Inside the containment building is a thick-walled room containing the pebble reactor. Fuel replacement is a continuous process where pebbles are recycled from the bottom of the reactor to the top. The center pebbles are pure graphite to act as moderators to slow down and reflect neutrons into the pebbles containing fuel. The inner wall of the reactor container has a graphite lining to also reflect neutrons back into the reactor. A pebble will recycle through the reactor ten times over its normal three-year life and is examined and tested for integrity when removed from the bottom of the reactor. If expended of fuel or damaged, the pebble is removed to a nuclear waste area and replaced by a new one. Unlike spent fuel rods, it is exceedingly difficult to extract plutonium from a pebble. A 165 megawatt plant will produce about 32 tons of spent fuel pebbles per year of which 1 ton is spent uranium. Storage is easier than spent fuel rods from conventional reactors as no safety cooling system is needed to prevent fuel failure. A pebble reactor plant facility will have sufficient storage for spent pebbles to cover its forty-year operational life.

The potential cost savings in modular design where plant components are built at a single site for transport by truck or rail to the facility site is no longer restricted to the pebble reactor. The proposed Westinghouse (now a division of British Nuclear Fuels) AP600 design of 600 megawatts of electricity output represents the latest generation of light water reactors. The Westinghouse plant has a simpler design incorporating standardization and modularity to reduce costs. The plant has both passive and active safety means to shut down the reactor. The passive safety means depend on natural driving forces such as gravity flow, natural circulation, and pressurized gas to react to a hazardous condition with less operator intervention than active systems. Westinghouse is also offering an improved version of an existing design called System 80+, which has an output of 1,350 megawatts. Whereas Westinghouse is noted for its pressurized water reactors that require a steam generator to produce the steam that powers the turbines, General Electric is known for its boiling water reactors where steam from the reactor directly feeds the steam turbines. This eliminates the need for a steam generator but results in low level radioactivity of the steam turbines. As a result of General Electric's partnership with Hitachi and Toshiba of Japan, an advanced boiling water reactor of 1,350 megawatts of electricity generation has been introduced with improvements in efficiency, safety, reliability, and cost.

Thirty-two reactors are listed in twenty-three applications for new nuclear plants in the United States, six are the U.S. version of the EPR, fourteen are Advanced Pressurized Water Reactor manufactured by Westinghouse, two are Economic Simplified Boiling Water Reactors manufactured by GE-Hitachi, four are Advanced Boiling Water Reactors manufactured by GE, and the remainder are yet to be determined.

## FUSION POWER

Whereas fission is the splitting of heavy atoms, fusion is the uniting of light atoms. The sun and other stars produce heat when hydrogen atoms fuse to form helium, transforming matter into energy. Thus, for fusion to work on Earth, an environment equivalent to being in the center of the sun has to be created, requiring temperatures over 15 million degrees Celsius and pressures over 340 billion times greater than atmospheric pressure. Hydrogen fusion on Earth is obviously quite a technological challenge, but fusion of deuterium and tritium, isotopes of hydrogen, is less demanding than hydrogen. Deuterium can be extracted from seawater and tritium is a byproduct of fission. The challenge is to design a magnetic field strong enough to contain plasma, a heated mix of electrons and ions, under conditions conducive to fusion (100 million degrees Celsius, much hotter than the center of the sun, to compensate for the sun's much higher pressure).

Neutrons are produced when fusion takes place and become a source of heat when trapped in a stainless steel containment vessel wall. This heat is transferred to water to produce steam to run an electricity generator. Once fusion is triggered, it has to be controlled and kept self-sustaining by adding more fuel from a surrounding blanket of lithium in which neutrons react with lithium to produce tritium and helium. Leakage of plasma from the magnetic field is a major problem because this can stop the fusion process. So far, more energy (electricity) is consumed to maintain the plasma than is extracted from fusions. If and when this technical challenge is overcome, it is estimated that half of the electricity produced by fusion will be consumed to contain the plasma within the magnetic field.

The fusion process is inherently safe. A hydrogen bomb environment cannot be created because any "runaway" condition stops the fusion process by removing the plasma. The trick is knowing how to keep the plasma together long enough for fusion to occur. Alternative approaches to magnetic confinement as a means of trapping the hot plasma are lasers or particle beams. The energy source for fusion is virtually inexhaustible. Radioactivity is limited to high-energy neutron bombardment of the containment system. This radioactivity is short-lived (100 years) compared to the radioactivity of a fission reactor (thousands of years). An additional health hazard is the possibility of tritium leaking into the environment. Tritium, with a half-life of 12.4 years, is easily absorbed by the human body and, once ingested, remains a serious threat to human health for a long time. The advantage of the deuterium-deuterium fusion process is that no tritium is involved.

In 1989 there was great excitement over the possibility of cold fusion, creating energy in a test tube (so to speak), which turned out to be either a case of vain hope or scientific sleight of hand. The idea of cold fusion is trying to get back in the limelight. Researchers at a U.S. Navy laboratory announced that there is significant evidence of cold fusion (low-energy nuclear reaction) producing neutrons and other subatomic particles at room temperatures.[10] Research in nuclear fusion is being conducted in the United States, Russia, various European nations, Japan, Korea, China, Brazil, and Canada. In 2005, France was selected as the host nation for a $10–$13 billion experimental nuclear fusion reactor, the ITER (International Thermonuclear Experimental Reactor), to be funded by the European Union, the United States, Japan, South Korea, Russia, and China. Its goal is to produce 500 megawatts of power for hundreds or thousands of seconds at a time. Construction began in 2006 for completion in 2013. It may take as long as twenty-five years before an acceptable design for a commercial fusion plant can be developed.

The National Ignition Facility is a consortium of government and private organizations dedicated to creating conditions found in the cores of stars for fusion to occur. Housed in a ten-story building covering an area of three football fields, a spherical plastic capsule the size of a small pea filled with 150 micrograms of two heavy isotopes of hydrogen, deuterium and tritium, will be exposed to the combined output of 192 giant lasers of 500 trillion watts lasting 20 billionth of a second. For 10 billionth of a second, the capsule will be compressed to a density 100 times greater than lead and heated to 100 million degrees Celsius, hotter than the center of the sun. It is hoped that fusion will result producing ten to one hundred times the energy consumed. If this project is successful, the world energy problem will be potentially solved, but the solution will take time. The project would have to be scaled up to prove that fusion can safely generate enough energy for commercial electricity generation and fusion plants would have to go through the long drawn-out process of receiving permission to be built.[11]

## FUTURE OF NUCLEAR POWER

In spite of new plants under construction, most expect nuclear power output either to level off as older plants are phased out, something already in progress, or on a more optimistic note to maintain its share as a source of energy. Yet, at the same time, global demand for electricity continues to rise, although not as rapidly as in the past. In the 1950s annual growth averaged 8.7 percent, 7.3 percent in the 1960s, 4.1 percent in the 1970s, 2.6 percent in the 1980s, and 2.1 percent in the 1990s with a continued growth of about 1.8 percent per year. Even a modest 1.8 percent annual growth would require the addition of about 190 gigawatts of new electricity-generating capacity net of plant retirements per year out to 2030. Roughly 130 new electricity-generating plants of about 1.5 gigawatts each will have to be constructed annually to meet this demand.[12] Large plants of this order of output are invariably coal-fired or nuclear powered. There are plentiful domestic reserves of coal to meet the challenge, but coal has its environmental problems, unless clean-coal technology takes hold. Although wind will play some role, it is unrealistic to expect wind power to fulfill a significant portion of this shortfall in base-load demand.

It is difficult to imagine building this much electricity-generating capacity with no contribution from nuclear power. Moreover, the hydrogen economy will require large numbers of nuclear power plants to produce hydrogen through electrolysis of water. Producing the requisite electricity by burning fossil fuels defeats the whole purpose of the hydrogen economy, which is to do away with carbon dioxide emissions (unless they can be sequestered). The potential generation of electricity from carbon dioxide-free hydro, wind, solar, and geothermal energy sources is not even close to meeting the demands of the hydrogen economy.

The public should become aware that something has to be done before the lights go out. Those opposed to large electricity-generating plants, be they nuclear or coal, do not have a viable alternative other than wind and solar power. Certainly wind and solar power should be encouraged, but even here environmentalists have stopped the building of wind farms off the coasts of Massachusetts and Long Island. Yet no one, including the environmentalists, is advocating letting the lights go out. If nuclear power plants are to play a role in satisfying the demand for electricity, a technology should be selected that makes it possible to reduce capital costs by building a large number of essentially identical plants from modules built in a centralized manufacturing facility. The learning curve of building standard designed nuclear plants can generate further cost savings by eliminating the mistakes and inefficiencies associated with the construction of the first plants in a series. Siting and licensing have to be streamlined, and a cadre of well-trained operators has to be created. Having the same basic nuclear plant design would ease training requirements and allow operators to be easily transferred from one plant to another. Moreover, plants of a standard design are not only cheaper to build but also less expensive and safer to run because equipment, skills, and experience can be shared among the plants.[13] However, the problem of disposing of spent fuel has to be resolved and serious consideration should be given to reprocessing to reduce the quantity of radioactive waste and extend the effective life of uranium reserves. What is needed is public support for nuclear power, which can only come about if doubts over safe operation can be resolved.

The U.S. Energy Policy Act of 2005 provides significant incentives for ending the thirty-year moratorium on licensing new nuclear power plants. The most important is a 1.8 cents per kilowatt hour production tax credit for the first eight years of plant operation. This is a substantial tax credit, considering that the average U.S. retail price of electricity was 9.75 cents per kilowatt hour in January 2009.[14] A tax credit is not a cash subsidy, but a reduction in tax payments that the government would otherwise receive. The tax credit is for a maximum of 6 gigawatts of new plant capacity (six new plants of 1-gigawatt or 1,000-megawatt capacity) of not more than three separate designs. Financial support for certain specified delays caused by litigation or delayed Nuclear Regulatory Commission (NRC) approvals is also available. While the Obama administration initially included nuclear power and clean-coal technology in its green energy plan during the 2008 election campaign, both were surreptitiously dropped in 2009 from the green energy plan without public comment. Clearly, the future of nuclear power has shifted from the United States to China, India, and Europe.

## HYDROPOWER

Dams have a long history of supplying water to meet human needs. Ancient dams in Jordan, Egypt, Yemen, Greece, and Turkey were built to supply water for human and animal consumption, irrigate crops on land too dry to sustain agriculture, and control flood waters; the same purposes for building dams now. What is new is using hydropower to generate electricity. A few of these ancient dams have been in more or less continual operation for two or more millennia. The ruins of the Jawa Dam built around 3000 BCE still stand in Jordan. The Ma'rid Dam in Yemen in operation today was originally constructed over 2,700 years ago. Beginning in the first century, the Romans built a number of dams to impound river waters around the Mediterranean such as the Cornalvo and Proserpina dams in Spain still in service after 1,700 years.

Waterwheels turned by running water have lifted water for irrigation and ground grain since Roman times; a definite improvement over tread wheels operated by humans or animals. The first waterwheels were horizontal and drove a vertical shaft to rotate millstones that ground grain on a floor above the waterwheel. Vertical waterwheels were vastly superior to horizontal waterwheels because they could more efficiently translate the momentum of moving or falling water into power. Gearing was now necessary to change the direction of a rotating shaft from horizontal to vertical in order to operate millstones, something that different societies found not always technically feasible. Over the centuries waterwheels were applied to a variety of tasks such as sawing wood, crushing ore, stamping, cutting, grinding, polishing, and powering bellows to force air into a furnace to refine metals. In the 1680s, a large installation of waterwheels pumped water to supply the fountains at the palace at Versailles, France. Factories in England and New England, the first centers of industrialization, continued to be powered by waterwheels long after the invention of the steam engine. Waterpower had the virtue of being free, but steam from burning coal eventually overtook waterpower in the nineteenth century because steam could deliver a lot more power with greater reliability.[15]

There are 45,000 dams in the world with a vertical distance of fifty feet or more. These dams catch 14 percent of precipitation runoff, provide 40 percent of water for irrigated land and more than half of the electricity for sixty-five nations.[16] Many of these are in developing nations in Central and South America, Africa, and Asia. Central America is nearly fully reliant on hydropower. The Gilgel Gibe III hydroelectric dam being built in Ethiopia will rise 240 meters above the Omo River and have an upstream reservoir 150 kilometers long to accommodate the river's annual flooding. The dam will control the river's flow downstream of the dam and will produce 1.8 gigawatts of electricity, doubling the nation's generating capacity. When completed in 2012, the dam will solve Ethiopia's energy (electricity) problems and allow Ethiopia to become an energy exporter to Sudan and Kenya. The dam faces criticism over its potential environmental impact on Lake Turkana, the world's largest desert lake that depends on the river for 80 percent of its water inflow and on the people who depend on the river for their livelihoods.[17] Africa is home to two dams with the world's largest reservoirs: the Owen Falls Dam in Uganda whose reservoir goes by the name Lake Victoria and the Kariba Arch Dam on the border of Zimbabwe and Zambia whose reservoir is known as Lake Kariba.

One hundred and fifty dams are considered major in terms of generating electric power, reservoir capacity, and height. As a group they generate 40 percent of the energy produced by hydropower, but not all dams generate electricity. Some are built to provide water for some combination of human consumption and recreation, irrigation, and flood control. Flood control dams contain heavy rains and snowmelt to reduce flooding of low-lying areas such as those built by the Tennessee Valley Authority (TVA) in Appalachia. Smaller dams span rivers to allow navigation of larger-sized vessels. Ships sailing on major rivers, such as the Mississippi and its tributaries and the Danube, bypass the dams via locks that raise and lower a vessel to the height of the water on either side of a dam. Large vessels could not navigate these rivers were it not for these dams eliminating rapids and controlling the depth of the water.

Hydroelectric dams raise the level of water to create a hydraulic head to power electricity-generating turbines. Reservoirs compensate for fluctuations in the inflow and outflow of water. Inflow is determined by the amount of rainfall in a dam's watershed. Spillways and gates control the discharge of excess water from the reservoir while intake valves control the flow of water through a tunnel (penstock) to the hydraulic turbines that drive the electricity generators. Long-distance transmission lines are generally necessary as many dams are located far from population centers. A few hydroelectric dams have locks that allow ships to pass around them and others have steps, called ladders, to allow fish to get to and from their spawning grounds. Some small, low-powered hydroelectric dams are being dismantled as the economic benefit of restoring fisheries destroyed by the dam now outweigh the value of generated electricity.

The principal advantage of hydropower is that it utilizes a cost- and pollution-free renewable source of energy. However some environmentalists maintain that hydroelectric dams built in tropical regions contribute to carbon dioxide emissions since pre-existent forests now covered by their reservoirs no longer absorb carbon dioxide. Though hydropower has no fuel cost and a low operating cost, it has a high capital cost and is site-specific. Unlike fossil-fueled plants, hydropower dams are not built where they are needed. Prospective dam sites require ample supplies of water plus favorable geological conditions suitable for building a dam whose reservoir is sufficiently large with a bottom that limits water absorption. The capital cost of a dam includes the preparation of a site, the construction of the dam, and the installation of an electricity-generating plant and long-distance transmission lines. From a fuel standpoint, hydropower is environmentally friendly, but other environmental concerns still have to be addressed such as the impact of dams on fish and wildlife, resettlement of people living upstream of the dam, and the potential of catastrophic structural failure for those living downstream.

With tens of thousands of dams, some fail each year, mostly without catastrophic results other than local flooding. The 1889 Johnstown flood was caused by the failure of the South Fork Dam with a loss of over 2,200 lives. The rich folk living along the reservoir, which served purely as a recreational lake, did not bother to spend the money necessary to fix a deteriorating dam. Nor were they held financially responsible for the consequences of their neglect. In 1928, the two-year-old St. Francis Dam in California failed, leaving more than 450 dead. This occurred twelve hours after the builder (always a good source for an unbiased opinion) declared the dam safe, even though water was passing through the dam in spots where it was not supposed to. The cause of the dam failure turned out to be the unsuitable geology of the site. In 1975, unprecedented rainfall caused the Shimantan Dam in China to fail and its floodwaters destroyed the downstream Banqiao Dam. The combined deluge of water and dam debris carried away other downstream dams and dikes, drowning over 85,000 people. In 1976, after seven months of filling the newly constructed Teton Dam in Idaho, with the reservoir only three feet below the spillway, three leaks were found: one at the bottom of the gravel-filled cement dam, another alongside one of its abutments, and still another about 100 feet below the top of the dam. Less than two hours later, the dam was breached and water poured through the dam. In a matter of hours the breach widened, carrying away a large portion of the dam and emptying a seventeen-mile-long reservoir over a wide area of Idaho with a loss of fourteen lives.

Heavy rainfall can cause dams to fail, but dams are also affected by a lack of rainfall or a drought that fails to replenish the waters they hold. The California energy crisis in 2001 was sparked by a drought in Oregon and Washington that curtailed the export of hydroelectricity to California. That same year Brazil suffered power disruptions from a drought that significantly cut hydroelectricity generation, the primary source of that country's electricity. Hydropower in Brazil and other nations with a high dependence on hydropower fulfills both base and variable load. Hydropower is amenable to satisfying variable power because its output can be easily controlled by varying the flow of water through the turbines. In the United States, base-load electricity demand is satisfied primarily with coal and nuclear power. A large coal-fired plant takes days to reach full power and days to shutdown. Since coal and nuclear power cannot handle quick changes to power demand easily, these plants generally run at full power to satisfy base-load demand while hydropower (despite its free energy) and natural gas primarily satisfy variable demand.

Unlike other forms of energy, electricity cannot be stored. Electricity capacity must be able to meet peak demand without consumers experiencing brownouts or blackouts. Batteries cannot store sufficient quantities of electricity to smooth out the operations of an electric utility by supplementing supply when demand is high and being recharged when demand is low. Hydropower provides a way to "store" electricity through pumped storage plants. These plants have reversible pump-turbines that pump water up to a storage reservoir during periods of low demand. During periods of high demand, water flows from the storage reservoir through reversible pump-turbines to generate electricity. Motors that pump water to the storage reservoir become generators to produce electricity. Pumped storage plants reduce variability in electricity demand by pumping water to the reservoir during periods of low demand and by generating electricity during periods of high demand. This increases the base-load demand and reduces the need to invest in costly peaking plants.

The first commercial site for generating electricity was New York City's Pearl Street station built by Thomas Edison in 1882. The plant produced direct current electricity from generators driven by coal-burning steam engines and was the progenitor of other plants to electrify the city. The second commercial site for generating electricity was Niagara Falls, where a hydropower plant built by George Westinghouse produced alternating current electricity. Construction of a tunnel to divert water upstream of the falls to a downstream power plant began in 1890. Commercial sales started in 1895, and the plant's generating capacity was continually expanded until the 1920s. With increasing availability of electricity generated from hydropower, industry rapidly developed along the Niagara River.

The first recorded public outcry over the environmental consequences of energy was the ban on burning coal in London during the thirteenth century. At the turn of the twentieth century, New Yorkers demonstrated against black smoke emissions from the early electricity-generating plants. While the environmental movement can be traced back in time to a number of such public outcries over polluted air and water, the major thrust that propelled environmentalism to the forefront of public awareness was a dam powered by one of the cleanest sources of energy.

## The Saga of the Hoover and Glen Canyon Dams

The Hoover and Glen Canyon dams mark the beginning and the end of a dam-building spree in the United States. When built, the Hoover Dam ranked first in the world in size and power generation. Although the Glen Canyon has the same electricity-generating capacity as the Hoover Dam, and is similar in size and structure, a few far larger dams were built in the thirty-year interim separating the two.[18] The Hoover dam was built during the Great Depression in the 1930s to jump-start the U.S. economy as were dams built in Appalachia under the Tennessee Valley Authority. Other major dam projects were the Shasta Dam across the Sacramento River and the Grand Coulee Dam across the Columbia River. The Shasta and Grand Coulee dams supply water for irrigation and flood control, but of the two only the Grand Coulee Dam generates electricity; more than twice the combined output of the Hoover and Glen Canyon dams.

The Hoover and Glen Canyon dams straddle the Colorado River, discovered by Coronado in

1540 in his quest for the fabled seven cities of gold (actually Cardenes, a member of Coronado's party, was the first to discover the Colorado River from the rim of the Grand Canyon). Coronado named the river after the Spanish word for "red," the color of the silt-laden river. Coronado did not explore the Colorado River; in fact, the Colorado River presented an insurmountable barrier to further exploration. Exploring the river would not take place for another 300 years, when a daring individual led the first recorded expedition down the river.

The Colorado River falls 14,000 feet from the Rocky Mountains to sea level in the Gulf of California and carries more silt than any other river in the world, including the "muddy" Mississippi. The original time estimate for Lake Powell, the reservoir in back of Glen Canyon Dam, to fill up with silt was 400 years, but this was subsequently revised to 1,000 years by later estimates of the silt-capturing capacity of other dams upstream of where the Colorado River enters Lake Powell. The primary advantages of the Colorado River from the point of view of dam building are that the river flows through a canyon whose geology is ideal for damming and through a region desperate for water. The disadvantage of the Colorado is its relatively low average water flow, which varies from a summer trickle to a springtide flood that carries away the snowmelt of a large area of the Rocky Mountains.

In the early part of the twentieth century, the original idea was to build a dam at Glen Canyon first, followed by three more downstream dams whose construction would be made easier by building the upstream dam first. The problem was that the Glen Canyon reservoir would serve Arizona, which had a small population at the time. Population growth was centered in California, and by the 1920s it was clear that further development hinged on having an adequate and dependable supply of water to support agriculture and urbanization. California politicians prevailed at deliberations as to where to build the first dam—it would be built at Boulder Canyon, whose reservoir water could be easily diverted to California. It was understood at the time that another dam would eventually be built to serve Arizona.

The name Boulder Dam stuck after the original site was changed to a better location in nearby Black Canyon, about thirty miles southeast of Las Vegas. Boulder Dam was renamed Hoover Dam in 1930 after the president who authorized its construction. In 1933, New Deal bureaucrats decided that the world's most monumental dam project should not be named after the president who presided over the onset of the Great Depression and changed the name back to Boulder. The dam was completed in 1936 and another six years were to pass before its reservoir, Lake Mead, was filled. In 1947, a Republican-controlled Congress under President Truman passed a law to reinstate the name Hoover.

Dams and other capital-intensive projects cannot be funded from private sources; too much money is at risk. The risk private investors shun is accepted by the government because the risk of loss can be spread among the taxpaying public. Moreover, government cooperation is needed for land condemnation to clear the way for the reservoir, particularly when much of the land is already in the public domain. The responsibility for dam building fell under the auspices of the Bureau of Reclamation of the Department of the Interior. "Reclamation" was interpreted to mean "reclaiming" unproductive land for agricultural use by building dams to provide water for irrigation. Earlier reclamation projects were financial failures because the revenue from growing crops on irrigated land fell far short of justifying the cost of building a dam. It was the discovery that dams could also generate electricity that changed the financial equation in favor of dam building. The Department of Interior was also the administrative home for the Bureau of National Parks Service, charged with preserving and protecting wilderness areas, and the Bureau of Indian Affairs, which establishes and administers American Indian reservations. One bureau built dams whose reservoirs, at times, submerged lands set aside by a sister bureau to preserve wilderness areas or by another to establish American Indian reservations. Talk about dichotomy of purpose!

There are marked similarities between the Hoover and Glen Canyon dams. Both generate 1.3 million kilowatts or 1,300 megawatts or 1.3 gigawatts of output, enough electricity to supply a U.S. city of 1 million people. Both rise 587 feet above the riverbed, although the Hoover Dam is taller by sixteen feet when measured from bedrock. Like most dams, both had huge tunnels built around the dam site to divert the waters of the Colorado River at full flood during Dam construction. These were eventually plugged when the dams were completed to start filling the reservoirs, although both have diversion tunnels to reduce excessively high reservoir levels. Each required the building of a new town for the construction workers, one that started out as a disorganized tent city at the Hoover Dam site and the other an equally disorganized trailer park at the Glen Canyon Dam site. Tents and trailers were eventually replaced by carefully laid-out company towns for the construction workers and both survived the completion of the dams as Boulder City, Nevada, and Page, Arizona.

The reservoir behind Hoover Dam (Lake Mead) holds two times the annual flow of the Colorado River; enough to irrigate 1 million acres of farmland in southern California and southwestern Arizona and 400,000 acres in Mexico, and supply more than 16 million people with water in Los Angeles and portions of Arizona and southern Nevada. Lake Mead is 110 miles in length with 550 miles of shoreline. The reservoir behind Glen Canyon Dam (Lake Powell) covers 252 square miles, is 186 miles long, and has 1,960 miles of shoreline. Considering the area and the length of Lake Powell, its average width can only be slightly over a mile of flooded canyons. Lake Mead was named after Elwood Mead, a commissioner in the Bureau of Reclamation. Lake Powell was named after John Wesley Powell, the one-armed Civil War veteran who in 1869 successfully led the first recorded expedition of ten men in four boats down the Colorado River. Although Powell did mention developing the area along with the need for preserving its natural beauty, what he had in mind in terms of development was far different than the development posed by the lake that bears his name. Mead is a fitting name for a dam's reservoir; Powell is not.

Both dams were built in a similar fashion—in blocks, the smallest being the size of a house. One-inch copper pipes for pumping refrigerated water through the wet cement were incorporated in the construction of the dam to speed up curing from an estimated 150 years to nineteen or so months. Most dams built before the Hoover dam were gravity dams; pyramidal in shape (thick at the bottom and narrow at the top), so that the weight of the dam held back the water. They were commonly cement or masonry on the outside and filled with rock or gravel. Arch dams of pure concrete or masonry, first built in the late nineteenth century, were thin in comparison with gravity dams. A gravity dam depends on its massiveness to hold back the pressure of the water in a reservoir whereas the arch dam transfers the pressure on the dam to thrust on the canyon wall abutments. The Hoover and Glen Canyon dams were an innovative combination of both the gravity and arch designs. Though curved, they are still pyramidal, thick at the base and narrow at the top. (A third type is the buttress dam where the face of the dam is supported by buttresses on its downstream side.) While similar, there are differences between the two. The intake towers at Hoover Dam were built on the canyon walls, and tunnels (penstocks) were cut through the canyon walls for water to flow to the turbines whereas the intake towers and penstocks were incorporated within the Glen Canyon Dam. One can drive across Hoover Dam, but there is a bridge for vehicle traffic alongside Glen Canyon Dam, whose construction was a feat in itself.

Parenthetically, Las Vegas was built on the electricity generated by Hoover Dam. The gangster Bugsy Siegel saw "easy-going" Nevada, with its legalized gambling, as a land of opportunity, and built the first gambling palace, the Flamingo. Bugsy saw before others that Hoover Dam could supply cheap and plentiful electricity for air conditioning and lights and water for casino fountains built in the middle of a hot, dry, inhospitable desert. The Flamingo was the first step in transforming a backwoods desert town into the gambling Mecca of the world and one of the fastest-growing cities in the United States.

Glen Canyon Dam, started in 1958, was completed four years later when the gates to the lower tunnel were closed to begin filling Lake Powell. While the reservoir was filling, much work remained. The generators and transmission lines had to be installed, and the tunnels that diverted the flow of the Colorado River had to be permanently sealed. The fill rate was slow because a minimum quantity of water must flow through Glen Canyon Dam to ensure an adequate supply of water to Lake Mead, which in turn supplies water to California and powers Hoover Dam's generators. With light snowfall in the Rockies in 1963 and 1964, Lake Mead was rapidly dropping while Lake Powell was hardly filling. The return of normal snowfalls sped up the fill, but a court injunction in 1973 temporarily stopped the filling of Lake Powell when its reservoir water was about to invade the Rainbow Bridge National Monument. A congressional law was subsequently passed that allowed water to flood land previously set aside as part of a National Monument, violating a prior agreement with environmentalists that allowed Glen Canyon Dam to be built. In 1980, seventeen years after the completion of the dam, Lake Powell was finally filled.

Hoover Dam was planned in the late 1920s in response to California developers who saw a lack of water as an impediment to further development of agriculture and urban areas. By harnessing a mighty river for the common good—making deserts bloom, lighting cities, and providing power to industry and commerce—Hoover Dam was "concrete" proof of America's engineering skill and industrial might. No one opposed the building of the Hoover dam. Supporters included the federal government via the Bureau of Reclamation, private construction companies, and California politicians and developers. Thirty years later the Glen Canyon dam was also viewed favorably by the same coterie of supporters, except the politicians and developers were from Arizona. But a new entity was involved: the first environmentalist group to capture the nation's attention, the Sierra Club.

The Sierra Club was formed in the late nineteenth century by John Muir, a naturalist, to preserve the Sierra Nevada Mountains in their original pristine condition. Ever interested in preserving nature, Muir persuaded Theodore Roosevelt to declare a portion of the Grand Canyon as a national monument, at the same time chiding Roosevelt for his habitual trophy-hunting of game animals. Sierra Club members were mainly conservative businessmen and academics dedicated to preserving the wilderness areas of the high Sierras. After Muir lost a fight to prevent building a dam on a national preserve in the Sierras, the Sierra Club vowed that they would never allow this to happen again—in the Sierras. The transformation of the Sierra Club to openly fighting for conservation and preservation of wilderness beyond the Sierras started in 1949 when the Bureau of Reclamation publicized its intention to build a dam across the Colorado in Dinosaur National Monument. This marked the beginning of a dramatic change in the makeup of the membership of the Sierra Club, from one of conservative businessmen and academics to a more politically active constituency that advocated the preservation of the wilderness and conservation of natural resources far beyond the high Sierras.

To its everlasting regret, the Sierra Club acquiesced to the building of the Glen Canyon dam on condition that no more dams would be built in national parks and that something would be done to prevent flooding the Rainbow Bridge National Monument. The ban on dams in national parks also included two more intended for the Grand Canyon between the Glen Canyon and the Hoover dams. These dams (Bridge Canyon and Marble Canyon) were to be smaller in size and less intrusive than their larger counterparts. They were intended to generate electricity to pump water over intervening mountains from Lake Powell to Tucson and Phoenix. With the agreement not to build these dams, a substitute source of electricity was needed. It was first proposed that a nuclear power plant be built (this was in the 1960s, when nuclear power was considered safe and cheap). In the end, the Navajo Generating Station was built near Glen Canyon with a 2.5 gigawatt output, about equal to the combined output of the Hoover and Glen Canyon dams. The plant, started in 1970 and completed in 1976, is fueled by Black Mesa coal strip-mined on Navajo reservation land and shipped in by rail. It is ironic that the environmentalists' success in preventing the building of two clean and sustainable hydropower dams led to the building of one of the world's largest coal-burning plants that spews carbon dioxide and other emissions into the atmosphere. It is also ironic that current attempts by environmentalists to dismantle Glen Canyon Dam ignore that Lake Powell draws far more tourists than Yellowstone and Yosemite Parks. The debate that continues to this day over Glen Canyon Dam has prevented any other large hydropower projects in the United States from moving ahead.

The building of the Glen Canyon dam marks a watershed in the change of attitudes toward large-scale industrial development. Once viewed as signs of the improvement of humanity's material well-being, dams became viewed as an irretrievable loss of wilderness. The Sierra Club gave birth to innumerable environmental groups dedicated to stopping not only dams but just about anything that can be stopped: from oil refineries in Texas to wind farms off the coasts of Massachusetts and Long Island. Environmentalists maintain that building one dam leads to the building of another because the industrial and agricultural development allowed by the construction of the first dam creates the demand for electricity and water to justify building a second, then a third, and a fourth, and so on until the entire wilderness is submerged in reservoirs.

This phenomenon of progress creating its own demand was first observed when Robert Moses built a parkway on Long Island to give New Yorkers easy access to the "country." Once built, so many New Yorkers moved to suburbia that the subsequent highway congestion created a demand for a second parkway. This opened access to other parts of Long Island, creating more urban sprawl, more road congestion, and the need for building yet another parkway until, presumably, all of Long Island would eventually be paved over. The same is true for power plants—building one allows a community to expand in population, commerce, and industry until there is a need for another. As one community experiences the economic benefits of a power plant, others copy it and the process continues until the nation is covered with power plants and the horizon cluttered with transmission lines. This is one of the chief complaints of environmentalists—progress continues until the last vestige of natural life is irretrievably lost. What the alternative vision of life under the rule of environmentalists would be like is left largely unanswered.

## Aswan High Dam

The environmental consequences of the Aswan High Dam best exemplify what environmentalists fear most—the consequences are largely unknown before something is built; once built, little can be done to counter them. The first Aswan dam, built in 1889 when Egypt was under British control, was to irrigate cash crops such as cotton. The height of the dam was increased in 1912 and 1933 to enhance its water storage capacity. The sluice gates of the original Aswan dam were opened during the flood season to let the floodwaters proceed unimpeded downstream. As the flood season neared its end, the sluice gates were closed, trapping water behind the dam for crop irrigation.

The Nile flood originates in the Ethiopian highlands, the source of the Blue Nile, during the monsoon season. Silt deposited by the floodwaters formed a thick, fertile layer of alluvium that made the Nile valley and delta one of the most productive agricultural regions on Earth. After the Egyptian revolt in 1952 brought Nasser to power, the Soviet Union sponsored the building of the Aswan High Dam, five kilometers long, one kilometer wide at its base, and rising 107 meters in height. This dam, called the Pyramid for the Living by President Nasser, permanently stopped the annual flooding of the Nile valley and delta.

The dam was supposed to be a major source of hydroelectric power for Egypt, but unfortunately this potential was never fully realized. Lake Nasser did not rise to its anticipated level because of its high rate of evaporation, the volume of water diverted to irrigate cropland, and possibly leakage through the reservoir bottom. Electricity was necessary, not only to supply the needs of the people, but also to provide energy for the production of fertilizer as a substitute for the alluvial deposits formerly left behind by the annual floods. The alluvial deposits were free, but fertilizer is not. In addition to affecting the productivity of the Nile valley and delta, agricultural land has been lost by erosion of the Nile delta by the Mediterranean Sea, which had previously been replenished by the annual inundations. Penetration of saline waters from the Mediterranean into the Nile delta further decreased productivity and reduced the local fish population. Agricultural land upstream of the dam, now part of Lake Nasser, was lost, along with the livelihoods for 120,000 Nubians, who had to be resettled, but this was more than made up by bringing into production other lands bordering on Lake Nasser.

There also appears to be a correlation between Lake Nasser's water level and earthquake activity. Some geologists feel that the weight of Lake Nasser is affecting underlying faults; a phenomenon that has been observed at other dam sites. The sediments that once fertilized the Nile delta now accumulate in the bottom of Lake Nasser, over time reducing the volume of irrigation water stored in the lake. The presence of large bodies of water behind dams can affect the local climate, although this can be benign. The Aswan High Dam has also been blamed for the spread of schistosomiasis, a parasitic disease that leads to chronic ill health that has also been associated with other large-scale water development projects. Where once the annual inundation of the Nile flushed the delta and river of snails that carry the parasite, now the snails are moving further upstream and affecting larger numbers of people.[19]

This avalanche of environmental objections over the building of the Aswan High Dam has to be counterbalanced by what the proponents say. They point out that the water in Lake Nasser saved Egypt from famine in 1972 and 1973 and maintained its agricultural output during nine successive years of drought between 1979 and 1987. Lake Nasser has provided irrigation for enough new land to be brought into cultivation and to partially support a doubling of the population; but not quite enough to prevent Egypt, once a net food exporter, from becoming a net food importer. Moreover, the dam protected the Nile valley from major floods in 1964, 1975, and 1988.[20]

## HYDROPOWER: TODAY AND TOMORROW

Hydropower once provided a significant portion of electricity-generation capacity in the United States (40 percent in 1920 increasing to over half during the 1930s). Since the Second World War, fossil-fueled and nuclear generating plants were built in large numbers, pushing hydropower to the background. North American hydropower development is now centered in eastern and western Canada. Hydropower plants in eastern Canada are built and operated by Hydro-Québec with 59 hydropower generating stations encompassing 560 dams and 25 large reservoirs with an installed capacity of 34.1 gigawatts.[21] The company has access to another 5.4 gigawatts of output at Churchill Falls plus 2.3 gigawatts of output from a nuclear and several conventional plants and another 1.8 gigawatts through purchase agreements with independent power producers including wind farm operators.

The company owns and operates a 33,000-kilometer transmission system with interconnections to other transmission systems in Ontario and Québec Provinces, the Midwest, Middle Atlantic,

Figure 8.4 **World's Largest Hydropower Producers** (Percent of Total Electricity Output)

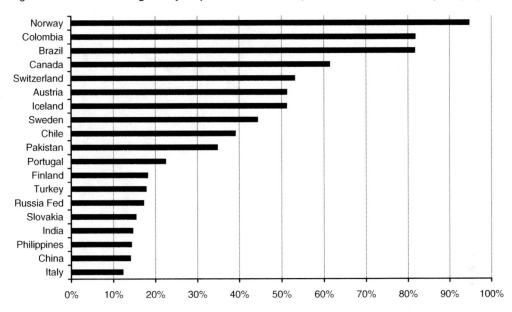

and New England states. This arrangement helps to even out the base load where the winter peak to heat homes and office buildings in Canada is balanced by a summer peak to cool homes and office buildings in the United States. The company has spearheaded technological advances in long-distance transmission to reduce transmission losses (an imperative considering the remote location of its hydropower plants), and shares its expertise by getting involved with hydropower projects in other lands. On the other side of Canada in British Columbia, BC Hydro, a government-owned company, produces 11 gigawatts of electricity of which 90 percent is hydroelectric at 30 integrated generating stations. Like Hydro-Québec, a significant portion of its electricity output is consumed in the United States.

The leading hydroelectric regional producers are Asia with a 29 percent share of which a 19 percent share is in China, Europe and Russia each with a 25 percent share, and North and South America each with a 21 percent share. Figure 8.4 shows those nations with the greatest dependence on hydropower for electricity generation.

Norway is almost entirely dependent on hydropower for electricity generation. Brazil, with a noteworthy 82 percent dependency on hydropower, had a national energy policy to become entirely dependent. In pursuit of this objective, the Itaipu hydroelectric power project was built between 1975 and 1991 with eighteen generating units for a total output of 14 gigawatts of electricity. This single dam complex has an output equivalent to about fourteen nuclear or large coal-power plants of 1,000 megawatts or 1 gigawatt each. Itaipu is a binational development project on the Paraná River between Brazil and Paraguay, not far from the border with Argentina, and provides 25 percent of the electricity supply in Brazil and 80 percent in Paraguay. The height of the dam is 643 feet (196 meters) with a length of nearly 5 miles (7.8 kilometers) and a reservoir 106 miles (170 kilometers) long. The dam has become a major tourist attraction as a construction marvel, much like Hoover and Glen Canyon dams. While being built, wet cement was refrigerated before pouring to decrease the setting time rather than installing refrigerated water pipes as was done at the Hoover and Glen Canyon dams. Whereas it took seventeen years to fill the Glen Canyon res-

Table 8.3

**World's Twenty Largest Dams in Terms of Electricity Generation**

| Name | Location | Rated Capacity (GW) | Built/Capacity Expanded |
|------|----------|---------------------|-------------------------|
| Three Gorges | China | 22.5 | 2009 |
| Itaipu | Brazil/Paraguay | 14.0 | 1984/1991/2003 |
| Guri–Simon Bolivar | Venezuela | 10.2 | 1986 |
| Tucurui | Brazil | 8.0 | 1984 |
| Grand Coulee | U.S. | 6.8 | 1942/1980 |
| Sayano-Shushenskaya | Russia | 6.7 | 1983 |
| Krasnoyarskaya | Russia | 6.0 | 1972 |
| Robert-Bourassa | Canada | 5.6 | 1981 |
| Churchill Falls | Canada | 5.4 | 1971 |
| Bratskaya | Russia | 4.5 | 1967 |
| Ust Ilimskaya | Russia | 4.3 | 1980 |
| Yacireta | Argentina/Paraguay | 4.1 | 1998 |
| Tarbela | Pakistan | 3.5 | 1976 |
| Ertan | China | 3.3 | 1999 |
| Ilha Solteira | Brazil | 3.2 | 1974 |
| Xingo | Brazil | 3.2 | 1994/1997 |
| Gezhouba | China | 3.1 | 1988 |
| Nurek | Tajikistan | 3.0 | 1979/1988 |
| La Grande-4 | Canada | 2.8 | 1986 |
| W.A.C. Bennett | Canada | 2.7 | 1968 |

ervoir, the Itaipu reservoir was filled in a matter of weeks—the water rose so fast that an intensive effort had to be made to save animals from drowning.

Brazil's dream of achieving full reliance on hydropower for generating electricity was shattered in 2001 when a severe drought lowered reservoir levels throughout the nation to the point of cutting electricity generation by 20 percent, causing widespread power disruptions and economic dislocations. Brazil is now pursuing a policy of energy diversification for electricity generation rather than total reliance on hydropower.

Dams are ranked all sorts of ways such as by height, reservoir size, and the material consumed in their construction. In terms of electricity-generating capacity, the Three Gorges Dam in China is by far the world's largest dam as shown in Table 8.3.[22] While currently at 22.5 gigawatts, the Three Gorges Dam will generate 25.6 gigawatts in 2011 when the whole project is completed.

On a global scale, hydropower supplied 18.5 percent of electricity between 1990 and 1997. Then a slow decline set in that reduced its contribution to 15.7 percent in 2008, which meant that other means of electricity generation were favored over hydropower. This trend may be reversed by hydropower projects in India and China. The potential for hydropower is enormous in both nations because their major rivers start 15,000 feet above sea level on the Tibetan plateau. The Indian government is a strong advocate of hydroelectricity as an alternative to coal-burning plants to reduce air pollution by utilizing a free source of clean energy. However, the government faces strong environmental opposition to its plans for hydropower and it is not clear how these projects will fare in the future.[23]

Three Gorges Dam on the Yangtze River stretches a mile (1.5 kilometers) across and towers close to 2,000 feet (600 meters) above the world's third longest river. Its reservoir will eventually cover land 350 miles upstream of the dam, forcing the resettlement of close to 2 million people. Its installed capacity of 22.5 gigawatts is the largest in the world, equivalent to twenty-three nuclear power plants, and will supply 6 percent of China's electricity needs. A system of locks allows ships to pass around the dam. The Three Gorges dam is also a flood-control measure for a river notorious for disastrous floods.

The benefit of flood control, along with the substitution of clean hydropower for dirty-burning coal in electricity generation, has made little impact on those opposed to the dam. Human rights organizations criticized the resettlement plans, archaeologists were concerned about the submergence of over 1,000 historical sites, and others mourned the loss of some of the world's finest scenery. Moreover, millions of Chinese downstream of the dam would be at risk if there were a catastrophic structural failure (memories of the Shimantan dam disaster still persist). The Three Gorges dam is but one project underway in China's quest to double its hydropower potential.

Large-scale dam projects are underway in Turkey at the headwaters of the Euphrates River to irrigate agricultural land, supply water to towns and cities, and generate electricity. These projects have strained relations with Iraq because the Euphrates is also the principal source for irrigation and drinking water in Iraq along with the Tigris River. Turkish dam projects have also spurred opposition from Kurds and other indigenous people who are being displaced by the reservoirs. Once fully operational in 2010, a grouping of five dams in Turkey and three in Syria have the potential to severely reduce the water flow to Iraq depending on the amount of water diverted for irrigation.

In mid-2009, what was feared most happened. The flow in the Euphrates River fell from 950 cubic meters per second to 230 cubic meters. Part of the decreased flow was blamed on the dams in Turkey and Syria plus the repercussions of a two-year drought, which also affected the flow in the Tigris River. Moreover, water-management practices in Iraq are generally poor resulting in wasteful consumption. The lack of water has destroyed a large swath of Iraqi agriculture and forced Iraq to import fruits, vegetables, and grain once homegrown. Poisonous snakes, losing their natural habitat in the reed beds, are now attacking cattle and humans. Desertification of once fertile land has begun. Although an appeal to Turkey to release more water was successful, Turkey is under no obligation to maintain the increased flow.[24] The problem of water flow will worsen with Turkey's plans to build the Ilisu dam on the Tigris, Iran's building of dams on tributaries to the Tigris, and Iraq's building of a 230 meter tall dam at Bekhme Gorge in a Tigris tributary in Kurdistan.

Another potential problem is the Nile River. Currently, Sudan is permitted 13 percent of the Nile flow with the remaining 87 percent for Egypt. Now other nations in the Nile basin (Burundi, Democratic Republic of Congo, Ethiopia—source of 85 percent of the Blue Nile— Eritrea, Kenya, Rwanda, Tanzania, and Uganda) want a share of the Nile waters. Some believe that access to water will be the next source of conflict between nations after oil. A water conflict has already erupted between Lebanon and Israel because some Israelis felt that a plan to divert the headwaters of a stream in Lebanon, used for irrigation and drinking water in Israel, was tantamount to an act of war.

Prospective sites for large hydropower projects are nearly exhausted in the United States and Europe. South America still has a great deal of potential that can be tapped as does Asia, the present world center of dam building. In contrast, mini and micro hydro plants are considered nonthreatening plants, not disruptive to people or the environment. Small may be back in style, but small dams lack the inherent economies of scale of megadams.

One potentially huge hydropower project under consideration is associated with the Dead Sea, 1,370 feet below sea level, the lowest spot on Earth. It is bordered by Israel and Jordan and the West Bank under the control of the Palestinian Authority. For thousands of years, the flow of the Jordan River was sufficient to replenish water lost to evaporation. Being "at the end of the road," the Dead Sea accumulates salts carried by the Jordan River. Whereas the world's oceans have a salinity content (salts of sodium, magnesium, calcium, potassium, and others) of 3.5 percent and the Great Salt Lake in Utah has a salinity of 27 percent, the Dead Sea's 33 percent is almost ten times that of ocean waters. Dead Sea waters are thought to have therapeutic properties and have an oily sensation. A person floating in the Dead Sea finds it hard to stand up and leaves the water caked with salt.

The problem is that the Dead Sea is no longer being replenished with water. The Jordan River and its tributaries have been thoroughly tapped by Israel, the Palestinian-controlled West Bank, Jordan, and Syria for the region's scarcest resource, which has cut the flow of the Jordan River by nearly 90 percent. What now flows into the Dead Sea is mainly sewage and other waste waters dumped into the Jordan River after its clean waters have been drawn off. Depending on where it is done, baptism by submergence in the Jordan River can be hazardous to one's health. The idea to build sewage-treatment plants to remove wastes being dumped into the Jordan actually worsens the problem. Once treated, the water would probably be diverted for irrigation, reducing the flow in the Jordan from a trickle to nothing.

With this massive diversion of water for irrigation, the Dead Sea is falling about 1 meter per year and its shoreline has retreated 500 meters over the last few decades, resulting in the loss of one-third of its area.[25] To counter this, the possibility of building a 108-mile (174-kilometer) system of canals and pipelines to bring seawater via gravity flow from the Gulf of Aqaba on the Red Sea to the Dead Sea has long been considered. Pipelines would siphon water over intervening highlands. Siphoning occurs when water leaves the pipeline at a lower elevation than where it enters the pipeline, eliminating the need for pumping. The end point of the Red-to-Dead project would be a hydropower plant with a hydraulic head of 500 or more meters, higher than most dams. The potential output of electricity, presently envisioned at 0.55 gigawatts, can be far larger depending on the flow of water from the Red Sea. Electricity generation can be partly dedicated to desalinizing water for human and agricultural use. The project requires the cooperation of Israel, Jordan, and the Palestinian Authority to arrive at a way of fairly sharing the electricity and desalinized water and its estimated $5 billion cost. The project has to deal with environmental objections over potential damage to coral reefs in the Gulf of Aqaba caused by diverting waters to feed the Red-to-Dead Project and potential chemical and biological consequences of pouring vast quantities of Red Sea water into the Dead Sea basin. On the other hand, doing nothing means another environmental calamity when, in about 150 years, continued evaporation transforms the Dead Sea into a supersaturated solution of salt incapable of further evaporation.

## NOTES

1. Information on nuclear reactors and other aspects of nuclear power from World Nuclear Association Web site www.world-nuclear.org/info/reactors.html.

2. Nuclear Energy Institute Web site www.nei.org.

3. *Federal Financial Interventions and Subsidies in Energy Markets 2007* (SR/CNEAF/2008–1, EIA, Washington, DC).

4. Edward S. Cassedy and Peter Z. Grossman, *Introduction to Energy* (Cambridge, UK: Cambridge University Press, 1998).

5. *World Energy Outlook* (Paris: International Energy Agency, 2008).

6. Figure 8.2 from World Nuclear Association Web site www.world-nuclear.org/info/reactors.html; Figures 8.1, 8.3, and 8.4 from *BP Energy Statistics* (London: British Petroleum, 2009).

7. The Generation IV International Forum Web site www.gen-4.0rg/index.html and the Nuclear Energy Institute Web site www.nrc.gov/reactors/new-reactors/col.html.

8. "Why the French Like Nuclear Energy" by Jon Palfreman Web site www.pbs.org/wgbh/pages/frontline/shows/reaction/readings/french.html; Areva NP Web site www.areva-np.com.

9. Pebble Bed Reactor topic in Absolute Astronomy Web site www.absoluteastronomy.com/ topics/Pebble_bed_reactor; safety issues from Web site web.mit.edu/pebble-bed/Presentation/ HTGRSafety.pdf; also, "A Future for Nuclear Energy: Pebble Bed Reactors" by Andrew Kadek (2005) and "Nuclear Power Plant Design Project" by Andrew Kadak and others (1998), Massachusetts Institute of Technology Web site www.mit.edu/pebble_bed.

10. "Scientists in Possible Cold Fusion Breakthrough," Newsmax.com (March 24, 2009) Web site www.newsmax.com.

11. National Ignition Facility and Photon Science Web site lasers.llnl.gov.

12. *World Energy Outlook* (Paris: International Energy Agency, 2008).

13. As a former engineering officer onboard a nuclear submarine, I could easily be transferred from one submarine to another because the reactor and steam-propulsion systems were essentially identical. There was only one plant layout and one set of manuals to learn for operating instructions and emergency procedures. Frankly, I always felt comfortable and secure with the power produced by a nuclear plant. It was safe, reliable, and gave me and other crew members confidence in a safe return (nuclear submarine casualties have been related to seawater pipe failures, accidental torpedo detonations, and navigational errors, not problems with the nuclear plant). The only time I felt nervous was when we secured the nuclear plant and ran on diesel power to ensure that the diesel engine would function if the nuclear plant became inoperative, which never (in my experience or knowledge) ever happened.

14. *Electric Power Monthly,* Web site www.eia.doe.gov/cneaf/electricity/epm/table5_6_a.html.

15. Vaclav Smil, *Energy in World History* (Boulder, CO: Westview Press, 1994).

16. Fen Montaigne, "Water Pressure," *National Geographic* (September 2002), vol. 202, no. 3, p. 29.

17. "Ethiopia: Ministers condemn Gibe III dam critics as Bank finalizes evaluation," Web site en.afrik.com/article15536.html.

18. Russell Martin, *A Story That Stands Like a Dam* (Salt Lake City, UT: University of Utah Press, 1999).

19. World Health Organization Web site at www.who.int/ctd/schisto/index.html.

20. International Commission on Large Dams Web site www.icold-cigb.net.

21. Hydro-Québec Annual Report for 2009 Web site www. hydro. qc.ca.

22. All-rankings.com Web site www.all-rankings.com/rank.php?r=82c27c146b.

23. An example of the opposition to hydropower projects is Friends of the River Narmada Web site www.narmada.org. For a rebuttal, go to International Commission on Large Dams Web site www.icold-cigb.net.

24. The Independent Web site www.independent.co.uk/environment/nature/as-iraq-runs-dry-a-plague-of-snakes-is-unleashed-1705315.html and Campbell Robertson, "Iraq, a Land Between 2 Rivers, Suffers as One of Them Dwindles," *New York Times* (July 14, 2009), p. A1; see also "Fertile Crescent will Disappear this Century" at Website www.newscientist.com/article/dn17517-fertile-crescent-will-disappear-this-century.html?DCMP=OTC-rss&nsref=climate-change.

25. Joshua Hammer, "The Dying of the Dead Sea," *Smithsonian Magazine* (October 2005), vol. 36, no. 7, p. 58.

# 9

# SUSTAINABLE ENERGY

This chapter discusses the meaning of sustainability and the principal sustainable energy sources: wind, solar, geothermal, and ocean (tidal, wave, and thermal). Their contribution to meeting world energy needs, along with their relative reliability compared to fossil fuels, will also be covered. Two sources of sustainable energy have already been dealt with: biomass in Chapter 3 and hydropower in Chapter 8. Some feel that nuclear power also qualifies as a sustainable energy source if reprocessing of spent fuel and breeding fuel can extend the life of uranium reserves for thousands of years.

## THE MEANING OF SUSTAINABILITY

Sustainability is a modern-day concept, but it has deep roots as expressed by the following quote from Thomas Jefferson:

> Then I say the earth belongs to each. . . . generation during its course, fully and in its own right. The second generation receives it clear of the debts and encumbrances, the third of the second, and so on. For if the first could charge it with a debt, then the earth would belong to the dead and not to the living generation. Then, no generation can contract debts greater than may be paid during the course of its own existence. (1789)

Actually, this refers to financial sustainability where the debts of one generation should not encumber the next. It is a poignant countermark to the trillions of dollars that have been piled on the national debt along with assumed government guarantee obligations, not only in the United States but throughout the developed world, to keep the global financial system afloat and prevent national economies from crashing. But is it fair for one generation to mortgage the future of several generations for its benefit? And how can layering of more debt on top of a system awash with debt that cannot be repaid by debtors be a sustainable solution?

Theodore Roosevelt provided his version of sustainability:

> The "greatest good for the greatest number" applies to the [number of] people within the womb of time, compared to which those now alive form but an insignificant fraction. Our duty to the whole, including the unborn generations, bids us to restrain an unprincipled present-day minority from wasting the heritage of these unborn generations. (1916)

The present population, representing a small minority of the generations that are to follow, should not waste the heritage given them by their forebears. This was best exemplified by Theodore Roosevelt's setting aside wilderness areas as national parks preserving the heritage of his generation for future generations.

Susceptible to becoming a buzzword with no precise meaning, sustainability was given a universally accepted definition in the 1987 Report of the United Nations World Commission on Environment and Development as:

> meeting the needs of the present without compromising the ability of future generations to meet their own needs.[1]

The concept of sustainable development can be pictured as being supported by three independent pillars: social progress, economic growth, and environmental improvement. Another view of sustainable development is three overlapping circles: society, economy, and environment, signifying the strong interdependence among the three. The latter view better exemplifies the holistic approach of sustainable development to influence human progress. Sustainable development should not be a single-minded focus on an individual issue such as population control, nutrition, preservation of ecosystems, conservation of natural resources, urban livability, redistribution of wealth, energy usage, economic progress, industrial activity, and pollution control. However, all of these may be elements of a sustainability development program. A sustainable society is not impossible. The Indians of the Americas with a population of tens of millions, kept in check by tribal warfare and short lives, had a sustainable society before the Europeans arrived. Indian culture and religion were concerned with preserving the ecosystem. Hunting animals, gathering wood for shelter and burning for warmth and cooking, and raising crops did not reduce the animal and plant population or the fertility of the soil. The Indians showed the Pilgrims how to fertilize naturally by burying a fish with each kernel of corn and helped them in other ways that ensured their survival.

The Aztec and Inca cities of Mexico and Peru were certainly livable and had no surrounding garbage dumps (the Conquistadors considered them engineering marvels of unimaginable beauty before putting them to the torch). Sharing material possessions without a sense of legal ownership or property rights obviated the need for redistributing wealth. This paradise, however, did not include all Indian tribes. The Aztecs taxed neighboring tribes so heavily, in addition to using them as a ready source of victims for human sacrifice, that they eagerly sided with Cortez. Without these tens of thousands of willing allies, and the ravages of European-imported smallpox (an unintentional example of biowarfare), Cortez would not have been able to bring down the Aztec empire. Nevertheless, Native Indian civilizations were sustainable, which meant they could have gone on forever. Indians view modern civilization as a temporary structure, intrinsically opposed to nature and ultimately unsustainable. As a Mohawk Indian leader once said, "Not until the last tree has fallen, the last river has been poisoned, the last fish has been caught, will man realize that money isn't edible!"

Without becoming a modern industrialized society, this is what happened on Easter Island as discussed in Chapter 1. When first populated, the earth was fertile to grow crops, animal life was plenteous, and palm trees provided more than enough nuts for food and logs for making canoes to fish in the surrounding waters. Generations passed with the earth maintaining its fertility, animal life its population, and palms their numbers. But, alas, came a day when the demands of a growing population caused fertility of croplands to decline along with the population of animals and the number of palms. Life on Easter Island was no longer sustainable. An ever-increasing population hastened the inevitable demise of a society that had no way to escape.

Haiti is a nonindustrialized nation that has become unsustainable. The only difference between Haiti of today and Easter Island of centuries ago is that the people can escape. Unsustainability is a growing issue in other nonindustrialized nations in sub-Saharan Africa plagued by disease, economic deprivation, and the anarchy of failed states. The population in a number of these states is falling—a true sign of an unsustainable society. Some maintain that the sustainability of the entire planet is threatened by consumption of irreplaceable vital resources of which fossil fuels are but one, and also include loss of topsoil and falling water tables affecting agriculture, destruction of forests removing a vital carbon sink, and "strip-mining" the oceans obliterating marine life. Pollution of the environment, species extinction, and growing stress among peoples and nations do not bode well for the future. All this can be linked to an expanding world population unwisely pursuing ultimately unsustainable objectives; but this is beyond the scope of this book!

Perhaps a better way to look at sustainability in a more restricted fashion is to examine sustainability programs. One such program established by Monmouth University (New Jersey) is first a commitment to renewable energy. A 454 kilowatt solar photovoltaic system was installed on four campus buildings—the largest such installation at an educational institution "east of the Mississippi." The installation will pay for itself in eight years primarily by a 60 percent subsidy by the state on the installed cost and by fixing the cost of a portion of electricity usage in an environment of steadily rising rates. Its environmental benefit over its 25-year life is a reduction in carbon dioxide emissions equivalent to planting 1,500 acres of trees, or the emissions savings of not driving automobiles 13 million miles, or taking 1,000 automobiles off the road. There is also avoidance of sulfur and nitrous oxide emissions by not having to generate electricity with coal. Besides this commitment to renewable energy, the sustainability program also involves energy conservation and efficiency such as lowering water heater temperatures, adding reflective material on windows and roofs to reduce the air-conditioning load, replacing mechanical equipment with more efficient models, and installing energy-saving light bulbs. Water-resource reduction includes installing water-saving devices and intelligent scheduling and application of irrigating water for lawns, plants, and shrubs. Waste management involves recycling of glass, aluminium, paper, and electronic devices; the use of biodegradable disposable service ware and "trayless" service in the cafeteria; energy efficient hand dryers to avoid paper towel waste; purchase of fuel-efficient hybrid vehicles; and participation in various EPA environmental stewardship programs. Committees of staff, faculty, and students have been established to examine opportunities to reduce energy demand through conservation and efficiency measures, increase the use of renewable energy resources, provide outreach programs to educate campus and community stakeholders in energy and environmental sustainability policies and practices, take actions to reduce greenhouse gas emissions, and measure and verify sustainability actions in terms of their success in meeting goals and in lowering operating costs. The driver in Monmouth University's award-winning sustainability program is an ongoing effort to reduce its carbon and ecological footprints. The elements of Monmouth's sustainability program are fairly common among other institutional programs.

Companies may have sustainability programs. Manufacturing is conducted in a way that minimizes greenhouse gas and other harmful emissions. The productive output of machinery and equipment is maximized through an effective maintenance program to reduce downtime and intelligent production scheduling for full utilization. Less machinery and equipment have to be purchased for a given output when a plant operates at full utilization. Maximizing product quality means that the product will last longer between replacements, reducing demand for material resources and energy. The product itself should emit less in emissions when in operation (if applicable). This is perhaps best exemplified by General Electric's locomotives and aircraft engines that operate with fewer emissions to reduce their environmental impact. Both in manufacturing and in product operation, emission reduction is achieved by greater energy efficiency. Cutting emissions by using less energy also cuts manufacturing and operating costs. Thus sustainability programs actually improve profitability by maximizing manufacturing and operating productivity and in enhancing sales through a product's energy efficiency, quality, and longevity.

Corporations are also embracing reverse logistics as a part of sustainability programs. An example of reverse logistics is a major retailer that sent all returns to a dumpsite. A company specializing in reverse logistics took over the handling of returns. Returned items were either sent back to the manufacturer for credit, repaired, or working components removed for resale to create value as a substitute for a loss. Using repaired items and salvaged components for resale also reduces the number that have to be manufactured. Companies that rebuild heavy construction equipment and diesel engines and recycle computers and other electronic products contribute to sustainability by cutting emissions associated with manufacturing new equipment and products. Corporate sustainability programs aimed at reducing their carbon and ecological footprints improve profitability just as institutional sustainability programs cut costs.

Housing two-thirds of the world's population, cities and towns are an important part of global sustainability. Increased urbanization will cause their share of global carbon emissions to grow from 70 percent in 2008 to 76 percent by 2030. Urban sustainability is focused on livability and on the reduction of a city's carbon and ecological footprints. The role model for urban sustainability is Europe, where cities tend to be more compact with much less urban sprawl than American cities. European cities generally rely more on public transport, bicycles, and walking rather than automobiles. They have greater control over land use and have a higher priority to improving the environment than cities elsewhere. Housing is diverse design-wise, not overly concentrated as in the monolithic high-rise rabbit-coop structures that plague many cities. Shopping areas, parks, and small city farms are interspersed in residential areas along with places of employment. Tree-lined roads are set aside for pedestrians and bicycles, and public transport systems rely more on trams than buses, essentially eliminating the need for automobiles. Historic sites are preserved rather than being bulldozed for high-density buildings.

Construction codes promote "green" urbanism by being less demanding on the environment in terms of consuming energy and generating waste along with encouraging architecturally attractive designs. Buildings with flat roofs may have either topsoil with gardens that act as insulation or solar panels for electricity or both. Zero-energy building designs, on balance, consume no energy by means of greater insulation, energy-efficient lighting and appliances, and solar water heating to reduce energy demand combined with solar panels and/or wind turbines for electricity generation. Zero energy means that the sales and purchases of electricity from and to a utility are about equal; that is, no net purchases of electricity. Industrial enterprises are designed to fit unobtrusively within city environs close to residential areas to allow employees to walk or bicycle or take a tram to work. The objective of urban sustainability development is for a city to become a self-contained unit, providing the economic means and the ecologically-desirable surroundings that allow residents to work and live within city limits on workdays and to rest and pursue leisurely activities on weekends. Urban sustainability is not a national or state program but a local program voluntarily undertaken by individual cities to improve their livability.[2]

Though European cities have been in the vanguard, they are not alone in reducing their ecological footprints as part of more encompassing sustainability programs. In 2005, the mayor of Seattle spearheaded the formation of the U.S. Conference of Mayors Climate Protection Agreement where cities pledge to reduce local greenhouse gas emissions to 7 percent below 1990 levels by 2012 as part of a wider program of urban sustainability. By 2008, 850 mayors representing 80 million Americans had signed the Agreement. In 2007, the mayor of New York City hosted the second C40 Large Cities for Climate Protection conference involving the world's forty largest cities and also spoke at the Bali Climate Change Conference on the role that cities can play in mitigating the effects of global climate change. Examples of city networks established for pursing sustainability goals are the Nottingham Declaration Partnership (U.K.), Partners for Climate Protection (Canada), Network of Cities for Climate (Spain), Kyoto Club (Italy), and Coalition of Local Governments for Environment Initiative (Japan). Individual cities have announced climate-change policy targets within more encompassing sustainability programs such as Toronto's 80 percent reduction of emissions from 1990 levels by 2050, London's 60 percent reduction from 1990 levels by 2025, Bristol (U.K.) 60 percent reduction from 2000 levels by 2050, Berkeley (U.S.) 33 percent reduction from 2000 levels by 2020, Tokyo's 25 percent reduction from 2000 levels by 2020, and Paris' 25 percent reduction from 2004 levels by 2020. San Jose (U.S.) plans to have all its electrical power from renewable energy sources within fifteen years and intends to take advantage of this demand to create new jobs in solar energy and make San Jose a center for companies pursuing clean technologies.

China's percentage of urbanization will increase from 40 percent to 60 percent by 2030. Its 11th Five-Year Plan calls for a 20 percent energy-intensity reduction by 2010. This effort is spearheaded at the national and provincial level, not at the city level, reflecting China's preference for centralized authority. With intense competition among cities to attract investment, city governments are taking the initiative to address concerns about energy security and local air pollution by limiting the role of coal, promoting industrial structural change from primary to less-polluting, more energy efficient, secondary industries, and improving public transport. Some Chinese cities are trying to develop low-carbon environments and new cities such as Dontang Eco-City, near Shanghai, are being built with an emphasis on clean energy and a clean environment as part of sustainability programs. A local air pollution control policy was effective in preparing for the 2008 Beijing Olympics. Following Beijing's example, Shanghai established emission-control measures to improve its air quality by prohibiting highly polluting motorcycles on its main thoroughfares, restricting the number of vehicle licenses, and taking action to develop public transport to enhance its future sustainability as a major world city.[3]

Sustainable development is not limited to reducing the ecological footprint of institutions, companies, and population centers in the developed world. In some respects, sustainable development will increase mankind's ecological footprint by its concern for the have-nots of the world: the 1.3 billion people without access to clean water, the 2 billion people without access to electricity, the 3 billion people (half of humanity) without access to adequate sanitation and who earn less than $2 per day. Sustainable development is also concerned with the inequality of wealth distribution where the top 20 percent of the world's population account for 86 percent of consumption, and the bottom 20 percent account for only 1.3 percent.[4]

Sometimes, improving the living standards of the world's poor as part of a sustainability development program can have undesirable consequences. Some years ago, women in India had to manually haul drinking and cooking water from wells until rural electrification allowed small electric water pumps to be installed that eased their plight. Then it was discovered that the water could also be used for irrigation to improve agricultural crop yields, but this required installing large water pumps. Reducing the manual workload for women and improving agricultural output are admirable goals in terms of sustainability development. But irrigation expanded to the point of being the largest consumer of electricity in the agricultural sector, which of itself accounts for nearly half of India's electricity consumption, much of which is powered by burning coal.[5] Along with the unfortunate consequence of added carbon emissions is a falling water table measured in hundreds of feet—a harbinger to a water crisis with a food crisis in its shadow.

Concerns about encouraging a sustainable society were first voiced at the 1992 Rio Earth Summit attended by 152 world leaders, but no real action plan to pursue sustainability was initiated in its aftermath. The follow-on 2,500-page 2005 Millennium Ecosystem Assessment concluded that the world faces a bleak future in meeting the goals of sustainability by various measures including the growing inability of nature to purify the amount of air and water polluted by mankind, the massive wave of species extinctions, and the general lack of progress in moving towards a sustainable world.

Focusing on the concept of sustainability with regard to energy, a sustainable source of energy should be renewable and environmentally benign. Though not environmentally benign, some consider nuclear power with reprocessing as a sustainable energy source. To be fair, no renewable energy source is entirely environmentally benign—even wind has its opponents who are concerned with bird kills, wind turbine noise, and the despoiling of the natural landscape. While sustainable energy sources may seem inexhaustible, there are capacity limits in terms of the number of wind turbines and solar panels just as there are capacity limits in the number of coal-fired generation plants. Growth in capacity is limited by capital, manufacturing and construction constraints, and an equally important constraint in the form of the willingness of society to build more capacity.

Biomass is a sustainable source of energy as long as a crop is grown, burned for its energy content, and replaced by another. Under these conditions, there is no net addition of carbon dioxide to the atmosphere because the carbon dioxide released from burning is absorbed in growing the replacement crop. But as noted in Chapter 3, ethanol from corn in the United States consumes about as much fossil fuel as the amount of ethanol produced and provides, at best, marginal reduction in carbon emissions while ethanol from sugar in Brazil effectively reduces fossil-fuel demand. Biomass is limited by the availability of arable land for raw materials. Deforestation for food and nonfood crops adds carbon dioxide to the atmosphere as more biomass is burned than is replenished and is not sustainable; at some point, the forests are gone. Biofuel crops that displace tropical forests have less capacity to absorb carbon dioxide even after taking into account the savings in biofuel carbon emissions. Since biomass, nuclear, and hydro as renewable energy sources have been covered in previous chapters this chapter concerns itself with alternative and renewable energy sources of wind, sun, heat within the earth (geothermal), and the movement of water (tides, currents, and waves).

A major difference between conventional and renewable sources of energy (other than geothermal) is reliability. Electricity can be generated at the dispatcher's whim up to a plant's rated capacity for a generator fueled by fossil and biomass fuels, nuclear power, and geothermal energy. This is not true for other sources. Hydropower depends on rainfall, which affects the water level behind a dam. Wind and solar power depend on whether the wind is blowing or the sun is shining. Though tidal energy is predictable, there is no guarantee that peaks in electricity generation coincide with peaks in electricity demand. Wind, solar, tidal, and wave sources can certainly be tied into an electricity distribution grid and contribute to the electricity pool "weather permitting," but they can only displace, not replace, conventional sources of energy unless backup sources of standby power are available to guarantee their reliability.

## WIND ENERGY

Wind results from differences in air temperature, density, and pressure from the uneven solar heating of the earth's surface. Like ocean currents, wind currents act as giant heat exchangers, cooling the tropics and warming the poles. Successful placement of wind turbines are in areas with persistent winds such as where geological formations force wind to flow through relatively narrow mountain passages as in California or along the east side of the Rockies, making the northern plain states ideal for wind turbines. Another area of desirable wind patterns are along coastlines where, during the day, air above land heats up more quickly than air over water causing a sea breeze of heavier, cooler air over water rushing in to take the place of rising warmer air over land. At night, a land breeze results from air cooling more rapidly over land than over water. Coastlines and offshore waters are high on the list for wind-development projects to take advantage of their fairly reliable wind patterns.

**Historical Development**

The history of wind as an energy source goes back to the dawn of history. Around 5000 BCE, the ancient Egyptians employed boats fitted with sails to move goods up and down the Nile River. The Phoenicians later adapted the sail for a more vigorous marine activity of trading between Mediterranean ports. Despite the apparent advantage of sail as a means of moving goods, it took millennia for wind power to replace those who performed what must have been the most tiring and tedious of jobs: that of oarsmen. Eventually, sail became the ubiquitous means of transport throughout the world until the appearance of coal-fired merchant ships in the nineteenth century. Their chief advantage over sail was being capable of keeping to a schedule. The Clipper ships were a dying technology's response to progress with the thought that speed would be a competitive edge over slower moving coal-fired vessels. But alas, speed was contingent on the wind blowing in the right direction. The 1869 opening of the Suez Canal was the death knell to Clipper ships on the Pacific tea trade as now slower, but steady-speed coal-fired merchant ships had a much shorter route to ply between Europe and Asia (sailing vessels had a difficult time navigating the narrow Suez Canal and had to pass around Cape of Good Hope to reach the Pacific). The era of the Clipper ship lasted only a few decades. Interestingly, the subject of sail-assisted merchant vessels has been revived in recent years whenever the cost for bunkers (ship's fuel), reflecting spikes in oil prices, consume half or more of voyage revenue. Sail is still used in the Middle East, Africa, and Asia for commercial fishing and local trade.

The first land-based windmills were developed in Persia and the Middle East around 500–900 CE (although there is a claim that China used wind power to pump water as early as 200 BCE).[6] These early windmills employed woven reed or wooden sails, adapted from sailing vessels, to either grind grain or pump water. Grinding grain requires a horizontal grinding stone that must be driven by a vertical axis. Early windmills with sails powered vertical shafts of reed bundles or wood. (Sail-powered vertical axis windmills can be found today in Crete pumping water for crops and livestock.) Returning merchants and crusaders from the Middle East and Persia brought the idea of the windmill to Western Europe. This evolved from a vertical-axis design to the more efficient horizontal-axis configuration for capturing wind energy, but this also required gearing to translate the motion of a horizontal axis to a vertical axis to drive a grindstone. The earliest illustration of these windmills, dating back to 1270, shows a four-bladed mill mounted on a central post or post mill with wooden cog-and-ring gears to translate the motion of the horizontal shaft to a vertical shaft to turn a grindstone. In 1390, the Dutch refined the design of the windmill with a horizontal post mill at the top of a multistory tower, which was translated to a vertical post mill that passed through separate floors for grinding and removing chaff and storing grain, with the bottom floor serving as living quarters for the wind-smith and his family. This refined windmill was also adapted for draining lakes and marshes in the Rhine River Delta to expand agricultural land, and later, with the building of dikes, to create a nation by taking land away from the sea. Holland had 8,000 windmills in 1650, England 10,000 windmills in the early 1800s, and Germany more than 18,000 windmills in the late 1800s.[7]

The process of perfecting the windmill sail and in making incremental improvements in efficiency and reliability took about 500 years. By the time the process was complete, windmill sails had all the essential features incorporated by designers of modern wind turbine blades. Windmills in Europe were eventually replaced with the convenience and reliability of coal-fired steam engines.

In the United States, windmills for pumping water were perfected during the nineteenth century beginning with the Halladay windmill in 1854 and continuing on with the Aermotor and Dempster designs still in use today. The original mills had thin wooden slats nailed to wooden rims with tails to orient them into the wind. An important refinement of the American fan-type windmill was the development of steel blades in 1870, which allowed for a more efficient and lighter design. Between 1850 and 1970, over six million small (1 horsepower or less) mechanical output wind machines were pumping water for livestock and home use.[8] Large windmills with blades up to 18 meters (59 feet) in rotor diameter (the circle swept by the tip of the blades) supplied the large water requirements of steam locomotives where water had to be pumped from below ground.

The wind turbine is the opposite of a fan. A fan consumes electricity to power a motor that turns a rotor with attached blades to move air. In a wind turbine, moving air turns the blades attached to a rotor that drives a generator. The first windmill to generate electricity was built in Cleveland, Ohio, in 1888 by Charles F. Brush. The Brush wind turbine had a post mill with a multiple-bladed rotor 17 meters (56 feet) in diameter and a large tail hinged to orient the rotor properly to the wind. A step-up gearbox turned a direct current generator at its required operational speed. This design did not work well and in 1891, the Danish entrepreneur, Poul La Cour, improved the design and developed the first electricity-generating wind turbine of 25 kilowatt (kw) output with four-bladed airfoil shaped rotors. The higher speed of the La Cour rotor made these machines practical for electricity generation. By the end of the First World War, cheaper and larger fossil-fuel steam plants started to replace the electricity-generating wind turbines that dotted the Danish landscape. By the mid-1920s, small electricity-generating wind machines (1–3 kw), developed by Parris-Dunn and Jacobs Wind-Electric, were popular in the Midwest and Great Plains to provide lighting for farms and charge batteries for powering crystal radio sets. Electricity from these wind turbines soon began to power an array of direct current motor-driven appliances including refrigerators, freezers, washing machines, and power tools. However, their sporadic operation when the wind ceased blowing was a problem. In the 1930s, the Great Depression spurred the federal government to sponsor the Rural Electrification Administration's program to stimulate depressed rural economies by extending the electricity grid throughout rural America, ending the days of wind-generated electricity. (History likes to repeat itself, but with a twist. One of the Obama administration's programs to stimulate the economy is the extension of transmission lines to isolated areas with persistent winds to promote wind-generated electricity or to areas with lots of sunlight to generate solar electricity.)

The development of bulk-power, utility-scale wind energy conversion systems was first undertaken in Russia in 1931 with the 100 kw Balaclava wind generator. This wind turbine operated for about two years on the shore of the Caspian Sea. Subsequent experimental efforts in the United States, Denmark, France, Germany, and Great Britain between 1935 and 1970 demonstrated that large-scale wind turbines worked, but they failed to produce a large practical electric wind turbine. In 1945, the largest wind turbine was the Smith-Putnam machine installed on a Vermont hilltop called Grandpa's Knob. This horizontal-axis design featured two-blades with 175-foot rotor diameter and generated 1.25 megawatts (MW) in winds of about 30 mph. Its power was fed to the local utility network, but after only several hundred hours of intermittent operation one of the blades broke off near the hub from metal fatigue, ending its life.

European developments continued after the Second World War when temporary shortages of fossil fuels led to higher energy costs. In Germany, Professor Ulrich Hutter developed a series of advanced, horizontal-axis designs of intermediate sizes that utilized modern, airfoil-type fiberglass and plastic blades with variable pitch to provide lightweight and efficient generation of electricity. This design sought to reduce bearing and structural failures by "shedding" aerodynamic loads rather than "withstanding" them. Hutter's advanced designs achieved over 4,000 hours of operation before the experiments were ended in 1968. In France, G.J.M. Darrieus began the development of vertical-axis rotors in the 1920s comprised of slender, curved, airfoil-section blades attached at the top and bottom of a rotating vertical tube resembling an eggbeater. The research ceased until two Canadian researchers took on major development work in the late 1960s.

## Government Involvement in Developing Wind Turbines

The popularity of using the energy in the wind has always fluctuated with the price of fossil fuels. Interest in wind turbines waned when fuel prices fell after the Second World War, but revived when oil prices skyrocketed in the 1970s. The U.S. federal government's involvement in wind energy research and development (R&D) began in earnest within two years after the 1973 oil crisis to refine old ideas and introduce new ways of converting wind energy into useful power. Many of these approaches were demonstrated in wind farms, a grouping of wind turbines located in a single area that fed electricity into a utility grid. Despite the speed with which it was initiated and the early show of promising results, this program ultimately proved to be ineffective with the withdrawal of government funding before final success could be achieved.

Nevertheless, other federal R&D activities such as at Sandia National Laboratories resulted in the design, fabrication, and testing of thirteen different small wind-turbine designs (ranging from 1–40 kw), five large (100 kw–3,200 kw or 3.2 MW) horizontal-axis turbine (HAWT) designs, and several vertical axis (VAWT) designs ranging from 5 to over 500 kw. Most of the funding was devoted to the development of multimegawatt turbines in the belief that U.S. utilities would not consider wind power to be a serious power source unless large, megawatt "utility-scale" turbines were available. Wind turbine development in the United States progressed from blade lengths of 5 to 10 to 17 meters (16 to 33 to 56 feet). The latter machine, commercialized by FloWind, used much of the technology developed by Sandia National Laboratories, but a real market for this technology never emerged.

While Canadian development was focused on a 4 megawatt (MW) Project Eole turbine on Magdalen Island in the St. Lawrence River, the National Aeronautics and Space Administration (NASA) Plum Brook Ohio facility became involved with wind turbines and started development of the 100 kw MOD-0 in 1975, and rapidly moved through several generations including the MOD-1 and the 100-meter (328-foot) diameter MOD-2 wind turbines. The program was plagued by not realizing the importance of "teetering" hubs essential for reducing dynamic loads in two-bladed machines created by the tower shadow. After initial failures, the first "real" NASA wind turbine was the MOD-2. Three of these machines operated for several years providing valuable engineering data to pinpoint and correct several design weaknesses. Unfortunately, these pitfalls were all that were needed to provide detractors with enough ammunition to end the program in 1981. Nevertheless, lessons learned on the MOD-2's were incorporated in the huge 3.2 MW MOD-5B wind turbine at the Makani Moa'e wind farm in Kahuku, Oahu, operated by Makani Uwila Power Corporation. The wind turbine had two blades with a rotor diameter of 320 feet and was the largest-sized wind turbine in the world until a few years ago when 3.6 MW turbines became commercially available. Wind turbines are getting larger in capacity to take advantage of economies of scale with the next generation of 5 megawatt turbines already in their testing phase.

Another federal effort started in 1976 was to develop a reliable wind turbine to perform as envisioned in a federal wind-application study. Within four years, thirteen wind-turbine designs were developed for five size-range categories including 1–2 kw High Reliability, 4 kw Small Residential, 8 and 15 kw Residential and Commercial, and 40 kw Business and Agricultural. This development work led to the 1–3 kw and 6 kw small wind turbines commercialized by Northern Power Systems and still being sold for remote power users and a three-bladed 40–60 kw wind turbine installed by the hundreds in California wind farms by Enertech. Wind farms in California were the vanguard in commercializing wind energy and were the result of both R&D efforts undertaken by the federal government and financial incentives established by the Public Utility Regulatory Policies Act (PURPA) of 1978. This Act required state regulatory commissions to establish procedures for nonutility companies to sell electricity to utilities generated from renewable energy sources, waste, and cogenerating plants run on natural gas. California state regulators, fearing that oil-fueled electricity-generating plants would be vulnerable to falling oil production in California and Alaska, were particularly aggressive in carrying out PURPA provisions. They required California utilities to buy electricity generated from wind farms at a premium over conventional sources to induce the development of wind energy. As a result, California would eventually become the home of over 17,000 wind turbines, which produce individually between 50–600 kw of electricity. For a measure of scale, a single wind turbine producing 600 kilowatts or 600,000 watts can generate enough electricity for 6,000 100-watt light bulbs. Major California wind farms are located at the mountain passes that experience persistent winds much of the time such as the Altamont Pass east of San Francisco, Gorgonio Pass near Palm Springs, and at Tehachapi south of Bakersfield. Wind farms in California made up most of U.S. wind turbine installations until the early 1990s. At the height of their power potential, these turbines had a collective rating of over 1,700 megawatts (1.7 gigawatts), sufficient in the United States to supply a city of 1 million people—but only when the wind was blowing at all their various locations. Fortunately, periods of high winds over the coastal hills correlated fairly well with timing of high commercial and residential air-conditioning loads in the summer. The key subsidies making wind-turbine investments financially attractive were a 15 percent federal energy credit, a 10 percent federal investment credit, a 50 percent California state energy credit, and a high electricity rate mandated by state regulators that had to be paid by utilities for electricity produced from alternative sources. The high rates paid for electricity produced by wind farms and the subsidy benefits provided by the federal and state governments were neatly packaged into investment products by private financial firms to garner the necessary capital from individuals and companies to build California's wind farms.

The beneficiaries of the heavy federal wind-energy funding programs were supposed to be the large U.S. aerospace and construction firms developing the MOD-2, MOD-5, and the intermediate sized MOD-6 wind turbines. But an increase in military expenditures reduced the interest of aerospace firms in risky new business challenges like wind turbines. The "counter-culture" wind-energy entrepreneurs at Rocky Flats, Colorado, founders of the American Wind Energy Association in the mid-1970s, became the driving force in the development of wind turbines. Unfortunately, a combination of design problems, the Reagan administration's attitude toward deregulation, and a period of low oil prices removed the incentives to pursue renewable energy sources and the wind energy business slowed considerably in the 1980s.

Nevertheless, there was still activity. In contrast to American companies that pursued two-bladed wind turbines, Danish firms developed three-bladed wind turbines based on the Gedser mill design. The design, considered somewhat primitive and inefficient, but well understood, was modernized with fiberglass blades. By 1986, the Danes captured 50 percent of the U.S. wind farm market replacing hundreds of inoperable U.S. turbines cluttering the California landscape. Design shortcomings became apparent when high California wind loads began to pulverize the poorly manufactured Danish blade roots, requiring an expensive "fix" for thousands of turbines. Even though wind farm operators were weighed down with high maintenance costs and constant repairs to keep their wind turbines running, the U.S. wind farm demand for new intermediate-size wind turbines was still alive. Then the wind farm operators were hit with the end of the federal energy credits in 1984 and the phase-out of California state credits shortly thereafter. Fortunately for the wind farm operators, California utilities were required to maintain artificially high buyback rates for the output of wind turbines into the 1990s, when many of the wind turbines had long since been paid off, thus making investments in wind turbines quite profitable. Although sales of small wind turbines during this period were slow, the volume was sufficient to provide business for several manufacturers of wind turbines designed for water pumping and electricity generation at remote locations such as Southwest Wind Power and Bergey Windpower. In general, however, the U.S. market lagged and gradually declined during the 1980s and into the 1990s.

**From Tiny Acorns to Mighty Oaks**

During this period, wind-turbine installations increased steadily in northern Europe. Denmark was the leader, drawing on its earlier role in wind energy. The higher cost of electricity and excellent wind resources in northern Europe created a small but stable market for single and cooperative-owned wind turbines. Driven by high utility power rates for wind power, the installation of 50 kw turbines rapidly gave way to 100 kw, then 200 kw, then 500 kw, and now 1.5 megawatt wind turbines by cooperatives and private landowners in the Netherlands, Denmark, and Germany. The installation of over 70,000 megawatts (70 gigawatts) of European wind capacity by 2009 supports a thriving private wind-turbine development and manufacturing industry.

In the 1990s, robust wind-development activity in Europe contrasted with the U.S. penchant for low utility rates based on cheap coal and natural gas, which when coupled with deregulation of the utility industry, virtually strangled wind energy development. In the 1990s, the California wind farm market was further pummeled by the expiration or forced renegotiation of once attractive power purchase contracts with the major California utilities—Southern California Edison and Pacific Gas and Electric. Despite this negative outlook, in 1999, "green power" initiatives in Colorado, Texas, and elsewhere spurred U.S. wind-energy development. New wind farms included a cluster of Zond Z-40 turbines operated for a southwest Texas utility, a wind farm of 46 Vestas machines at Big Spring, Texas, a 10 megawatt wind farm in northern Colorado with other turbines in the upper Midwest, plus "repowering" of California projects with larger and more modern units. Entrepreneur Jim Dehlsen founded the company that manufactured Zond turbines, now part of GE Wind. Vestas is the leading Danish wind-turbine manufacturer with a 20 percent global share of the wind-turbine market. Other major manufacturers are Gamesa and Acciona (Spain); Suzlon (India); Enercon, Siemens, and Nordex (Germany); and Goldwind and Sinovel (China).[9] Foreign wind-turbines manufacturers have set up factories in the U.S. to handle the resurgence in wind energy.

Perhaps the greatest incentive for the revival of wind energy was the fall in the price of electricity from wind turbines from $1.00 per kilowatt-hour in 1978 to under $0.05 in 1998, and $0.025 when new large wind turbines came online in the early 2000s. However, it is difficult to accurately compare the costs of wind farms and fossil-fuel plants because their respective cost drivers are so vastly different. Low installed-cost-per-kilowatt figures for wind turbines are misleading because the cost estimates are based on full-capacity operation. But wind is not reliable, and actual load factors vary between 25 and 40 percent of capacity compared to average load factors for fossil-fuel power plants of 50 to 70 percent of capacity with the ability to ramp up to 100 percent capacity at will, an option that wind turbines cannot replicate. Widely dispersing wind farms and placing them in areas where acceptable wind conditions are prevalent much of the time increase the reliability of wind power. Moreover, the cost estimates of wind-energy projects frequently neglect the need for backup sources of power in case the wind stops blowing and the need to construct transmission lines from generally remote areas amenable for generating wind energy to the electric power grid.

While fuel is free, wind turbines have operating costs such as insurance and maintenance. Film clips of wind farms always show a number of idle wind turbines, which gives an inkling of reliability. With the top of wind turbines a few hundred feet in the air, some method has to be devised to get repairmen up to where the electricity-generating equipment is located. On land, large cranes are necessary to hold ladders in place for the workmen to climb. In offshore waters, helicopters have to be employed to lower repairmen to the dome-shaped top of wind turbines. Repair costs have to reflect the use of large cranes or helicopters and the inherent danger of climbing hundreds of feet up a ladder in gusty winds or being lowered on a dome shape in windy conditions compounded by the helicopter's downdraft prior to fastening oneself to a safety line.

Like water flowing in a river, the amount of generated electricity is determined by the energy contained in the wind passing through the area swept by the wind turbine blades known as the wind-power density. Wind-power density depends on the cube of the wind speed (when wind speed doubles, the wind-power density goes up by a factor of eight) and also on air density and temperature (lower altitudes and cooler temperatures increase wind-power density). A turbine has four output phases depending on wind speed. No power is generated when wind is below a minimum speed. Above the minimum speed, electricity output rises rapidly with increasing wind speed until the wind speed attains a threshold level. Above this, electricity output is constant at the turbine's rated capacity even with increasing wind speed to avoid overstressing the wind turbine. Turbine blades are designed to rotate with a frequency that ensures optimum efficiency and maximum yield of wind-power density that can be converted to electricity with minimum tower oscillation, but are also designed to become less efficient at wind speeds that can damage the tower supporting the turbine or the blades themselves. When wind speed is too high, the wind turbine stops producing electricity and assumes a mode of operation that protects the blades and tower against physical damage. Large commercial wind turbines operate between 10 and 20 revolutions per minute (rpm) where the rate of rotation depends on the wind speed. The variable rate of rotation generates a variable-frequency electrical current, which is converted to direct current (DC). Electricity can be transmitted for long distances in the traditional manner as high voltage AC, but recent technological progress now allows high-voltage DC transmission. Either at the start or less frequently at the end of its transmission to an electricity grid, direct current is converted to a fixed frequency alternating current as required by the utility (e.g., 60 cycles per second in the U.S. or 50 cycles per second in Europe).

Electricity from wind is experiencing explosive growth. From the tiny acorns planted in the 1980s in California, mighty oaks are growing. Global wind-energy capacity totaled 120 gigawatts in 2008, representing a compound growth rate of 27 percent since 2000 when total output was 17.4 GW shown in Figure 9.1.[10]

Figure 9.2 shows 2008 installed wind-power capacity and planned capacity additions. The United States, which was in third place in 2003, is now in first slightly ahead of second place Germany. Future additions to U.S. wind-energy capacity have four major supports. One, the Obama administration is expected to establish a national renewable electricity standard (RES) of 25 percent by 2025, with a near-term standard of 10 percent by 2012. Although the RES applies to all forms of renewables (biofuel, wind, solar, geothermal, hydro and others), wind will be a prominent player

Figure 9.1   **Global Wind Power Installed Capacity** (GW)

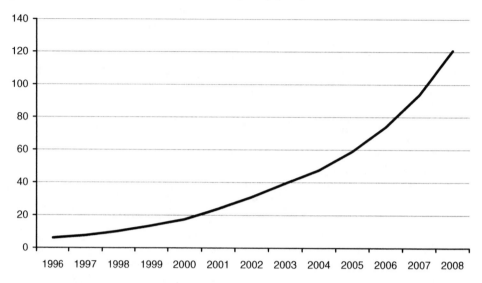

Figure 9.2   **Installed Capacity as of 2008 and Planned Capacity** (GW)

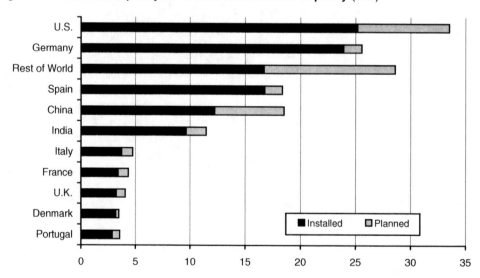

as its cost is more closely aligned to conventional forms of electricity. Two, the Obama administration is expected to support a high-voltage interstate transmission "superhighway" to tap the nation's vast renewable energy sources. Three, some form of cap and trade program is expected to be established with regard to carbon emissions for climate control. This will make fossil fuels more expensive and provide an additional economic incentive for investments in renewables.

Four, the American Recovery and Reinvestment Act of 2009, signed into law by President Obama in February 2009, is intended to jumpstart the economy by taking measures to modernize U.S. infrastructure, enhance energy independence, expand educational opportunities, preserve and improve affordable health care, provide tax relief, and protect those in greatest need. With regard to energy, the Act provides a 30 percent grant of the installed cost of renewable energy projects with a termination date for approving such projects of January 1, 2013. The grant replaces a 30 percent tax credit, which requires a firm to be profitable for the tax credit to be of value. The 30 percent grant is independent of a company's profit—it is a free gift to help fund a project that never has to be repaid. Moreover the grant is effective for four years, quite unlike past tax credits that turned "on and off" with frequent regularity, causing investors to shy away from investing in renewable energy sources.

The leading state from the point of view of both installed and planned additions is Texas, followed by Iowa at less than half that of Texas, with California in third place with very little in the way of capacity additions. Despite the allure to build wind farms, T. Boone Pickens, an oil man with his own solution to the oil problem, abandoned what would have been the world's largest wind farm (4 gigawatts) in the Texas Panhandle in 2009 citing doubts over the actual construction of a long-distance transmission system that would be necessary to connect the wind farm with the electricity grid, problems in obtaining financial support, and low natural gas prices. Wind farms supply electricity to meet variable demand, which is generally priced at the cost of electricity generated by natural gas during the day and coal and nuclear at night. A falloff in natural gas prices lowers daytime electricity rates, which cuts the revenue stream for wind farms. Pickens is still involved with other wind projects, but this particular project is now on hold until the global financial situation stabilizes along with some real progress in the government's intention of extending the transmission system to service wind farms.

Another favored area for wind farms is the offshore waters of New Jersey and Delaware. If there were wind farms about fifteen miles offshore along much of the coastline, electricity generation would make Delaware and New Jersey not only self-sufficient, but leading electricity-exporting states. As with any project, a hurdle for offshore wind farms is getting the requisite permissions. Shoreside residents may not wish to see the tips of wind turbines peeking over the horizon, much as shoreside residents in Cape Cod and Long Island have killed offshore wind projects for this reason despite their espoused economic and energy benefits. The northern Great Plains (Montana, the Dakotas, and Wyoming), self-dubbed the Saudi Arabias of wind energy, have the potential to supply the United States with all its electricity needs, weather permitting, on land that would take up about 10 percent of the area of just one state. But these states have not yet become the center of wind activity from a lack of a long-distance transmission system to get the electricity to market. If a transmission superhighway were authorized to be built that reached into the northern Great Plains, these states may well take the first steps to fulfill their self-proclaimed slogan.

Germany and Spain, in common with all nations desiring renewable sources of energy, have various subsidy programs in place to support the development of renewable resources. These subsidy programs have made it possible for parts of Germany (Schleswig-Holstein) to receive as much as 25 percent of their electricity from wind. Denmark, once the global center for wind-energy development, reached 25 percent saturation for wind energy and has essentially stopped adding capacity. Twenty-five percent appears to be an upper limit considering the reliability factor associated with wind. Denmark is still heavily involved with wind technology, being a major exporter of hardware (wind turbines) and software (knowledge and expertise) to other nations. A very large potential area for development of European wind energy is not coastlines but offshore waters. There are 150,000 square kilometers (58,000 square miles) of water less than 35 meters

(115 feet) deep available for development with more than enough potential to fulfill the continent's electricity needs, weather permitting. An acceptable location is one with an annual average wind speed of at least fourteen miles per hour; an ideal location is one with a persistent wind speed between twenty-five and thirty-five miles per hour. Like Pickens' project in Texas, a number of European wind projects have been placed on hold.

China and India have added a new wrinkle to the story. The Kyoto Protocol sets up the Clean Development Mechanism (CDM), which permits a company of a signatory nation (primarily European) to either reduce its carbon emissions or buy credits via CDMs where carbon emissions can be reduced at less cost than direct investment in carbon-emission controls at the company's facilities. An early example of a CDM was planting trees in developing nations in Africa, South America, and Asia. The carbon reduction of planting trees is a low-cost alternative that could be purchased by a carbon-emitting utility or industrial plant rather than investing in much more expensive means to reduce carbon emissions at their source. A better example today of CDMs is wind-energy development projects in developing nations. In 2009, there were 25 GW of wind power projects in the CDM pipeline including 17 GW in China, 5 GW in India, 1 GW in Mexico, and smaller projects in 18 other developing nations. The irony is that China and India, along with other developing nations, do not participate in the Kyoto Protocol. They do not want to be placed under a mandatory program of reducing carbon emissions because, in their minds, the industrial west is entirely responsible for the buildup of carbon dioxide in the atmosphere. The fact that they now number among the world's heaviest carbon and other pollutant emitters is irrelevant. Yet China, India, and other developing nations freely sell carbon-emission credits to participating Kyoto Protocol signatory nations, which helps to finance their wind and other carbon-reducing projects.

Wind projects are not concentrated in a few countries but are becoming widely dispersed as shown in Figure 9.1 under "Rest of the World," which includes Australia, Japan, Brazil, Canada, and many other nations. The most common-sized wind turbine is 1.5 megawatts, but increasingly 2 and 3.6 megawatt turbines are being installed, with the next generation of 5 megawatt turbines already in the testing stage. Two hundred of these turbines would generate the power of a nuclear or large coal plant, weather permitting.

For wind turbines to be efficiently employed, dispatchers should have a forecast of wind conditions in order to plan the next day's schedule of operation for the utility's generating resources. Unfortunately, dispatchers cannot schedule future production with confidence considering the reliability of weather forecasts. The average output of a wind turbine is only 25–40 percent of its rated output because of variance in wind speeds plus an allowance for downtime for maintenance. Thus 200 GW of wind capacity represent at most 80 GW of conventional electricity-generating plants. Even at the optimistic assessment of 80 GW, wind only represents 1.8 percent of global electricity-generating plant capacity of about 4,500 GW in 2009. Figure 9.3 shows the areas of the world where incremental wind projects are projected to be built.

Although wind projects are worldwide in scope, Figure 9.3 clearly shows that Asia (China and India) will be the area of greatest projected growth. Even if Pickens were to build the world's largest wind farm of 4 GW, the title would be short-lived. China has started construction on the Daliang Wind Station outside Anxi in Gansu Province. When completed, this grouping of six wind farms with an individual capacity of 10–20 GW each may propel China to first place in wind-generated electricity if its announced aggregate output of 100 GW is achieved by 2020. These titanic-sized wind farms will be connected to China's electricity smart grid by a low-loss high-voltage DC transmission system. China has a national goal of building a renewable energy infrastructure in order to become the world's dominant player in wind and solar energy.[11] By

Figure 9.3  **Projected Growth in Wind Capacity** (GW)

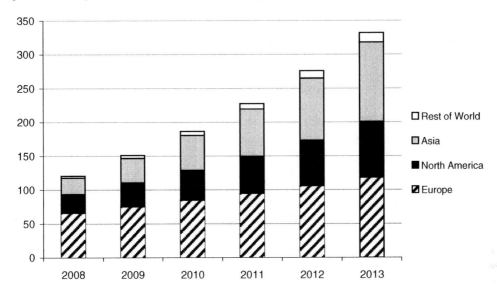

2013, world electricity-generating capacity is expected to be around 4,800 GW. With 330 GW of wind capacity contributing an actual output of 130 GW, wind will contribute 2.8 percent of world electricity-generating capacity. Despite acorns to mighty oaks, the total contribution of wind is not even covering marginal growth in electricity demand. The most it is accomplishing is reducing the growth rate for conventional sources of electrical power. Nevertheless, regardless of the size of the contribution, every watt contributed by wind energy is one less watt that has to be contributed by burning fossil fuels and that much less carbon dioxide and other emissions added to the atmosphere.

**Objections to Wind Power**

Not surprisingly, there has been little opposition to locating wind turbines on farmland, given the long history of windmills on American farms that lasted until the mid-twentieth century. Farming operations are minimally disturbed by the presence of wind turbines, which are normally sited in pastures or along edges of fields, and are viewed favorably by farmers as a source of incremental income. Much of the opposition to developing wind farms comes from suburbanites, real estate developers, and environmentalists for a variety of reasons.

Wind turbines are highly visible. In the 1980s, wind turbines were built with lattice-style structures of 50–300 kilowatt capacity and a rotor blade diameter of 15–30 meters (49–98 feet). In the 1990s, the tubular structure was adopted with turbine capacity of 300–750 kilowatts and a rotor blade diameter of 30–50 meters (98–164 feet). The popular sized GE 1.5 MW wind turbine has 3 blades with a rotor diameter of 77 meters (253 feet) and a hub height in four sizes varying from roughly 60 to 85 meters (197 to 279 feet). As a point of reference, a Boeing 747–400, which can carry up to 436 passengers, has a wingspan just over 211 feet (64.4 meters) and a length just under 232 feet (70.7 meters) and thus can fit within the rotor blade diameter of a large commercial wind turbine. The GE 2.5 MW wind turbine has a rotor diameter of 100 meters (328 feet) and a hub height in 3 sizes of 75, 85, and 100 meters ( 246, 279, and 328 feet). The 3.6 MW wind turbine has a rotor diameter of 111 meters (364 feet) and its hub height is site specific.[12] No matter what the size, suburbanites do not want to look at them and environmentalists object to locating wind farms in scenic areas or along coastlines.

Some of this opposition can be overcome by designing less obtrusive and/or more pleasing designs, such as foregoing lattice for tubular-style towers and blending a line of wind turbines with the contours of the land. Unsightly transmission lines can be removed by burying them. Some object to the swishing noise of the blade passing through the air, which can be heard within a few miles of a large wind farm and within several hundred feet for an individual wind turbine. Though noise from a wind farm is less obtrusive than normal motor vehicle traffic, the fact that a quiet night is no longer quiet bothers people. To counter this, increasing the separation between a wind farm and residential areas reduces noise levels. Larger wind turbines can be quieter than smaller ones, depending on the speed of the blade tip and the design of a blade's airfoils and trailing edges. Local opposition can be mollified if the citizenry receives a monthly stipend or a reduction in property taxes for permitting a wind farm to be built. Non-local opposition cannot be bought off so easily.

Another objection was locating early wind farms in mountain passes that turned out to be bird migratory paths. Birds were killed when they flew into the rotating blades. Siting wind farms now takes into account bird migratory paths. Even if built in a migratory path, migration is a seasonal phenomenon. Radar can be used to stop the wind turbines when a large flock of birds is about to pass through or near a wind farm. The leading cause of bird fatalities by human interference is not birds flying into wind turbines but into buildings, windows, high-tension lines, communication towers, and motor vehicles, plus fatal encounters with pet cats and pesticides. Wind turbines have the lowest kill rate among these fatal encounters.

Nevertheless, wind turbines pose a hazard for birds that cannot dodge a blade whose tip speed is over 200 miles per hour. A proposed design for wind turbines with no external blade would avoid killing birds. Wind enters a vertical cylindrical structure where airfoils direct the wind against blades on a rotating vertical shaft. The vertical shaft allows the generator to be at ground level for greater ease of maintenance and reduced interference with radio, television, and communication signals. The vertical axis wind turbine is shorter in height than the traditional wind turbine, less obtrusive in appearance, creates less noise from its lower speed of rotation, and has a surrounding wire mesh to prevent birds from entering the turbine. While the vertical axis wind turbine has an optimal wind speed similar to that of traditional wind turbines of 28–33mph, it can operate with wind speeds up to 70 mph versus 50 mph for traditional wind turbines. This higher range of wind speed increases the overall average output from 25–40 percent of rated capacity for traditional wind turbines to 40–45 percent.[13]

As with any utility project, there are a number of organizations a wind farm developer must successfully negotiate with before construction can begin. State governments have boards that require an environmental impact assessment for the wind farm and its transmission lines. Permits are required from land commissions before a project can move ahead. A public utility commission must grant a certificate of need. County- and community-planning boards ensure compliance with zoning ordinances and land use requirements. As with any real estate development, clearing land for access roads and wind turbine foundations must be done in a manner that avoids or minimizes soil erosion. These boards can also address the possibility that a wind farm might interfere with radio and television reception. If the wind project is on land, then the Bureau of Land Management or the Forest Service will be involved along with the Fish and Wildlife Service to ensure minimal hazard to birds and other wildlife.

The views of community groups greatly influence the permit process. Such groups can challenge a site proposal through the court system if they believe that laws, regulations, and legal procedures have not been properly followed. To ensure public support, it is important for project organizers to make the public aware of the benefits of wind power, including any contribution that the wind farm is making in the form of paying local taxes in addition to steps being taken to minimize environmental objections.

**Evaluating a Potential Site**

While a single wind turbine can have large fluctuations in power output from abrupt changes in wind speed and direction, a wind farm covering a wide area tends to dampen the aggregate impact of shifting winds. Wind patterns can be affected for days from passing storms and weather fronts and for months from seasonal variations (winds are generally more intense in winter and spring). What counts in determining the feasibility of a potential wind farm site is not short-term wind fluctuations or seasonal swings but the average speed throughout the year. The economic return of a wind farm is enhanced if the wind blows more during daytime when electricity is more highly valued. In addition to average annual wind speed, wind patterns near the ground are critical in selecting the height of the hub (center of the rotor). Wind shear is the change in wind speed with height, which is influenced by solar heating, atmospheric mixing, and the nature of the terrain. Forests and cities tend to increase wind shear by slowing the speed of air near the surface. A differential in air speed between the blade's lower and upper sweeps can damage the blade. Wind shear can be greatly reduced with an abrupt change in terrain height such as a sea cliff or mountain ridge. Cliffs and ridges also accelerate wind speed, as do mountain passes.

**Financial Incentives**

Tax shields to induce investment come in various forms such as accelerated depreciation and tax credits. A tax shield reduces a corporate or personal tax by the tax rate; for a corporation paying a tax rate on its profit of 35 percent, a $100 tax shield is worth $35 in reduced taxes. A tax credit is a far more powerful incentive than a tax shield because a tax credit is a dollar-for-dollar reduction in taxes; a $100 tax credit is worth $100 in reduced taxes as long as the corporation is paying taxes. In 1992, Congress enacted a production tax credit of 1.9 cents per kilowatt-hour for the first ten years of a wind turbine's life. For a tax-paying company, lower taxes can be viewed as a direct subsidy that covers the higher incremental cost of wind energy—up to 1.9 cents per kilowatt-hour more than conventional energy sources. If the installed cost of a wind turbine is no more than 1.9 cents per kilowatt-hour over that of a conventional source of electricity, then the 1.9 cents in tax credits make the wind turbine economically competitive with conventional plants. In the United States, the problem with production tax credits, both at the state and federal levels, is that they normally expire after a short period of time and require frequent legislative renewals, which are not always forthcoming.

When production tax credits expire, those units built before the expiration date keep their tax credits, but new units built after the credits expire do not receive the tax incentive. U.S. production tax credits expired in 1999, were renewed in 2000, expired in 2001, were renewed in 2002, and expired in 2003. This on-again, off-again tax credit has predictable results. Following the expiration of production tax credits in 1999, 2001, and 2003, installations of new turbines fell considerably in 2000, 2002, and 2004. The renewal of the production tax credit in 2004 (effective in 2005) was different in that eligible projects were expanded from wind to include solar, geothermal, micro hydroelectric, open-loop biomass, refined coal, livestock and municipal solid waste, and landfill gas. The renewal in 2004 would have expired at the end of 2005, but the Energy Policy Act of 2005 extended the expiration to the end of 2007. While an improvement, the stop-and-go tax credit still complicates the planning and investment process.[14] However in 2009, as previously mentioned, a 30 percent grant was authorized by the Obama administration that does not expire until 2013, giving the wind and other renewable energy source companies a degree of stability in terms of government support that had been previously lacking.

A successful way to encourage growth in wind energy and other renewable sources is for utilities to offer customers the option to pay a premium on their electricity rates that will support generation of electricity from renewable sources. The utilities enter into a contract to buy the output of a renewable power project at commercial rates that apply to conventional plants. Since this rate cannot economically support an investment in electricity produced from renewable energy, the utility has to find enough consumers willing to make up the difference in the form of a rate premium. Care has to be exercised to ensure that the amount of electricity that carries the premium rate covers, but does not exceed, the capacity of the renewable energy source. In the United States, more than 300 utilities offer their customers a voluntary premium rate that is applied to electricity generated from renewable energy sources. Utilities in the south generally favor solar power while those in the north favor wind power. Some utilities in the United States and abroad give consumers a choice of power supply such as solar, micro hydro, and wind, each with a different premium to cover their respective extra costs.[15] This method does not assure efficiency of operation, however, because the consumer is picking up the entire incremental cost associated with the capital and operating costs of a renewable energy electricity-generating plant.

The approach of the European Union is to set a goal to be attained, not by utilities, but by member nations. The 2001 EU Directive specified an overall EU target to increase renewables' share of electricity from 14 percent in 1997 to 21 percent in 2010. Europeans recognize that conventional power production from coal and nuclear power benefits from state aid, and there is no reason why renewable energy sources should be exempt. Wind energy is subsidized to make it competitive with coal and nuclear energy. The subsidy has only a modest impact on electricity rates when spread across the entire rate base. Germany and Spain went one step beyond and established a quota that had to be filled by wind power, coupled with an associated electricity rate that would spur its development.

Policy directives, consumers voluntarily bearing the extra cost, production tax credits, and quotas with a fixed price have their pros and cons, but they are not as effective as the renewables portfolio standard (RPS) approach. If energy from renewables is desirable because of security of supply or environmental concerns over fossil fuels, then a more forceful approach is warranted than tax gimmicks, appeals to a consumer's environmental conscience, and policy goals. In the United States, a number of states have some form of renewable power requirement where a certain percentage of the power generated by a utility must come from clean, renewable energy. The RPS starts low and slowly increases up to 10 or 15 or 20 percent or more of the utility's portfolio over a reasonable period of time. It is up to the utility to select the most economical form of renewable energy source. The RPS is essentially a quota system without a price. A quota with a set price does not provide an incentive to enhance efficiency. A quota without a set price creates a competitive environment among renewable energy providers to offer electricity at the lowest possible price by enhancing efficiency and improving technology. It is anticipated that a national RPS will be established by the Obama administration as part of its energy package, which would provide the nation with a common goal. Presumably a state could have a higher RPS, but not a lower RPS than that stipulated in federal legislation.

The gap between the cost of electricity generated by conventional and renewable sources has narrowed considerably with the tripling or quadrupling of natural gas prices and the doubling of coal prices in 2004 and 2005. However, the collapse of natural gas prices in the United States in 2009 has lowered electricity rates, and in so doing, taken away from the incentive for alternative energy sources. The gap has been further narrowed by technological progress in lowering the capital and operating costs of generating electricity from renewable energy sources, particularly wind turbines. Wind is clean and free and the cost of electricity generated by wind is not affected by OPEC but only by its capital, insurance, and maintenance costs. Wind farms are a hedge against rising fossil fuel prices and can be built in stages in response to growing demand, quite unlike large coal and nuclear plants that add large increments to capacity that may not be entirely usable during the early years of a plant's life.

Lastly, the wind industry is a source of employment. According to the American Wind Energy Association (AWEA), growth in the number of wind turbines created 35,000 new jobs during 2008, increasing total employment to 85,000. If wind energy provides 20 percent of the nation's electricity by 2030, the wind industry will support an estimated 500,000 jobs and perhaps as many as a million jobs counting indirect jobs such as accountants, computer systems analysts, and those associated with the integration of wind farms with the electricity grid, including the building of transmission lines. According to the European Wind Energy Association (EWEA), the wind industry employed 108,000 people directly and 150,000 in total counting indirect jobs in 2008, double that of 2002. As is also true for the United States, the EWEA cites shortages of project and site managers, engineers, and skilled operations and maintenance personnel. If present projections of wind-generating capacity hold true, direct employment in Europe will be 330,000 by 2020 and 375,000 by 2030, split with 160,000 associated with onshore installations and 215,000 with offshore installations. This suggests that nearly 60 percent of wind turbine capacity will be in offshore waters by 2030.

## Small Can Be Beautiful

As with hydropower, wind farms do not have to be large to be effective. Isolated areas that are not connected to electricity grids via transmission lines can be served by hybrid power systems consisting of a local distribution system to supply electricity from small wind farms coupled with diesel generators as backup when the wind is calm. In addition to small wind farms, there is an increasing effort to develop small wind turbines to allow individual homeowners, farmers, businesses, and public facilities to generate their own clean power to reduce electricity bills or for use in areas not served by an electricity grid. Wind turbines for individuals have a capacity of 1–10 kilowatt hours, while intermediate wind turbines of 10–100 kilowatt hours can serve villages and can be augmented by solar power when the sun is shining. Battery storage is a form of backup, but diesel power backup is still needed for those times when the battery has a low charge and the wind is not blowing and the sun is not shining.

## SOLAR ENERGY

Like wind, solar energy is also free, but like other free sources of energy, particular conditions apply. Solar power can only be generated during daylight hours, with peak output on clear days when the sun is directly overhead. Several factors affect the efficiency of solar power: cloud cover, which markedly reduces solar output; times of day when the sun is near the horizon (early morning and late afternoon); seasons during which the sun does not rise high in the sky (winter at high latitudes). As with wind, solar power can contribute to power generation, but cannot be relied upon without a backup. Solar power is more expensive and its overall contribution is smaller than that of wind. Solar power has one advantage over wind—it is produced only during daylight hours when electricity demand is highest, reducing the need for peaking generators.

There are two types of solar energy. Thermal solar is a source of hot water that can be used for heating or for making steam to generate electricity. Photovoltaic solar is the direct conversion of solar energy to electricity.

## Historical Development

Sunlight sustains life on Earth, and the sun was an object of worship in early religions. The Chinese and Greeks were the first to apply technology to the sun in the 7th and 6th centuries BCE with the "gnomen," a vertical stick or stone in the ground that would trace the sun's shadow to show meal times first and foremost, but also mark the solstices (important for planting and harvesting) and determine latitude and true North. They also began using crude magnifying glasses to focus the sun's rays to light fires for light, warmth, and cooking. The Chinese were the first to use mirrors (reflective metals) to light fires, and later mirrors were used by the Greeks and Romans to light torches for religious processions. In the fifth century BCE, the Greeks incorporated passive solar design in their buildings by allowing the southern sun to penetrate the interiors for warmth in the winter. In 212 BCE, Archimedes focused sunlight with polished bronze shields on a Roman fleet attacking Syracuse and succeeded in setting ships afire (this was successfully repeated in 1973 by the Greek navy setting fire to a wooden boat 50 meters away from the reflectors). During the first four centuries of the Common Era, the Romans improved on Greek passive solar technology practices with large, south-facing windows in public bathhouses to capture the sun's warmth and greenhouses for growing exotic plants. The Justinian Code (529–534) included laws regarding "sun rights" to ensure that houses and buildings had continued access to sunlight after their construction. In the thirteenth century, the Anasazi Indians in the U.S. Southwest built their dwellings in south-facing cliffs to capture the warmth of the winter sun. In 1515, Leonardo da Vinci proposed the use of parabolic reflectors to supply energy for a cloth dyeing factory.[16]

Capturing the thermal energy of the sun in a more dynamic way began with Auguste Mouchout, a French mathematics instructor, who converted solar radiation into mechanical steam power in 1860. The arrival of cheap coal from England stopped further progress in capturing solar power, but he was also able to demonstrate the use of solar energy in pasteurization and making ice. In 1883, John Ericsson, an American, invented a solar-powered steam engine that used parabolic trough construction to concentrate solar energy similar to Mouchout's engine. Ericsson also noted prophetically that in a couple of thousand years, a drop in the ocean of time in his opinion, coal fields will be completely exhausted and the heat of the sun will have to be their substitute. He was off in his timing but right in his concept. In 1878, an Englishman William Adams constructed a reflector of flat silvered mirrors in a semicircle to track the sun's movement and concentrate the radiation on a stationary boiler to heat water. He was able to power a 2.5 horsepower steam engine, much larger than Mouchout's 0.5 horsepower steam engine. He advocated the use of solar energy as a substitute for fuel in tropical countries. His basic design, known as the power tower concept, is still in use today. Charles Tellier, in 1885, installed the first solar-energy system for heating household water on his rooftop. Henry Willsie was the first to build a solar plant capable of storing power for nighttime use at his two electricity generating plants in California in 1904, but was unable to compete with low-cost power from fossil fuels. In 1912, Frank Shuman built parabolic solar collectors near the Nile River capable of tracking the sun. The reflectors produced enough steam to power a series of water pumps totalling 55 horsepower capable of lifting, for the time, an astonishing 6,000 gallons of water per minute a height of 33 feet to irrigate a large tract of desert land. His dream of building 20,000 square miles (!) of reflectors in the Sahara desert for irrigation purposes died when his Nile River installation was destroyed during the First World War. Passive solar buildings became popular during the Second World War when energy became scarce. In the 1950s, Frank Bridgers designed the first commercial building with solar water heating, now listed in the National Historic Register. Giovanni Francia, an Italian, invented the Fresnel reflector in 1964, which can substitute flat glass for curved glass in focusing solar energy. In 1969, a "solar furnace" was constructed in Odeillo, France, featuring an eight-story parabolic mirror.[17]

Capturing solar energy in the form of electricity began with Edmund Becquerel, a French physicist, who studied the photovoltaic (electricity from light). In 1838, he noticed that an electrical current through two metal electrodes submerged in a conducting medium increased when exposed to light but did not pursue the matter further. In 1873, Willoughby Smith, an Englishman, experimented with the photoconductivity of selenium. The first solar cell is credited to an American, Charles Fritts, who coated the semiconductor selenium with a thin layer of gold in 1883 to produce the first working photovoltaic (PV) solar cell.

A PV solar cell is made up of two layers of semiconductor material that can convert sunlight to electricity. One layer has an abundance of electrons and the other a shortage. Sandwiching these together forms an electrical field at the interface, which acts as a battery when exposed to sunlight. PV solar cells produce direct current, which has to be converted to alternating current for home use or feeding into an electricity grid. However, the high cost and low efficiency of 1 percent for converting solar energy to electricity left the Fritt's idea dormant until 1941 when another American, Russell Ohl, used silicon to improve the conversion rate to 5 percent at a far less cost. Russell Ohl received a patent for what is recognized as the first modern solar cell. In 1954, three scientists at Bell Laboratories were able to design a silicon solar cell with a greater conversion rate of solar energy to electricity of 6 percent along with another reduction in cost, opening the door to the commercialization of solar cells. The first commercial solar cells made their debut in 1956 to power radios and toys but were very expensive at $300 per watt. AT&T built the first solar arrays to power the earth satellite Vanguard I launched in 1956. Hoffman Electronics improved the conversion rate of silicon cells to 10 percent in 1960. In 1963, Japan built the largest ground-based PV array installation of 242 watts with a storage battery to supply electricity for a lighthouse. The energy crisis in 1973 provided the incentive to increase funding on solar technology with the result that the price of solar cells dropped dramatically to about $20 per watt (today it is $4–6 per watt). In 1973, the University of Delaware built "Solar One," a roof-installed integrated photovoltaic/thermal hybrid system that supplied heated water to a home as well as electricity. The excess output during the day was sold to a utility that supplied the home with electricity at night and during times of cloud cover.

## Thermal Solar Energy

Thermal solar energy can heat water for space heating, household appliances, swimming pools, and for various commercial and industrial processes. Solar water heaters with copper collector tubes in a glazed housing can be installed on the roofs and sides of homes most exposed to sunlight. When the sun is shining, water is pumped through the collector and the heated water is stored in a tank. A thermosiphon solar water heater has the storage tank above the collector tubes, eliminating the need for a pump. Although thermal solar energy is associated with warming a house, heated water can drive an absorption or desiccant air-conditioning system for cooling a house. For colder climates, a water/glycol mixture is pumped through the collector, which then requires a heat ex-changer to heat water for appliances and space heating. Backup substitute power is required for cold, cloudy, blustery days when snow and ice cover the thermal panels.

Harking back to the days of the Greeks and Romans, buildings can be designed for passive solar energy by having large south-facing windows complemented with building materials that absorb and slowly release the sun's heat. There are no mechanical aspects to passive solar heating, and a well-designed system can significantly cut heating bills. Passive solar designs also include natural ventilation for cooling during hot weather. Hybrid lighting concentrates sunlight and feeds it through fiber optics into a building's interior. "Hybrid" means that a backup power source for interior lighting is necessary for times of little or no sunlight, and certainly for nighttime illumina-tion. Thermal solar output for heating water, including a small portion for electricity generation, was nearly 70 GW in 2001. China led with 22.4 GW of solar thermal capacity followed by the United States with 17.5 GW, Japan with 8.4 GW, Turkey with 5.7 GW, and Germany with 3.0 GW.[18] This dwarfed the installed output of 1.1 GW of photovoltaic output at that time (in 2007, photovoltaic output was about 8 GW).

Solar thermal energy can also heat water for conversion to steam for driving turbines to gener-ate electricity. The types of thermal solar power systems that can generate electricity are parabolic troughs, power towers, and dish/engine systems. These technologies are normally hybridized with fossil fuel (natural gas) to maintain electricity output when the sun is not shining or covered with clouds. This gives the system the necessary reliability required by dispatchers and enhances the economic performance of the system (the generator is producing revenue whether or not the sun is shining). Natural solar power provides 2.7 megawatts per square meter per year. While this may sound impressive, it is actually a low rate of energy transfer considering that this is over a year's time. Thus, solar thermal systems require a great deal of area for mirrors to collect and concentrate the requisite solar energy. However, the land area does not compare unfavorably with coal-fired plants when mining and storage areas are taken into consideration.[19]

Solar thermal energy for electricity generation requires a location where there is sunlight much of the time and sufficient available space for mirrors. The ideal location is a desert. The first system to commercially convert solar thermal energy to electricity was built in the 1980s in the Mojave Desert in California. Nine solar thermal electricity-generating plants have a combined output of 354 megawatts (one-third the output of a large coal-fired or nuclear power plant), the world's largest installation of solar power. Trough-shaped parabolic mirrors automatically follow the sun and focus the sun's rays at thirty to sixty times their normal intensity on a receiver pipe filled with synthetic oil. The oil is heated to 735°F and passes through a heat exchanger to produce steam for a conventional steam turbine electricity generator. Natural gas serves as a supplemental fuel for cloudy weather and nighttime operation.[20]

The modern power tower, also developed in California, stores solar energy in the form of molten-salt. A circular field array of heliostats (large mirrors) individually tracks the sun. The heliostats focus sunlight on a central receiver mounted on top of a tower to heat molten salt, such as a mixture of sodium and potassium nitrate, to 1,050°F for storage in the "hot" tank. As power is needed, molten salt flows from the hot tank through a heat exchanger to produce steam for electricity generation. Then, it travels to the "cold" tank, where it remains molten at 550°F until needed for heating in the tower. Depending on the size of the hot tank and its insulation properties, a hot tank can supply energy to generate electricity for some hours after sunset, an advantage over trough-shaped parabolic mirrors. Moreover, the system is more reliable because dispatchers can depend on the system to produce power even when clouds temporarily cover the sun by generating electricity from energy stored in the hot tank. To further enhance reliability, the system can be hybridized with a fossil fuel, such as natural gas, to produce power when needed by a dispatcher at any time.

Trough-shaped parabolic mirrors and power towers require water to generate steam, a commodity in short supply in a desert, but no water is required for the dish/engine solar energy system. Parabolic dish-shaped mirrors, mounted on a single support frame, focus solar energy on a receiver to heat a transfer fluid to nearly 1,400°F. The heated fluid transfers its heat to a gas such as hydrogen or helium to power a Stirling engine, which is similar in construction to an internal combustion engine, or to a Brayton engine, which is similar to a gas turbine engine (sometimes referred to as a micro-turbine). In neither case is there combustion; the engines run off the energy of the heated gas and drive an electricity generator. Solar dish engines have the highest efficiency of thermal solar systems, converting nearly 30 percent of solar energy to electricity. Trough-shaped parabolic mirrors and power towers best serve an electricity grid whereas solar dish engines best serve isolated areas beyond a power grid. However, there is nothing that precludes connecting dish engine arrays to a grid.

The latest idea, based on one first advanced by Leonardo da Vinci, is a solar power tower shaped like a chimney that directs hot surface air up to cooler air at higher altitudes. One company plans to build such a tower that will direct heated surface air up the circular tower to cooler air almost 3,300 feet (1,000 meters) above the Australian outback. The power driver is the air temperature differential between the bottom and the top of the tower. The tower is surrounded by sunlight-absorbing material that further heats the incoming air. Air rushing in the bottom of the tower passes through wind turbines that can generate up to 200 megawatts of rated capacity, enough to supply electricity to 200,000 Australian homes.[21] Table 9.1 lists the thirteen largest thermal projects in existence or under construction.[22]

## Photovoltaic Energy

The earth receives an average of 1,367 watts of energy per square meter (about 11 square feet) at the outer edge of the earth's atmosphere. The atmosphere absorbs and reflects most of the X-ray and ultraviolet radiation, reducing the energy that reaches sea level at high noon on a clear day to a maximum of about 1,000 watts per square meter. One hour's worth of solar energy striking the earth is greater than all the energy consumed by the world's population in one year. Desert land 100 miles on a side (10,000 square miles, which is equivalent to 9 percent of the area of the state of Nevada) could generate enough electricity to supply the United States, weather permitting (the Southwest could become the Saudi Arabia of solar power!). However, the intent is not to concentrate the nation's solar power in one location, but to install solar power plants on rooftops and over parking lots throughout the nation to reduce reliance on electricity from conventional sources.[23]

Many nations are pursuing the solar option and research is being conducted under a wide assortment of public and private programs sponsored by governments, universities, and private enterprises. The objective is to make electricity from solar power competitive with conventional sources by reducing front-end costs such as material costs for semiconductors, manufacturing and installation costs of solar arrays, and enhancing efficiency. The greater the efficiency in converting sunlight to electricity, the smaller the solar array has to be to deliver a given amount of electricity.

Most commercial PV solar cells are made of crystalline silicon cut in wafers as thin as 200 microns, usually between two and three square inches (12.5 to 20 square centimeters) in area. Single-crystal PV cells are grown and have a commercial efficiency that ranges between 15–18 percent in converting solar energy to electricity. Solar cells have a higher efficiency if surrounded

Table 9.1

**World's Thirteen Largest Solar Thermal Power Projects**

| Location | Size | Type | Solar Co. | Utility | Start |
|---|---|---|---|---|---|
| Mojave Desert, US | 500 MW to be expanded to 900 MW | Power Tower | BrightSource Energy | Pacific G&E | 2011 |
| Mojave Desert, US | 500 MW possibly to 850 MW | 20,000 Parabolic Dishes over 4,500 acres | Stirling Energy | San Diego G&E | 2011 |
| Upington, South Africa | 100 MW possibly to 600 MW | Power Tower | Eskom | Eskom | Not yet finally approved |
| Mojave Desert, US | 553 MW | 1.2 million mirrors, 317 miles vacuum tubing, 6,000 acres | Solel | Pacific G&E | 2011 |
| California, US | 400 MW | 3 Power Towers | Solar Partners | Southern California Edison and Florida Power & Light | Not yet started |
| Mojave Desert, US | 310 MW | 400,000 mirrors on 1,000 acres | | | World's largest operating built 1984–1991, Solar Energy Generating Systems (SEGS) |
| Seville, Spain | Now 11 MW being expanded to 300 MW | Power Tower | Abengoa and ALTAC | | 2013 |
| Florida, US | 300 MW | Flat Fresnel Reflectors substitute for Parabolic mirrors | | Florida Power & Light | 2011 |
| Arizona, US | 280 MW | Mirrors on 1,800 acres | Abengoa | Arizona Public Service | 2011 |
| Negev Desert, Israel | 250 MW | | | Gov't of Israel | Seeking bids |
| Mojave Desert, US | 250 MW | 500,000 parabolic troughs on 2,000 acres | | Florida Power & Light | 2011 |
| California, US | 177 MW | Fresnel Reflectors | Ausra | Pacific G&E | 2010 |
| Mildura, Australia | 154 MW may be expanded to 5,000 MW by 2030 | Power Towers | Solar Systems | TRUenergy | 2013 for the 154 MW |

by cool rather than warm air. The space program normally uses more expensive PV cells made of gallium arsenide, whose efficiency in transforming solar energy to electricity can exceed 30 percent.[24] Multicrystalline PV cells depend on a less-expensive melting and solidification process, but have a marginally lower commercial efficiency of 14 percent. An even lower-cost solar cell is a film of extremely thin layers of PV semiconductor materials such as amorphous silicon, copper-indium-gallium-diselenide, or cadmium telluride, deposited on a backing of glass, stainless steel, or plastic. While cheaper to make, thin-film PV arrays have a lower efficiency that ranges between 7–13 percent, so they have to cover more area to produce the same output than conventional solar panels. The advantage of thin films is avoiding the glass covering and mechanical frames of conventional solar panels. Thin films on a plastic covering can be made to look like roofing material and designed to fulfill the twin roles of protecting the roof from weather plus generating electricity from the sun. The savings in not having to install roofing reduces the cost of the solar power system. There is also research on employing nanotechnology to produce organic solar cells of molecular polymers and other esoteric materials. Progress in thin films technology has spurred their growth from 6 percent of PV capacity in 2005 to 13 percent in 2007; the remaining is primarily wafer design.

A PV, or solar, cell is the basic building block, small in size, and capable of producing 1 or 2 watts of power. These are combined into larger units, called modules or panels, which produce 50–300 watts of power, which are then joined together to form solar arrays sized to meet the desired power output. Solar arrays are particularly useful for serving isolated buildings in sunny climates such as lodges in national parks, lighthouses, and other buildings and facilities far from an electricity grid. Smaller solar modules can light signs, streets, gardens, pools, and provide power for remote telephones or automatic teller machines, or any need with similar power requirements. These applications normally have an associated battery that is charged by day in order to supply power at night or during times of inclement weather.

Solar arrays are given serious consideration by government bodies to help launch economic development in areas too remote and/or sparsely populated to justify building an electricity grid. An independent solar-power system, with a battery to store electricity for times of cloud cover or at night, in isolated locations obviates the need for building a generation, transmission, and distribution system. A good example of this is a $48 million solar-power project on the island of Mindanao in the Philippines. The project, funded by the Spanish government and built by BP Solar, will supply electricity to 400,000 people in 150 villages plus provide electricity for irrigation and drinking water systems and for schools and medical clinics.[25]

Solar power can bring electricity to a remote area at less cost than building a conventional generation, transmission, and distribution system, including the purchase of normally imported fuel. Solar and wind power, either singly or together, with a diesel backup, are viable means of supplying electricity on a local or distributive basis to the 2 billion people who live in isolated communities far from electricity grids or in areas of low population density. One of the chief benefits of introducing hybrid renewable electricity to remote locations is improving the health of the people. Females in some parts of the world spend nearly every waking hour collecting and transporting dung and wood on their heads or backs for cooking and heating. Some have to walk twenty miles a day, rising early in the morning and going to bed late at night, ruining their health in the process. Moreover, cooking with biomass in closed environments is a major health hazard that shortens life expectancy. Electricity from renewable sources eliminates these time-consuming and onerous tasks and their adverse health consequences. Electricity allows women to sleep longer, improving their health; and, when they are awake, have the energy to improve their lifestyle.

If an electricity grid is available, solar arrays can be connected into the grid for a power sup-

Figure 9.4  **Growth in Solar Photovoltaic Power** (GW)

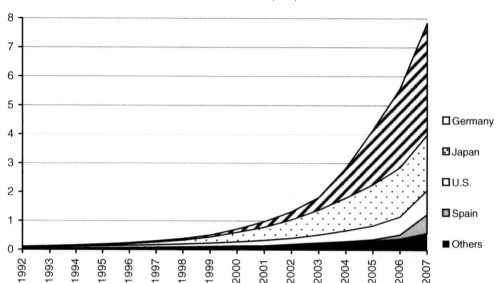

ply by night or on cloudy days, eliminating the need for a battery. Arrangements can be made for excess production of a solar array to be fed into the grid, the revenue of which can be part of the economic decision to install a solar power system. In addition to the solar panels, the capital investment also includes the cost of a mounting structure and the installation of the array, an inverter to convert the direct current output to alternating current, a storage battery for off-grid solar systems, along with a charge controller for battery operation or modifications to an existing electricity grid to allow the sale or purchase of electricity.[26] As Figure 9.4 shows, growth in solar power is exponential, similar to wind, but in comparing Figure 9.4 with Figure 9.1, solar provides less than 10 percent of wind power's contribution.

Three-quarters of the 50 percent growth in solar PV power in 2007 took place in Germany and Spain, and the figure is 90 percent by adding in Japan and the United States. The two major subdivisions of solar power are off-grid and grid-connected. Off-grid installations are at remote locations where homes and buildings are not connected to an electricity grid. Off-grid installations serve remote telecommunications stations, navigational aids, and other needed functions. Solar-powered emergency phones can be found along major highways. Grid-connected installations also serve homes and buildings, but are also connected to an electricity grid for service when the sun is not available and for sale of unneeded electricity back into the grid. In 1992, about 75 percent of installations were off-grid and 25 percent were grid-connected. In 2007, the ratio was 5 percent off-grid and 95 percent grid-connected. Table 9.2 shows the thirteen largest PV projects. The United States plays a less dominant role in PV projects than thermal projects listed in Table 9.1.

The development of solar power, as with wind, started in the United States (California, to be precise) as a result of PURPA legislation. Since the mid-1990s, Japan and Germany have become centers of solar energy development. The largest suppliers of PV cell production are located in Japan with a 38 percent share, Germany 35 percent, United States 11 percent, Norway 6 percent, and Spain 5 percent. The largest corporate suppliers of PV cell production are Q-Cells (Germany) with a 16 percent share, Sharp (Japan) 15 percent, Kyocera (Japan) 9 percent, Sanyo (Japan) 7 percent, Deutsche/SolarWorld (Germany/U.S.) 6 percent, Scancell (Norway) 6 percent, Mitsubi-

Table 9.2

**World's Thirteen Largest Solar Photovoltaic Power Projects**

| Location | Size | Solar Co. | Utility | Start |
|---|---|---|---|---|
| New Mexico, US | 300 MW | New Solar Ventures and Solar Torx on 3,200 acres | | 2011 |
| Arizona, US | 280 MW | Abengoa on 1,900 acres | Arizona Public Service | Not yet finally approved |
| Victoria, Australia | 270 MW | Solar Systems (company intends to build 270,000 MW to fulfill Australia 20% goal for renewable by 2020) | TRUenergy | 2013 |
| California, US | 80 MW | Cleantech and California Construction Authority on 640 acres | | 2011; California also has legislation calling for solar panels to be installed on 1 million roofs by 2018 |
| Leipzig, Germany | 40 MW | Juwi Solar | | 2009 |
| Murcia, Spain | 20 MW | 120,000 PV panels on 247 acres | Atersa | Operating since 2008 |
| Alicante, Spain | 20 MW | 100,000 PV panels | City Solar | Operating since 2007 |
| Sinan, Korea | 20 MW | 109,000 PV panels | SunTechnics | Operating since 2008 |
| Nevada, US | 14.2 MW | 90,000 PV panels on 140 acres | Sunpower | Operating since 2008 |
| Salamanca, Spain | 13.8 MW | 70,000 PV panels | Kyocera | Operating since 2007 |
| Murcia, Spain | 12.7 MW | 80,000 PV panels | Ecostream | In operation |
| Bavaria, Germany | 12 MW | 1,400 sun-tracking PV panels | Solon AG | Operating since 2006 |
| Alentejo, Portugal | 11 MW | 52,000 PV panels on 150 acres | | Operating since 2007 |

shi (Japan) 5 percent, First Solar (U.S./Germany) 5 percent, and Isofoton (Spain) 4 percent. The largest suppliers dominating the solar photovoltaic grade silicon market are Wacker (Germany), REC Solar Grade Silicon and Hemlock Semiconductor (U.S.), and Tokuyama (Japan). The U.S. is a major provider of PV grade silicon in the PV supply chain. A large number of companies are involved with other aspects of solar power including supplying semiconductor materials, producing PV modules, and installing solar panel arrays. In addition, there is a great deal of entrepreneurial effort by companies trying to establish a niche in this emerging business.

Significant government monies are being invested in the development of solar power. In 2007, the four nations that spent the most for solar energy research and development were the United States ($138 million), Germany ($61 million), Japan ($39 million), and South Korea ($18 million). Japan, Germany, United States, and other nations offer incentives for individuals and businesses to install solar energy. Like those provided for converting to wind and other alternative sources of energy, these come in various forms such as a direct grant or rebate paid to the individual or business for installing solar panels, various tax benefits, soft loans at below market interest rates and long payout periods, the right to sell excess production back to the utility at above-market rates (feed-in tariffs), and sustainable building standards that require installing PV panels. In the United States, most states have some sort of program to encourage the development of solar energy, ranging from personal, corporate, sales, and property tax exemptions plus loan and grant programs as a means of inducing homeowners to install solar power. Significant rebates of the order of 50 and 60 percent are offered by various states such as New York and New Jersey. In addition, the government has a production tax credit that can be applied against corporate taxes for companies that install solar power and other forms of renewable energy plus, as with wind, direct grants provided by the 2009 American Recovery and Reinvestment Act.

## Economics of Solar Power

The economics of solar power depend on many variables. For example, an energy-efficient 2,000-square-foot home needs about 2 kilowatts of output from a solar array mounted on the roof. If the cost of installation is $16,000 and if there is a rebate available for $8,000, the net cost to the consumer is $8,000. The amount of electricity that the solar array can produce is 100,000 kilowatt hours over its twenty-five-year life, assuming that the sun is shining an average of 5.5 hours per day (2 kilowatts per hour × 5.5 hours per day × 365 days per year × 25 years). The 5.5 hours per day takes into consideration reduced output when the sun is near the horizon and during times of cloud cover. At higher latitudes, three hours per day might be a closer approximation for the equivalent of sunlight directly overhead with no cloud cover. If the average cost of electricity over the next twenty-five years were ten cents per kilowatt hour, then the avoidance of the need to purchase 100,000 kilowatts from a utility would equal the net investment of $10,000, including accrued interest. Without the rebate, there is no economic justification for installing solar power.

Solar power works better if electricity rates are based on time-of-day metering when rates track actual demand. This would improve the economics of solar power immensely since the day rate for electricity is much higher than the night rate, reflecting marginal rates charged by base-load electricity providers. If electricity rates during daylight hours were sixteen cents per kilowatt hour, then the investment of $8,000 (after the rebate) will generate savings of $16,000 in avoided electricity purchases over a twenty-five-year period, providing a 2.8 percent return on the investment. If there were no rebate, the savings would only compensate for the investment, assuming the money has no time value. If it is profitable to install solar power, then one can consider oversizing the array and selling the excess power back to the utility. Regardless of the economic analysis, one may still choose solar power just for the satisfaction of having a home that does not require burning a fossil fuel or relying on nuclear power.

Installing a 454-kilowatt solar array for Monmouth University in New Jersey had a capital cost, including installation, of $2,860,000. A substantial rebate was available from the state of New Jersey in the amount of $1,715,000 (60 percent of capital cost). This reduced the capital investment to $1,145,000. Table 9.3 shows the economic analysis of the installation assuming a cost of purchase of ten cents per kilowatt-hour, with 3 percent escalation over the twenty-five-year life of the solar panel.

The net capital investment of $1.1 million earns a healthy return, primarily in the form of avoided electricity purchases. Any hike in electricity rates above ten cents per kilowatt-hour, which occurred as a consequence of much higher natural gas prices for the utility, increases the rate of return on the investment. As the analysis plainly shows, the internal rate of return is positive only because of the significant commitment on the part of the government to support the development of solar

Table 9.3

**Economic Analysis of Actual Solar Energy System**

|  | Aggregate Savings (Costs) over 25-Year Life of Project |
| --- | --- |
| Avoided Electricity Purchases | $2,415,000 |
| Avoided Transformer Losses | $50,000 |
| Estimate of Sales of Excess Electricity Back to Utility | |
| First 4 Years Only | $315,000 |
| Maintenance of Solar Energy System and Roof | ($110,000) |
| Aggregate Savings | $2,670,000 |
| Cost of System net of Rebate | $1,145,000 |
| Internal Rate of Return over 25 Year Period | 8.3% |

power. A review of the project in 2009 showed that its profitability was greater than originally anticipated because of subsequent hikes in electricity rates. The solar installation provided a fixed electricity rate that lowered the overall cost of electricity. A new building on campus was not fitted with solar panels pending a study on the feasibility and economics of a thin-film solar installation that would be applied directly to the building without the need for frames to hold solar panels.

One of the over 300 utilities that offer electricity from renewable energy to consumers is Arizona Power Service. Located in the Southwest, where the company can take advantage of the 300 days of sun, and with plenty of available desert land for installing solar arrays, the utility has become a leader in promoting solar power to its customers. The company intends to build two thermal solar systems totalling 0.6 GW and offers homeowners a free installation of rooftop solar panels that fixes the cost of their electricity for the next twenty years. The company's objective is to make Arizona the "Solar Capital of the World."[27]

Further government support for solar power occurred at the end of 2005 when the California Public Utilities Commission unveiled a plan to install 3 gigawatts (3,000 megawatts) of capacity over the next eleven years. This plan would double the existing global solar power capacity and would supply 6 percent of California's peak electricity demand. The California Solar Initiative provides $3.2 billion in rebates over the next eleven years with the objective of installing solar panels on 1 million homes and public buildings. Funding would also be eligible for solar water heating along with other solar power technologies. The new initiative is actually an expansion of an existing program that adds a surcharge to consumer utility bills with the proceeds dedicated to rebates for solar power installations. In 2009, Public Service Electric & Gas of New Jersey announced a $0.5 billion plan to place small solar panels costing $1,000 each on telephone poles and rooftops in equal numbers to feed directly into the grid. The plan will add about 80 megawatts of power by 2013, making New Jersey second to California in solar-power generation. The U.S. Bureau of Land Management is examining 1,000 square miles of land on twenty-four tracts of public land in the Southwest to identify a potential site of three square miles for the generation of 100 GW of solar power (present U.S. output is less than 1 GW!). Four solar power plants (1 solar array and 3 thermal) are under review for construction in Nevada and California totalling 2.4 GW. Progress in obtaining regulatory approval is impeded over species protection, availability of water for thermal solar projects, and the greatest barrier of them all, a maze of multiple government agencies' regulations with overlapping jurisdictions. Things are not much better on the state level—regulatory requirements are as much an impediment for adding renewable energy capacity as they are for fossil fuels.

One idea on the table is to convert 30,000 square miles of public lands into thin-film module arrays for the generation of 2,940 GW. This would require an increase in thin-film module conversion rate of solar energy to electricity from the present 10 percent to 14 percent and another 16,000 square miles for thermal solar systems with an increased conversion rate from the present 13 percent to 17 percent to generate 558 GW, plus the building of 100,000–500,000 miles of new high-voltage DC transmission lines to connect the Southwest with the nation's electricity grid. The cost of electricity will be near current rates if the indicated conversion-rate improvements can be achieved. Such a system could provide nearly 70 percent of the nation's electricity by 2050 and could be further expanded to provide 100 percent by 2100.[28]

## GEOTHERMAL ENERGY

Geothermal energy, from the Greek words *geo* (earth) and *therme* (heat), takes advantage of hot water or steam escaping from hot spots in the earth. Geothermal sources are located where magma is relatively close to the surface of the earth and where the rock above the magma is porous and filled with subsurface water with access to the surface. Geothermal sources are found near tectonic plate boundaries that are separating (the rift valley in east Africa and in Iceland) or colliding creating subduction zones (Japan) or sliding by one another (California). Geothermal energy sources are also found near volcanoes (Mount Vesuvius in Italy, the island of Hawaii, and the caldera at Yellowstone), where magma protrusions lie relatively close to the earth's surface. The Maoris in New Zealand and Native Americans used water from hot springs for cooking and medicinal purposes for thousands of years. Ancient Greeks and Romans had geothermal heated spas. The people of Pompeii, living too close to Mount Vesuvius, tapped hot water from the earth to heat their buildings. Romans used geothermal waters for treating eye and skin disease. The Japanese have enjoyed geothermal spas for centuries.

The earth's crust insulates us from the hot interior of the mantle. The normal temperature gradient is about 50°F–87°F per mile or 17°C–30°C per kilometer of depth and higher where the crust is relatively thin or near plate boundaries and volcanoes. Magma trapped beneath the crust heats up the lower rock layers. If the hot rock is porous and filled with continually replenished subsurface water with access to the surface, then the result is fumaroles of escaping steam and hot gases, geysers of hot water, or pools of boiling mud. As a geothermal source, the earth becomes a boiler and escaping hot water and steam, called hydrothermal fluids, are tapped for hot spring baths, heating greenhouses (agriculture), heating water for marine life (aquaculture), space heating for homes, schools, and commercial establishments, heating streets and sidewalks to prevent ice formation, and as a source of hot water for industrial use or steam for generating electricity. Some cities have district heating using geothermal hot water to heat an entire area, best exemplified in Reykjavik, Iceland, where 95 percent of the city receives hot water from geothermal sources.

There are three types of geothermal power plants for generating electricity. The first is a dry-steam geothermal reservoir in which emitted steam directly spins a turbine. These are relatively rare and were the first dedicated to generating electricity. One in Tuscany has been in operation since 1904 and The Geysers, 90 miles north of San Francisco, has been in operation since 1960. The Geysers represents the largest single source of tapped geothermal energy in the world and generates enough electricity to supply a city the size of San Francisco. A falloff in steam pressure in the 1990s was successfully countered by water injection to replenish the geothermal reservoir. Injected water was waste treatment water from neighboring communities, an innovative and environmentally safe method of disposal. Some thought has been given to tapping the world's most productive source of geothermal energy, Yellowstone, the caldera of a supervolcano that last erupted 600,000 years ago. (Another eruption of that magnitude would wipe out half of the United States and emit an ash cloud large enough to send the planet into a "volcanic" winter.) But Yellowstone, as a national park, cannot be commercially developed.

The second and most common form of geothermal power plant is driven by geothermal reservoirs that emit hot, pressurized water between 300°F–700°F. The drop in pressure inside a separator allows the liquid to flash to steam, which is then directed into a turbine. Any gases in the geothermal water such as carbon dioxide, hydrogen sulfide, and nitrous oxides pass to the atmosphere, but these are a tiny fraction of the emissions from a coal-burning plant with an equivalent power output. Water and steam remaining after flashing and passing through a turbine are usually reinjected to replenish the water in order to maintain the reservoir's pressure. If reservoir pressure can be maintained, then geothermal becomes a sustainable source of nearly nonpolluting clean energy.

Shallower sources of geothermal energy in which the water temperature is between 250°F–350°F require a binary power plant where a heat exchanger transfers the heat of the geothermal water to a second or binary fluid such as isopentane or isobutane. The binary fluid boils at a lower temperature than water and its vapors pass through a turbine and are then condensed to a liquid for recycling. Binary plants are closed systems in which the hydrothermal fluid, along with any entrapped gases, is reinjected into the reservoir. A binary system may be necessary for water with a high mineral content to prevent forming a harmful scale on the turbine blades. Hybrid plants, part flash and part binary, are also available such as the one that supplies 25 percent of the electricity for the island of Hawaii.

As of 2005, there were 490 geothermal power plants with 9 gigawatts (GW) of installed capacity, equivalent to the production of nine large-sized nuclear or coal-fired plants, enough to supply the electricity needs of 9 million people.[29] The United States leads with 2.9 GW, mostly in California and Nevada, whose 209 operating plants supply 0.5 percent of the nation's energy needs. The second largest producer is the Philippines with 57 operating plants of 1.9 GW of capacity sufficient to meet 19 percent of the nation's electricity demand. The third largest is Mexico with 36 operating units of 0.95 GW, representing 3 percent of the nation's electricity. The fourth largest is Indonesia with 15 operating plants of 0.8 GW sufficient to satisfy nearly 7 percent of the nations' electricity needs. Italy is the fifth largest producer with 32 plants of nearly 0.8 GW of electricity or 2 percent of the nation's electricity needs (one center of activity is near Mount Vesuvius on the outskirts of Naples). Other nations have smaller outputs, but their generating capacities make a meaningful contribution in satisfying the nation's electricity needs such as El Salvador (22 percent of electricity is geothermal), Kenya (19 percent), Iceland (17 percent), Costa Rica (15 percent), and Nicaragua (10 percent). It is interesting to note that Central America is largely dependent on renewable sources, hydro and geothermal for electricity generation. Thermal uses, distinct from generation of electricity, total another 16 thermal GW for hot springs, agriculture and aquaculture, and district heating.[30] Geothermal heat pumps use the constant underground temperature either for cooling or heating residences. Heat pumps are effective over a limited range of temperatures and require supplemental cooling and heating to handle more extreme variations in temperature.

Geothermal sources are limited primarily to porous hot rock permeated with subsurface water that can escape to the surface. If water is trapped by a cover of impermeable caprock, then the geothermal reservoir must first be discovered before it can be exploited. The same technology for discovering oil fields and drilling wells to tap oil and natural gas reservoirs can be applied for discovering and developing geothermal reservoirs. The future of geothermal energy is limited in so far as current efforts are, for the most part, restricted to developing known sources of geothermal energy, not in discovering new ones.

Hot rock underlies the entire crust. Its usefulness is a matter of depth and whether it is porous rock filled with subsurface water. But the presence of subsurface water and porous rock is no longer necessary. The feasibility of drilling two wells deep into the earth's crust to reach hot rock, and then fracturing the rock separating the two employing methods practiced by the oil industry, has been demonstrated. Water is then pumped down one well under pressure and forced through the fractured hot rock, where it is heated and rises to the surface via the other well as pressurized hydrothermal fluid. This can be flashed to produce steam and drive electricity generators or heat another liquid medium in a hybrid plant.

Hot rock from a magma protrusion of up to 570°F was discovered two and three-quarter miles below the surface in southern Australia. Geodynamics, a start-up company that raised $150 million in capital, has drilled two wells 14,000 feet down to the hot granite. These wells, when fractured to allow the flow of water from one well to the other, will be able to generate geothermal energy. A small generator is scheduled for completion in 2009 followed by a larger one. It is hoped that these generators will establish the feasibility of generating geothermal electricity on a commercial basis. If successful, large-sized electricity generators will be installed with the possibility of supplying a potential of 10 GW of electricity. A transmission system would have to be built to connect the geothermal-generating plant to the nation's electricity grid. It is possible that this hot rock formation may one day supply most of Australia's electricity needs.[31]

Another geothermal project had a far different outcome. The Swiss Deep Heat Mining Project near Basel, Switzerland, was to pump water down three-mile deep boreholes to hot rocks of 200 degrees Centigrade. The returning superheated steam would be sufficient to supply electrical power to 10,000 homes and hot water heat to another 2,700 homes. The project, partly backed with financial support by the Swiss government, was considered a safe and sustainable alternative to a nuclear power-plant project opposed by the Swiss people. Basel is prone to earthquakes, with one in 1356 strong enough (6.5 on the Richter scale) to raze the city. Pumping water down the boreholes was held responsible for setting off tremors measuring 3.3 on the Richter scale up to ten miles away from the site. The project was suspended. State prosecutors began looking into the possibility of criminal negligence on the part of the promoters despite support from the Swiss government.[32] Nevertheless, there are a number of geothermal projects in various stages of development in India, Nevada, and California.

A more esoteric idea is to mine heat from magma as a geothermal ore in places where it is accessible by current drilling technology. For this, a hole is drilled through the crust and a sealed pipe with a concentric inner pipe is thrust into the magma. Water is pumped down the inner pipe and is transformed into high-pressure hydrothermal fluid by the magma surrounding the bottom of the sealed pipe. From there, the hydrothermal fluid flows up the outer pipe to the surface to be flashed to steam to power electricity generators. A major obstacle to overcome is drilling all the way through the crust. The deepest bore hole ever drilled was in Russia 7.5 miles into crust 30 miles thick. Even if a bore hole were drilled into magma, precautions would have to be taken to prevent creating a mini-volcano if magma escapes to the surface. Another major obstacle is finding materials that can withstand the extreme high temperatures, pressures, and corrosive properties of being thrust into magma.[33] But if the inner heat of the planet could be tapped, geothermal energy could conceivably satisfy the world's electricity demand.

## OCEAN ENERGY

The oceans cover over 70 percent of the earth's surface and represent an immense reservoir of energy in the form of tides, currents, waves, and temperature differentials. Tides result from the gravitational interaction of the earth and the moon, with about two high and two low tides each day. The time between high tides is twelve hours and twenty-five minutes. The shift in maximum power output on a daily basis, while predictable, may not correspond to the timing of peak demand for electricity. Tides are also affected by the relative placement of the sun and moon with respect to the earth, which causes spring (maximum) and neap (minimum) tides. The elliptical path the earth traces around the sun, plus weather and other influences, affect tides, as does the topography of the shoreline. Unfortunately, coastal estuaries that can create tidal rises of up to fifty feet are located at high latitudes, far from population centers. Tidal power output must be viewed as a supplemental power source available only about eight to ten hours a day.

The concept of tidal power is fairly old; waterwheels powered by tidal currents ground grain in eleventh-century England. Tidal power is tapped by building a dam with sluice gates across an estuary at a narrow opening to reduce construction costs. The sluice gates are opened to allow an incoming tide to increase the height of the water. When the tide turns, the sluice gates are closed, entrapping the water. As the tide goes out, the water level differential on either side of the dam widens until there is a sufficient head for water to pass through specially designed turbines to generate electricity.

A tidal dam must be located where there is a marked difference between high and low tides. One favored area proposed for building a tidal dam is the Bay of Fundy in eastern Canada, where the difference in water level between tides is over fifty feet, the highest in the world. Other areas with pronounced tides in the northern hemisphere are Cook Inlet in Alaska, the White Sea in Russia, and the coastline along eastern Russia, northern China, and Korea. In the southern hemisphere, potential sites are in Argentina, Chile, and western Australia. With electricity production limited to between eight and ten hours a day, a tidal dam has an effective output of only 35 percent or so of rated capacity and the timing of its maximum output may not correspond to the timing of peak demand. Moreover, a substantial investment is necessary to transmit the generated electricity from remote sites conducive to tidal dams to population centers.

The only major source of tidal energy in the world is the tidal dam at La Rance estuary in France, built in the 1960s, capable of producing 240 megawatts of electricity. It has a maximum tidal range of twenty-six feet, operates at 26 percent of rated capacity on average, requires low maintenance, and is in service 97 percent of the time. Three other such dams are far smaller; an 18-megawatt tidal dam at Annapolis Royal, Canada (Bay of Fundy), which serves the local area, a 3.2-megawatt dam in eastern China at Jiangxia, and a 0.4-megawatt dam in the White Sea at Kislaya, Russia. One proposal under consideration since the 1980s is to build a sixteen-kilometer (ten-mile) dam across the Severn estuary in the United Kingdom. It would have a maximum output of 8.6 gigawatts, employing 214 electricity-generating turbines, and would be capable of supplying about 5–6 percent of the United Kingdom's electricity demand.[34] Another under consideration since 1990 is a 48-megawatt tidal dam near Derby in northwestern Australia, but little progress has been made to date. South Korea is nearing the completion of what will be the world's largest tidal dam. An existing seawall between Sihung City and Daeboo Island created saltwater Lake Sihwa. Without an outlet, Lake Sihwa was becoming polluted. Constructing an outlet through the sea wall to flush the lake also allowed for the installation of turbines to take advantage of tidal flows. When in operation, the output of 254 MW will make it larger than the tidal dam at La Rance, France. South Korea has also embarked on another tidal dam at Inchon, near Seoul. The project, to be completed in 2014, will consist of a 4.8 mile barrier connecting four islands and containing turbines capable of generating 812 MW when the tide is flowing.[35]

A more effective way to harness tidal power is channeling tidal flow through a restricted waterway so that the tidal current powers turbines during incoming and outgoing tides. This "double flow" system provides electricity generation whenever the tides are running but not during a change in tides when the tidal current reverses. Though the double flow system has a higher effective output than the tidal dam, electricity generation is still not continuous and may not be timed to accommodate demand. One proposal, now defunct, was to build a tidal fence two and a half miles long (four kilometers) in the San Bernardino Strait in the Philippines between the islands of Samar and Dalupiri. The tidal fence would contain 274 turbines capable of generating 2,200 megawatts (2.2 gigawatts) at peak tidal flow. The Race Rocks Ecological Reserve off the coast of Vancouver Island has built a small power plant powered by tidal current in addition to a solar panel to supply most of its electricity demand by renewable sources. A larger installation has been built in Strangford Narrows, Northern Ireland, by Marine Current Turbines. When the tide is running, the tidal stream turbine powers a 1.2 megawatt generator sufficient to power 1,000 homes. Means to supply power when the tide is turning can be a battery charged when the tidal current is running. Another interesting solution is to use some of the generated electricity to compress air in a sealed cavern. During times when the tide is turning, or when the wind isn't blowing for wind turbines, the compressed air becomes a motive force to generate electricity.

The "double basin" method of tidal power provides a continuous supply of electricity because the water flows continually from a higher basin to a lower basin. Water in the upper basin is replenished during high tide and water accumulating in the lower basin is drained during low tide. Continuous power is possible by installing a turbine in a river as proposed for the Mississippi and the Niagara where power generation would not be interrupted by changing tides. Tidal or river currents with an optimal speed is 4.5 to 6.7 miles per hour (2 to 3 meters per second) turn a propeller that drives a generator whose output is transmitted to shore via underwater cables. In principle, this is similar to a wind turbine. The major difference is that water is 850 times denser than air, which allows a smaller propeller to generate electricity at a lower rate of rotation. (Fish learn to live with the rotating propellers whose speed is slow enough for them to escape contact.) A tidal turbine with thirty-four-foot-long blades has been built in Hammerfest, Norway, capable of generating 300 kilowatts of electricity when the tide is running to supply the local community of 35 homes. The European Marine Energy Centre describes tidal devices being built or proposed to capture tidal energy such as the horizontal axis turbine (one is installed in the East River of New York City), the vertical axis turbine, the oscillating hydrofoil, and other designs along with a list of over fifty companies in various stages of developing tidal power.[36] The largest water current electricity-generating scheme ever devised is the proposal to dam the Mediterranean at Gibraltar where the waterway is about ten miles wide. There are two currents at Gibraltar; a surface current of outgoing water and a deeper current of incoming water (submarines during the Second World War would "sneak" into the Mediterranean by drifting in this lower current).[37] The net flow of water is incoming as the Mediterranean and Black Seas evaporate more water than is entering via the Nile, Danube, Dnieper, and other rivers. Obviously gates would be necessary for the passage of ships. Enormous turbines would be installed in the dam powered by the incoming water current. The electricity-generating potential is enormous, but cost and obvious concerns over its environmental impact have stymied the project.

Waves are caused by wind and their enormous energy potential can be tapped by using hydraulic or mechanical means to translate the up-and-down motion to rotate a generator. Calm weather and severe storms affect the operation of these devices, but when in operation, electricity can be delivered to shore via underwater cables. While one may feel that this energy source is futuristic, tens of thousands of navigational buoys have long relied on wave motion to power their lights. The height of a column of water in a cylinder within the buoy changes with the up-and-down motion of the buoy, creating an air-pressure differential that drives a piston powering a generator to supply power for the lights, sound signals, and other navigational aids of the buoy. A battery is kept charged by the wave motion in case of calm weather. One wave-power system has been in operation since 1989, producing 75 kilowatts for a remote community at Islay in Scotland. Pelamis Wave Power builds sausage looking semisubmerged, articulated cylindrically shaped wave generators where internal hydraulic rams, driven by wave motion, pump high pressure oil through hydraulic motors to drive generators. Electricity is collected in a single underwater cable for transmission on shore. Load control maximizes output in quiet seas and limits output in dangerous weather. Precautions have to be taken to keep ships away from wave generators. Ocean Power Technologies produces a conventional looking buoy capable of converting wave energy to a mechanical stroking action that drives an electricity generator for servicing a shore community. Small generating buoys are deployed off the coast of New Jersey and Hawaii. A 1.4 megawatt installation is being built offshore northern Spain with a planned project for a 5 megawatt installation offshore U.K.[38] An entrepreneurial professor of electrical engineering has invented a simple "wave-energy converter" with only one moving part. The buoy consists of an outer cylinder with copper wires wound on its inside tethered to the bottom so that it remains stationary. Inside the cylinder is a float free to move with the wave motion. The magnet in the float generates a current as it moves up and down within the cylinder, and the generated electricity is transmitted to shore by an underwater power cable.[39]

The last method of extracting energy from the ocean is to take advantage of temperature differentials. The warm temperature of ocean surface water can be used to vaporize a working fluid, such as ammonia, which boils at a low temperature, to drive a turbine to generate electricity. The working fluid is cooled and condensed for recycling by deeper cold water. The warmed cold water must be pumped back into the ocean's depths to prevent cooling the surface. Ocean thermal systems are located in the tropics, where warm surface waters lie over deep cold waters. This provides the greatest temperature differential for operating a turbine; even so, the efficiency of heat transfer at these relatively small temperature differentials is only 5 percent, a technical challenge that requires building and operating a heat exchanger large enough to produce a significant amount of electricity. Demonstration plants have been built, including one in Hawaii that produced up to 250 kilowatts of electricity for a number of years. However, technical problems associated with ocean thermal energy still pose a significant barrier to developing this source of energy on a commercial scale.

One idea is to have "grazing plants" located far from shore where temperature differentials are the greatest. This precludes having an underwater cable connecting the grazing plant to the shore. The generated electricity would produce hydrogen by electrolyzing water. Hydrogen then becomes a stored form of electricity that can be shipped from the grazing plants in specially designed vessels to shore-based terminals for further distribution as an energy source for fuel cells in automobiles and homes.

## NOTES

1. Environment and Development (also known as the Brundtland Commission), 1987.

2. "Energy Use in Cities" Chapter 8, *Global Energy Outlook* published by the IEA, Paris, 2008; and "Emission Control Measures in Shanghai, China" published by Institute for Global Environmental Strategies Web site www.iges.or.jp/APEIS/RISPO/inventory/db/pdf/0031.pdf.

3. "Energy Use in Cities" Chapter 8, *Global Energy Outlook* published by the IEA, Paris, 2008; and "Emission Control Measures in Shanghai, China" published by Institute for Global Environmental Strategies Web site www.iges.or.jp/APEIS/RISPO/inventory/db/pdf/0031.pdf.

4. Anup Shah, "Sustainable Development Introduction" Web site www.globalissues.org/article/408/sustainable-development-introduction 2005.

5. India Climate Solutions Web site www.indiaclimatesolutions.com/pump-sets-irrigation-and-human-power.

6. Darrell M. Dodge, *Illustrated History of Wind Power Development,* Web site www.telosnet.com/wind/index.html. Unless otherwise indicated, this is the chief source of information on the development of windmills and wind turbines.

7. Vaclav Smil, *Energy in World History* (Boulder, CO: Westview Press, 1994).

8. As a child I lived on an estate dairy farm on Long Island that had a large wooden windmill, perched on top of a tall stucco and brick tower, that was used for pumping and storing water; but by then, the windmill was no longer operable and the tower had been converted to a silo for corn.

9. Web site energy.sourceguides.com/businesses/byP/wRP/lwindturbine/byB/mfg/byN/byName.shtml contains a full listing of wind turbine manufacturers.

10. Figures 9.1, 9.2, and 9.3 data are from Global Wind Energy Council's Web site www.gwec.net, along with the American and the European Wind Energy Associations Web sites www.awea.org and www.ewea. org, respectively.

11. Keith Bradsher, "Drawing Critics, China Seeks to Dominate in Renewable Energy," *New York Times* (July 14, 2009) p. B1.

12. General Electric Web site www.gepower.com/prod_serv/products/wind_turbines/en/15mw/index.htm.

13. Terra Moya Aqua (TMA) Web site www.tmawind.com.

14. *Outlook 2005 for Wind Power,* American Wind Energy Association Web site www.awea.org.

15. For example, the Australian joint venture utility company ActewAGL offers the GreenChoice Program, Web site www.actewagl.com.au/environment/default.aspx.

16. Solar Energy Technologies Program of the U.S. Department of Energy, Energy Efficiency and Renewable Energy Web site www.eere.energy.gov/solar/solar_time_7bc-1200ad.html.

17. Solar Energy History Web site www.facts-about-solar-energy.com/solar-energy-history.html; and Solar Panels Plus Web site www.solarpanelsplus.com/solar-energy-history; and Solar Energy History Web site www.solarevents.com/articles/solar-energy/solar-energy-history; and Ausra "A History of Solar Power" Web site www.ausra.com/history/index.html.

18. United Nations Development Program (UNDP), "World Energy Assessment: Overview 2004 Update," New York, 2004.

19. National Renewable Energy Laboratory's Web site www.nrel.gov.

20. Energy Efficiency and Renewable Energy Solar Technologies Program Web site www.eere.energy.gov/solar/csp.html.

21. Enviromission Company Web site www.enviromission.com.au.

22. Data for Tables 9.1 and 9.2 obtained from ECO Worldly Web site ecoworldly.com.

23. Solar Energy Technologies Program of the U.S. Department of Energy Efficiency and Renewable Energy Web site www.eere.energy.gov/solar/pv_cell_light.html.

24. PV Power Resource Web site www.pvpower.com.

25. For more information on BP Solar installations in remote locations, see Web site www.bp.com/genericarticle.do?categoryId=3050422&contentId=7028813.

26. International Energy Agency Photovoltaic Power Systems Program 2007 Report, Web site www.iea-pvps.org.

27. Arizona Power Service solar program is described on Web site www.aps.com/main/green/choice/choice_82.html.

28. "Solar Grand Plan," *Scientific American* (January 2008), p. 65–73; also available at Web site www.scientificamerican.com/article.cfm?id=a-solar-grand-plan.

29. Geothermal Education Office Web site geothermal.marin.org.

30. Geothermal Resources Council Web site geothermal.org.

31. Geodynamics Ltd. Web site www.geodynamics. com.au.

32. "Swiss Geothermal Project Causes Earthquakes" published online by *Scitizen* (September 12, 2007), Web site http://www.scitizen.com/.

33. Wendell A. Duffield and John H. Sass, *Geothermal Energy–Clean Power from the Earth's Heat,* Circular 1249 (Washington, DC: U.S. Geological Survey, U.S. Department of the Interior, 2003).

34. For the current status of this project, see Web site www.reuk.co.uk/Severn-Barrage-Tidal-Power.htm.

35. Environmental & Energy Research at the Washington University in St. Louis, Web site www.eer.wustl.edu/McDonnellMayWorkshop/Presentation_files/Saturday/Saturday/Park.pdf.

36. European Marine Energy Centre (EMEC) Web site www.emec.org.uk.

37. The 1981 movie *Das Boot* shows a submarine taking advantage of this current.

38.Palamis Wave Power Web site www.pelamiswave.com; Ocean Power Technologies Web site www.oceanpowertechnologies.com. See also European Marine Energy Centre for description of wave generating devices and companies involved with this technology Web site www.emec.ort.uk.

39. "Catching a Wave" by Elizabeth Rusch, *Smithsonian* (July 2009), vol. 40, no 4, p. 66.

# 10

## LOOKING TOWARD THE FUTURE

This chapter deals with the hydrogen economy, climate change, the impact of fossil fuels on the environment, legislative acts to deal with air pollution, and energy efficiency and conservation.

### THE HYDROGEN ECONOMY

Hydrogen is the most abundant element in the universe, making up 75 percent of its mass and 90 percent of its molecules. Hydrogen, when burned as a fuel, emits only water and heat, the cleanest source of energy by far. Though plentiful in the universe, there is no free hydrogen here on Earth. While a portion is locked away in hydrocarbons and other chemicals, most of what there is has already been burned and its product of combustion is all around and in us: water.

Curiously, human progress in energy has been marked with decarbonizing fuel sources. For most of history, humans burned wood, which has the highest ratio of carbon to hydrogen atoms, about ten carbon atoms per hydrogen atom, in comparison to fossil fuels. This means that burning wood emits more carbon dioxide than burning fossil fuels for an equivalent release of energy. Coal, the fossil fuel that sparked the Industrial Revolution, has about one or two carbon atoms per hydrogen atom, which means it emits less carbon dioxide than wood. Next is oil, with one half of a carbon atom per hydrogen atom (or one carbon atom for every two hydrogen atoms), and natural gas is last, with one-quarter of a carbon atom per hydrogen atom (or one carbon atom for every four hydrogen atoms). Thus, as people have learned to use new fuels, each one was a step down in carbon dioxide emissions for an equivalent release of energy. The ultimate step is hydrogen, which has no carbon atoms and, therefore, no carbon dioxide emissions, no emissions of carbon monoxide, sulfur, nitrous oxides and other progenitor chemicals that create smog, and no metallic emissions (mercury, arsenic); hydrogen produces only plain water and heat.

Henry Cavendish discovered "inflammable air" in 1766 and Antoine Lavoisier renamed it hydrogen. Hydrogen is colorless, odorless, has no taste, and burns with a pale blue flame virtually invisible in daylight. In the 1870s, Jules Verne thought that water would be the fuel of the future. In 1923, John Haldane predicted that future energy would be in the form of liquid hydrogen. Rows of windmills would generate electricity to produce hydrogen by the electrolysis of water. Hydrogen gas would then be liquefied and stored in vacuum-jacketed underground reservoirs until needed to generate electricity when recombined with oxygen. Although his idea was ridiculed at the time, Haldane's prediction is essentially where we are headed today.[1]

The fuel for the engines on German-made Zeppelin dirigibles that carried passengers between European cities and across the Atlantic Ocean to the United States varied from diesel fuel to a mixture of benzene and gasoline, augmented by excess hydrogen blow-off as a booster fuel. The crash of the *Hindenburg* in 1937 ended the days of dirigibles filled with hydrogen, which was replaced with helium. The *Hindenburg* gave hydrogen a reputation for being a dangerous fuel. It was originally thought that an atmospheric electrical charge called St. Elmo's Fire, a blue glow sometimes seen around church spires, sailing masts, and airplane wings during stormy weather, ignited the hydrogen. More recent investigations into the cause of the tragedy point to other possibilities such as an electrical discharge that ignited not the hydrogen, but the highly combustible coating of aluminized cellulose acetate butyrate dopant, a component of rocket fuel, which saturated the outer cotton fabric. Another possibility was leaking fuel from a propulsion engine dripping on a hot surface that started a fire within the internal structure of the dirigible. These investigations concluded that design faults and operating deficiencies made the *Hindenburg* a bomb waiting to be detonated. Regardless of the specific cause of the fire, once the hydrogen ignited, the end came quickly.

Hydrogen also has gotten a bad rap by being associated with the hydrogen bomb, which, of course, has nothing to do with combustion. On the other hand, hydrogen aficionados maintain that a tank full of hydrogen in an automobile presents no more of a hazard to a passenger than a tank full of gasoline. They argue that it may be less hazardous because a ruptured gasoline tank spills its contents on the ground, which, if ignited, will almost completely combust. If a tank filled with pressurized hydrogen were to rupture, a large portion of the fuel may escape to the atmosphere before ignition takes place. Hydrogen, the lightest of all elements, has a very high diffusion rate and disperses four times faster than natural gas and ten times faster than gasoline vapors. Moreover, hydrogen radiates relatively little heat compared to burning petroleum, and personal injuries are confined to those in direct contact with the flame. On the downside, hydrogen can burn when its concentration in air is between 2–75 percent, whereas the flammable range of gasoline vapors is between 1.4–7.6 percent. This means that gasoline vapors cannot ignite if their concentration is less than 1.4 percent (too little vapor to ignite) or greater than 7.6 percent (too little oxygen to support ignition). For natural gas, the flammable range is 5–15 percent. These are much more restrictive ranges than hydrogen. Not only does hydrogen have a wider flammable range and "ignites" easier than gasoline or natural gas, its nearly invisible flame in daylight is another element of danger. Whatever the virtues of supposedly being less hazardous than commonly used gasoline, propane, or natural gas, this is not the public's perception of hydrogen. There are real safety concerns when one is dealing with hydrogen, as is the case with any flammable substance.

Yet hydrogen has a long history of use. Hydrogen was a component of coal-derived town or manufactured gas along with methane, carbon dioxide, and carbon monoxide. This mixture of gases was burned in homes and businesses long before the discovery of natural gas fields and continued to be burned as late as the 1950s before being fully replaced by natural gas. Hydrogen has been an industrial commodity for over fifty years with about 50 million tons of hydrogen produced annually worldwide. Most hydrogen is a byproduct of reforming naphtha in oil refineries and is largely consumed within the refinery to increase the yield of more valuable light end products from the heavy end of the barrel with a relatively small portion pipelined to nearby petrochemical plants.

Only about 5 percent of hydrogen consumed by industry is merchant hydrogen, specifically produced (mostly by steam reforming of natural gas) for commercial purposes. It is transported either in pipelines as a compressed gas or in tanks carried by rail, barge, and truck as either a compressed gas or a cryogenic liquid at a temperature of minus 253°C, only twenty degrees above absolute zero. Merchant hydrogen is used by the food industry for hydrogenation of edible organic oils and in making margarine, by the fertilizer industry for producing ammonia for nitrogen-based fertilizers, and by the semiconductor industry. The aerospace industry relies on merchant hydrogen for fuel cells aboard manned space stations to produce electricity and potable water. The oil industry and producers and consumers of merchant hydrogen have an excellent safety record because of their understanding and appreciation of its inherent risks.

In the area of transportation, a number of experimental vehicles including submarines and torpedoes ran on hydrogen in the 1930s and 1940s. The 1973 oil crisis awakened the public to the possibility of hydrogen as a motor vehicle fuel. In 1988, the Soviet Union and the United States experimented with airplanes fueled by liquid hydrogen. The first hydrogen-fueled buses were in operation in Belgium in 1994, and in 1995 the city of Chicago tested hydrogen-fueled buses. A small number of hydrogen-fueled buses currently operate in several European and American cities, mainly for testing and demonstration purposes. A motor vehicle engine can be converted fairly easily from gasoline to natural gas or hydrogen. For hydrogen-fueled vehicles the problem is fuel availability, cost, and storage, not engine design. But the role of hydrogen is not limited to its potential as a motor vehicle fuel. In 1992, the first solar home that relied on hydrogen as a means to store electricity, rather than a battery, was successfully demonstrated in Germany. In 1999, Iceland announced a long-term plan to become the world's first hydrogen economy by totally eliminating fossil fuels by 2050. Icelandic motor vehicles and fishing vessels will run on hydrogen produced by electrolysis of water with the required electricity generated from hydro and geothermal sources.[2]

The problem is how to produce hydrogen. Reforming it is a three-stage process that begins with the hydrocarbon (mainly natural gas, but coal can be used as well as various petroleum products) in an endothermic (heat-absorbing) reaction in the presence of a catalyst to form hydrogen and carbon monoxide. The second stage is combining carbon monoxide with steam in an exothermic (heat-releasing) reaction to form additional hydrogen and carbon dioxide. Heat released by the exothermic reaction can be recycled to supply a portion of the heat for the endothermic reaction. The third stage is the removal of carbon dioxide and trace amounts of carbon monoxide through an adsorption process to separate the hydrogen. "Black" hydrogen results if the waste-product carbon dioxide is released to the atmosphere. An owner of a hydrogen-fueled automobile who proudly announces that he or she is not polluting the environment is suffering from a case of self-delusion if the automobile is running on black hydrogen. Hydrogen from reforming is quite expensive and efforts are underway to find a different technology such as advanced ion transport membranes to reduce the cost of separating hydrogen from hydrocarbons.

"Green" hydrogen results if the carbon dioxide emissions from steam reformers are sequestered such as in an integrated coal-gasification combined cycle (IGCC) plant. The U.S. government-sponsored FutureGen project (shelved by the Bush administration for cost overruns in 2007 but reinstated by the Obama administration in 2009) employs ultra-low emissions technology, coupled with sequestering carbon dioxide emissions, where coal produces electricity and hydrogen with virtually no emissions to the atmosphere. Green hydrogen can be produced from ethanol, which opens up biomass as a hydrogen fuel. While this process releases carbon dioxide, growing crops to supply ethanol removes an equivalent amount of carbon dioxide from the atmosphere. This makes hydrogen from biomass essentially carbon dioxide neutral as long as energy from biomass fuels, not oil, is consumed in the growing, harvesting, and processing of biomass crops. Another way to produce green hydrogen is electrolysis of water, in which the source of electricity is not a fossil fuel (unless carbon dioxide emissions are sequestered), but nuclear, hydro, wind, solar, geothermal, tidal, or grazers (proposed floating plants on the world's oceans generating electricity from thermal differentials).

Electrolysis is the flow of direct-current electricity between a positive and negative electrode in pure water that contains an electrolyte to enhance conductivity. Electricity splits the water molecule into its elements, oxygen, which collects at the anode, or positively charged electrode, and hydrogen, which collects at the cathode, or negatively charged electrode. The gases are drawn away from the electrodes, dried, and stored. Hydrogen can be a fuel for specially adapted conventional motor vehicle engines or for fuel cells. Oxygen can be pressurized in bottles and sold for industrial use or released into the atmosphere. One proposal is to install solar panels on hospital rooftops to generate electricity for the hospital and for electrolysis to produce oxygen and hydrogen. Oxygen can supply patients who need breathing assistance and hydrogen can supply fuel for ambulances and/or be sold to owners of hydrogen-fueled motor vehicles.

Only 4 percent of the world's output of hydrogen is by electrolysis because of the high cost of electricity compared to steam reformers that strip hydrogen from fossil fuels. A cost differential of three or four times puts hydrogen by electrolysis at a severe disadvantage. If hydrogen is to reduce carbon dioxide emissions, electricity for electrolysis cannot come from fossil-fueled plants (other than coal-burning IGCC plants that sequester carbon dioxide emissions). From a practical viewpoint, the generation of the enormous quantities of electricity necessary for the hydrogen economy would have to depend largely on nuclear power and IGCC plants augmented by hydro, wind, and solar sources. The capacity of this combination of power sources could be expanded to the point of satisfying peak electricity demand. As electricity demand from consumers, businesses, and industry moves off its peak, excess electricity-generating capacity would be dedicated to hydrogen production. This combination of electricity-generating plants operating at full capacity would eliminate carbon dioxide emissions from electricity generation as well as the need for building generators to satisfy transient electricity demand. The uniform charge for electricity to consumers and to hydrogen producers would be the same low base rate, eliminating marginal electricity rate differentials for operating at less than base load. The prospect of nuclear power and coal for IGCC plants playing a major role in the hydrogen economy is viewed disdainfully by environmentalists but not necessarily by hydrogen enthusiasts. These two groups should not be at odds with one another because both share a mutual desire to eliminate carbon dioxide emissions.

**Hydrogen Stores Electricity**

Energy (heat) generates electricity for producing hydrogen by electrolysis of water. Fuel cells reverse electrolysis by reuniting hydrogen with oxygen, producing electricity, heat, and water. Electrolysis consumes electricity when converting water to hydrogen and oxygen, and a fuel cell generates electricity by converting hydrogen and oxygen to water. A fuel cell represents a twofold generation of electricity—once to produce hydrogen by electrolysis of water and again when the fuel cell converts hydrogen back to water. Hydrogen can be produced any time there is available electricity then distributed, stored, and converted back to electricity when and as needed by fuel cells. Although one might say that hydrogen fulfills the same role as a battery, there is a major difference. A battery stores chemical energy that is converted to electricity until the chemical energy is exhausted. As such, a battery is a finite source of energy that must be recharged or discarded when the chemical energy is gone. A fuel cell converts chemical energy (hydrogen) to electricity continually up to its rated capacity as long as supplies of hydrogen are available. Hydrogen, quite unlike a battery, never runs down, never is exhausted, and never has to be recharged. Hydrogen is far more effective in storing electricity than a battery.

Sir William Robert Grove invented the hydrogen fuel cell in the 1830s, but, without practical use, the fuel cell faded from view. It was revived in the 1960s when General Electric developed a workable fuel cell as a power supply for the Apollo and Gemini space missions. Hydrogen, the fuel for fuel cells, must be uncontaminated and can be supplied from tanks pressurized with hydrogen gas or from associated reformers that extract hydrogen from natural gas, propane, methanol, gasoline, or other types of hydrocarbons. A fuel cell consists of a proton-exchange membrane (PEM) at its center, surrounded on both sides by a catalyst. On the outside of each catalyst is an anode or a cathode electrode connected by an electrical circuit that passes through a motor or a light bulb or any electrical load. Hydrogen, passing through a flow plate at one end of the fuel cell, enters the anode catalyst, where the hydrogen is split into protons and electrons (a hydrogen molecule is two atoms of hydrogen each of one proton and one electron). The PEM only allows protons to pass through to the cathode catalyst, where they establish an electrical charge to induce the flow of the electrons from the anode electrode through the electrical load to the cathode electrode. Once through the PEM, protons pass to the cathode catalyst, where they are reunited with the returning electrons from the cathode electrode and with oxygen from the air to form water and heat. The waste products, which may contain a trace of nitrous oxides from protons reacting with nitrogen rather than oxygen atoms in the air, pass through the flow plate on the other end of the fuel cell. A fuel cell stack of individual fuel cells is connected to others to form a fuel cell module that produces a desired output of electricity. Fuel cells have no moving parts and are about two to three times more efficient than an internal combustion engine in converting fuel into usable power. In addition to PEM fuel cells, there are also phosphoric acid fuel cells, molten carbonate fuel cells, and solid oxide fuel cells that have different operating temperatures and performance characteristics for specific applications.[3]

Water waste poses a problem when operating a fuel cell exposed to freezing weather. Waste heat prevents water from freezing during operation, but when a fuel cell is shut down, residual water can turn to ice and damage the fuel cell. This, along with costs, presents a challenge for manufacturers of fuel cell-powered motor vehicles. Although there has been progress in reducing costs, fuel cells are still expensive to manufacture and to operate, given the cost of hydrogen. Further technical breakthroughs are necessary to make fuel cells competitive with gasoline engines. About 60 companies worldwide are in some phase of fuel cell manufacturing, of which 32 are in the United States, 7 in Canada, 6 in the United Kingdom, 5 in India, 2 in Singapore, with single company representation in eight other nations.[4] The current market for fuel cells is primarily as backup power supplies for critical communications and computer systems where a power loss can have severe operational repercussions. These fuel cells, for the most part, have associated reformers that strip hydrogen from hydrocarbons. Fuel cells also supply electricity and potable water on manned space missions.

Major automobile companies are dedicating considerable resources to developing hydrogen-powered fuel cell cars such as Audi, BMW, Chrysler, Daihatsu, Fiat, Ford, GM, Honda, Hyundai, Kia, Mazda, Mercedes, Mitsubishi, Nissan, Peugeot, Renault, Suzuki, Toyota, and Volkswagen plus newly formed independent companies.[5] In addition to funding from private sources, there is also public funding such as the U.S. Department of Energy (DOE) research program to develop FreedomCAR, a motor vehicle powered by a hydrogen fuel cell or other technologies such as advanced hybrid propulsion systems. To hasten the development process, the FreedomCAR has teamed up with the U.S. Council for Automotive Research (USCAR), a collaborative research effort of Ford, Chrysler, and GM. California, with its tough air quality laws and calls for zero-emission vehicles, has become a national testing ground for battery-powered and hydrogen-fueled motor vehicles.

Hydrogen's low density, however, presents a serious logistics problem. Hydrogen contains only about one-third the energy content of natural gas when compressed to the same pressure. Once in an automobile as a compressed gas, the small molecules of hydrogen can more easily leak through cracks, porous material, and faulty fittings and gaskets than the larger methane molecules. The integrity of fittings and gaskets is an even greater technical challenge when hydrogen is compressed to 5,000 or more pounds in order to store a sufficient volume for a 200–300-mile driving range in a normally sized automobile fuel tank. Liquefied or cryogenic hydrogen at atmospheric pressure would require three times the volume required by gasoline, thus, three times the tank size, to deliver the same amount of energy. The reason why hydrogen-fueled buses have preceded automobiles is that large tanks can be mounted on top of buses to accommodate the storage requirements. Research is being conducted on solid-state storage using metal hydrides (magnesium, lanthanum and nickel, sodium aluminum, or lithium boron). Hydrogen is stored within the molecular structure of metal hydrides and released by heating the storage medium.

Hydrogen-fueled motor vehicles represent the classic chicken-and-egg situation. No one is going to build hydrogen refueling stations without hydrogen-fueled cars, and no one is going to build hydrogen-fueled cars without refueling stations. In 2005, there were only seventy hydrogen refueling stations worldwide, and in 2009, there were 191.[6] California is the national trendsetter with its hydrogen highway initiative program that plans to install hydrogen service stations from Vancouver, BC, to Baja California. There are 38 hydrogen filling stations in California with another 15 planned to serve a current population of about 150 hydrogen-fueled automobiles. Michigan is in second place with 9 hydrogen filling stations, followed by New York with 7. There are a total of 82 filling stations in the United States, with another 17 planned in addition to the 15 planned for California. There are 109 hydrogen-filling stations outside the U.S. with 26 in Germany, 24 in Japan, and 10 in Canada. Another 32 stations are planned with 9 in Denmark and 6 in Norway. Canada is planning to have a hydrogen highway between Vancouver and Whistler in British Columbia in time for the 2010 Winter Olympics, when fuel cell automobiles will shuttle people between events at both locales. The Scandinavian Hydrogen Highway links the hydrogen highways in Sweden, Norway, and Denmark. The European Union Hydrogen Highway will link the Scandinavian Hydrogen Highway with Germany, the Netherlands, Belgium, France, Austria, Italy, Spain, and the U.K. The Japan Hydrogen Highway will connect cities around Tokyo Bay (Tokyo, Kawasaki, and Yokohama).

California, Canada, Scandinavia, Europe, and Japan are attacking the chicken-and-egg situation by ensuring an adequate number of refueling stations along highly travelled automobile corridors for hydrogen-fueled vehicles. These vehicles will have to be owned by those whose driving patterns are more or less confined to a 100–150-mile-wide strip on either side of the highway (assuming a 200–300-mile range between refuelings). Once a stretch of road can serve hydrogen-fueled vehicles, then the population of hydrogen-fueled vehicles can expand in communities along the hydrogen highway. As the population of hydrogen-fueled vehicles grows in areas adjacent to the hydrogen highways, more refueling stations can be added, increasing the area that can serve hydrogen-fueled vehicles, allowing for another step up in the population of hydrogen-fueled vehicles and encouraging the opening of more hydrogen refueling stations. Once started, this process feeds on itself and could mark the start of the era of hydrogen-fueled vehicles and the end of the era of gasoline-fueled vehicles.

If this process sounds vaguely familiar, it is. The first automobiles did not have gas stations for refueling. Gasoline (naphtha and other light-end products) was purchased in tins. The first gas stations were in city centers where the first automobiles were sold. Building gas stations and roads around city centers expanded the market for automobiles, which, in turn, expanded the market for gas stations and for roads. This process continued until the nation, and eventually much of the world, became blanketed with automobiles and gasoline stations and paved with roads and parking lots.

While the probability of a massive switch to hydrogen-fueled vehicles may seem remote at this time, there are serious bets being made that hydrogen will eventually come out a winner. Right now the problem is cost. The hydrogen fuel cell, which once was a hundred times more costly than a comparable internal combustion engine, was ten times more costly in 2005 with costs continuing to fall. A forty-passenger fuel cell-powered bus costs between $1 and $2 million, about ten times more than a conventional diesel-powered bus. Huge developmental efforts are still necessary to improve manufacturing processes and the expected life and reliability of fuel cells, particularly those exposed to low winter temperatures. Some believe that an entirely new fuel cell technology may have to be created for another tenfold reduction in costs. On the other hand, the automobile companies are convinced that the necessary cost reduction and performance enhancements can be achieved with present-day technology. Several automobile companies plan to have hydrogen cars available for sale to the public around 2012.

On top of the large capital investment is the cost of fuel. Hydrogen was about five times more expensive in energy equivalence than gasoline in 2004. Thanks to the escalation of oil prices, it was about three times more expensive in 2005, but more expensive in late 2008/09 with the fall in crude prices. If another oil crisis occurs and gasoline prices approach $10 per gallon, hydrogen may prove cheaper. The odds of hydrogen becoming the fuel of the future depend on what happens in the oil patch.

### Tomorrow's World of Hydrogen

While hydrogen will most likely come from stripping hydrogen from hydrocarbons, black hydrogen will eventually have to give way to green hydrogen to reduce carbon dioxide emissions. The problems in transporting hydrogen over long distances, associated with its low density and propensity to leak through fittings and gaskets, can be overcome by generating electricity and producing hydrogen locally in small plants. Each community, or group of communities, would have its neighborhood nuclear or IGCC power plant, augmented as much as possible by sustainable energy sources. The nuclear and IGCC plants would produce electricity for the electrolysis of water augmented by direct hydrogen production from IGCC plants. A distributed generation system would supply electricity locally and excess electricity would be dedicated to generating hydrogen, which would be sold at nearby motor vehicle refueling stations. This would be a return to Thomas Edison's original idea for neighborhood electricity-generating plants. Electricity generators would operate close to full capacity in order to sell electricity at a low base rate for consumption by individuals, businesses, and industry or for electrolysis of hydrogen. This would negate the need to invest in generators that only operate part of the time in response to transient changes in electricity demand and also the need for marginal electricity rates. This concept, if carried to its logical conclusion, would make Westinghouse's idea of large centralized power stations with long-distance transmission lines obsolete.

The next step toward the hydrogen economy would be for every building and home to be fitted with a solar array and/or a wind turbine, an electrolysis unit, a hydrogen storage medium, and a fuel cell module. The solar array or wind turbine would provide electricity to the building. Excess electricity would be fed to the electrolysis unit to produce hydrogen, which would be stored in a tank or storage medium. Hydrogen would be fed to the fuel cell module to generate electricity when the sun was not shining and/or the wind was not blowing. Waste heat, in the form of hot water generated when hydrogen is converted to electricity, would be recycled for personal use, running appliances, and space heating.

The ultimate dream of the hydrogen aficionados is to increase the amount of electricity generated by solar energy, which would depend on vastly improving the efficacy of converting sunlight to electricity. If solar power could be significantly stepped up, then the electricity output might be great enough to produce enough hydrogen for a fuel cell-powered motor vehicle. Motor vehicles for personal use operate only about 5 percent of the time, which means that their fuel cells are idle 95 percent of the time. This is not an efficient use of any capital investment. Once parked at its destination, a hydrogen-fueled automobile would be plugged into the electricity grid to generate electricity as long as there is enough hydrogen left for the return trip. If sufficient numbers of these mobile generators are available and if a sufficient volume of hydrogen can be generated from the sun and wind, this could conceivably eliminate most of the neighborhood nuclear and IGCC plants.

Utilities would still be needed for power generation to cover shortfalls and serve as backup, but their primary purpose would be providing the physical connections for millions of automobiles, homes, and buildings to plug into the electricity grid where every home, building, and automobile is both an electricity-generating utility and a consumer. If the aggregate output of sustainable power sources were large enough, there would be no need for backup generators. Once this occurs, then the distributive utilities could become as obsolete as their centralized kin for electricity generation. However, they would remain as "virtual" utilities, overseeing the buying and selling of electricity among millions of users and generators and providing the technical means to dispatch and control millions of micro-generators. The transformation of an electricity grid with a few large generators into an interactive electricity network of millions of microgenerators would require advanced computer technologies, millions of sensors, and sophisticated software to allow electricity to flow exactly where and when it is needed at the lowest rate in a world where everyone is electrically and electronically connected to everyone else. Cooperatives could be set up for buying and selling electricity among their members, possibly even taking over the utility's role of providing an interactive electricity network modeled after the worldwide communications Web. If the cooperatives also took over the responsibility of servicing and installing electrical wires and cables and connections, then the entire concept of a utility becomes obsolete.

If all this sounds esoteric, it is. It may hold true a century or two from now, but not from today's perspective. Significant technological advances have yet to be made to bring about the hydrogen economy. Other than those who are alarmed over its cost, few are against the concept. Hydrogen is virtually pollution-free with an unlimited supply. But for hydrogen to become a major energy source in the coming decades, sustainable sources of energy (hydro, wind, solar, geothermal) will not be enough. Nuclear power and coal-burning IGCC plants with sequestered carbon dioxide emissions will have to play a major role in generating the requisite amounts of electricity.

## CLIMATE

First and foremost there is no such thing as a "normal" climate.[7] Climate change is continual, with warm and cold cycles, and within these cycles weather patterns change significantly. Treating climate change as something abnormal is an oxymoron. Ancient Carthage in North Africa was sustained by agricultural activities on land that is now desert. Cave paintings in the Sahara portray vibrant animal life on grasslands where there are now only sand dunes. Satellite photographs, employing a technology that can see through sand, reveal a world of dried riverbeds and streams. Thus, climate change does not have to take millions of years. Dramatic changes can occur in a few thousand years as when most of the greenery in North Africa gave way to an inhospitable desert. It only required a few centuries for agricultural activities around ancient Carthage to disappear. Climate change can also occur overnight—woolly mammoths were instantly frozen about 20,000 years ago and can be found today "fit for eating" with their flesh and stomach contents intact.

With modern weather record keeping barely two centuries old, a method had to be developed to track the history of climate. The first such method, counting tree rings, was devised in the early part of the twentieth century. The width of annual tree rings is a record of the weather. Wide tree rings mark years of favorable growing conditions with plentiful rainfall, whereas narrow tree rings mark years of unfavorable growing conditions such as drought and extremes in temperatures. The first trees analyzed were ponderosa pine and giant sequoia in northern California, where overlapping sequences of cores taken from living and dead trees provided a history of climate going back 3,000 years. From this record, along with carbon-14 dating of wood in the Anasazi cliff dwellings in the U.S. Southwest, it was shown that this 500-year-old advanced Native Indian civilization collapsed in the 1200s as a consequence of a twenty-six-year drought.

The next method for analyzing the history of climate was the examination of lake and ocean sediment. Several techniques had to be devised to make this time capsule of climate change readable. One was the discovery that certain types of plankton thrive in warm waters, others in cold, and the ratio of their calcium carbonate skeletons is a good indicator of water temperatures. Another was improving the technique to bring up deep cores from lake bottoms and ocean floors with minimum distortion to the sedimentary layers. Areas of ocean floors had to be found that were least disturbed by burrowing worms and other marine life whose activity blurs the distinction between layers. The discovery of radioactive carbon dating in 1947 was followed by the discovery of the ratio of two oxygen isotopes sensitive to changes in temperature. These two measuring sticks made it possible to obtain a record of major climate changes in terms of ocean temperatures and the waxing and waning of ice sheets going back many thousands of years.

Just as tree rings showed that a severe twenty-six-year drought brought an end to the Anasazi civilization, the analysis of sediments from the bottom of a Yucatan saline lake showed that three periods of extreme drought within a 150-year dry spell brought an end to the 3,000-year-old Mayan civilization in the ninth century. The Maya, capable of devising a highly sophisticated calendar to keep track of time and of building massive temple complexes, had an estimated population of 15 million in the centuries before the dry spell. A similar situation is thought to be the cause of the demise of the Khmer Empire in present-day Cambodia. The capital of the Khmer Empire, Angkor, at its height covered an area of almost 400 square miles (the size of all five boroughs of New York City) with a population of about 750,000 inhabitants of which 40,000 lived in the city center. The constricted growth rings in a rare type of cypress trees called po mu showed back-to-back mega-droughts lasting from 1363–1392 and again from 1415–1440 that spelled the end of this civilization.[8] Droughts of unusual severity can occur even when climate is reasonably stable, for example, the 1930s Dust Bowl in the U.S. Southwest and the ongoing desertization in sub-Saharan Africa.

Advances in analyzing sediment layers in lakes and oceans to detect the history of climate change were accompanied by advances in analyzing annual snowfalls that formed distinct layers in stationary ice packs in Greenland and Antarctica. The first 1,000-foot core of ice was removed from the Greenland ice pack in 1956 and cut into segments for transport to labs in Europe and the United States for analysis. Technical advances in drilling allowed cores to be withdrawn from deeper depths in a more pristine state, and in 1966 a 4,500-foot-long core that extended down to bedrock was extracted from the Greenland ice pack. In the 1980s another core, 6,600 feet long, was extracted, followed in the 1990s by a core over 9,800 feet in length, both down to bedrock. Sediment from lake bottoms and ocean floors and cores from Greenland have provided a record of climate change for the past 100,000 years, and subsequent cores drilled in Antarctica have pushed back the record to about 400,000 years.

Before the extraction of sediment and ice cores, the theory of climate change was based on the earth's elliptical orbit and its slight wobbling about its axis (precession), which induced periods of reduced solar radiation every 22,000 years in the northern hemisphere. It was thought that this would create a 22,000-year cycle of relatively short ice ages, interspersed by long periods of a stable and warm climate. This early theory on climate was in concert with a general belief that change in the natural world was gradual and resulted from existing forces operating uniformly over eons of time. This gave animals and plants ample opportunity to shift their habitat in response to the slow pace of climate change.

The record of climate gleaned from the lake and ocean sediments and the Greenland and Antarctica ice packs dashed the belief in gradual and uniform change as well as the implied ability to forecast general climate conditions within reasonable bounds. The record better supports chaotic and catastrophic change, leaving little time for animals and plants to adapt to shifting climate conditions. The story locked in sediment and ice cores is that there is no such thing as a normal climate. The only predictable behavior regarding climate is change itself, but not its direction or magnitude. Significant shifts in the ratio of oxygen isotopes testify to large changes in average temperatures over relatively short periods of time, sometimes accompanied with heavy layers of volcanic ash. The analysis of gas entrapped in the ice core showed cyclical fluctuations in methane and carbon dioxide concentrations. With the exception of the past 10,000 years, variations in temperature were much more severe, transitions between cooling and warming trends were swift (about 1,000 years), and the earth was a decidedly much colder place to live. The warmest part of the temperature cycle would be similar to today's weather, but it did not last long before the world plunged into another frigid ice age. About 14,700 years ago, the earth warmed and the climate stabilized for about 2,000 years before there was a sudden reversion to a 1,000-year ice age. Then, for inexplicable reasons, the climate suddenly reversed direction and an era of unusual warmth with relatively stable temperatures began that has lasted about 12,000 years (named the Holocene Epoch); a phenomenon not experienced during the previous 400,000 years.

While some might consider this evidence of the transition from Genesis 1:2 to 1:3, others feel that the cause of the sudden warming was civilization. According to this hypothesis, people have been affecting the weather for at least 8,000 years, since the advent of agriculture, much longer than the 200 years, since the advent of the industrial age, as normally thought. Analysis of ice cores shows that the concentration of methane in the atmosphere rose and fell over the past 250,000 years fairly closely following the 22,000-year cycles in solar radiation. During this cycle, solar radiation in the northern hemisphere varied between 440–520 watts per square meter with methane, a greenhouse gas, tagging along and varying between 400–700 parts per billion as measured from Vostok (Antarctica) ice cores. Methane follows the 22,000-year solar radiation cycle because warm spells encourage plant life. When dead plants decay in anaerobic (without oxygen) water, copious releases of methane (swamp gas) add to natural gas seeps from underground coal, oil, and natural gas fields, increasing its concentration in the atmosphere.

This trend lasted until 5,000 years ago, when solar radiation fell as part of its normal 22,000-year cycle and methane, rather than falling to an expected 450 parts per billion, rose to nearly 700 parts per billion. This unexpected rise in the methane concentration is hypothesized to be the result of agricultural practices, especially growing rice and breeding herds of domesticated animals. The anaerobic decay of rice stalks in flooded rice paddies and the digestive processes of grazing animals are both major contributors to atmospheric methane. Thus, the earth did not cool as expected from a fall in solar radiation from changes in the earth's orientation with the sun because the rise in methane, a greenhouse gas twenty times more effective than carbon dioxide, inhibited the escape of infrared red radiation from the earth into space.

Carbon dioxide cycles are more complex than methane. For the last 400,000 years, carbon dioxide concentrations peaked at about 280–290 parts per million every 100,000 years, with a number of minor cycles contained within each major cycle. The discovery that carbon dioxide concentrations bottomed out at about 200 parts per million in the depths of an ice age was the first evidence linking carbon dioxide with climate. Carbon dioxide peaked around 10,500 years ago, at the end of the last ice age, and began its expected retreat as it had done in the past. About 8,000 years ago, however, the retreat became an advance. By the start of the industrial era, the concentration of carbon dioxide was back to 280–290 parts per million, the "normal" peak during the previous 400,000 years. This was an estimated 40 parts per million higher than one would predict on the basis of past patterns and could be attributable to our use of biomass fuel. Methane, about 250 parts per billion, and carbon dioxide, about 40 parts per million higher at the start of the Industrial Revolution, compensated for a falloff in solar radiation reaching the earth's surface. Had it not been for these additional concentrations of greenhouse gases, the earth might have experienced another period of glaciation with the reduction of solar radiation caused by earth's orientation to the sun. Thus, it is conceivable that humanity's activities have helped to stabilize climate for the better![9]

**Climate Changes During Recorded History**

There have been significant changes to the climate within recorded history. The period 900–1300 CE was called the medieval warm period with a warming trend similar to what is happening now. Agricultural output soared, as did the human population by an estimated 40–60 million. Vineyards sprouted in England, and English wine gave French wine a run for its money. Greenland was not misnamed as some have thought by a real estate charlatan trying to induce prospective settlers to buy frozen land. Its green coastline would have allowed Vikings to establish communities where, as archaeological evidence shows, they supported themselves by farming the land for food and crops to feed grazing herds of livestock, augmented by fishing and trading.

The start of the Little Ice Age in 1300 CE, known as history's Big Chill, saw average temperatures fall between 4°F–7°F. While this might not sound like much of a change, it was sufficient to bring an end to the greenery in Greenland along with the Viking settlements, and grape vineyards in England. Agricultural output plunged, as did the population from starvation and malnutrition, which weakened resistance to disease. Between 1371 and 1791 there were 111 recorded famines in Europe, with one famine in Russia claiming a half million lives in 1601. Part of the blame for the Black Death, which wiped out about one-third of the population of Europe, was rats seeking warmth in human habitations to escape the cold. The coldest period during the Little Ice Age was between 1645 and 1715, a period of minimum sunspot activity and reduced solar radiation, which lowered the average temperature by another 3°F. Alpine glaciers began to advance rapidly, swallowing up farmland and villages, and the Thames River froze over, starting a tradition of annual ice festivals that lasted until the early nineteenth century. Further hardships were in store for the people from sparse harvests, which contributed to social unrest, perhaps even to the French Revolution.[10]

There are three explanations for the Little Ice Age. The first is that it resulted from a 0.5 percent reduction in solar radiation, whose cyclicality may also be affected by periodic changes in sunspot activity and magnetic field intensity. Variation in solar radiation, coupled with variations in the earth's orbit and precession about its axis, induced severe cold spells. The second explanation is the slowing of the Gulf Stream conveyor belt. Normally, the Gulf Stream is more saline than the water in the North Atlantic. After warming the northern European atmosphere, whose latitude is the same as Newfoundland, the saline, cooled, and heavy Gulf Stream waters sink to the bottom of the Atlantic and return to the Caribbean. The sinking of the Gulf Stream waters is thought to be the driving force behind the immense conveyor carrying warm Caribbean waters to the North Atlantic. Thus, the preceding medieval warm period may have caused polar ice to melt, releasing vast quantities of freshwater along with a greater outpouring of freshwater from Siberian rivers. The freshwater emptying into the Arctic Ocean would eventually flow into the North Atlantic, diluting the salinity of the Gulf Stream. Less saline waters decreased the density of the Gulf Stream, reducing its capacity to sink and power the conveyor belt. As the Gulf Stream weakened, the weather in northern Europe cooled.

The third explanation is that there were several major volcanic eruptions during the Little Ice Age; the worst being the 1815 eruption of Tambora in Indonesia, which had the force of 100 Mount St. Helens. Whereas Mount St. Helens blew off 1,300 feet of its top in 1980, 4,200 feet of Tambora's top was blasted thirty miles into the stratosphere, reducing its height from 13,500 feet to 9,300. The eruption left behind a five-mile-wide caldera three-quarters of a mile deep, the largest on Earth within recorded history. An estimated 120,000 people were killed either by instant carbonizing in the 2,000°F pyroclastic flows rushing 100 miles per hour down the volcano's slopes or, more slowly, by starvation. This was just the start of the death count as Tambora, as with other large volcanic eruptions, affected global climate. The enormous plume of 200 million tons of sulfur contained in 100 cubic kilometers of ash blanketed the earth, which prevented solar radiation from penetrating the earth's atmosphere. Sulfur combined with oxygen to form sulfur oxides and then with water vapor to form an aerosol of sulfuric acid that covered the upper surfaces of clouds, which reflected incoming sunlight. With ash shading the earth and an aerosol mist reflecting sunlight, the earth cooled by an average of 2°F. However, in the northeast United States and Canada, and northern Europe, the cooling was about 10°F, making 1816 the year without a summer. It snowed in North America and northern Europe was drenched in cold rain, preventing crops from maturing. The eventual death toll from starvation and disease brought on by malnutrition, mostly concentrated in Europe, is thought to be several times that of the death toll in Indonesia. In New England, the year without a summer caused a migration of farmers to begin anew in the Midwest.

Volcanoes are "natural coal burners," releasing huge volumes of ash, sulfur, sulfur oxides, aerosols, and carbon dioxide that can affect global climate, but the amount of carbon dioxide released by volcanoes is far less than man's contribution. However, the eruption of Mount Pinatubo in the Philippines in 1991 released more particulate pollution into the atmosphere in a few weeks than civilization had released since the start of the Industrial Revolution, and brought about a couple of years of cooler weather.

In 1850 the Little Ice Age abruptly ended, inaugurating a general warming trend still in progress. There are four explanations for this change: no major volcanic eruptions of the order of Tambora (notwithstanding the 1883 Krakatoa eruption); an increase in solar radiation influenced by increased sunspot and magnetic field activity; the restoration of the Gulf Stream conveyor belt; and the addition of carbon dioxide to the atmosphere by the Industrial Revolution. Each of these explanations has been advanced with no consensus as to which or what combination was responsible for a warmer climate.

## Where Is Climate Headed?

The evidence that the warming trend continues is ample: Glaciers are continuing their retreat, although there are counterexamples of some glaciers advancing; the Arctic ice cap is thinning and covering less area; the thawing of permafrost is marked by "drunken" trees bending in all directions in Alaska, Canada, and Siberia; roadbeds resembling roller coasters; and buildings structurally damaged from shifting and sinking foundations.[11] Other evidence of climate change is the record-breaking temperatures nearly every year for the last decade up to 2005, although average annual temperatures have been cooling for the last few years. Record-breaking wet and dry spells have accompanied the record-breaking temperatures, spawning floods in some areas and droughts and wildfires in others. The sea level rose eight inches from the nineteenth century, partly from melting of the Greenland and Antarctica ice packs and partly from thermal expansion of warmer ocean waters. Melting of the Arctic polar cap is sometimes cited as a cause of rising ocean levels, but floating polar ice has already displaced seawater and its melting does not affect ocean levels. This can be seen by filling a glass with ice cubes and then with water to its brim, letting the ice cubes protrude above the top of the glass. A paper towel under the glass will remain dry as the ice melts, showing that the water level has not changed as the ice melted. Of course, this observation does not hold true for melting snow and ice on land, whose waters flow into the oceans.

Unfortunately the reduction of the surface area covered by polar ice decreases the earth's reflectivity, or albedo. Sea ice reflects up to 80 percent of the sunlight that strikes it, but reflectivity is reduced when white ice gives way to dark water. Greater absorption of solar energy by open ocean water leads to higher temperatures and more ice melting, creating larger areas of reduced albedo, an example of a positive feedback system. In tropical ocean waters, higher average temperatures from a warming Earth spawn hurricanes and cyclones. The intense hurricanes that have struck the United States in the last few years are partly caused by record water surface temperatures in the Gulf of Mexico that can transform a low-level tropical storm entering the Gulf into a Category 5 hurricane in two days' time. In 2005, Katrina struck in August, Rita in September, and Wilma in October in one of the worst hurricane seasons ever recorded. However, global warming may not be the only cause of the increasing frequency of hurricanes because hurricane activity is itself cyclical over a period that spans several decades. Moreover, history records devastating hurricanes and typhoons and tornadoes in the past when average temperatures were lower. For instance, a hurricane in the Caribbean in 1780 sank 1,200 ships drowning their crews; the Galveston hurricane in 1900 killed over 6,000 people; 1955 was an extremely active year for hurricanes and tornadoes; and the 1970 typhoon killed over one-quarter of a million people in Bangladesh.[12]

A 1973 study of the carbon dioxide concentration of the atmosphere measured atop Mauna Loa, Hawaii, showed that the carbon dioxide concentration had climbed steadily from 316 parts per million in 1959 to 330 parts per million in 1972. In 1980 an analysis of Antarctic ice cores established that the concentration of carbon dioxide was around 280–290 parts per million at the start of the Industrial Revolution, already at its cyclical peak for the previous 400,000 years. For the first time in 400,000 years, carbon dioxide did not decline from its peak, but continued to rise. It reached around 300 parts per million in 1900 and a century later 370 parts per million; by 2004 the concentration of carbon dioxide had reached 377 parts per million and in 2009, 387 parts per million and still climbing. Carbon dioxide concentration increased at a faster pace during the twentieth century than the nineteenth, correlating well with our greater consumption of fossil fuels.

Similarly, the rise of methane concentration is also accelerating. From 1000 to 1800 CE, methane was about 700 parts per billion. It rose 100 parts per billion during the nineteenth century to 800 parts per billion. In the twentieth century methane leaped by 900 parts per billion to 1,700 parts per billion. This rise is almost entirely attributable to human activities: increased rice growing and other agricultural activities, a far higher population of domesticated grazing animals, a higher methane-emitting termite population from deforestation, greater volumes of methane escaping from landfills, and from increased coal mining and oil and gas activities. And, of course, vast quantities of methane entered the atmosphere from venting of natural gas in oil fields in the U.S. Southwest before construction of the long-distance natural gas pipelines. More methane entered the atmosphere from venting natural gas in Africa and the Middle East before the 1973 oil crisis.

Thereafter, natural gas was reinjected into oil fields when it was finally recognized that venting and flaring were equivalent to burning money.

Projections vary, but depending on what actions are taken to reduce carbon dioxide emissions and which computer model is selected, the most likely projected level of carbon dioxide by 2100 is 450–550 parts per million, with the outside possibility of 1,000 or more parts per million. Again, depending on the selected computer model, the projected rise in average temperatures is between 1°C–5°C, or between 2°F–9°F.[13] If the low-end estimates are correct, we will survive. If the high-end estimates are correct, we will be facing severe problems on all fronts. Shifting weather patterns may affect rainfall over the grain-growing regions, seriously affecting agricultural production. Sea levels may rise as much as ten feet (three meters), flooding coastal regions including highly populated areas (New York City, London, the Louisiana delta, and Florida) and large parts of nations (Bangladesh and the Netherlands). Increased storm activity and severity completes the climate doomsday scenario.

Yet there are climatologists, looking at the same temperature statistics of those who advocate global warming, who come to an opposite conclusion. Though they agree that the earth did warm between 1977 and 1998, they maintain that the temperature since then has been relatively stable with statistical evidence that we may currently be in a cooling trend. The basis for this contention is a 100-year low in sunspot activity since 2007. Sunspot activity is linked to the radiation given off by the sun. The Maunder Minimum, a period of very low sun spot activity, occurred between 1645 and 1715, the coldest period of the Little Ice Age.[14] Though a low in sunspot activity only accounts for a reduction of 0.5 percent in solar radiation, this can significantly affect climate. The prognosis is that the cooling period should already be in progress. And the evidence suggests just that—the winter of 2007/08 had the deepest snow cover in the northern hemisphere since 1966 and the coldest temperatures since 2001. The winter of 2008/09 surpassed the winter of 2007/08 in both snow depth and cold temperatures. In response to this, advocates of global warming state that variations in solar radiation and in volcanic activity were not sufficient to cause the warming in recent decades and that the only explanation left is the anthropogenic one of mankind's burning of fossil fuels adding to atmospheric carbon dioxide. The recent cooling trend, they maintain, is nothing more than a statistical aberration contained within a long upward trend in temperatures.

One may ask how is it that highly intelligent people can look at the same data and come to an opposite conclusion? Part of the explanation is that temperature data are choppy; that is, they exhibit volatility that makes it difficult to come to a definitive conclusion. Part is the choice of where to start a trend line. To illustrate this point, a record of annual degree-days in the United States since 1992/93 is plotted in Figure 10.1. Degree-days measure how cold the weather is from a reference temperature of 65 degrees Fahrenheit. If the average temperature for a day is 60 degrees, then this adds 5 degree-days to the annual measure; 50 degrees adds 15 degree-days. The downward slope of the trend line indicates fewer degree-days, hence supports the contention of a warming climate. In Figure 10.2, the chart starts from 1998. Its upward slope of increasing degree-days supports the contention that a cooling trend has set in.

Which trend line do you select? This is an important decision because carbon dioxide control measures such as cap and trade or a carbon tax will cost taxpayers billions of dollars and have a significant impact on the level and direction of economic activity.

## CARBON DIOXIDE CONUNDRUM

As previously noted, burning coal releases more carbon dioxide for a given quantity of energy than other fossil fuels. There is nothing that can be done about this, other than sequestering, as

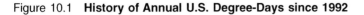

Figure 10.1   **History of Annual U.S. Degree-Days since 1992**

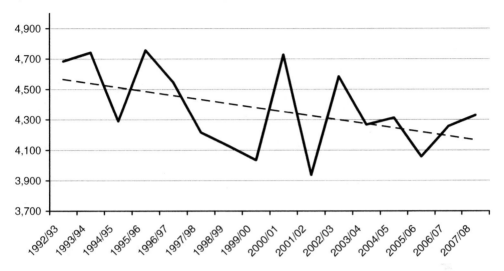

Figure 10.2   **History of Annual U.S. Degree-Days since 1998**

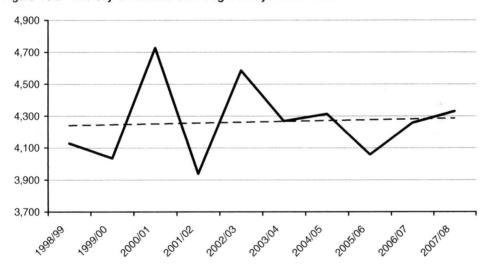

this is a chemical property of coal with its higher ratio of carbon to hydrogen atoms. Natural gas, with its relatively low ratio of carbon atoms to hydrogen atoms, is the cleanest-burning fossil fuel, releasing the least amount of carbon dioxide on an energy-equivalent basis plus water. According to the International Energy Agency, burning coal in terms of the energy release of 1 metric ton of oil equivalent (toe) produces 1.14 metric tons of carbon, burning 1 metric ton of oil releases 0.89 tons of carbon, and burning natural gas equivalent to 1 metric ton of oil releases 0.73 metric ton

Table 10.1

**Calculating Carbon Release**

|  | World Consumption in Billions TOE | Percent Fuel | Carbon Release Factor | Carbon Release in Billion Tons | Percent Carbon Emissions |
|---|---|---|---|---|---|
| Coal | 3.304 | 33.2 | 1.14 | 3.767 | 40.7 |
| Oil | 3.928 | 39.4 | 0.89 | 3.500 | 37.8 |
| Natural Gas | 2.726 | 27.4 | 0.73 | 1.990 | 21.5 |
| Total | 9.958 | 100 | 2.76 | 9.257 | 100 |

of carbon, all of which enters the atmosphere as carbon dioxide. With these figures as guidelines, Table 10.1 calculates the global release of carbon from burning of fossil fuels for 2008.[15]

Table 10.1 excludes biomass, which has a higher carbon release factor than coal. However, plants and trees absorb carbon dioxide before being cut down for wood or eaten by animals. Rounding to take into account some net carbon release from deforestation, the approximate amount of annual carbon release into the atmosphere caused by human activities burning fossil fuels, including non-sustainable burning of biomass (deforestation), is a little over 10 billion tons, which works out to about 40 billion tons of carbon dioxide.[16] As noted in Table 10.1, coal adds a proportionally greater amount of carbon dioxide to the atmosphere than the other fossil fuels, representing 33 percent of fossil fuels consumed in terms of energy release and 41 percent of carbon dioxide emissions. Moreover, old coal-burning electricity-generating plants in some parts of the world, particularly India and China, are energy inefficient compared to those in developed nations. Replacing these coal-fired plants with new natural gas energy-efficient plants would reduce carbon dioxide emissions in two ways—natural gas releases less carbon dioxide than coal for an equivalent output of energy and less fuel would be burned for an equivalent output of electricity. Furthermore, natural gas does not emit sulfur and nitrogen oxides or heavy metals, nor does it desecrate the landscape or affect water supplies. One can see why nations prefer to abandon coal in favor of natural gas. But the reality is that the supply of natural gas is not sufficient to replace coal, and its higher price compared to coal would add to energy costs.

Before we become too enthralled with our capacity to influence the weather, the 40 billion tons of carbon dioxide we add to the atmosphere per year is dwarfed by nature's recycling program. It is estimated that 2,000 billion tons of carbon dioxide are locked up in partially decayed plant matter in the soil, peat bogs, and permafrost. Living plant life absorbs 120 billion tons, about that released to the atmosphere by decaying plant life. As a point of comparison, agriculture and land use by humans releases and absorbs less than 2 billion tons, a rounding error in what nature recycles. The atmosphere is estimated to contain 730 billion tons of carbon in the form of carbon dioxide, of which about 90 billion tons are exchanged with the oceans, which contain 3,800 billion tons of carbon in the form of dissolved carbon dioxide. In comparison, the burning of fossil and biomass fuels adds about 10 billion tons of carbon. With a total of 200 billion tons of carbon exchanged naturally between vegetation and the oceans with the atmosphere, scientists ponder why a paltry 5 percent addition to nature's recycling program is making such a big difference to the atmospheric concentration of carbon dioxide.[17]

A higher concentration of carbon dioxide, in itself, should spur plant growth, which would absorb greater quantities of carbon dioxide from the atmosphere. The 12,000 species of diatoms in oceans and lakes are another sink, or source of natural removal, of carbon dioxide. Diatoms are single-celled algae that convert carbon dioxide, water, and sunlight into food and release oxygen. Unlike other phytoplankton, diatoms also absorb carbon dioxide to create microscopic shells that sink to the bottom of the lake or ocean when they die. It is estimated that diatoms remove about half as much carbon dioxide as photosynthesis, a huge volume of carbon dioxide. One potential way of reducing carbon dioxide would be expanding the population of diatoms.[18] However, diatoms cannot absorb all of the higher levels of carbon dioxide in the atmosphere. Some of the additional carbon dioxide absorbed by the ocean from its higher partial pressure is transformed to carbonic acid, which is estimated to have lowered the pH of ocean from 8.2 to 8.1. While this does not sound like much, the acidification of ocean water has already affected coral reefs and shellfish. With the mixing of surface waters with deeper levels, perhaps plankton, the first step in the food chain ladder for marine life, may be affected.

If a higher concentration of carbon dioxide is causing global warming, which leads to greater evaporation, one would think that greater cloud cover, through reflectivity, would reduce the heating effect of sunlight on the earth's atmosphere. If this were true, then greater cloud cover would be a negative, or self-correcting, feedback system. But water vapor in the atmosphere is itself a greenhouse gas with a much greater warming impact than carbon dioxide and, as such, is a positive feedback system. While cloud cover reduces air temperatures from reflectivity, water vapor warms air temperatures by capturing reflected radiation. Atmospheric water vapor as both negative and positive feedback systems indicates the complexity of modeling climate. Although the ice pack in West Antarctica is melting along its coastal regions, about 75 percent of Antarctica's land mass is experiencing increased precipitation that is thickening the interior ice pack, keeping sea levels from rising at a faster pace! Another puzzle for one to ponder is that, with a carbon dioxide concentration far in excess of that of the medieval warm period, temperatures are still less than what they were when greenery flourished along Greenland's shores. Others point out that there was a general cooling trend from the 1940s to the 1970s, with carbon dioxide continuing its inexorable uptrend. How can that be if global warming is caused by increasing concentration of carbon dioxide?

The cacophony of voices about global warming is caused in part by the availability of government and private grants for research in support of anthropologic global warming with relatively little in funds that do not support this view. Scientists and researchers go where the money is, which can bias research activities and results. Moreover, some advocates of global warming stand to personally gain if greenhouse-warming programs such as cap and trade programs are initiated by their advocacy.

To add to the confusion, there are those who say that the rise in carbon dioxide in the atmosphere is a lagging indicator of global warming; that is, increasing carbon dioxide is a consequence of global warming and not the cause. These advocates point out that warming of the oceans during interglacial warm periods causes oceans to give up some of its carbon dioxide just as carbon dioxide is released from warmed carbonated beverages. When oceans cool during the subsequent ice age, they are able to absorb a greater quantity of carbon dioxide, which reduces the level of carbon dioxide in the atmosphere. Thus carbon dioxide concentrations follow, not lead, changes in global temperatures.

To add even more to the confusion, there are those who advocate taking a paleoclimate view covering hundreds of thousands of years. During these long stretches of time, in rough numbers, ice ages last about 100,000 years with interglacial periods of about 12,000 years. This rhythm of climate stems from three Milankovich cycles of variation in the shape of the earth's orbit that has a period of 100,000 years, variation in the tilt of the earth that has a period of 41,000 years, and the precession of the equinoxes, the earth's wobble, that has a period of 26,000 years. These three periods, working together, are responsible for variation in the degree of solar radiation falling on the northern hemisphere resulting in 100,000-year cycles of ice ages interspersed with 12,000-year periods of interglacial warming. Paleoclimate advocates criticize the anthropogenic global warming view of focusing on a timeline measured in decades, not hundreds of thousands of years. They maintain that the real risk is that we may be at the end of the Holocene period of interglacial warming and about to plunge into the next ice age (a view, by the way, that was nearly as popular in the 1970s as global warming is today). If so, pumping carbon dioxide into the atmosphere may turn out to be a virtue rather than a vice.

## PROJECTING THE FUTURE

There are three projections for future climate—it will stay about the same; it will get a lot warmer; it will get a lot colder. The advocates of a much warmer Earth are worried about global warming reaching the point where the permafrost in Alaska, Canada, and Siberia thaws, which could release enormous volumes of methane currently entrapped within an ice lattice (methane hydrates). Being twenty times more effective as a greenhouse gas than carbon dioxide, massive releases of methane could conceivably set in motion runaway global warming. Rising temperatures would release even greater volumes of methane, along with the carbon dioxide locked in the oceans and in the partially decayed plant matter frozen in the permafrost.

Those who predict that the earth will get a lot colder look to the introduction of vast quantities of freshwater into the North Atlantic from melting Arctic and Greenland ice caps, an increased flow of Siberian rivers, and increased freshwater runoff from the thawing permafrost. This could dilute the salinity of the Gulf Stream and slow down the conveyor belt sufficiently to cause another ice age to set in. The reflectivity of the earth, its albedo, increases once ice begins to cover wider areas of the earth, further reducing temperatures, causing more snow to fall, enlarging areas covered by snow and ice, and increasing reflectivity, thereby inducing even lower temperatures. If the ice covers a sufficiently large area of the earth, then an irreversible trend may set in where the earth becomes a snowball with glaciers and frozen oceans covering the entire planet. There is evidence that the earth has been a global snowball twice, once about 2.2 billion years ago and again about 0.5 billion years ago. It is thought that the effects of extreme volcanism ended the frozen state by introducing vast quantities of carbon dioxide to the atmosphere, which initiated global warming, and by volcanic ash decreasing the earth's albedo.

Both runaway global warming and cooling are examples of positive feedback systems; once started, nothing can stop the trend from worsening other than some massive external intrusion such as extreme volcanism.

We believe in linear systems. Tugging a rope attached to a wagon causes the wagon to move, whose speed can be estimated by taking the force of the tug and the wagon's resistance to movement into account. But climate is a nonlinear system, which is akin to tugging on a sleeping dragon's tail. Nothing happens tug after tug. Then that one tug, which may be weaker than the others, awakens the dragon. Now something happens. While nonlinear systems may lend themselves to statistical analysis, probabilities become quite meaningless if a set of circumstances (variations in the sun's radiation, variations in the earth's orbit and precession, variations in greenhouse gas concentrations) all line up to induce climate to move from one point of equilibrium to another. The shift between equilibrium points can be relatively swift, with dire repercussions for life on earth, as the frozen woolly mammoths in Siberia plainly attest.

Our climate may be warming or about to cool from a naturally occurring cyclicality in solar radiation, variations in the earth's orbit and precession, Chandler's wobble (variations in atmospheric and oceanic density and snow accumulation affecting the orientation of the earth's poles), increasing greenhouse gas concentrations, volcanic activity, or some combination thereof. Having a carbon dioxide concentration at a level never experienced in 400,000 years, which is continuing to rise, is a cause for worry. It is not absolutely clear how much of this increase is caused by burning fossil fuels or by something else that is affecting nature's capacity to recycle carbon dioxide. Others believe that global warming, at least in part, is caused by greater solar radiation before the latest cessation of sunspot activity, and point to the melting ice caps on Mars as possible confirmation that the sun was emitting more energy. However, there may be other reasons why Mars's polar regions are retreating since weather patterns on Mars are even less understood than those on Earth.

The risk we face is that adding carbon dioxide and methane to the atmosphere, in concert with other natural forces that are affecting the global climate, may be the tug that awakens the sleeping dragon, initiating a major shift in climate. The new equilibrium point may make life difficult for Earth's inhabitants. Such a shift may not be triggered by heightened carbon dioxide concentrations but, perhaps, by heightened gamma ray bursts from outer space, which also affect global weather patterns. We just do not know what the trigger point for climate change is. What makes this such a challenge is that the trigger point may not be a single combination of conditions, but a number of different combinations in which heightened levels of greenhouse gases may play an indeterminable role in triggering radical climate change.

## ENVIRONMENT

Speculation concerning climate change during the next hundred years tends to mask what is happening to the environment now, best epitomized by the Asian brown cloud.[19] The Asian brown cloud encompasses thousands of square miles and can be seen from space. It originates primarily in China and India and results from burning coal and biomass without environmental safeguards as required in developed nations. In the developed world, electrostatic precipitators capture over 99 percent of the fly ash, the solid particles in combustion emissions, which is trucked to a disposal site or consumed in the production of cement. Desulfurization units (sulfur scrubbers) remove a large percentage of the sulfur. In India and China, much of the particulate residues and sulfur emissions from burning a generally low-quality coal enter the atmosphere as ash, soot, and sulfur dioxide. Burning coal is not entirely to blame; other major contributors are burning biomass and exhaust fumes from a rapidly growing population of motor vehicles throughout Asia. Some motor vehicles made in Asia (but not in Japan) have substandard environmental safeguards compared to those produced in the West, and cannot be exported because they would fail pollution emission standards. These vehicles contribute to airborne pollution more than Western-made motor vehicles. The two-cycle gasoline engines found on small motorcycles throughout Asia are horrific polluters. However, China is embarking on a program to enhance the emission standards of its domestically manufactured motor vehicles, not only to try to clean up its environment, but also to open up export markets in the West.

The Asian brown cloud that hovers over mainland Asia and the island nations of Southeast Asia affects the health of millions of people. Air in major metropolitan areas noticeably affects the eyes, nose, and throat. At times the overhanging haze is so thick that one can look directly at the diffused light of the sun. The two-mile thick Asian brown cloud reduces the amount of sunlight reaching the ground by 10–15 percent. Sunlight warming the lower atmosphere, or troposphere, rather than the earth's surface increases the frequency and strength of thermal inversions, which trap large amounts of pollution near the earth's surface. Those immersed in a cloud of pollution suffer from an increasing incidence of acute respiratory infection, pulmonary disease, lung cancer, tuberculosis, and asthma. Combined with outdoor pollution is indoor pollution from burning bio-mass fuels (wood and dung) and coal inside dwellings. Indoor pollution in India is felt to cause a half million premature deaths of children below the age of five annually. With less sunlight reaching the earth's surface, the Asian brown cloud reduces evaporation and affects the amount and pattern of precipitation, reducing photosynthesis and agricultural productivity. Rice production in India is estimated to be down by about 5 percent from air pollution.

Depending on the season, prevailing winds over India spread pollution to Nepal in the Himala-yas or over much of the Indian Ocean. Seasonal prevailing winds over China spread pollution to otherwise isolated, idyllic, and pristine tourist Meccas in the Pacific Islands, where it is noticed, or at times as far away as Los Angeles, where it goes unnoticed. The Los Angeles basin frequently suffers from a temperature inversion that traps pollution near the surface, where it is unable to escape over the surrounding mountains. Early explorers noted overhanging smoke from native Indian fires, but now it is caused by the hydrocarbon emissions of motor vehicles. As late as the 1930s, the probability of having a very clear summer afternoon, with a visual range in excess of thirty-five miles was 21 percent, but by the 1940s the increased population of automobiles had dropped the probability by a factor of 100 to 0.2 percent.

Various types of pollution seem to conflict with one another. Carbon dioxide and methane hinder the escape of infrared red radiation from the earth to space, heating up the atmosphere. An aerosol mist of sulfuric acid collects on cloud tops, increasing their albedo, or reflectivity, reducing the amount of sunlight that enters the atmosphere. Acid rain inhibits wetland bacteria from producing methane (swamp gas) from decaying plant matter, a major contributor to green-house gases. Soot from burning coal and biomass and diesel engine emissions collect on glaciers, reducing their albedo and accelerating their melting. This same soot is responsible for "global dimming," which is no longer limited to Asia. Records over the past thirty-five years of a declin-ing rate of water evaporation on the surface of the earth, despite higher average air temperatures, confirm that less sunlight is reaching the surface. Solar radiation reaching the surface of the earth, measured in watts per square meter, has declined on average from 191 in 1958 to 190 in 1965 to 182 in 1975 to 176 in 1985 to 171 in 1992, an accelerating trend.[20] Reduced solar radiation at the earth's surface would mean less evaporation, and perhaps, less cloud cover, which if true, means more incoming solar radiation that would increase air temperatures. Some combination of these conflicting environmental factors may be behind the heightened activity and severity of storms experienced in recent years.

Some climatologists think the connection between rising levels of carbon dioxide in the atmo-sphere and global warming is tangential, at best, and should be regarded with caution. Spending huge sums of money to reduce carbon dioxide emissions takes away from programs to relieve poverty and, in that sense, the fight against carbon dioxide may be deleterious, not beneficial to society. Russian climatologists nearly unanimously deny any anthropogenic linkage between human activities and global warming. They believe that variation in weather patterns reflects the normal cyclicality of climate. Western climatologists are nearly unanimously opposed to this opinion and believe that there is a direct anthropogenic link between global warming and our consumption of fossil fuels. The Russian climatologists look at drunken forests, roads that resemble roller coasters, and collapsing buildings in Siberia and blame only nature. Western climatologists look at drunken forests, roller coaster roads, and collapsing buildings in Alaska and blame only ourselves. Some cynics suggest that some Western climatologists may be guilty of purposely arousing public fear over global warming in order to win more grants to conduct research. The uneasy feeling that we may be taking the wrong path has made its way into fiction, which, on occasion, has turned out to be fact.[21]

## U.S. Clean Air Acts

The United States has been criticized for not being environmentally responsible for refusing to sign the Kyoto Protocol. These critics conveniently forget that the United States was the first nation to pass legislation specifically aimed at improving the environment. Before a series of Clean Air and Clean Water Acts beginning in the 1950s, industry was free to pollute, degrading the environment for all, with no cost to itself. This represents a market failure. Markets supposedly establish a clearing price that matches supply with demand, taking into consideration all the factors that affect costs. The market mechanism clearly failed when no cost was ascribed to the damage from environmental pollution. The Clean Air Acts, in concert with the Clean Water Acts, established regulatory regimes to reduce air and water pollution. The Acts set forth standards that industry was expected to comply with or face punitive action, either in monetary terms or cessation of operation.

Unfortunately, one consequence of such actions to improve the environment in the United States has been to export pollution to areas where environmental restrictions are largely nonexistent. For example, to reduce sulfur emissions, high sulfur coke from U.S. oil refineries is prohibited for use as a boiler fuel in the United States. As a consequence, the U.S. price for high sulfur coke fell substantially in relationship to the world price, making it attractive for Far Eastern cement manufacturers to buy the coke. The consequence of the Clean Air Act, which was intended to reduce sulfur emissions in the United States, has been to increase sulfur emissions in Asia. Pollution simply changed location and, once in the atmosphere, wind currents assured its global distribution.

Some industrial enterprises, such as electricity-generating plants, cannot move, and must comply with air pollution restrictions. Even for companies that could move, but stayed and complied with the regulations, the cost of compliance could make their product prices uncompetitive in a world marketplace where competitors, mainly in developing nations, operate with virtually no restrictions on pollution, and, as well, on wages and working conditions. Pollution abatement, for all its merits, has contributed to the deindustrialization of the United States and Europe.

The 1990 Clean Air Act differed from its predecessors by internalizing an externality. The externality was environmental degradation, which affects everyone. Internalizing makes environmental degradation a cost directed at those responsible for pollution emissions. Once a cost is placed on pollution, whether in the form of acquiring allowances that permit pollution emissions or as a direct tax, industry then has an economic incentive to do something about reducing pollution. The process for internalizing an externality—the reduction of sulfur dioxide emissions—set up by the 1990 Clean Air Act has been adopted by the Kyoto Protocol as a primary means of reducing greenhouse gas emissions.

The first legislative act was the Air Pollution Control Act of 1955, "an Act to provide research and technical assistance relating to air pollution control." While the Act recognized air pollution as a national problem, its scope of action was limited primarily to providing research grants. The Clean Air Act of 1963, "an Act to improve, strengthen, and accelerate programs for the prevention and abatement of air pollution," called for a more specific recognition of problems associated with burning high sulfur coal and oil and motor vehicle emissions. The Act recognized two general categories of pollution: stationary sources (utility and industrial plants) and mobile sources (motor vehicles, trains, and aircraft). Mobile sources are more difficult to control than stationary sources because their movement affects pollution over a wide area.

The first tailpipe emission standards for motor vehicles were established in California in 1959 to take effect for the 1966 model year. Realizing that state regulation would result in automobile manufacturers having to comply with as many as fifty different sets of pollution emission standards, the 1963 Act established the principle of a national standard for automobile emissions. One standard of pollution emissions would apply to all motor vehicle manufacturers (domestic and foreign), regardless of where a vehicle was sold in the United States. The first federal emission standards adopted in 1965, as amendments to the 1963 Act, applied to the 1968 model year. These standards were virtually identical to those adopted by California for 1966 models. The 1990 Clean Air Act, a counterexample to establishing uniform regulations, established gasoline standards to deal with automobile exhaust emissions that varied both in time of year and place. This complicated the refining and distribution of gasoline in the United States, a situation made even more complex by the right of states to impose standards on gasoline sold within their jurisdiction.

California has always been a frontrunner in state-inspired initiatives to cut pollution and a model for other states and for the federal government. California, along with New Jersey and Illinois, passed state laws to force the cleanup of aircraft engine emissions over their airspace, which were subsequently adopted by the Clean Air Act.[22] The state has been particularly vigorous in setting tough standards on gasoline sold within its jurisdiction. In 2005, California again seized the initiative by setting standards for automobile exhaust greenhouse gas emissions for future model years. This legislation does not violate the Clean Air Act's uniform set of standards for automobile emissions because these standards covered specific pollutants, not greenhouse gases. If other states follow California's example, then the federal government may be forced once again to take action to set a uniform standard for automobile greenhouse gas emissions throughout the nation. The first step for federal regulation of a uniform set of standards for greenhouse gas emissions was taken in April, 2009, by declaring carbon dioxide along with five other heat-entrapping gases to be pollutants subject to EPA regulation.

Carbon dioxide and the other greenhouse gases will be added to the six recognized forms of pollution in the Clean Air Act: sulfur and nitrous oxides, carbon monoxide, volatile organic compounds, particulate matter, and lead. Sulfur oxides come from burning high sulfur coal in electricity-generating plants plus emissions from papermaking and metal processing, and burning motor vehicle fuels with a high sulfur content. Nitrous oxides come from both mobile (gasoline and diesel fuel engine exhaust) and stationary sources (smokestack emissions from industrial boilers and utility plants). Sulfur and nitrous oxides damage the lungs and, when combined with water in the atmosphere, form acid rain, acid snow, fog, mist, and dust. Acid rain can have a devastating impact on marine life in lakes and streams, depending on the type of bottom. Lake bottoms of sedimentary rocks like limestone neutralize acid rain, whereas granite and similar rocks do not. Acid rain has caused extensive damage to forests in the northeastern United States, Canada, and Europe (the Black Forest in Germany), and has eaten away limestone and marble in outdoor statues, frescoes, and facades of buildings.

To avoid local pollution, Midwest coal-burning utility plants built high smokestacks to let prevailing winds carry sulfur and nitrous oxide pollution aloft. The prevailing winds not only carried pollution away from the Midwest, but also transformed it to acid rain that eventually fell on the U.S. Northeast and Canada. This is an example of market failure because the harm to marine life and forests and damage to stone facades far from the high sulfur coal-burning utilities was in no way reflected in the emitters' costs, other than what they spent to build higher stacks.

Carbon monoxide results from the incomplete combustion of fuels. It reduces the ability of blood to deliver oxygen to body cells and can result in death in a confined space. Volatile organic compounds (VOCs) are released from burning motor vehicle fuels in the form of benzene, toluene, and other hydrocarbons and also from solvents, paints, and glues. Ground-level ozone, the principal component of smog, results from "cooking" VOCs and nitrous oxides in the presence of sunlight. Ozone reduces visibility, damages plant life, irritates lungs and eyes, and lowers resistance to colds and other infectious diseases. Particulate matter (dust, smoke, and soot) comes from burning fuels and agricultural activities. The finer the particulates lodged in the lungs, the more hazardous they are to health, aggravating or causing bronchitis, asthma, and other respiratory diseases. Lead found in leaded gasoline, which was subsequently phased out by 1985, is also emitted by lead smelters and processing plants. Lead harms the brain and nervous systems, particularly in children.

Amendments to the Clean Air Act in 1967 divided the nation into Air Quality Control Regions (AQCRs) to monitor air quality. AQCRs that meet or exceed Clean Air Act standards are designated attainment areas, whereas those that do not are designated nonattainment areas requiring special attention. Enforcement of pollution standards is primarily carried out by the various states' environmental agencies. Each state develops a state implementation plan (SIP) that outlines how it will enforce compliance with the pollution standards set forth in the Clean Air Act. Although states have the right to set tougher standards than those imposed by the Act, they are obligated to meet its minimum standards. The Environmental Protection Agency (EPA) approves each SIP and has the right to take over enforcement if the SIP is unacceptable. The issuing of environmental permits under the Clean Air Act includes information on the type and quantity of pollutants being released, how they are being monitored, and what steps are being taken to reduce pollution. The EPA does not specify how to reduce pollution, but requires that the Maximum Available Control Technology (MACT), changed to the Best Available Control Technology (BACT) by the 1990 Act, be used to ensure an effective means of pollution abatement.

The Clean Air Act of 1970 described itself as "an Act to amend the Clean Air Act to provide for a more effective program to improve the quality of the Nation's air" and was an essential rewrite of the previous Act. The Act established National Ambient Air Quality Standards (NAAQS) for the cited pollutants and also included New Source Performance Standards (NSPS) that strictly regulated emissions from new factories, including electricity-generating and other industrial plants. The Act set standards for hazardous emissions and gave individuals the right to take legal action against any organization, including the government, for violating emissions standards.

Rather than set guidelines that were normally not complied with, as in the previous Clean Air Acts, the 1970 Act required the EPA to perform compliance tests, enforce performance warranties from manufacturers, and impose a per vehicle fine for those that did not meet Clean Air Act standards. The 1977 amendments to the Act established a policy of Prevention of Significant Deterioration (PSD), which defined areas such as national parks where there was a general prohibition from doing anything that would result in significant deterioration of the environment. A long string of amendments, or EPA granted extensions, was necessary to give motor vehicle manufacturers time to comply with emission standards. In the meantime, lead was removed from gasoline. Oil refiners had to invest in refinery improvements to produce a lead-free gasoline whose performance standards were similar to leaded gasoline and to meet lower sulfur specifications imposed on gasoline and diesel fuel. Diesel engine manufacturers had to build engines that cut particulate emissions. These additional costs borne by industry were eventually passed on to consumers as higher prices.

Congress once again drastically amended the Clean Air Act in 1990, which described itself as "an Act to amend the Clean Air Act to provide for attainment and maintenance of health protective national ambient air quality standards, and for other purposes." The Act recognized that pollution in many metropolitan areas could not be restricted to a single state. People live in one state and work in another. Trucks frequently pass over state borders. Thus, air pollution from motor vehicles cannot be handled under a single state jurisdiction when cars and trucks spread pollution throughout an entire metropolitan region. The 1990 Act set up interstate commissions responsible for developing regional strategies to clean up the air. Pollution crossing the national borders in either direction between the United States, Mexico, and Canada was addressed in a special annex to the North America Free Trade Agreement (NAFTA). The Act mandated that all power plants had to install continuous emission monitoring systems (CEMS) to keep track of sulfur and nitrous oxide (SOx and NOx) emissions. Pollution permits required every power and industrial plant to specify a schedule for meeting emission standards.

The 1990 Clean Air Act introduced reformulated and oxygenated gasoline. Reformulated gasoline combats smog by emitting a lower level of VOCs that mix with nitrous oxides to form ozone, the primary ingredient in smog. Oxygenated gasoline burns more completely, particularly during engine startup in cold weather, reducing carbon monoxide emissions. Reformulated and/ or oxygenated gasolines were required for certain nonattainment areas of the nation that suffer from high levels of ozone and/or carbon monoxide pollution for particular periods of the year. As described in Chapter 3, the Energy Policy Act of 2005 substituted a minimum quantity of ethanol and other biofuels in the gasoline stream for the oxygenate requirement contained in the 1990 Clean Air Act.

The 1990 Act contained mandatory reductions in sulfur emissions on a timetable that permitted industry to adapt to the new standards in an orderly fashion. A cap was established on aggregate sulfur emissions that stepped down in time. This cap became a maximum allowance or limit for the principal sulfur dioxide emitters. Reducing sulfur emissions on an individual company basis can be done in a number of ways. One way was for a sulfur emitter to buy a particularly rundown, outmoded, inefficient, obsolete, cheap sulfur-emitting smoker in order to establish its baseline for sulfur emissions, then shut the plant down, thereby fulfilling its sulfur-reduction obligation. The more prevalent way was the method used by utilities in the Midwest and Northeast, which shifted from high-sulfur Appalachian coal to low-sulfur western coal. This caused low-sulfur coal prices to rise in relation to high-sulfur coal prices, establishing a price differential, which, if wide enough, provided an economic justification to install scrubbers. Scrubbers remove sulfur in exhaust fumes and enable the plant to burn cheap high-sulfur coal while keeping within mandated sulfur emission allowances. Retiring old coal-fired plants and replacing them with clean-burning natural gas plants, or, better yet, with sustainable solar and wind power plants, are ways for an industrial concern or utility to reduce sulfur emissions.

These actions are pedestrian compared to the innovative part of the 1990 Clean Air Act, which internalized an externality; instituting an economic benefit to encourage pollution abatement through emissions trading. (Installing scrubbers based on a coal price differential could be considered an economic incentive, but emissions trading takes a more direct approach.) Although the beginning of emissions trading can be traced back to the 1977 Act, the 1990 Act brought it to the forefront. The Act introduced a market-based system for the buying and selling of rights or allowances to release pollution emissions. A pollution-emitting plant could invest in environmental equipment to decrease its emissions. If the equipment installation lowered sulfur emissions below the cited allowance or authority of a company to emit a pollutant, the company had the right to sell emission allowances (or rights to pollute), up to its maximum allowance, to companies that exceeded their mandatory emission allowances. The value of these emission allowances was to be determined by the market forces of supply and demand just like the value of corporate shares and commodities.

Buying and selling pollution emission allowances does not in any way abrogate the reduction in total emissions required by the Act. It simply redistributes the amount of allowed pollution among emitting plants. This gives companies flexibility to reduce emissions either by taking direct action to do so by investing in pollution-reduction equipment or by buying excess allowances from other emitters. At the end of a compliance period, every emitter must have EPA issued and purchased allowances equal to its pollution emissions or face stiff fines. This ability to buy allowances is called allowance trading, or cap and trade. Cap and trade means that there is an aggregate emissions cap, or a maximum limit, on total allowable emissions. The overall cap on emissions is initially set lower than the historical level of emissions, which gives value to allowances. As the overall cap is progressively lowered with time, so is each individual pollution emitter's allowance limit. If a company's emissions are less than its allowance limit as determined by the EPA, then the company has the right to sell the difference. If a company's emissions are above its allowance limit, then it must buy the difference or reduce operations to cut pollution or pay stiff fines. Cap and trade allows companies to act in the most economical way to reduce pollution by investing in pollution-abatement equipment, by buying allowances from a company that has, by reducing operating levels, or any combination thereof that best serves their financial interests.

Rights to pollute have a positive impact in that plants that go the full mile to reduce pollution are rewarded for beating their individual allowance limit by making money selling their excess emission allowances. Plants that have not fully complied with their individual allowance limits now have a financial incentive to do so because of the cost of buying emission allowances above their allotted allowances. A plant can use the revenue from selling excess emission allowances to justify its investment in reducing pollution emissions below the legal requirement. A plant buying sulfur-emission allowances can use the cost to justify investing in emission-abatement equipment. As the aggregate cap on emissions shrinks with time, these allowances, or rights to pollute, are apt to gain value to the greater benefit of those who are below their allowance limit and to the detriment of those who are above. Bonus allowances are rewarded to power plants that install clean-coal technology to further reduce pollution emissions, use nonpolluting renewable energy sources such as wind and solar, or encourage energy conservation to reduce the amount of power that has to be generated. The proceeds from selling bonus allowances can justify taking more costly actions to reduce pollution. Allowances can also be stored for future use.

Since 1997, between 15–25 million tons of sulfur allowances have been traded annually at a generally increasing price of $100 per ton in 1997 to a little over $200 per ton in early 2004. The price escalated sharply in the second half of 2004, reaching $485 in the fall of 2004, $700 in early 2005, and broke through $1,000 in October 2005 peaking at $1,600 at the beginning of 2006, and sharply falling thereafter to $500 in mid-2006, and to a little below $400 in the first half of 2008. Prices fell to $150 per ton in July 2008 and to less than $100 per ton in March 2009 as demand for sulfur allowances waned in the wake of reduced electricity output caused by the economic recession. The 1990 Clean Air Act's establishment of a cap and trade program has succeeded in reducing sulfur emissions despite growing coal consumption at a lower cost than a command requirement. A command requirement dictates that a company must reduce sulfur emissions by a set amount regardless of cost. Cap and trade has the benefit of lowering the overall investment in pollution-control equipment by making it possible for companies to avoid high pollution-abatement costs by buying excess allowances from companies with low pollution-abatement costs. However, at $1,600 per ton, companies must have taken a second look at investing in pollution-control equipment rather than buying excess allowances whereas their thinking probably changed when allowances fell to $100 per ton in 2009.[23] Nevertheless, the cap and trade emissions-trading program is estimated to have reduced the overall cost of pollution abatement by about one-third over a cost-indifferent command requirement. This has resulted in smaller electricity rate hikes for consumers, who, ultimately, foot the bill for pollution abatement.

In 2005, the EPA issued the Clean Air Interstate Rule (CAIR) to reduce air pollution that moves across state boundaries. Under the ruling, CAIR caps sulfur dioxide and nitrous oxides in twenty-eight states and the District of Columbia, covering nearly every state east of the Mississippi. When fully implemented in 2015, CAIR will reduce sulfur dioxide emissions by 70 percent and nitrogen oxides by 60 percent, resulting in projected health benefits of the order of $100 billion per year. The reduction in health costs is estimated to be twenty-five times greater than the cost of instituting CAIR. The EPA will set up a state's emission budget for both pollutants letting the states decide what measures are to be taken to reduce pollution and whether to have power plants participate in an EPA-administered interstate cap and trade program. The reduction in sulfur dioxide emissions represents an acceleration of that contained in the Clean Air Act for the affected states.[24]

Reducing nitrous oxides is a greater technical challenge than removing sulfur oxides. Sulfur is removed as an impurity from gasoline and diesel fuel during the refining process and is barely present in motor vehicle fuels with low-sulfur specifications. Nitrogen is not an impurity that can be removed; it is part of the molecular structure of oil. Sulfur impurities are not removed from coal prior to combustion, but sulfur oxides are technologically easier to remove from smokestack fumes than nitrous oxides. The government requirement to remove nitrous oxides acts as an incentive for entrepreneurs and corporations to find a cost-effective way of doing that. The technology to remove noxious oxides does not have to be sold; the market has already been created by government mandate.

In a closely related ruling, the EPA also issued the Clean Air Mercury Rule (CAMR) to cut mercury emissions for the first time. Mercury contamination harms the central nervous and reproductive systems of adults. Pregnant mothers eating mercury-laden fish have a greater risk of bearing children with brain disorders and learning disabilities. The largest source (40 percent) of mercury is coal-burning power plants that emit about 48 tons of mercury each year. The CAMR calls for an ultimate reduction of nearly 70 percent from 1999 levels with an initial cap of 38 tons in 2010 and 15 tons in 2018. A cap and trade program will be set up for mercury emissions to aid utilities in attaining their allowance limits.

The Clean Air Act of 2004 called for a reduction of nonroad diesel sulfur content from 3,000 parts per million (ppm) to 500 ppm. In 2006, the EPA issued rules that 80 percent of highway diesel fuel must be ultra-low sulfur content of 15 ppm and 20 percent low sulfur with a maximum content of 500 ppm. In 2010, 100 percent of highway diesel must be ultra-low sulfur diesel. Diesel for nonroad diesel engines also has to be ultra-low sulfur diesel by 2010 and locomotives and marine diesels by 2012. Sulfur reduction in diesel fuel has to be considered an ambitious and successful program from a starting point of 3,000 ppm in 2004 and an ending point of 15 ppm only six years later. This reduction required close collaboration with diesel engine manufacturers and oil refinery operators.

The public was largely unaware of global warming when the Clean Air Acts were originally legislated and for that reason did not include carbon dioxide and other greenhouse gas emissions as air pollutants. In April 2009, the EPA declared that carbon dioxide and five other greenhouse gases endangered public welfare and human health as a consequence of global warming. This is a prelude to establishing a national cap and trade program in GHG (greenhouse gas) emissions. One might argue that a national GHG emission program was perhaps in reaction to regional consortia of Canadian provinces and U.S. states (e.g., Western Climate Initiative and the Midwest Greenhouse Gas Regional Accord) taking the initiative to set up GHG emission reduction programs.[25] A single standard for the entire nation would be preferable to states having differing standards.

The Clean Air Acts have proven to be contentious, complicated, and difficult to administrate. The succession of acts and amendments to the acts manifest the challenges faced by the federal government in trying to improve the quality of the air in fifty states. While one can argue that the environment is far from pollution-free and we still have a way to go for a clean air environment, nevertheless, the Clean Air Acts have also been effective in reducing pollution. Between 1970 and

2000, sulfur dioxide emissions were down by 27 percent, carbon monoxide by 31 percent, VOCs by 42 percent, particulate matter (soot, smoke) by 71 percent, and lead emissions by a whopping 98 percent, the greatest single achievement of the Clean Air Acts.[26]

## Montreal Protocol

Ozone is a molecule of three oxygen atoms, not the normal two, and is constantly being created and destroyed in the stratosphere, nine to thirty miles above the earth. In an unpolluted stratosphere, the natural cycle of production and decomposition is at the right equilibrium to maintain a protective layer of ozone to filter out harmful ultraviolet B-rays that can cause skin cancer. But manmade chemicals such as chlorofluorocarbons (CFCs) affect the ozone layer. CFCs are a refrigerant in refrigerators and air-conditioning units, a propellant in aerosol sprays, and are used in solvents and foam-blowing agents. CFCs escape into the atmosphere through leaks in refrigerators and air-conditioning units for buildings, rooms, and motor vehicles, and from the failure to remove CFCs from disposed units. As an aerosol propellant, CFCs ultimately end up in the atmosphere where they rise to the stratosphere and decompose releasing chlorine, which acts as a catalyst speeding up the decomposition of ozone. This thins the ozone layer to the point of creating an ozone hole, first noticed over Antarctica, where it grew in size to include the southern tip of South America. Those caught in the ozone hole were exposed to ultraviolet B-rays and began to suffer from a higher incidence of malignant melanoma, a dangerous form of skin cancer. While the ozone hole was mostly restricted to Antarctica, there was also evidence of thinning of the ozone layer over the Arctic that could potentially affect those living in northern Europe.

The Montreal Protocol on Substances That Deplete the Ozone Layer is a landmark international agreement for controlling air pollution on a global scale.[27] Originally signed in 1987 and substantially amended in 1990 and 1992, the Montreal Protocol made it obligatory on the part of signatory nations to phase out production of CFCs and substitute other chemicals that fulfill the same function without affecting ozone. The Protocol's timetable calls for an 85 percent phase-out of CFCs by 2007, an 100 percent phase-out of CFCs and halons (used in fire extinguishers) by 2010, and an 100 percent phase-out of methyl bromide (a fumigant) by 2015. The Montreal Protocol was very successful in reducing CFCs and the size of the ozone hole. Its success encouraged world leaders to proceed with the Kyoto Protocol to reduce greenhouse gas emissions for countering global warming.

## Kyoto Protocol

The Kyoto Protocol is an international agreement signed in 1997 to reduce carbon dioxide and other greenhouse gas emissions. The Protocol calls for a reduction in greenhouse gas emissions to an average of 5 percent below 1990 levels to be achieved between 2008–2012. Greenhouse gases are defined as carbon dioxide, methane, nitrous oxides, hydrofluorocarbons (HFCs), perfluorocarbons (PFCs), and sulfur hexafluoride. Table 10.2 shows the relative strength of the greenhouse effect of these gases compared to carbon dioxide and their lifetime once in the atmosphere.[28]

HFCs and PFCs represent two families of similar chemicals, which explains the wide spread in their global warming factors and lifetimes. Table 10.2 is a bit unsettling in that carbon dioxide has a lower impact on global warming compared to the other greenhouse gases. A given volume of methane has twenty-one times the impact as the same volume of carbon dioxide. One unit of volume of sulfur hexafluoride has the warming potential of 23,900 units of volume of carbon dioxide. Of course, there is far less methane and other greenhouse gases in the atmosphere than

Table 10.2

**Global Warming Potential and Atmospheric Lifetime of Greenhouse Gases**

| Greenhouse Gas | Global Warming Potential for 100 Years | Atmospheric Lifetime in Years |
|---|---|---|
| Carbon Dioxide | 1 | 50–200 |
| Methane | 21 | 9–15 |
| Nitrous Oxide | 310 | 120 |
| Hydrofluorocarbons | 140–11,700 | 1.5–264 |
| Perfluorocarbons | 6,500–9,200 | 3,200–50,000 |
| Sulfur Hexafluoride | 23,900 | 3,200 |

carbon dioxide. The lifetime of carbon dioxide varies between 50 and 200 years before it is removed from the atmosphere by natural processes (photosynthesis by plants and absorption by the ocean and marine shells), whereas methane has a much shorter lifetime of nine to fifteen years before it is removed by decomposition. But HFCs and PFCs and sulfur hexafluoride, once in the atmosphere, remain forever from a human perspective. The largest greenhouse gas emitters in 2008 were China, responsible for 22 percent of global emissions, followed by the United States with 20 percent, the European Union with 15 percent, the former Soviet Union with 9 percent, and India and Japan each with 4 percent.

Voting for the ratification of the Kyoto Protocol was both a straight vote by nation and a weighted vote, depending on a country's volume of greenhouse emissions. The United States, the world's greatest contributor to greenhouse gas emissions at that time, had a single vote as a nation and the largest weighted vote based on emissions. The ratification of the Kyoto Protocol required the approval by a minimum of fifty-five nations, representing an aggregate contribution of 55 percent of greenhouse gas emissions.[29] In 2002, over ninety individual nations had ratified the Protocol, but their aggregate contribution to greenhouse gas emissions was only 37 percent. The ratification of the Protocol was in doubt. The principal objection to the Kyoto Protocol was that, if ratified, only thirty-eight developed nations were obliged to take action to reduce their greenhouse gas emissions. The obligor nations were mainly in Europe, including those in transition to a market economy in central and eastern Europe, plus the Ukraine and Russia. Nations outside Europe obliged to reduce their greenhouse emissions were the United States, Canada, Japan, Australia, and New Zealand. Although developing nations could vote in favor to ratify the Protocol, they were exempt from taking any action to reduce greenhouse gas emissions.

The rationale for limiting the obligation to reduce greenhouse gases to thirty-eight nations (actually thirty-seven since one signatory was the European Community, whose members were separate signatories) was that these nations were most responsible for the presence of greenhouse gases already in the atmosphere. Since the developing nations were not responsible for creating the greenhouse gas problem, they should not be held responsible for decreasing their emissions. The counterargument to the obligation being limited to developed nations was that China, India, Mexico, and Brazil, representing 40 percent of the world's population, had become major greenhouse gas emitters in their own right and were expected to be the largest contributors to projected gains.

In 2003, the United States and Russia announced that they would not sign the Kyoto Protocol. Both nations feared the adverse economic impact of complying with the Kyoto Protocol on their respective economies and the accompanying economic advantage that would accrue to nations that did not have to comply. The combined voting power in terms of greenhouse gas emissions of Russia and the United States was sufficient to prevent the Kyoto Protocol from coming into force, but either one switching would swing the vote the other way. In 2004, with 123 nations having ratified the Protocol, representing 44 percent of total emissions, Russia signed the Kyoto Protocol under pressure from European nations, bringing the Protocol into force in February 2005. Australia, a long-time holdout by virtue of being a coal-dominated economy, signed in 2008. Excluding the United States, the remaining thirty-six nations became responsible for putting into place policies and procedures to reduce their greenhouse gas emissions to 95 percent of their 1990 levels sometime between 2008 and 2012. (Australia agreed to reduce its 2000 emissions by 60 percent by 2050.)

The United Kingdom and Germany are already close to compliance because of their switch from coal to natural gas for electricity generation since 1990. Other nations have a tougher row to hoe. Compliance can come about by reducing methane, nitrous oxides, HFCs, PFCs, and sulfur hexafluoride rather than focusing on carbon dioxide since these greenhouse gases have a much greater impact on global warming than carbon dioxide on a unit volume basis. Thus, a relatively small reduction in these gases counts the same as a relatively large reduction in carbon dioxide emissions at potentially less cost. Greenhouse gas emissions can be reduced by building nuclear and sustainable power plants (hydro, wind, solar, tidal), switching from coal to natural gas, and by creating carbon dioxide sinks.

A cap and trade program for greenhouse gases in terms of tons of carbon was set up by the signatory nations to the Kyoto Protocol. Its structure is similar to the cap and trade program established by the U.S. Clean Air Act of 1990 for sulfur oxide emissions in terms of tons of sulfur. The emissions-trading program for the EU is built around a National Allocation Plan, whereby each member nation is assigned an annual allotment of greenhouse gas emissions. These are broken down and reassigned to an estimated 12,000 greenhouse gas emitters targeted for emission reduction. These include power and heat-generation facilities, oil refineries, coking ovens, and production facilities for ferrous metals, cement, glass, brick, porcelain, pulp, and paper, which, in the aggregate, are responsible for nearly half of European carbon emissions. Similar to the U.S. program, the targeted companies can participate in an offset program, which compensates for additional emissions from a new plant or an expansion of an existing plant. Targeted companies can select a downstream emissions program, which focuses on reducing greenhouse gas emissions at the point of release to the atmosphere such as during combustion, or an upstream program, which focuses on the characteristics of a fuel such as substituting natural gas for coal.

The estimated cost of a greenhouse gas emissions program is of the order of 15 billion euros net of the savings achieved through a cap and trade program.[30] To achieve this savings, an effective emissions-trading program has to be set up by first establishing an aggregate limit or cap on emissions that is stepped down over time. For trading to be successful, individual participants must have divergent compliance costs in order to create a cost-savings benefit. Companies that can reduce their emissions at a lower cost than others should do so to the maximum practicable extent. This allows the companies to profit from selling emission allowances that are below their stipulated maximum allowances to those facing a high cost for lowering emissions. By purchasing these allowances, companies can avoid making a costly investment in pollution-abatement equipment. Accurate monitoring of actual emissions and effective enforcement are also part of an emissions-trading program to ensure that every greenhouse gas emitter holds enough emission entitlements and trading allowances to cover its actual emissions or face stiff fines.

Exchange markets have been established, with others in the process of being set up, in Europe and the United States for trading emission pollution allowances for SOx, NOx, and carbon dioxide. Emissions trading requires a properly organized exchange market to provide ease of trading, transparency of market information to ensure that all participants know the price and volume of every transaction, and standardization of contracts between buyers and sellers to simplify ownership transfer and settlement of disputes. A well-organized market provides access to speculators and traders, whose participation adds depth (volume) to the market. This gives hedgers an opportunity to take a position against an adverse change in the price of greenhouse gas emission rights. Hedging is important if the future value of greenhouse gas emission rights is financially supporting the purchase of pollution-abatement equipment.

An alternative to cap and trade is baseline and credit, a method in which an emissions baseline is defined. A participant takes actions to reduce emissions below the baseline. If successful, an emitter is granted credits for the difference between actual emissions and the baseline at the end of the compliance period. These credits can then be sold to those emitters requiring credits to meet their emission baselines or banked for future use or sale. Borrowing involves the use of allowances or credits on the basis that they will be credited in the future when, for instance, emission-control devices have been installed. Banking and borrowing can be similar to the workings of a commercial bank where banked credits (deposits) are borrowed at some "interest" charge.[31]

In addition to emissions trading, the Kyoto Protocol established the Clean Development Mechanism (CDM) as another means of reducing greenhouse gas emissions. This allows nonparticipants, that is, nongreenhouse gas emitters, to earn carbon credits by implementing a program that reduces emissions or creates a greenhouse gas sink. Carbon credits can then be sold to emitters in need of emission allowances. The economic basis for the CDM is that the reduction of carbon dioxide at its source may cost $15 to $100 per ton of carbon, whereas developing a carbon dioxide sink may cost as little as $1 to $4 per ton.

The World Bank is a proactive investment banker for carbon finance, and manages a large portfolio of "carbon" loans. The World Bank has set up the Prototype Carbon Fund to demonstrate how to reduce greenhouse gas emissions through the use of CDM in a cost-effective fashion. The Community Development Carbon Fund and the Bio Carbon Fund are designed so that small rural communities can benefit from carbon finance by selling credits in sustainable energy projects.

An example of carbon financing is a project to substitute charcoal for coal in pig iron production in Brazil. A plantation of eucalyptus trees is to be established on degraded pastureland where the growing trees are treated as a carbon dioxide sink. After seven years, the trees are harvested and transformed into charcoal as a substitute for coal. The financing is based partly on the economics of the project in the form of revenue generated by selling eucalyptus trees for charcoal production and partly on the sale of carbon credits generated by the plantation as a carbon sink. Another example is an electricity-generating plant fueled by methane emissions from a landfill. The project could not be financed solely on the sale of electricity. By selling the project's carbon credits through a World Bank facility to a company obliged to cut gashouse emissions in accordance with the Kyoto Protocol, enough incremental revenue can be earned for the project to obtain the necessary financing. The financing draws on both the economic benefit of the project to generate electricity and on its environmental benefit of lowering methane emissions to the atmosphere.[32] As of 2009, there are over 1,660 registered projects with another 84 in the pipeline that run the gamut of conceptualization, approval, validation, registration, and implementation. The leading nations for registered projects are China (35 percent), India (26 percent), Brazil (10 percent), and Mexico (7 percent). Renewable energy projects make up 60 percent of registered projects followed by 17 percent for waste handling and disposal and 7 percent for emission controls of fossil fuels. Other projects involve increasing manufacturing efficiency, agriculture, and forestation.[33]

Nonparticipating nations to the Kyoto Protocol are at least partially fulfilling the objectives of the Protocol indirectly. China, with much of its population submerged in a heavy haze of pollution, is paying more than lip service to cleaning up its air. China is trying to reduce its reliance on coal and is taking action to cut exhaust emissions of its domestically produced automobiles, a necessity if China wants to become a major world exporter of automobiles. China's largest automaker has teamed up with Toyota to assemble fuel-efficient hybrid automobiles in China. Beijing was able to significantly reduce air pollution for the 2008 Summer Olympics, and Shanghai has taken action along a same vein.

Several states in the United States are requiring companies to report on their carbon dioxide emissions, a possible precursor to setting up a program to place a limit on or decrease emissions. A few states require either a carbon cap or an offset requirement for new plants, a few more have set up committees to explore the possibility of carbon sequestration, and a fair number are developing climate action plans. Many states have instituted some means of keeping track of greenhouse gas inventories and/or have issued mandates for renewable energy to play a specified role in meeting electricity demand. Nine participating states in the Northeast, with five observing states including California, have a goal of setting up the Northeast Regional Greenhouse Gas Initiative to design a regional cap and trade program for carbon dioxide emissions from power plants. As noted, mayors of 850 U.S. cities representing 80 million people have responded to an idea put forth by the mayor of Seattle to have cities contact greenhouse gas emitters to take an inventory of gas emissions. Once the amount of greenhouse gases is known, then it would be possible to establish a goal for cutting emissions by about 7 percent. Some utilities are initiating actions to cut greenhouse gases. One utility gave land to the U.S. Fish and Wildlife Service for incorporation in the national refuge system to grow trees as a carbon sink to counter its carbon emissions. Others are looking into carbon sequestration as a means to reduce their carbon emissions. Companies emitting greenhouse gases may one day face potential public and/or shareholder approbation for failing to take some sort of action.

In 2005, the California Air Resources Board adopted the first rules in the United States to reduce greenhouse gas emissions from automobiles sold within its jurisdiction. The new rules require automakers to cut greenhouse gas emissions by as much as 25 percent, beginning in the 2009 model year and increasing to 34 percent for 2016 models. Although this unilateral action appears to be in defiance of a provision in the Clean Air Act that requires one set of automobile pollution emission standards for the nation, the Clean Air Act did not originally deal with greenhouse gases until 2009 when greenhouse gases were declared to be air pollutants, therefore subject to EPA regulation. The EPA has not promulgated regulations on greenhouse gas emissions but if history is prologue to the future, California's rules may form the basis of these regulations.

Automobile manufacturers have warned that reducing greenhouse gas emissions increases the cost of automobiles because the engine, transmission, and air-conditioning systems would have to be redesigned. But this same warning was given to reduce pollution emissions stemming from the Clean Air Acts. Like all corporate costs, the incremental costs of pollution abatement are passed on to the consumer in the form of higher prices. If carbon emission legislation is established in the United States, then automobiles imported into the world's largest market will also have to abide by these rules. Once a company's automobiles marked for export have reduced their greenhouse gas emissions for sale in the United States, it may be cumbersome to have differently designed automobiles marked for domestic consumption. Thus, what California initiated for reducing greenhouse gas emissions from automobiles sold within its jurisdiction may end up not only with the federal government setting uniform standards for the nation, but may affect the entire global automobile manufacturing industry.

Mandatory programs for reducing carbon dioxide emissions in the United States would likely result in an active carbon-emissions-trading program. This would be a boon for solar and wind power providers because their sale of carbon credits would aid in financing new sustainable energy projects and would be a financial burden to coal-burning electricity generators and to agriculture, a heavy user of fossil fuels. A number of carbon-trading exchanges have already been established in the United States and are in operation ready for any cap and trade program set up by the government.

## Copenhagen Climate Change Conference

The United Nations Framework Convention on Climate Change (UNFCC) was signed in 1992 and has subsequently been ratified by 184 nations. These nations have agreed to work together to stabilize concentrations of greenhouse gases in the atmosphere at a level to prevent dangerous human-induced interference with the global climate system. The primary mechanism of carrying out this mission is the UNFCC's 1997 Kyoto Protocol that sets forth steps to reduce greenhouse gas emissions from 2008 to 2012. In 2007, the Intergovernmental Panel of Climate Change (IPCC) published its Fourth Assessment Report which gave a clear signal that climate change is accelerating caused primarily by anthropogenic greenhouse gas emissions. This led to the Climate Change Conference in Bali where developed and developing nations agreed to step up their efforts to combat climate change promulgated in the Bali Road Map, which included a long-term cooperative action plan to be defined at the December, 2009 Climate Change Conference in Copenhagen. The overall mission of the Copenhagen Climate Change Conference was to agree on a plan to stabilize greenhouse gas levels with 2020 and 2050 emissions-reduction targets; delineate an effective means of measuring, reporting, and verifying emissions performance; provide incentives for a dramatic increase in financing deployment and development of low-emissions technologies; and provide a means to finance forest protection.

Two proposals analyzed by the International Energy Agency (IEA) are the 450 and the 550 Policy Scenarios where carbon dioxide concentration, now at 387 ppm, will level off at either 450 or 550 ppm by 2020. Both these policies call for draconian and immediate action to succeed involving major changes in power production away from coal, except for IGCC plants, with a major emphasis on nuclear, hydro, biomass, wind, solar, and geothermal. Besides power plants, energy-intensive industrial sectors such as iron and steel, cement, aluminium, paper and pulp will be targeted to be encouraged to use the best available technology to cut emissions. Aircraft engines are to be redesigned to reduce fuel requirements, and hybrid-electric and pure electric motor vehicles are to be favored over fossil-fueled vehicles. The analysis concluded that energy efficiency and conservation will have important roles to play to reduce carbon dioxide levels. It also advocated a cap and trade program on carbon emissions to provide an economic benefit along with Clean Development Mechanism (CDM) to provide less costly equivalent means of reducing carbon emissions.

The critical fault in the Kyoto Protocol will have to be addressed—that of undeveloped nations excusing themselves from participation because of the fact that the buildup in carbon dioxide was primarily caused by the industrialized powers. Though true, it begs the question as to the role that the undeveloped world is now playing in contributing to greenhouse gas emissions. According to the Energy Information Administration, in 1980, the United States emitted about 4.5 billion tons of carbon dioxide emissions, with China at about one-third this level. In 2005, China surpassed the United States. In 2030, the projected greenhouse gas emissions for China is a little over 11 billion tons and the United States at 8 billion tons. For China and other major and rapidly growing greenhouse gas emitters such as India, Brazil, and Mexico to be excluded from any solution on greenhouse gas emissions borders on the ludicrous. China has been vocal in the past of not having carbon-emissions standards imposed on developing nations. Now China is advocating a plan to reduce carbon dioxide emissions per unit of GDP activity, but not in terms of an absolute reduction in carbon dioxide emissions. This may be in response not just to public pressure, but to China becoming the largest global investor in clean energy technology. The Copenhagen Conference ended on a sour note with the United States insisting on transparency and verification, and with China resisting what if considers intrusions on its national sovereignty.

## EFFICIENCY AND CONSERVATION

Efficiency is giving up an SUV that gets ten miles to the gallon for a hybrid that gets fifty miles to the gallon. Thus, driving an automobile the same distance consumes less gasoline. Conservation is driving the automobile fewer miles by combining trips, carpooling, and eliminating unnecessary travel. Efficiency is adding insulation to a house to keep it at the same temperature, thereby consuming less heating oil or natural gas. Conservation is lowering the temperature. Efficiency implies that the same function can be accomplished with less energy. Conservation implies less need for a function.

Energy conservation is a particular way of thinking, or having a mindset, about energy, if individuals are to undertake a whole range of energy-saving actions. These can take the form of wearing sweaters rather than tropical short-sleeved shirts during the winter to lower room temperatures, cleaning furnace filters, sealing air leaks around windows and doors, and installing insulation. During the summer the largest source of energy savings is relying less on air conditioning and more on natural air circulation, perhaps enduring higher, but not uncomfortable, temperatures. Regardless of the season, turning off unnecessary lights and electronic equipment (televisions, computers) when not in use, running dishwashers and washing machines with full loads, and a host of other practical actions can save energy. Though each act saves only a smidgen of energy, the aggregate impact of many individual acts by tens or hundreds of millions of individuals can have a significant impact on energy demand, energy prices, and pollution emissions. Both energy efficiency and conservation have an economic benefit by lowering energy costs by reducing demand and an environmental benefit by reducing pollution emissions. However, the very success of energy efficiency and conservation programs in lowering energy costs has the perverse effect of increasing energy consumption (drive an energy-efficient car on longer trips because of low gasoline prices). Energy prices have to remain high for energy efficiency and conservation to have a lasting impact.

### Energy Star Program

The major impetus to energy efficiency in the United States is the Energy Star program, established by the EPA in 1992 to reduce greenhouse gas emissions by encouraging energy efficiency.[34] Computers and computer monitors were the first products to carry the Energy Star label, which was extended to other office equipment and residential heating and cooling equipment in 1995. In 1996, EPA partnered with the Department of Energy (DOE) for those products that fell under the DOE domain for enhancing efficiency (dish and clothes washers, refrigerators, room air conditioners, light bulbs, and windows). The Energy Star program now has thousands of partnerships with private- and public-sector organizations to deliver the technical information and tools necessary for organizations to select business solutions and management practices that enhance energy efficiency. Companies that produce energy-efficient products are provided the means to break down market barriers and alter decision-making patterns so that more consumers will buy energy-efficient products.

The Energy Star label is issued when the additional cost of enhancing energy efficiency compares favorably with the benefit of lower energy costs throughout the product's life. At times, there is no additional cost such as reducing energy demand when office equipment and home electronics (e.g., personal computers) are automatically placed in a standby mode. The Energy Star label provides consumers with a straightforward determination of whether or not to purchase an energy-efficient product. The goal of the Energy Star program is to have all manufacturers offer Energy Star-labeled products, making it impossible for consumers to buy cheap energy-inefficient products.

The primary focus of the Energy Star program is to enhance efficiency in order to reduce pollution from residential and commercial sources, which account for 35 percent of greenhouse gas emissions in the United States, equally divided between the two. The remaining sources are industrial (30 percent), transportation (27 percent), and agriculture (8 percent). Greenhouse gases are estimated to be 85 percent carbon dioxide, 13 percent methane and nitrous oxides, and 2 percent HFCs, PFCs, and sulfur hexafluoride. Methane emissions come primarily from agricultural activities, while nitrous oxides stem mainly from electricity generation and transportation.

In 2008, there were over 12,000 Energy Star partners comprising 2,000 manufacturers who offer 40,000 different products with the Energy Star label; 1,000 retail partners carrying Energy Star products plus providing educational services to the public; 5,000 building partners who build Energy Star houses; 3,000 public-sector and private businesses investing in energy efficiency and reducing energy consumption in buildings; 550 utilities relying on Energy Star products to improve energy efficiency of homes and buildings; plus hundreds of energy providers, architects, and building engineers promoting energy efficiency through the Energy Star program. Americans have bought an aggregate of 2.5 billion Energy Star products, which, in 2008, saved $19 billion in utility bills and avoided greenhouse gas emissions equivalent to 29 million cars. One hundred and twenty thousand new homes were built in 2008 with the Energy Star Label bringing the total to 840,000 homes. Sixty-two thousand buildings comprising 55 percent of hospital space, 52 percent of supermarket space, 31 percent of school space, and 24 percent of hotel space have taken advantage of the EPA's energy performance rating system. A total of 4,000 buildings have received the Energy Star recognition for energy efficiency by using 35–50 percent less energy than comparable buildings.

### Light-Emitting Diodes and Compact Fluorescent Light Bulbs

An incandescent bulb, as the name suggests, heats a filament in a vacuum until it glows, releasing a large amount of waste heat. Light-emitting diodes (LEDs) are semiconductor materials that emit light. They have been around since the 1960s when LEDs emitted only red, green, and yellow light. In the 1990s, blue LEDs were developed, which, when combined with red and green, resulted in white light. Since then, improvements have been made to reduce their manufacturing costs and improve their brightness. Compact fluorescent lights (CFL) consist of a bulb filled with argon gas with a tiny amount of mercury. A charge across the bulb induces electrons to flow through the inert gas vaporizing the mercury. Mercury vapor gives off photons that interact with the phosphor powder coating on the inner surface of the bulb to give off white light. Other colors are possible by switching argon with neon or other rare earth gases. Both consume 75 percent less energy than an incandescent light bulb of the same brightness. CFLs are more expensive than incandescent bulbs, and LEDs are more expensive than CFLs. Based on three hours a day usage, a CFL can last around nine years and a LED in excess of twenty-two years. CFLs take one second to turn on with some delay before achieving full output, whereas the LED turns on instantly. A CFL is cooler than an incandescent bulb, and an LED is cooler than a CFL. At this time CFLs are replaceable like ordinary incandescent light bulbs, whereas LEDs are part of a fixture where the fixture has to be replaced in case of a failed LED.[35]

The Energy Independence and Security Act of 1970 calls for light bulbs to be 25–30 percent more efficient in 2012 for 100-watt bulbs and above and in 2014 for 40-watt bulbs and above. This spells the end of incandescent bulbs. CFLs already meet this criterion. By 2020, light bulbs are to be 70 percent more energy efficient than incandescent bulbs, a condition still satisfied by CFLs.

The fall in electricity demand will lower energy costs, cut pollution emissions, and reduce the need to build large generating plants to satisfy base load. Less capital spending for electricity generators and transmission lines can be dedicated to fulfilling other needs. The fly in the ointment is that most lighting is needed at night, when electricity demand is at its lowest. CFLs/LEDs reduce nighttime base-load demand, not higher daytime (daylight) demand. Thus, the fall in base demand still necessitates generators to handle daytime demand. CFLs are a government-mandated market representing little risk for manufacturers since consumers do not have an alternative product. CFLs are manufactured primarily by machine with little labor input. Why then are CFLs made in China? The labor cost differential between American and Chinese workers on a per bulb basis must be minuscule and the bulbs have to be transported halfway around the world. Perhaps CFLs can cast light on the reasons for the retreat (if not the rout) of American manufacturing.

## U.S. Green Building Council/LEED

The U.S. Green Building Council (USGBC) is a non-profit organization dedicated to sustainability through cost-efficient and energy-saving green buildings. The organization comprises 78 local affiliates, over 20,000 member companies and organizations, and more than 100,000 accredited professionals. Its membership includes builders and environmentalists, corporations and nonprofit organizations, elected officials and concerned citizens, teachers, and students. The USGBC maintains that buildings are responsible for 39 percent of carbon emissions, 40 percent of energy consumption, and 13 percent of water consumption. Greater building efficiency can satisfy 85 percent of projected incremental energy demand, reducing the need to build more electricity-generating plants. USGBC has an educational outreach certification program called Leadership in Energy and Environmental Design (LEED), which provides a framework for identifying and implementing practical and measurable green building design, construction, operations, and maintenance to owners and operators. LEED's internationally recognized certification system measures how well a building performs in terms of energy savings, water efficiency, reduced greenhouse gas emissions, improved indoor environmental quality, and resource stewardship. Its rating system has become a nationally accepted standard for the design, construction, and certification of environmentally friendly "green" buildings that cut energy demand by half and water demand by a third. Structure, materials, insulation, heating and cooling systems, windows and doors, water usage, shade trees and landscaping, and disposal of construction debris are some of the areas scrutinized in a LEED certification.[36]

## CAFE STANDARDS

The Energy Policy Conservation Act of 1975 established the Corporate Average Fuel Economy (CAFE) standards for automobiles and light trucks, administered by the National Highway Traffic Safety Administration (NHTSA) under the Secretary of Transportation.[37] As originally structured, CAFE standards applied to the sales-weighted average fuel economy of a foreign and domestic manufacturer's fleets of passenger cars and light trucks of less than 8,500 pounds in gross vehicle weight sold in the United States. The original near-term goal was to double new car fuel economy by model year 1985. The EPA is responsible for calculating the average fuel economy for each manufacturer. CAFE standards have been set at the maximum feasible level consistent with technological and economic practicality, along with the need to conserve energy.

The objective of doubling gas mileage did not occur. The initial standard for passenger cars for the model year 1978 was an average eighteen miles per gallon, increasing to twenty-seven and one half miles per gallon for model year 1990 and thereafter. Light truck standards originally applied to vans and pickup trucks, commonly used in place of automobiles for personal travel in the United States in addition to their commercial use. Manufacturers earn CAFE credits for models that beat CAFE standards, which can be applied to models that exceed standards, or face monetary penalties if average fleet performance does not meet CAFE standards. Light and other truck designations above 8,500 pounds, which includes nearly all commercial trucks, were outside the purview of CAFE standards. CAFE standards have barely changed from the mid-1980s to 2011. The Energy Independence and Security Act, signed into law under President Bush in 2007, called for annual step-ups to a combined average fuel economy for the fleet of passenger vehicles of 35 miles per gallon to be achieved by 2020. For individual makes of trucks, standards will be assigned in accordance with a vehicle "footprint," the product of the average track width (the distance between the center line of the tires), and the wheelbase (the distance between the centers of the axles). In 2009, the Obama administration proposed that the 35 mpg standard be reached four years earlier in 2016 with proportionately greater step-ups (4.5 percent rather than 3.3 percent per year) in fuel efficiency starting in model year 2012. Moreover a greenhouse gas emission standard will be incorporated for the first time that will be met if the vehicle attains CAFE mileage standards with the proviso that air conditioners, whose use consumes vehicle fuel, does not cause greenhouse gas emissions to exceed the proposed standard. No advanced hybrids, plug-in hybrids, electric and alternative-fuel vehicles are to be incorporated in calculating fuel performance. Proposed legislation will ensure that there is one standard set for the nation forbidding different federal agencies (e.g., Department of Transportation and Environmental Protection Agency) or any state (e.g., California) from setting their own.

Critics of the original CAFE standards point out that the automobile manufacturers already had in the pipeline a number of technological improvements to enhance automobile gasoline mileage when the CAFE standards were instituted. These improvements responded to the public demand for fuel-efficient automobiles in the wake of high gasoline prices in the late 1970s and early 1980s, which gave a tremendous boost to fuel-efficient Japanese and European automobile imports. Thus, the move to higher-mileage automobiles was not driven by a government mandate but by market forces. A more damning criticism can be leveled at the decision to classify sports utility vehicles (SUVs) as light trucks rather than automobiles. As light trucks over 8,500 pounds, the low-mileage, heavier SUVs avoided compliance with CAFE standards until recently.

The popularity of SUVs has grown rapidly since 1980. In 2007 when 14.9 million motor vehicles were sold, 7.6 million were automobiles and station wagons and 7.3 million were pickups, vans, and SUVs. Sales of SUVs totaled 4.3 million, or 29 percent of total sales. The fleet of SUVs grew from only about 2 percent in 1980 of the total motor vehicle fleet to close to 30 percent in 2007.[38] The relatively low mileage of SUVs plus the growing popularity of pickups and vans for personal transportation increased gasoline demand in the 1990s and early 2000s when gasoline prices were relatively low.

CAFE standards are a subject of intense discussion whenever the U.S. energy policy is under review, when gasoline prices spike, and during elections. In the past, U.S. labor unions have kept a wary eye on CAFE standards because they see small fuel-efficient cars as a potential loss of jobs compared to the jobs generated by manufacturing larger, more fuel-inefficient SUVs. U.S. labor unions also feel that pushing the market toward fuel-efficient cars would open up marketing opportunities for foreign makers of small cars, another threat to domestic jobs. Automobile companies kept a wary eye on CAFE standards because profit margins on large cars were greater than small cars. On top of this is a continuing debate over the role of the government in determining fuel standards or of passing the responsibility from automobile manufacturers to automobile buyers through higher-priced gasoline.

Some feel that higher CAFE standards will be satisfied mainly by building smaller and lighter-weight cars, which will lead to higher highway deaths in car accidents. However, studies have shown that death rates are more closely related to the type and make of car and not its weight. The discriminating factor in death rates by automobile model is engineering safety design (particular models of SUVs have the worst record for fatalities). Another argument against lighter-weight cars, particularly hybrids, is that fuel-efficient automobiles use less gasoline and, therefore, pay less in highway taxes. One proposal has been made to tax fuel-efficient automobiles in order to ensure that their contribution to highway trust funds remains equivalent to that of less fuel-efficient automobiles (punish the good guy tax). Another proposal has been to install a GPS on every car that will permit authorities to track each car in order to obtain its annual mileage and tax according to mileage, not gallons of fuel purchased. This would also permit the government to track every single vehicle in the nation. Some would be in favor of such surveillance as a means of combating crime; others would view it as a major infringement on an individual's right to privacy.

CAFE standards mandate government intrusion in the design of automobiles. Another way to get Americans to buy fuel-efficient automobiles is by keeping a high price on gasoline by means of a gasoline tax. In 2008 with gasoline prices $3–4 per gallon, there was a marked shift to buying hybrids and avoiding SUVs and reducing miles driven per vehicle. This shows the economic benefit of high-priced gasoline, still less than half of what Europeans pay, on fuel efficiency (buying hybrids over SUVs) and conservation (driving less). When gasoline prices dropped with the collapse of oil prices, SUV sales went up and hybrid sales went down. High-priced gasoline is necessary for the fuel savings of a hybrid to justify its higher cost and in carrying the extra costs associated with biofuels and other alternative fuels. Gasoline tax revenues can replenish highway trust funds and help fill empty government coffers. Low gasoline prices simply set the stage for another oil crisis.

## NOTES

1. Jeremy Rifkin, *The Hydrogen Economy: The Creation of the Worldwide Energy Web and the Redistribution of Power on Earth* (New York: Jeremy P. Tarcher/Penguin Group, 2002).

2. For details, visit the Icelandic New Energy Web site at www.newenergy.is.

3. The workings of fuel cells and their present commercial uses are well described online at Plug Power, Inc. Web site www.plugpower.com, and Ballard Power Systems www.ballard.com. More information on hydrogen can be found at the U.S. Department of Energy Office of Fossil Energy Web site www.fossil.energy.gov.

4. See Web site energy.sourceguides.com.

5. Web site www.hydrogencarsnow.com lists every model, their technical specifications, and stage of development including a listing of hydrogen filling stations.

6. See Web site www.fuelcells.org/info/charts/h2fuelingstations.pdf.

7. John D. Cox, *Climate Crash* (Washington, DC: Joseph Henry Press, 2005).

8. "Answers From Angkor" by Richard Stone, *National Geographic* (July 2009), vol. 216, no. 1, p. 26.

9. William F. Ruddiman, "Did Humans Stop an Ice Age?" *Scientific American* (March 2005), vol. 292, no. 3, p. 46.

10. Brian M. Fagan, *The Little Ice Age: How Climate Made History (1300–1850)* (New York: Basic Books, 2001).

11. *Impacts of a Warming Arctic: Arctic Climate Impact Assessment* (Cambridge, UK: Cambridge University Press, 2004), Web site www.acia.uaf.edu.

12. "Looking Back" and "Making Records" from the January/February 2006 issue of *Weatherwise* magazine, vol. 59, no. 1, pp. 10, 48.

13. *Impacts of a Warming Arctic: Arctic Climate Impact Assessment* (Cambridge, UK: Cambridge University Press, 2004), Web site www.acia.uaf.edu.

14. "Solar Variability: Striking a Balance with Climate Change" by Robert Calahan Web site http://www.nasa.gov/topics/solarsystem/features/solar_variability_prt.htm, May 2008.

15. Degree-days from Natinoal Climatic Data Center, Web site www.nedc.noaa.gov; carbon release from fossil fuels from BP Energy Statistics (London: British Petroleum, 2009).

16. The atomic weight of carbon is 12 and is 16 for oxygen. The atomic weight of carbon dioxide of one carbon atom and two oxygen atoms is 44. Thus a ton of carbon, when burned, produces 44/12 tons of carbon dioxide.

17. "The Case of the Missing Carbon," *National Geographic* (February 2004), vol. 205, no. 2, p. 88.

18. "Gas Guzzlers" by Deborah Franklin published in the February 2004 issue of *Smithsonian,* vol. 34, no. 11, p. 25.

19. The *Asian Brown Cloud: Climate and Other Environmental Impacts* published by the United Nations Environment Program (UNEP), 2002.

20. G. Stanhill and S. Cohen, "Global Dimming: A Review of the Evidence," *Agricultural and Forest Meteorology* 107 (2001), p. 255.

21. Michael Crichton's, *State of Fear* (New York: HarperCollins, 2004) is one such book of fiction.

22. Environmental Protection Agency, *The Plain English Guide to the Clean Air Act* (Washington, DC: Author, 2006); see Web site at www.epa.gov/oar/ oaqps/peg_caa/pegcaain.html.

23. Federal Energy Regulatory Commission Web site www.ferc.gov/market-oversight/othr-mkts/emiss-allow/othr-emns-no-so-pr.pdf.

24. EPA Clean Air Interstate Rule at Web site www.epa.gov/interstateairquality.

25. Federal Energy Regulatory Commission Web site www.ferc.gov/market-oversight/mkt-electric/overview/elec-ovr-ghg.pdf.

26. "Clean Air Act Timeline" published by *Environmental Defense,* Web site www.edf.org/documents/2695_cleanairact.htm.

27. United Nations Environmental Programme at www.uneptie.org/ozonaction.

28. Intergovernmental Panel on Climate Change (IPCC), National Greenhouse Gas Inventories Programme at www.ipcc-nggip.iges.or.jp/index.html.

29. The Convention and Kyoto Protocol is available online at the United Nations Web site at www.unfccc.int/ resource/convkp.html.

30. *Emissions Trading and Utilities: What's the Impact?* (Albuquerque, NM: UtiliPoint International, 2005).

31. *A Guide to Emissions Trading* (New York: United Nations Environmental Programme, 2002).

32. The "Carbon Finance Annual Report for 2005" and other information can be found on the World Bank Web sites at www.worldbank.org and www.carbon finance.org.

33. Clean Development Mechanism Web site cdm.unfccc.int/Statistics/index.html.

34. Information on the Energy Star Program and the Annual Report of the Energy Star Program for 2004 are available online at www.energystar.gov.

35. Energy Star Web site www.energystar.gov/index.cfm?c=fixtures.pr_fixtures.

36. More information on this organization is available at the U.S. Green Building Council Web site at www.usgbc.org.

37. National Highway Traffic Safety Administration Web site at www.nhtsa.dot.gov/cars/ rules/cafe/overview.htm.

38. *Transportation Energy Data Book* (Oak Ridge, TN: Center for Transportation Analysis, Oak Ridge National Laboratory, 2008).

# 11

# AN ENERGY STRATEGY

## WE NEED TO IDENTIFY THE RELEVANT GOAL

I will have to admit that I've changed my mind as to an appropriate energy strategy since the publication of the first edition. The objectives of an energy strategy have not changed, but the overall strategic goal has. I have become convinced that we are on Easter Island. I do not believe that climate change is even a relevant issue. The relevant issue is that we are exhausting our fossil-fuel resources at an alarming rate. As a case in point, we have long since exhausted our reserves of anthracite coal—exhaustion of resources can occur. This was not fatal as vast quantities of a second-rate substitute, bituminous coal, were available.

The reserves-to-production ratio for oil is about 40 years, 60 years for natural gas, and 120 years for coal. That is, at our present rate of production (where production is essentially equal to consumption), in 40 years we will run out of oil, in 60 years natural gas, and 120 years coal. Civilization, as we know it, is about 6,000 years old. What is 100 years in human history? What about the presumably remaining thousands of years of civilization? The percentage of people living to 80 or 90 or more years is increasing thanks to advances in medical technology. So 100 years can fit into a single lifetime. Babies born today may still be alive when oil and natural gas are gone, and coal is down to its last seams.

Take a close look at our civilization. We are utterly dependent on coal and natural gas for most of electricity generation and oil for just about all transportation fuels. Oil and natural gas are indispensable for petrochemical feedstock to produce a wide variety of consumer products. They are also vital in agriculture for pesticide and fertilizer production and fuel for operating farm machinery and for processing and distributing food. Life in suburbia depends on automobiles. The world's highways are congested with a billion automobiles, trucks, and buses and are becoming more so. What happens if oil were to run out? It would be nothing like the disruption envisioned by Theodore Roosevelt—it would bring about utter social chaos. Our way of life is not just threatened—it's gone.

## MOTOR VEHICLE FUELS

Theodore Roosevelt was proven wrong. Rather than running out of oil, discoveries made after his death created an enormous surplus that oil companies had to contend with for decades. Oil company executives today say that there is plenty of oil; the problem is not under the ground but above the ground. Drilling restrictions, xenophobia among producers, difficulties in negotiating contracts, and rescinding contracts without restitution are some of the above-ground challenges faced by oil companies. Below ground, oil companies have improved technology for finding oil

Figure 11.1   **Per Capita Energy and Oil Consumption from 1965 to 2008** (Barrels per Year)

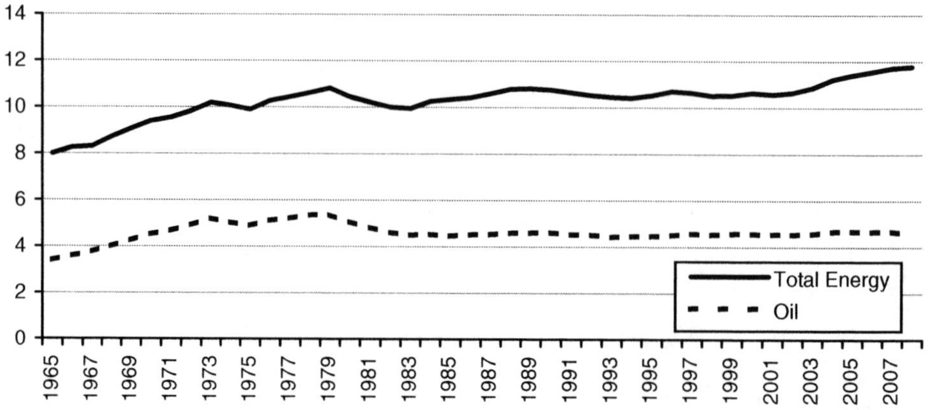

and developing oil fields in difficult locations such as two miles below the ocean surface and then another five miles into the ocean bottom, in tight sands and shale that heretofore were out of reach for commercial development, and by tertiary means of recovery that drain as much as half of the oil in an oil field. Superficially, with constant reserves to production ratio of forty years, we appear to be adding oil reserves at the same rate we are drawing down on reserves. So the conclusion one can reach is that there is no problem.

The fact that no giant oil field has been discovered in about forty years is disconcerting. Exploration keeps reducing the probability for finding a giant oil field as each well drilled eliminates another potential site. Existing giant oil fields are showing distinct signs of aging, which is another way of saying we're exhausting our oil reserves; a concept in financial accounting known as a wasting asset. A giant oil field may yet be discovered in largely unexplored Iraq or in the South China Sea where conflicting littoral jurisdictional claims by coastal nations discourage drilling. Relying on a yet-to-be made discovery of a giant oil field (actually a series of giant oil fields) to maintain oil reserves and keep motor vehicles fueled is like a single large bet at a roulette wheel. What if you lose? While there is a certain degree of comfort that oil reserves to production is constant, an examination of recent reserve additions shows that about one-third is from developing new oil fields and two-thirds from writing up existing reserves. Writing up existing reserves may be valid since reserves can be better estimated as oil is pumped out of a field. Nevertheless, it is still disheartening to see new additions from oil discoveries significantly lagging consumption.

The greatest concern for the nature of reserves is OPEC, responsible for 45 percent of world production and 76 percent of world reserves. OPEC nations have a strong incentive not to write down reserves despite their enormous oil drawdowns year after year. Production quotas are based on reserves. If an OPEC nation reduces its reserves, its production quota is cut affecting its oil revenues. Indeed, the huge write up in reserves in the mid-1980s described in Chapter 6 may be viewed more as political jockeying to determine future production quotas rather than reflecting an upward revision of actual reserves. OPEC does not mean infinite oil—Indonesia, a founding member of OPEC, is now a non-OPEC oil importing nation.

Has oil peaked? Figure 11.1 shows per capita consumption of energy and oil in barrels per year. While per capita consumption in energy is rising, oil has essentially leveled out since the early 1980s. Oil share of the energy pie has declined from 44 percent in 1980 to 39 percent in 1990 through 2000 and then down to 35 percent in 2008, with coal and natural gas shares rising to fill the gap. Since per capita oil consumption is rising in India, China, the Middle East, and South America, there has to be an offset for per capita consumption to level out. Part of this is a long-term decline in per capita consumption in Europe and, in the last few years, joined by North America and Japan. Most of the remainder is the growing economically deprived portion of the world population whose consumption of oil is nil. And it is going to remain nil because many third world nations with little in the way of hard currency reserves can afford oil imports. High oil prices coupled with high food prices, partially caused by food being diverted to fuel, have disastrous consequences for the world's poor. Some view the slight rise in overall oil production between 2005 and 2008, despite positive global economic growth accompanied by a fall in spare oil capacity and a sharp spike in oil prices, as a strong indication that oil production has peaked. Others view the same data and conclude that the problem lies in political maneuverings that stymie oil exploration and development, the root cause for spare capacity falling to dangerously low levels. They maintain that if we would only let the oil companies do what they are supposed to do—concentrate on the problems below the ground— then prices will fall as new discoveries restore spare capacity. On the other hand, it appears that the world's oil companies were busy exploring and developing oil fields throughout 2005 and 2008, though perhaps not in all the places where they would like to be actively involved. Yet during this period when oil production barely advanced and oil prices zoomed through the roof, there didn't seem to be any evidence of idle oil exploration and development rigs other than those that were becoming or had become technologically obsolescent from the increasing challenge of extracting oil from this planet. With production only slightly rising and every rig working coupled with spare capacity falling and prices rising to historically high levels, are these not the signs of oil peaking?

Let's take another tack. In 2043, the earth's population is projected to be 9 billion people. With a population of 6.7 billion and oil consumption of 84.5 million bpd in 2008, the projected oil consumption in 2043 is 113.5 million bpd with no change in per capita oil consumption. Considering that Saudi Arabia produced 10.8 million bpd in 2008, the projected gain in demand of 29 million bpd is equivalent to 2.7 more Saudi Arabias within the next thirty-three years. This estimate would be higher if there were economic growth in addition to population growth. But it is not just adding three more Saudi Arabias that is the only problem, there is also the problem of making up for the depletion of existing oil fields including those in Saudi Arabia in the interim. Some existing giant oil fields will have been in operation for a century from the perspective of 2043. Creating some number of Saudi Arabias to compensate for expected declines of wasting assets, plus another three Saudi Arabias to handle incremental demand within a generation of time just to preserve the status quo does not even sound feasible.

## Biofuels as a Substitute for Gasoline

Biofuels (ethanol and biodiesel) currently make up a few percent of global motor vehicle fuels. Biofuels is a sustainable source of motor vehicle fuels only when a relatively small amount of fossil fuels is consumed in their production. Moreover, agricultural crops should not be diverted to fuel production. One statistic should show its futility—about 30 percent of the U.S. corn production is dedicated to providing 3 percent of its gasoline demand. Ethanol from corn affects food availability and prices and only has a marginal impact on greenhouse gases since the savings in carbon emissions from corn ethanol is about equal to the carbon emissions of fossil fuels consumed in growing and processing corn and distributing ethanol. Ethanol from sugar in Brazil, for reasons discussed in Chapter 3, is far more efficacious as a biofuel both environmentally and economically. In 2008 and 2009, U.S. ethanol producers were caught in a negative biorefinery spread where the revenue from selling ethanol did not compensate for the costs of buying and processing corn. While some U.S. ethanol producers went bankrupt, Brazil's ethanol producers remained profitable demonstrating the economic advantage of producing ethanol from sugar over corn.

Brazil should be encouraged to transform underutilized grazing land to sugar production by removal of the discriminatory tax applied against Brazilian ethanol imposed by the United States. It is ironic that Venezuela, no friend of the United States, can export crude oil to the U.S. without an import tax whereas Brazil, a friend of the United States, faces a discriminatory import tax for ethanol. U.S. corn ethanol production should be limited to that of a price support mechanism to avoid the government having to pay farm subsidies to corn growers. Less costly ethanol from Brazil should take its place, and Brazil should be encouraged to expand sugar production dramatically to raise the overall ethanol content in U.S. gasoline to 10 percent as a step in reducing dependence on Middle East oil imports.

Ethanol from cellulosic material holds great promise, but technological hurdles have to be overcome before cellulosic ethanol is commercially feasible. Cellulose feedstock for making ethanol are fast-growing trees and grasses utilizing non-agricultural or marginal lands and can also include wood, lumber, forest, and municipal waste. Algae are another promising biofuel source where biodiesel, bioethanol, and nutritious animal feed are the outputs with smokestack emissions and polluted water as inputs. An alga in coastal waters of the Mediterranean introduced by an accidental intrusion of a common aquarium plant (*Caulerpa taxifolia alga*) is strangling native marine plants and emitting a toxin that affects young fish. If the proper technology were available, the plant-like alga that grows profusely to ten feet in length and is rapidly spreading to new areas, could be harvested and processed on specially fitted floating factories to transform this menace to a feedstock for biofuels and animal feed. Perhaps a genetically modified alga can be developed that grows fast, can be easily harvested, and produces a great deal of oil. Jatropha, a weed, bears a non-edible oil seed that can be converted to biodiesel along with other oil-bearing non-edible seed plants grown on land unfit for agriculture. This would be a boon to farmers who can obtain another cash crop from unusable or marginal land. Mali, Bangladesh, and a host of other impoverished nations can transform themselves from petroleum-importing to biofuel-exporting nations, bettering the lives of their people.

Fats and offal from slaughterhouses, used tires, and municipal waste can be converted to biofuels using current technology. While trucks can burn biodiesel with little in the way of modifications, most warranties on gasoline engines are void if more than 10 percent ethanol (E10 gasohol) is consumed. In time, engines should be built to accept higher levels of ethanol and maintain their warranties as in Brazil. Biodiesel is very promising given the developed state of its technology and the amount of nonagricultural land in Africa, South America, and Asia that could be dedicated to jatropha and other nonfood oil seed-bearing plants. The advantage of biodiesel is that it can be handled by the current infrastructure. As discussed in Chapter 3, ethanol has its logistical challenges but these can be overcome as demonstrated in Brazil.

The advocacy of natural gas as a substitute for gasoline and gas to liquids projects, while possibly having short-term benefits, ultimately just moves the problem from a fossil fuel with forty years of reserves to another with sixty years. Large-scale consumption of natural gas in the United States as a substitute for oil only substitutes gas imports for oil imports. It does little to promote energy independence.

## Electricity as a Substitute for Gasoline

Recent developments in electric hybrids and pure electric automobiles seem to indicate that they will be the most likely replacement for gasoline-fueled automobiles. More technological progress has to be made in reducing the cost and increasing the capacity of batteries for the electric car to become something more than a curiosity. Technological enhancements to the fuel cell are necessary before the hydrogen fuel cell can be considered a viable alternative to the gasoline internal combustion engine. Looking far, far into the future, it is possible to have a world where biodiesel fuels aircraft, trucks, and locomotives; bioethanol fuels automobile hybrids; and electricity, stored in batteries or as hydrogen, fuels electric cars.

Many decades and a great deal of restructuring of the electricity-generating and transmission infrastructure will be required to make the transformation to electric or hydrogen cars even if we start in earnest today. The electric car, whether battery or hydrogen fueled, is a much greater challenge than switching from petrofuels to biofuels. Besides the technical challenges still to be overcome, and ignoring for now the load that electric cars will place on the electricity transmission and distribution grid, the key question is what fuel will be used to generate the enormous quantities of electricity required by millions of electric or hydrogen cars. This leads to the question of what role coal, by far the most important fuel for electricity generation, will play in the future. As discussed in Chapter 4, other than coking coal for steelmaking, nearly all coal is consumed in generating electricity. From a carbon-emissions perspective, generating electricity from coal to produce hydrogen or to power the electric car is self-defeating. From a fossil-fuel perspective, transforming a 120-year wasting asset to a sixty or so year wasting asset by markedly increased consumption is not a viable proposition. Coal cannot be the incremental energy source if the goal of an energy policy is ultimately not to burn coal. Clean-coal technology with carbon sequestration actually makes the problem of coal as a wasting asset worse because about one third more coal has to be burned to generate the same amount of electricity as today's conventional plant.

Sustainable sources of energy for electricity generation are hydro, wind, solar, geothermal, river and tidal currents and ocean waves. River and tidal currents and ocean waves will be marginal contributors under any foreseeable scenario. Geothermal has the potential to power the world, but not nearly enough effort is being dedicated to transform geothermal into something other than a marginal contributor to energy supply. More effort in developing geothermal energy is warranted. Solar power will make a more meaningful contribution, particularly if a material can be found or developed that markedly increases the conversion rate of solar energy to electricity to cut the cost of solar-generated electricity. Nevertheless, solar power is expected to grow and hopefully make more than a marginal contribution. At this time, wind is the closest to being competitive with conventional sources of energy for electricity generation. The prime sources for both wind and solar energy are remote from population areas. Large-scale investments in transmission systems are necessary before wind and solar can achieve their full potential. Even so, there appears to be an upper limit of around a 25 percent contribution to total electricity demand, given the relatively poor reliability associated with dependence on wind conditions and degree of sunlight for electricity generation. Batteries could be used to store the output of wind turbines and solar arrays when there is a lack of demand; but as noted, advances have to be made in battery technology in terms of cost and capacity before such large-scale storage of electricity is possible. Using spare electricity to compress air stored in caves and then using the compressed air to generate electricity when needed has been proposed. A better solution in terms of storage capacity is to dedicate excess electricity generation to electrolyzing water to produce hydrogen, which is a stored form of electricity that can be consumed as needed in fuel cells.

Assuming an upper limit of 25 percent from wind and solar energy, where then will the remaining 75 percent come from given that it can't be coal? Natural gas cannot be a substitute for coal because switching from a fossil fuel with reserves to production ratio of 120 years to one of sixty years is jumping from the frying pan into the fire. Only two alternatives are left: hydro and nuclear power. Hydropower is more or less fully developed in the United States and Europe, although there is room for expansion in Canada along with the building of micro-hydropower facilities in the United States and Europe. Hydropower has a great deal of potential to expand in South America and in India and China, where headwaters of their major rivers are 15,000 feet above sea level on the Tibetan plateau. Environmental opposition to major dams has effectively halted hydropower projects in India, but China is moving ahead with the construction of other dams following the completion of the Three Gorges Dam. Unfortunately, hydropower cannot fill the bill—there aren't that many suitable dam sites left.

This leaves nuclear power to fill the yawning gap between energy supply of hydro, wind, and solar and energy demand for electricity generation in place of coal and natural gas. As discussed in Chapter 8, a nuclear plant program should adopt the European model where one central authority controls the industry with one basic reactor design and a limited number of output capacities. The "cookie cutter" approach to nuclear design, construction, and licensing is the only way to control construction costs and schedules. Of all reactor types, the pebble bed reactor has the greatest simplicity of design; lowest cost of construction, operation and maintenance; and most of all, the greatest inherent safety. A core meltdown, the worst type of reactor accident, cannot occur in a reactor that has no core. These plants are small in size from 100 to 250 megawatts to ensure passive safety (the highest achievable temperature from a loss of coolant is less than the melting temperature of the ceramic cladding surrounding each of the 10,000 or more fuel microspheres within each pebble). A collection of six or so of the larger plants would be necessary to equate to a single large 1,500 megawatt (1.5 gigawatt) plant. Though this is perfectly feasible, it is also possible to build these plants to serve the needs of local communities in a distributive form of electricity generation without the need for long-distance transmission lines as originally envisioned by Thomas Edison.

Conventional pressurized water reactors permit the recycling of spent fuel rods. Reprocessing spent fuel not only reduces nuclear waste by 97 percent in volume but also extends the life of uranium reserves. Reprocessing is not possible with the pebble reactor. The integrity of the ceramic casing surrounding the tiny uranium fuel microspheres in a spent pebble is so great that spent pebbles cannot be easily reprocessed. To compensate, nuclear fuel reserves can be extended by taking advantage of plentiful thorium reserves that are larger than uranium reserves. The building of thorium reactors espoused by India in a three-stage reactor program outlined in Chapter 8 should be pursued. A carefully crafted program of pebble bed reactors, conventional reactors with reprocessing of spent fuel, thorium and fast breeder reactors that produce more fuel than consumed can make nuclear power sustainable by extending fuel reserves to thousands of years.

Conversion to nuclear power will take time. There are currently 44 reactors under construction with a total capacity of 39 gigawatts (GW). If these are completed within five years, the world is adding about 8 GW per year. In a world of 4,500 GW of electricity capacity, this will not do. Even if this were twelve-times greater at 100 GW per year, and in a future world of 5,000 GW of demand which is satisfied, say, 35 percent with hydro, wind, and solar, it would take a full generation of construction to fill the gap. But if electric cars become prevalent, electricity demand will double, or triple, or more, calling for an unbelievable demand for wind, solar, and nuclear installations stretching one's imagination to the breaking point. Yet this is what will be necessary to essentially eliminate the use of coal and natural gas in electricity generation.

One advantage of electric cars is that they would flatten the electricity-demand curve. Timing of recharging automobile batteries or for producing hydrogen would be controlled in a manner that essentially eliminates variable demand. With electricity-generating units running close to full capacity, electricity rates will fall to base rates; perhaps low enough for electricity to substitute for heating oil and natural gas in heating and cooling homes and buildings. For this to occur, the electricity grid has to continue being converted to smart meters to let consumers select when to run appliances to take advantage of lower electricity rates and to control loads during times of peak demand. Smart meters coupled with smart grids will be necessary to accommodate the recharging of electric cars and/or the electrolysis of water for hydrogen in a world of distributive systems of renewable energy sources (wind farms and solar arrays) coupled with pebble bed reactors serving local communities.

## THE PROBLEM IS THE MAGNITUDE OF THE PROBLEM

We consume prodigious quantities of oil, natural gas, and coal and essentially eliminating their use will not be an easy task. (Exceptions will be made for oil and natural gas to produce petrochemicals, pesticides, and fertilizers, coal for steelmaking, and natural gas for uses other than electricity generation and heating and cooling homes and buildings.) We have to proceed in steps. For the United States, there should be a concerted effort to eliminate Middle East imports first and foremost in order to redirect funds supporting military activity to energy development as discussed in Chapter 6. Development of unconventional sources of crude oil (syncrude) such as oil sands in Canada, oil shale in Colorado, and bitumen lying on the surface in the Orinoco region of Venezuela should be actively pursued as also described in Chapter 6. Potential unconventional oil reserves dwarf Middle East reserves. Unconventional oil has its drawbacks, not least being the amount of energy consumed to produce syncrude. Venezuela is unfortunately off-limits for investment at this time, but there is no reason not to continue the development of Canadian oil sands and U.S. shale reserves relying on yet-to-be more fully developed technologies for *in situ* conversion to crude oil. *In situ* conversion eliminates many of the environmental objections lodged against the current practices of transforming oil sands and oil shale to syncrude.

The transmission highway should be built to allow for the construction of large-scale wind farms in the Northern Plains and elsewhere, such as Texas and large-scale solar installations in the Southwest. The Northern Plains should live up to their self-proclaimed slogan of becoming the Saudi Arabia of wind power and the Southwest the Saudi Arabia of solar power, and parenthetically, Brazil the Saudi Arabia of ethanol. The price of electricity has to be increased to justify this massive conversion process away from fossil fuels. A carbon cap and trade program is suboptimal for a system intended to divorce mankind from fossil fuels. A cap and trade program allows an electric utility to continue operating a coal-burning plant as long as it can purchase carbon credits, such as planting trees in sub-Saharan Africa. This does not deal with the goal of eliminating coal. Cap and trade is great for Wall Street intermediaries, as money paid by utilities and companies for carbon credits is funneled to tree farms in developing nations (to be fair, wind farms are being partially financed in China and India by European utilities and manufacturing companies buying carbon credits). A carbon tax provides direct revenue to the government, which can then be spent to fund, for example, the transmission highway. A carefully crafted carbon tax creates a world where utilities look at wind turbines, not natural gas generators, as an economically viable means of replacing coal-fired units. A carbon tax deals directly with the phaseout of fossil fuels, whereas a carbon cap and trade program finds alternatives to phasing out fossil fuels. A carbon tax, which will increase the price of gasoline and electricity, will provide an incentive not just to utilize alternative fuels, but to be more efficient (using less energy to accomplish the same purpose such as buying a hybrid over a SUV or adding insulation in a home) and more conservative (driving a hybrid less miles by making more intelligent driving decisions or wearing a sweater in order to lower room temperatures in winter). The latter years of the 1980s and the 1990s amply demonstrated that energy efficiency and conservation fall by the wayside when energy is cheap.

## ARE ENERGY COMPANIES ENDANGERED FROM SUCH A TRANSFORMATION?

If fossil fuels are wasting assets, so are the companies in the fossil-fuel business. But this does not endanger energy companies, as it will take decades to make the transformation. Every existing fossil-fuel plant, every plant in construction, and every plant on the drawing board will have a full life of operation supplying needed electricity before they are exposed to a meaningful decline in the availability or demand for fossil fuels. This gives energy companies plenty of time to redirect their considerable financial assets and technical knowledge and expertise from fossil fuels to bio-fuels and sustainable energy sources such as wind, solar, geothermal, hydro, and nuclear power. Moreover by eliminating fossil fuels, the dreams of those who believe in sustainable energy will be fulfilled along with those who want to drastically decrease the carbon and ecological footprints of modern society built on fossil fuels. Getting rid of fossil fuels should make everyone happy . . . but, of course, it won't. Environmental objections over wind farms, perhaps solar installations, and certainly nuclear power plants will still be present. If these objections are effective in stopping the conversion process, as they've been in the past, then turning away from fossil fuels cannot occur. By stymieing progress in finding a solution to the fossil-fuel problem, perhaps the more extreme environmentalists' solution of eliminating 90 percent of the world population in order to save the planet Earth may become more than just a talking point.

## THERE IS ALWAYS AN ALTERNATIVE

The alternative is very simple. Do nothing—which is what we've been doing for the past forty years. It is remarkable that this book contains nothing new, had it been written in the late 1970s, other than technological progress in manufacturing wind turbines and hybrid cars and in exploring and developing oil fields, and in other technical areas. Europe and Japan have adopted energy policies, and other nations are in the beginning stages. That is a sign of progress, but their energy strategies do not have as a goal the phaseout of fossil fuels. Europe's goal is to minimize gasoline and coal consumption with greater reliance on diesel oil, natural gas, and nuclear power including development of solar and wind power. Japan's goal is to diversify types and sources of energy so as not to be overly reliant on any one type or source, with an emphasis on nuclear power and development of solar power. Other than as noted, both regions are still firmly wedded to fossil fuels. For most of the rest of the world, there are either no coherent national energy policies or, if there are, no effectual action plans to accomplish them.

Just about every concept in this book was known back in the 1970s, and obviously we have not learned our lesson. We have essentially spent the last forty years drifting, with regard to our dependence on fossil fuels. The consequence of drifting is that we are consuming more fossil fuels than ever before. Between 1973 and 2008, world oil consumption has climbed 50 percent, natural gas 160 percent, and coal 110 percent. We can drift for the next forty years consuming more and more fossil fuels, but I don't think this luxury will be available. I don't think we have the capability of adding three more Saudi Arabias to oil production, which would be necessary just to stay where we're at with no allowance for production declines in existing fields or economic growth. We have to be blind not to see how close we are to a major world conflict over oil, when in fact we have been in continual conflict in the Middle East for a generation. It is perfectly conceivable that a major global confrontation over oil can shut down not just the United States but also Europe, China, Japan, India, and others without a steady flow of imported oil to fuel their economies. The risk of industrial powers becoming third world nations is the risk we are taking when we continue drifting with no policy and no effectual means to reduce our dependence on fossil fuels. When the infrastructure of refineries, pipelines, storage tanks, and filling stations of the most vulnerable of the fossil fuels runs dry, then what will we do?

# INDEX

*Italic page references refer to tables and figures.*

# ABOUT THE AUTHOR

**Roy L. Nersesian** has spent most of his professional career observing the energy industry as part of his involvement in energy transportation. He is an adjunct professor at Columbia University at the Center for Energy, Marine Transportation, and Public Policy in the School of International Public Affairs, and a professor at the Leon Hess School of Business at Monmouth University, West Long Branch, New Jersey. He brings a fresh perspective to the energy business—where it was and where it is heading.